Apollos Old Testament

COMMENTARY

23

OBADIAH, JONAH & MICAH

TITLES IN THIS SERIES

EXODUS, T. Desmond Alexander
LEVITICUS, Nobuyoshi Kiuchi
DEUTERONOMY, J. G. McConville
JOSHUA, Pekka M. A. Pitkänen
RUTH, L. Daniel Hawk
1 & 2 SAMUEL, David G. Firth
1 & 2 KINGS, Lissa Wray Beal
PROVERBS, Paul Overland
ECCLESIASTES & THE SONG OF SONGS, Daniel C. Fredericks and Daniel J. Estes
DANIEL, Ernest C. Lucas
HOSEA, Joshua N. Moon
OBADIAH, JONAH & MICAH, Elaine A. Phillips
HAGGAI, ZECHARIAH & MALACHI, Anthony R. Petterson

APOLLOS OLD TESTAMENT
COMMENTARY

23

OBADIAH, JONAH & MICAH

Series Editors
David W. Baker and Gordon J. Wenham

ELAINE A. PHILLIPS

Apollos
London, England

APOLLOS (an imprint of Inter-Varsity Press)
36 Causton Street, London SW1P 4ST, England
Email: ivp@ivpbooks.com
Website: www.ivpbooks.com

Inter-Varsity Press, England, publishes Christian books that are true to the Bible and that communicate the gospel, develop discipleship and strengthen the church for its mission in the world.

IVP originated within the Inter-Varsity Fellowship, now the Universities and Colleges Christian Fellowship, a student movement connecting Christian Unions in universities and colleges throughout Great Britain, and a member movement of the International Fellowship of Evangelical Students. That historic association is maintained, and all senior IVP staff and committee members subscribe to the UCCF Basis of Faith. Website: www.uccf.org.uk.

Scripture quotations are the author's own translations.

First published 2022

British Library Cataloguing-in-Publication Data
A catalogue record for this book is available from the British Library.

ISBN: 978–1–78974–378–4 (print)
ISBN: 978–1–78974–377–7 (digital)

Set in Sabon 10/12pt
Typeset in Great Britain by CRB Associates, Potterhanworth, Lincolnshire
Printed and bound in Great Britain by TJ Books Ltd, Padstow on paper from sustainable sources

CONTENTS

To my beloved husband, Perry,
who embodies Micah 6:8

EDITORS' PREFACE

The Apollos Old Testament Commentary takes its name from the Alexandrian Jewish Christian who was able to impart his great learning fervently and powerfully through his teaching (Acts 18:24–25). He ably applied his understanding of past events to his contemporary society. This series seeks to do the same, keeping one foot firmly planted in the universe of the original text and the other in that of the target audience, which is preachers, teachers and students of the Bible. The series editors have selected scholars who are adept in both areas, exhibiting scholarly excellence along with practical insight for application.

Translators need to be at home with the linguistic practices and semantic nuances of both the original and target languages in order to be able to transfer the full impact of the one into the other. Commentators, however, serve as interpreters of the text rather than simply its translators. They also need to adopt a dual stance, though theirs needs to be even more solid and diversely anchored than that of translators. While they also must have the linguistic competence to produce their own excellent translations, they must moreover be fully conversant with the literary conventions, sociological and cultural practices, historical background and understanding, and theological perspectives of those who produced the text as well as those whom it concerned. On the other side, they must also understand their own times and culture, able to see where relevance for the original audience is transferable to that of current readers. For this to be accomplished, it is not only necessary to interpret the text; one must also interpret the audience.

Traditionally, commentators have been content to highlight and expound the ancient text. More recently, the need for an anchor in the present day has also become more evident, and this series self-consciously adopts this approach, combining both. Each author analyses the original text through a new translation, textual notes, a discussion of the literary form, structure and background of the passage, as well as commenting on elements of its exegesis. A study of the passage's interpretational development in Scripture and the church concludes each section, serving to bring the passage home to the modern reader. What we intend, therefore, is to provide not only tools of excellence for the academy, but also tools of function for the pulpit.

David W. Baker
Gordon J. Wenham

AUTHOR'S PREFACE

It was providential to encounter David Baker at Tyndale House in Cambridge in the spring of 2018. At some point in the course of daily conversations in the Commons over coffee and tea, he generously offered me the opportunity of writing for the Apollos Old Testament Commentary series on Obadiah, Jonah and Micah. I am grateful for the privilege. To be candid, I did not know as I started what an undertaking this was going to be. It sent me back to engage again with what I thought were familiar texts, and it has deepened remarkably my love for the rugged and passionate prophetic poetry and narrative in the HB. In the interval, it has been most helpful to try out ideas in teaching venues addressing prophetic literature. Not only has the undergraduate student context been helpful; I am also grateful for the opportunity to team-teach Micah with my husband for Boston's Park Street Church Christian Formation classes.

Speaking of my husband, to him I offer loving thanks for the encouragement, support, wisdom, prayer, sacrifice, humour, tech assistance and so much else. I am grateful that we have been partners in a small part of God's kingdom for now almost half a century. He is a gift from the Lord and a consistent source of incarnational love. Above all, we share joy and hope as participants in that great throng that the Lord has drawn to Mount Zion through the atoning and shepherding work of the One born in Bethlehem.

This final season of writing has been in the shadow of the 2020–22 pandemic. No matter how one parses all the complexities, several things are certain: I have been blessed and assisted by members of the library staff at Gordon College who have done yeoman's labour in acquiring interlibrary loan texts, allowing reference works to accompany me home, and generally cheering me on. Likewise, the library at Gordon-Conwell Theological Seminary has been a haven for research and writing. These have been bolstered by small but effective armies of praying friends whose encouragement and faithful intercession have been sources of renewed purpose. I am equally grateful for the patient direction, corrections, suggestions and occasional refocusing provided by David Baker. Philip Duce and Thomas Creedy of Inter-Varsity Press both offered guidance and encouragement. The meticulous editing skills of Eldo Barkhuizen were already the stuff of legend when he received my manuscript; I have benefited immensely from his keen eye, expertise, patience and gracious comments. As many authors are wont to acknowledge, the labours of all these scholars have prevented me from straying afield.

Above all, thanks be to God who daily provides his children with strength and help.

'He whose heart is kind beyond all measure, gives unto each day what he deems best. Lovingly, its part of pain and pleasure, mingling toil with peace and rest' ('Day by Day', C. W. Sandell, 1865; tr. A. L. Skoog).

ABBREVIATIONS

TEXTUAL

1QpMic	Qumran Micah pesher
1QS	Qumran Community Rule
4QMic	Qumran Cave 4 Micah fragment
4QXIIa/f/g	Qumran Minor Prophets
8ḤevXIIgr	Greek Minor Prophets scroll (Naḥal Ḥever)
b.	Babylonian Talmud, Soncino edition, ed. I. Epstein, London: Soncino, 1969
DSS	Dead Sea Scrolls
HB	Hebrew Bible
Hebr.	Hebrew
K	Kethibh
LXX	Septuagint
m	Mishnah
MS(S)	manuscript(s)
MT	Masoretic Text
MT^{A}	Masoretic Text, Aleppo Codex
MT^{C}	Masoretic Text, Cairo Codex of the Prophets
MT^{L}	Masoretic Text, Leningrad Codex
Mur	Murabba'at 88
Ned.	Tractate Nedarim of the Babylonian Talmud
Q	Qere
Qum	Qumran
Sanh.	Tractate Sanhedrin of the Babylonian Talmud
Sym	Symmachus, translation of OT into Greek
Syr	Syriac
Tg	Targum
Vg	Vulgate

HEBREW GRAMMAR

abs.	absolute
acc.	accusative
act.	active
adj.	adjective
adv.	adverb(ial)

art.	article
coh.	cohortative
conj.	conjunction
const.	construct
dat.	dative
def. art.	definite article
demonst.	demonstrative
fem.	feminine
gen.	genitive
hiph.	hiphil
hith.	hithpael
hithpal.	hithpalel
hithpol.	hithpolel
hoph.	hophal
impv.	imperative
inf.	infinitive
interr.	interrogative
juss.	jussive
masc.	masculine
niph.	niphal
pass.	passive
pi.	piel
pl.	plural
plupf.	pluperfect
pol.	polel
prep.	preposition(al)
pron.	pronoun/pronominal
ptc.	participle
pu.	pual
qat.	qatal
reflex.	reflexive
rel.	relative
sg.	singular
subst.	substantive/substantivally
suff.	suffix
voc.	vocative
wayyiq.	wayyiqtol
weqat.	weqatal
weyiq.	weyiqtol
yiq.	yiqtol

MISCELLANEOUS

Anab.	Xenophon, *Anabasis*
ANE	ancient Near East(ern)
Ant.	Josephus, *Antiquities of the Jews*
AV	Authorized (King James) Version
BoT	Book of the Twelve
C. Ap.	Josephus, *Contra Apionem*
ch(s).	chapter(s)
ESV	English Standard Version
ha	hectares
HCSB	Holman Christian Standard Bible
Hist.	Herodotus, *Historiae*
J. W.	Josephus, *Jewish War*
km	kilometre(s)
l	litre(s)
m	metres
Marc.	Tertullian, *Adversus Marcionem*
NASB	New American Standard Bible
NIV	New International Version (2011)
NKJV	New King James Version
NLT	New Living Translation
NRSV	New Revised Standard Version
NT	New Testament
OT	Old Testament
pts	pints
v(v).	verse(s)

JOURNALS, REFERENCE WORKS, SERIES

AASOR	Annual of the American Schools of Oriental Research
AB	Anchor Bible
ABD	D. N. Freedman (ed.), *Anchor Bible Dictionary*, 6 vols., New York: Doubleday, 1992
AJA	*American Journal of Archaeology*
ANET	J. B. Pritchard (ed.), *Ancient Near Eastern Texts Relating to the Old Testament*, 3rd ed., Princeton: Princeton University Press, 1969
AOTC	Apollos Old Testament Commentary
ASOR	American Schools of Oriental Research
ATR	*Anglican Theological Review*
BA	*Biblical Archaeologist*
BAR	*Biblical Archaeology Review*
BASOR	*Bulletin of the American Schools of Oriental Research*

BBR	*Bulletin for Biblical Research*
BDB	F. Brown, S. R. Driver and C. A. Briggs, *The Brown-Driver-Briggs Hebrew and English Lexicon, with an Appendix Containing the Biblical Aramaic*, Boston: Houghton, Mifflin, 1906; repr. Peabody: Hendrickson, 2012
BHQ	A. Gelston, *The Twelve Minor Prophets, Biblia Hebraica Quinta* 13, Stuttgart: Deutsche Bibelgesellschaft, 2010
BHS	K. Elliger and W. Rudolph (eds.), *Biblia Hebraica Stuttgartensia*, Stuttgart: Deutsche Bibelgesellschaft, 1983
Bib	*Biblica*
BibInt	*Biblical Interpretation*
BibOr	Biblica et Orientalia
BibRes	*Biblical Research*
BR	*Bible Review*
BTB	*Biblical Theology Bulletin*
BTC	Brazos Theological Commentary
BZAW	Beihefte zur Zeitschrift für die alttestamentliche Wissenschaft
CBQ	*Catholic Biblical Quarterly*
CJ	*Concordia Journal*
COS	W. W. Hallo and K. L. Younger Jr. (eds.), *The Context of Scripture*, 4 vols., Leiden: Brill, 1997–2016
CTA	A. Herdner (ed.), *Corpus des tablettes en cuneiforms alphabétiques découvertes à Ras-Shamra-Ugarit de 1929 à 1939*, Mission de Ras Shamra 10, Paris: Geuthner, 1963
CTQ	*Concordia Theological Quarterly*
DCH	D. J. A. Clines (ed.), *Dictionary of Classical Hebrew*, 8 vols., Sheffield: Sheffield Phoenix, 1993–2008
DJD I	D. Barthelemy and J. T. Milik, *Qumran Cave 1: Discoveries in the Judean Desert*, Oxford: Clarendon, 1955
DJD IIa/b	P. Benoit, J. T. Milik and R. de Vaux, *Les Grottes de Murabbaʿat*. Oxford: Clarendon, 1961
DJD VIII	E. Tov, *The Greek Minor Prophets Scroll from Naḥal Ḥever (8ḤevXIIgr)*, Oxford: Clarendon 1990
DJD XV	E. Ulrich, F. M. Cross, R. E. Fuller, J. E. Sanderson, P. Shekan and E. Tov (eds.), *Qumran Cave 4: Discoveries in the Judean Desert*, Oxford: Clarendon, 1997
EBC	*The Expositor's Bible Commentary*, T. Longman and D. Garland (eds.), 13 vols., Grand Rapids: Zondervan, 2008

EEC	Evangelical Exegetical Commentary
EJ	F. Skolnik and M. Berenbaum (eds.), *Encyclopedia Judaica*, 2nd ed., Jerusalem: Keter, 2007
ErIsr	*Eretz-Israel*
EvQ	*Evangelical Quarterly*
FOTL	Forms of the Old Testament Literature
GBS	Guides to Biblical Scholarship
GKC	E. Kautzsch (ed.) and A. E. Cowley (ed., rev. and tr.), *Gesenius' Hebrew Grammar*, 2nd ed., Oxford: Clarendon, 1910
HALOT	L. Koehler, W. Baumgartner and J. J. Stamm, *The Hebrew and Aramaic Lexicon of the Old Testament*, tr. and ed. under supervision of M. E. J. Richardson, 2 vols., Leiden: Brill, 2001
HAR	*Hebrew Annual Review*
HCOT	Historical Commentary on the Old Testament
HS	*Hebrew Studies*
HSM	Harvard Semitic Monographs
HTR	*Harvard Theological Review*
HUCA	*Hebrew Union College Annual*
IBHS	B. Waltke and M. P. O'Conner, *Introduction to Biblical Hebrew Syntax*, Winona Lake: Eisenbrauns, 1990
ICC	International Critical Commentary
IDB	G. A. Buttrick, T. S. Kepler, J. Knox, H. G. May, S. Terrier and E. S. Bucke (eds.), *Interpreter's Dictionary of the Bible*, 4 vols., New York: Abingdon, 1962
IEJ	*Israel Exploration Journal*
IES	Israel Exploration Society
Int	*Interpretation: A Journal of Bible and Theology*
JANES	*Journal of the Ancient Near Eastern Society*
JBL	*Journal of Biblical Literature*
JETS	*Journal of the Evangelical Theological Society*
JHS	*Journal of Hebrew Scriptures*
J-M	P. Joüon, tr. T. Muraoka, *A Grammar of Biblical Hebrew*, Rome: Pontifical Biblical Institute, 2005 corrected edition.
JNES	*Journal for Near Eastern Studies*
JNSL	*Journal of Northwest Semitic Languages*
JPOS	*Journal of the Palestinian Oriental Society*
JSOT	*Journal for the Study of the Old Testament*
JSOTSup	Journal for the Study of the Old Testament Supplement Series
JSS	*Journal of Semitic Studies*
JTS	*Journal of Theological Studies*

KTU	M. Dietrich, O. Loretz and J. Sanmartín (eds.), *Die keilalphabetischen Texte aus Ugarit*, AOAT 24.1, Neukirchen-Vluyn: Neukirchen Verlag, 1976; 2nd enlarged ed.: *The Cuneiform Alphabetic Texts from Ugarit, Ras Ibn Hani, and Other Places*, Münster: Ugarit-Verlag, 1995
LCL	Loeb Classical Library
LHBOTS	Library of Hebrew Bible / Old Testament Studies
LS	H. G. Liddell and R. Scott, *A Greek–English Lexicon*, Oxford: Clarendon, 1843 (9th ed. 1940; supplement 1968)
NAC	New American Commentary
NEAEHL	E. Stern (ed.), *The New Encyclopedia of Archaeological Excavations in the Holy Land*, 5 vols., Jerusalem: Carta, 1993
NIB	L. E. Keck (ed.), *The New Interpreter's Bible*, 12 vols., Nashville: Abingdon, 1996
NIBC	New International Biblical Commentary
NICOT	New International Commentary on the Old Testament
NIDOTTE	W. VanGemeren (ed.), *New International Dictionary of Old Testament Theology and Exegesis*, 5 vols., Grand Rapids: Zondervan, 1997
NIVAC	The New International Version Application Commentary
NSBT	New Studies in Biblical Theology
OTL	Old Testament Library
PEQ	*Palestine Exploration Quarterly*
PTR	*Princeton Theological Review*
ResQ	*Research Quarterly*
RRJ	*Review of Rabbinic Judaism*
SBLDS	Society of Biblical Literature Dissertation Series
SHBC	Smyth and Helwys Bible Commentary
TA	*Tel Aviv*
TDOT	G. J. Botterweck, H. Ringgren and H.-J. Fabry (eds.), *Theological Dictionary of the Old Testament*, 15 vols., Grand Rapids: Eerdmans, 1974–2006
TOTC	Tyndale Old Testament Commentaries
TrinJ	*Trinity Journal*
TWOT	R. L. Harris, G. L. Archer Jr. and B. K. Waltke (eds.), *Theological Wordbook of the Old Testament*, 2 vols., Chicago: Moody, 1980; repr. as one vol. 2003
TynB	*Tyndale Bulletin*
UF	*Ugarit-Forschungen*
VT	*Vetus Testamentum*
VTSup	Supplements to Vetus Testamentum

WBC	Word Biblical Commentary
ZIBBC	J. H. Walton (ed.), *Zondervan Illustrated Bible Backgrounds Commentary*, Grand Rapids: Zondervan, 2009
ZAW	*Zeitschrift für die alttestamentliche Wissenschaft*

GLOSSARY

alliteration words in close proximity that begin with the same sound
assonance repetition of similar vowel sounds
athnach the major disjunctive accent, separating two parts of the verse
chiasm, chiastic rhetorical structure in which the ideas presented initially are inverted and represented (ABCBA)
cognate accusative a verbal form followed by a noun deriving from the same root
colon, cola (pl.) a single line of poetry; bicolon; bicola (pl.) – two parallel lines of poetry
ellipsis, ellipses (pl.) omission of one or more words in a sentence; they need to be supplied for the structure to be grammatically complete
gemara the material in the Talmud that expands on the Mishnah
hapax (legomenon) a word that occurs only once
hendiadys two words joined by 'and' that express a single idea
inclusio similar material at the beginning and end that frames the entire section
intertextuality recognizing the interconnectedness of texts, both within a canonical text and outside that text
***lex talionis* (Latin for 'law of retaliation')** punishment should be equivalent to the crime
merismus two parts that may be opposite are representative of the whole; example: 'heaven and earth'
metathesis the transposition of letters or syllables in a word
metonymy one word stands in for another, often larger conceptually, with which it is closely associated
middle voice when the verb form combines both pass. and act. aspects and affects both the subject and the object
midrash exposition of one or more biblical texts that are woven together with intertextual connections
paragogic (word-extending) nun the Hebr. letter (nun) attached to certain finite verb forms; its significance is not certain
paranomasia wordplay; the use of words that sound similar but have different meanings
parashah a section of the HB, generally dealing with one topic
pericope a passage of Scripture
qînâ Hebr. term for 'lament'
rabbinic written materials reflecting Jewish responses in Late Antiquity and beyond to their traditional texts

Rashi Rabbi Shlomo ben Yizhaq – eleventh-century Jewish Bible and Talmud commentator
redact/redaction edit/edition
stanza two or more lines of a poem that are marked by shared patterns
stich a line of poetry
terminus ad quem the latest possible date for an event or composition
vaticinium ex eventu prophecy written after an event, but presented as if it were stated prior to that event

GENERAL INTRODUCTION

1. APPROACH AND METHODOLOGY

The threesome of Obadiah, Jonah and Micah is unusual among the texts in the BoT because it includes both challenging poetic gems as well as the familiar story of Jonah. Questions related to historical context, authorship, date, coherence, genre and purposes have unique aspects when it comes to each text. Approaches to these questions have been reworked by successive generations of scholars as the methodological winds continue to shift. Here, I will make general observations regarding hermeneutical issues, focusing on guiding principles. I will address particulars in the introductions to each book.

There is a growing cadre of scholars who engage the study of Scripture from both a rigorously critical and an unabashedly confessional stance, affirming the interweaving of historical integrity, literary artistry and theological/ideological import. This stance commences with the components of text criticism and builds incrementally with literary analysis, historical contextual study and ideological discernment (Petterson 2015: 36–39). As Bartholomew outlines his agenda for a robust trinitarian hermeneutic, data from the whole range of academic disciplines are essential, among them historical assessment, narrative theology, philosophy and postmodern perspectives (2015: 9–12). Primary emphases and conclusions broaden as geographical contexts and presumed sociopolitical setting(s) receive more attention. Canonical contexts, intertextual connections and audience perspectives likewise come into play. Each of these focuses will surface in the introductions to the individual books. A substantial Bible atlas will be a helpful auxiliary resource.

Above all, elucidating the timeless messages is the primary focus. It is my concern that readers and students of the living Word of God foster a vibrant sense of its unique nature. These are words of God, mediated through real people in a real time and place. Their messages were spoken into those contexts with rhetorical force and passion; the circumstances demanded powerful words. These words were recorded to be read and reread, studied for their lasting effectiveness; the rereading audiences are a steady emphasis in the commentaries of Ben Zvi on the texts (1996, 2000, 2003). The literary messages are equally dynamic. Focusing solely on arrangements of forms and structures, however, risks losing the sense of real tragedy, trauma and hope into which the prophets spoke as they lived with God's people. These words were, are and will be timely – *lĕʿôlām wāʿed* ('for ever and ever') if you will. The basic contours of human experience always require challenging and consoling words from heaven.

All translations, unless otherwise noted, are my own. As I translated each section, I initially produced a very rugged English representation of the Hebr. In some cases, it was just wrong! In others, terribly awkward. But I did not want to be influenced by well-known smooth English renditions, particularly when the text is uneven. Whether prose or poetry, the temptation to offer felicitous English dampens the force conveyed by the sound and structure of the Hebr. For that reason, the translations that commence each unit are a compromise. They are intentionally shaped to reflect as closely as possible the Hebr. meaning and forms without verging on incomprehensible. To be sure, translations in pew and study Bibles must be as accessible as possible in the receptor language, and it is essential to read this commentary along with a suitable English translation, preferably more than one. See further below regarding characteristics of Hebr. poetry and prose that are intrinsic to the message. Alter (2019: 52) warns against 'airbrushing' the Hebr. vocabulary and syntax. His approach has been refreshing and affirming as he critiques translations that water down the impact of the Hebr.

At the outset, I was compelled to wrestle with how to represent the covenant Divine Name (the Tetragrammaton). My inclination has always been to avoid writing or pronouncing a direct representation of those letters, based on the solemn warning in the Ten Words as well as the fact that we really don't *know* how to pronounce it; that is for a reason. Just as our Jewish colleagues and friends have used one form of circumlocution or another (HaShem, Adonai, AdoShem), I have in the past tended to write it as Lord. Where this gets cumbersome, however, are the places in the text where we have Lord (Adonai) in combination with Lord. For this series, I have elected to use YHWH, both in the 'Translation' and the

'Comment' sections. That maintains the sense of the inherent distance; it too cannot be pronounced as is.

In those places where the English versification is different from Hebr., the English will appear in square brackets following the primary reference in the HB. Terms that are less familiar appear in bold in the text and are defined in the glossary.

2. RHETORICAL AND LITERARY CONSIDERATIONS

Language matters, and all aspects of language matter when the message is the authoritative word of YHWH intended to persuade, warn and console. These prophetic words were meant to be both heard and read. The frequent command to 'Hear!' is a hint as to how important sound is in conveying the messages. At the same time, from the eighth century on, writing became increasingly important as these texts were a growing repository of divine revelation (Goldingay 2021: 12–15). The writing process would involve further structuring of the messages. There is a possible hint to this effect in Mic. 3:1, which inserts a quick 'So I said' before continuing to record the message. Perhaps more extensive preaching over longer periods of time was condensed and structured as written text. In the Second Temple period, interpretation of texts supplanted hearing oracles. Those who were 'curators' shaped the prophetic corpus so that it would continue to function authoritatively in new circumstances (Biddle 2007: 154–166).

Through the lenses of discourse analysis, Block (2013: 9–10) explores how the rhetoric in these written texts works to convey principle theological points that are significant both within the book and in the wider canonical context. Whole units and structural interconnections are important components of the messages, whether they were already in the oral pronouncements as the result of deeply embedded cultural structures or are part of the compositional artistry. Subsequent generations of readers and hearers continue to absorb and actualize the authoritative texts even as historical circumstances develop, and further prophetic oracles speak into ever-modulating contexts (Renaud 1977: 421–423).

Of particular interest are the oracles targeting foreign nations. Both Obadiah and Jonah fall into this category and raise their own genre-specific questions. Raabe (1996: 236–257) addresses the presumed purposes and goals of these oracles, ostensibly oral pronouncements to or about these nations, but also conveying messages for YHWH's people. On a macro level, the reality of impending judgment humbles the proud and destroys the wicked. Those outcomes mean deliverance for Israel, intended to encourage their trust in YHWH and disavowal of impotent false gods. The last part of Obadiah depicts an ideal future, possibly viewed through eschatological lenses.

Challenges arise as subsequent generations grappled with the written text. Some of these are evident in the ways the early versions wrestled with difficulties. The HB is a relatively small sampling of the language, spanning centuries. A word may be used only once in a terse poetic line. Even if it appears elsewhere, the contexts may be different. Words have wide semantic ranges that expand and modulate across those centuries; the rich potential also means potential ambiguity. Seemingly awkward or rugged syntax may bedevil exegetes, but it carries a significant part of the message for Hebr. hearing and reading audiences.

Further, the 'rules' for poetry are different from those for prose; poetry is evocative and relies on the combined impact of unusual vocabulary and word order along with irregular grammar and syntax. These literary markers would make original audiences sit up and take notice. Prophetic discourse, somewhere between prose and poetry, adds further complexity, especially in the quest for metrical regularity and thematic coherence. Freedman (1983: 141–158) distils the issue: to what extent can we render the configurations of Hebr. words in prophetic oracles into comprehensible English? A first principle is to wrestle with the MT as we have it rather than immediately resorting to emendations.

2.1. Poetic considerations

The long-standing expectations associated with the label 'poetry' have entailed a presumption that certain metrical patterns should define each line or set of lines. Focusing primarily on metrical analysis, however, has occasionally led to an overenthusiastic tendency to emend lines that do not fit with the anticipated metre. Imposing rigid grammatical and formal standards may rob the poetry of its force. Oral discourse is especially prone to grammatical infelicities. Their presence may be an argument for authenticity of the spoken oracle; we rarely speak without grammatical and syntactical lapses. Linguistic turbulence is part of the message. Later literary composition preserves these features (Andersen 1995: 147–148).

That does not mean syllables and stresses are unimportant, but they are part of a significantly richer understanding of poetry. The lament (***qînâ***) form, for example, generally is characterized by three stresses in the first line, followed by two in the second. Garr (1983: 59) observes that the *qînâ* metre is enhanced by syntactic features that create a 'sobbing effect'. After addressing the complexities of syntactic, semantic/lexical and phonological features, Alter (2019: 94–95) affirms the rhythmic qualities of Hebr. poetry. Most lines have two halves that he labels 'versets'; some have three parts. Versets commonly have three accented syllables. Commentaries from previous generations of scholarship characteristically start with notes on the nature of the **cola**, **bicola**, **stiches** and **stanzas**. Given that the analytical terminology is less familiar to many readers, I will substitute the term 'line' for 'colon' and 'parallel lines' for 'bicolon'.

Equally important will be the distinction between 'clause' (an expression that has a verbal element) and 'phrase' (a verbless utterance). Verb forms in poetry have a 'timeless quality' and translating them woodenly does not work (Lessing 2007: 192). The language of poetry draws together particular historical contexts with an 'archetypal horizon' (Alter 1985: 146). I label the characteristic verb forms as qat., yiq., weqat. and wayyiq. to avoid having to choose between 'perfect', 'imperfect', 'conversive' and 'consecutive'.

The dominant feature of Hebr. poetry, parallelism, has been part of the analytical canon for more than two centuries. Following the distinctions proposed in the eighteenth century by Lowth, categories of parallel lines were labelled 'synonymous', 'antithetical' or 'synthetic' and were said to respond to the initial idea in different words, primarily for emphasis. Kugel (1981: 49–54) challenges the prevailing assessment of Hebr. poetry that tends to assign passages to one of the three categories based primarily on semantic considerations. He prefers to call the phenomenon 'seconding' rather than 'parallelism' because each second line supports, augments, counters and presses forward the implications of the first. He references the succinct summary by Hrushovski-Harshav (1971: 599): parallelisms in adjoining lines may be semantic, syntactic, morphological or phonological, or a combination; generally, they overlap with no one aspect dominating; and the dynamic combinations result in 'free rhythm', based on clusters of changing aspects. The phonological aspect includes such devices as **assonance**, **alliteration**, puns, chains of repeated sounds and root repetitions (**cognate accusatives**). An additional commonplace feature is the shift from second to third person when the poetry is addressing YHWH, either in speaking intimately with him or in describing his mighty acts of deliverance. While readers of standard Western literature find this last characteristic jarring, it ought not to be so. It may be analogous to communal prayer directed to the Lord that occasionally embeds sermonettes intended for the hearing gathered community.

Kugel claims that semantic parallelism is only vaguely present or even entirely absent from a significant amount of what we think of as poetry in the HB. Instead, lines of poetry are rich combinations, balancing and interweaving all the possible aspects. Terseness does not necessarily mean a text is poetic, a label imposed from Hellenistic literature. Instead, he argues for a continuum (1981: 85–87). For her part, Berlin (2008: chs. 3–5) challenges this radical dismissal of poetry as a recognizable genre, and instead sorts through the interweaving of grammatical (morphological and syntactical), lexical, semantic and phonological aspects along with the levels at which we encounter them. The first line takes on additional meaning in the light of the second, and it is necessary to circle back and revisit the first. That makes the process dynamic, especially as the parallelisms of all kinds set up comparisons; they are the 'stuff' of metaphor (Berlin 2008: 99–102). The result is an enriched understanding of how parallel lines both disambiguate and sustain ambiguous tensions. As just one example, Miller (2007: 41–60) focuses on verbal gapping between two parallel lines and the instances when those lines are coordinated with a waw (a single letter attached to the following word and serving as some form of conj.). It turns out that the waw is more frequent when there is verbal gapping, suggesting that its presence assists in processing how the two lines fit together structurally. It may be overreading its presence to presume that it serves to emphasize or intensify.

In sum, the array of poetic possibilities is rich. Robinson (1988: 83–97) encourages students of poetic texts to retain the poetic dynamism by keeping in balance the following factors: embedded reflections of the natural and historical worlds and cultural contexts; indicators of genre; and evidence of ironies that emerge against the backdrop of the canonical and theological world views. The closing admonition: do not be hasty to impose patterns or monolithic structures that make the prophetic utterance static. They may be there, but they are also likely to be interrupted; that is part of the message.

2.2. Elements of narrative

Biblical narratives, in contrast to ANE epics, employ prose characterized by relatively simple diction and vocabulary (Alter 2019: 53–55). Readers of biblical narratives encounter the power of repeated key words, reversals, **chiastic** patterns – both large and small – and surprising interruptions to those patterns. Repetitions at every level drive stories forward (Alter 1981: 92–94). The most basic – and important – of these repetitions is the succession of 'imperfect' (yiq.) forms to which the waw-conj. ('and') is attached (yielding wayyiq.). These are generally rendered as past tense. This narrative feature marks the steady progression towards whatever the end happens to be. In the case of Jonah 1, it evidences the terrifying rush of the characters coping with the storm. Reshaping translations with subordinating clauses or presumed causations loses the dynamic created by the simple sequential placement of the phrases or clauses. At the risk of the translation sounding overly repetitive, I will maintain that feature as much as possible.

Additional syntax features help readers know what is important. For example, starting a clause with the subject interrupts the steady progression of wayyiq. forms and calls attention to that subject. Alter (2019: 28–32) calls the latter 'syntactical fronting'. Further repetition in the form of **cognate accusatives** – verbal forms followed by a noun from the same root – likewise adds to the emphatic colouring of the narrative.

Dialogue features prominently in HB narrative; Alter suggests it subtly demonstrates humanity imaging God, for whom the creative and operative Word is vital (1981: 178–185). A character's first words are important, and the order of those words is likewise significant. A characteristic of Jonah is the repetition in dialogue of the phrases and sentences of the narrator.

Contrast portrays ambivalence, depth and conflict. Sometimes the last is evident between two characters, notably between YHWH and Jonah in Jon. 4. In other instances, characters themselves are a bundle of contrasting emotions and motives. The narrator may lead readers to expect one set of outcomes while the reality of the plot development heads in a different direction. The narrator also creates suspense and illusion by leaving gaps. Some of these are of major proportions, such as not telling readers at the outset what Jonah's affirmation reveals in 4:2. Other times, they are smaller, created with shifting or absent verb forms or other **ellipses**. These leave space for the imagination of readers and hearers of the text. 'Minimal representation can give maximum illusion' (Berlin 1983: 136–137).

2.3. The Book of the Twelve

There is ongoing discussion regarding the extent to which the arrangement of the individual texts within the BoT reflects intentionality. House (1990: 64–73) surveys the history of interpretation, notes the importance of literary and chronological considerations and adopts a theological rubric shaped by both covenant and cosmic themes. These themes appear in the BoT with sequential emphases on sin, punishment and restoration – in that order. Israel's culpability primarily characterizes Hosea through Micah, whereas the focus on punishment and restoration is muted in those texts. Because Hosea, Amos, Jonah and Micah are traditionally assigned to the eighth century based on the named ruling kings, their role was to call out the disobedient covenant people. The MT includes Joel and Obadiah with these four, even though they may fit better in the sixth century. That suggests additional criteria beyond a chronological framework for the arrangement in the MT.

With an interest in intentional connections among the individual books in the BoT, Nogalski pursues major themes that recur (2007: 125–136). He articulates particularly the day of YHWH, fertility of the land, the fate of YHWH's people and theodicy. These are, however, general categories. He brings more focus by noting the targets, time frames and means of judgment in specific texts. Schultz (2003: 27–33) pursues networks of quotations, allusions and catchwords linking individual books to those that precede or follow. Reuse of and dependence on Exod. 34:6–7, YHWH's self-revelation to Moses, are integral.

Major themes – such as day of YHWH and judgment – are sufficiently general to characterize most of the prophetic literature. Does their presence in the BoT warrant the conclusion that it is a **redacted** whole? There are no book introductions that make explicit connections with other BoT texts. The same is true of conclusions; they are by and large unique for each book. Ben Zvi (1996: 125–156) further questions the reliability of catchword analysis because lexical links also appear in books that are not proximate. In sum, collection is not the same as coherence. The threads that seem to be possible connectors are occasionally tangled or interrupted. Claiming that Jonah was added later to the BoT, Kaltner et al. note that its placement between Obadiah and Micah interrupts some catchwords (2020: 166).

While determining intentional shaping of the entire BoT corpus may prove to be elusive, there are thematic and lexical connections that are significant for the placement of these three – Obadiah, Jonah and Micah. Amos 9:12 closes that book with the reference to possessing the remnant of Edom. Not only is Edom the sole focus of Obadiah; the closure of that book states a series of reversals for Yhwh's people and among them a reference to those in the Negev possessing Mount Esau (Obad. 19). Edom receives special attention. It was not just another foreign nation; it should have been an ally for struggling Judah against the superpower, Babylon. While the position of the book does not make sense chronologically, it does thematically. Obad. 1–14 may be a commentary on Joel 4:19[3:19], and Obad. 15–21 on Amos 9:12 (Wolff 1986: 17).

In addition to content connections, the visionary aspect of Amos 7 – 9 may point ahead to the vision that commences Obadiah. Nogalski (2012: 89–107; followed by Sieges and Werse 2020: 151–163) suggests that this vision in Obadiah was intentionally altered from Jer. 49 to establish more continuity following Amos 9. Obadiah in its entirety has structural elements that echo Amos 9. Each has five *ʾim* clauses (starting with 'if'); compare Obad. 4–5 with Amos 9:2–4. 'From there I will bring you down' appears only in Jer. 49:16, Amos 9:2 and Obad. 4. Further parallels between the end of Amos and Obadiah are pronounced: Amos 9:11 and Obad. 15 both address 'the day'. There are restoration parallels in Amos 9:14–15 with the closing verses of Obadiah (vv. 19–21).

Shifting to Obadiah and Jonah, both deal with God's intentions towards the Gentile world but in very different ways. Jonah's audience – once he gets there – is a large, pagan and brutal foreign city in the superpower of the day.

Micah, reflecting the real horrors of Assyrian subjugation in the eighth century BC, follows Jonah's message of Yhwh's mercy to Assyrian Nineveh just a generation prior, and it precedes the subsequent development in Nahum. The three perspectives jostle against each other echoing a turbulent century in geopolitics. Kessler (2020: 176–185) observes that Micah occupies a central place in the BoT with the stark description of Zion's utter destruction (3:12) at the pivotal point. Before this, Samaria has a higher profile, both in the BoT and in Micah; Jerusalem is on the margins. The sins of the house of Israel are not articulated in Micah; they are expected to be known by reading Hosea and Amos. The references to 'images' and prostitution in Micah depend on Hosea to understand the judgment at a more profound level.

Biddle (2007: 154–166) explores the dynamic 'debate' among the prophetic voices. Competing ideologies seem to be held in tension regarding the nations and Jerusalem. From the geopolitical perspective, some come to attack while others come in pilgrimage; Mic. 4 is a microcosm. Through another interpretive lens, Jonah is a key in dealing with YHWH's mercy offered outside the covenant community. Jonah is also a step into new prophetic territory as it wrestles with matters of fulfilment and contingency. Authentic prophecy is not necessarily tied to accurate prediction of actual events. 'Instead, its authenticity depends upon whether it correctly outlines a contingency that is appropriate to current realities' (Biddle 2007: 165). If a nation continues its evil path, the consequences are judgment. The prophetic statement is God's 'position' vis-à-vis the circumstance. The editors of the BoT selected a range of materials that serve the future with a whole range of contingencies.

In the HB (MT), Micah is sixth; the LXX has it third after Hosea and Amos. It seems that the compilers of the LXX rearranged the MT order to reflect their perception of the chronological 'order'; they did that with other parts of the HB canon as well, notably repositioning Ruth after Judges, and Chronicles and Ezra–Nehemiah into their 'historical contexts' after Kings. In the LXX, Joel, Obadiah and Jonah follow in the same order as they are in the MT. The oldest fragmentary MS from Qumran (4QXIIa, dating to the mid-second century BC) has Jonah at the end after Malachi (Fuller 1997a: 221–222). Placement of individual prophetic texts in the BoT was apparently still fluid, however, for that community; in the fragments of 4QXIIf (50 BC) Jonah may precede Micah (Fuller 1997a: 268).

3. BIBLICAL THEOLOGY SERVING THE CHURCH

Jesus taught his followers to pray 'Thy kingdom come' (Matt. 6:10). YHWH as King is the centrepiece of both narratives and poetry in the HB. That royal imagery is inseparable from YHWH as Shepherd. He is the enthroned Shepherd who goes before his people (Mic. 2:13). He both scatters and gathers them (Mic. 4:6–8). He threatens their enemies and enables his often fickle and wayward people to pummel the forces gathered against them. Not limited to the land or the people of his inheritance, he draws peoples from afar to his footstool, Mount Zion (Mic. 4:1–4).

The nations are not monolithic. There is a motley crew of sailors (Jon. 1), a population of wicked and, at the same time, clueless Ninevites (Jon. 3), nations who presumed to gather and revile YHWH's people (Mic. 4), and Edomites who carry a long grudge (Obadiah). Those

Edomites lived with an arrogant but false sense of security, thinking they could hide out of YHWH's reach. We may learn from YHWH's message to them: even though we create all sorts of ways of 'hiding' from the Lord, it's just not an option. Their hideouts may be paralleled with the best defensive weapons or top of the line house security systems.

Obadiah closes with the timeless declaration 'the kingdom is YHWH's' (v. 21). This King is *our* King, equally mystifying in his grim warnings and boundless grace. YHWH is not blind to the abuses heaped on his people whether individuals or the whole nation. Justice will be done. There is always the promise of restoration after judgment, even when it is as overwhelming as the day of YHWH.

4. TEXT AND NOTES

The commentary is based on the Hebr. text represented in the *BHQ*. See Gelston 2010: 5–9 for complete descriptions of the textual witnesses. The MT of the Leningrad (St Petersburg) Codex is foundational; differences that appear in the Aleppo and Cairo codices are in the apparatus. The text of the Murabba'at fragment (Mur) is close to that of the MT.

The 'Notes' section for each unit provides the foundation for translation decisions, including parsing, definitions and explanations from standard Hebr. dictionaries and grammars. When they elucidate a challenging passage, readings from early versions are indicated. 'Form and structure' observations have primarily to do with features that characterize the prose and poetic forms and contribute to the force of the message. As noted above, I have not focused on technical metrical analyses of the poetry. The 'Comment' sections address matters of canonical and historical concern that illuminate each passage. 'Explanations' tease some of these latter out more, turning finally to ways the truths touch the lives of God's people, both in the past and continuing into the present.

OBADIAH

INTRODUCTION

1. TITLE, AUTHOR AND AUDIENCE(S)

The title of this book, 'a vision of Obadiah', is as succinct as its contents. Obadiah means 'servant of YHWH'. While it could be both a personal name and a description – similar to Malachi ('my messenger') – the frequency with which Obadiah appears in the pages of the OT suggests that it refers to a named individual (Wolff 1986: 44; Renkema 2003: 109). The question is, which one? There are twelve additional Obadiahs; most of them simply make cameo appearances, notably in the genealogies at the outset of 1 Chronicles. Only one, the faithful servant in the house of Ahab (1 Kgs 18:1–16), appears fleshed out in a narrative.

The 'vision' of Obadiah and the spoken word of YHWH interface with the words of a messenger. This combination is a microcosm of the complexity of divine authoritative revelation as it is conveyed to and through human consciousness and memory. The richness increases exponentially once the message that was originally seen and heard is preserved both orally and in written form. See further discussion: '5.3 Oral discourse / written intertextuality'.

Edom is the stated object of and presumed audience for this authoritative word (v. 1). The subsequent direct address (vv. 2–5) is likely a rhetorical device, designed to indicate that YHWH has taken particular notice of Edom's egregious treatment of Judah, and will effect justice on behalf of his people. Judah, greatly in need of assurance, is clearly a significant intended audience, especially because the final discourse unit addresses additional geopolitical entities in relationship to Judah and Jerusalem in the 'day of YHWH'.

2. GUIDING QUESTIONS

Our track forward will address the following questions.

1. How did the long-standing sibling relationship that is foundational to this prophetic discourse develop through the centuries between the events recorded in Genesis and the period of the divided monarchy?
2. What does an understanding of basic geography contribute to the interpretation of these historical narratives as they underlie the prophetic voice?
3. What marks both continuity and discontinuity between recognizable sections of the book?
4. When might the prophetic discourse(s) have been shaped into literary unit(s)?
5. What are the most prominent theological issues? What should audiences expect in terms of fulfilment? Are aspects of the prophecy eschatological in some sense?

3. HISTORY OF A TROUBLED RELATIONSHIP

3.1. Jacob and Esau

When Rebekah's unborn twins were restless in her womb, Yhwh responded to her enquiry with a far-reaching prophecy. The offspring of these children would become two people groups, one stronger than the other. The descendants of the older child would serve the younger (Gen. 25:22–23). From the start, the brothers themselves entered the realm of tension and hostility, culminating with Rebekah's coaching Jacob in the deception to obtain Isaac's blessing (Gen. 27). That blessing included the declaration 'be mighty over your brothers, and may the sons of your mother bow down to you' (27:29; see also v. 37). Subsequently, Isaac's words to Esau set the trajectory for the ongoing relationship: 'by your sword you will live, and your brother you will serve; when you become restless, you will break his yoke from your neck' (27:40).

3.2. Israel/Judah and Edom

Fast-forward some four hundred years. After the extended wilderness sojourn, Moses sent messengers from Kadesh, requesting permission to cross through the territory of Edom (Num. 20:16–17). Edom refused and threatened Israel (20:18), following up with a show of force (20:20). The Israelites turned away (20:21) and journeyed around Edom and Mount

Seir (21:4; Deut. 2:1). As they made their way through Transjordan, the foreign prophet Balaam was summoned to curse Israel. Instead, he spoke of the star and sceptre from Jacob and Israel who would crush the heads of Moab and conquer Edom (Num. 24:17–19).

The troubled history continued. Saul's foes included Edom (1 Sam. 14:47). David subdued Edom and the Edomites (1 Chr. 18:11–13). The growing opposition to Solomon festered after an earlier hostile encounter. David's general, Joab, had trounced Edom, staying there for six months and killing all the Edomite men. Hadad, from Edom's royal line, escaped to Egypt along with some Edomite officials. There he bided his time until the deaths of David and Joab (1 Kgs 11:14–22).

Geopolitical realities shifted with breathtaking speed, and Edom was often tangled in them. Most germane to the investigation of possible historical contexts for Obadiah was Jehoram's attempt to subdue an Edomite uprising. He failed when they surrounded him; their rebellion lasted 'until this day' (2 Kgs 8:20–22; 2 Chr. 21:8–10). Ahaz of Judah faced continued aggression from Edom among others (2 Chr. 28:16–18).

The biblical narrative sources regarding Edom's hostility are silent after this point as they primarily focus on the onslaught of the Assyrians, followed by that of the Babylonians. While the historical books do not accuse Edom of participating in the sack of Jerusalem and the temple by the Babylonians in the sixth century, there are allusions, especially in Ezekiel, to Edom's involvement.

3.3. Edom in the Prophets and Psalms

Edom is mentioned in the latter prophets more often than either of its counterparts Moab and Ammon (see Raabe 1996: 33–45). In the eighth century BC, Amos inveighed against Edom, both for their participation in what sounds like a well-oiled slave trade (Amos 1:6, 9) and for violent aggression against 'his brother' (Amos 1:11). Amos 9:12 looks ahead to the restoration of the house of David who will possess the remnant of Edom; the book of Obadiah follows logically. In Isaiah's extended pronouncement of eschatological and cosmic judgment, all the nations are in the crosshairs (34:2–3), but Edom is high profile (34:5–13). That judgment motif reappears in Isaiah 63:1, 'Who is this that comes from Edom . . . from Bozrah?'

As Judah spiralled down in the late seventh century, the prophetic rhetoric ratcheted up. Jeremiah castigated Edom among the surrounding nations (9:24–25[25–26]; 25:15–28). When God commanded Jeremiah to don a yoke, the symbolic action was not solely for Judah's consumption: he was to convey the message to the kings of Edom, Moab, Ammon, Tyre and Sidon that they would be subjugated to Nebuchadnezzar (27:1–15). A possible subtext here is that these small political entities attempted to form an alliance against the juggernaut of Babylon. This same combination of small ethnicities hostile to Israel appears in Ps. 83:5–9[4–8], a psalm of Asaph. As Judah and Jerusalem neared their end, their enemies chased and ambushed them. Edom, mentioned twice, was exultant, but their time was coming. The cup would be passed to them as well (Lam. 4:18–22). After the destruction and the appointment of Gedaliah as governor, Jews who had fled to surrounding countries returned. Among them were some from Edom (Jer. 40:11).

Ezekiel's oracles are equally damning. Edom and the Philistines acted with vengeance against Judah and Jerusalem (25:12–17). Mount Seir would be destroyed because it nursed the ancient hostility – clearly referencing the brothers' animosity – and delivered the Israelites over to the sword at the time of the latters' disaster. Making a play on the words for 'blood' and 'bloodshed' (*dām*), 'their calamity' (*ʾêdām*) and Edom (*ʾĕdôm*), YHWH swore it would be utterly destroyed and promised a measure-for-measure response to Edom's glee at the devastation and potential possession of God's land; as it had done, so the nations would rejoice at its destruction (Ezek. 35:1 – 36:7). A microcosm of Edom's hostility is distilled in Ps. 137:7 – 'Remember, YHWH, against Edom the day of Jerusalem; how they said, "Lay bare, lay bare, down to her foundations!"' See also Joel 4:19[3:19]. This sober tone continues well into the post-exilic life of the people; in the middle of the fifth century BC, Malachi indicates Edom has been devastated, and they are a people against whom YHWH's fury will rage for ever (Mal. 1:2–5).

The apocryphal text *4 Ezra* (1 Esdras) claims that the Edomites burned the temple when the Babylonians were attacking (4:45). There is no evidence for this in the biblical historical narratives in Kings or Chronicles. Because the authorship responsible for *4 Ezra* was living long after the Babylonians were off the scene, they might have substituted the current threat (Idumeans) into the narrative about burning the temple, echoing into their own tragedy of the destruction of the temple. By that time, the Idumeans, the Hellenized form of 'Edomites', had long since migrated westwards across the Aravah, into the Negev, and were established in the Shephelah between Judea and Philistia. First Maccabees 4:15 called the region around Marisa 'the plains of Idumea', and as Josephus describes the subjugation of Idumea by Hyrcanus, he mentions the cities of Marissa and Dora (*Ant.* 13.9.1). An Idumean named Herod was beholden to Rome for his position as puppet king of Judea.

While this cumulative picture seems unequivocally to point to a grim reality behind Obadiah's prophecy, Bartlett (1982: 13–24) suggests that the hostility has been overstated: the declarations in Ezek. 35 and Ps. 137:7 should be read as stock phrases. This points to several macro-level hermeneutical issues. First, while the Genesis narratives seem to underlie the ongoing tensions in the relationship between the two small nations, some sound a cautionary note against allowing those narrative details to affect unduly the interpretation of the prophetic oracles lest the methodology suffer from circularity (Renkema 2003: 116). Further, is the special focus on Esau and Edom in Obadiah a call for justice in the face of kinship betrayal, does Edom more broadly epitomize all of Israel's enemies, or is it a combination of the two (Raabe 1996: 40–44)?

4. GEOPOLITICAL EDOM

Geopolitical Edom was south-east of the Sea of Salt (Dead Sea), between Wadi Ḥesa (biblical Zered) at the south-east end of the Sea of Salt and the northern tip of the Gulf of Aqaba. The relatively narrow western highlands where elevations exceed 5,000 feet (1,524 m) stretch from the Wadi Ḥesa to the east–west divide at Wadi Feinan (preserving the biblical name Punon), called the Punon embayment. Edom proper was only about 12 miles (19 km) wide with one line of north–south settlements along the mountain spine. Sela, the capital, was near Bozrah, north of the Punon embayment, and Petra (Rekem) was south. Teman is likely a regional name instead of a city and refers to the region north of the embayment. See Baly 1974: 233–240 and Rainey and Notley 2006: 41.

The modern concept of fixed national boundaries does an injustice to ancient geopolitical contexts, notable here in the case of southern Transjordan and the Negev in the second and first millennia BC. The term *gĕbûl* refers to the border around a region as well as the region itself. Edom frequently extended its control westwards across the Aravah into the Negev, thus enlarging the region thought of as 'Edom'. Based on archaeological data, that expansion is clear in terms of seventh and sixth centuries BC (Bartlett 1989: 141–143). Nevertheless, the process might have begun already in the second millennium BC; it is evident in Moses' appeal to the king of Edom, made from Kadesh, that the Israelites were on the 'edge of your territory' (*qĕṣēʾ gĕbûlekā*). See Rasmussen 2010: 107. The degree to which the Pentateuchal accounts (in this case Num. 20:14–21 and Deut. 2:1–8) reflect the facts on the ground in the second millennium BC is debated. Bartlett (1989: 90–93, 140–141) thinks these passages indicate instead the situation in the late monarchy. Nevertheless, there is evidence that eighteenth- and nineteenth-dynasty pharaohs, Thutmose III and Ramses II, made military forays into and through the Negev in the second millennium BC. The latter got as far as Dibon in Moab (Rainey and Notley 2006: 68, 98). The route across the Negev, called later the King's Highway (Num. 20), was a plum that the inhabitants of geopolitical Edom would secure for their own gain. It controlled, among other advantages, the lucrative spice trade.

Edom's cultural penetration and occasional military aggression westwards increased during the Iron Age (Israelite Period), evidenced by a considerable amount of Edomite pottery in the Negev from the late Iron

Age (Bartlett 1982: 15). Several of the ostraca discovered in the Iron Age Israelite fortress at Arad shed additional light on Judah's defensive posture to Edomite presence. Located in the eastern basin of the biblical Negev, Arad was strategically positioned to guard the south-eastern approaches into the Judean highlands and eventually to Jerusalem. One of the key ostraca from the Eliashiv archive (no. 24) obliquely references a threat to the city of Ramath-Negev (ll. 5–6) and the fear that Edom may come (l. 9). Aharoni (1970: 16–42; 1981: 5, 46–47) interpreted this as anticipation of an Edomite attack. Ramath-Negev was a fortress, identified as Horvat Uzza, just about 6 miles (9 km) south/south-east of Arad and positioned at the head of a wadi that would have been a principal route to and from Edom. Na'aman (2011: 83–93) reassessed several of the pertinent ostraca and suggested that the collapse of the Negev fortresses was gradual: growing tensions between Judah and Edom led to Edomite attacks even before Jerusalem fell. Judah's attempts to defend the south-eastern front failed.

The wider geopolitical context of Obad. 19–20 includes the Negev, along with the Shephelah between the Philistine plain and the Judean hills. In the wake of Nebuchadnezzar's destruction and deportations, Edomite presence was even more pronounced in the Negev and southern Shephelah regions. Jer. 13:18–19 may be an allusion to Edom's incursion into the Negev after the exiles departed Judah. Josephus (*Ant.* 10.9.7) records a campaign of Nebuchadnezzar against Ammon and Moab in 582 BC, but Edom is not mentioned. That may be because they submitted to Babylon, which then gave them freedom to expand across the Aravah (McCarter 1976: 89). Geopolitical Edom experienced its own cultural shifts; in 553 BC, Nabonidus was responsible for aggression against Edom (Goldingay 2021: 352). Archaeological evidence is meagre, but suggests that major cities, including Bozrah, were destroyed prior to the Persian period, making way for the Nabatean takeover in 312 BC (Bartlett 1989: 157–159; Block 2013: 27). McCarter (1976: 89) suggests that the place of foreigners 'where there is no understanding' (v. 7) could allude to Arabian tribes coming in, paving the way for the later Nabatean arrival in 312 BC. That assessment places the book significantly later, in the post-exilic period.

5. LITERARY AND RHETORICAL CONSIDERATIONS

5.1. Structure and unity of the text

Three sections follow the introductory verse. YHWH first pronounces the sentence against Esau (vv. 2–10), including criticism of Edomite pride (vv. 2–7) and threats of cutting off (vv. 8–10). The second section centres on the condemnation of Esau's complicity and participation in the violence against the house of Jacob (vv. 11–14). Having the sentence precede the condemnation is unusual, but these details of Edom's culpability connect with the third section, the anticipated judgment and subsequent restoration on the day of YHWH (vv. 15–21).

Networks of conceptual and lexical connections contribute to the overarching coherence of the text. Each section is joined with the next by catchwords that serve to bridge between the shifting topics. Ben Zvi (1996) uses the terms 'terrace pattern' and 'cross references' to indicate these rhetorical repetitions of key words from the preceding section as a new one gets underway. As an example, v. 10 serves as a hinge, continuing the thought from the end of v. 9 and pressing forward the previous beginning emphasis on 'day'. The same is true of v. 15, which shifts to the day of YHWH for the nations but circles back to Edom's crimes, all under the umbrella of the ***lex talionis***.

5.2. Prophetic rhetoric

Obadiah's rhetoric is marked by vivid descriptions, 'interruptions', accusations thinly veiled as admonitions, the centrepiece reversal in vv. 15–16, and a series of hopeful future scenarios. Block (2013: 36–37) suggests this text lands somewhere on the continuum between poetry and prose. Grammatical, lexical, semantic and phonological parallelisms weave through the verses. At the same time, the repeated drumbeat of 'day', 'disaster' and 'do not . . .' in vv. 12–14 drives the rhetoric steadily forward. Voices merge, and it is not always clear which voice is speaking. **Ellipses** are quite frequent, creating tensions and ambiguities.

The imagery captures a vivid sense of the place where the Edomites live, surrounded by seemingly impregnable rocks, with watching birds nesting high up and the cutting of clusters of the grape harvest. It also captures their fears – theft, loss of security, betrayal (vv. 3–5). Additional poetic characteristics surface in the ambiguity of verb tenses and implied tenses (vv. 2, 13–14), the occasional absence of explicit verbs (vv. 19–20), and embedded ironies. An example of the last will suffice for now: YHWH brings down the arrogant from presumably inaccessible heights (vv. 3–4).

5.3. Oral discourse / written intertextuality

Questions of authorship, audience and date are complicated by the interface between the initial oral discourse and the text that is preserved. The text is sparse in details, allowing it to fit a range of contexts; most commentators faithfully summarize the attempts to do so. Ben Zvi (1996: 113–114) sidesteps the complexity of dating the spoken oracles, making the case that the primary audience(s) were highly literate and competent readers. He styles them readers and 're-readers'. He emphasizes attention not so much to the *Sitz im Leben* (life setting) for a given text but to the *Sitz im Buch* (literary context). Generations of (re)readers would know the canonical traditions of Israel. They would be aware of subsequent fulfilments of the prophetic words and would appreciate the artistry as the authorship wove together layers of literary features – allusions, sounds and double meanings. Because of the cultural significance of the written word, they would be especially attuned to discourse elements that engaged and re-engaged that word. Every feature that contributes to ambiguity is especially noteworthy, including placement of words, multiple meanings of prepositions, additional multiple meanings of words and grammar, and the wealth of canonical connections.

Regarding the last, it is not surprising that much of Obadiah echoes authoritative texts (Biddle 2007: 161; Block 2013: 37–41). Covenant stipulations and sanctions define the prophetic messages, notably when the focus on foreigners has consequences for YHWH's own people as is the case for Obadiah's message (Lev. 26:31–45; Deut. 32:7–9, 35–43). Furthermore, words of Ezekiel, Jeremiah, and Isaiah merge in Obadiah's repertoire. Front and centre is the extensive correspondence between Obadiah and Jer. 49. That is one factor in the discussion of dating the composition of the text.

5.4. Obadiah and Jeremiah 49

In the comparison that follows, I have translated the Hebr. as literally as possible – in spite of the woodenness – in order to indicate the divergences. The section of Jeremiah is in a wider context of oracles against other nations including Philistia, Moab, Ammon and Syria. It starts by pointing to Edom, indicating it is bereft of wisdom and understanding (49:7b). That is followed by a warning to flee and hide in caves because disaster and the time of visitation are coming to Mount Esau (49:8). Then we have the troops of thieves and grape gatherers (49:9) and the taunt that the hidden things will be uncovered (49:10). The general theme of drinking the cup appears briefly in conjunction with the destruction of Bozrah and all her towns (49:12–13). It is only then that Jeremiah and the messenger announce the call to arms against Edom. Segments are reordered.

> [1]The vision of Obadiah:
> Thus says Adonai YHWH concerning/to Edom.
> Jer. 49:7a – concerning/to Edom, thus says YHWH of Hosts:
> An announcement we have heard from YHWH; a messenger has been sent [*šullāḥ*] among the nations. 'Rise up!' 'Let us rise up against her for battle.'

Jer. 49:14 – An announcement I have heard from YHWH; and
a messenger has been sent [*šālûaḥ*] among the nations.
'Gather together and come against her and rise up for battle!'
2Behold! I have made you small among the nations; you are
greatly despised.
Jer. 49:15 – For behold; I have made you small among the
nations, despised among humankind [*'ādām*].
3The arrogance of your heart has deceived you;
Jer. 49:16a – Your horror [a **hapax**] has deceived you – the
arrogance of your heart;
the one who settles in the clefts of the rock,
Jer. 49:16b – the one who settles in the clefts of the rock,
the height of his habitation;
Jer. 49:16c – the one who grasps the high hill.
the one who says in his heart, 'Who will bring me down to earth?'
4If [*'îm*] you build high like the vulture; if among the stars your
nest is placed, from there I will bring you down – an utterance of
YHWH.
Jer. 49:16d – though [*kî*] you lift up your nest like the vulture,
from there I will bring you down – an utterance of YHWH.
5If thieves came to you; if the destroyers at night – how you
have been cut off! – would they not steal only enough for them?
Jer. 49:9b – if thieves at night, they would destroy only enough
for them;
If gatherers came to you, would they not leave gleanings?
Jer. 49:9a – If gatherers came to you, they would not leave
gleanings.
6How Esau is ransacked! His hidden treasures [**hapax**] are
exposed [*nib'û*].
Jer. 49:10a For I have stripped Esau naked; I have uncovered his
secrets [*mistārāyw*].

Obad. 7d–9 addresses the perishing of wise men from Edom, understanding from Mount Esau and mighty men from Teman. These images are conflated earlier in Jeremiah's discourse unit (Jer. 49:7b). The fluid arrangement seems to point to a vibrant oral tradition that was woven into each prophet's declarations. Ben Zvi's conclusion (1996: 50–85, 99–114), albeit tentative, is that neither Obadiah nor Jeremiah depended on the other work, but that they both were thoroughly schooled in the traditions and source materials underlying both. Wolff likewise concludes that both texts derived from a previous proclaimed text: the insertion of rhetorical questions indicates 'the character of living speech' (Wolff 1986: 40). Nevertheless, some scholars do give priority to Jeremiah, suggesting that Obadiah refined the message for the singular opponent of Edom (Renkema 2003: 118; Block 2013: 58).

5.5. Fulfilment and prophetic discourse

Prior to returning to the complex issues surrounding the possible historical circumstances shaping the prophecy, one additional matter warrants some consideration. The very nature of prophecy implies fulfilment at some future point; this established the authenticity of the prophet (Deut. 18:21–22). See Block 2013: 110–111 regarding the authority and authenticity of Yhwh's true prophet.

The question may be addressed from several angles. There is first the matter of time and timelessness in conjunction with God's revelation. Prophets were called to speak into particular historical circumstances, but their words – mediating God's eternal Word – transcend time in ways that we recognize. The invasive plague of locusts in Joel provides a telling example; at some point a devastating onslaught of locusts morphs into the invasion of enemy armed forces and then remorphs to a cataclysmic and eschatological 'day'. Even when we determine to the best of our ability the original setting, those words are intended to be read and reread.

A second perspective involves the grammar and syntactical features of the prophetic discourse. Verbs are central to this pursuit as they are lodged in some kind of time frame. One illustration of this is the so-called prophetic perfect. Recognizing that it points towards a time future to the prophet, it should be rendered as future; in Yhwh's timetable that future event is already a done deal. Nevertheless, the punctiliar nature needs to be acknowledged. We see an example in the ambiguity of Obad. 2. Is that form indicative of Yhwh's already having diminished Edom, or is it pointing to a definitive, but still future, humiliation? See 'Comment'.

There are equal complexities with the *ʾal* plus juss. forms in vv. 12–14. In theory, they anticipate a situation where Edom *may* do such things and needs to be warned not to. In actuality, these powerfully portray the abominable attitudes and actions that have already manifested themselves.

Finally, the three verses that close Obadiah cast a longer view, seemingly well beyond the points of Edom's hostilities against Judah and its own judgment within several centuries. Taken as a whole, the book both rests within a given historical context and stands outside that context, pointing to the fate of all enemies of God's people.

6. POSSIBLE HISTORICAL CONTEXTS

An overarching matter for consideration is the changing relationship between Edom/Esau, Yhwh and Judah/Jacob. The first oracle condemns Edomite pride; the second depicts their hostile actions against a beleaguered Judah; the third shifts to national hopes for restoration.

With these factors on the table, the proposals for dating Obadiah's prophecy, or at least parts of it, may be summarized as follows:

1. During the reign of Jehoram in the second half of the ninth century BC, Edom rebelled and there were renewed and continuing hostilities (2 Kgs 8:20–22; 2 Chr. 21:8–10, 16–17).
2. In the wake of the Syro-Ephraimite war during the reign of Ahaz (2 Chr. 28:16–21), Edom attacked and carried off prisoners.
3. Obadiah was in a position to witness the fall of Jerusalem (587 BC), and the destruction and resultant demoralization of the population was fresh in his mind as he prophesied during the early exile.

By the middle of the fifth century, Edom had already experienced the judgment; through these interpretive lenses, the book is ***vaticinium ex eventu***. A number of scholars posit that the text reached its final form in the post-exilic period. This presumes that the text was not originally a single unit.

While the third option is widely held and is the one that underlies the commentary in the following pages, there are advocates for a pre-exilic context. In brief, that case rests on the following observations. First, the placement of Obadiah in the MT between Amos and Jonah, both of whom are traditionally eighth-century prophets, suggests that he was viewed as representative of that general time frame as well. Second, the language of Obadiah lacks the depth of emotion that reverberates through Jeremiah, who lived through the trauma of the destruction. Jeremiah is then thought to have depended on Obadiah's already inscribed prophecy. Third, the negative commands of vv. 12–14 make sense if the possibilities are still in the future; this would not be the case after the fall of Jerusalem. See Niehaus 1993: 499–502 for a presentation of this position. The third argument seems to miss the rhetorical significance of that repeated syntactical form.

The case for dating Obadiah shortly after the horror of the destruction of 587 BC does have several wrinkles. Obadiah does not specifically note Babylon's attack on Jerusalem or its destruction of the temple, and there is no evidence of Edom's destruction at that time. Further, the final verses indicate a future land-oriented restoration. This last matter raises the issue of multiple time periods represented in the text. If the catastrophe of 587 signals the primary time frame, the canonical form may represent a two-staged composition, the first part pre-exilic and the second, developed in exile and revisiting the judgment themes. This suggestion presumes that Obadiah witnessed the devastation and deportation. Reflecting that context, he might have been among those of the poorer classes left in the land (2 Kgs 25:12; Jer. 40:7). The practice of removing the upper strata of society had begun already with the exile of Jehoiachin in 597 BC (2 Kgs 24:14).

Assis (2014: 209–221) observes the first segment is relatively benign in terms of relations between the two ethnic entities and therefore may reflect pre-587. In contrast, the second reverberates with the visceral pain of

Jerusalem at the hands of her attackers in 587, among whom Edom was complicit. The expressions are sufficiently raw that it could easily be dated just after the fall of Judah. The third segment may be significantly later, especially as it reflects a time when neighbours of Judah had encroached into the margins of Judahite territory. In addition, the prospect of return from a range of diaspora locations may seem like a possibility once the community was re-established in Judah. These suggestions make good sense on the surface. The next question is when they came together and what that compiled text continued to reflect to and for its readers. However the redaction process might have unfolded, the final text demonstrates literary coherence (Werse 2013: 115). In response to the complexity of these challenges, Hassler (2016: 241–254) proposes that the entire book may be read through eschatological lenses, indicating that 'in that day' binds it together.

Ben Zvi (1996: 38–39, 249) suggests a different 'role' for Obadiah. To wit, the readership would have had in their minds the Obadiah who was well known as the official in Ahab's court. (This was the interpretive position in Jewish tradition; see *b.* Sanh. 39b.) This does not mean the text was written at that point, but that 'Obadiah' is a literary/theological figure who had prophetic visions spanning three centuries. Whenever it was composed – likely in the Achaemenid period in Ben Zvi's formulation – the readers who were steeped in the narratives of Israel's history would read Obadiah's message through a long-distance lens that draws attention to the importance of Zion and Zion theology, the tragedy of the destruction of the temple and the abused kinship relationship between Jacob and Esau. This allows Ben Zvi to avoid making connections to specific historical contexts for any parts of the text, a particularly challenging matter when it comes to a presumed time frame for vv. 12–14 as well as the 'day of Yhwh'.

In the wider company of scholars who presume Obadiah's words reflect in some way the crisis of 587, Wolff's position bears special mention (1986: 18–20). The vivid language in vv. 11–14 not only reflects Obadiah's experience of those wrenching conditions, but Wolff suggests Obadiah was a cult prophet who, in the aftermath of destruction, was called to give the broken remaining congregation some semblance of hope. The whole text, however, is not one unit. Instead, the message developed through the citation of previously known sayings.

7. THEOLOGICAL CONNECTIONS

7.1. Placement in the canon

While the initial six texts in the BoT are not chronologically sequential, there are theological themes that bind them together. Amos 9:11–12 promises that the fallen tent of the house of David will possess the remnant of

Edom. Part of Yhwh's judgment on Edom is articulated in the final three verses of Obadiah: remnants of Israel will repossess territories that had been absorbed by Edom and others.

Obad. 15 picks up on the theme of the 'day of Yhwh' from Joel 1:15, 2:1–2, 11 and Amos 5:18–20, and interweaves it with the ***lex talionis*** as justice unfolds for the nations and for Edom.

Both Obadiah and Jonah address foreign threats to Yhwh's people. To be sure, those threats come from very different entities, the respective messages are couched in quite different genres, and both have radically unexpected outcomes. Edom was relatively insignificant in the ANE political scheme of things, but its judgment will be severe. Jonah expands the perceived range of Yhwh's kingship, the final declaration in Obadiah, to embrace the brutal and terrorizing might of Assyria.

7.2. Primary theological emphases

The kingdom of Yhwh is a defining theme through the whole of Israel's tradition. When Moses and the Israelites sing of Yhwh's complete triumph over the enemy forces of Pharaoh, each descriptive line moves towards the culmination of their jubilation: Yhwh will reign unto eternity and beyond (Exod. 15:18). Centuries later, Obadiah's message is a microcosm of that theme. Yhwh rules over the nations – all of them. That declaration is the foundation for everything else that is said in the book.

The way to the triumphant closing verse is, however, through the tumult of the day of Yhwh, at the centre of the book (vv. 15–16). On that day, enemies of Yhwh will drink the cup of his wrath. It will be a day of disaster and calamity, commensurate with the succession of calamitous days befalling Zion (vv. 12–14).

The day of Yhwh has its primary roots in Israel's prophetic tradition, expressed initially in the expectation that Israel's enemies will get their comeuppance (Isa. 2:12–21). It is a dynamic symbol, modulating and developing its significance through prophetic usage (Werse 2013: 109–124). There is also a wider cultural backdrop of portrayals of extraordinarily mighty kings winning an entire war in a single day (Stuart 1976: 159–164). In the eighth century BC, Amos shifts the attention of his audience. Yhwh's own disobedient and complacent people will face the prospect of judgment on that day (5:18–27). The sixth-century prophets continue to make it clear that the people of Judah need to sit up and take notice. They portray it in ominous tones. It will be a day of darkness, accompanied by symbolic cosmic disturbances (Joel 2:1–2, 11; Zeph. 1:14–18). These latter features are not evident in Obadiah; the day of Edom's recompense focuses on measure-for-measure justice.

The defining principle of Yhwh's justice is the ***lex talionis***: all judgment will be in appropriate measure according to the crime. All wrongs will be set right; the high and proud will be brought down and humiliated. ***Lex talionis*** is embedded in the wordplays in the book that juxtapose the identities of Esau and Jacob, Edom and Judah. The text is threaded through with the names of the brothers Esau and Jacob; the violation of those kinship bonds is reprehensible in the extreme. 'Small' and 'great' echo the context of their birth narrative, as do the images of high and low.

Shifting to national identities, Edom will be repaid for its evil deeds in measure. 'Cutting off' and drinking indicate both its evil deeds and the nature of the punishment. YHWH's chosen people, on the other hand, having had their turn at drinking the cup, will be restored (Anderson 2010: 247–255). The 'houses' of Esau and Jacob also interface with the significance of 'mount'. Mount Esau has trampled Mount Zion, which is not only central to Judah's identity but particularly the location of YHWH's house. In that regard, the land as inheritance is part of the 'house' and relationship picture as well.

Through the window of this small text, there is powerful symbolism in Edom as representative of enemies of YHWH. Its characteristic arrogance is likewise representative of the state of all humanity (Gen. 3); even the name Edom sounds like *ʾādām*. Edom's abuses of kinship also have long roots, stretching even before the brothers Esau and Jacob, all the way to the hostility manifested by Cain against Abel (Gen. 4).

The emphasis on apparently harsh retributive justice is a theme that does not always settle well with contemporary, twenty-first-century Western audiences. Nevertheless, it is vital that this message of justice not be dismissed. Just as there were devastating abuses against YHWH's people in sixth-century BC Jerusalem, so also there are 'modern-day Edoms' wreaking havoc in the lives of God's people where and when they are vulnerable. The prospect of assured judgment brings hope to broken people. Obadiah's message is double-edged: there will be judgment for those who choose to be enemies of God's people. God's people are soberly warned not to depart from the way of obedience lest they are given the cup of judgment first (Wolff 1986: 57).

That does, however, draw us back to the beginning and end of the matter – the kingdom is YHWH's. From the post-resurrection perspective, that points to the anointed King, Jesus Christ, the Lord of heaven and earth to whom every knee shall bow (Isa. 45:23–25; Phil. 2:9–11). In Jesus, God incarnate, all promises of and hopes for justice are completely fulfilled.

8. TEXTS

The MT represents three nearly complete tenth-century MSS – Cairo, Aleppo and Leningrad – named for the cities where they were kept for significant amounts of time. Obadiah, however, is missing from the Aleppo

Codex. Many earlier fragmentary texts come from the Dead Sea region. These include 4QXIIg from the Cave 4 library, dating to the last third of the first century BC (Fuller 1997a: 272). The condition of the MS is poor; it has portions of Obad. 1–5, 8–12, 14–15 (Fuller 1997a: 308–309). A second scroll (Mur) containing the Twelve and dating to the second century AD was found about 10 miles (16 km) south of Qumran in a cave in Wadi Murabbaʿat (DJD IIa: 67–69). Obadiah is nearly complete albeit somewhat damaged (DJD IIa: 189; IIb: Plate LIX). A cave just south in Naḥal Ḥever yielded a Greek MS (8ḤevXIIgr) but Obadiah is not represented (DJD VIII).

It may be that text issues underlie the difficulties in vv. 7 and 20 (Raabe 1996: 5–6). There are also textual challenges in the last section (vv. 19–21).

9. OUTLINE

Introduction (v. 1)
Condemnation of Edom's pride (vv. 2–4)
Thievery and betrayal (vv. 5–7)
Judgment of Edom's violence by cutting off (vv. 8–10)
Condemnation of Edom's sins 'on that day' (vv. 11–14)
The day of YHWH and the ***lex talionis*** (vv. 15–16)
Ascendancy of house of Jacob over house of Esau (vv. 17–18)
Restoration of possessions and kingdom of YHWH (vv. 19–21)

TEXT AND COMMENTARY

OBADIAH 1

Translation

[1]The vision of Obadiah:
Thus says Adonai YHWH concerning Edom.
An announcement we have heard from YHWH: that a messenger has been sent among the nations. 'Rise up!' 'Let us rise up against her for battle'.

Notes on the text

1. *ḥāzôn* conveys the sense of extraordinary 'seeing' (*DCH* 3:183), notably in contrast to the more widely used forms of *rʾh*, which imply both prophetic visionary experiences as well as normal sight (*DCH* 7:341–362).

The perf. *ʾāmar* ('he said') is the customary introduction to the word of YHWH: the word is firmly established. It is the characteristic messenger formula, also called a 'citation formula' (Block 2013: 50).

The prep. *lĕ-* in relation to Edom may be understood as 'about', 'concerning' or 'to' (*IBHS* §11.2.10). *šĕmûʿâ* ('announcement') is a pass. ptc. cognate acc. with the verb 'we have heard'. A woodenly literal rendition is, 'that which is heard we have heard'. The LXX has the sg., perhaps to match Jer. 49:14. The waw commencing the clause about the messenger could be a simple conj. 'and' (*IBHS* §39.2.1c), pointing to two separate actions. It seems best, however, to translate it as 'that', indicating that this is part of what Obadiah has heard (Renkema 2003: 118). The pu. (*šūllāḥ*) ('sent') intimates the actions of YHWH, who is behind the summons to the nations, arousing them against Edom.

The LXX and Vg read the equivalent of 'against him' (*ālāyw*) instead of 'against her' (*ālêhā*). Edom can be fem.; see Mal. 1:3–4, where both occur. *ʿālêhā* may be fem. for the sake of assonance, or because national entities may be represented as fem. (*IBHS* §6.4.1c). The pronouns shift to masc. sg. in v. 2.

Form and structure

The declarative fabric of this opening verse is rich; it is also ambiguous because it has more lines than are customary. Prior to the content of YHWH's words to or concerning Edom is some human recipients' perspective. 'We have heard' is a parenthetical insertion with two parallel introductions: the 'report from YHWH' and the 'messenger sent among the nations', perhaps to encourage *that* audience to 'rise up!', to which they respond with enthusiasm. From a macrostructural perspective, the nations initially clamour to join the surge against Edom, but both will be judged for the atrocities they committed against Mount Zion.

Generally, 'thus saith YHWH' is followed directly by the content of YHWH's declaration. Block (2013: 47) notes that Obadiah includes 'surprises' such as this misplaced clause that would more logically fit after the next two clauses.

Comment

1. *ḥāzôn* ('vision') is incorporated into the 'titles' of the books of Nahum, Isaiah and Obadiah. While YHWH and the heavenly realms are the objects of visions, the experience is also interwoven with verbal communication (Hab. 2:2a – 'write a vision and describe on the tablets'). Jeremiah accuses the false prophets of speaking a false vision (Jer. 14:14); they are speaking a vision from their hearts, not from YHWH (Jer. 23:16). There is no single English word that captures the nature of this experience that fuses the audible with the visual. Hebr. often associates a range of sensory experiences with eyes (Jepsen, *TDOT* 4:280–290). Here, Obadiah *sees* the future of Edom through a series of dramatic images.

Adonai YHWH is used 7 times in the book and 134 times in the OT; it emphasizes YHWH's authority (Block 2013: 51). It combines the title (my lord) and Name (YHWH) of the sovereign God.

Edom (see 'Introduction') is the subject of the report and call to arms; thus, the prep. may be translated 'concerning Edom'. There are additional instances in prophetic addresses where *lĕ-* indicates 'about' or 'concerning'; see Jer. 46:2; 48:1. At the same time, what follows in vv. 2–7 is rhetorically the direct address *to* Edom. See the similar expression in Jer. 49:7. That constitutes part of the 'report' as well, especially since Edom's relationship with Judah and the surrounding nations will be front and centre. Put another way, the audience (Judahites) is invited to listen to a message that is 'to Edom'. See Goldingay 2021: 354, n. 12. Both meanings are important; together they raise the question in readers' minds regarding how YHWH relates to Israel and Edom in the sphere of revelation (Ben Zvi 1996: 24–25). Front-loading the direct object, 'a report', puts emphasis on the announcement; this is urgent. The individual making that announcement is 'sent'. It is both vision and revealed word from YHWH.

Diverging from the parallel in Jer. 49:14, Obadiah uses 'we' instead of 'I' as the subject hearing the announcement. It is not clear who 'we' includes; Goldingay (2021: 358) summarizes the range of possibilities. Perhaps it reflects Obadiah's perception that he is part of a group of like-minded prophets for whom he serves as an authoritative spokesperson (Renkema 2003: 117; see also Wolff 1986: 45). This may indicate his allegiance to Israel (Jenson 2008: 12) or his identification with YHWH's purposes (Niehaus 1993: 513–514). Related to the last suggestion, it may represent Obadiah's self-perception as identifying with the divine council (Ben Zvi 1996: 40–41).

ṣîr is an unusual word for 'envoy' or 'messenger' and is used only in poetry (*DCH* 7:119). It appears in the parallel statement in Jer. 49:14. Its only other uses are regarding messengers (parallel to the more common *mal'ākîm*) sent across the sea (Isa. 18:2) and far off (Isa. 57:9), and the salutary benefits of sending faithful messengers (Prov. 13:17; 25:13). Considered in conjunction with the 'vision' component, Obadiah might have been privy to a vision into the heavenly realms that has some similarity to 1 Kgs 22:19–23. In that context, Micaiah saw YHWH on his throne deputizing one of the surrounding heavenly hosts to be a lying spirit in the mouths of Ahab's prophets because YHWH had decreed disaster for Ahab (Block 2013: 53). Possibly the 'messenger' refers to an earlier oracle – perhaps Jer. 49 or a previous underlying source – rather than a personage (Biddle 2007: 161–162).

The impv. (*qûmû*) ('rise up') and the following coh. (*wĕnāqûmâ*) ('and let us rise up') emphasize the intentionality of this declaration (GKC §108d; *IBHS* §34.5.1–2). It may be the envoy associates himself – and perhaps YHWH as well – with the call to arms against Edom (Ben Zvi 1996: 35–36; Raabe 1996: 116; Goldingay 2021: 359). On the other hand, that syntactical shift could point to a shift in speakers. Just one command ('rise up!') from the envoy may prod the nations to respond with a hearty 'Let's go!'

(Renkema 2003: 102; Block 2013: 49, 54). Grievances are pent up and burst out in response to the messenger's arrival to arouse the nations.

Explanation

šlḥ ('send') is a technical term for YHWH's commissioning prophets. This messenger is directly sent by YHWH, which removes the necessity of identifying a human role for him (Renkema 2003: 119). While the layers of 'messenger' and 'report' may seem thick to twenty-first-century readers, that was a time where literacy was rare. It is important to indicate both the messenger's role as a faithful carrier along with the sender (YHWH), especially because these will be difficult words to absorb (Baker 2006: 165). Prophets were not the political commentators of their day: their task was to transmit the words of YHWH (Renkema 2003: 111–112). Because the introduction declares that Edom will be punished, the obvious next question is 'Why?' That sets the stage for what is forthcoming.

When Amos hears the 'lion roar' and 'Adonai YHWH speak', his response is inevitable: 'who can help but prophesy?' (3:8). Obadiah sees and hears this summons from YHWH. Even though leonine imagery is not evoked, YHWH's sovereign purposes will be accomplished, no matter what nations are dominant at a given point in time. Isaiah will see and hear the powerful summons for the day of YHWH against Babylon, and it will cause tumult and disruption in every sphere (Isa. 13). Obadiah's announcement is intended to propel the nations to rise up against Edom. The one-word command to 'Rise up!' is a compression of Jeremiah's exhortation (49:14). Once the nations are summoned, they muster their corporate will to engage in war, possibly suggesting that the audience for Obadiah's words is ready to see Edom trounced (Renkema 2003: 120).

In Jeremiah, this oracle is one of many against foreign nations. Here Edom is the sole focus and Obadiah develops the discourse into an eschatological reversal. Edom is the foil against which Judah will be restored. While Jer. 49 develops the theme of Edom's pride as the basis for the coming punishment (v. 16), it does not expand on Edom's treatment of Judah as the basis. The ***lex talionis*** theme is not as pronounced in Jeremiah, who focuses more on drinking the cup (of wrath) that will come to all nations (cf. Jer. 25).

OBADIAH 2–4

Translation

2 In point of fact, least I have made you among the nations; you are greatly despised.

[3]The arrogance of your heart has deceived you, the one who settles in the clefts of the rock, the height of his habitation; the one who says in his heart, 'Who will bring me down to earth?'

[4]If you build high like the vulture; if among the stars your nest is placed, from there I will bring you down – an utterance of YHWH.

Notes on the text

2. *hinnēh* ('behold'; rendered above 'in point of fact') indicates the need to pay immediate attention to the next words: they are the words of YHWH. *hinnēh* connects what is coming with the 'visionary' aspect that commenced the message (see BDB 243–244). Miller-Naudé explores the nuances of *hinnēh* as a pointer to a development or object that is noteworthy and perhaps unexpected (Miller-Naudé and Merwe 2011: 53–81).

qāṭôn is a standard way of expressing the superlative and may be translated 'least' or 'smallest' among the nations (Jenson 2008: 13). The qat. verb form (*nĕtatîkā*) could also be rendered as an assured future – 'I will make you least among the nations' – representing a complete and independent future state (*IBHS* §30.5.1e). Both the Tg and LXX translate the verb as an already established state.

'I have made you': the object 'you' is masc. sg. as is the following pron., 'you'. This contrasts with the fem. pron. suff. with *ʿal* in the MT of v. 1.

3. On the form of *šōkĕnî* ('the one who settles'), see GKC §90lm. The ḥireq-yod represents an archaic const. relationship, called the ḥireq compaginis. There are other instances in the HB where a prep. (here it is *bĕ-*) comes between two nouns in the const. relationship (Niehaus 1993: 517). The prep. 'in' controls both 'clefts of the rock' and 'height of his habitation' (GKC §119hh). Sela is a place name, representing the capital of ancient Edom. It also describes the predominant geographical context. The shift from the voc. (*šōknî*) to 3 masc. sg. (*šibtô*) is not unusual in the HB (GKC §144p).

The root *zyd* means presumptuous and arrogant behaviour, based on patently false self-perceptions; it may apply to both individuals and nations (Smith, *NIDOTTE* 1:1094–1096).

4. *ʾim . . . miššām* ('if . . . from there') echoes the pattern in Amos 9:2–4. Generally, *gbh* in hiph. does not mean 'soar' (BDB 147). *DCH* 2:298 suggests, however, that this passage, along with Job 5:7, 39:27 and Ps. 113:5, can mean to 'arise' or 'raise oneself'. Because the hiph. suggests an object, perhaps there is an **ellipsis** at this point, and it refers to building the nest high. *nešer* is a broad term, designating both 'eagle' and 'griffon vulture'. Its translation depends on the context. Most of the twenty-six OT uses draw metaphorically on its capacity for flight and its devouring prey. See Kiuchi, *NIDOTTE* 3:200–201; Kronholm, *TDOT* 10:77–85.

The LXX, Vg, Syr and Tg read *śîm* (MT and Mur) as if it were *tāśîm*. *śîm* is best interpreted as a pass. ptc. – 'your nest is placed' (see Num. 24:21).

nĕʾūm (a pass. ptc. serving as a noun in const.) is a fixed technical expression ('utterance').

Form and structure

Contrasting images of high and low are part of the ongoing reversals. The sentence structure is important; both the descriptive adjectives 'small' and 'despised' introduce their respective clauses (v. 2). Arrogance of *heart* at the beginning of v. 3 is mirrored by 'saying in his *heart*' at the end. The answer to the rhetorical question at the end of v. 3 is delayed until the close of v. 4, creating suspense. The repetition of similar sounds binds together the heart's 'deception' (*hiššîʾekā*) – an internal state – with the inaccessible dwellings (*šōknî* and *šibtô*).

nĕʾūm-YHWH often marks the end of a unit of discourse, emphasizing the authoritative status of what has been articulated; it serves as a 'signatory' (Block 2013: 61–62).

Comment

2. The qat. form *nĕtatîkā* ('I have made you') has been variously translated, although the predominant rendering is as a future event (ESV, HCSB, NASB, NIV, NRSV), implying that YHWH has yet to make Edom small, but it will assuredly happen. Goldingay (2021: 355, n. 14) indicates that the qat. designates what YHWH has already determined and started; he translates it with the English present tense. Niehaus (1993: 515–516) translates it as past tense, but with the implication that it anticipates an event yet to come. Block (2013: 59) renders it as a past tense and suggests that 'small' has mainly to do with sociopolitical status. That status reduction, however, is woven together with reduction in territory. While Edom does penetrate westwards, that will be reversed (Renkema 2003: 122). When the declaration is translated and interpreted as a past event, it is a powerful backdrop for its unrealistic arrogance. 'Small' is already their position whether they admit it or not. That sense carries over into the next verbless clause. Whichever the translation choice, the divine Subject is entirely responsible for the repositioning of Edom.

There is a further dimension to the 'smallness': it implies shame. Both the adjectives 'small' and 'despised' introduce their respective clauses, emphasizing that Edom's status is quite at odds with its self-perception. The second clause indicates the nature of Edom's character. It is not the result of YHWH's judgment (Ben Zvi 1996: 50).

3. 'Heart' (*leb*) in the world view of the HB reflects the centre of the will and intentionality. There is confirmation of this in the words of Jesus as he responds to a query about the greatest commandment. Deut. 6:5

urges the people of YHWH to love him with all their 'heart' (*lēbāb*), their 'life' (*nepeš*) and their 'strength' (*mĕʾōd*). The evangelist records Jesus as saying, 'You shall love the Lord your God with all your heart and with all your soul and with all your mind and with all your might' (Mark 12:30), introducing for the first-century AD audience the central elements behind *leb*.

Edom's 'heart' is characterized as *zādôn*, emphasizing their insolence and arrogance (Deut. 17:12; Prov. 11:2; 13:10). These are the dangerous accompaniments of pride, never a static trait. Edom has a false sense of security that will be deleterious; their activities (vv. 10–14) are the upshot of their arrogance (Jenson 2008: 13). Jer. 49:16 substitutes a different word (*tiplaṣtĕkā*), which is a **hapax**, likely meaning 'your shuddering in terror'.

'Deceive' is the most fitting translation of the hiph. of *nšʾ*, even though an alternative could be 'beguile'. The latter implication makes the matter of overweening pride sound seriously seductive. If the qat. form is translated as a past tense, it implies they have been deceived over the long haul, and the whole situation is resulting in YHWH's judgment. On the other hand, it may represent the present ongoing state of misplaced trust (Renkema 2003: 124).

šōkĕnî ('the one who settles') may also refer to God (Deut. 33:16). 'Clefts' is used only in Song 2:14, the parallel in Jer. 49:16, and here. It is always in const. followed by *selaʿ* ('rock'). Jer. 49:16 reads 'you who settle in the clefts of the *selaʿ*', with the def. art. That may signify the capital city (Sela). The indefinite use in Obadiah could point more broadly to the expanses of presumably secure natural fortresses within which the Edomites lived (Renkema 2003: 129).

The second descriptive phrase uses 'height', signalling Edom's ongoing exaggerated self-perception. YHWH accuses them of presumptuously reaching into the heavens as part of their identity and security. The rhetorical question at the end of the verse circles back to the arrogant heart. It anticipates the response 'No one!' but is the foil for what comes next.

4. *ʾim* with the yiq. form expresses a contingency of which there is little question (GKC §159l). The image of the vulture with its nest among the stars is a vast backdrop; in spite of their presumably building above the reach of any attack, they will be brought down. That is the answer to the rhetorical question closing v. 3. *ʾim* forms a bridge into v. 5.

Given the parallel images in the first line, *tagbîāh* ('raise up') should refer to the vulture's both building and placing the nest among the stars. Nevertheless, the grammar is ambiguous. There is not a direct object immediately following the verb. Instead, there is likely an **ellipsis** at that point. Jer. 49:16 compresses the declaration 'you have raised like a vulture the nest'. The idea of the 'soaring' bird likely comes from a parallel description in Job 39:27–28, and numerous English translations have followed that image (ESV, NIV, NKJV, NRSV). Here, however, both raising up and building apply to the nest: the vulture builds and lives in high and safe places. 'Among the stars' is the same kind of embellished description as the previous 'the height of his habitation'. Pride and the inaccessible nest are both brought down. The double emphasis on height makes the declaration of Yhwh that much more forceful (v. 4). It begins with 'from there', starting Yhwh's response to Edom's question. In spite of all the flourishes in regard to the security of heights, they will not stand a chance.

Explanation

The notions of small and despised could reflect both Edom's diminutive geographical advantages and its status. For the preceding centuries, at least through the HB lenses, Edom had existed on the margins of Israel's prominence and was geopolitically 'small', albeit elevated and 'safe'. Their settlements were nestled high among crags, particularly notable from a Judahite's perspective, looking eastwards towards the formidable eastern scarp of the Rift Valley. Sela was the capital of the Edomite kingdom in the OT period (Rainey and Notley 2006: 41). Settlements through the ANE depended on two things – water sources and natural defences that could be enhanced. The higher and more isolated, the better. In their arrogant self-perception, they were not 'small'. Yhwh would disabuse them of that notion, both rhetorically and in their prophetic future. From a geopolitical perspective, Edom's withdrawal from the anti-Babylonian coalition (c. 593 bc; cf. Jer. 27) was really self-preservation, and they likely presumed it was possible given their geographical circumstances. By the fifth century, Malachi attests to the dissolution of Edom (1:3) and the absence of any hope of recovery (1:4–5). By 312 bc, the Nabateans had overtaken the old Edomite kingdom. Nevertheless, Idumea carried on the Edomite identity, just shifting it geographically westwards across the Aravah.

The use of the hiph. verb meaning 'to deceive' often refers to deceiving through a seemingly reasonable and convincing speech or argument (2 Chr. 32:15; Isa. 36:14; Jer. 4:10). Along with the possible meaning 'to beguile', it echoes the deadly combination of pride and deceitful seduction that is the foundation for the serpent's words in Gen. 3:13. It may be associated with wrongful wisdom (Ben Zvi 1996: 55).

Edom is rhetorically depicted as an enemy of Yhwh, their thought processes representing their presumption of God's inability to act against them. 'He says in his heart' indicates prophetic awareness of Edom's 'reflective soliloquy' (Wolff 1986: 49). They are insolent in heart (v. 3) and they articulate that arrogance *in [their] heart*: 'who will bring me down?' The extent of Edom's ascending pride and presumption of security reaches cosmic proportions: 'among the stars' suggests a vertical and mythical dimension (Jenson 2008: 14). This descriptor increases the drama of

Edom's downfall from the *stars* to the earth (Block 2013: 58). There are possible echoes here of Isaiah's prophetic description of the Babylonian king: 'I will ascend to heaven; above the stars of God, I will exalt my throne' (Isa. 14:13). The same imagery surfaces in Ezekiel's lament over the arrogance of the king of Tyre (Ezek. 28:11–19). While these initial verses focus heavily on Edom's pride as the causative factor behind the forthcoming judgment, it will be equally (if not more) based on their heinous conduct (Renkema 2003: 126–127).

Job 39:27–28 draws together the powerful bird of prey, likely the vulture, and its inaccessible nest: it is on the 'tooth of a rock' (v. 28). While Western twenty-first-century culture tends to have a negative view of vultures, that was not necessarily the case in the ANE. There is evidence from both Egypt and Mesopotamia of a vulture cult and the vulture's occupying a place similar to a royal eagle (Kronholm, *TDOT* 10:79–80).

OBADIAH 5–7

Translation

[5]If thieves came to you; if destroyers at night – how you have been cut off! – would they not steal only enough for themselves? If gatherers came to you, would they not leave gleanings?

[6]How Esau is ransacked! His hidden treasures are exposed.

[7]To the border they have sent you – all the men of your covenant;

They have deceived you; they have brought you to an end, the men of your peace.

Your bread they will place as a snare behind you.

There is no understanding in it.

Notes on the text

5. *ʾim* may be conditional ('if') or temporal ('when'). See *DCH* 1:301. The verbal root *dmh* has multiple translation possibilities: (1) 'to establish a likeness'; (2) 'to cease' or 'be silent'; (3) 'cut off' (*DCH* 2:447–448; see also *HALOT* 225–226). *nidmêtâ* is a niph. 2 masc. sg., reflecting the third sense (see BDB 198). The niph. means 'to be destroyed' (Isa. 6:5; 15:1; Jer. 47:5).

The masc. pl. ptc. of *šdd* suggests 'those who destroy'. Nevertheless, the fact that they are active at night indicates a closer parallel with the preceding 'thieves' (Renkema 2003: 133–134). In other contexts, *šdd* is associated with noontime, not night (Ps. 91:6; Jer. 15:8).

There is a connection between *bōṣrîm* ('those who gather by cutting off') and Bozrah (*boṣrâ*), a significant fortified city in Edom located close to

Sela (see Isa. 34:6; 63:1). The root means to 'cut off', 'make inaccessible', with the connotation of gathering grapes (BDB 130–131; *DCH* 2:246–247). *ōlēlôt* ('gleanings') is an intensive fem. pl. noun, always figurative of a remnant (BDB 760) and associated with the process of cutting off (see Judg. 8:2).

6. Both verbs are qat. masc. pl. niph. forms. The first presumes that Esau's inhabitants will be searched out – perhaps like those who were robbed (v. 5). The second verb refers to something happening to the 'hidden things'. *nibʿû* is generally understood as a niph. form from the root *bʿh*, 'to be searched out' (BDB 126). That meaning, however, is based primarily on the occurrence here in parallel with the preceding verb, *neḥpĕśû*, translated 'ransacked'. The only other use in the niph. is a vivid description of a falling wall bulging at the instant before it collapses (Isa. 30:13; *DCH* 2:236). In this context, it has the sense of exposure. The noun *maṣpūnāyw* is a **hapax**, but the verbal root means 'to hide or treasure' (*DCH* 7:150–151). The mem prefix often indicates place; here, that would suggest a 'place of hiding'.

The shift from second to third person is a common stylistic device, heightening the effect of the poetry.

7. In the second part of the verse, the vocalization of the MT is *laḥmĕkā* ('your bread'). It was difficult for early interpreters. The ancient versions understood it as some sort of trap: the LXX reads 'ambush'; Tg has 'snare'; Vg reads 'ambush' (or 'treachery'). Perhaps they understood it as *lōḥămêkā* ('your fighters') and left out any reference to 'bread' (Nogalski 1998: 67). 'Fighters' fits better if *māzôr* (a **hapax**) is read as *māṣôr* ('siege works' or 'entrenchment') or *māṣôd* ('net spread out for hunting'). The alteration of consonants, especially resh (ר) and daleth (ד), may explain most of those changes. The LXX, Tg and Syr also read the equivalent of a qat. form for the verb (*śāmû* instead of *yāśîmû*). A wooden translation of the MT would be 'they have placed your bread as food [under you or behind you or after you]'. See 'Comment'.

Form and structure

ʾim connects these sets of hypothetical threats with the preceding recital of attempted defences. It likewise links with Amos 9:2–4. The connotation of the particle shifts, however, from a scenario of the inevitable consequences of YHWH's intervention in v. 4 to two socio-agricultural illustrations that serve as a backdrop against which to view their hopeless estate. YHWH as destroyer gives way in these verses to human perpetrators. Each hypothetical 'if' is followed by the qat. form.

V. 5 knits together compact metaphors that both compare and contrast, and are interrupted by a brief outburst of lament, introduced by *ʾēk*, 'How?' The rhetorical effect of the latter emphasizes the overwhelming horror: the prophet jumps the gun as it were. That outburst has also to do with 'cutting off' in one form or another.

Each verb in v. 6 describing Edom/Esau shifts to third person and is pass. It may indicate Obadiah's distancing himself from the land of Edom. It may also hint at YHWH's implicit activity and the intended audience of Judah.

Perhaps for rhetorical effect, each succeeding description of the allies in v. 7 is shortened by one word. The first was three words (*kōl ʾanšê bĕrîtekā*; 'all the men of your covenant'); the second is two (*anšê šĕlōmekā*; 'the men of your peace'); the last one is 'shorthand' as it is only one word (*laḥmĕkā*). 'Those who eat' is implicit before 'your bread'. The **ellipsis** is intentional. See 'Comment'.

Comment

5. Irony is lodged in the first hypothetical case: the impenetrable defences of Edomites will be broken through by thieves who come at night. The addition of night-time destroyers may intentionally raise the ominous spectre of national disaster (Jenson 2008: 15; although see Renkema 2003: 133–134). Both are dreaded; Edom would be better off facing those circumstances than what is actually forthcoming. Only taking 'enough for them' depicts the thieves as being curbed by the loot they can carry.

Likewise, those cutting the clusters will leave some gleanings. The latter was an expected and beneficent practice on the part of landholders (Deut. 24:19–22). The outcomes from both ventures – the first illicit, the second sanctioned – mean something is left. In contrast, Edom will lose everything. The prospect is so grim that, even before the stated conclusion, the first description is interrupted with a return to the image of 'cutting off', either by silencing or destroying. A similar image appears in Isa. 15:1 – because of 'destroyers of the night', both Ar and Kir, cities of Moab, will be cut off. Zeph. 1:11 also has an ominous parallel between 'silenced' and 'cut off'.

Rhetorically, *hălôʾ* establishes the certainty of a matter by virtue of posing it as a question, 'Is it not?' (Brown 1987: 201–219; Moshavi 2011: 91–105). It is used by the prophet to jog the audience's memory about something they already should know.

Putting the images together, if the audience has not yet got the point, cutting off is the underlying motif.

6. The preceding exclamation 'How you [masc. sg.] are cut off!' is echoed here. 'How they are searched out!' shifts to pl., no doubt referring to the whole of Esau. The name change to Edom at this point begins to draw on the long tradition of sibling enmity. Obadiah's message will make clear that Esau's descendants have ill-treated the descendants of Jacob (v. 13); they will suffer in kind.

Obadiah's rendition expands that of Jeremiah with the above interjection, an extra phrase describing the havoc brought by thieves, and posing each conditional description as a rhetorical question (*hălô'*). In addition, Obadiah reorders the two images, starting with destruction that thieves bring about and following it with the gleaners who, if they follow proper protocol are expected to leave something. Jeremiah's reference to the thieves destroying is embedded in the parallel line in Obadiah about 'destroyers of the night'.

The figures of 'hiding' and 'hunted' work well in the topographical context, laced through with clefts and high rock walls; it is a perfect place of concealment. While the text does not indicate the nature of the plunder, Edom's control of this portion of the Transjordanian and King's highways, noted for the transport of spices and other goods, may suggest there are goods stashed away that are worth pillaging. On the semantic level, the verbs simply refer to searching out; perhaps pillaging and plunder are reading in a bit more than is warranted.

7. The passive description of Esau's vulnerability to outside enemies ransacking its stored treasures (v. 6) gives way to a scenario of 'insider' treachery. The combination of descriptors suggests a relationship in which it has trusted. The use of 'deceive' here links with v. 3. Trust in oneself and in faulty alliances proves lethal. The first two parallel lines have to do with those who apparently are allies of Edom; to wit, 'all the men of your covenant [*bĕrît*]' and 'the men of your peace [*šālôm*]'. The two terms *bĕrît* and *šālôm* occur together (Num. 25:12; Isa. 54:10; Ezek. 34:25; 37:26) to represent a 'pact by which the parties declare their solidarity, friendship, and commitment to seek one another's well-being' (Block 2013: 65). The reference to *gĕbûl*, meaning either 'boundary' or 'territory that lies within borders', suggests this might have been a geopolitical arrangement to the effect that Edomites could flee to the presumed allies in the face of an impending invasion. To their horror, they are now turned back. See Wolff 1986: 50–51 and Renkema 2003: 141–144. The situation worsens as both are deceived and overpowered by those who have presumably been party to the agreement. On the significance of *yākōl-lĕ-*, see Gen. 32:26[25]; Num. 13:30; Judg. 16:5; 1 Sam. 17:9. It is a common idiom intimating physical force. Reading the two verbs together as a **hendiadys** packs a singular punch (Baker 2006: 171).

That geopolitical scenario informs the difficult third line; it may point to partaking of a meal in covenant-making (Gen. 31:51–54; Exod. 18:10–12; 24:1–11). Before emending the text to read 'fighters' as some of the earlier versions do, it is important to explore the possibilities that may be found in conjunction with 'bread'. The MT reads 'they have placed your bread as a trap under you [or behind you or after you]', not the most intelligible image. Several options involve revocalizing the text so that 'your bread' becomes a pl. ptc. ('those eating') with a 2 masc. sg. suff. In that case, it could be a third articulation of the subject after 'the men of your covenant' and 'the men of your peace'; i.e. 'those eating your bread place a trap under you'. While that initially seems as if it might work, the normal syntax requires that the suff. on *leḥem* be a direct object. In other words, it cannot be 'those eating *with* you [your bread]'. At the same time, 'those eating you' is not the best understanding for obvious reasons. If, however, there is an **ellipsis** in the third component, then the 'men of your peace' is followed by '[those who eat] your bread'. This pair is found in Ps. 41:10[9], specifically regarding betrayal by someone who is trusted because of his or her relationship. The conceptual sphere of treaty components may be helpful at this point. Several OT passages demonstrate that providing bread to an army constitutes an act of political alliance (1 Sam. 21 – 22). Melchizedek's meeting Abram with bread and wine has relationship overtones (Gen. 14:18; see again Exod. 24:1–11). In Edom's situation, 'bread' could be understood as a metaphorical synonym for 'covenant'. Perhaps Obadiah is condemning the political alliances and saying the Edomites will end up being entrapped by them. They will suffer at the hands of those who have previously joined in alliance (Nogalski 1998: 68–71). The treacherous 'allies' have sent them back, deceived and prevailed against them and set a trap (Renkema 2003: 146–147; Block 2013: 65–66).

The word *māzôr*, indicating what is placed under them, adds to the challenge. Its derivation is dubious, and it is often left untranslated (BDB 561). With two emendations, it could read *māṣôd*, which encompasses within its semantic range a kind of net or hunting implement (BDB 844–845). While the interchange between resh (ר) and daleth (ד) is a likely possibility, the shift from ṣade to zayin is less conceivable. Another option is the Mishnaic Hebr. root *mzr*, which means 'to twist' or 'weave' (Jastrow 1950: 756). Three other occurrences of this word signify 'sore' or 'wound' (Jer. 30:13; Hos. 5:13 [twice]). While that does not fit the context, later readers of the text might have had that connotation in mind as part of the complex socio-emotional picture behind this brief vignette (Ben Zvi 1996: 91).

From another perspective, *māzôr* may follow the familiar pattern of nouns derived from middle weak verbs intimating place. *zwr* means 'to be strange or foreign', and this would then mean a 'place of strangers'. The prep. indicating the placement of this item allows significant freedom. It could be 'under', 'behind' or 'in your stead'. The first two options fit in the covenant-betrayal context; the meal is used as a trap. 'In your stead' fits the future prospects of the Edomites being forced out by deteriorating political circumstances (McCarter 1976: 87). A minor modification of this interpretation reads the word as *mûzār*, a hoph. ptc., 'one who has become a stranger' (see *HALOT* 256). In other words, the former partners with Edom have replaced Edom with a foreign entity (Ben Zvi 1996: 90–91; Renkema 2003: 148–150). For additional summaries and critiques of interpretations that have been put forward, see McCarter 1976: 87–91 and Davies 1977a: 484–487.

The final line of v. 7 initially seems unconnected with what precedes it, no matter how the prior clause is translated. It may be another one of Obadiah's exclamations that punctuate the messages. He marvels at the obtuseness of the Edomites. Dumbfounded at what is happening, 'they just don't get it'. Rhetorically, this connects with the substance of v. 8; *těbûnâ* connotes the insight necessary to deal effectively with the circumstances, but Edom no longer has any vestiges of it. There is no understanding, because Yhwh will remove wise men from Edom and understanding from Mount Seir. Similar expressions appear in Deut. 32:28 and Prov. 21:30. In both cases, the context has to do with opposition to Yhwh.

Explanation

Given the nature of Edom as an emporium for trade and an area that had natural resources, the prospect of robbers and thieves would be unsettling. The exclamation with which Obadiah interrupts his discourse hints at how disturbing this is, especially as it portends to be significantly worse than common thieves, who at least have some sense of boundaries (Baker 2006: 169–170). On the horror expressed with *ʾêk* (How!), see Prov. 5:12 regarding the dissolute person at the end of his days bewailing the consequences of hating discipline. See also the lament in Jer. 9:18[19] from the women of Zion, 'How we are destroyed [*ʾêk šūdādnû*], deeply shamed; for we have left the land, for they have cast us from our homes'. It appears as well in Mic. 2:4 and Zeph. 2:15.

Gleaning was a practice implemented in Israel for the care of marginalized populations, but no doubt the surrounding agriculturally based societies had similar socio-economic safety nets. While the 'gleaners' precede the 'thieves' in Jeremiah, Obadiah reverses the order of the images. Those folks who just do their job are a stark foil for the treacherous predators on the prophetic horizon.

It is not clear who has been party to a treaty with Esau: they are called 'men of your covenant' and 'men of your peace'. The resulting image conforms readily to our own conceptual realm, by presenting a picture of betrayal from within. It is not too much of a stretch to reflect on contemporary illustrations of 'breaking covenants', all the way from personal betrayals to international backstabbing. The effects of doing so are deleterious and have ripple effects beyond one given situation. One's word should sufficiently seal a covenant, whether it is a marriage vow, a promise to deliver work on time, a stated agreement to abide by institutional practices or a guarantee of timely payment of debt.

OBADIAH 8–10

Translation

[8]And in that day – an utterance of Yhwh – will I not cause to perish wise men from Edom and understanding from Mount Esau?

[9]And your valiant men will be in terror, O Teman, because every man will be cut off from Mount Esau.

On account of slaughter

[10][and] violence against your brother, Jacob, shame will cover you and you will be cut off for ever.

Notes on the text

8. On *hălôʾ* as the vehicle for a powerful assertion, see 'Comment' on v. 5.

The hiph. weqat. form points to Yhwh's forthcoming activity (GKC §112p).

ḥākām ('wise') is an adj. used subst. in the pl.

9. The verb *wĕḥattû* can mean both 'to be dismayed' and 'to be shattered' (*DCH* 3:337; *HALOT* 365–366). The lxx has 'to be dismayed or terrified'. The 2 masc. pl. suff. on *gibbôr* ('valiant man') means that Teman is in a voc. position. The last word of the verse, *qeṭel* ('slaughter'), is a **hapax** but the root is a familiar one. On the basis of the lxx and Vg, Goldingay (2021: 356, n. 23) reads it with the first word of v. 10; so also, BDB 881. In other words, slaughter and violence against Jacob would result in Edom's complete end. Hence, its position in the translation above. Based on the three occurrences of the verb form (Job 13:15; 24:14; Ps. 139:19), a translation of 'murder' is not too strong: it is intentionally committed by Edom.

10. *ḥāmās* is 'violence' unleashed by stronger parties against weaker, whether on the international, community or individual levels. It is motivated by hatred and greed (Swart and Van Dam, *NIDOTTE* 2:177–180). *mēḥămas ʾāḥîkā* is an objective gen. (GKC §128h), pointing to violence 'against your brother'. It may more specifically be labelled a gen. of disadvantage (*IHBS* §9.5.2e).

Form and structure

There are features that mark continuity and those that create disjunction. The first line of v. 8 starts with *hălôʾ*, establishing continuity with v. 5. Nevertheless, the connection is immediately and awkwardly interrupted. The syntax serves to keep the audience waiting for what Yhwh will do after he speaks. At the same time, 'in that day' signals a new development ('day of Yhwh').

'Says Yhwh' (v. 8) seems premature, as the expression often closes an authoritative declaration. Here again Obadiah surprises his audience with the disjunction. At the same time, *tĕbûnâ* in the last clause echoes the absence of 'understanding' at the end of v. 7.

The final word of v. 9, *miqqāṭel* ('on account of slaughter'), dangles awkwardly. The prep. *min* looks both backwards – Edom itself will be judged severely – and forward; the judgment will be 'on account of' their murderous treatment of Judah (Ben Zvi 1996: 124–128). V. 10 moves from the preceding summary of the already-articulated future punishments to a presumed recital of past events, styled as a series of warnings against engaging in these activities (vv. 11–14). The order of these two sections reverses the expected sequence.

Comment

8. There is an increasing emphasis through the rest of the prophecy on 'day'. Its starting point is Yhwh's destruction of the underpinnings of effective government. *ḥākām* has a wide semantic range but includes a class of people who would have been responsible for guidance in political crises (*DCH* 3:219–222). With governance structures in tatters, all diplomacy and political endeavours will end (Wolff 1986: 52). Wisdom associated with Edom may surface in the description of Solomon's legendary wisdom: he was wiser than all the men of the east (1 Kgs 5:10[4:30]), a designation that could include Edom. A further allusion appears in Job 2:11; the famed Eliphaz arrived from Teman, synonymous with Edom (Obad. 9), to 'instruct' Job. Job himself lived in Uz, generally associated with Edom, given the parallel in Lam. 4:21. Yhwh would also bring understanding to an end on Mount Esau. This designation is used for Edom or Mount Seir only in Obadiah, and surfaces here in preparation for the mention of Jacob. The reader is repeatedly reminded of the sibling relationship.

9. What would cause 'powerful men' (*gibbôrîm*) to be dismayed – or even possibly shattered – in terror? These are not simply military men. That would be *ʾanšê-hamilḥāmâ* ('men of war'). This refers to the crack troops; it is the same term used regarding David's famed 'mighty men' (2 Sam. 20:7; 23:9).

Teman is likely the mid-region of Edom, south of the Punon embayment. It may be thought of as the geopolitical backbone of the country. On the basis of Amos 1:12, the name has also been associated with a location near Bozrah (Rainey and Notley 2006: 123). The direct address to Teman is a warning: they will not be able to rely on the valiant men. While *lĕmaʿan* generally indicates purpose, it may also express the consequences (J-M §169g). Because the mighty men of Teman will be immobilized in terror, every man will be cut off from Mount Esau. The passive (niph.) signals that YHWH is the moving force, but does not name him as the originator of the destruction. The declaration draws together the results for the whole population, the special forces as well as the ordinary folk.

If the last word of v. 9 is read with v. 10, then both vv. 8 and 9 end with Mount Esau, a fitting parallel. That does alleviate the question as to how to address *miqqāṭel* as a closure to v. 9, and makes it quite clear that the combination of slaughter and violence against 'your brother Jacob' refers again to Edom's culpability and accounts for the utter shame that will accompany being cut off. On the other hand, if its position of closing v. 9 is retained, it could specify *how their* being cut off would occur – i.e. from slaughter (Jenson 2008: 18), YHWH being the one doing that action of judgment.

10. 'Violence' (*ḥamas*) is a strong term, especially when the litany that follows is heavily weighted on the side of Edom's being the classic 'bystander' without getting involved – at least initially – in helping the descendants of Jacob in their time of need. It is a reminder that violence is not limited to overt brutality. Their standing aside allows hostile forces to strike lethal blows. Obadiah is not hesitant about reminding his audience that Edom has violated the kinship relationship. Shame will *cover* Edom, a figure that speaks to public and comprehensive humiliation. It echoes vv. 2–3 and is directly followed here by the grim prospect of being cut off for ever. The absence of a legacy is one of many facets in loss of honour.

The measure-for-measure principle resurfaces. The rhetoric of the next verses articulates Edom's humiliation of Judah, as the latter are suffering the horrors of defeat at the hands of the Babylonians. Edom will suffer in kind, and it will be a harbinger of the day of YHWH (cf. Ezek. 7:18). This creates the expectation of divine retribution against the perpetrator (Ben Zvi 1996: 130). Its final declaration that 'you will be cut off for ever' suggests closure. On the other hand, it makes the connection with 'your brother Jacob' that will shape the accusations going forward.

Explanation

All human might and wisdom at enmity with YHWH will perish. The loss of moral strength and integrity culminates in disaster. The threats have escalated through the first verses of the book, and they are YHWH's response to Edom's pride, utter self-deception and self-absorption. The humiliation of being small leads to Edom's being plundered and betrayed, which in turn spell loss of governance and finally the extermination of their population (Wolff 1986: 52). The work of YHWH on the day of judgment will cause a major component of their national security to disintegrate. When the military (or police) framework designed to protect the citizenry fractures, those folks are worse than vulnerable.

A critical component of wisdom is the definitive counsel that guides through times of crisis without being swayed by lobbyists, self-interest groups, revisionist history, cancel culture or whatever other temporary intellectual fad surfaces. Pride and persistent self-absorption ruin individuals, organizations, national and international polities and are accompanied by blind spots of monumental proportions. Wisdom that is necessary for constructive political decisions interfaces with theological and ideological wisdom (Ben Zvi 1996: 121–122). The dearth of foundational governing wisdom echoes Micah's sarcastic observation a century prior to the fall of Jerusalem: 'Is there no king in your midst? Has your counsellor perished?' (Mic. 4:9).

OBADIAH 11–14

Translation

11On the day when you stood aloof; on the day when strangers removed his strength to exile, and foreigners entered his gate, and cast the lot over Jerusalem; also you were like one of them.

12Don't gape on the day of your brother, on the day of his foreignness; and don't rejoice over the sons of Judah on the day of their perishing, and don't enlarge your mouth on the day of distress.

13Don't come into the gate of my people on the day of their calamity; don't gape – yes, you – at his disaster on the day of his calamity, and don't loot his wealth on the day of his calamity.

14Don't stand at the crossroad to cut off his fugitives; and don't imprison his survivors on the day of disaster.

Notes on the text

11. The two initial inf. const. forms (*ʿămādĕkā* and *šĕbôt*) with 'on the day' indicate a time frame in which they do this: 'when you stood aloof' and 'when they removed to exile'. The latter is a **hapax** as an inf. const. but has a common root, *šbh* ('to take captive').

ḥēlô, 'his [Judah's] strength, army, wealth' (BDB 298–299; *DCH* 3:212–214) may refer to a social class of the population rather than possessions, because the exiles will not be carrying much with them as they leave (Jenson 2008: 20).

zārîm and *nokrîm* are synonymous, referring to someone or something that is foreign, strange or forbidden. Political enemies are among those designated as *zārîm* (Konkel, *NIDOTTE* 1:1142–1143). *nokrî* likewise indicates foreigners who are perceived to be hostile and should be excluded (Konkel, *NIDOTTE* 3:108–109).

The K is *šaʿărô* ('his gate') whereas the Q, followed by the LXX, Vg and Syr, is *šĕʿārāyw* ('his gates'). The Tg reads 'his cities'.

The verb in conjunction with *gôrāl* ('lot'), *yaddû* ('they cast'), appears only in Joel 4:3[3:3], Nah. 3:10 and this passage.

12. Day of his *nōkrô* ('foreignness') is unusual, used only here and in Job 31:3. Even though modern translations opt for some representation of misfortune (ESV, HCSB, NASB, NIV, NRSV), the ancient versions (LXX and Vg) retain the element of 'foreign', pointing in the direction of Judah's exile to foreign lands. The sg. pron. suff. refers to 'your brother'. It shifts in the next line ('their perishing'); the referent is 'sons of Judah'.

śmḥ implies spontaneous exuberance in expressing joy (Grisanti, *NIDOTTE* 3:1251–1254). 'To enlarge the mouth', occurring elsewhere only in Ezek. 35:13, is a vivid portrayal of arrogant challenge.

13. *ʾêd* means 'calamity' or 'disaster'. The sg. pron. suff. has as its referent the collective 'my people'. 'Do not send' (*ʾal tišlaḥnâ*) is a fem. pl. juss. The standard idiom has 'hand' as the direct object of *šlḥ*; it is implicit here. The larger complication is determining the subject of the fem. pl. verb as the MT has preserved it. Interpretive possibilities have included reading *nāʾ* (a particle of entreaty) instead of the attached *-nâ*. The verb form would then be masc. sg. Another option revocalizes the first syllable so that it is pass. (*tušlaḥnâ*), with 'hands' as the subject. Ben Zvi (1996: 156–157) explores further nuances.

14. The uncertainty about the meaning of *pereq* is evident in the early versions. It is a collective. The Vg has 'exits'; the Tg reads 'crossroads'; LXX – 'ways through'; but Symmachus has 'places of refuge'.

Form and structure

These verses move seamlessly between what Edom has already done (v. 11) and warnings not to gaze disdainfully, taunt or otherwise harm Judah in the time of their distress (vv. 12–14). The yiq. forms initially suggest that the latter are yet to come. Nevertheless, it is apparent that they are part of the recital of Edom's known offences for which they will pay. This is a powerful rhetorical tool, re-entering the past to hammer home in multiple ways the appalling ways that Edom committed violence against Judah in the day of the latter's distress and to serve notice for the future (Block 2013: 74).

The second-person juss. with *ʾal* shapes vv. 12–14; it recurs eight times and indicates urgency (*IBHS* §34.2.1b). See 'Explanation' regarding the theological significance of 'eight'. Patterns of three dominate especially vv. 12 and 13. Each has three admonitions (*ʾal* plus juss.) followed by 'on the day of'. The repeated sound of *bĕyôm* ('in [the] day') contributes to a crescendo of foreboding. All of them point to and connect with v. 15 – 'the day of YHWH is near for the nations'.

Comment

11. Their first offence is standing aside while hostile enemy forces enter the gate (of Jerusalem). The adv. *minneged* can mean physically 'standing out of the way' (2 Kgs 2:7), 'indifference' (2 Sam. 18:13) or 'failing to provide help' (Ps. 38:12[11]). *ḥēlô* ('his strength') may pointedly refer to nobility. In 597 BC, the upper classes were carried off into exile (2 Kgs 24:10–17). The later capture and deportation of Zedekiah (2 Kgs 25:4–7; see also Jer. 39:4–10) could likewise be behind this (Renkema 2003: 165). The hostile strangers are the Babylonians. 'Foreigners' emphatically precedes the verb form; they penetrated the gate and doled out the plunder of Jerusalem.

Each context where *yaddû gôrāl* ('cast the lot') is used refers to those who violently attacked a captive population. Here there are several interpretive options: (1) gambling for the loot (Achtemeier 1996: 246); (2) dividing the city into sectors in which looting privileges were granted; or (3) determining who would go into exile and who would remain (Block 2013: 74). Nah. 3:10 connects lot casting with men of high social standing.

The final clause starts with *gam-ʾattâ* ('also you'). It is as if to say, 'This picture includes you' (Merwe 1993: 35–38). Their 'standing aside' is merely a temporary pretence of non-involvement. Their hearts are oriented in the same way as those of the pillaging forces.

12. Although *rʾh* means 'to see', here in combination with the prep. it includes the object of seeing – their downfall – as well as the emotional state of those looking. It may be purposeful and greedy, looking to determine how much loot may be accessible as a result of the devastation (Renkema 2003: 172–173) as well as gloating (Emerton 2001: 186).

Attitude changes to action; the rhetorical admonitions build on that. Having initially stood aloof while the foreigners entered the gate, now their ill motives are activated. The question is how to address the shift in the time frame for 'that day'. On the grammatical level, the *ʾal* plus juss. implies present or future. Nevertheless, the deeper level presses it to be understood as past, linked with the specific mention of 'Jacob' in v. 10 and 'your brother' here (Werse 2013: 120–121). The author projects himself into the past, looking back at Jerusalem's ruin and using it as a platform for a contemporary warning (Bartlett 1982: 21).

While 'day of his foreignness' may be a veiled allusion to the dislocation of the exile, there is ambiguity in the expression. It could also be a subtle reference to the now-broken kinship relationship. Edom has treated his brother as a foreigner. The day of Judah's downfall is the final severing of the fraternal relationship (Renkema 2003: 174). That is painfully evident in the rejoicing and excessive boasting that breaks forth. Neither is benign (Ps. 137:7). *ṣārâ* ('distress') is a place of narrow straits, pressured from all sides (*DCH* 7:158); Judah is defenceless. *yôm ṣārâ* is used twenty-five times in the OT; the parallel expression in

Ezek. 35:5 is *ʾēd* ('calamity' or 'disaster'); both imply final punishment (Block 2013: 75).

13. Of the twenty-four occurrences of *ʾêd*, eight are in conjunction with 'day' and refer to God's vengeance against his enemies (Van Dam, *NIDOTTE* 1:371). Nothing about this disaster is happenstance: it is part of YHWH's judgment upon Judah. Accompanying each notice of 'day' is the increasingly aggressive activity of Edom vis-à-vis Judah. First, Edom breaks through the gate – no more standing to the side. Once there, they assess how best to exploit their brother's 'misery' (*rāʿātô*). 'You, yes you!' catches them in the act of that covetous looking. And then they begin in earnest to loot whatever they can lay their hands on. Three times 'day of their/his calamity' (*ʾêd*) echoes through v. 13, closing each negative imperative. Lexically, this is the day of Jacob's disaster, but the phonological parallel between *ʾēdām* and Edom is not to be missed. The symbol also points to the forthcoming judgment day for Edom: there is one day of YHWH (Wolff 1986: 55; Raabe 1996: 181; Baker 2006: 182; Werse 2013: 121–123).

14. The frenzied nature of the hostility escalates. *pereq* is used only here and in Nah. 3:1; the verbal root means to 'tear away' or 'tear apart'. BDB (830) suggests 'parting of ways' for this context and 'plunder' for Nah. 3:1. Following suit, *DCH* 6:781 reads plunder for Nah. 3:1, but is ambivalent regarding this context, offering 'crossroads', 'narrow pass' and 'escape route' as equally viable options, perhaps based on the early versions. Plunder as a derived meaning from 'tear away' makes sense but does not fit this context. Perhaps instead of standing 'at the *pereq*' to cut the survivors off, the prep. *ʿal* should be read as 'against'. If so, *pereq* may be parallel to both *pĕlîṭayw* and *śĕrîdayw*: they are not to stand against the torn and broken survivors. See the use of *šeber* in Ezek. 32:9 (Ben Zvi 1996: 161).

The main point is what occurs there. Those who are close to escaping are cut off; it is a repeated theme. The hiph. of *krt* suggests execution, not simply being stopped. No doubt the Edomites position themselves where they can ambush those fleeing. The verbal root *plṭ* has a range of meanings, depending on the conjugation. In qal, it generally means to 'escape to a place of safety'. It appears most frequently in pi., meaning 'to bring out', 'deliver' or 'save'. In hiph., it means 'bring to safety' (*DCH* 6:690–692; see also *HALOT* 930–931). That is the basis for the related noun that means 'fugitive' (*DCH* 6:694; *HALOT* 932). It is synonymous with *śārîd* in the next line. Both terms are used in conjunction with the day of YHWH's anger (Lam. 2:22).

Not all the refugees are murdered; some are imprisoned. The root *sgr* means 'to close'; the hiph. *ʾal-tasgēr* suggests handing over (Block 2013: 79), perhaps for later sale. In sum, what was initially hateful arrogance has morphed into vicious brutality. Nevertheless, these disasters could not happen unless YHWH had given the refugees up. See Deut. 32:30.

Explanation

Motive, attitude, action and YHWH's judgment are woven together. The initial reluctance of Edom to get involved may be politically motivated. They already have control of the eastern biblical Negev which was close to the Babylonians' sphere of operations. They may be biding their time to see if Nebuchadnezzar will respect their annexation of southern Judah or simply take it all. It may be described as 'opportunistic politics' (Renkema 2003: 164–168). Esau's status as brother should mean the Edomites' actions are in marked contrast to those of the foreigners, but that is not the case. Edom follows the hostile foreigners through the gate of Jerusalem, gawks at the potential loot and then starts in with glee.

Don't gape; don't rejoice; don't enlarge your mouth; don't enter; don't gape; don't send; don't stand; don't cut off. These eight prohibitions are unique for their number in the OT. Generally, the number seven suggests perfection and completeness in the human sphere. There are, however, significant occurrences of eight, particularly representing divine perfection. They range from literary expressions (the acrostic pattern in Ps. 119) to ritual. The latter are particularly telling as they unfold in the sphere of approach to God: purification of the tabernacle (Lev. 9:1); the eighth day of Sukkoth (Deut. 31:10–13); circumcision on the eighth day (Lev. 12:3); eight divisions of priests ministering in the temple (1 Chr. 4:24). In this wider theological context, Obadiah's rhetoric reflects the indignation of YHWH in the face of these abuses (Renkema 2003: 170–171). The series of presumed prohibitions not only captures a sense of the heinous deeds of the past; it also serves as warnings that these transgressions are viewed by YHWH as reprehensible no matter who the perpetrators and when.

Obadiah hammers at the same accusations that Ezekiel articulates against Mount Seir. They harbour enmity (35:5); they revile and mock YHWH's people (35:12); they 'made their mouths great' against YHWH (35:13). Even though Ezekiel's rhetoric may employ conventional stock phrases that were used of enemies of God and God's people (Bartlett 1982: 20), there is an unsettling reality that underlies them, evident in contemporary expressions of anguish. 'YHWH fully vented his wrath . . . he kindled a fire in Zion, and it consumed its foundations. The kings of the earth did not believe . . . that oppressor or enemy could enter the gates of Jerusalem' (Lam. 4:11–12; see also Ps. 79:1–2).

'Day' is steadily present, creating the ominous trajectory towards the 'day' of reckoning that is forthcoming. These initial 'days' are Judah's disaster at the hands of those whose 'day' is still coming. The multiple indications of extreme distress that characterize Jacob's 'day' develop in intensity. Ps. 137:7 appeals to YHWH to remember 'the day of Jerusalem' when Edom's voice called for Zion's utter destruction. When there are contemporary strident voices clamouring for attacks against God's precious people, it is imperative that our prophetic voices be heard in opposition. In Ezekiel's vision of the spiritual wreckage of Jerusalem just before 587 BC, only those who cry out against what is happening are marked to be spared. The rest are executed by the angels of destruction (Ezek. 9:1–11). It does not get much more sobering than that.

OBADIAH 15–16

Translation

[15]For near is the day of YHWH against all the nations; as you have done, so it will be done to you. Your recompense will return on your head.

[16]For just as you have drunk on my holy mountain, all the nations will drink continually, and they will drink and totter, and they will be as if they were not.

Notes on the text

15. After *kî* ('because'), the next word is *qārôb* (*near* is the day of YHWH), emphasizing its imminence. *gĕmûl* can mean 'recompense' for good or for ill (Carpenter, *NIDOTTE* 1:871–873; *HALOT* 196). The second-person forms in the verse are sg.

16. The first word is again *kî*, but the pron. shifts to 2 masc. pl., introducing ambiguity as to whether those who have drunk are Edomites, Judahites or more vaguely the larger collection of nations on whom YHWH's judgment day is coming.

More than twenty Hebr. MSS read *sābîb* ('round about') instead of *tāmîd* ('always'), suggesting a continuation of the spatial dimension indicated by 'my holy mountain' (Renkema 2003: 196). Mur is unclear at the end of that line and not helpful either way (DJD IIa: 189).

lāʿû could mean either 'to speak rashly' or 'to gulp down, swallow' (*DCH* 4:556), both fitting in terms of excessive drinking. Goldingay (2021: 356) translates it as 'jabber'. The implications for speech may be elucidated by Job's description of his words in the throes of his calamity (6:3). Additionally, it may also mean 'to sip or slurp', both reflecting an onomatopoeic sense (*HALOT* 533). BDB (534) suggests the possibility of reading *nāʿû* ('tremble' or 'totter'), which appears in images of the earth and nations tottering and reeling as if drunken (Isa. 24:20; 29:9). The LXX interprets it as 'to fall down', another result of drinking to excess.

Form and structure

As with earlier section breaks, whether to include v. 15 with the preceding unit or attach it to what follows is up for grabs. It brings the theme of 'day' into a new dimension – the future and imminent 'day of YHWH'. Both vv. 15 and 16 start with *kî*, connecting what has been with what is forthcoming. Translating *kî* as an indication of a causal connection between the fraternal hostility and the very next declaration about the day of YHWH against all peoples has prompted numerous interpreters to shift the first and second lines of v. 15. That is not necessary, however, if *kî* is read as a particle of emphasis (*IBHS* §39.3.4e; Muilenburg 1961: 135–160). The point of connection is that when the preceding kinds of activities are done – no matter who does them – the judgment of YHWH will be at hand. In addition, reordering the two lines imposes a particular logic on them that then robs the declaration of its power to unsettle.

Comment

15. The preceding verses build the tension around the word 'day': now that day is 'near', and it is the 'the day of YHWH for the nations'. This single verse is central in shifting from the preceding agonizing description couched in powerful rhetoric to a declaration of universal proportions: justice will be done for all people. *qārôb* precedes *yôm YHWH* in significant descriptions of that day (Isa. 13:6; Joel 1:15; 4:14[3:14]; Zeph. 1:7, 14). Its imminence is the definitive characteristic; the contemporary audience is to rouse itself from its lethargy.

The shift in the first part of the verse to 'the nations' is initially jarring, but the judgment of YHWH has universal implications; it is always so. What Edom will experience is to be viewed as only a part of that wider and assured picture. Thus, the scope is expanded to capture the breadth of what is forthcoming. It is an 'uneven' expansion, as v. 15b states the principle of ***lex talionis*** in terms of a singular offender. The 2 masc. sg. pron. is laced through the second half of the verse, and measure-for-measure is apparent in the matching verbs as well as the 'recompense' (*gĕmûl*) on 'your head'. This is a standard phrase for just retribution. See also Joel 4:4–7[3:4–7] and Ps. 7:17[16]. Implicit in this declaration is judgment coming against Edom under the very large umbrella of *yôm YHWH*. The niph. form again intimates that this is judgment from YHWH without directly attributing that judgment to him.

16. The parallel seems evident at the outset; the previous verse declares, 'as you have done', and continues with the expected 'it will be done to you'. This one starts with 'as you have drunk' but then the reader must pause. Now 'you' is pl. And the payback is not quite in kind. 'You' (pl.) have drunk on YHWH's holy mountain, but 'they' will drink. How is that ***lex talionis*** for Edom? Does this instead leave Edom to the side? If so, who is the subject? Because Obadiah characteristically refers to Edom with sg., the pl. marks a shift. This is another of Obadiah's surprises. Perhaps the referent is Judah, and this is not describing a carousing bunch of Edomites defiling Mount Zion in that manner. Instead, attention shifts to drinking the cup of YHWH's wrath on Zion. Judah is the first to undergo that purging (Jer. 25:15–29); Edom's turn is coming (Ben Zvi 1996: 181–182; Raabe 1996: 203–204; Baker 2006: 190–191; Block 2013: 87–88). On the other hand, if Edom is indeed the subject, how does this judgment against Edom come to occur on 'the mountain of my holiness?' Up to this point, Edom's judgment is in the context of their own land. That, however, may be the point; Obadiah envisions that Edom will experience the figurative cup of wrath in Israel, particularly notable because they have absorbed a significant part of Judah by this time (Renkema 2003: 190–194; see also Isa. 34:5–9).

If the MT's *tāmîd* ('always') is retained, the description takes on an eschatological flavor. If *sābîb* ('round about') is the correct reading, then the location of Zion is the primary focus. Emending the word to *tāmîm* suggests drinking it to completion – on and on and on, for ever (Renkema 2003: 195).

Multiple drinking images are embedded in the ambiguity of *lā'û*; these drunkards gulp, slurp, babble and stagger, depending on how we treat this unusual word. A related noun, which is a **hapax** (*lōa'*), seems to mean 'throat' in Prov. 23:2. Job 6:3 and Prov. 20:25 suggest excessive verbiage; drinking affects speech. The consonantal modification to *nā'û* connects with the tottering in Isa. 24:20; 29:9. Prophetic descriptions of the coming 'cup of YHWH's wrath' use the imagery of complete loss of control, utter shame and humiliation, and the horrors of madness. This may be 'shorthand' for all the deleterious effects of total inebriation (Block 2013: 89). See Isa. 51:17–23; Jer. 25:15–16.

Three of the four clauses in v. 16 contain a form of the verb 'drink' and the fourth declares the upshot of that – 'they will be as if they were not'. The end of the drunkards in Obad. 16 is the annihilation of person and memory, a terrifying prospect (Ps. 88:6[5]).

Explanation

This is the first mention of *yôm YHWH* in Obadiah, but the prospect of a significant day of judgment is embedded in Israel's tradition. See 'Introduction'. Woven into the very fabric of the day of YHWH is the completion of justice – measure-for-measure (***lex talionis***). This principle was widely acknowledged outside Israelite culture. The Code of Hammurabi (196–200) cites specific cases for application of the ***lex talionis*** (*ANET* 175). There would be no avoiding it for Judah at this point. The principle is spelled out after a long statement of YHWH's judgment of Babylon in Jeremiah (51:56): 'because YHWH is a God of retribution he will surely repay [*šallēm yěšallēm*]'. After this point in

Obadiah, the justice shifts from retributive to distributive; in other words, Judah's fate will now be shared by the nations (Block 2013: 86). Whoever has defiled YHWH's sanctuary in the day of its destruction will drink themselves into the judgment of oblivion, imbibing YHWH's wrath. All the nations are under judgment (Anderson 2010: 253–254); the nations' hostility is always part of the backstory. See Pss 79:1; 83:5–8[4–7]. 'More than any other text, Obadiah makes it comprehensible why from 587 onwards, Edom should have become the prototype of all enemies of God's people' (Wolff 1986: 63). Even after the abominations that his own people brought to Zion (Ezek. 8) and the desecration of 587 BC, YHWH still claims Zion (Joel 4:17[3:17]) and calls it 'his holy mountain' (Block 2013: 88).

It is telling that in Gethsemane Jesus pleaded with the Father to remove the cup (Matt. 26:39). The image in the HB is full and frightening. The final punishment poured out on unrepentant idolaters will be 'the wine of God's fury' (Rev. 14:9–10).

OBADIAH 17–18

Translation

17But on Mount Zion there will be those who have escaped, and there will be holiness. And the house of Jacob shall possess their inheritance.

18And the house of Jacob will be a fire, and the house of Joseph a flame, but the house of Esau stubble. And they will ignite them and devour them, and there will not be a remnant to the house of Esau, for YHWH has spoken.

Notes on the text

17. The root *yrš* can mean both 'possess' and 'dispossess' (*DCH* 4:302). If *môrāšêhem* is the noun *môrāš* with the 3 masc. pl. pron. suff., then the 'house of Jacob' (Judah) will possess (again) its possession; i.e. its own land. If, on the other hand, this is a hiph. ptc. (*môrîšêhem*) from *yrš*, then it refers to the house of Jacob's possessing those who had dispossessed them; i.e. Edom. The LXX, Vg and Syr readings reflect the hiph. ptc. reading as does Mur (DJD IIa: 189), one of the few places where Mur differs from the MT (Goldingay 2021: 357, n. 30). Renkema (2003: 201–202) and Goldingay follow the hiph. ptc. reading. Block (2013: 91) opts for the MT: they will again possess what had been theirs. Ben Zvi (1996: 189) suggests that the ambiguity of the consonantal text invites both options – the dispossessors will themselves be dispossessed as well as the rightful possessors again inhabiting their inheritance.

Form and structure

V. 17 starts with Mount Zion, emphasizing the forthcoming contrast to the previous degradation of 'my holy mountain'. The juxtaposition of brothers continues; 'house of Jacob' appears twice as does 'house of Esau', but the outcomes are radically different. The 'house of Joseph' is nestled between those two sets of pairs and is part of the process of consuming the 'house of Esau'. There are sound parallels, starting with the cognate acc.: *yrš* and *môrāšêhem* regarding the 'house of Jacob', followed by its being characterized as *ēš* ('fire'). That in turn is followed by the semantic parallelism with *lehābâ* ('flame'). The opposite description of the 'house of Esau' as *qaš* ('stubble') continues the phonological similarities.

Comment

17. The waw conj. could be 'and' or 'but'. If the former, it would continue the emphasis on the effects for Mount Zion on the day of YHWH. Read as an adversative, it emphasizes the contrast between the previous consequences of drinking and the holy remnant.

The noun *pĕlêṭâ* may refer to a delivered remnant who will be secure on Mount Zion after all the trauma of drunkenness and judgment. If it connects with those beleaguered few attempting to escape who were being systematically cut off (v. 14), perhaps some have survived. Depending on how the previous verses are interpreted, this may refer to Judah, who experienced the wrath of YHWH, escaped the intervening dread and now will be secure on Zion. Viewed through eschatological lenses, those who escape, those whom YHWH calls, will be on Mount Zion and in Jerusalem (Joel 3:5[2:32]). At the same time, the attribution of 'holiness' to the place indicates that Mount Zion itself needs deliverance to be restored to its proper place as the dwelling of YHWH.

How to interpret the final line depends on the grammatical issue noted above. It may describe the house of Jacob's simply possessing again their inheritance (*môrāš* as a noun) after having been driven out by the combined enemy forces. *yrš* ('possess' or 'dispossess') occurs frequently in Deuteronomy, linking the covenant past with the future. The noun forms vary: *yĕrûšâ* is the common term in Deuteronomy; Ezekiel uses *môrāšâ*, while here we read *môrāš* (Wolff 1986: 60; Block 2013: 91). On the other hand, this expression may imply again bringing measure-for-measure judgment on Edom, who had dispossessed Judah. Either way, the prophetic word about YHWH's people possessing continues in v. 19. There they will extend their 'possessions' beyond earlier territorial holdings of Israel.

18. The 'house of Joseph' is an unusual insertion in addition to 'house of Jacob'. It is the only place where the two are used together. Here the latter refers to Judah, while the 'house of Joseph' is an allusion to the northern kingdom (Renkema 2003: 205; Jenson 2008: 24). 'Stubble' or 'chaff' (*qaš*) signifies both Esau's utter worthlessness to start with as well as their end in complete destruction. Just as those drinking themselves to oblivion on Mount Zion would be no more, now the 'house of Esau' would be consumed. See the same imagery in Ps. 83:14–15[13–14] regarding the destruction of Israel's enemies. Only in Obadiah is Israel the flaming instrument (Wolff 1986: 66). It is revenge on the 'house of Esau' by the 'hand of my people Israel' (Ezek. 25:14).

That escaped 'remnant' (*pĕlêṭâ*) is negatively reflected in v. 18 – there will *not* be a 'shred' (*śārîd*) left. The annihilation suggested by the image needs to be read with the closure in v. 21. The 'house of Esau' – used only here – intentionally echoes the brothers' narratives in Gen. 25–36.

Explanation

While Zion was viewed by some as inviolable – even up to the crisis of 587 BC – that was a theologically unsound position. The ethical demands of the covenant were repeatedly violated, and the devastation by the Babylonians was the fulfilment of YHWH's covenant sanctions. Jeremiah emphasizes this theme (see 9:11–15[12–16]; 25:1–11). Nevertheless, these two verses present a remarkable picture. A mere remnant – just shreds of what has been – will become a mighty flame, empowered by YHWH, effecting his justice. The notion of Zion as a restored place of refuge means that the audience will need to see beyond their current perceptions of Zion.

Burning stubble is an important action in getting land ready for restoration. First it is ignited and then completely consumed. The basic meaning of the second verb is 'to eat', but it expands to include consumption. Fire consumes offerings (Lev. 6:3); fire from YHWH consumed Nadab and Abihu in judgment (Lev. 10:2); the sword devours (Jer. 2:30). YHWH's judgment by fire builds on the metaphor of his being a consuming fire (Deut. 4:24). The image is compelling and terrifying: flames consume swiftly and thoroughly.

There are additional prophetic references to the reunification of the two 'houses'. Isaiah describes a second occasion when the Lord (Adonai) will gather the remnant that remains from places as far away as Mesopotamia, Egypt and the islands of the sea. The descendants of both Judah and Ephraim will together expand to the plains of Philistia to the west and take Edom, Moab and Ammon to the east (Isa. 11:11–14). After the exile, Zechariah declared YHWH will restore the houses of Judah and Joseph and bring back those he scattered to Egypt and Assyria. They will inhabit Gilead to the east and Lebanon to the north (Zech. 10:6–10).

Just as the oracle against Edom commences with 'thus saith YHWH', so it ends with 'for YHWH has spoken'. Edom's end will be as the sovereign YHWH decrees. The rest of the book serves as a prophetic postscript about the restoration of YHWH's people in the land.

The severity of YHWH's wrath against evil in every form is a constant that is both sobering and heartening. It should drive God's people to our knees as we live in contemporary environments that call evil good and good evil (Isa. 5:20). It should drive us to public platforms as we hold officials at every level accountable. The societal consequences are far-reaching and happen with blinding rapidity – endorsing the termination of infant lives and the dissolution of marriage, turning a blind eye to buying and selling sex slaves, paying for political and judicial favours. The list goes on and on. See Baker 2006: 193.

OBADIAH 19–21

Translation

[19]And the Negev will possess Mount Esau; and the Shephelah, the Philistines. And they shall possess the field of Ephraim, and the field of Shomron; and Benjamin, the Gilead.

[20]And the exiles of this host of the sons of Israel [will dispossess] Canaanites unto Zarephath; and the exiles of Jerusalem who are in Sepharad, they will possess the cities of the Negev.

[21]And the deliverers will go up on Mount Zion to judge Mount Esau, and the kingdom will be YHWH's.

Notes on the text

19. The regional names point to the Israelite inhabitants of those areas, indicated by the masc. pl. verb *wĕyāršû*. The direct-object marker *ʾet* prior to 'Mount Esau', 'the Philistines' and 'the Gilead' indicates directional expansions of YHWH's people. Mount Esau is **a hapax** that stands in for Mount Seir. When people are the object of the verb *yrš*, it means to 'dispossess'. If land is the object, then 'possess' is the implication (Block 2013: 97).

Because the single mention of one small tribe, Benjamin, is unusual, Achtemeier suggests reading *bĕnê ʿammôn* ('the sons of Ammon') instead of *binyāmîn* (1996: 251).

20. The Hebr. is awkward; Achtemeier declares it a corrupt text (1996: 251). The critical apparatus does not include any evidence from versions or MSS that would help sort it out. *haḥēl-hazzeh* has prompted some emendations, but see below. It seems that the verb at the end 'they will possess' governs both segments of the verse.

Instead of *ʾăšer*, a rel. pron., the text might have read *yiršû ʾēt* ('they will possess' followed by the direct object marker), which would maintain the consistent parallelism through the verse.

21. The MT reads *mōšīʿîm* as a hiph. masc. pl. ptc., meaning 'those who are delivering' or 'saving'. Multiple Greek versions and Syr read 'those who rescue' as if it were pass.: 'those men who have been saved'. The MT reading is supported by Vg and Tg.

Form and structure

The style shifts noticeably: the pronouncements are longer descriptions that employ the third-person weqat. forms in vv. 19 and 21. The subjects of the first (v. 19) are the Negev and the Shephelah. These two geographical names serve as **metonymies** for the inhabitants of those regions. The objects are respectively Mount Esau and the Philistines. The second line is not as clearly balanced in the MT. The masc. pl. subjects who will possess the fields of both Ephraim and Shomron are unnamed. The closing weqat. form (v. 21) sets those who are on Mount Zion over those on Mount Esau. In between (v. 20) are two clauses that commence with *wĕgālūt*, likewise a metonymy for those who were exiled. After that word, each part of the verse moves into its own syntactical and geographical territory.

Comment

19. When Judah was under duress – which happened on more than one occasion – they were often pressured from the south-east by Edom and from the west by the Philistines. The Edomites had filtered westwards across the Aravah and into the Negev even by the time YHWH brought the Israelites out of Egypt (Num. 20:14–21). They were a persistent thorn in the flesh of the south-eastern flank of Judah, especially in the late Iron Age. See the 'Introduction'. On the presence of Edomites in the Negev and farther west, see Anderson 2010: 250–251. By the fourth century BC, the Idumeans controlled the whole of the Negev as well as a good part of the Shephelah (the foothills to the west and south-west of the tribal area of Judah). The OT city of Mareshah, Marisa in the Intertestamental period, was Idumean. This first territorial reversal means not only push-back into the Aravah; it declares that the inhabitants of the Negev will possess Mount Seir, the heartland of Edom south-east of the Dead Sea.

The Philistines historically made incursions from the western coastal plain through the buffer zone of the Shephelah into Judah proper, starting in the period of the Judges, escalating in the early monarchy under Saul and David, and continuing into the eighth century BC. The formerly beleaguered populations on the vulnerable western front will reverse that picture. Obadiah is not the only prophet to voice a death knell for the Philistines; see Jer. 47:4–8; Zeph. 2:4–7. By the time of the Persians, Philistia was assimilated and after the conquest of Alexander the Great, all that remained was the name Palestine (Baker 2006: 197).

The second half of the verse lacks a named subject for 'they will possess'. One suggested emendation has been to remove the direct-object marker before 'field of Ephraim', making it the subject and 'the field of Samaria' the object. That, however, is not a particularly helpful emendation because the two expressions overlap. Allen (1976: 70, n. 37) reads 'fields of Samaria' as a gloss; Stuart (1987: 407) emends 'field of Ephraim' to 'the mountainous area [*har*] of Ephraim', following the LXX; *har Ephraim* is the common expression regarding Ephraim, which in turn points to the northern kingdom. When all is said and done, however, the geopolitical implications of this segment are not clear.

The subjects who will possess Ephraim and Samaria may be Judahites. If so, this may be an allusion to a future turnaround from previous history when the characteristically stronger northern kingdom made life miserable for the south on occasion (2 Chr. 28:5–8). While the entire house of Jacob will be reunited in the future, the vestiges of the former southern kingdom will more than hold their own.

A second option is to read Ephraim as the subject who will at some point occupy the 'fields of Samaria'. If the latter name refers to the historic capital of the northern kingdom, several scenarios suggest themselves. The name itself smacks of the foreignness introduced by the Omri dynasty (1 Kgs 16:21–33). Further, echoes of 2 Kgs 17 may underlie this; the inhabitants of that region transplanted from across the Assyrian Empire will no longer be there. In any case, a place whose name bears traditionally negative associations will be repossessed.

The final allusion to Benjamin seems initially opaque, but the geographical context sheds light on the matter. Even though Benjamin was a small tribal area, it was formidable in terms of its geopolitical significance. It was sandwiched between the north and south, and the major east–west and north–south routes met in Benjamin at Ramah. During the period of the Judges, the tribal area was overrun by Ammonites coming through Gilead and across the Jordan Valley to fight against Judah, Benjamin and Ephraim (Judg. 10:9). The unsavoury events at the end of the book of Judges established a connection between the tribe of Benjamin and Jabesh in Gilead (Judg. 21). On behalf of Jabesh-Gilead, the new king Saul went to war from the centrally located Benjamin against Ammon (1 Sam. 11:1–11). Small as it was, the tribe was repeatedly contested between north and south. In the aftermath of Jerusalem's destruction, a makeshift government was established at Mizpah in Benjamin. It was the locus of turbulence as the shreds of Jewish settlement attempted to reestablish some form of continuity (Jer. 40 – 41). In anticipation of a future restoration, Benjamin would be an excellent location for gathering to move out triumphantly. It was centrally located, proximate to the cities of Judah and the hill country, and easily connected with the Shephelah and the Negev. These same geographical allusions appear in Jeremiah's words of future restoration for the people (Jer. 32:44).

20. The first line is syntactically more difficult and lacks a finite verb, but the proper names suggest that the first *gālût* refers to the exiles from the north. The second group of exiles is associated directly with Jerusalem. Appended after the major disjunctive accent is an additional brief indication that 'they [unnamed again] will possess the cities of the Negev'. Because this is the only verb, it governs the first clause about the exiles who are in northern regions, the second, addressing the exiles of Jerusalem and this final clause.

While the syntax is rugged and the name Sepharad is a conundrum, the intent of the verse is clear. Those who have been exiles from both north and south are coming back. But how does it work? Each use of the sg. term *gālūt* has a locational connection, but both lack clarity. The disruption of exile is possibly even embedded in the rhetoric as the movements both to and from exile are interrupted. In the first case, *haḥēl hazzeh* has been read by some as a proper name, Halah – a possible, but unidentified, destination of the northern exiles in 722 BC. It may represent the most distant location imaginable in that context (Renkema 2003: 212). The LXX has read it as 'this first captivity', presumably from *ḥll* in the hiph. ('to begin'), likewise pointing to the exile of the northern kingdom. *haḥēl* could also be a shortened form of *ḥayil* (*ḥēl*), a formidably large group. Followed by 'children of Israel', this would indicate the larger of the two exiles. *ḥayil* may mean 'upper class', a social stratum that was exiled (*HALOT* 311–312; see 'Comment' on v. 11). The presumed object of 'they will possess' is 'the Canaanites', specified by the mention of Zarephath, a city in Phoenicia near Tyre and Sidon. The designation of 'Canaanites' continued in common parlance into the first century; compare the Gospels of Matthew and Mark regarding the Syro-Phoenician woman. Matthew's term is 'Canaanite' (Matt. 15:22) while Mark identifies the region as Syro-Phoenicia (Mark 7:24–26). In the absence of some form of *yrš*, the rel. pron. *ʾăšer* has been emended to read *yiršû* or *tirāš* with either an indefinite masc. pl. subject or *gālūt* as the subject (Gray 1953: 53; see also Ben Zvi 1996: 216–221).

The second part of the verse addresses the waves of exiles deported from Jerusalem (2 Kgs 24:10 – 25:12). They would reclaim the cities of the Negev from the Idumeans. The result of the two population movements would be resettlement in the entirety of an expanded land. The challenging question is what to do with *ʾăšer bispārad*. Even though Sepharad was the standard name for Spain in the Syr and Tg, those are later texts; there is no evidence of Jewish settlement there prior to AD 70. Several locations have been suggested. The name *Çparda* appears in Persian inscriptions as a land subject to the great king. In that context, it occurs in conjunction with 'Jaunâ', peoples called 'Ionians' (Greeks). The Behistun Inscription has it in proximity to Media, Armenia and Cappadocia, which implies somewhere in Asia Minor. The drawback is the later date of these inscriptions (Schrader 1885, 2: 145–146). Sardis in western Asia Minor had a long-standing Jewish population, indicated by a sizable synagogue and an Aramaic inscription from Daskyleion that is either fifth or fourth century BC (Cross 1966: 7–10).

A second option is the site of Hesperides (ancient Berenice near Benghazi in Libya), which fits in terms of consonantal similarity. In addition, there were Jewish settlements on the northern coast of Africa. The *Letter of Aristeas* references Jewish prisoners in the late fourth century BC that Ptolemy Lagos settled in Egypt and Cyrene; see also Josephus, *C. Ap.* 2.44. The case for Libya has been made by Gray (1953: 57–59), who notes the parallel geographical movements: those Jews coming from Mesopotamia returned to the north, and those who would settle in the Negev arrived from the far west. To be sure, by the first century AD, there was a Jewish presence in Cyrene (Luke 23:26; Acts 2:10). For a review of all three options, see Pons 2014: 297–313 and Lipinski 1973: 368–730. Sardis seems the most likely.

21. With the territorial resettlements in place, attention turns once more to Mount Zion, no longer buffeted by enemies but restored as the nexus between heaven and earth. The symbolism of 'going up' echoes the Zion visions in Mic. 4:1–5 and Isa. 2:2–4. To that location all nations will ascend, and there YHWH will judge and settle disputes among the nations. Likewise, in Obadiah the kingdom belongs to YHWH and judgment will occur. The question is the identity of those who go up and how they function. 'Deliver' and 'judge' appear together in the summary description of the period of the Judges (Judg. 2:16–18). Othniel is called a *môšîaʿ* ('one who delivers'), who went on to rule (Judg. 3:9–10). Following suit, subsequent judges delivered their people (6:15; 8:22; 10:1; 12:2). The two concepts merge here with the rich connotations of deliverance and justice. The implications of YHWH's sovereignty are expressed in the absolute rule emanating from the centre of his kingdom.

Because there has been such a focus through the book on the tensions between Jacob and Esau, Israel and Edom, Mount Zion and Mount Esau, and all that these oppositions mean, the book could not conclude with people from Jerusalem inheriting only Negev settlements. Something exceedingly important is reserved for Zion and Jerusalem. YHWH delegates regency to the deliverers over his restored dwelling on Mount Zion.

Explanation

When the Assyrians overran the northern kingdom in 722 BC, their policies of exile and population exchange severed the connections of people with their homeland. The Babylonians continued that foreign policy as they dealt with conquered people. The returnees of Obadiah are coming from geographical locations to which they were dispersed. The first three named inheritors of v. 19 are nearby; in contrast, Sepharad is viewed as at 'the ends of the earth' (Ben Zvi 1996: 223). Perhaps *haḥēl* is intended the same way if it meant a location (Halah) far to the east. These specific indicators fit into the grander picture of regathering from the four corners of the earth that is threaded through the prophets along with representative samples of the hymnic tradition (Ps. 107:3; Isa. 60:4–10).

Isaiah prophesied that the remnant would be gathered in the day that the root of Jesse raised a banner. That united remnant would press westwards against Philistia, east into Gilead, and take over Moab, Edom and Ammon (Isa. 11:10–14). Ezek. 37:15–28 also conveys the picture of the reunited houses of Judah and Ephraim. Although Edom is not specifically mentioned, Seir appears in the brief oracle following the description of Babylon's fall (Isa. 21:11). Accompanying it is Dumah which could be a play on the name Edom.

It is initially a surprise that the exiles of Jerusalem will not possess Jerusalem, and raises the question as to who will. V. 21 is the answer. The final line is an **inclusio** with the introduction. It echoes the ancient declaration in the song of YHWH's victory as he brought his people out of Egypt, out of the house of bondage and across the sea (Exod. 15:18); Moses and all the people sang it. It echoes David's blessing at the end of his life as he was about to hand over the earthly kingdom to Solomon (1 Chr. 29:11): all Israel witnessed it. Now, these words of YHWH assure the justice he will surely bring about for his people, even as they have endured just punishment for their own deeds. What remains of Edom after judgment will be under the rule of YHWH. The human 'saviors' will be delegated representatives of the kingship of YHWH. The def. art. on 'kingship' points to its absolute nature in contradistinction to all current political endeavours. Israel's future rule on Mount Zion will be only because they have been delegated by the Master of the universe (Block 2013: 102–103).

Closing thoughts

Stepping back to survey the ground Obadiah has covered in these twenty-one verses, what messages rise to the surface? Surely the disastrous effects of deceived self-perceptions and arrogance are right up at the top. When these effects are combined with opportunities to wreak havoc, the results are heartbreaking, especially when they destroy relationships.

At the same time, what appears to be hopeless will be turned around by YHWH on his day. Just as Israel's oppressors will be overcome, so will ours, whoever and whatever they may be. Attention to Obadiah's words creates a community waiting in expectant hope for the kingdom of YHWH, aware of the cup and fire of judgment that are on the way to Mount Zion (Wolff 1986: 70–71).

As the supreme – and only – antidote to pride, we remember that the enthronement of Jesus was on the cross. There he took on the cup and fire of judgment. It was there that he was declared King of Israel, adorned with a crown of thorns, and earlier dressed in the royal colour of purple. Isaac Watts's venerable hymn text says it best:

> When I survey the wondrous cross, on which the Prince of Glory died;
> My richest gain I count but loss and pour contempt on all my pride.
> See from his head, his hands, his side, sorrow and love flow mingled down.
> Did e'er such love and sorrow meet, or thorns compose so rich a crown?

JONAH

INTRODUCTION

These four chapters both captivate and bewilder. The prophet seems like a caricature of our own foibles – magnified. His experiences are off the charts. Is he – are they – for real? How do we read this as part of authoritative Scripture when every chapter leaves us scratching our heads? Who is this God who sends his servant into the jaws of a violent city, chases him down with a destructive tempest, nearly drowns him, burps him back to land via a fish, gives him a message to broadcast that could get him skewered, and in the end aggravates him with persistent questions? What is the point of it all?

The main characters, God and Jonah, do not lodge in singular historical and literary contexts. Our exploration will range well beyond Israel in the eighth century, even though the narrator intends audiences initially to connect the text with the prophet named Jonah, son of Amittai, who lived in the northern kingdom at that time. Naming Nineveh is also purposeful: it points to the threatening spectre of Assyria. Nevertheless, the time frames expand. When was the book written, and how were its messages read by subsequent generations of God's people? What kind of story is this?

1. APPROACH TO THE TEXT

The affirmation, articulated in the 'General Introduction', that the Word is powerful and is authoritative for God's people across generations and cultures shapes our investigation. That does not impose a straitjacket of only one interpretive scheme on this narrative. It rather underscores that the Scriptures are rich with possibilities. A robust approach to the Jonah narrative presupposes that the doctrines of revelation and inspiration will result in literary artistry and sound theological applications, interwoven within a historical narrative that is not divorced from reality, even when that reality is laced with divine interventions. Even though it is de rigueur in some circles to dismiss historical questions in favour of narrative pursuits, it is a methodological error not to ask those questions when a text presents itself within a space–time context.

Three principles – admittedly simplified here – shaped much critical methodology in the nineteenth and twentieth centuries: scepticism towards sources; presumption that present human experience limits what qualifies as historical in the past; determination that all historical events are simply the result of natural forces or human agency. The result was suspicion about the historical veracity of biblical narratives. The primary targets of this scepticism were the accounts narrating supernatural interventions. These were deemed to be the product of ideological thinking and not accurate presentations of what happened. Nevertheless, records of divine interventions are not limited to the HB; they are evident in ANE texts as well. Regnant world views in the ANE accepted the supernatural as a matter of course. Just as the biblical text credits YHWH with divine intervention, so for example do the scribes of Shalmaneser III (858–824 BC) ascribe his victories to Ashur (*ANET* 276–279). A century later, Sennacherib and his son Esarhaddon regularly credit the god Ashur with victories for the Assyrians (*ANET* 287–294). Accounts of these victories are mined for historical details. What makes the HB unique is the teleological nature of God's involvement. Furthermore, the text presents a uniquely monotheistic focus. Leaders of Israel are routinely evaluated and critiqued through the lenses of obedience to the covenant, not in terms of their power and politics. See Provan et al. (2015: 102–152) and Lessing (2007: 4–8). In contrast, Assyria and Egypt minimized or ignored military defeat and royal weakness in their historical records (Siddall 2013: 98). Jonah is not exempt from the thinly veiled criticisms of the narrator.

Studies of Jonah elucidate the complexity of the text and its primary characters. It is important to explore *how* the story is told. The interwoven forms and content are the launch points into assessment of the suggested genre labels. The book does not permit a singular focus. It is not only a theological treatise regarding the nature of YHWH, or the portrait of a self-centred rebel, or a satire of one sort or another designed to skewer Israel and Israel's prophetic office. Each of those 'freezes' the characters and sets them outside the tangled nature of human existence. The narrative, whenever it was written, vividly portrays the challenges caused by abruptly articulated commands, by fear, by rapidly modulating circumstances and by new developments that are entirely unexpected. All the improbabilities jammed together force readers to stop and, if nothing else, consider whether they acknowledge the sovereign rule of YHWH over all of reality. We must allow Jonah to reflect the volatility of emotion that is human and not subject him to scrutiny as 'the failed prophet of YHWH'. In sum, I offer a sympathetic reading of Jonah.

2. IDENTITY OF JONAH

The character and mission of Jonah are located in the historical context of 2 Kgs 14:23–27. Jonah, the son of Amittai, is called the 'servant of YHWH', the characteristic term for a prophet of YHWH. Jonah's home town was Gath-Hepher in Galilee, near one of the interior routes connecting Acco on the Mediterranean Sea with the Sea of Galilee. Gath-Hepher was just a few miles east of Nazareth, a datum of interest eight centuries later when Jesus references 'the sign of Jonah' (Matt. 12:38–42; 16:4; Luke 11:29–32). Jonah was prophesying when Jeroboam (II), son of Joash, was king of the north (793–753 BC). If Jonah functioned within that court scene in Samaria, his claim to worship YHWH reflects an unusual stance in the northern kingdom. It is reminiscent of the Obadiah who, just about a century earlier, remained faithful to YHWH even in Jezebel's reign of terror (1 Kgs 18:3–16). Jeroboam was an evil monarch, and his own kingdom was ripe for judgment. Nevertheless, Jonah prophesies not only a 'stay of execution' for the northern kingdom but the prospect of robust territorial expansion – at least for a time. These developments are based on YHWH's mercy for his people. It is not stated how Jonah's seemingly quite disparate prophetic activities, one in Israel proper and the other on the streets of Nineveh, interface in terms of the time frame.

Jonah's activities and words do not lend themselves to a single character assessment. In some quarters, he is pilloried as disobedient, unrepentant of that disobedience, self-pitying and angry (Fretheim 1977: 32–33). Pressing it further, his character represents the angry and suffering posture of Israel against the backdrop of evil powers (Wolff 1986: 165–176). The label 'nationalistic bigot' captures the least charitable expression of this approach to Jonah (Nogalski 2011a: 442). The fact that he is not called a prophet in the text intimates that he was not a good prophet, even though not a false one (Hoyt 2019: 417, n. 26).

At the same time, his message is wildly successful, in spite of himself. Generally, YHWH's prophets were rejected because of their stern messages; Jonah's story clearly turns that on its head. He seems to reject the recipients of his message, even before he proclaims it. Jonah is faced with deeply disturbing dissonances. His understanding of YHWH along with his own role leave him with two seemingly unacceptable options. Come to think of it, he is like most of God's people when faced with the need to choose 'the lesser of two evils'. His fear, flight, stubbornness, excuses, interspersed with bursts of genuine gratitude and joy, resonate with us. Jonah's story is illustrative of the pervasive effects of fear and anxiety in a world fraught with violence and uncertainty.

There are differences of opinion regarding whether Jonah's names have symbolic significance. Venturing in the direction of allegory, *yônâ*, meaning 'dove' (Lev. 5:7, 11) and one who is beloved (Song 2:14; 5:2; 6:9), could allude to Israel. It is a short step to connecting Jonah with disobedient Israel (Wolff 1986: 98–99). Doves, after all, are flighty (cf. Hos. 7:11); so also is Israel in its allegiance to YHWH. His surname, Amittai, may combine *ʾemet* ('faithful') and the abbreviated form of the divine Name (Yah). Jonah is 'son of the Faithful One'. YHWH's faithfulness and Jonah as rebellious Israel come together in the turbulence of the narrative (Ben Zvi 2003: 43).

There are additional potential symbolisms. The *yônâ* was also a sacrificial guilt offering for the common folk (Lev. 5:8; 12:8; 14:22). The meaning encoded in Jonah's name may not be a flighty, timid bird that moans and laments, but one that is suitable for an atoning sacrifice. The salvation of two groups of Gentiles occurs at Jonah's expense, the first on board the ship and the second in Nineveh. When Jonah arrives in the city, he takes on an ambivalent role, potentially destroying his own life by uttering a prophecy he assumes will turn out to be false (Frolov 1999: 95–97). Finally, *yônâ* can also mean 'oppressiveness' (Zeph. 3:1); the double meaning may be intentional as the commission of Jonah will involve future oppressions against YHWH's people (Sweeney 2000: 307–308). While these connections are of interest, most names in the HB are not invested with weighty symbolism. When all is said and done, it is not overly fruitful to construct levels of symbolic meaning from 'dove' and 'faithful' (Stuart 1987: 431).

3. HISTORICAL CONTEXTS

Multiple layers of context warrant exploration. The connection with 2 Kgs 14:23–27 suggests the geopolitics of eighth-century Israel vis-à-vis Nineveh and Assyria as the starting point in terms of the narrated events. The subsequent historical pictures are less definitive but equally significant as the text is read and studied in post-Assyrian cultural contexts.

3.1 Assyrian geopolitics in the ninth and eighth centuries BC

Under the aggressive military policies of Ashurnasirpal II (883–859 BC) and his successor, Shalmaneser III (859–824 BC), Assyrian armies ranged westwards into the Levant, including Syria, Palestine and eastern Anatolia. The royal inscriptions of both rulers provide a significant cultural, geopolitical and religious backdrop for ninth-century Assyria. Recurring themes include brutality in repeatedly massacring whole cities (*ANET* 275–281).

Contrary to the opinion that Assyria started to take interest in regions to the west only in the eighth century BC (Goldingay 2021: 370), the Levant was already important for Assyria from an economic standpoint, being a source of metals, timber and manufactured goods. Further, campaigning to the Mediterranean Sea signalled military might and domination. Ashurnasirpal received tribute from Tyre, Sidon, Byblos and other cities on the Great Sea (Grayson 1976, 2: 143, 149; Siddall 2013: 63). In the mid-ninth century BC, Shalmaneser III defeated Hadadezer of Damascus along with a twelve-king coalition and received tribute from Jehu of Israel (*ANET* 280–281).

From the end of the ninth to the mid-eighth century, however, the empire was characterized by general instability, weakened kings (Shamshi-Adad V and Adad-nirari III) and the resultant decentralization, a situation that spiralled further down in the decades between the death of Adad-Nirari III (783) and the rise of Tiglath-Pileser III in 746 (Wilson 1918a: 453; Olmstead 1923: 174; Alexander et al. 1988: 78–81; Page 1995: 204–205; Timmer 2011: 92–94). Although inscriptions are few, there are several stelae from that period referring to the power held by regional governors (Lawrence 1986: 123; Ferguson 1996: 301–305; Rainey and Notley 2006: 211). They were installed in secondary administrative posts in turbulent areas, notably in the northern and western parts of Assyria; i.e. the greater Nineveh region (Siddall 2013: 58–59, 100–102).

During the reign of Asshur-Dan III (771–754), the Eponym Chronicles indicate there was ongoing plague and possibly internal revolt extending from his sixth to twelfth years. These problems were exacerbated by a solar eclipse in 763 (Lemanski 1992: 40–49). It was viewed as a portent of disaster both for the country and for the king. Protocol for a total eclipse included proclaiming a fast, followed by the king stepping off his throne, removing his royal garments and handing them over to a substitute king until the danger passed. The echoes in Jon. 3 are unmistakable (Wiseman 1979: 45–51; Stuart 1987: 490–493; Walton 2018: 101). In this context, the term 'king of Nineveh' did not imply power; rather, the subtext is impotence (Judisch 1999: 154).

Although Nineveh was not officially the capital until 705, when Sennacherib elevated it to that position, it was a venerable city and was especially noteworthy after Tiglath-Pileser resuscitated the empire in 745 BC. It retained that reputation until it was destroyed in 612 BC, prophesied by Nahum (see also Zeph. 2:13–15). Accompanying the Greek troops who were engaged in battle along the Tigris River, Xenophon bore witness in 401 BC to the wholesale ruin of both Calah and Nineveh (*Anab.* III.iv.6–12).

Two sticking points in terms of the accuracy of the narrative details in Jonah are the expression 'king of Nineveh' (3:6) and the indication of three days' journey regarding its being a 'great city' (3:3). It is argued that the text must have been written much later when the name Nineveh was only a mythic representation of a threatening enemy from the past. Under those circumstances, the author did not bother with the detail regarding just when Nineveh became the capital and whether the king of the empire resided there. If the narrative was composed close to the presumed date of the events, the ruler would have been properly called 'king of Assyria' (Allen 1976: 186), the designation that recurs through 2 Kgs 18 – 20.

That argument can, however, go both ways. No matter when the narrative was written, the authorship would have been aware of the title as it appears in 2 Kgs 18 – 20. Perhaps the author chose to use 'king of Nineveh' to set off *this* particular situation from considerations of the wider empire. During the turbulence of the mid-eighth century, the regional governors controlling the western, northern and eastern flanks of the central part of Assyria wielded considerable power (Lawrence 1986: 124–131). If the local ruler in Nineveh had limited power, he would seek support for significant edicts, as evidenced in Jon. 3:7. Considerations of the size of Nineveh will be addressed in the 'Comment' on 3:3.

The geopolitical situation in eighth-century Israel is equally important (Rainey and Notley 2006: 215–217). Adad-Nirari III engaged in a successful war against a north Syrian alliance, in which he significantly weakened the power of Damascus, the rest of Syria and Israel (*ANET* 281–282). Joash of the northern kingdom took control of contested lands between Israel and Aram-Damascus (Siddall 2013: 41–43, 66–70). After Adad-Nirari's death in 783, the combination of weakness in Assyria and Syria gave Jeroboam, son of Joash, freedom to expand in accordance with the word of YHWH through his servant Jonah, son of Amittai (2 Kgs 14:24–27). Therefore, at the time that Jonah was commissioned to go to Nineveh, the northern kingdom was in a good place geopolitically even though the king was remembered as wicked. At some point during the reign of Jeroboam, there was a memorable earthquake (Amos 1:1; Zech. 14:5). One wonders how far the tremors and aftershocks spread, both geographically and socioreligiously. The breathing space closed with the death of Jeroboam in 753 BC and the subsequent rise of Tiglath-Pileser III (also called Pul) in 745. The northern kingdom quickly spiralled downward, going through multiple kings (2 Kgs 15). Samaria capitulated in 722 to Sargon II (Alexander et al. 1988: 81; *ANET* 284–285).

3.2 Compositional time frames: overview

While the basic narrative does not necessitate an eighth-century composition, the audience is primed to hear the story in that historical context. The narrative follows those of Elijah and Elisha in 1–2 Kgs; Jonah was at the pivotal point between those prophets and the written oracles of Hosea and Amos. If Jonah's story was recorded prior to the devastation of Samaria and the north in 722 BC, the brief heyday under Jeroboam II (2 Kgs 14:25) was within the memory of readers. How rapidly their circumstances shifted to the harsh realities of the encroaching forces of Tiglath-Pileser III! It is a bitter backdrop for a narrative about sparing Nineveh.

Most scholars tend to date the book at some point in the exilic or post-exilic periods. See Allen (1976: 186–188); Fretheim (1977: 30–37); Alexander et al. (1988: 52–63); and Sasson (1990: 26–27) for representative presentations. The *terminus ad quem* for composition is the mid-third century BC because 'the twelve prophets' (presumably including Jonah) are mentioned in Ben Sirach 49:10. The translator's prologue to Ben Sirach mentions the 'thirty-eighth year of Euergetes' (132 BC), and the translator happens to mention the fact that Jesus ben Sirach was his grandfather, intimating that the book was written approximately 200 BC.

The brutality of the Assyrian Empire lived on in the corporate memory of Israel (mentioned in Judith and Tobit), even though Nineveh was overrun by Babylon in 612 BC and was left as a ruin. The catastrophic fall of Jerusalem and destruction of the temple in 587/588 BC, the exile and the return of a small number of Jews to Judah also left their mark on the recipients of every prophet's message. Once the book was written, readers at specific points in time and in particular places would read the narrative through their own lenses. Ben Zvi (2003: 6–10) describes these readers (and rereaders) as a knowledgeable elite living primarily in a post-monarchical context. They would have been aware of the whole sweep of their national traditions, and that dynamic inevitably shaped each successive generation's readers.

3.3 Possible compositional contexts: reflections

If the book was composed in Jonah's lifetime, the northern kingdom was thriving, at least on the surface. If Jonah was a presence in the court, he would have been aware of diplomatic exchanges between Israel, Syria and Assyria and be more sensitive than others regarding the delicate work necessary to maintain the international power balance. The title 'king of Nineveh' may indicate awareness on the part of the authorship of the mid-eighth century fracturing of Assyria. From the Nineveh perspective, Jonah's deputation to Nineveh might have been initially perceived as a customary arrival of a foreign attaché (Wiseman 1979: 42–44).

If the narrative was written in the century between the fall of the north and the impending tragedy for the south, the overthrow of Samaria instead of Nineveh would be the dominant concern. Jonah's prophecy regarding the 'overturning' of Nineveh, however it was understood (see below), would read like an ugly falsehood in every respect. By 705, Nineveh had been made the capital of Assyria by Sennacherib. It was a mighty city; Nahum's picture of the violence is vivid. None of the geopolitical or personality factors seem to fit the narrative of Jonah 3.

Once several additional centuries intervened between the presumed events of the narrative and their possible inscripturation, the world stage would have been radically reset. Later audiences, knowing of Nineveh's fall in 612 and the canonical backdrop of Nahum, would expect the Jonah of 2 Kgs 14:23–27 to prophesy judgment against Nineveh, a legendary locus of wickedness and violence. As the narrator presents Jonah, his commission to go to Nineveh was unambiguous and dangerous. That Jonah's prophecy results in repentance indicates that the narrator makes the theological connection between Jon. 3:8–10 and Jer. 18:7–11, a sixth-century prophecy (Wolff 1986: 98–100).

Those commentators who presume post-exilic composition point out historical vagueness in addition to linguistic and cultural peculiarities (see Allen 1976: 186-188; Alexander et al. 1988: 52–61; Sasson 1990: 22–27; Ben Zvi 2003: 7–9; Jenson 2008: 29–32; Youngblood 2019: 34–35). The alleged vagueness is of a piece with the intertestamental books of Judith and Tobit, where the historical details are fuzzy at best. The first chapter of Tobit has the hero of the story living from the time of the split in the kingdom (931 BC) until the reign of Sennacherib's son, Esarhaddon (681–669 BC). The story of Judith places the events in the twelfth year of Nebuchadnezzar, who ruled over the Assyrians in Nineveh. Nebuchadnezzar did not come to power until his aged father died in 605 (Rainey and Notley 2006: 262). The interwoven names create a sense of dread but one that has become legendary over time. Through a post-exilic lens, the text of Jonah reflects a Nineveh long gone (Bolin 1995: 110–113).

Additional factors have been noted as supportive of post-exilic composition (Page 1995: 206–209). One is the presumed late language, including Aramaisms (Bewer 1912: 12). Examples include the words *ṭaʿam* ('decree'), *mallāḥ* ('mariner'), *sĕpînâ* ('ship'), the rel.pronoun *š*-, *štq* ('to still') and *mnh* ('to appoint'). These claims, however, were already put to rest by Wilson (1918a: 280–298), who surveyed the biblical usages of each word, comparing them with the translations into Aramaic and the surrounding language contexts. Just because a word is a **hapax** does not automatically render it late. Many of the verbs and nouns in Jonah are also represented in texts deemed by critics to be eighth century BC or before. Presumably later linguistic features are not uniformly late. They are not sufficient to determine the date of a text, notably because the HB represents a limited sample of the much more extensive living language. Additionally, features formerly thought to represent Aramaisms and late language may be connected with Canaanite and Phoenician contexts, perhaps to the extent of representing a northern kingdom dialect (Alexander et al. 1988: 52–55; Sasson 1990: 22–23; see also Lessing 2007: 16–17; Hoyt 2019: 341–348).

A second factor has to do with customs that appear to reflect a Persian context. These include trappings of mourning worn by animals and the participation of nobles along with the king (Allen 1976: 186–188). Those details, along with the presumed inaccuracies, may indicate historical distance from the eighth century. The participation of nobles, however, seems to have been already a part of the Assyrian eighth-century geopolitical context (see above; and Lawrence 1986: 130–132). Perhaps the mourning 'costumes' were as well.

An additional criterion to which scholars have appealed is the matter of intertextual dependency, thinking it may be possible to demonstrate borrowing on the part of the author of Jonah. There are indeed significant connections with Joel, Jeremiah and the psalms. Similarity with significant themes and theological declarations in the canon, however, is not determinative in terms of dependency. See further below.

Arguments from silence are vulnerable, but it seems that a post-exilic author would allude to some of the drastic developments for YHWH's people (Ferguson 1996: 302), just as the initial pronouncement of Jonah against Nineveh evoked the ancient overthrow of Sodom and Gomorrah (Youngblood 2019: 48–49). The juxtaposition of Jonah's narrative and the condemnation of Nineveh by Nahum poses a challenge. It is certainly part of the subsequent interpretive tradition, but the narrative of Jonah closes simply with the expression of YHWH's mercy for Nineveh. Jonah's interaction with foreigners may also be read against the backdrops of Joseph, Daniel, Esther and Mordecai, all of whom manifested a positive presence in foreign courts (Ben Zvi 2003: 127), and all of whom are the subjects of compelling stories.

4. LITERARY ARTISTRY

4.1 Macrostructures

The four chapters may be divided into two mirroring sets that are characterized by both similarity and contrast. Each of the two major sections commences with the command of YHWH to go to Nineveh (1:1–3 and 3:1–3). While they are almost identical commands, the subtle differences are significant and are followed by quite different responses from Jonah. The next parallel development is the prominence of foreigners who, unlike Jonah, are remarkably responsive to what they are learning about God, even though it is pretty much on the fly for each foreign 'community'. The sailors in ch. 1 seem to be a motley crew with distinct allegiances to their own deities; the Ninevites operate (oddly enough) in unison. YHWH miraculously intervenes, both on behalf of each group of foreigners and to nudge Jonah where he needs to be. Those interventions initiate communications (2:3–10[2–9] and 4:2) to YHWH from Jonah. Geography plays an important part in establishing contrasts. It ranges from places on terra firma – such as Nineveh, Joppa and Tarshish – to the more numinous locations of Sheol and the very bottom of the sea.

4.2 Narrative features

How the story is told matters (Magonet 1983: 6). Wayyiq. forms drive the story forward. These are accentuated by **cognate accusatives**, the verb form emphatically followed by the cognate noun (GKC 117q). It is a form of repetition that, especially in a heard text, would be compelling. 'Conventional language is used in an unconventional way' (Limburg 1993: 65). These cognate forms are artfully linked together in ch. 1 where the drama and emotion, like the sea, run high. As an example, the sailors initially fear (v. 5) but as the situation escalates out of control, they 'feared a great fear' (v. 10). By the end of their ordeal, they 'feared a great fear – YHWH' (v. 16). The adjective 'great' appears frequently.

Word pairs link characters, heightening potential comparisons and contrasts. There is an interplay between *zʿq* and *qrʾ* as the sailors 'cry aloud' (*zʿq*, 1:5), the captain commands Jonah to 'cry out' (*qrʾ*) in prayer (1:6), YHWH commands Jonah to 'proclaim' (*qrʾ*) judgment (1:2) and warning (3:2), and the king 'proclaims' (*zʿq*) a decree (3:7). 'Turning [away]' (*šûb*) and 'change' (*niḥam*) draw together the pagans and YHWH (3:8–10). Anger and pity on the parts of Jonah and YHWH are matched (Magonet 1983: 20–21, 25–26). Cooper (1993: 151) points out additional pairs that connect sections of the text: the storm on the sea contrasts with the desert hot wind and sun; the Phoenicians and Assyrians represent two potential threats; the great fish contrasts with the tiny worm.

Key words and concepts are both rich in meaning and potentially and intentionally ambiguous. A signature case is *rāʿâ*, which is used in multiple ways, each usage interacting with the others. The connotations range from moral evil to misery, displeasure, misfortune, disaster and calamity (*DCH* 7:521–524). Of the nine appearances of the word in Jonah, only two specifically imply moral evil (3:8, 10). While YHWH's characterization of Nineveh as *rāʿâ* (1:2) initially suggests to the reader a strong moral component, that may not necessarily be the case. It poses a hermeneutical problem for Jonah. Should he hear 'evil' as a descriptor of the city's wickedness, or focus on the 'calamity' that Nineveh was experiencing in the tumultuous eighth century (Stuart 1987: 437)? The answer is not definitively forthcoming. Battered at sea, the sailors label the 'evil' or 'misfortune' (1:8) of the great storm for what it is: they are in danger of losing their lives. When Jonah accepts responsibility for the storm, he does not label it *rāʿâ*. Between chs. 3 and 4, the obvious evil of the Ninevites is juxtaposed with the not-so-obvious evil afflicting Jonah. The latter has to do with Nineveh apparently getting away with evil. The final occurrence refers to Jonah's own misery (4:6). A central theme of the book is how God deals with 'evils', some natural, some systemic and others individual. The interface of Nineveh, YHWH and Jonah regarding *rāʿâ* is dynamic (Magonet 1983: 22–25). When God sees that the Ninevites turn from *their* disastrous way, he determines to change course regarding the concomitant punishment, called 'the evil' (3:10). This principle reverberates through Scripture: evil acts result in catastrophic punishment (2 Sam. 12:7–15; 1 Kgs 21:17–19; 2 Kgs 21:9–12; Mic. 2:1–5), always indicative of YHWH's justice (Sasson 1990: 76). Equally in the balance, however, is YHWH's mercy. Through his own emotional lenses, Jonah perceives that merciful turn of events as a 'great evil' (4:1), perhaps because the outcome is a commentary on his role in this unsettling process. In frustration, he declares that he knew ahead of time YHWH would respond by turning from the evil (4:2).

The built-in ambiguity of *nehpāket* ('overturned') poses a second major interpretive challenge. Destruction first comes to mind. Lying behind that interpretive choice is the ancient narrative regarding Sodom and Gomorrah, combined with the dominant sense of *rāʿâ* as applied to Nineveh. Nevertheless, the niph. form could also be reflex.: Nineveh would 'overturn itself' and experience a major reformation. To what extent does Jonah hear the ambiguities and double entendres? Recognition of the double meaning has a long history. The Talmud (*b.* Sanh. 89b) posed the conundrum: in regard to 'overturned', Jonah was told 'Nineveh *nehpāket*', but he did not know if for good or for evil.

Contrasts are powerful narrative vehicles. Jonah's character is contrasted with the pagan sailors and captain and his wrath with God's mercy. He sings thanksgiving in the midst of trauma (Fretheim 1977: 51–54). Contrasts contribute to the irony that is laced through the book. What would be expected of an Israelite prophet is countered repeatedly by Jonah. He abandons the task, sleeps on board the ship, does not pray even when exhorted to do so and is angry at repentance. There are also inconsistencies in Jonah's own actions. He flees and yet prays; he preaches with great success even though he does not want to; and he wishes for death in the face of great success (Lessing 2007: 23–25).

Narrative gaps set the stage for later surprise reversals (Sternberg 1985: 312–320). The audience does not know at the beginning just why Jonah makes his radical decision to disobey God, and consequently tends to fill in motivations and character traits. This initial gap controls the narrative for the whole book. It also prompts assessments of the relationship between YHWH and his prophet. Sternberg's reading has Jonah as compassionate and not wanting to issue judgment against Nineveh, as well as being concerned for the sailors' lives. God, on the other hand, is menacing in the extreme in the way he pursues Jonah relentlessly, endangering the mariners on the way. Having set in readers' minds the impression of a God of judgment, the narrator has us ready for Nineveh's destruction, when

'Surprise'! Nineveh repents, the words are ambiguous after all, and Jonah is made out to be unmerciful in the extreme. Sternberg calls the narrative developments 'informational thunderbolts' (319) that destroy the readers' perceptions, cleverly manipulated by the narrator from the beginning. By leaving out what Jonah said when he was still in his country (see 4:2), the audience has been pointed the wrong way. At the end, God and Jonah are still opposites, but their oppositions have shifted 180 degrees.

Dialogue plays a powerful role in biblical narrative (Alter 1981: 70). Direct speech advances the plot, expands the scene and reveals important character details. God not only commands; he also feels pity and compassion. Questions serve rhetorical purposes (Craig 1993: 162–165). In ch. 1, questions elicit a slender thread of information from Jonah and express the mariners' inner worlds of panic-driven, long-shot hope. Not all the questions garner responses. The king poses his own question (3:9), reaching for a hopeful connection with God, whose power and authority he clearly recognizes. In ch. 4, YHWH advances the moral formation of his prophet through questions, some of them adopting Jonah's own language to prod him a bit.

Reported prayers, both long and short, give depth to the characters and propel the narrative forward. There are seven references to prayer. Jonah's two prayers are interwoven in the poem of ch. 2. The cry of the sailors, the content of the king's edict and Jonah's response to YHWH in ch. 4 are equally significant. They all address God in a manner that is evocative of Israelite prayer patterns but also transcends them: crying out to God is a universal response to crisis. It is noteworthy that Jonah does not pray when it might have been expected during the crisis on the ship (Craig 1993: 83–92). In the first three chapters, the threat of death prompts the prayers. Jonah reverses that pattern in ch. 4, longing for death after witnessing deliverance.

4.3 Poetry

The psalm of thanksgiving in ch. 2 sounds like snatches of what Jonah remembers from his liturgical heritage. Parallel lines of poetry and less familiar vocabulary replace narrative patterns. It is a rich fabric, weaving together lyric and liturgical phrases in new ways specifically for Jonah's unique situation. The metaphors in these texts come to life in his terrifying reality. As the tumult sweeps Jonah downward, the unusual words and brief clauses depict the horror. It has a steady downward descent until he reaches the extreme parts of the underwater terrain, nearly dying in unknown depths (Magonet 1983: 49–52). Traditional language gives way at this point. It may be an adumbration; just as Jonah crosses the bars between life and death, he will soon cross from the familiar land of Israel into enemy territory.

Wilson (1918a: 437–443) counters the claim that the psalm was a later insertion by exploring where each of the words in Jonah's psalm appears elsewhere. These expressions include 'belly of Sheol', 'heart of the seas', 'river encompassing me', 'I have been cut off', 'I will add to look to your holy temple', 'seaweed bound to my head', '*tĕhôm* ['depths'] encompassing me', 'the bars of the earth', 'the roots of the mountains' and 'when my soul fainted within me'. This is a theologically profound hymn. Key words in the psalm set the stage for Jonah's prayer in 4:2 even while the latter draws on Exod. 34:6–7.

4.4 Intertextual connections

The intertextual connections evident in Jonah range from Genesis narratives to Torah, and into the historical, prophetic and liturgical texts. The primary connection is with 2 Kgs 14:23–27: the two accounts inform each other. In both cases, human behaviour and divine response seem at odds, especially as Israel's national wickedness seemingly gets a 'pass' (Ben Zvi 2003: 55). Further, what happens when this prophet who spoke of success for his Israelite king apparently shifts his allegiance and interests elsewhere?

Beyond the explicit connection with 2 Kgs 14:23–27, there are echoes of the Elijah narrative from 1 Kgs 17 – 19. Both prophesied in the northern kingdom, Elijah in the ninth century. Just as Elijah ventured into the foreign territory of Phoenicia, Jonah is called to Nineveh. Elijah fled in fear from the fury of Jezebel. Jonah also flees; the question will be just what he fears. Elijah's 'one day journey' from Beersheva is echoed in Jonah's one day's walk into Nineveh. Both men sat under plants, although the circumstances of the arrival and demise of Jonah's plant are extraordinary. Elijah expressed his desire to die as does Jonah. When he arrived at Mount Horeb, Elijah had a conversation with YHWH that started with a divine question; Jonah experiences likewise as he sits east of Nineveh, but the conditions and consequences vary considerably.

Underlying the prophecy of doom pronounced on Nineveh is the Genesis narrative of the overturn of Sodom and the other cities of the plain (Gen. 19). This narrative of judgment shapes how Jonah's words are heard, just as much as the nearer historical contexts in 1–2 Kgs do (Allen 1976: 176).

YHWH's self-revelation of his covenant character in the aftermath of the golden calf debacle (Exod. 34:6–7) is the foundation of Jonah's expressed knowledge of YHWH's graciousness, compassion, long-suffering, abundant *ḥesed* ('covenant love') and forgiveness in 4:2. This affirmation appears in a number of prophetic contexts. One of the most complete is Joel 2:13–14. Joel and Jonah are the only two prophetic texts that add 'and changing concerning the evil', drawing together Exod. 34:6–7 with Moses' prior plea in Exod. 32:12 (change concerning the evil) and YHWH's immediate response. On Jonah's lips, however, confession becomes an accusation (Dozeman 1989: 215–216). See also Schultz 2003: 38–40. The venture out to sea and the tumultuous storm remind the audience of Ps. 107:23–32 and Ezek. 27.

Jonah was not alone in his refusal to accept his prophetic commission. To be sure, none of the others outright turned and fled, but even Moses raised every objection he could think of, topping them off with 'Please send someone else!' At that, the anger of YHWH burned, but he did not let Moses off the hook; Aaron was appointed as spokesperson (Exod. 4:13–16). Jeremiah and Amos responded to YHWH's call with wariness and unease (Jer. 1:4–6; Amos 3:8; 7:14–15). Ezekiel went 'bitter and with a burning spirit' (3:14).

4.5 Unity of the text

For a review of nineteenth-century approaches to the unity of the whole book, see Bewer 1912: 13–21. Nogalski (2011a: 427) offers a succinct summary of the differences that have contributed to the varied scholarly conclusions (see also Alexander et al. 1988: 64–69). The contrast between rebellious and gloomy Jonah (chs. 1, 3, 4) and pious Jonah singing from the fish's belly (ch. 2) is dramatic. Could this possibly be the same person? Instead of sleeping, he is alert. His apparent avoidance of prayer, even when called upon to do so, is transformed into well-informed liturgical prayer. Along with others, Wolff (1986: 78–79, 128–130) concludes that ch.2 is a later addition, primarily because the character of Jonah is so altered, and the story works without ch. 2 (Bewer 1912: 21–24; Wolff 1986: 128–132). To be sure, the narrative does not come unhinged if ch. 2 is removed. Nevertheless, the parallel macrostructure of the four chapters is ruptured if it is excised; key features in ch. 2 are necessary to connect the whole narrative. The ship has taken Jonah into the chaos of the sea 'from the presence of YHWH', but the fish brings him back. He has been shown mercy and given another chance. His response of thanksgiving is important to understand his compliance in ch. 3. It is also the foil for ch. 4; only against the backdrop of his gratitude for YHWH's mercy are his own hard heart and deep internal trauma painfully evident. Jonah's character is alive; he is profoundly affected by his circumstances. Further, while he has been chastened, the audience learns that Jonah still thinks he is correct regarding Nineveh. There are additional examples, both in the HB and outside, where poetry 'interrupts' the narrative. Among them are the songs of Moses and Miriam (Exod. 15:1–22), the victory song of Deborah (Judg. 5) and the recounting in 2 Sam. 22 of David's exploits (Stuart 1987: 470–473; see also Nogalski 2011a: 429).

4.6 Genre and why it matters

A wide range of labels has been proposed to capture the nature of the book and thereby get a better handle on what its intended messages may be. Summaries and justifications for selecting given labels are presented by Wolff (1986: 80–85) and Bolin (1997: 46–51; see also Alexander 1985: 36–37; Lessing 2007: 3–7). Those that have surfaced more frequently include satire, parody, **midrash**, legend, novella, tragedy, didactic fiction, allegory, parable, historicized fiction and historical narrative. Satire and parody draw on the stinging ironies in the book, and often presume the message is aimed at the prophetic office as it emerges in the uncomplimentary picture of Jonah. Wolff suggests the text is 'God's loving laughter over narrow-minded piety', notes that it is misguided to become slaves of 'historicity' (1986: 12) and labels it satire that is filled with irony (1986: 84–86). Ben Zvi (2003: 21–23) ups the ante, calling the book a 'satire within a satire', the targets of which are Jonah as a prophet and those who hold YHWH to 'deadlines' in terms of fulfilment. Parody is closely related; both are intended to ridicule (Jenson 2008: 33; see also Sweeney 2000: 304). There is, however, nothing in the book indicating that it was intended to be funny, whether satire or parody (Stuart 1987: 485). 'Jonah is not painted with the brush of mockery or disdain, but drawn with the pencil of deep and sympathetic insight into human weakness' (Goitein 1937: 74).

Sharp (2008: 177–186) presses the rich possibilities of ironic implications well beyond the expected focus on the persona of Jonah, who contrasts radically with the genuine mariners and an ethically sensitive king. Additional ironies may be noted: YHWH in his sovereignty compels the whole of creation to serve his purposes but apparently does not change the heart of his angry prophet; while Jonah is disobedient, he is right; in spite of Jonah's affirmation of YHWH's merciful character (4:2), YHWH does not seem to treat Jonah himself very mercifully. These are thought-provoking connections and reversals. Nevertheless, irony is sufficiently vague and all-pervasive as to contribute very little to the discussion of genre.

There have been scholars who have viewed Jonah as **midrash**, developing the connections between 4:2 and Exod. 34:6–7 in conjunction with 2 Kgs 14:25. Depending on the scholar in question, base texts have ranged from 2 Kings and Exod. 34 to include Jer. 18:6–11, Joel 2:13–14 and Obadiah (Wolff 1986: 81; Page 1995: 210–211). A note of caution is in order, however, because the term 'midrash' has sometimes been adopted without understanding its range of meanings. It involves exposition of one or more biblical texts, either narrative or instructional. These are then woven together with intertextual connections expanding the exploration (Neusner 2004: vii–viii). Generally, the product is not an extended story. There is nothing about the narrative of Jonah that suggests it is a commentary on other parts of Scripture (Stuart 1987: 436–437). Trible's conclusion is that the book defies any label and should be free to 'move among genres' (1996: 472–474).

Even though some have explored the range of allegorical connections (see those cited and dismissed by Allen [1976: 181]), there is no place in the allegory for God and yet he is the major character. In addition, ch. 4 does not rest comfortably in the allegorical camp (Page 1995: 212–213).

Novella, didactic fiction and historicized fiction are ways to get around the same conundrum – how does the audience deal with extraordinary miracles, exaggeration and 'surprise' in the text? Didactic fiction is set somewhat apart from the novella or historicized fiction by the adjective 'didactic', presuming it teaches theological themes (Limburg 1993: 36). The obvious improbabilities include YHWH's pursuit and 'capture' of a prophet by hurling a storm and appointing a fish, Jonah's living and praying in a fish that subsequently disgorges Jonah at just the right place, wholesale change of an entire large metropolis, fasting animals and an unnamed and weirdly withering plant. In the wake of modernist thinking, the miraculous elements are presumed to be impossible as they are narrated. That is, however, a sorry perspective; a sizable piece of the biblical narrative is centred on the miraculous, culminating in the resurrection of Jesus (Stuart 1987: 440). To dismiss supernatural interventions is contrary to the entire fabric of covenant history. The events in Jonah do indeed surprise readers; that is as it should be. How else would the often-dulled attention of readers be gripped? If we affirm that these remarkable episodes occurred under the sovereign direction of YHWH, the Master of the universe, shaping the message of the book, it then becomes 'didactic history' (Page 1995: 213–219). See below.

The favoured fallback alternative to the presumption that Jonah is a historical narrative is to call it a parable. That avoids the uneasy looseness of the allegory label, the connotations of 'fiction' and the demand for belief in the miraculous (Alexander 1985: 38–40). Strictly defined, however, a parable is a comparison drawn from ordinary life that is familiar to the audience. The Hebr. word *māšāl* has a wide semantic range, from the title of the book of Proverbs to something that verges on a taunt (Mic. 2:4) or a riddle (cf. Ezek. 17). These draw on the familiar but do so in quite different ways. A parable serves as a vehicle for ethical instruction. Generally, parables are brief and do not frequently mention God. In contrast, God or YHWH is the major character in the book of Jonah (Judisch 1999: 148–149). When the parable label is pressed into service in this context, it has a fuzzy boundary with allegory, especially as the explanation presumes the grudging, narrow-minded Jonah is a caricature of a group of people (Allen 1976: 177–179). Further, biblical parables are generally anonymous unless the names are intrinsic to the point of the narrative (Luke 16:19–31; Stuart 1987: 436). This is true for both OT parables (2 Kgs 14:9–10; Ezek. 17 and 24) and the parables of Jesus (Matt. 13).

That leaves historical narrative. When Jesus is asked by some scribes and Pharisees for a sign, he declares that just as Jonah was in the belly of the fish, so also the Son of Man will be in the heart of the earth (Matt. 12:38–41). The allusion is not as compelling if it is not based on YHWH's intervention to bring Jonah back alive, the implication being that the Son of Man will likewise exit the heart of the earth. Just as Jonah's time in the fish was deliverance from the horror of near-death in the sea, so also Jesus' three days in the grave will be a rest after the horror of experiencing God's wrath outpoured while he is on the cross. He declares 'It is finished!' (John 19:30) before being removed to the tomb of Joseph of Arimathea – from which he rises on the third day.

Scholars who prefer to call Jonah a parable maintain that Jesus' reference does not require Jonah's experiences to be factual. Jesus simply adopts a popular Jewish understanding to make a comment about himself (Allen 1976: 180). The claim, however, that Jesus uses a fictional character and event does not fit well with the idea that this is a 'sign'. 'Signs' are divine interventions in a given historical context that point forward, authenticating a forthcoming event that will be equally lodged in history. The miracle of Nineveh's repentance is the second point of connection that Jesus makes. Jonah's very existence was the basis for claiming 'One greater than Jonah is here' (Alexander et al. 1988: 91–94; Judisch 1999: 155–156). That in turn suggests additional potential connections. Jesus accuses his interlocutors of representing a 'wicked and adulterous' generation, echoing the description of Nineveh. The latter repented whereas the generation to whom Jesus refers is sufficiently hardened that they will only be given the 'sign of Jonah', and it may not break through their hardness.

Centuries of interpreters understood that the author's intent was to narrate an event that actually occurred, employing literary conventions to great effect (Alexander 1985: 58). These interpreters were comfortable with the exaggerated surprises in the story, perhaps because they are more common in life than is acknowledged in the narrow dimensions of literary analysis. The improbabilities contribute to the force of the message. The use of 'great' is an example: readers are to think 'big'. Foreigners repent in droves immediately, but God has difficulties with his own people (Fretheim 1977: 66). The book is redolent with surprising elements – a call to go to Nineveh of all places, a prophet who has the brazen effrontery to refuse the call of YHWH and then experiences one adventure after another, all of which were intended to arrest the audience's attention (Allen 1976: 176).

Given the HB concern not to trivialize God, the central character, a caution regarding fictionalizing may be in order. The narrative details that fit the eighth-century BC context suggest that this is not a parable constructed centuries later to make theological points (Youngblood 2019: 50–51). Instead, it is both a window into God's self-revelation in time and space (Stuart 1987: 440) and a message that transcends spatial and temporal boundaries for communities of believers.

4.7 Narrative theology

While the story is disarmingly simple, the questions it raises are complex, and suitable answers seem always to lie just out of reach. The book 'reverberates with a cacophony of theologies. Sovereignty, freedom, creation, retribution, vindictiveness, violence, repentance, mercy, pity, and caprice sound major dissonances' (Trible 1996: 488). How we read the complexities and ambiguities of the narrative shapes both our perceptions of Jonah's character and where we pause in the story to find the lessons. Each read pushes us to see the story and the characters of YHWH and Jonah from new angles (Magonet 1983: 85–87).

We know God is sovereign by virtue of his remarkable engagement with the whole of his creation, his command of the sea and all that is in it, the dry land, the winds over both sea and land, the hearts of motley seamen and hardened urban pagans. He hurls, appoints, turns, changes and questions. God rescues, an important message for those in distress, and he cares for all people, both foreigners and Israelites. Through all the narrative developments, God is the inaugurator. YHWH has the first and the last words in the book (Wolff 1986: 81). Nevertheless, YHWH does not seem entirely benign: to accomplish his purposes, he apparently endangers innocent sailors and hounds his prophet (Trible 1996: 484–485).

The names for the divine Person shift between Elohim when foreigners are the focus and YHWH in relationship to Jonah; that is straightforward. More challenging are the subtle fluctuations in ch. 4, where Jonah's actions and pique draw forth divine provision, gentle rebuke and temporary punishment. The process starts with YHWH's challenging Jonah's angry despair with a question (v. 4). Once Jonah signals his autonomy by exiting the city and building his own shelter (v. 5), the divine stance and name are noticeably different. YHWH Elohim appoints a plant (v. 6). YHWH is still part of the name; he is providing relief for Jonah. The name combination is reminiscent of Gen. 2, where YHWH Elohim cared for Adam and later Eve in the garden. With the appointment of the worm to cut down the plant, however, the formal and distant 'the Elohim' is the subject (v. 7). Elohim likewise appoints the raking east wind that brings Jonah to the end of himself (v. 8). God repeats the question from v. 4 about Jonah's anger, but this time distanced with Elohim. The final rhetorical question contrasting Jonah and YHWH and their respective capacity for compassion comes from YHWH (Magonet 1983: 33–38). This vignette in ch. 4 displays the sensitivity of the narrator for the emotional connections and distance between YHWH and his struggling and troubled prophet.

For his part, Jonah is called a 'servant of YHWH' (2 Kgs 14:25), implying his submission to the commands of YHWH. He exercises the responsibilities of that prophetic role, seemingly in quite public circumstances. The main question for readers is, why does Jonah flee? The question does not garner uniform responses. He may be afraid for his life: returning to the court in Samaria after Nineveh's about-face will be a most uncomfortable re-entrance. At a deeper level, however, he knows YHWH's character all along. Even as he appears to capitulate, he continues to resist because he does not want to see reprieve for Nineveh (Trible 1996: 481).

Servants of YHWH did not always obey the command of YHWH immediately, but none pushed off and went the other direction or pushed back at YHWH by reciting his own self-revelation. Jonah is indeed an atypical prophet. What was the *rāʿâ* that troubled Jonah so, both as it was intrinsic to Nineveh's existence (1:2) and as that existence was prolonged right before Jonah's eyes (3:10 – 4:1)? It seems that we must seek for something more than self-absorption, petulance, possible embarrassment, anger or bad orthodoxy combined with self-righteous hypocrisy. This is the character assessment, give or take a few factors, at which numerous commentators arrive; Hoyt (2019: 458–470) is representative. The 'greatest evil in the book . . . is Jonah' (Lessing 2007: 360). That is harsh. Slightly softening the tone, Fretheim (1977: 19–24) suggests that Jonah disobeys based on what he believes. His prayer and faith demonstrate that he knows God but is unwilling to be part of God's love for enemies. Even though he *experiences* God's judgment and deliverance in the sea and knows what judgment is like, he determines that God should be stricter with the vicious and cruel city. As a contrast, instead of castigating Jonah as a narrow-minded, bigoted prophet, Goldingay (2021: 406–407) recognizes the real conflict that Jonah encounters in his circumstances. He has known life under an imperialistic aggressive power and cannot understand the message he is commissioned to give. It is not necessarily disjunctive to rejoice in his own deliverance (ch. 2) while landing firmly in the court of judgment for brutal enemies.

If we are to take his words in 4:2 at face value, his knowledge of YHWH is his motivating factor, and it does not seem to be reducible to 'bad orthodoxy'. Is he concerned for miscarriage of justice: is this a commentary on the capriciousness of God (Cooper 1993: 149–152)? Or is he concerned that Israel will suffer? Or for his own reputation (Magonet 1983: 85–87)? YHWH's character is tied with his people, rebellious as they are. So is Jonah's. Do readers' own circumstances affect how they interpret Jonah's perceived fear, his apparent desire for death and his concern for his people's future as YHWH's people? Profound fear is knit into the narrative character of Jonah at every turn. This ought not to surprise us: fear enters the human experience in Gen. 3 in the immediate aftermath of disobedience. From that point on, the objects of fear multiply, shifting away from healthy fear of YHWH to dread of everything else. YHWH makes the point to Isaiah: don't fear and dread what these people dread. Let YHWH of Hosts be your Fear and Dread, and he will be your Sanctuary (Isa. 8:12–14).

As an aside, while the fish is not a central character, it is also not entirely ancillary to the point of the book. When Jonah goes to Nineveh, he is likely accompanied by his own miracle narrative. That may be critical in persuading the Ninevites to turn (Bickerman 1967: 30).

5. BRIEF HISTORY OF INTERPRETATION

The history of interpretation, spanning from the first century to modern scholarship, has been succinctly reviewed by Bickerman (1967: 15–18), Alexander et al. (1988: 74–77) and extensively by Bolin (1997: 14–67). The last commences with the earliest pre-modern interpretations, notably Josephus' rendition of the story (*Ant.* 9.10.1–2) and Jesus' didactic use as recorded in the NT (Matt. 12:38–41 // Luke 11:29–32; more indirectly, Matt. 16:1–4). Jonah appears frequently in rabbinic texts; the references are gathered in Levine 1978: 105–106. Those of greatest interest address both Jonah's motive for fleeing from the presence of YHWH when he knew that was impossible and his dismay at the results in Nineveh.

Significant voices represent the church fathers. Tertullian took the Marcionites to task regarding the nature of God as represented in changing his decree concerning Nineveh (*Marc.* I.154–155). Augustine and Jerome wrangled over the nature of the plant and the fish. At the same time, the larger concern of purpose appears: Jerome declares that Jonah was sent to Nineveh as condemnation to the Israelites. From literary and theological perspectives, Jerome read the story as adumbrating the rejection of Jesus by the Jews. For both Jerome and Augustine, Jonah was the personification of now-rejected Judaism.

Among Reformation scholars, the names Luther and Calvin stand out. Luther read the text against the backdrop of his own context. God's long-suffering with Nineveh had nothing to do with their fasting and repentance: they first believed in God and the outward signs followed. Calvin emphasized that Jonah was a type of Christ because he returned to life again; the book had little to do with the call to and conversion of Gentiles. Jonah's disobedience was due to fear (1847: 21–28). Modern study has ranged over issues of historicity, linguistic considerations in conjunction with dating the book, unity and genre(s) of the text, literary approaches that divorce the text from its original context(s), and the array of potential messages conveyed or embedded in the narrative.

6. PRESUMED PURPOSES: AN OVERVIEW

If Jonah is didactic, it ought to be possible to articulate purposes that underlie its presence in the canon. Among the recurring suggestions are the following: (1) the prophetic office and the matter of apparent unfulfilment; (2) the nature of repentance – a primarily Jewish interpretation;

(3) polemic against narrow nationalism – a primarily Christian reading; (4) a theological treatise on divine justice and mercy; (5) a window on God's sovereignty (Jenson 2008: 36). The last, however, ends up being so general it fits most of the canonical texts. Bolin (1997: 58–61) revises the list, front-loading three views: (1) polemic against Jewish exclusivism; (2) critique of the prophetic office as a failing institution; (3) exploring the relationship between YHWH and Jonah. These merit further exploration.

6.1 Polemic against Jewish exclusivism

[The author] 'wants to teach the narrow, blind, prejudiced, fanatic Jews of which Jonah is but the type that "the love of God is wider than the measures of man's mind"' (Bewer 1912: 64). The anti-Semitism is hardly veiled! A softer expression of this approach is that of G. A. Smith (1929: 500–505), who interprets Jonah as a type for Israel, fleeing from the duty that God had given to them to be a light to the nations. If the story was designed to inveigh against perceived Jewish nationalism and exclusivism, the Jonah depicted in 2 Kgs 14:23–27 was ideal for the enterprise. Add in the possibility of a post-exilic Judean audience and it is a perfect recipe for unsettling and inflaming sentiments against what was by that time Samaria. Jonah after all had prophesied favourably regarding the northern kingdom (Allen 1976: 179–180). Nevertheless, portraying Jonah as a rigid nationalist over-reads Jonah's 'anger' in ch. 4 and fails to account for significant emphases of the narrative. Ironically, Jonah is berated for his lack of mercy by commentators who extend little mercy to him (Bolin 1997: 50). Goitein (1937: 65–66) suggests that modern commentators are so concerned with the author's context instead of with the prophet that they simply read it as a protest against some presumed – but incorrect – version of post-exilic Jewish ideology. That robs the narrative of its robust characters and does a disservice to the complexities of Judaism during those tumultuous centuries.

6.2 Commentary on the prophetic role

Ben Zvi suggests the text is 'meta-prophetic' because it is foundational for understanding how to read all the other prophets (2003: 85). The reigning paradigm regarding true and false prophets, especially during the united and divided monarchy, is based on Deut. 18:18–22. If the words of the prophet do not come to pass, YHWH has not spoken through that prophet. Jonah's words, however, are overturned and apparently unfulfilled (Allen 1976: 175; Alexander et al. 1988: 84–85; Bolin 1997: 66–67). The additional factor of chastisement is significant: the prophet's words are intended to draw YHWH's people back to him (Lev. 26:40–42; Deut. 30:1–4). When the people pay heed to prophetic warnings of judgment and repent, YHWH responds with constancy in the context of his covenant; the principle is articulated in detail in Ezek. 18. What about non-Israelites? The text of Jonah ventures into new territory. It is the narrative form of Jer. 18:1–11; whether 'a nation [*gôy*] or a kingdom [*mamlākâ*]' responds to the word of YHWH with repentance or recalcitrance is determinative of its future. If the nation 'turns from its evil, YHWH will change from the evil that he planned to do'. These sound very like significant clauses in Jonah where the key word is *niḥam*, which Lessing (2007: 292–293) aptly interprets as 'change the verdict'. While Jonah and Jeremiah both squirm and baulk at their uncomfortable places in YHWH's scheme of things, it turns out that it is not about them in the end. YHWH's final parting shot suggests it is not even about human repentance (Ben Zvi 2003: 28). Instead, his mercy and pity extend to those who do not know any better – for whatever reason.

6.3 Relationship with YHWH

On the surface, the story is about God's faithful pursuit of Jonah, both across the sea and through the dark places of the prophet's burning resentment. The prospect of YHWH's changing in response to repentance, particularly of non-Israelites, is not part of Jonah's credal affirmation (Exod. 34:6–7). He is called to act in accordance with an unsettling doctrinal development that has fearsome potential consequences. Against that backdrop, Jonah flees his post as servant of YHWH, struggling between his belief about YHWH's character and obedience to YHWH's summons (Fretheim 1977: 78). To gather his errant prophet back into service, YHWH employs the storm, the lots and the fish, and then personally commissions him a second time. YHWH's patience has a high profile even when Jonah retreats from Nineveh in silent dudgeon. Jonah alludes to YHWH's long-suffering in his longer rehearsal of what he knows about YHWH (4:2), but does not seem to reflect on the need for that patience in terms of his own recalcitrance. Instead, the prospect of YHWH's patience with Nineveh fills him with fear, especially after he witnesses YHWH changing the verdict, mentioned three times (3:9–10; 4:2). The book is a personal raw confession (Goitein 1937: 74). Jonah or someone close to the story writes about his failings and hardness as a prophet. Nevertheless, ch. 4 does not allow Jonah to stay in that place. With questions, YHWH reorients his prophet and the readers. Depending on how we read the final verse, YHWH's final utterance may tutor Jonah and us to think about YHWH's characteristics as they are worked out through even the small and humble aspects of his creation. In the end, YHWH leaves Jonah (and the readers) with a question.

6.4 Additional reflections: justice and mercy

Alexander et al. (1988: 88–91) frame the 'message question' as a matter of theodicy. Put simply, how can a righteous God extend mercy to violent and wicked people? Is compassion evidence of injustice? The expected course of action for God in the face of blatant evil is retributive justice. What is the effective role of repentance vis-à-vis divine sovereignty, justice and mercy? It is reminiscent of Abraham's question 'shall not the One judging all the earth do justice?' (Gen. 18:25c). Abraham's context was the forthcoming destruction of Sodom and Gomorrah on account of their sin – which did happen. Nineveh was eventually destroyed because of its rapacious and oppressive evil (Nah. 3:1); the judgment was just on a different timetable. The story is about Yhwh's freedom to exercise mercy and 'change the verdict'. Even that, however, is not a certainty: the very last verse of Jonah, if read as a declaration and not a question, emphatically states that Yhwh will not have mercy. Read in the canonical context that includes Nahum, that was ultimately the case. For later reading audiences, the substantial question could be, why did Yhwh eventually destroy Nineveh if he had forgiven them? The message is that God is free not only to love whom he will but also to change (Bolin 1995: 115–119). The sailors already articulated this awareness: Yhwh 'does as he pleases' (1:14).

This interfaces with and develops the second interpretive approach above since prophetic preaching was to draw God's people back to faithful covenant living and, in that sense, repentance would erase the need for judgment. Reading the narrative solely in those terms, however, runs the risk of locking God in. The closing message is that God is free to do as he wills, defying any attempts to predict his decisions and actions (Cooper 1993: 144–163). The book ends with a new theological word (*ḥûs*) that moves the discussion beyond judgment to compassion and pity. The story carries two theologies of grace; the first is based on repentance; the second is inexplicable (Trible 1996: 483–488).

In the meantime, Jonah is too hasty in presuming how Yhwh should respond to evil. There are parallels with the ending of Job: both Jonah and the poetic response from Yhwh to Job end with questions, leaving open the tangle of issues. Neither Job nor Jonah really has to do with theodicy; they have to do with Yhwh's wisdom, and that is never reducible. The matters of justice and innocence, dealing with gratuitous and moral evil are only a part of the dynamic interface of both divine and human freedom. The solution to Job's dilemma comes in the very act of Yhwh's revealing himself; so also with Jonah. To be sure, clemency for wicked people – in this case, Ninevites – seems to fall far short of justice, but that is exactly what happened on the cross, also by Yhwh's sovereign design (Youngblood 2019: 151). How very often the church arrogates to itself that divine prerogative of determining who deserves mercy – or not. The story pokes at *our* own tendency towards self-righteous moralism.

Central to Jonah's declaration (2:10[9]) is the affirmation that God is faithful to his character. The first chapter may be said to explore the 'theology of disobedience': why YHWH allows his children to go astray, especially when that straying may endanger others (Hoyt 2019: 451). YHWH expects obedience, even from intrinsically flawed human beings, but also deals bountifully in compassion. Jonah's story addresses the mystery of sovereignty and contingency. Repentance, profiled primarily in ch. 3, is a significant theme, as evidenced by the place afforded the text in the Day of Atonement ritual, but it does not carry over into ch. 4 (Alexander et al. 1988: 81–83). That God should choose to make his actions contingent on human repentance is no limitation to his sovereignty. The closure to the book expands the understanding of God's sovereignty as he 'tends' his creation (Allen 1976: 192–193). At the same time, it is ambiguous, leaving the audience to ponder. Hymn texts capture the wonder:

> Holy, holy, holy, Lord God Almighty;
> Holy, holy, holy, Merciful and mighty.
> ('Holy, holy, holy! Lord God Almighty!', R. Heber, 1826)
>
> He saw me ruined in the fall and loved me notwithstanding all;
> He saved me from my lost estate,
> His lovingkindness is so great.
> ('Awake, my soul, in joyful lays', S. Medley, 1782)

7. AMONG THE TWELVE

Jonah's role is different from the other BoT prophets. Its placement among them indicates it was viewed as prophetic. Nevertheless, its primarily narrative structure and the absence of characteristic prophetic motifs distinguish it. There are no allusions to covenant blessings and curses regarding Israel's obedience, no eschatological promises of return, no mention of the day of YHWH. Its narrative develops a theme rarely evident in the canonical prophets: mercy for repentant enemies of Israel (Nogalski 2011a: 405).

In the MT, Jonah is fifth, following Obadiah. The Muraba'at MS has it in the same place. If there was an ordering 'principle', it might have drawn those two together based on their both addressing foreign nations. The 'envoy sent among the nations' (Obad. 1) could possibly connect with the role Jonah was called to play; this is a rabbinic tradition (Sasson 1990: 14). In the LXX, Jonah follows Obadiah, and Nahum is directly after Jonah as if to say the questions at the end of Jonah did not represent the end of the story of divine justice. Nahum also concludes with a rhetorical question, but the implications for Nineveh have shifted radically. Fuller (1997a: 221–222) describes a second-century BC fragment from Qumran (4QXIIa), in which Jonah appears to follow Malachi. See also Nogalski 2011a: 405. That seems to be an anomaly, however, because 4QXIIf (c. 50 BC) has Jonah prior to Micah (Fuller 1997a: 268).

8. TEXT AND TRANSLATION

Goldingay (2021: 16–17) summarizes the textual tradition, starting with the three Masoretic MSS from approximately the tenth century AD. They are named for the cities where they were kept for centuries – Cairo, Aleppo and Leningrad (St Petersburg). The MT as represented in the *BHQ* serves as the basis for the translation and commentary that follow. See also Sasson 1990: 9–11 regarding collections of variant readings.

The text of Jonah is represented in fragments from the Qumran library in Cave 4. Four of five fragments in 4QXIIf have Jon. 1:6–8, 10–16 (Fuller 1997a: 267–270). 4QXIIg, dating to the last third of the first century BC, is poorly preserved but has portions of Jon. 1:1–9; 2:3[2] – 3:3; 4:5–11 (Fuller 1997a: 272, 309–313). 4QXIIa preserves significant parts of ch. 1, but just a few fragments of lines of chs. 2 and 3. There is nothing from ch. 4 (Fuller 1997a: 229–232).

A second scroll (Mur), containing the Twelve and dating to the second century AD, was found about 10 miles (16 km) south of Qumran in a cave in Wadi Murabba'at (DJD IIa: 181–184). The text of Jonah is nearly complete (DJD IIb: 190–193; Plates LX–LXI). A cave just south in Naḥal Ḥever yielded the Greek scroll of the BoT (8ḤevXIIgr) (DJD VIII: 28–33). In spite of almost a millennium of time lapse between these texts and the MT, it is evident that the MT preserves the text tradition remarkably.

Two complete Greek MSS (Sinaiticus and Vaticanus) date from the fourth century AD; Alexandrinus is fifth century. The Greek version is cited as LXX when most versions agree; otherwise, Aquila, Symmachus and Theodotian are noted. Additional ancient versions include the Aramaic Targum of Jonathan, Jerome's Latin Vg and the Syr.

The translation that follows attempts to forge a combination of faithfulness to the Hebr. and readability. Occasionally, that goal proves elusive, but I have wrestled with the MT as we have it rather than emend it to support an easier reading. On a very basic level, it means representing the wayyiq. forms as they drive the narrative steadily forward. When the ancient versions diverge, they might have been offering 'good guesses' for difficult texts rather than using a Hebr. *Vorlage* we no longer have (Sasson 1990: 13).

9. OUTLINE

I. Jonah's commission and flight (1:1 – 1:3)
II. Jonah at sea (1:4 – 1:16)
    Responding to imminent disaster (1:4–7)
    Accusatory questions and Jonah's confession (1:8–12)
    The valiant sailors (1:13–16)
III. Jonah and the great fish (2:1–11)[1:17 – 2:10]
    Preparation (2:1–2)[1:17 – 2:1]
    Prayers (2:3–10)[2:2–9]
    Reprieve (2:11)[10]
IV. Jonah's second commission and the responses (3:1–10)
    YHWH's proclamation to Nineveh through Jonah (3:1–4)
    Revival in Nineveh: belief and repentance (3:5)
    The king's proclamation to Nineveh: repentance and appeal to God (3:6–9)
    God's response (3:10)
V. How to handle a disgruntled prophet (4:1–11)
    A. Jonah's complaint and YHWH's first response (4:1–4)
    B. Jonah broods and YHWH appoints and reproves (4:5–11)

TEXT AND COMMENTARY

JONAH 1:1–3

Translation

[1:1]The word of Yhwh came to Jonah, son of Amittai, saying,
[2]'Get up! Go to Nineveh, the great city, and preach against it, because their evil
has risen up before me.'
[3]But Jonah got up to flee to Tarshish from Yhwh's presence, and he went down
to Joppa, and he found a ship going to Tarshish, and he paid its fare, and he went
down into it to go with them to Tarshish away from Yhwh's presence.

Notes on the text

1:1. *wayĕhî* (lit. 'and it was') starts a number of canonical books including Joshua, Judges, 1–2 Samuel, 2 Kings, Ezekiel, Ruth and Esther. Only two of them, Ezekiel and Jonah, are prophetic. Because Jonah follows Obadiah, *wayĕhî* may pick up from the preceding oracle to a foreign nation (Wolff 1986: 75). *lēʾmōr* ('saying') is the equivalent of the opening quotation mark. Youngblood suggests 'as follows' (2019: 53).

2. *qûm* ('get up') followed by *lēk* ('go') is a common imperative combination (GKC 120g), often rendered as a singular idea expressed with both words (a **hendiadys**). In this context, however, both terms contribute to the backdrop for Jonah's disobedient movement.

'The great city' is in apposition to Nineveh.

The prep. *ʿal* ('against') is significant because it contrasts with the summons in ch. 3 where Jonah is commanded to 'call to her' (*ʾēlêhā*).

The pron. suff. on *rāʿâ* is masc. pl. in the MT, but both the LXX and Vg have fem. sg., 'her evil', referring to the city. It is generally understood as 'their evil has come up' (Sasson 1990: 75).

3. The succession of wayyiq. forms drives the narrative forward. Jonah is intent on getting out of YHWH's presence. 'Flee' plus *millipnê* suggests complete removal; see *IBHS* §11.3.1a.

The vocalization of *ʾoniyyâ* ('ship') is unusual; generally, the word is spelled *ʾŏniyyâ*.; see vv. 4, 5. Of equal interest is the verb *bāʾâ*, a fem. sg. ptc. meaning 'coming'. It may be that the ship has just arrived from Tarshish. Of the three occurrences of Tarshish in this verse, this one does not have the locative *hê* ('to Tarshish') as the other two do. *ymʾ* is a frequent translation of Tarshish in Tg (Gelston 2010: 92*). The pron. suff. on *śākār* ('fare') is fem. sg. referring to the ship. See 'Comment'.

Form and structure

Trible sketches the chiastic structure of this verse (Trible 1994: 129):

> 'to flee to Tarshish from the presence of YHWH'
> 'he went down to Joppa'
> 'Tarshish'
> 'he went down into it'
> 'to go to Tarshish from the presence of YHWH'

'What words proclaim the structure subverts' (Lessing 2007: 91). Jonah's presence is surrounded by mentioning the presence of YHWH twice. After v. 3, there is an information gap: readers are not told why Jonah makes such a radical choice to flee. His reasoning surfaces only in 4:2.

Comment

1:1. 'Word of YHWH' is the formal expression to commence a prophetic message. Goldingay (2021: 376) renders *wayĕhî dĕbār* YHWH as 'Yahweh's message became a reality'. Combining *wayĕhî* with 'the word of YHWH *to Jonah*' is unique as an introduction to a prophetic book. The narrative is about YHWH and Jonah – in that order. The substance of this brief introduction is that the word of YHWH is rejected by his prophet, Jonah. That tension remains throughout. Jonah is blatantly disobedient from the outset. Identifying Jonah in connection with his patronym follows the pattern of other writing prophets (Isa. 1:1; Jer. 1:1; Ezek. 1:3; Hos. 1:1;

Joel 1:1; Zeph. 1:1; Zech. 1:1). *wayĕhî* suggests that this narrative is linked with something prior to it – the prophesying activities of the Jonah in 2 Kgs 14:25. While many scholars have disavowed a historical identification of these two individuals, the canonical and literary connection is intended by the narrator (Bolin 1997: 74–75; Judisch 1999: 152). To be sure, other than the name, no additional narrative elements connect the two (Ben Zvi 2003: 46–47). Some suggest the book's contents were brought together from a larger collection of Jonah stories (Sasson 1990: 85).

With the 2 Kgs 14 context as the background, readers know that Jonah was prophesying when Jeroboam (II), son of Joash, was king of the north (793–753 BC). Jeroboam was an evil king in a succession of evil kings. His own kingdom was ripe for judgment. Jonah's home town was Gath-Hepher in Galilee, near one of the east–west routes connecting Acco on the Mediterranean Sea with the Sea of Galilee and just a few miles east of Nazareth. See 'Introduction'. When Jesus refers to the 'sign of Jonah', he draws on the local heritage, additionally interesting in the light of the derogatory comment from some Jerusalem chief priests and Pharisees that no prophet arises from Galilee (John 7:52). The capital of the northern kingdom was Samaria, just about 30 miles (48 km) south of Gath-Hepher. It is possible that Jonah was a regular presence in the royal court.

2. The implications of *ûqĕrāʾ* range from 'call out' to 'proclaim'. If *ʿal* is understood as 'against', this could refer to audible preaching of judgment. It could, however, be somewhat ambivalent if *ʿal* means 'concerning' (*IBHS* §11.2.13fg). The use of *ʿal* in contrast to the summons to call 'to her' (*ʾēlêhā*) in ch. 3 suggests that God's stance towards Nineveh changes, especially since 'evil' or 'calamity' does not occur in that context. If so, this initial proclamation carries warning of judgment. Assessment of both prepositions as they are used with 'call out' indicates that their meanings overlap; both can be used in terms of judgment and for positive outcomes. They appear synonymously in Jer. 18:11 in the context of YHWH's planning judgment. Nevertheless, *ʿal* in conjunction with a positive calling is rare (Hoyt 2019: 422–423); the expression carries a sense of impending doom. See also Deut. 15:9; 24:15; 1 Kgs 13:2, 4; 2 Kgs 23:17.

The reason for Jonah's proclamation is the great *rāʿâ* of Nineveh. While this key word has a wide semantic range that depends on the context for its interpretation, the audible proclamation issued 'against her' tips the balance regarding the nature of YHWH's summons. Nineveh's condition clearly necessitates repentance; this becomes clear in ch. 3. At the same time, Jonah is aware that YHWH is long-suffering, and an announcement of judgment could prompt repentance, thus short-circuiting the punishment (Jer. 18:7–11). See 'Introduction'.

Nineveh had a long history and reputation as a major city of Assyria, evident in Gen. 10:11–12, where the expression 'the great city' initially surfaces, possibly referring to the urban combination of Nineveh and

Calah. Whenever that annotation was written, the point is the long-standing traditional connection between Assyria and Nineveh. While Nineveh did not become the capital of the Assyrian Empire until Sennacherib's rule in the late eighth century, it was already a formidable presence in the ninth century (Grayson 1976, 2: 182–193). The heyday of Assyria in the ninth century, however, was followed by a period of decline with military setbacks, uprising, famine (765 and/or 759) and earthquake, along with a solar eclipse in 763. The whole picture might put a superstitious population on edge (Wiseman 1979: 44–46; Stuart 1987: 440; Hoyt 2019: 353–354). See 'Introduction'.

Assyria's legendary brutality would be an understandable cause for consternation on Jonah's part. His prompt disobedience may stem from his concern for the immediate future of Israel. Nineveh was rife with bloodshed and deceit, as later reflected in Nah. 3:1. Even after its fall in 612 BC, the name would evoke bitter memories as a centre of savage power. The same perception continues into the intertestamental period, as evidenced in both Tobit and Judith. No matter when Jonah's narrative was written, the image of 'the great city of Nineveh' prompts associations with everything opposed to Israel's own identity as the people of YHWH. A later reading audience would know the book of Nahum in which judgment of the violence and wickedness of Nineveh is front and centre. Unlike Nahum and other prophets who utter oracles against foreigners from the safety of the land, however, YHWH calls Jonah to take the message to that city, a dubious distinction (Allen 1976: 203). Ironically, it is Jonah who prophesied expanded boundaries for Jeroboam, an evil king. Now he is called to cross that border heading for enemy territory with a message that might have a complicated outcome in terms of the political developments between Assyria and the northern kingdom (Youngblood 2019: 61).

3. From Jonah's perspective, Tarshish is far from Israel, in the opposite direction from Nineveh, and at the edges of recognizable named locations (Isa. 66:19). His movements indicate he has already determined to head as far away from YHWH as possible even before he arrives at Joppa to find a ship. His good theology – which will become clear later – is not connecting with his thoroughgoing apprehension at the implications of YHWH's command. Jonah likely takes this deliberate step to remove himself from the prophetic role: if he gets out of Israel, he will no longer hear from YHWH (Hoyt 2019: 417–418). He would not have been simple-minded enough to think he could escape YHWH's territory. Instead, by fleeing he is leaving the position of standing in the presence of YHWH, a role that prophets fulfilled (Youngblood 2019: 57–58). 'Standing in the presence' meant submission to service (1 Kgs 17:1; 18:15; 2 Kgs 3:14; 5:16; Jer. 15:19). Against the backdrop of the whole array of prophetic figures (among them, Moses, Samuel, Elijah and Elisha), Jonah's choice to disobey YHWH's Word is shocking (Alexander et al. 1988: 101; Lessing

2007: 91). Perhaps he presumes this will buy enough time for YHWH to commission an alternative (Stuart 1987: 450–453; Jenson 2008: 45).

Joppa was not under Israelite control during the monarchy period, but would have been a significant seaport for the northern kingdom. Further, it had a long history prior to Israelite presence in the land. The name appears in Egyptian inscriptions as well as the Amarna letters (Rainey and Notley 2006: 66, 73, 82). The coast of this part of the Levant was not conducive to seafaring endeavours as there were no natural harbours. Joppa was north of Ashdod. The next major ports to the north would have been Dor and then Acco. If Jonah was frequenting Samaria, as is suggested by 2 Kgs 14:23–25, Joppa is the logical coastal city from which to set out. For his purposes, it would also have been the first step away from the presence of YHWH.

An *ʾŏnîyyâ* was a sea-going vessel. Solomon's ships ('going to Tarshish') sailed along with those of Hiram of Tyre to points across the Mediterranean Sea and perhaps even around the African continent. That range is suggested by the indication that the ships arrived once every three years and their cargo included such exotic items as apes, ivory and peacocks (2 Chr. 9:21). Although ships are not specified, tribute was sent, presumably to Solomon, from the 'kings of Tarshish' (Ps. 72:10). Jehoshaphat made 'ships of Tarshish' to sail to Ophir for gold. Unfortunately, they were shipwrecked at Ezion-Geber (1 Kgs 22:49–50[48–49]; 2 Chr. 20:36–37). Unless the seafarers were portaging across the Negev from Gaza to Ezion-Geber and back, we may surmise they were sailing the long, circuitous route. Ezek. 27 is a lament for Tyre and her extensive seafaring mercantile ventures. These vessels were powered by rowers (Ezek. 27:26–29). In a separate oracle against Tyre, Isaiah takes note of Tarshish three times; the context suggests it was across the sea (23:1–14). Isaiah's vision of future glory and restoration includes 'ships of Tarshish' serving as vessels returning YHWH's children (Isa. 60:9).

While the customary interpretation is that Jonah pays a single fare for himself, the rabbis interpreted the grammar quite strictly: he pays for the whole ship (*b.* Ned 38a). If the boat has just arrived, paying 'her hire' could mean that Jonah pays to have the ship turn around and head back out again. Because it would normally take some time to prepare a ship to relaunch (Hoyt 2019: 414, n. 12), a subtext could be that they are somewhat ill-prepared to head out but are pressured to do so. Trible (1994: 130, n. 27) likewise suggests this is indicative of the magnitude of his intended disobedience. Lessing (2007: 76–77) concurs; this would shed additional light on Jonah's having access to the innermost part of the ship and may be a further factor in the sailors' reluctance to pitch him overboard right away. Perhaps in the course of bargaining for the ship, he divulges what the narrative reveals only in v. 10 – that he is fleeing from the presence of YHWH. See also Wolff 1986: 97. Handy (2004: 32) notes there was no such thing as a passenger ship: people travelled on large cargo vessels. Normally, arranging passage for Tarshish – wherever it was – would take a long time. The captain and crew would load cargo, watch for good weather and winds, make sure the omens were in order and offer sacrifices.

Explanation

Vv. 1–3 introduce all the arenas in which the narrative takes place and the tension between divine command and human contradiction that continues throughout (Wolff 1986: 96). Given the wide-ranging implications of *rāʿâ* (see 'Introduction'), the nature of Jonah's message as commissioned by YHWH modulates from intent to judge to invitation to repent. Nothing about this story is static. A related question has to do with the readership's perception of YHWH's purposes. If subsequent generations of readers presume that YHWH intends all along that Nineveh will repent at this point, to what extent will this proclamation be a bona fide declaration of judgment? How does that fit with the eventual destruction of the city as prophesied in Nahum? See Ben Zvi 2003: 35–39.

'To Tarshish from the presence of YHWH' occurs twice. The name Tarshish was attached to more than one location in antiquity. The sixth-century BC description in Ezek. 27 of the merchandise coming to Tyre seems to locate a Tarshish along the coast of Cilicia (Ezek. 27:12; see also Isa. 23:1–10). Josephus likewise identified Cilicia as the location of Tarshish (*Ant.* 9.10.2). A Phoenician text found on the island of Sardinia, west of Italy, also bore this name. The place appears to have migrated along with the increasing range of the Phoenician ships from an original location in the area of Cilicia to Tharros in Sardinia and eventually to Tartessos in Spain (Aharoni et al. 1993: 88; Rainey and Notley 2006: 28). Alexander et al. (1988: 99–100) cite evidence in favour of a location in present-day Spain even as early as the first millennium BC.

Going down to the sea has layers of implications. The sea was an ominous location for Israelites because the ultimate feared enemy was there (Ps. 74:13–14; Isa. 27:1). It was characterized by turmoil and darkness. Jonah's heading out to sea is a sign of his desperation to avoid the commission (Page 1995: 229–230; Lessing 2007: 94–95). This is an adumbration of ch. 2, where the term Sheol is part of Jonah's description (2:3[2]). The sea was his avenue to the west, likewise a great unknown. Ps. 107:23–32 celebrates the enterprise and courage of those who go down to the sea in ships while Ps. 48:8[7] describes the wreckage of ships of Tarshish by the east wind.

Jonah's identity is clear: he is YHWH's prophet who disobeys the command of YHWH. But why? It takes the narrative and poem to discover that he hates – or fears – those who have done evil, even though YHWH remarkably loves them enough to give them a second chance (Stuart 1987: 453). It also takes the entire narrative to drive home the point that standing in

Yhwh's presence and doing his bidding are uncomfortable (Youngblood 2019: 62–63). With Jonah, prophetic protest is elevated to prophetic flight (Bolin 1997: 77).

JONAH 1:4–7

Translation

[4]But Yhwh hurled a mighty wind to the sea, and there was a huge storm on the sea, and the ship was on the verge of being broken apart.

[5]And the seamen were afraid and each one cried out to his gods, and they hurled the containers that were in the ship to the sea to lighten it from their [weight], but Jonah went down into the hold of the boat and lay down and slept deeply.

[6]The chief of the linemen approached him and said to him, 'What are you doing sleeping? Get up! Call to your god. Perhaps that god will have pity on us, and we will not perish.'

[7]In the meantime, each man was saying to his fellow, 'Come on; let's cast lots so that we can know on whose account this great evil is upon us.' And they cast lots and the lot fell on Jonah.

Notes on the text

1:4. The three independent clauses (introduced by *wa-*) leave freedom in terms of how they should be combined. It is the translator's /interpreter's choice as to whether or how to subordinate the second and third.

Yhwh and 'the ship' both stand first, following the waw, in their respective clauses, emphasizing their roles. *hēṭîl* is a 3 masc. sg. hiph. from *ṭul*, meaning 'to hurl'. Generally, it is followed by *ʿal*, implying 'towards', but here (as well as vv. 5, 12, 15) the prep. is *ʾel*, either 'into' or 'to'.

ḥiššĕbâ is a pi. fem. sg. qat. form. The basic meaning is 'to think' or 'consider' (BDB 363; *DCH* 3:328). Generally, persons (human or God) are the subject (1 Sam. 18:25; 2 Sam. 14:13–14; Jer. 26:3; 29:11). This is the only place where an inanimate object, the ship, is the subject. The MT indicates a pause after 'the ship'; the personification is emphatic. Tg reads 'sought to break up'. The LXX translates the verb 'ran the risk'.

lĕhiššābēr is a niph. inf. const. from *šbr.*

5. The sequence of wayyiq. verbs suggests consecutive developments, but it may also indicate concurrent actions. In the chaos of the storm, the sailors try everything simultaneously (Hoyt 2019: 426, n. 66).

While there has been a tendency to identify *mallāḥîm* with the word *melāḥ*, meaning 'salt' (Nogalski 2011a: 418), there is no connection. Instead, *mallaḥ* is from Sumerian, and refers to ship handling. It is a general term, applied to all sailors (Sasson 1990: 97). It is used only here, and in Ezek. 27:9, 27, 29 regarding the mariners engaged in Tyre's shipping enterprises.

'îš is used distributively, 'each one'.

kēlim is a general term meaning 'articles', 'utensils', 'implements' or 'vessels' (BDB 479). The LXX reads *tōn skeuōn*, a term as general as *kēlim*. Based on Acts 27:19, some suggest the meaning 'tackle', but that is likely the last set of materials they would cast overboard.

lĕhāqēl is a hiph. inf. const. from *qll*, 'to lighten'. It has no direct object, but is simply 'from upon them'. Some suggest this may be an oblique reference to their attempt to appease the gods of the sea since that is the most recent antecedent (Trible 1996: 495–496). The prep. *'el* may likewise point in that direction (Sasson 1990: 94–95).

Breaking into the wayyiq. sequence, a disjunctive clause with Jonah as subject precedes the verb *yārad*. The waw is best translated as 'but'. The qat. may reflect a pluperf. or another action simultaneous with the sailors' activities. Because the verb sequence is interrupted, Wolff (1986: 109) thinks it should read as a pluperf.; the narrator seems to have a predilection for that stylistic move. On the other hand, Jonah's disappearance as the storm grows increasingly terrifying is another commentary on his character (Lessing 2007: 103)

sĕpînâ is used only here. The root *spn* means 'to cover'. Presumably Jonah descends below the deck covering the ship (*DCH* 6:181). That sheltered place is called the *yarkĕtê* of the ship. *yarkâ* means the side, perhaps intimating the recesses of the interior (BDB 438; *DCH* 4:299). More specifically, it may refer to the place where two angles of the ship's sides joined (Sasson 1990: 100). On the form in construct, see GKC 95i.

rdm is used only in niph. and means 'to be in a deep sleep'.

6. A *ḥōbēl* is one who pulls ropes or lines (*ḥăbālîm*). Here it is used as a collective and the *rab* is the captain. It may be a **metonymy** for those men who worked the sails (Jenson 2008: 50). It is used in parallel with *mallāḥîm*; both terms appear only in Jonah and Ezek. 27:27, 29.

mâ lĕkā is idiomatic, in this case suggesting an emphatic 'why?' (*IBHS* §18.3b). It appears in contexts where one who has a superior role poses an accusing question to the lesser party (Gen. 20:9; Isa. 3:15; 22:1; Ezek. 18:2). A literal English rendition would be, 'What with you that you sleep?'

nirdām is a niph. ptc. that describes the state – sleeping – in which the captain finds Jonah (GKC §120b). It could also serve as a voc., 'O sleeper!' (Sasson 1990: 103). The LXX renders it 'you snoring' (LS 1567). It occurs only in niph. and implies a deep sleep (*DCH* 7:421). See 'Comment'.

The captain's order to 'get up and call' echoes YHWH's initial command (v. 2). It adumbrates the second command from YHWH to Jonah in 3:2.

yit'aššēt is a hith., likely meaning to 'give a thought to' (BDB 799; *DCH* 6:624). One occurrence in qal seems to mean 'devise' or 'plan'

(Jer. 5:28). The LXX renders it as the possibility that God will save them; the Tg, that there will be mercy; the Vg, if God will think of them (Sasson 1990: 104).

The def. art. in *hāʾĕlōhîm* refers to Jonah's God, *ĕlōhêkā*, 'that god of yours' (GKC 126a).

wĕlōʾ nōbēd (juss.) may suggest 'lest we die' or a result, 'so that we don't die' (GKC 109g).

7. *lĕkû*, the masc. pl. impv. of this verb of motion, heightens the effect of the pl. coh. that follows it (*IBHS* 34.5.1a).

nappîlâ is a hiph. 1 pl. coh. from *npl*, meaning 'to cause to fall'. The conclusion of the process is marked as the singular lot falls (qal) on Jonah.

gôrāl is generally sg.; it appears only eight times, in the pl.

bĕšelmî combines the lamed of possession with *š* to make *šel* (*IBHS* §19.4, n. 15) and adds the *bĕ-* prep. in the beginning and the interrog. at the end. Put together, it means 'on whose account'.

Form and structure

The definitive concepts 'getting up' and 'going down' are augmented by 'hurling'. Both YHWH and the sailors will hurl, a powerful movement on the part of each. In addition, the sea with all its turbulence is the surface on to which YHWH hurls the storm and the sailors hurl the shipping containers.

From the rhetorical perspective, Jonah's continued silence through the raging storm, the accusation and challenge of the captain, and the ominous process of lot-casting raises the tension and suspense. While his words are not recorded through any of these moments of heightened horror, v. 10 intimates that at some point he muttered something of his misguided flight from YHWH.

V. 4 employs three rhetorical devices: prosopopoeia, onomatopoeia and assonance. The first of these indicates that human characteristics are given to an object: in this case, the ship 'thinks'. Onomatopoeia uses the sounds of words to convey what is happening: the sibilant (š) sounds like ship planks grinding and shattering. Finally, assonance is another sound effect, joining in proximity the same sounds (Trible 1994: 131–132). The repeated sounds in the juxtaposition of *ḥiššĕbâ* and *lĕhiššābēr* emphasize the hissing turmoil of the waters around the ship. V. 5 has sound connections between *rdm* and *yrd*.

This narrative unit highlights contrasts between Jonah and the mariners. The three responses of the sailors in v. 5 are matched, quantitatively, by three of Jonah. The latter are intent on staying alive, and they appeal to their gods for assistance and revelation. Jonah seems all too eager to die, he does not pray in this set of dire circumstances, and his acknowledgment of *his* God appears only under duress (Youngblood 2019: 73). Casting lots, noted three times in v. 7, moves from 'causing the lots to fall' as the mariners cast them to the singular lot falling (qal); i.e. 'going down'. It is another indicator of YHWH's sovereign control.

Comment

1:4. The wind (*rûaḥ*) is matched in ferocity by the storm (*sa'ar*). Both are described as 'great'. The word for storm appears in conjunction with disturbances often at the nexus of heaven and earth. YHWH's appearance to Job is heralded by a *sĕ'ārâ* (Job 38:1); Ezekiel's vision of the cherubim breaks in with a *rûaḥ sĕ'ārâ* (Ezek. 1:4) and reappears to destroy a whitewashed and flimsy wall (13:13). YHWH raises the fearsome storm (*rûaḥ sĕ'ārâ*) encountered by the enterprising mariners (Ps. 107:25). Storms are a means of bringing judgment. The chronicler declares that the wreckage of Jehoshaphat's joint shipping with Ahaziah is due to YHWH's displeasure with that alliance (2 Chr. 20:35–37).

The object of 'hurl' may be a weapon, such as a spear (1 Sam. 18:11; 20:33), things (Jon. 1:5), persons such as Pharaoh (Ezek. 32:4) or Jonah (1:12, 15), or this storm (*DCH* 3:361). While *'al* and *'el* are interchangeable to a degree, *'el* in this context may be intended to bolster the impression that the sea is not an object of God's judgment but his instrument.

The condition of the ship is the focus: *'ŏnîyyâ* starts the third clause. Tossed about by the terrible storm, it acts as if it has a mind of its own; the personification leaves no doubt as to the significance of the ship's groaning. For someone on board, shuddering just prior to shattering would convey that sense. It is 'on the verge of being broken up'. Ancient mariners believed that ships had guardian spirits. Portrayed as sentient, the ship became YHWH's 'accomplice' in thwarting Jonah's intention instead of Jonah's means of escaping YHWH's commission (Youngblood 2019: 75). Isaiah describes the 'ships of Tarshish' as 'howling' (Isa. 23:1). Ironically, Jonah does not 'consider', but the ship does (Lessing 2007: 100). Brody (1998: 63) indicates that ships were thought to be endowed with divine spirits; hence they often carried a figure on the prow and apotropaic eyes were emblazoned on them.

5. The sailors were accustomed to being at sea, but this tempest is far beyond their confidence level. Their fear drives them to appeal to the supernatural powers they perceive to be the source of the terrifying storm. *'îš* ('each') individualizes their response even in the growing pandemonium. 'Elohim' could indicate the plurality of each sailor's pantheon, or it could indicate a crew with diverse backgrounds. It is unlikely that they are appealing to the sovereign Elohim of the HB at this point. Their fear escalates through the chapter as they do not manage to attract the attention of the 'right god'.

At the same time the sailors are crying out, they are flinging everything overboard that can be spared. If the term *kēlîm* refers to 'vessels', it would likely be ceramic storage jars for the merchandise on board. These seagoing vessels also carried bronze vessels (Ezek. 27:13). This was the container ship of antiquity. No doubt the cargo was weighty. Brody (1998: 40–41) describes 'sacred anchors' that were kept on ships and thrown overboard in storm emergencies to secure or slow a vessel. That, however, does not directly relate to their intent to 'lighten' the ship. Because the hiph. of *qll* does not have a specified object, the verb may be interpreted 'appease' or 'lighten the hand' of the sea as a deity (Trible 1994: 136). Lessing (2007: 102) raises the same possibility in the light of 1 Sam. 6:5, where Philistine priests and diviners recommended sending an offering back with the ark so that YHWH would 'lighten his hand from upon' them. See also v. 12.

The next waw is an adversative. Attention shifts to Jonah's response in contrast to the panic of the sailors. If Jonah is our man from Gath-Hepher (2 Kgs 14:25), he is not likely to be comfortable with life on board a boat, even a large one. Gath-Hepher was thoroughly landlocked. This raging storm sends him below decks as far away as possible from the crashing waves. It is not necessary to translate *yārad* as a plupf., suggesting that he headed to a comfortable sleeping spot immediately on boarding the ship. Instead, the terror of the storm drives him there. Possibly he is growing increasingly mindful that he is not particularly successful in evading YHWH. He may seek a location that is least apt to be pounded by the alarming waves. If he did purchase the entire ship for his getaway, he would have access to the innermost parts. Fretheim (1977: 82–83) presses the interpretation a bit further: Jonah's sleep in the face of this disaster is evidence that he has made himself comfortable in his disobedience. Wolff (1986: 109) adds this is another indication the narrator is poking fun at Jonah who, although running from YHWH, is the instrument through which YHWH will bring the sailors to worship.

The description of Jonah's protected spot mirrors other hidden places. The same word is used to describe the innermost part of the cave where David was hiding when Saul entered the front of the cave (1 Sam. 24:4). It appears as well in Isa. 14:15 regarding the 'innermost parts of the pit'. Jonah's deep sleep contrasts with the preceding verse, where the ship itself is sentient: the narrator reimagines him as an object, replacing the containers the sailors have jettisoned (Trible 1994: 135).

The 'deep sleep' is what Adam experienced as a prelude to the creation of Eve (Gen. 2:21). Prior to cutting the covenant, sleep 'fell' upon Abram and was accompanied by thick darkness (Gen. 15:12). The Canaanite general Sisera was fast asleep and oblivious to Jael's approach with a lethal tent peg and hammer (Judg. 4:21). Eliphaz's description of numinous and terrifying night-time revelations has them occurring during deep sleep (Job 4:13). This is no ordinary nap for Jonah.

6. The narrative is spare; we do not know how the ship's chief officer finds Jonah tucked away in the darkness or how he manages to wake him up. Perhaps they discover his sleeping form as they are feverishly hauling containers on deck to hurl them overboard (Hoyt 2019: 434). The captain's voice rises above the roar of the sea. Whether he addresses Jonah as 'Sleeper!' or includes the unlikely state of sleeping through the tumult as part of the question, the captain orders Jonah to get up and join the appeal, focusing first on 'your god' among the gods of the other mariners. The double imperative 'get up and call' was no doubt unsettling. Those words echo YHWH's commissioning statement from which Jonah is fleeing.

The three utterances of the captain move from accusatory question to imperative to a long-shot expression of hope. *yitʿašēt* may be interpreted as a parallel with 3:9 in which case it could have the connotation of 'have pity' as the versions have read (Lessing 2007: 106). A possible glimmer in the captain's thinking of hierarchy among the gods may account for the shift to a designated god. If this god is more powerful and would listen, the logical result will be that they will not perish. On the other hand, it may simply be the captain's attempt to command Jonah to pray to *his* god, the one they seem not to have reached yet. The summons to 'call out' to his god would have been the obvious directive: the divine was woven into the ANE world view. Further, in the face of life-threatening disaster, there are few atheists!

7. The subtext at this point is that Jonah ignores the captain's order (Jenson 2008: 51). The sailors for their part pause from wholesale crying and flinging to probing the possible cause of the impending disaster. To do so, they appeal in a different and presumably more focused way to the divine. While casting the lot was a common practice in Israelite culture, there is no parallel expression outside the HB. It acknowledges the need for wisdom beyond human reasoning to arrive at a determination. It may be that the narrator reshapes the sailors' actions in Israelite form, parallel to the portrayal of the Ninevites' fasting in ch. 3 (Strawn 2010: 71–74). The frequent use of the verb *npl* ('to fall') in conjunction with 'lot' suggests that the lots fell after a container was agitated (Kitz 2000: 213–214). In this case, they expect whatever deity may be in control of the sea to respond. In the Israelite cultural context, lot casting was the means of arriving at land-allocation decisions (Josh. 18:6), determining a guilty party (Josh. 7:14–26) or settling disputes (Prov. 18:18). A number of verbs are associated with the process, among them the qal and hiph. forms of *npl*. Both appear in this context. The causative points towards divine oversight.

The narrative slows down, building the tension. First the sailors exhort each other to 'cause them to fall' to know; both verbs are coh. They cast the lots (pl.), and the lot falls on Jonah. That implies that he has arrived on deck at some point, most likely at the prodding of the captain. Nevertheless, Jonah continues to maintain his silence.

Explanation

All of YHWH's creation serves his bidding in reeling in his errant prophet: the sea surges, the wind rages and the ship has its own cooperative persona (Youngblood 2019: 76). For those whose lives were shaped by the sea, it is not surprising that each movement and sound of their ship would seize their attention. That Jonah's ship would 'consider' is not a surprising descriptor. Isaiah's summons to the 'ships of Tarshish' to 'howl' (*hêlîlû*) is an evocative onomatopoeic word suggesting mighty winds raging through sails (Isa. 23:1).

Wolff (1986: 112) emphasizes the continuing irony: the sailors pray and work; Jonah does neither. Even more pointed, the pagan captain urges the Israelite prophet to pray (Bewer 1912: 33), posing the possibility to Jonah that his god may consider them. The psalmist clings to the same hope expressed by the captain; he is poor and needy but expresses confidence that the Lord (Adonai) will consider him (Ps. 40:18[17]). Jonah's descent into the bowels of the ship where he lies down metaphorically hints at death – which Jonah wants (Ezek. 32:21, 27–30; Ps. 88:4–5[3–4]).

Figures commissioned to perform a task and who survive tempests at sea constitute a familiar narrative motif outside the Israelite context. See 'The Shipwrecked Sailor' (Lichtheim, *COS* 1:83–84) and 'The Report of Wen-Amun' (Lichtheim, *COS* 1:89–93). Recall also the journey of the apostle Paul (Acts 28).

The word *yām* ('sea') is used eleven times in the first chapter, where pagan sailors are the major players. Yam was a key figure in the Canaanite pantheon, a son of El the head of the deities. Texts from Ugarit give a window into the cultural perceptions of divine conflicts in the tumultuous spheres of sea, storm and death. When Yam (sea) requested the divine assembly to give powerful Baal (master of thunder, rain and storm) over to him, it did not finally go well with Baal. Conflict ensued and Yam lost and ended up subservient to Baal. In a later text, Baal's consort (Anath) claimed she subdued Yam. In the end, Mot (death) kills Baal, and that's only part of the story (Grisanti, *NIDOTTE* 2:461–466). This was the world view of the sailors if they were from eastern Mediterranean regions.

Ezekiel's depiction of the cargo ships of Tyre (Ezek. 27) gives a good sense of ship construction and the types of cargo. A variety of wood types was used in the ships, from straight and tall cedar masts to pine decks and planks (vv. 5–6). Both oars and sails were employed (vv. 6–7); this fits well with the captain being called a 'chief of linemen'. The exchange of merchandise was extensive and represented ports around the Mediterranean – ivories, precious metals, fabrics, food stuffs and spices, horses and livestock (vv. 12–25).

Marine explorations of shipwrecks more than 30 miles (48 km) west of Ashkelon reveal the size of these eighth-century BC shipping vessels, the nature of the containers and the range of cargoes (Ballard et al. 2002:

151–168). Two ships were initially discovered in 1997 and explored in 1999. Their location suggests that they were on a straight line from their departure port to either Egypt or the newly founded Carthage. That would indicate they did not stay close to the shore on their sea routes, perhaps because the waters off northern Sinai are among the most treacherous in the eastern Mediterranean. The ships were seaworthy, the length being just about three times the width. The primary cargo was fine wine, shipped in standard-sized ceramic jars that could be tied together for better transport. The maritime archaeologists also found cooking pots. An incense stand suggests the possibility of ritual prayers to the mariners' gods. Comparative ceramic assessment indicated that these vessels originated in Phoenicia. These may resemble the 'ships of Tarshish' of the biblical text. The authors suggest it might have been an unexpected and fierce east wind that sank the ships as they departed for points west (Ps. 48:8[7]; Ezek. 27:26).

JONAH 1:8–12

Translation

8 And they said to him, 'Tell us, we beg you, on whose account this great evil has come to us! What is your mission? From where are you coming? What is your country? And from what people are you'?

9 And he said to them, 'I am a Hebrew, and I fear YHWH, the God of the heavens, who made the sea and the dry land.'

10 And the men feared even more, and they said to him, 'What is this you have done'? For the men knew that he was fleeing from before the presence of YHWH, because he had told them.

11 And they said to him, 'What shall we do with you, so that the sea will be quiet from against us'? For the sea was surging and raging.

12 And he said to them, 'Lift me up and hurl me into the sea, and the sea will cease from upon you, for I know it is on account of me that this great storm is upon you.'

Notes on the text

1:8. The extremity of the situation requires translating the particle of entreaty *nâʾ*, and with something stronger than 'please!'

baʾăšer lĕmî is not used elsewhere in the HB. The expression echoes and expands *bĕšelmî* from v. 7. Some MT MSS and the LXX have omitted it (see Allen 1976: 209, n. 31; *BHQ* 93*). Nevertheless, it is present in Mur, supporting the MT reading.

The noun meaning 'work' or 'occupation' (*mĕlāʾkâ*) is similar to the word meaning 'messenger' (*malʾāk*). They might have been asking Jonah what kind of diplomatic 'mission' he was on, especially as their questions continue to probe his identity in relation to people and land. 'From where are you coming?' may be seeking to learn what has compelled a person to travel (Judg. 17:9; 19:17) (Sasson 1990: 114).

ʾē-mizzeh is a 'directional locative' (*IBHS* §18.4b) meaning 'from which'?

ʿam indicates a group that shares kinship as well as culture, both of which were tied to land, although blood relationship is not necessary to be considered part of this community. Both sg. and pl. may refer to a collective entity (O'Connell, *NIDOTTE* 3:429–432).

The succession of the interr. particles is alliterative: *lĕmî*, *mâ mĕlaʾktĕkā*, *mēʾayin tābōʾ*, *mâ ʾarṣekā*, *ʾē-mizzeh*.

9. The subject and object of each successive clause precede the verb in Jonah's answer, emphasizing his Hebr. identity and YHWH as the one he fears.

The LXX has 'servant of the Lord', *ʿebed* (*YH*), instead of *ʿibrî*. It may be a conscious connection with 2 Kgs 14:25, where Jonah is called 'servant of YHWH' (*BHQ* 93*).

The *ʾăšer* clause brings more definition to 'God of the heavens'. The 'sea' is of greatest concern: it comes first. In place of the expected 'land', Jonah substitutes 'dry land', a contrast to the raging sea and in anticipation of 2:11[10].

10. 'They feared a great fear' conveys the escalation in their terror from the point described in v. 5.

11. The sailors ask what they should do 'to' or 'for' (*lĕ-*) Jonah (see Williams 2007: 107). The wayyiq. form following their question is a result clause (GKC §166a; *IBHS* §33.4b; 39.2.2). The root *štq* ('to be quiet') is infrequently used. It occurs only in this context, in Ps. 107:30 (the waves dying down) and in Prov. 26:20 – strife being quiet (see *DCH* 8:579).

hôlēk ('going') followed by an additional masc. sg. ptc., *sōʿēr* ('storming'), is an idiom indicating the increasing intensity of the storm (GKC §113u; *IBHS* §37.6d). The horror of their experience is conveyed effectively by translating both verbs. Both the ptc. and noun forms of *sʿr* appear in this verse and v. 12.

12. Usually, *nśʾ* does not refer to lifting a person up as it does here. Instead, it frequently is accompanied by 'voice' or 'face', the latter indicating showing favour.

This is the third use of 'hurl' (previously in vv. 4, 5). The same pattern of the result clause (*wĕyištōq*) shapes Jonah's answer.

Form and structure

This unit rests within the larger framework of vv. 4–16; v. 9 is the centrepiece and is the first time Jonah speaks. He confesses his allegiance to YHWH, creator of the sea and dry land. The narrative has embedded dialogue interspersed with the narrator's presentation of pertinent conditions, states of mind and prior motives. There was likely more dialogue at that point than the narrator chose to include. They know, after all, that Jonah is fleeing from the presence of YHWH whether he told them earlier or divulges the information at this point. Added dialogue would have slowed the compelling forward movement of the narrative. The multiple questions in v. 8 may adumbrate the questioning dialogue of ch. 4 (Trible 1994: 140, n. 57). The apparent redundancy of the questions reflects the real-time verbal chaos.

Cognate accusatives (GCK §117pq) abound – fearing a great fear (vv. 10, 16), sacrificing a sacrifice and vowing vows (v. 16). In addition, seven *kî* clauses jostle against each other in this section and into the next. Together, they drive forward the increasingly ominous impressions that are converging.

Comment

1:8. As the lot falls on Jonah, it unleashes a verbal pandemonium from the sailors not unlike their frenzied actions earlier. They have just determined by lot who is responsible and are circling round, irate. The first recorded bluster may not be intended as a question but serves to point a very accusing finger at Jonah. If it is indeed a question, it reflects their quest for some degree of certainty in this messy set of circumstances. It is not necessarily redundant. It may reflect the sailors' attempt to be certain they have located the right culprit (Allen 1976: 209); it could reflect their concern that they have not done something ill against this mystery figure or have aided and abetted him in a crime (Stuart 1987: 460). Through another lens, it may indicate their concern to determine which *deity* was behind the calamity. Their subsequent questions, each of which is linked in ANE thinking to the divine authority behind this individual, bolster this interpretation as does Jonah's response (Youngblood 2019: 80). It also could be interpreted as an appositional phrase – 'you on whose account this evil has come upon us' (Bolin 1997: 82–83).

The questions overlap as they tumble out, driving at what may underlie the current dire straits. These are sailors and their spoken dialects may not quite have accorded with prophetic, archival and court language (Wilson 1918a: 285). Enquiring about 'your mission' first is important because they need the framework to understand their predicament. Most occurrences of *mĕlā'kâ* refer to occupation and the men may be enquiring about his trade. The same word appears in Ps. 107:23 regarding the work of those engaged in the shipping enterprise. Nevertheless, if he hired the ship solely for himself, their suspicions that something is amiss are confirmed by the lot falling on Jonah. They are intent on discovering the nature of his commission, and the most important avenue into that will be where he is headed. The network of relationships leading up to this point will help reconstruct the nature of the current dilemma. Their questions ascertain his ethnic, geopolitical and religious identities. Land and people are inextricably linked.

9. Jonah answers their last question. For the purposes of the narrative, it is all that is necessary. His response links his Hebr. identity with YHWH, God of the heavens. Those two data points help this crew of non-Israelites locate him. The term 'Hebrew' characteristically appears in narratives where God's people are identified within a larger, external culture. It is notable in conjunction within the Egyptian context (Gen. 39:11–17; 40:15; 41:12; 43:32; Exod. 1:15–19) and vis-à-vis the Philistines (1 Sam. 4:5–9; 13:19; 14:11, 21). See GKC §2b for a full list of occurrences. If Jonah were identifying himself to other Israelites, he would have named his tribe.

Jonah's declaration that YHWH made the sea and the dry land adds those dimensions to the title 'YHWH God of the heavens'. Jonah shapes a traditional affirmation – found in multiple psalms – for his non-Israelite audience (Ben Zvi 2003: 108, n. 31). The men on the ship resonate and likely quake at hearing 'heavens' and 'sea'. Those are the places they perceive as the sources of their immediate danger. By adding 'dry land', Jonah effectively covers all the spheres known to them. The last is what they long to see again. It is Jonah's way of saying he is rightfully afraid of the One who controls everything. It also is firmly lodged in his own tradition (Pss 95:5; 135:6).

Jonah's dissonances are evident in his declaration that he fears God while he is still very much on the run and in his posture of disobedience (Fretheim 1977: 85). Wolff (1986: 116) suggests that Jonah's reference to fear may be more in the context of traditional worship, significantly removed from visceral dread of holiness and thus devoid of confession. He inserts the allusion to fear into the affirmation of God's might and power, all the while maintaining his stubborn silence until the lot 'outs' him. What this means for understanding the humanity of Jonah is left shrouded, but it is not outside the realm of reality to say what is expected and continue to live in the opposite manner. By way of contrast, the sailors are experiencing heart-stopping terror.

10. Now these toughened mariners are simply called 'men' instead of sailors. Their growing horror contrasts with Jonah's fear of YHWH, a description that sounds calm by contrast. Their accusing question 'What have you done?' may be an exclamation of horror and not a real enquiry. The intensity of that question echoes all the way from Gen. 3:13 – what had Eve done to upend the whole fabric of human relationship with YHWH (Lessing 2007: 110)? On the other hand, perhaps the sailors determine that his prior answer is not fully satisfactory and circle back to it – 'What have you really done?' The timing of the third clause – 'because he told them' – is of interest. Most likely, he elaborates on what he said in v. 9 and, although it is not recorded, they know (Sasson 1990: 120–121). All of this leads to their question in v. 11. Now they are putting together the apparent magnitude of Jonah's disobedience: it has truly alarming consequences for them. Jonah's God is a much more significant deity than they have anticipated. From their perspective, Jonah's flight from his God is going to drag them down to their watery deaths; there does not seem to be any way out of it. Thus, their question practically vibrates with outrage.

11. The mariners know they must address the core of the problem, and that is Jonah. The Hebr. prep. attached to Jonah's name may mean 'to' or 'for'. If it implies 'to', then it seems they think sacrificing him in some way may be the answer. They might have perceived that option as a very real alternative to certain death for everyone. On the other hand, perhaps it should be 'for', suggesting that they are intent on finding a way to save his life *from* the sea, return him to a place where he can resume his vocation, and thus appease the wrath of his God (Hoyt 2019: 441–442).

It is not clear if the final descriptive clause about the growing intensity of the sea is part of what the sailors said or is commentary by the narrator (Sasson 1990: 122). The latter seems more likely as the sailors do not need to describe for Jonah the raging of the sea, but for the alternative interpretation, see Hoyt (2019: 442).

12. With his response to the sailors' query, Jonah's words echo what they have already done with the vessels on board the ship – they must hurl him into the sea. Earlier, he has been a substitute for the discarded vessels of the ship; now he will join those containers being hurled overboard (Trible 1994: 146).

While Hoyt (2019: 443–444) intimates repeatedly that Jonah is cowardly, self-centred and seeking 'sailor-assisted suicide' in his continued rejection of his commission, the situation is more complicated. Jonah knows that all his attempts to flee the presence of YHWH have failed utterly. He recognizes that only his intentional removal from the ship that is currently preserving his life will stop the storm. Jonah's response starts with detailed instructions. 'Lift up' is an important part of them. The sailors were not simply to push him overboard; Jonah tells them to engage in an action that will make them come to grips with their own responsibility (Sasson 1990: 124) exercised before the God of the heavens, sea and dry land. At the same time, he declares his culpability. His previous downward trajectory is reversed with 'lift me up' whether he is fully appreciative of that pivot or not.

Assessments of Jonah's motives and intentions are varied. Through one set of lenses, Jonah has two options at this juncture. One is to tell the sailors to turn back and, presuming that this signifies his belated obedience to the command of God, will result in the storm's abating. The second, which he chooses, is to tell them to pitch him overboard to bring about the cessation of the storm. This is not to be construed as an offering to the sea. That would be far from his own orthodox framework. It is also not the same as a despairing longing for death. In fact, once he is swirling in the tortuous sea, he joins the company of voices who recognize the evil of that kind of death and pray for deliverance (Landes 1967a: 23–24). The latter choice, however, is still brimming with interpretive challenges. For whatever reason, Jonah offers his life, but does not articulate any form of repentance (Fretheim 1977: 88). Is Jonah self-centred and rebellious to the end, his declaration reflecting his final attempt to flee the responsibility that YHWH imposed on him by effecting his own demise (Wolff 1986: 118; Trible 1996: 499; Lessing 2007: 130; Shemesh 2010: 15)? Or is he manifesting a profound awareness that his own sacrifice, as the guilty party, is necessary to save the lives of the mariners (Bolin 1997: 85–86)? Or something else?

Explanation

The sailors have worked their way through a tumultuous progression of responses. They have hurled the cargo overboard, cried out to their gods, cast lots and frantically interrogated the culprit. These actions escalate in intensity because their lives hang in the balance. The expression 'God of the heavens' would be familiar to Phoenician-based sailors, who knew Baal Shamen as a deity responsible for storms (Röllig 1999: 149–151). When Jonah declares YHWH to be God of the heavens, he offers a radical corrective to their understanding of the cosmos. Their gods have obviously failed. Even from his disobedient posture, he offers a window of hope: YHWH indeed controls all three spheres of the cosmos. In the world views of the ANE, the sea represented the abyss by virtue of its depth, darkness and turmoil. It was chaotic and unknown. The mighty storm on the surface would be matched by the tumult swirling around Jonah in ch. 2.

Craig (1993: 132–133) summarizes the differing interpretations of Jonah's instructions to the mariners to hurl him overboard. Wolff (1986: 118) reads it primarily as a death wish, parallel to what he expressed in 4:3, 8. Allen's assessment (1976: 211) is that Jonah realizes the extent of his guilt before YHWH. Another possibility – Jonah offers himself for the sake of the sailors (Bolin 1997: 85–86). No one reading, however, does justice to the dynamic portrayals of the inner life of characters in the narrative. Another possibility – Jonah was so desperate that Nineveh be judged that he was willing to die to accomplish this. Without his presence in the city there would be no prophetic warning to avert Nineveh's comeuppance (E. Barkhuizen, private communication, April 2022).

JONAH 1:13–16

Translation

13Nevertheless, the men dug in with their oars to return to the dry land, but they were not able because the sea was surging and raging against them.

[14]Then they called out to YHWH and said, 'Please, O YHWH, do not allow us to perish with the life of this man, and do not hold against us innocent blood, for you, O YHWH – as you please, you do.'

[15]And they lifted Jonah up and hurled him into the sea, and the sea stood still from its raging.

[16]And the men even more greatly feared YHWH and they offered a sacrifice and fulfilled vows.

Notes on the text

1:13. The initial wayyiq. form suggests a contrast with the preceding circumstances (*IBHS* §33.2.1): 'nevertheless' is an appropriate translation. The second waw is an adversative – 'but they were not able'.

ḥtr means 'to dig' (*DCH* 3:337). Seldom used, it refers to breaking through a wall (Ezek. 8:8; 12:5). This is the only place it is used regarding water.

šûb is a verb of motion that has to do with positions and relationships. This is a hiph. inf. const.

14. *nōʾbĕdâ* is a coh. from *ʾbd* ('perish'). Preceded by *ʾānnâ* Yhwh *ʾal-nāʾ*, the entreaty is powerful.

The prep. *be-* with *nepeš* could mean either 'with' or 'on account of' (*IBHS* §11.2.5de).

YHWH is voc.

The order of the verbs in the final clause is instructive. The desire of YHWH is determinative of what he does. Wolff (1986: 120) calls it a 'confirmatory perfect', describing a state that already exists and continues to exist. See *IBHS* §30.4b.

15. The wayyiq. resumes the sailors' action from v. 13 following their petition in v. 14.

ʿmd can mean to 'stand', 'stop' or 'be silent'. In coming to a standstill, the sea loses any power it had to damage.

zaʿap ('rage' or 'fury') is a rare word; it refers to the raging of YHWH (Isa. 30:30; Mic. 7:9), kings or Israelites (2 Chr. 16:10; 28:9; Prov. 19:12). Here, the sea is personified.

16. *ʾet-*Yhwh is a second object of 'fear'.

Form and structure

The instructions of Jonah (v. 12) are mirrored in the actions of the sailors and the result (v. 15): they lift Jonah up, hurl him into the sea and it ceases from its raging. The verb 'to hurl' appears for the fourth time; each one refers to the sea. YHWH hurls the storm on to the sea; the men hurl containers overboard; Jonah instructs the men to hurl him overboard; finally, they hurl Jonah to his certain death.

The number of Hebr. words in each clause of v. 16 decreases from five to three to two, just as the sailors fade from view (Trible 1994: 151). There is very likely a time gap in the middle of v. 16. The sailors row to shore where they acquire the necessary provisions for sacrifices.

Comment

1:13. Early in the narrative, the seamen are identified specifically as such. They are mariners (*mallāḥîm*) and 'linemen'. No doubt very little fazed them. By v. 10, they are like anyone else in their terror. Here the text continues to call them 'men'. Fear levels the playing field. It also makes them dig in with their oars, breaking the waves. Despite Jonah's instructions, the sailors make a valiant effort to bring their ship to land. They are not, however, able to do so. This is a brief shift of focus back to the ship. Ezek. 27:26–29 indicates that oars supplemented sail-power. Sails are useless with the tempest.

If we read this as any kind of realia, they make what could have been a foolish choice. Heading for shore in a hurricane-force storm is unwise even along the straight coastline of the eastern Mediterranean because it is lined with jagged reefs and ridges of calcified sandstone. Perhaps they reason that God will be pleased at their efforts to get Jonah back on track as soon as possible and not allow them to be harmed even in the vicinity of crashing breakers. Preserving Jonah's life is their initial priority and getting to shore seems the fastest option. Safely landing would be for them a demonstration of YHWH's complete sovereignty over these dangerous circumstances (Sasson 1990: 142).

The connotations of *šûb* range widely from physical turning to metaphorical and theological change. The hiph. is rarely used in the sense of returning to a point of departure. It does not have a stated object in this context and could imply returning *Jonah* to shore (Wolff 1986: 119). The centrality of *šûb* to the process of repentance is much more common (Thompson and Martens, *NIDOTTE* 4:55–59).

14. The perceptions of the men on board shift radically. To this point, they cry out 'each to his own god' as they hurl goods overboard. As they put together the implications of the tempestuous sea, Jonah's own confession of YHWH as sovereign over sea and land, and their inability to do anything to save themselves, they plead with Jonah's YHWH, invoking the Name two times. Affirming YHWH's unmatched power and his relationship with Jonah does not necessarily mean the sailors jettisoned their belief in other gods. They might have moved comfortably into henotheism, recognizing the supremacy of this one god among others.

Their petition acknowledges the double edge to their predicament. If they keep Jonah on board, they perish; if they become guilty of innocent blood, they perish (Trible 1994: 148). Because the focus of the second part is on the possibility of their moral culpability, it is likely that the first plea addresses simply their survival – 'let us not perish *with* the life of this man'. Wolff (1986: 119), however, interprets it in the opposite way, noting it is better to read 'on account of', because that serves as a better parallel to the request that follows regarding 'innocent blood'.

dām nāqî means the 'blood of an innocent person'. Almost exclusively, the expression refers to the blood of the person who has died or will die (Hoyt 2019: 446, n. 133). It surfaces in Jer. 26:12–15, where the prophet is defending himself against an angry mob. The contrast between that situation and the conundrum facing the mariners is marked. Do the sailors construe Jonah as 'innocent', even after his confession? That seems unlikely in the light of what has happened: he has jeopardized their lives. Nevertheless, the possibility that they will be held guilty of murder underlies this; they plead not to perish 'on account of' what they are about to do with Jonah. They have made up their minds that there is no way out of this other than to do as Jonah advises because he is culpable, but that jeopardizes their own innocence as he will die because of their intervention. They have not observed anything akin to 'due process' and are pleading for leniency as they commit an inescapable crime (Wolff 1986: 120; Sasson 1990: 134). A slightly altered understanding of the syntax might have them asking that *they* not perish *with* the life of this man (*bĕnepeš*) – that YHWH not take *their* own innocent blood.

The sailors' prayer echoes Pss 115:3 and 135:6. Their final declaration submits to the divine authority as they perceive it: YHWH does as he desires. It is their hope that he will desire they live.

Ben Zvi (2003: 72–75) poses the possibility that the sailors understood Jonah as a runaway slave because he identified himself as a servant of his God. They were intent on returning him to land so his Master would not be angry with them. They knew they were innocent and wanted to show that. This reflects a view that God is geographically limited. On the other hand, they might have determined that God is Master of the sea, Jonah is his prophet and Jonah's directive about tossing him overboard is the way to go. Nevertheless, they try to counter God's direction and get Jonah *out* of the sea, God's territory.

15. Perhaps initially in the minds of the sailors, Jonah will be an offering to the raging sea as they follow his instructions to the letter. The continuation of the narrative implies the sea responds immediately. It ceases; lit. 'the sea stood from its raging'. The personification of the sea fits into the drama of the sailors' previous world view. It seethes and roars, just like an angry deity, until they invoke the Name of YHWH and obey the words of the prophet of YHWH. What the sea does in 'standing' is different from what the sailors, echoed by Jonah, have asked for. They ask it would be quiet, but the result is more dramatic: the power of the personified sea is constrained by the Master of the sea (Sasson 1990: 137). It is small wonder that their views of the deities are reshuffled as Jonah's form disappears beneath the surface.

16. Fear of YHWH leads to worship. There is no doubt that their prior ways of thinking have been overturned entirely; they fear YHWH and offer sacrifices to YHWH. The point is not to determine whether or not these pagans make their way to a temple structure or a shrine in order to offer sacrifices and pay vows. That would have been the customary activity in the ANE (Stuart 1987: 464–465), but little about this narrative fits traditional patterns. Might they have made their way to Jerusalem? Perhaps. Needless to say, it is doubtful that they cobble together materials for a sacrifice while they are still on board since they had pitched everything overboard.

There were shrines built on seaside promontories that marked particularly dangerous areas. Evidence from harbour temples and seaside shrines along the Levantine coast includes votive offerings of a nautical nature (Brody 1998: 40–42, 55). One of these might have been the destination for the sailors as they offered sacrifices and fulfilled vows. The practice of making sacrifices is evident throughout the ANE. It along with vows would have been easy next steps for the sailors to express their thanksgiving to YHWH (Averbeck, *NIDOTTE* 1:1066–1073). Generally, vows were made in the face of danger and stressful situations; when those had been alleviated by God, the vow was completed. It was optional to make a vow, but once it was made, it was incumbent upon the individual to pay that vow (Wakely, *NIDOTTE* 3:37–42). Reading between the lines, the vows of the sailors may point forward: they are promising that in the future, grateful sacrifice to YHWH will continue to be front and centre in their radically revised world view. This is a hint that their response is not only a burst for the moment. They have witnessed and lived through a profoundly transformative experience (Stuart 1987: 465). In the poetic perspective, Ps. 116:17–18 reflects both sacrifices of thanksgiving and completion of vows in the presence of YHWH's people. The conversion of the sailors is presented in terms that are the fabric of Israelite revealed religion.

Explanation

As the storm rages on the sea, these natural phenomena serve as mighty instruments in the arsenal of God. They combine to stop Jonah's headlong flight; they bring wizened mariners to fear. The tumult of furious waters echoes into a familiar Gospel narrative (Matt. 8:23–27; parallels in Mark 4:35–41; Luke 8:22–25). Evening storms are a frequent occurrence on the Sea of Galilee. Through one particularly alarming tempest, Jesus sleeps until he is awakened by his disciples, fearful they are going to perish. When the sea obeys his command to be calm, they recognize they are in the presence of the Master who controls the wind and the waves (Ps. 107:29). The parallels are notable. The tempest is of seismic proportions; Matthew's term is *seismos*. It nearly swamps the boat, terrifying the disciples who pray that they will not perish. Against the backdrop of those similar circumstances, the contrast between the two sleeping passengers could not be more striking. While Jonah does not even invoke his God, Jesus rebukes the waves and they stand still in the presence of the Master. Mark calls it a 'great calm', followed by the 'great fear' of the disciples (Mark 4:39, 41).

At the close of this part of the drama, the sailors have fallen to their knees in dread and gratitude, and Jonah has sunk beneath the waves. After being depicted as remarkably exemplary, the sailors disappear from the drama; we do not know the extent and substance of their belief. They have been the positive cast of characters among whom Jonah, less than a paragon of faithfulness, has endured the dramatic spotlight. Their activity and prayer are contrasted with the absence of those characteristics in Jonah. They work diligently to preserve Jonah's life while he seems to disregard it. Nevertheless, it is in Jonah's place of failure that YHWH uses him (Wolff 1986: 122–123).

Jonah's next experiences will bring to 'life' the possibly predictable affirmation of fearing YHWH that he previously offered to the audience of sailors. It is relatively simple to disparage Jonah's character at this point. At face value, he has not come out well in contrast to the mariners. That interpretation, however, creates a frozen picture of a complex person wrestling with the maelstrom created by calling and circumstances far beyond his control. At least, Jonah has come to the point of sacrificing himself to save the lives of the crew whatever motives might have driven him to that point. Part of his response seems to have been based on his fear of YHWH and the now-experienced knowledge that there is no possibility of escaping his assignment to Nineveh. In the meantime, his concern for the sailors, belated as it seems, is sufficient that he cannot be accused of xenophobia.

The importance of fear cannot be overstated, especially in contexts where an aversion to speaking of such a 'negative emotion' predominates. While panic and anxiety are indeed at odds with our life in fellowship with God, a healthy fear is salutary. It is notable that the exhortation to fear YHWH surfaces more frequently than the admonition to love him. It seems that God knows his children well! It is fear that compels a straying person to return in repentance, so that we are not left in gnawing anxiety and dread. Deut. 10:12 captures the emotional and spiritual trajectory: 'And now, O Israel, what does YHWH your God ask from you except to fear YHWH your God, to walk in all his ways and to love him and to serve YHWH your God with all your heart and all your *nepeš*.' The psalmist's perspective is likewise refreshingly honest: 'If iniquity you are counting,

O YH, O Lord, who could stand? But with you there is forgiveness; therefore, you are feared' (Ps. 130:3–4). YHWH readjusts Isaiah's perspectives in the face of what sound like overwhelming pressures. To paraphrase: Don't get all caught up in conspiracy theories and succumb to the fears of those around you. Instead, be sure that you sanctify YHWH of Hosts so that you fear and dread him – and he will be a sanctuary (8:11–14a). It is only when we properly fear YHWH with all the concomitant obedience that we truly find safety.

> 'Twas grace that taught my heart to fear;
> and grace my fears relieved . . .
> ('Amazing Grace', John Newton, 1779)

JONAH 2:1–2[1:17 – 2:1]

Translation

2:1[1:17]And YHWH prepared a great fish to swallow Jonah, and Jonah was in the belly of the fish for three days and three nights.

2[2:1]And Jonah prayed to YHWH his God from the belly of the fish.

Notes on the text

2:1[1:17]. The chapter division in the MT is after the sacrifices of the sailors, and ushers the appointed fish on to the scene. In English, ch. 2 starts with Jonah's prayer from inside the fish.

wayĕman ('and he prepared') is 3 masc. sg. pi. shortened (apocopated) wayyiq. from the root *mnh*; see GKC §75bb on the adjusted vocalization. This wayyiq. form may be intended to represent concurrent action. The fish is prepared even as the sailors are engaged in their encounter with YHWH. It may best be interpreted as 'in the meantime', and translated as a pluperf. (AV, NLT). This is the first of four occurrences of the word in the book. YHWH is always the subject, but his name changes each time.

bl' ('to swallow up', 'engulf') as it is used in the HB is never benign. It always has overtones of malevolence. See references in BDB 118.

'Belly' (*mē'eh*) includes the inward parts of a creature, generally a person. It is used in parallel with *beṭen* (Ezek. 3:3).

Dāg appears both in its masc. form (here) as well as fem. (v. 2). It is a general term for 'fish' of the sea.

2[2:1]. The fem. form (*dāgâ*) is most often a collective. This is the only instance where it has a sg. referent and may serve as a stylistic device to avoid exact repetition.

Form and structure

The descriptions utilizing 'great' continue. Everything in this narrative is oversized, the fish as well. The beginning of the chapter has Jonah swallowed down; at the end he is vomited up.

Comment

2:1[1:17]. The timing of YHWH's appointment of the fish is worth exploring. Perhaps YHWH prepared it (pluperf.) so that it is waiting to gulp Jonah down. On the other hand, it may arrive at the last moment after Jonah has been swirling in the depths and is at the point of expiring. Collins (1995: 127–128) articulates three criteria for determining that a wayyiq. form is indeed to be understood as a pluperf.: (1) there is an explicit pointer back to a prior event; (2) the logic of the referent requires that the action took place prior to the event represented by the immediately prior verb; or (3) the verb begins a new section. Jon. 2:1 fits with the third as it shifts from the sailors back to Jonah.

The fish does not chew Jonah but simply gulps him down, bringing him to rest for three days and three nights somewhere in the inner parts. While the floor of the sea was spatially as far down as Jonah could go, there is an even further descent into this undefined and unexperienced gastric pool. Inside the fish is like the darkness of the tomb (Jenson 2008: 60) but ironically, it is Jonah's rescue and deliverance from the watery grave. The prophetic concepts of judgment and salvation are intertwined for Jonah: he is preserved through this judgment (Trible 1996: 482–483; Youngblood 2019: 88). From a different perspective, Wolff (1986: 133) does not think the fish is portrayed as a source of rescue. Instead, three days are mentioned because that indicates sufficient time to *die*. Besides, swallowing imagery is associated with danger. Qal forms of *blʿ* appear in narrative contexts of unsettling miraculous events (Gen. 41:7, 24; Exod. 7:12; Num. 16:30–34) or poetry where the symbolism has a threatening tone (Exod. 15:12; Job 20:15; Pss 21:10[9]; 35:25; 69:16[15]; Prov. 1:12; Isa. 28:4; Jer. 51:34). The image is an ambiguous one: Jonah is both swallowed into darkness and delivered from the swirling abyss. The pi. form appears in Isa. 25:7–8; YHWH swallows death for ever. The word itself is onomatopoeic, with the final consonant resembling a sudden gulp. In Ugaritic texts, Mot (death) is a voracious monster who 'swallows' the moisture of Baal, who then dies (CTA/KTU 5.i, 15–35; 5.2.ii, 2–13). See De Moor 1987: 69–73 and Wyatt 1998: 116–120.

Because the miraculous element is the centrepiece of this narrative, identifying the fish and tracking stories of whales supposedly swallowing humans are not particularly relevant enterprises.

The expression 'three days and three nights' appears in full only one additional time in the HB (1 Sam. 30:12); it implies three *full* days. There are numerous additional references to three days, and many of them describe the length of either distress or a journey. Outside the Israelite context, the Sumerian legend about Inanna's descent into the underworld includes this specific time indicator. Landes (1967b: 446–450) has suggested that the phrase might have implied the travelled separation between the nether regions and terra firma. Perhaps the narrator here employs it to indicate that the fish is appointed by God to enable Jonah's journey across the vast separation and back from Sheol to dry land. Several HB references to three days address the ominous approach to or encounter with death: Abraham journeys to Mount Moriah to offer Isaac as a sacrifice (Gen. 22:4); the sons of the prophets search unsuccessfully for Elijah for three days after his whirlwind departure to the heavenly realms (2 Kgs 2:15–18); Hos. 6:1–2 declares that on the third day after they are wounded and torn, YHWH will heal Israel. Through NT lenses, three days is an indicator that a person was truly deceased (John 11:6, 14). It culminates in 'the sign of Jonah' evoked by Jesus (Matt. 12:38–41).

2[1]. This mention of prayer introduces stanzas that draw on the rich tradition of the psalms. From a literary standpoint, Jonah's prayer departs from the conventions of prose narrative. It is also a contrast in terms of Jonah himself. The rebellious character of ch. 1 sings his gratitude in ch. 2.

The shift from the masc. form for 'fish' to the fem. is likely stylistic. Nevertheless, it has prompted creative suggestions, all the way from **rabbinic midrash** to theologically motivated symbolism. The rabbis, for whom every lexical item was significant, indicated that Jonah was initially swallowed by a male fish but was too comfortable in that environment. Thus, he was regurgitated and swallowed by a pregnant fish. Those close quarters contributed to his distress (Levine 1978: 71–72). Trible (1996: 479–480) links the fem. form of 'fish' with 'internal parts', implying a possible maternal connection with the womb and life, but one that is dangerous. Through another lens, the masc. form represents judgment, while the fem. form points to the deliverance of Jonah (Youngblood 2019: 108). The same complex of factors is suggested as an underlying factor in the appearance of both divine names at this point. When the emphasis is on the disciplinary divine activity, Elohim is used; when those actions are merciful and beneficial, YHWH appears. Here they are together as Jonah is in between. See Magonet 1983: 33–38.

Explanation

Jonah experiences 'baptism' in the sea and deliverance to dry land, parallel to Israel. Paul develops the latter typology in 1 Cor. 10:1–2 (Lessing 2007: 110). One of the ancillary implications of 'three days and three nights' is that Jonah's time in the fish was a rest after experiencing the depths of Sheol. In the same manner, Jesus' three days and nights in the grave were a rest (Luke 23:43) after enduring the wrath of God against all human sin while crying out 'My God, why have you forsaken me?'

'Three days' has an even wider set of connections. The risen Jesus explained to the gathered band of followers that the Scriptures pointed forward to his suffering, dying and rising on the third day (Luke 24:46). 'According to the Scriptures' (1 Cor. 15:3–4) means telling all of Israel's covenant story as the story of Jesus: he embodies the history of national Israel. His mission is fundamentally the Exodus narrative – revelation and redemption. Passages about Israel's national narrative that mention three days are viewed as pointing forward to Jesus.

JONAH 2:3–10[2:2–9]

Translation

3[2]And he said,
I called out from my distress unto YHWH, and he answered me;
from the belly of Sheol I shouted aloud, and you heard my voice.
4[3]You cast me deep in the heart of the seas, and the river surrounded me.
All your breakers and your waves went over me.
5[4]And [then] I said, 'I am driven from before your eyes;
nevertheless, surely I will look again to your holy temple.'
6[5]The waters surrounded me to the neck, the deep surrounded me;
reeds were bound to my head.
7[6]To the extremities of the mountains I went down;
the earth with her bars behind me for ever;
but you brought me up from the pit of my life, O YHWH my God!
8[7]In the fluttering away from me of my life, I remembered YHWH,
and my prayer came to you, to your holy temple.
9[8]Those who attend to utter emptiness [idols] are forsaking their *ḥesed*.
10[9]But I with a voice of thanksgiving, I will sacrifice to you;
that which I have vowed I will fulfil. Salvation belongs to YHWH.

Notes on the text

2:3[2]. *qārāʾtî* ('I called'), introduces a prior prayer. The 3 masc. sg. ('YHWH answered') of line one shifts to 2 masc. sg. ('you heard my voice') in the second line.

Sheol is personified with *beṭen* ('belly').

ṣārâ suggests narrowing in addition to distress, perhaps alluding to experiencing the grave (Jenson 2008: 62).

šiwwaʿtî means 'to cry out for help'; it is loud. It may be related to the root *yšʿ*, meaning to 'save' or 'deliver' (BDB 1002).

4[3]. *wattašlîkēnî* is generally translated 'and you cast me', but the verb in hiph. could also mean 'to abandon' (*DCH* 8:395–399).

mĕṣûlâ (*ṣwl*) is frequently pl. used in construct with 'sea'. The sg. (as here) means the 'deep sea' (*DCH* 5:448–449). BHS suggests deleting either this word or the following *bilbab yammîm* ('in the heart of the seas'), but that is not necessary.

yammîm (pl.) is emphatic. The combination of *lēbāb* plus *yammîm* is unique to Jonah. Generally, the idiom is *bĕlēb yammîm* – frequently in Ezek. 27.

sbb ('to surround') in qal frequently intimates something hostile and threatening.

nāhār generally means a river above ground and is often used to name the Euphrates. It also refers to sea currents (Pss 24:2; 93:3; Isa. 44:27), possibly alluding to a mythical river of chaos and death (Wolff 1986: 134; Nogalski 2011a: 430; see *DCH* 5:632–633). In the Ugaritic Epic of Ba'al and Anat, 'house of Yam' and 'palace of judge Nahar' appear repeatedly in parallel (De Moor 1987: 29–34; Wyatt 1998: 49–69).

5[4]. At the centre of describing the harrowing circumstances, Jonah recalls a moment of dreadful self-perception, introduced by the emphatic 'And I, I said'.

nigraštî is an infrequently used niph. qat. form. Two additional prophetic texts employ the niph. form of *grš*. One likens the wicked to the sea, which is *nigrāš* (Isa. 57:20), and the second declares the earth is both *nigrāš* and sinks (Amos 8:8). In these two contexts, the niph. implies being tossed about. That could fit here as well; the previous verse describes tumult. The root appears more frequently in qal and pi., where it means to be driven away (BDB 176–177).

ʾak represents an affirmation that contrasts with what precedes (BDB 36; see J-M §164a). In this context, there are differences of opinion as to whether it poses a contrast or continues a sense of despair. The LXX has *ʿara*, which can be equally ambiguous, depending on whether it is in the context of a question or an affirmation (LS 232–233). The Greek text of Theodotian reads *pōs*, the equivalent of *ʾêk* ('how'). The variant is understandable: it involves the presence (or not) of a yod between the 'aleph and kaph.

ʾôsîp (1 sg. hiph.) along with the hiph. inf. const. of *nbṭ* means 'to continue to look' or 'to look again'.

6[5]. In addition to this context, *ʾpp* ('to surround') is found only in the psalms (18:5[4]; 40:13[12]; 116:3) and 2 Sam. 22 (parallel to Ps. 18).

Generally, the expected expression is *ʿad māwet* ('to death'). Here it is *ʿad nepeš*, perhaps an **ellipsis** indicating until life vanished. *nepeš* has a wide semantic range, including throat, neck, appetite, life, breath, soul (*DCH* 5:724). *IBHS* 11.2.12c n.103 suggests 'to the throat'. Once the neck and throat are constricted, the possibility of life wanes.

sûp ('reed') is a collective. The Tg seems to have associated it with *yam-sûp*: the Red Sea was wrapped around Jonah's head (Cathcart and Gordon

1989:107). The LXX reads it as *sôp*, the end or last (*eschatē*). *sûp* is a general term for sea vegetation; in some contexts, it was deep underwater and in others, it is closer to shore, notably the 'sea of reeds'.

ḥābûš is a qal pass. ptc. ('wrapped'). It is followed by the lamed prep.: the reeds are bound to Jonah's head.

7[6]. *qṣb* means 'to cut off' or 'to cut down'. While *qeṣeb* appears in 1 Kgs 6:25 and 7:37, those contexts refer to the shaping of the cherubim for the temple and do not help here. This form (pl. in constr. with 'mountains') is a **hapax**, translated 'extremities' (BDB 891; *DCH* 7:278). The Tg reads 'to the roots of the mountains'. The accent marking (*zaqep qatan*) suggests that 'I went down' should be read with 'to the roots of the mountains'.

ʾereṣ has two general referents – land and territory: earth and world. In a smaller number of instances, it may refer to the underworld (Job 10:21; Ps. 71:20; Isa. 44:23; Jer. 15:7). See *DCH* 1:582 and Craig 1993: 15, n. l.

běrîaḥ refers to a heavy bar that is part of a city gate and fortress structures (Deut. 3:5; Judg. 16:3). The earth was shut against Jonah. This word shares the root letters of *brḥ*, 'to flee'. This is the end of Jonah's headlong flight from the presence of YHWH.

baʿădî is the subst. *baʿad*, signifying 'separation from', with the 1 pron. suff. It generally accompanies verbs that define the nature of the separation (BDB 126). In this verbless clause, Jonah's separation is in relation to the 'bars' of the earth.

lěʿôlām indicates long duration beyond the span of measurable time.

wattaʿal could be either 2 masc. sg. or 3 fem. sg. qal or hiph.; the context determines that it is Jonah's addressing YHWH.

šaḥat ('pit') is from the root meaning to 'sink down' and is parallel to Sheol (Ps. 16:10). It was a place of decay and complete destruction. The word order is significant: 'from the pit' follows directly 'you brought up'.

8[7]. The inf. const. (*běhitʿaṭṭēp*) has a temporal sense: 'when'. The three roots associated with *ʿṭp* include being enfeebled or faint, something curling around or enveloping, and turning aside (*DCH* 6:350–351). It does not in this context necessarily have to do with losing consciousness (Sasson 1990: 193). Whatever condition it represents for Jonah, it is accompanied by his remembering and is followed with 'then' of the wayyiq. form.

nepeš is best understood as 'life' in this context.

YHWH as direct object precedes 'I remembered'.

The directional prep. (*ʾel*) with 'you' and 'your holy temple' indicates Jonah's sense of the efficacy of his prayer.

9[8]. *měšammĕrîm* is a masc. pl. pi. ptc., a **hapax** but from the common root *šmr*, meaning 'to keep' or 'guard'. The qal form appears in a similar context in Ps. 31:7[6] – 'I hate those who keep empty idols.'

hablê-šāwʾ is emphatic; the first word in sg. means 'breath' or 'vapour', a natural phenomenon. Here it serves as an adj. in const. with the second noun, the concept to which vapour points: 'emptiness', 'nothingness'. See *IBHS* §14.5b; J-M §141m. The words together mean 'utter emptiness'.

The yiq. form of the final verb shifts attention to an anticipated outcome for those described at the beginning of the verse. They will be in a state of forsaking.

The 3 masc. pl. pron. suff. on *ḥesed* could refer both to those who abandon their obligation to offer *ḥesed* to one another and to those abandoning the Source of faithful love.

10[9]. Placing the personal pron. first along with the finite form of the verb emphasizes the contrast between those described in v. 9 and Jonah. His closing utterance is characterized as a 'sound' (*qôl*), suggesting a song as well as words that express gratitude.

ʾezbĕḥâ ('I will sacrifice') is a coh., as is *ʾăšallēmâ*. *šlm* is best understood as 'fulfil' or 'complete' rather than 'pay'. It did not involve monetary transactions.

yĕšûʿātâ is a longer form of *yĕšûʿâ* ('salvation').

Form and structure

The arrangement of the segments of the chapter is complex. Jonah's 'prayer' – introduced in v. 2 – contains snatches revisiting his cries of distress when he was still swirling through the watery depths. The shifting tenses are not meant to be lodged in specific time frames: there is a timelessness and blurring of temporal boundaries as Jonah captures his experience with embedded hymnic phrases. Sasson (1990: 162–167) translates most of the qat. forms with the present tense: it conveys the sense of Jonah's immediate experience.

Jonah's prayer may be expected to be a lament and frantic plea for rescue. Yet it is primarily Jonah's expression of thanksgiving, a formal surprise. 'Dissonance triumphs' (Trible 1994: 171). The prayer is a link between rebellious Jonah of ch. 1 and compliant Jonah in ch. 3. It is also the backdrop for the prophet's complaint in ch. 4 (Youngblood 2019: 99, 105–106).

While the descriptions of distress share phrases and clauses with other parts of the liturgical tradition, Jonah's prayer is unique in that it has geographical coherence. The movement is downward, from the surface waves and breakers to the very roots of the mountains. It demonstrates within the poetic development a narrative direction, culminating in descriptions of horror and hopelessness (Magonet 1983: 40–41, 49; Limburg 1993: 68). The drama of reversal is midpoint in v. 7; in contrast to heading steadily downward, now YHWH brings him up. Jonah names him fully: YHWH my Elohim.

There are generally four parts to psalms of thanksgiving and Jonah's prayer exemplifies them: introduction that summarizes the deliverance, description of the personal crisis and appeal for help, the divine deliverance and a vow to praise (Allen 1976: 215; see also Youngblood 2019: 105). The primary structural challenge for the poem rests on how to read *ʾak* in 5b. If it serves as an emphatic particle (J-M §164a), Jonah's assurance despite the surrounding circumstances is emphasized.

There is no scholarly agreement in regarding the number of stanzas in the poem; suggestions range from three to seven. Lessing (2007: 184) suggests three, comprising vv. 3–5, 6–8, 9–10. If four can be defined, then there is a possible chiastic structure: 2:3 (A); 2:4–5 (B); 2:6–8 (B'); 2:9–10 (A') (Trible 1994: 163–171; 1996: 506–507).

Parallelism shapes most of the chapter as Jonah weaves together phrases and clauses adopted from the hymn and prayer traditions. There are places, however, where he departs from those patterned expressions; one of them is *ʿad-nepeš* (v. 6), which may be an indication of his horror. The tenses shift, particularly at major junctures throughout the poem. Likewise, second-person address to YHWH interfaces with more general descriptions for an audience. This is a familiar pattern from the psalms.

There is some conceptual tension between Jonah's poetic representation and the narrative of ch. 1. Jonah declares that YHWH cast him into the sea; technically it was the sailors although it is not necessary to quibble in the face of YHWH's sovereignty. Jonah further claims he has been driven away, but the storyline is that he fled. These details bump into each other, giving a richness and complexity to his 'character', however readers construe it through the lens of the poem.

Comment

2:3[2]. The 'belly of Sheol' is unique to Jonah; it seems to echo both the deepest part of the ship from the preceding chapter and the fish's innards. Thomas (1953: 222–224) suggests that Sheol may be used as a superlative: this is the lowest and worst possible place. While Sheol does refer to the grave in HB prose (Gen. 37:35; 42:38; Num. 16:30–33), it is primarily a poetic concept. The parallel poetic lines transport the reader to more numinous regions, characterized by dark and fearsome places of the underworld. In his taunt against the king of Babylon, Isaiah declares that Sheol below is quaking to meet him, the Rephaim wake up, and as his corpse arrives, worms will cover it (Isa. 14:9–11). There is a finality to the journey that leads to Sheol (Job 7:9). It has bars (Job 17:16), ropes and snares (Ps. 18:5–6[4–5]) as well as personified features – an unquenchable appetite and big mouth (Ps. 49:15[14]; Prov. 27:20; Isa. 5:14). Cross (1983: 159–167) explores connections with the mythic underworld in Ugaritic texts; notably chaotic waters and monsters with gaping jaws and an insatiable belly. Sheol is far beyond any hope that accompanies the presence of YHWH (Ps. 88:11–13[10–12]). Nevertheless, it is not beyond the span of YHWH's sovereign reach (Ps. 139:8). The appalling irony for Jonah is that he has tried to run as far away from YHWH as possible and here, from that most terribly distant place, he cries out to YHWH (Sasson 1990: 172). His disobedience identifies him with the wicked, who are destined for Sheol (Pss 9:18[17]; 31:18[17]) but even here at the brink of death, he cries out and is rescued.

Jonah's initial prayer from the depths is not recorded. He presumably uttered it from the desperate straits in which he swirled. That prior prayer has been answered, and he embeds it within this poem of thanksgiving. That is parallel to the revelation in 4:2 that he spoke to YHWH about his reason for not heading to Nineveh.

4[3]. While the sailors 'hurled' Jonah, they were the instruments of YHWH's divine action; the result was Jonah's sense that God had abandoned him (Hoyt 2019: 457). The same figure appears in Mic. 7:19 regarding YHWH's casting all of Israel's *sins* into the 'deepest places' of the sea. The expression includes both the literal deep waters (Pss 68:23[22]; 107:24) and the extremities of distress (Ps. 88:7[6]). Here Jonah himself has been cast to that point. Following the divine action, the turbulence of the sea, from the top with its waves and breakers to the very bottom, takes over in Jonah's description (cf. Ps. 42:8[7]). The implication of 'river' is the movement of the currents that sweep around and around Jonah. The heart of the seas is tumultuous and unfathomable as is the streaming river. The same word in pl. refers to the ancient waters on which YHWH founded the earth (Ps. 24:2). Youngblood (2019: 111) adds several possible interpretive angles. Part of the experience of crossing into the netherworld in ancient Mediterranean thought was traversing a river that flowed through the depths of the sea. A further cultural connection could be the 'river ordeal' in which an accused person had to undergo submersion in a tumultuous river. If he survived, he was deemed not guilty.

5[4]. Jonah is 'driven' by YHWH to the place where he wanted to be: away from the presence of YHWH and beyond a sight line that included YHWH. Nevertheless, from the swirling depths, he expresses both his desolation and radical hope; this recurs in v. 10. The psalmist poses the same despair: 'I said in my alarm, "I was cut off [*nigraztî*] from your sight"' (Ps. 31:23[22]). Like Jonah, the psalmist was heard.

The matter of Jonah's 'sure hope' is not uniformly affirmed by scholars. His outcry interrupts the harrowing description that returns unabated in v. 6. Based on the alternative reading of 'how' instead of 'surely', some suggest v. 5 simply continues his horrified realization that he is apparently for ever cut off. It may be that *ʾak* ('surely') commences a rhetorical question without an accompanying interrogative particle (GKC §150a; Sasson 1990: 180). Because *ʾôsîp* suggests continuity in terms of gazing at the sanctuary of YHWH, that seems beyond Jonah's expectation in his current distress.

hêkal is from a Sumerian word meaning 'imposing residence' (Sasson 1990: 181; Ottosson, *TDOT* 3:382–388). It was viewed as YHWH's dwelling and resting place (Ps. 132:5–8). Depending on when and how the narrator situated this story, this could mean the Jerusalem temple. Perhaps Jonah was drawn to it even as a northern kingdom resident. Two centuries earlier, Solomon's dedicatory prayer when the temple service was inaugurated included the plea that repentant sinners could petition towards the temple, be heard and be forgiven (1 Kgs 8:46–50). Jonah's role as YHWH's prophet could mean he was countercultural in that northern context. In this crisis, he turns his focus to the temple (Wolff 1986: 135; Timmer 2011: 86, n. 18).

On the other hand, given Jonah's near-death situation, it is equally likely he is casting his vision towards the heavenly realms at this point, especially as a contrast to the belly of Sheol (see Mic. 1:2; Hab. 2:20). *ʾak* may shift attention to that transcendent temple: on the cusp of life and death, Jonah is gazing to realms beyond. The boundary between earthly representations and heavenly realities of the divine dwelling was not sharply drawn (Page 1995: 52). See Ps. 132:7–8.

6[5]. *ʾpp* is rarely used and always in poetic expressions that resonate with the grim reality of impending death. Here the waters are the subject. Equally ominous are the waves of death, accompanied by torrents of destruction, cords of Sheol and snares of death (2 Sam. 22:5–6 // Ps. 18:5–6[4–5]). In like manner, evils without number (Ps. 40:13[12]) and the cords of death (116:3) surround the psalmists.

Reading *ʿad nepeš* as 'to the throat' or 'to the neck' suggests the breathing apparatus and the effects of choking. Isa. 5:14 describes Sheol's enlarging its *nepeš* in parallel with opening wide its mouth. See also Ps. 69:2[1] – 'the waters have come to my *nāpeš*'.

tĕhôm represents the vast and dark unknown regions beneath the surface of the waters. The pl. conveys the sense of the ultimate abyss: Pharaoh's army was covered by the *tĕhōmōt* as they sank into the depths (Exod. 15:5). These depths exist everlastingly: 'darkness was on the face of the deep' (Gen. 1:2; see also Prov. 8:27). The entanglement of reeds has puzzled some commentators; they are generally thought of as shoreline or river vegetation (Wolff 1986: 136; Sasson 1990: 185). If, however, this experience is conceptually connected with the submarine river of v. 4, the described presence of *sûp* makes sense (Youngblood 2019: 112). Generally, the Israelites were distant from sea experiences; they would not be parsing the botanical labels.

7[6]. The great reversal for Jonah occurs in this verse. He has gone down and down into the 'abyss' (the Greek tr. of *tĕhôm*) and beyond to the very roots of the mountains, and now YHWH raises him up. Before that dramatic turnaround, however, he describes two additional realities of drowning – navigating the tangled underwater mats of seaweed (v. 6) and bumping against the very bars between this existence and the next. The verbless clause leaves the audience suspended in the watery grave along with Jonah. The syntax imitates gasping – 'the earth, her bars, my separation for ever'. Bars and gates are figures for the nexus between the earth and the shadows beyond. Geography, myth and metaphor are all woven together – a bit like seaweed – in these figures. The narrative emphasized Jonah's deliberate choices to 'go down'; now the poem declares that he descended right to the very bottom, and it is not his doing. That final descent is framed by images of the unfathomable – roots of mountains and bars closing him off from the earth. In what has been shaped as an 'anti-pilgrimage' (Youngblood 2019: 113), Jonah sings as he descends to the very depths of Sheol, the opposite of making pilgrimage to Zion and singing songs of ascent on the way. The 'root' of the mountains is the subterranean context for the intrepid miner in quest of the elusive wisdom (Job 28:9).

The term *hā'āreṣ* generally refers to the land of covenant promise; here it indicates the space of exile away from YHWH. Nevertheless, in one action YHWH brings him up from destruction. 'Pit' has powerful connotations of death and decay. In the Israelite period, those who could not afford rock-cut tombs were deposited in pit graves when they died (Magness 2011: 157–158). These lines convey the continuing visceral memories of the harrowing experience interspersed with affirmations of deliverance, even after acknowledging the reality of that rescue. Horror permanently invades all memory. While Jonah has directed his words to YHWH through the prayer, it is not until this point that he names his God – 'O YHWH, My God'.

8[7]. The tone changes to Jonah's 'commentary' on his life-threatening crisis. He remembers YHWH even as his life, breath, throat, soul (all possible understandings of *nepeš*) turn against him, or faint, or feel completely curled up (likewise possible interpretations of *bĕhit'aṭṭēp*). See Pss 142:4[3] and 143:4 on the use of the verb in contexts where the psalmist's spirit or breath (*rû'aḥ*) is deeply affected by distress. This ambiguous introductory clause expresses the difficulty of describing in words what that loss of connection to the outside 'world' feels like. In v. 5, it was uncertain as to whether he expected to see YHWH in his sanctuary again. Here his confidence increases: his prayer has 'come' (*wattābô'*) into that holy temple.

Youngblood (2019: 114–115) views with suspicion Jonah's declaration that he remembers YHWH, stating that if Jonah's focus were proper, he would have gratefully affirmed that YHWH remembers *him* instead of the other way around. Jonah's presumably misplaced focus is only exacerbated by his pious affirmation that his prayer has come into YHWH's presence. Jonah's lack of repentance, absent from this psalm of *thanksgiving*, and his confidence in his own piety have him pilloried. This overconfidence prompts the abrupt outburst against idolaters in v. 9.

9[8]. The shift in v. 9 to censuring idolaters initially seems off course. Perhaps it is intended as a parenthetical commentary to a congregation gathered for worship. If so, it is the sole hint in the book that there is an intended audience – perhaps Israelites – who are deemed in need of firm correction as to where they have placed their loyalty (Limburg 1993: 69–70). On the other hand, it may simply indicate Jonah's posture vis-à-vis foreigners whose allegiance is entirely misdirected. Indirectly, it serves to reinforce readers' perceptions that this Jonah, recalcitrant as he is in terms of obedience, has a trained sense of orthodoxy.

It is not clear how this snippet connects directly with what has gone before, particularly since some of the vocabulary is compressed. Perhaps the declaration is intended to reflect Jonah's observations about the sailors (Sasson 1990: 195). After all, he does not know the outcome of their voyage and observed only their frantic appeal to a whole selection of gods. *hebel* is used in Jer. 8:19 in parallel with 'images', suggesting those idols are empty. The same combined idiom 'breath of nothingness' as the object of 'those who keep' appears in Ps. 31:7[6]. See Deut. 32:21, where the expression is parallel with *lōʾ-ʾēl* ('not God'). It characterizes how utterly invalid and empty these idols are. It is also ironic: there is nothing to guard, and yet they do it assiduously as they worship this vacuity (Jenson 2008: 67). Jonah along with the psalmist may subtly be contrasting his own presumably substantially robust belief with that of the pagans (Timmer 2011: 87–88). On the other hand, this may not be a smug or self-conscious observation. After the horror of experiencing the extremities of existence, YHWH draws him back up and, now devoid of any self-dependence, he offers a retrospective on his own pursuits that have been empty and close to losing the *ḥesed* of God (Magonet 1983: 51).

The systemic patterns that keep guardians in bondage to nothingness mean they abandon the real substance of what their lives could be. *ḥesed* in the covenant framework is unfailingly loyal love. It is the characteristic of acting benevolently, especially towards those of lower estate (1 Sam. 20:14–15), to preserve and nurture life and alleviate all ills. It has a strong relational component and represents not only God's love for humans, but also self-sacrificial love among people. There is a powerful ethical component to it (Clark 1993; Baer and Gordon, *NIDOTTE* 2:211–218).

Within that wider framework, it could refer to the previous idolaters, who will abandon their loyalty to false gods when they are exposed (Alexander et al. 1988: 117). More likely, however, it focuses particularly on YHWH's enduring loving relationship with his people (Pss 100:5; 118:1–2; 136; 144:1–2); people quickly forget the unspeakably rich benefits of YHWH's *ḥesed* (Wolff 1986: 183). Lessing (2007: 201) translates it as 'the One who loves them', shifting into an act. verb the rich connotations of *ḥesed*. Clinging to their idols blinds them to anything except their own self-gratification. Greed, after all, is idolatry (Col. 3:5).

Jonah might have been mentally contrasting his own deliverance and robustly traditional response with what he might have *thought* happened to the mariners. After all, his last sight of them was as they hurled him overboard into the surging waves. He would not know the response of fear and dread that brought them to their knees before YHWH when the storm stopped. He would also not know they were a bit ahead of him with sacrifices and vows.

10[9]. Jonah's prayer closes with strong echoes of Ps. 116:17–18. It also mirrors what the sailors did at the close of *their* harrowing experience with the sea, offering sacrifices and fulfilling vows. Singing with joy is a natural response to a deliverance as remarkable as his. See Pss 50:14; 107:22; 116:17; 118:14–17.

Some commentators make a point regarding the absence of penitence on the part of Jonah, declaring that he needed to be educated further towards conformity with YHWH's merciful nature (Hoyt 2019: 469–470; Youngblood 2019: 117). The narrative 'gap', however, may not warrant this theological insertion. Jonah is presented in human, not flawed iconic, terms. His closing declaration is substantial: salvation of the sailors, of Jonah and of Nineveh is entirely and solely YHWH's. (The closest psalm parallel is Ps. 3:9[8].) Does he understand the full import of its going forward? Probably not; neither do we at any given point.

Explanation

The shift from prose to a psalm of thanksgiving has prompted numerous scholars to suggest it did not belong with the narrative initially. Apart from the different vocabulary and form, the scenes underwater and in a fish seem too far-fetched, even if they are viewed as imaginative embellishments. Nevertheless, Jonah's about-face and his perception of YHWH's deliverance are the necessary backdrop for his subsequent obedient trek to Nineveh. They are even more pointedly the foil against which his own lack of mercy is stunning (Stuart 1987: 473).

Following the calm introductory 'and Jonah prayed', the words that tumble forth are a turbulent interweaving of psalm texts. At the outset, they echo David's words of penitence (Ps. 51:13[11]). Recognizing the appalling nature of his guilt, David prays, 'do not cast me away from your presence'. Jonah adopts the same image to describe what has happened. The horror of Jonah's watery grave is vivid and echoes segments from Pss 42:8[7]; 68:23[22]; 88:8[7]; 107:25–26.

The language is familiar from other contexts of distress. YHWH asks Job if he has any idea whatsoever about the 'gates of death' (Job 38:17). As the psalmist pleads for mercy from YHWH, he juxtaposes his being lifted from the 'gates of death' with his intention to sing YHWH's praises in the gates of the Daughter of Zion (Ps. 9:14–15[13–14]; see also Ps. 30:4–5[3–4]). Hezekiah came face to face with death before his miraculous recovery and names the foe. He starts with 'I, I said', and continues with the sense that he has been treading towards the 'gates of Sheol', that he will no longer see 'Yah, Yah, in the land of the living' (Isa. 38:10–11).

Some see Jonah's prayer in its entirety as an expression of his self-righteousness, self-absorption, lack of confession of guilt and repentance, and judgmental attitude tempered only by the facts that he demonstrates his knowledge of theology, and is honest (Trible 1994: 171–172; Lessing 2007: 212–224; Timmer 2011: 88–89; Hoyt 2019: 452–471; Youngblood 2019: 115–116, 123–124). Perhaps, however, a more charitable assessment is in order. Equally unsettling expressions characterize the wider lament tradition, but those authorships are not subjected to the same censure.

While Jonah evinces deep fear and instinctual self-preservation, that is no more than would be expected from a person in these straits. Including a verse acknowledging his own guilt and need for atonement may be asking too much of our prophet. If we take the narrative backdrop as representative in any way of human responses to rapidly deteriorating circumstances that are unearthly and appalling in the extreme, perhaps we can cut him some hermeneutical slack. There is a conceptual and literary parallel between the confessions of Jonah in this psalm and the realization of all the characters of ch. 1 that salvation, rescue and freedom come only after reaching the nadir of hope and life (Bolin 1997: 119–120). Perhaps the interpretive pendulum has swung too far towards accusing Jonah of hypocritically mouthing traditional platitudes in this psalm only because we arrive at a static composite portrait of Jonah at the end of the book. That may be blindness to a fully human person in unimaginably perilous circumstances. How about revisiting Jonah as a person who was really trying to reconcile what he knew of YHWH's goodness juxtaposed with palpably felt evil?

No matter how these matters are parsed, the message for the reader is powerful. Excerpts from the psalms continue to echo through Jonah's prayer; he knew them in order to depend on them in a time of extreme crisis. Those reading and rereading the text for millennia to follow know that in desperate straits, the inspired words of Scripture are the best vehicles for carrying terror, anxiety and dread into the presence of the Master of the universe. Further, these truths of Scripture infuse the long tradition of hymns of the church. Those who memorize and sing them know the power to restore that lies in those words. All of this, of course, suggests that planting them firmly in our hearts and minds is a valuable lifelong discipline.

The end of the psalm reflects an authentically jubilant Jonah, genuinely reflective of joy in his restored relationship with YHWH, who has saved him (see Ps. 118:14, echoing Exod. 15:2 and Isa. 12:2). He declares he will fulfil his vows, which may reflect his intent to head to the temple (Ps. 5:8[7]). YHWH will remind him there is an unfinished task (Magonet 1983: 52–53). Never mind that he will wobble from this path again very soon. That too is the reality of our own fleeting allegiance to the 'God of our salvation'.

JONAH 2:11[10]

Translation

[11[10]]And YHWH said to the fish . . . and it spewed Jonah forth on to the dry ground.

Notes on the text

Generally, *ʾmr* is followed by what the subject said; otherwise, *dibber* is more commonly the verb. Here the message is left aside (cf. also Gen. 4:8); how, after all, does YHWH speak to a fish? The results are the more important matter.

wayyāqēʾ can be either qal or hiph. (BDB 883 has it under both) from *qyʾ* ('to vomit'). Most likely it is qal here with the fish as the subject. If it is read as hiph. (so *DCH* 7:247), then YHWH causes this latest indignity for his prophet.

Form and structure

This verse reverses the descent into the belly of the fish (v. 1). Jonah is ejected from the belly, where the polarities of death and life were resting undigested. '[N]o wonder the fish vomited' (Trible 1994: 159).

Comment

The temptation is to translate the verb delicately, but that is not the intent of the verse. Readers are to associate the foul sight and smell of vomit with what the fish spews forth. It is messy – and humiliating. That is Jonah's state as he erupts from the fish's innards, completely indigestible (Wolff 1986: 139).

Equally disgusting images are drunken Moab splashing into his own vomit (Jer. 48:26) and the vomit (*qēʾ*) of dogs drawing them back to circle around it (Prov. 26:11). This is also the picture behind the image of the land throwing out its inhabitants because they made it so foul with their sin (Lev. 18:28). Nevertheless, this vomiting gives Jonah a second chance (Strawn 2012: 454).

ʾel-hayyabāšâ ('to the dry land') is the same objective that the sailors had when they were rowing with all their might. The fish manages to propel Jonah to safety; we have no idea where that might have been. The point all along is the miraculous nature of the preservation and rescue to get Jonah back on track towards Nineveh.

The image of the great fish as benign is a contrast to most of the depictions of monstrous creatures of the sea in the HB. Isa. 27:1 practically vibrates with the hostility between 'Leviathan . . . the monster of the sea' and YHWH. See also Job 7:12; 26:12; 41:1–34; Pss 74:13–14; 89:11[10]; Isa. 51:9.

Explanation

The figure of dry ground has important canonical connections, particularly in terms of YHWH's provision for his people. Crossing from bondage in Egypt to freedom in Sinai occurred on miraculously dry ground; it is mentioned three times in the narrative (Exod. 14:21–29). The poetic backdrop of the depths and tumult of the waters of the sea (Exod. 15:4–10) echoes here as well. On the other side of the wilderness experience, the children of Israel again crossed on dry ground (Josh. 3:17), moving into the land of their inheritance. Never mind that they squandered and polluted that gift. When YHWH escorted his servant Elijah on his final homeward journey, Elijah and Elisha passed over the Jordan on dry ground (2 Kgs 2:8).

JONAH 3:1–4

Translation

3:1 And the word of YHWH came to Jonah a second time, saying,
2 'Get up! Go to Nineveh, the great city, and proclaim to her the proclamation
that I am speaking to you.'
3 And Jonah got up and he went to Nineveh according to the word of YHWH.
(Nineveh was a large city, important to God, a walking journey of three days.)
4 And Jonah began to enter the city, the first day's walk. And he preached, saying,
'Yet only forty days and Nineveh will be overturned.'

Notes on the text

3:1. *šēnît* ('second') is a fem. ordinal adj. that serves in this context as an adv., joining two narratives (Sasson 1990: 225). It appears in Jer. 1:13 and 13:3 as well, but both of those instances involve something new; this command is a repetition, emphasizing that Jonah has received a prophetic second chance (Limburg 1993: 75).

2. In the MT (Leningrad Codex), the impv. (*qĕrā᾽*) is preceded by a waw with both a hireq beneath it and a dagesh indicating *ûqĕrā᾽* – 'and proclaim'. This is an error: the Cairo Codex simply has *û* (Gelston 2010: 63).

Proclaiming the proclamation is another cognate accusative. The noun *haqqĕrî'â* appears only here in the HB. YHWH's command is the same as 1:2 until *'el* ('unto') replaces *'al* ('against').

The LXX renders the ptc. (*dōbēr*, '[I] am speaking') in the past tense, but the present sense is a subtle contrast to the negative connotations in ch. 1.

3. The description of Nineveh interrupts the narrative. *hāyĕtâ* does not necessarily put this solely in terms of Nineveh's past glories (Wilson 1918a: 454–455; Sasson 1990: 228; contra Bewer 1912: 28–29; Allen 1976: 221). It serves to express facts established long before, the effects of which remain (GKC §106g).

mahălak is not intended to represent a straight-line walk (Sasson 1990: 230).

4. *wayyāḥel* is a hiph. 3 masc. sg. from *ḥll*. The root is used only in hiph. and with the inf. of another verb implying the start of an ongoing process. This is an unclear stem, reflected in the BDB entry (319–321). The syntax that follows is somewhat awkward.

The range of possible meanings of *'ôd* suggests continuance and persistence (BDB 728–729).

nehpāket is a niph. fem. sg. ptc. from *hpk* (to 'turn' or overturn'). When it refers to destruction of a city, it appears in qal; Sodom and Gomorrah are parade examples (Gen. 19:21, 25, 29; Isa. 13:19; Amos 4:11). Destruction is not, however, the only meaning. The qal form also describes YHWH's changing the curse of Balaam to a blessing (Deut. 23:6[5]) and mourning to joy (Jer. 31:13). The niph. perf. is used to describe the heart of YHWH turned over despite Ephraim's waywardness (Hos. 11:8). See *IBHS* §23.2.1 regarding the implications of the niph. expressing the middle voice and the equally viable possibilities associated with a reflex. understanding (*IBHS* §23.4). No occurrences of the niph. have to do with destruction other than possibly this passage (BDB 245–246). All the early versions (LXX, Vg, Tg) interpret the pronouncement in terms of Nineveh's being destroyed.

The LXX reads 'three days' instead of 'forty', perhaps influenced by the preceding description of Nineveh's size or is the result of an intent to make more sense of the length of time that Jonah would subsequently sit outside the city waiting for its destruction.

The message is five words in two segments, linked by a conj.

Form and structure

The introduction to Jonah's recommissioning echoes the preceding call with the addition of 'a second time', intimating the radical nature of the second chance for Jonah. The first verb of v. 3 is the same as in ch. 1, but the second departs from Jonah's previous flight pattern. The direction is the correct one, but before Jonah begins the proclamation, the narrator pauses to describe Nineveh. The interruption keeps the audience in suspense as to whether he is fully obedient. It also shifts the focus to Nineveh.

Comment

3:2. The change in prep. from 'against' (1:2) to 'unto' has occasioned considerable comment regarding a shift in tone from YHWH himself. This time, YHWH does not mention Nineveh's great evil, a description that fits with 'against' in the first summons (ch. 1). Some suggest that Jonah's mere five words in Hebr. in v. 4 are a distillation of a more fulsome declaration (Alexander et al. 1988: 120–121), but the words 'which I am speaking' seem to preclude that interpretation. YHWH gives him the precise words, which, ironically, hold a truly significant ambiguity.

3. The first time around, Jonah got up to flee (1:3). This time he gets up and goes according to the command of YHWH. *lēʾlōhîm* may simply be a way of indicating extraordinary size. Nevertheless, this is the only place in the HB where the prep. *lĕ-* precedes the divine name in a superlative expression; that suggests something unusual about the claim. See *IBHS* §14.5b; Allen 1976: 221. While it could allude to the multiplicity of gods worshipped in the city, the direction of the narrative is not concerned with those idols. In his study of all the instances in the HB where the divine names are used in what appears to be a superlative construction, Thomas (1953: 216–219) concludes that the expression indicates that the person or thing is drawn into relationship with God. Thus, it indicates that Nineveh is not only extraordinarily large; it is also under the sovereign authority of God and belongs to him (Stuart 1987: 486–488; Alexander et al. 1988: 119; Lessing 2007: 11, n. 54, 279–281). Because the inhabitants of Nineveh were evil, this is a significant declaration and anticipates what YHWH will do (Sasson 1990: 228–229).

mahălāk means 'a walking journey'. This may be a figure of speech indicating great size (Halton 2008: 193–196) and dramatically emphasizing the remarkable response of this vast city to Jonah's one-day, half-hearted effort (Wolff 1986: 148; Sasson 1990: 231). Oppenheim (1964: 140) notes that the city was upwards of 1,850 acres (749 ha) in the first millennium BC. That translates to approximately 3 square miles (5 km); it would not take three days to go around it. For the sake of comparison, Israel's capital, Samaria, with which Jonah was familiar, was significantly smaller. It is generally thought that the urban area surrounding the acropolis during the Israelite period was about 185 acres (75 ha) (Master 2013: 329–336).

The expression could represent the amount of time it would realistically take to walk through the city, pause, issue YHWH's pronouncement, and then move on to the next podium. Just as 'three days and three nights' (2:1[1:17]) emphasizes an extraordinarily long time in those circumstances, so three days here indicates a very long time of winding through its thoroughfares. Further, if Jonah were approaching as a recognized foreign envoy, the three days might have represented the time necessary to address diplomatic protocols (Stuart 1987: 487–488; see also Wiseman 1979: 37–39). Alexander et al. (1988: 57) questions this interpretation because the text uses the expression in terms of the size of the city, not Jonah's mission. From another angle, a symbolic connection may be instructive: the three-day journey recalls Jonah's sojourn in the fish's belly and his proximity to death in that context. Perhaps Nineveh was balancing on the edge of the netherworld and destruction because of its rampant evil (Youngblood 2019: 138).

4. 'To enter the city' followed by the indication of one day's walk suggests that it took but one day to reach the centre of the city from which the message would spread rapidly (Wolff 1986: 144). All we have is that one day's worth; where it transpired and Jonah's tepid preaching are left aside. The message was five words in Hebr., eight in succinct English: 'Yet forty days and Nineveh will be overturned.' It is not clear when within that period the overturning would occur, but it was perceived as a window during which change was possible (Stuart 1987: 489). The message does not start with a validation statement, 'Thus says YHWH', nor does it articulate grounds for judgment or an exhortation to change their behaviour to avert the disaster. The narrator has left the exhortation to the king. Youngblood (2019: 139) points to these gaps and suggests they hint of Jonah's ambivalence and possible alteration of YHWH's words. Fretheim (1977: 107–109) dismisses Jonah's message as vague, blunt, offensive and graceless.

In the temporal context of Jonah's dire five-word 'sermon', *ʿôd* could mean either 'at the end of' or 'during' (Trible 1994: 180; Hoyt 2019: 480). The ambiguity of the adverb adds to the possibilities regarding *nehpāket*. 'Forty' is a conventional number, appearing frequently in the history of Israel, often in conjunction with a period of separation. It was the number of days Moses spent on Mount Sinai on two occasions (Exod. 24:18; 34:28). The first time, he was receiving the instructions for the worship system. The second was in the aftermath of the golden calf debacle. The circumstances could not have been more different. The journey of the spies into the land lasted forty days (Num. 13:25), and the Israelites were sent to wander in the wilderness for forty years, one year for every day of the spying mission (Num. 14:33–35). For a detailed set of categories with accompanying references, see Hoyt 2019: 481–482. It is reflected in the life of Jesus, whose experiences echo those of national Israel (Matt. 4:2; Mark 1:13; Luke 4:2).

The niph. fem. sg. ptc. *nehpāket* describes the forthcoming consequence for Nineveh. It is central to the message but is stunningly ambiguous.

On the one hand, later reading audiences would be reminded that Sodom and the surrounding region were utterly overturned in the cataclysmic destruction (Gen. 19:21, 25, 29; Deut. 29:22). The appalling nature of Sodom and its overthrow were unmatched. The names Sodom and Gomorrah were bywords for wickedness (Isa. 1:9–10; 3:9; 13:19; Jer. 23:13–14; Ezek. 16:56–57). However Jonah's words would translate into the Ninevites' context, they heard destructive judgment for their wickedness (Sasson 1990: 236–237).

On the other hand, the niph. ptc. might have middle or reflex. implications. When Pharaoh heard the Israelites had fled, his heart was changed (Exod. 14:5). Samuel informed Saul that the Spirit of YHWH would come upon him in power, and he would be changed (1 Sam. 10:6). See also Hos. 11:8 and Esth. 9:22. In this context, it may suggest Nineveh will overturn itself, pointing to the reformation that Jonah witnesses.

Given these two hermeneutical possibilities, how does Jonah understand the words as he utters them? His prophetic word will be fulfilled no matter what Nineveh does (Fretheim 1977: 139; Trible 1994: 180; Bolin 1997: 125; Hoyt 2019: 478–479). Within the ambiguous interpretive sphere, Jonah chooses the set of meanings that best support his expectations regarding YHWH's just retribution against the evil city as described in ch. 1. The subtle shift in prepositions from *ʿal* to *ʾel* may be something Jonah does not want to hear. If he senses that Nineveh overturning itself could be the upshot, his consternation is understandable. This complex of issues sets the stage for Jonah's extreme dismay in ch. 4 and is crucial to the theological messages of the narrative (Sasson 1990: 234–345, 267–268). The niph. ptc. indicates the freedom of YHWH and prefigures *niḥam* that is forthcoming (Lessing 2007: 299).

This complexity has a long and venerable interpretive history. The double meaning surfaces in the Babylonian Talmud (*b*. Sanh. 89b). The **Gemara** explains, 'in regard to "overturned", Jonah was told "Nineveh *nhpkt*", but he did not know if for good or for evil'. **Rashi's** commentary (eleventh century) on Jon. 3:4 states:

> *nhpkt*. *nḥrbt* ('destroyed'). But he did not say 'destroyed' because *nhpkt* serves two meanings, evil and good. If they did not repent, then it would be destroyed. If they did repent, then *nhpkt* refers to the men of Nineveh, that they will be turned (*yhpkw*) from evil to good. [Rashi attributes this observation to a marginal note of Rabbi Aqiva.]

There are those who contend that the double meaning was not part of the original intent (Allen 1976: 222). Wolff states that the only way to understand this is as unambiguous judgment. No options or conditions are offered. It is 'impermissible to turn Jonah's saying into the equivocal oracle' (1986: 149). Lubeck (1988: 41–45) poses a provocative alternative interpretation. Jonah sabotages the message, choosing the word himself to make it an unconditional prediction that he wants to see fulfilled.

This raises additional questions: Is Jonah's declaration a prophetic prediction or a warning? That connects in turn with the wider themes of true and false prophecy, repentance, grace and YHWH's freedom (Page 1995: 262–263). See 'Introduction'. A bottom line: if readers 2,500 years later catch the double meaning, certainly Jonah does. Whether he wants to hear it is another question. The observation of the psalmist is thought-provoking: 'one thing [or once] God spoke; two things [or twice] I have heard', and the text goes on to balance those utterances, notably between *ḥesed* and recompense (Ps. 62:12–13[11–12]).

Explanation

The reasons for Jonah's unquestioning obedience this time are left unarticulated. He may be sufficiently chastened and fearful of another radical divine intervention. He may be temporarily grateful and ready to be magnanimous. YHWH does not lecture Jonah on the merits of obedience; instead, he issues the command again. Jonah may conclude that his message will be fully prophetic in the sense that he will now see Nineveh destroyed, as, in his assessment, it ought to be. Whatever the case, it seems that his prior notion that Nineveh deserves judgment remains unchanged. Jonah consistently has a robust understanding of YHWH's sovereignty over heavens, earth and sea; what he has not come to grips with (and perhaps never does) is YHWH's comprehensive mercy (Youngblood 2019: 138).

His message is a parade example of minimalism. It is understandable that he would be ill at ease. The reputation of the Assyrians for excessive brutality towards enemies was well known and advertised. Preaching judgment could get him executed on the spot. If he survived that, heading back to Samaria with a message of reprieve for the arch-enemy of the kingdom of Israel would likewise not be received with joy on the part of the folks back home.

Jonah's one day of preaching does not seem to be foot-shuffling reluctance; instead, he is now ready to do what YHWH has asked him to do, whether enthusiastically or just to dispense with the task. This is an ironic backdrop for his subsequent negative reaction as he waits and waits (Sasson 1990: 236–237).

Scholars have addressed the side issue of how the Ninevites would have understood Jonah. Was he speaking Aramaic, the lingua franca? Because this is not a necessary detail for the impact of the story, the narrator has not seen fit to include it – unlike those instances where the language difference *is* important (see Gen. 42:23 and 2 Kgs 18:26–37). It may be that

Jonah, who prophesied regarding the northern kingdom, had command of the language of the political entity to whom they were paying tribute (Sasson 1990: 232). That is just as likely as Sennacherib's men knowing sufficient Hebr. (*yĕhûdît*) to address the defenders at the walls of Jerusalem (2 Kgs 18:26). Stuart translates the gist of the message into Assyrian; there are sufficient cognate forms that the words are recognizable. The same ambiguities that reside in the Hebr. are in the translation (Stuart 1987: 489; see Wiseman 1979: 49).

The message of this book is robbed of its impact if readers fail to appropriate it for contemporary contexts. Wherever systemic evils of lies, perversions, hatred, disregard for human dignity and violence flourish, it is there that God's servants are called to go, preaching the words God gives. Despite the potential ambiguities, Jonah's words end up being a call to repentance. A paradigmatic NT counterpart is the apostle Paul, called to preach in one foreign and often hostile context after another.

JONAH 3:5–9

Translation

5But the men of Nineveh believed God, and they proclaimed a fast, and they put on sackcloth, from their greatest to their least.

6And the word reached the king of Nineveh, and he got up from his throne, and he removed his royal robe from upon him, and he covered [himself] with sackcloth, and he sat on the ashes.

7And he arranged for a proclamation to be issued in Nineveh by the decree of the king and his nobles, 'No person, domesticated animal, herd or flock may taste anything; they may not feed; they may not drink.

8And let them cover themselves with sacks, both man and animals, and let them cry out unto God with strength, and let each one turn from his evil way and from the violence which is in their hands.

9Who knows if he will turn, and this God will change and turn from the burning of his anger, and we will not perish.'

Notes on the text

3:5. *ʾmn* ('believe') appears primarily in niph. and hiph. It frequently takes the prep. *bĕ-* to indicate the object of belief; it is not necessarily belief 'in' (*DCH* 1:316). Generally, the object is YHWH; only here and in Ps. 78:22 is Elohim the object, and in the latter case they did *not* believe.

ṣôm is the word most frequently used for abstention from food and drink (Way, *NIDOTTE* 3:780–783).

The 'greatest to the least' may include size, age and social status. The comparative superlatives are adjectives; the pron. suff. makes them definite (GKC §133g; *IBHS* §14.5c).

6. The root *ngʿ* means 'to touch' and thus, 'to reach'. It suggests that some impact is part of the 'reach'. The subject of the verb is 'the word' or 'the matter'; either the content of Jonah's proclamation or the reaction of the city reaches the king (Alexander et al. 1988: 122).

wayyaʿăbēr is a hiph. form; perhaps the king has assistance in removing cumbersome royal robes. The phrase is unique in Scripture. In hiph., the verb occurs in contexts where things are put aside that are offensive to YHWH (Wolff 1986: 151; *DCH* 6:240). See 1 Kgs 15:12; Zech. 3:4.

The royal robe (*ʾadderet*) comes from the root *ʾdr*, meaning to be majestic or glorious (*DCH* 1:136–137). It is the word that describes what Achan coveted and hid in his tent, incurring the wrath of YHWH (Josh. 7:21).

waykas ('and he covered') is a pi. lamed-hê apocopated form of *ksh*. The root in hith. reappears (v. 8) as part of the decree.

ʾēper means not only 'ashes', but also loose soil or dust (Hayden, *NIDOTTE* 1:483–484). The latter may work better in this context lest it imply the ashes of sacrifice along with the penitential activities (Sasson 1990: 251). It sounds like *ʿāpār* ('dust'). The two words are used together only in Gen. 18:27; Job 30:19; 42:6. See also the actions of Mordecai upon learning of Haman's empire-wide edict against the Jews (Esth. 4:1–4).

7. The LXX and Vg have the decree starting after *lēʾmōr* ('saying'), in keeping with the punctuation of the MT that suggests 'and he said in Nineveh' is still part of the narrator's set-up. The major disjunctive accent of the verse (***athnach***) appears with *lēʾmōr*.

The foundational meaning of *zʿq* is to utter a loud agonized cry from the circumstance of dire distress or crisis (Hasel, *TDOT* 4:112–122).

ṭaʿam has a range of meanings, often having to do with 'taste'. It is not just 'feeding' in general, but also has to do with 'tasting delicacies' (1 Sam. 14:29; 2 Sam. 19:36[35]). Wider connotations also include judgment, reason and discernment regarding leadership roles (Job 12:20; Ps. 119:66; Prov. 11:22). The sense of 'decree' appears only here (BDB 381, 1094) and in Aramaic passages (Ezra 4:19–21; Dan. 3:10). This is not a particular problem, however, as Aramaic was already becoming the lingua franca of the ANE in the eighth century. Linking the two meanings, the contents of the decree (*ṭaʿam*) involve not tasting (*al yiṭʿămû*).

8. Each verb form is a juss. The hith. masc. sg. of *ksh* is reflex.: each person was to cover himself. In the LXX and Old Latin, the edict ends in v. 7 while v. 8 fleshes out the description. The MT, however, reads v. 8 as continuing the edict (Sasson 1990: 256–257).

Both humans and animals are to cry out in addition to wearing sackcloth; the outcry will be powerful – 'with force' (*bĕḥozqâ*) may suggest it is to be ongoing as well as loud.

The decree is individualized with *ʾîš* ('each') along with the m. pl. The 'wicked ways' is a general description, while the 'violence' (*ḥāmās*) in their hands particularizes the practices. The masc. sg. pron. suff. on *derek* ('way') matches the collective sg. *ʾîš*. The dual form of 'hands' has a pl. suff., suggesting lots of pairs of hands engaged in evil (Sasson 1990: 259).

9. *mî* plus the ptc. is a rhetorical exclamation expressing a desire (§GKC 151a). Of the ten occurrences of the expression 'Who knows?' in the HB, five expect that the outcome will change for the good; the others are less sanguine. This verse is in the former category (Crenshaw 1986: 274–275). The mandated about-face is followed with the hope that *hāʾĕlōhîm* will 'turn' (*yāšûb*) and 'change' (*wĕniḥam*) and 'turn' (*wĕšāb*). *niḥam* may be either pi., meaning 'to comfort/console', or niph., with the implications of being sorry, comforted, moved to compassion, change or repent (BDB 636–637; Butterworth, *NIDOTTE* 3:81–83). Lessing (2007: 292–293) translates it as 'change the verdict'.

The idiom *ḥărôn ʿāp* always refers to divine anger (BDB 354; *DCH* 3:314–315).

The king's hopes for divine turning are expressed threefold: if all those alterations happen, perhaps 'we will not perish'.

Form and structure

The sequence of wayyiq. forms conveys the haste with which the inhabitants of Nineveh engaged this citywide repentance followed by the urgency of the king's responses. His movements are parallel opposites: he gets up from his throne, puts off his royal robes, covers himself with humble sackcloth, and sits down on ashes. There are phonological connections. *ʾēper* ('ashes') in v. 6 would remind the audience of *ʿāpār* ('dust'). There is a subtle sound parallel between *waykas* ('and he covered') and *mikkisʾô* ('from his throne') earlier in v. 6.

There is some question regarding the logic of the king's decree when the people have already spontaneously started the fasting in the hope of averting disaster. Wolff (1986: 145) places the king's edict prior to v. 5, indicating this is the equivalent of a flashback. Nevertheless, it is not at all surprising that the national or regional leader would codify and attempt to convey authority and order in what might have looked like a panicked urban response. As the king has adopted the people's spontaneous actions, now he commands them to engage those actions along with him. See Trible 1994: 184–186 and Sasson 1990: 254–255. The king's response matches three prohibitions with three positive actions. The prohibition against grazing (*ʾal-yirʿû*) is phonetically related to the word for 'evil' (*rāʿâ*), just as *ṭaʿam* is phonetically related to the verb for tasting (*yiṭʿămû*).

Comment

3:5. The narrator is specific that the men of Nineveh 'believed'. Because it directly follows the description of Nineveh's vast size, this is presented as an astonishing miracle. Their response contrasts with that of the sailors. While the mariners likewise come into some sense of relationship with the God whose power they observed, their responses are great fear, sacrifices and fulfilling vows. Trappings of repentance are not part of the picture. No surprise there: they were in crisis at sea. In the context of Nineveh, belief is followed by donning sackcloth and engaging in a fast.

If the declaration about their belief is intended to mark trust in Yhwh (Lessing 2007: 283–285), that raises the question as to the content of the Ninevites' belief and whether it constitutes 'conversion' to Yhwh or not. Wolff (1986: 149) claims the expression is used only of Israel. No matter the subject, the listening audience would be expecting a radical change (Sasson 1990: 243). Even the most restrictive understanding of Nineveh's 'believing' makes it clear that Nineveh responds to Jonah's message by judging it true and reacting accordingly. Nevertheless, their return to violence within decades is a commentary on short-lived cultural reversals (Timmer 2011: 101–104).

The verb *qrʾ* ('to proclaim') often appears in conjunction with 'fast', but Joel 'sanctifies' the fast in conjunction with summoning the people to Zion (Joel 2:15). Fasting is the opposite of life-sustaining activity: it aligns the penitent with the sphere of death because that is what is deserved (Jenson 2008: 75). Fasting engages the whole body in supplication, emptying oneself to appeal to God for mercy and filling (Cary 2008: 111–112).

In times of national emergency, the Israelite community was summoned to fast. Notable examples include military threat (2 Chr. 20:3), locust plague (Joel 1:14; 2:15–16) and the edict that evil Haman promulgated against Jews in the Persian Empire (Esth. 4:16). The verb *ʿnh* has a more severe and expanded set of implications beyond *ṣôm*: it means 'to afflict oneself'. It is the word used in conjunction with the Day of Atonement (Lev. 16), which is the only corporate fast enjoined on the people of Israel. Both terms appear in Isa. 58:3–8 as God reminds the people that ritual activities must be accompanied by radically altered behaviour. Jeremiah alludes to what seems to have been a last-ditch fasting effort during the reign of Jehoiachin to forestall disaster, but makes it clear that it was futile (Jer. 14:11–12; 36:9); their disobedience had passed the tipping point.

The populace of Nineveh donned 'sackcloth' (*śaq*). Sackcloth, ashes and/or dust were customary practices for grieving, despair and supplication (2 Kgs 6:30–32; 1 Chr. 21:16; see also Job 16:15; Isa. 58:5; Joel 1:8). The *śaq* was intentionally uncomfortable, worn next to the skin. Made from goatshair, its darker colour was symbolic (Isa. 50:3). See Carpenter and Grisanti, *NIDOTTE* 3:1270.

6. The title 'king of Nineveh' appears only here. In the historical books, the ruler is called 'king of Assyria', twenty-two times in 2 Kings alone. Jenson (2008: 76) suggests the narrator might have coined this title as a literary tactic to indicate this is a fictional account, made to look as if it occurred during the reign of Asshur-Dan III – the time indicated by 2 Kgs 14:25. Equally likely, however, is that the expression points to the author's awareness of the geopolitical situation at that time. Regional governors held more sway, and one in particular was responsible for Nineveh and its surroundings (Timmer 2011: 109; Youngblood 2019: 142; see 'Introduction'). It diminishes the anticipated imperial sense that would be conveyed by 'king of Assyria'.

The king's motions come across as stiff and formal, perhaps verbally reflecting court protocol. 'He caused his cloak to pass away from upon him.' The contrast of the next clause is striking; there is an ellipsis where the object would be expected: 'He covered [himself] sackcloth.' The pi. form of *ksh* appears in contexts of confessing transgressions (Job 31:33; Ps. 32:5; Prov. 17:9; Sasson 1990: 251). The movement of the king from his throne to the ashes is highly symbolic: the king himself is 'overturned' (Trible 1994: 184). In Ezekiel's pronouncement against Tyre, the 'leaders of the sea' stepped down from their thrones, took off their garments and sat on the ground (Ezek. 26:16).

7. It is not entirely clear where the decree begins because there are two words that may introduce it: *wayyōmer* ('and he said') and *lēʾmōr* ('saying') both function that way. The punctuation in the MT suggests that 'and he said in Nineveh' is still part of the narrator's set-up. If that is so, the text of the edict starts with *hāʾādām* following *lēʾmōr* (Wolff 1986: 144). Others think it commences after 'and he said', indicating that the requirements will be implemented 'in Nineveh' (Sasson 1990: 253). The hiph. ('to cause to cry out') introduces another layer, indicating that the king prepared for a formal proclamation (*DCH* 3:128), a process that would necessitate criers in that socio-urban context. Given the dire warning, there is a deeply emotional component to the outcry. The hiph. form of the verb appears in contexts in the book of Judges when the people are in desperate straits (Judg. 4:10, 13).

The formalities of bringing the decree (*ṭaʿam*) to official status involve several layers. It is caused to be proclaimed and said; both the king and the 'great ones' are involved. The language may convey a byzantine court communication structure. While the king is the final authoritative voice, he is joined by his nobles, a practice that was evident in later Persian decrees but not so evident in extant Assyrian edicts. While this has been one of the bases for assigning a post-exilic date to the book, that is not a foregone conclusion. It may reflect the weakness of the 'king of Nineveh' at that time (Stuart 1987: 493). As a rare but necessary step in the face of this most unusual circumstance, it could add to the authenticity of the record (Alexander et al. 1988: 123); this 'king' is king in title only and the 'great ones' are a force with which to be reckoned and must be acknowledged in any public proclamation. The eighth-century geopolitical lay of the land as mined from inscriptions of powerful governors of regions surrounding Assyria warrants such a conclusion (Lawrence 1986: 130–131).

The def. art. prior to each class of creatures adds to the emphasis. The nouns are sg. collectives; the accompanying verb forms are pl. with the negation *ʾal*. All human beings are prohibited, but in case there is a question as to how to assess the animal populations, the larger class of domestic 'creatures' (*bĕhēmâ*) is divided in terms of the herds as well as those that are in flocks. The latter are primarily sheep and goats. This is a **merismus**: the four categories cover all the bases. None are allowed to taste, feed or drink.

These four categories have the appearance of a checklist that moves from the general to the particular. That is one reason for suggesting that the decree begins with this list. The edict says not to enjoy; altogether it implies demonstrating the utmost piety (Wolff 1986: 152–153). Three of the four categories have to do with animals; this unusual focus continues the role that the non-human world has already played in the narrative and additionally prepares for the lesson that will conclude the book (Sasson 1990: 255). While the participation of animals amuses a modern Western audience, these details also appear in solar eclipse omen texts (Wiseman 1979: 46–47; Stuart 1987: 491–492). Their participation would not be perceived to be that unusual.

Noting 'water' before the stated prohibition on drinking again indicates the severity of the fast. Three days without water is exceedingly taxing (cf. Exod. 15:22–25). No doubt a veritable outcry arose from the animals – reaching the very heavens. This fast is reminiscent of the fast Esther called in the extremity of her situation (Esth. 4:16). The prohibited activities are listed in this verse; the obligations follow in v. 8.

8. Following the series of prohibitions associated with the fast, the decree shifts to publicly visible and audible signs of penitence. While there are no Assyrian records of animals being clad in mourning trappings, the practice does appear in the Persian period (Herodotus, *Hist*. ix.24; Judith 4:10). In extreme circumstances, it is not outlandish, especially since there was a closer proximity of humans and animals in everyday existence (Stuart 1987: 493; Shemesh 2010: 18). The 'strength' (*bĕḥōzqâ*) of the outcry echoes from Judg. 4:3; 8:1; 1 Sam. 2:16; Ezek. 34:4. It may even connote a harsh outcry (Lessing 2007: 288).

Both fasting and sackcloth were outward signs of mournful penitence that could be institutionalized by decree. They were to be accompanied by a radical and deliberate turn from evil, a matter far less amenable to decree. This would first be a determination to change; over time, it would become evident in the cessation of egregious activities. This connects conceptually with the reflex. meaning of *nehpāket* (3:4). The pervasive ugliness of Assyria's whole sociopolitical structure is evident in the general use of 'wicked ways' and the practice of violence. The latter term recognizes the singular connection between unethical and immoral world views and the resultant ruthless attacks on fellow humans (Gen. 6:11; Judg. 9:24; Obad. 10; Mic. 6:12). The summons to the people to turn from their evil ways is a steady drumbeat through the Hebr. prophets. The narrator presents foreigners as being better at Israelite practices than the Israelites themselves (Limburg 1993: 83).

9. Four of the five passages in the HB that include 'Who knows?' in a hopeful sense have God as the intended subject. They are 2 Sam. 12:22, Ps. 90:11, Joel 2:14 and this text. Even though they hold out hope in the face of feared destruction, a positive outcome is not a done deal. In the case of David's son, the child does die. It may be, therefore, that the king is not at all hopeful that the divine edict can be turned around.

The matter of YHWH's 'relenting', 'changing' or 'being compassionate' – the most common renditions of *niḥam* – is a challenging one. YHWH is the subject in half of the occurrences of *niḥam*, no matter what the form is. When it is niph., more than two-thirds have YHWH as subject. There is a tendency to translate that combination as YHWH's 'changing his mind' (cf. 1 Sam. 15:29; Ps. 110:4, NIV), which raises questions regarding the nature of God. 'His mind', however, is not in the Hebr. In this context, *niḥam* is best understood as turning from activities that are contemplated but not fulfilled; thus, 'relent' or 'change the verdict' is the best interpretation. All occurrences of *niḥam* in Jon. 3 fit this pattern.

If the three divine changes take place, the result will be sparing the Ninevites. The def. art. with Elohim may be an oblique throwback to Jonah's message. The king has taken the pass. *nehpāket* in its grimmest sense, but he has also noted that it does not have a subject – just 'the gods'. Who knew which one would be out to compound their already disastrous situation (Stuart 1987: 494)? It seems a long shot: 'the god' may turn, have pity and turn away from his wrath. Just as Nineveh could possibly be overturned in the sense of changing, YHWH likewise may be 'overturned' in terms of his intended judgment. But even that may be only a temporary forestalling of the deserved judgment, an outcome that did occur in 612 BC.

Explanation

'Belief [in]' implies confidence that the message is trustworthy. In this case, something about Jonah's message that a god is preparing to turn the city upside down is convincing. Perhaps part of the unwritten backstory was their hearing the drama of how Jonah got there. In any case, the implication of the prophetic statement is that they will be turned – whatever it means – even if only for a short time. YHWH is not named, all of which may suggest their actions upon believing the message serve only as a 'stay of execution'. The culture at large likely remains polytheistic (Stuart 1987: 497; Walton 1992: 53–54). The same postponement happens for Judah when Josiah's reform, short-lived to be sure, staves off judgment until after his death. At the end of the Judean monarchy, YHWH does punish 'on account of the sins of Manasseh' (2 Kgs 23:26; 24:3–4; Jer. 15:4). The boundless mercy of YHWH, however, resounds from Nineveh's repentance centuries forward. When first-century Jews, having seen miraculous demonstrations of God's incarnate presence among them, still asked for a 'sign', Jesus replied they would have no sign but the sign of Jonah. Further, the men of Nineveh will 'rise up at the judgment' because they repented at the preaching of Jonah (Matt. 12:41). Often overlooked in the discussions regarding the fish and the 'sign of Jonah', Nineveh's repentance was equally miraculous. Both powerful and miraculous signs point to the One who is greater than Jonah.

There is considerable speculation as to why the Ninevites make such a quick about-face. Unlike the sailors, whose lives were obviously and immediately at stake, the Ninevites are simply confronted with words. Regardless of the interpretive ambiguities in the participle *nehpāket*, the Ninevites hear impending destruction, plain and simple. That may be why the text explicitly says, 'and they believed'. It is one thing to engage in pleas for divine assistance when the danger is at hand; it is another to trust that it is coming because of what someone says. This 'gap' in the narrative opens space for imaginative thinking. One possibility is that the contrast between the sailors in the first chapter and the Ninevites at this juncture argues against creating monolithic stereotypes of foreigners (Trible 1994: 182).

Additional scepticism surfaces as to the likelihood of such a mass conversion. It could be viewed as the stuff of myth and legend (Trible 1996: 516), especially as there are no Assyrian records to confirm it, and the royal behaviour is exaggerated in the extreme. Nevertheless, for ideological reasons, imperial records from the ANE studiously avoid any negative reflection on the rulership. The HB accounts, by contrast, are self-critical (see Provan et al. 2015: 85–92). In addition, there is evidence in Assyrian omen texts as to why a king might be prompted to take measures that would seek deliverance from the gods. These impending catastrophes would include foreign invasion, a solar eclipse, famine or flooding. There were even provisions to instal a 'substitute king' to stave off some ominous looming events. Perhaps the king's actions in this context reflect that practice (Wiseman 1979: 44–47; Walton 2018: 101). If, in YHWH's providential timing, Jonah arrived in one of these ominous periods, the superstition would reverberate through all the social levels up to the king and his nobles. As representatives of the gods, they were responsible for maintaining all forms of order. The king and his nobles would get on board (Stuart 1987: 490–491).

There are similarities between the actions of the Assyrian king and traditional responses of Israelites when crises loomed. In the face of yet one more Philistine threat, Samuel gathered the people at Mizpah with fasting and confession (1 Sam. 7:5–11). In the same spirit of fasting and petition, Jehoshaphat faced a coalition of Ammonites and Moabites coming from Edom (2 Chr. 20:1–12). As Sennacherib threatened Jerusalem in 701 BC, Hezekiah and his court donned sackcloth and appealed to Isaiah for prayers (2 Kgs 19:1–2). More than two centuries later, in the Persian capital of Susa, Mordecai chose the same route, followed subsequently by Esther (Esth. 4:1–17). These responses are recorded with the conventional language patterns including 'cry out', 'turn' and 'turn from evil' (Trible 1994: 193). In contrast, the customary Assyrian responses to unsettling news tended towards libations and sacrifices to the gods (Walton 1992: 47).

The participation of animals in mourning is not unique to this decree. An Assyrian text has animals participating in religious ceremonies, including prayer (cited in Shemesh 2010: 18–19). Joel 1:18–20 references the moaning and suffering of creatures without basic sustenance and YHWH's attention to them. See also Pss 104:21; 147:9. These domestic creatures would have lived in the home structures of the people. Thus, this is not necessarily intended as satire.

Read solely through Western lenses that are sharpened by personal autonomy, a culture-wide conversion seems an impossibility. Even in twentieth- and twenty-first-century contexts, however, there are instances of major popular movements. With that in mind, the belief and radical change, even if temporary, are noteworthy in the context of eighth-century BC geopolitics, especially once the repentance reaches the level of state policy. In addition, Nineveh is ripe for divine intervention (Stuart 1987: 490–491). The bottom line is that YHWH Elohim brings about the radical change in the hearts of these evil people. That is a source of hope in every geopolitical context, even in the face of human propensity to shift back to old and destructive patterns.

This is the pivotal point in the narrative where the king of a brutal empire is moved to appeal to the Master of the universe. All the details of ch. 1 are necessary to remind the audience both that Nineveh is evil and that the power of YHWH can crush that wicked human power. The narrative contrasts between the foreign sailors and the Ninevites are marked. The sailors are not described as wicked from the outset; Nineveh is. When the sailors pray, it is to YHWH; the Ninevites appeal to Elohim. After the deliverance, the sailors make sacrifices and fulfil vows; the Ninevites simply disappear off the scene (Trible 1994: 191).

Of greatest theological import is YHWH's response, both as expected by the righteous Israelite prophet and as the long-shot hope of hardened and ruthless Ninevites. What would their sudden and entirely off-the-charts repentance accomplish? That links directly with the larger question of biblical prophecy that remains 'unfulfilled' when changed humans prompt YHWH to change. What is the balancing point between the claim that YHWH does *not* change (Num. 23:19; 1 Sam. 15:29) and his change towards mercy? At this point, a robust understanding and affirmation of divine sovereignty is imperative. The sovereign immutability of YHWH encompasses the significance of human choices and historical contingencies as they unfold in the context of YHWH's unchanging covenant promises (Timmer 2011: 112).

An added wrinkle is introduced with the alternative understanding of 'overturned'. If it is to be interpreted as 'overturning itself', then the prophecy has not failed. Through Jeremiah, YHWH declared that he would change forthcoming deserved judgment against any nation or kingdom if they repented (18:7–10); it is the paradigmatic text for this situation. 'Paradoxically [Jonah's] prophecy is both true and false' (Trible 1994: 190). Closer to home, not too long after Jonah's words regarding Nineveh, Micah utters stark words against the mountain of YHWH's house: it will be utterly destroyed (Mic. 3:12). Jer. 26:18 records, however, the power of the message of Micah. Somewhat parallel to the situation in Nineveh, King Hezekiah is struck with the need for repentance. As a result, the destruction of Jerusalem is put off at least for a time (2 Kgs 19). There will likewise be a temporary reprieve during the time of Josiah in response to his reform efforts (2 Kgs 22:8–20). Those temporary reprieves, whether for Nineveh or disobedient Israel and Judah, also carry within them the hope that YHWH himself may be 'overturned' in response to human repentance and prayer. See further in 'Introduction'.

JONAH 3:10

Translation

10 And God saw their actions, that they turned from their evil way, and God changed the verdict concerning the destruction that he had spoken to do to them, and he did not do it.

Notes on the text

The title *hā'ĕlōhîm* (with the def. art.) continues from the preceding verse.

The syntax of 'from their evil way' matches the expression in the edict (v. 8).

Form and structure

There are three words related to *'śh* in the verse, drawing an emphatic line under the importance of deeds (Sasson 1990: 264). Their way has been evil and destructive; the adjective is *rā'â*. The intention of God to punish them is in like measure; *hārā'â* is a noun in this context. *rā'â* needs to be translated in a way that the measure-for-measure is evident. Justice is balanced.

Comment

Following immediately on the remarkable change in Nineveh, God changes or, as already suggested above, overturns his own stated verdict. This verse, with its five clauses, interweaves God's observation, expansion of that perspective, resultant revision of a previously stated intention and, finally, conclusive mercy. Initially, God sees their actions. The second clause, starting with *kî*, specifies the underlying message of those public demonstrations. It is not the fasting and sackcloth alone but what they convey about the change of the people. They turn from their way, the collective sg. possibly indicating the whole fabric of the pagan world view. God will not be manipulated but as they turn, so does he.

The third clause starts with *wayyinnāḥem*. The waw may suggest several related nuanced interpretations. One rendition may be 'then God changed', implying God does not change until he sees the evidence. At the same time, it emphasizes consequences: because they turn from their evil, God is doing the same. In this context, *rā'â* is not moral evil but divine justice that destroys sinful humankind. Only here and in Exod. 32:12 does the HB combine YHWH's both turning from burning anger and changing his verdict (Lessing 2007: 318–320). The fourth clause revisits the previous 'edict' of God: it is what he says he will do. 'Justice is better served by reformed characters than by corpses' (Allen 1976: 226).

Explanation

God has published the warning of judgment through Jonah to spare the guilty in the end. YHWH operates through the power of his word and Spirit; these are dynamic in the change from judgment to grace (Lessing 2007: 321). Jonah is a sign to the Ninevites (Matt. 12:39–41; Luke 11:29–32) not because he has been in the fish, but because he goes as a prophet and preaches the word that leads to repentance.

The question moving forward is, when does Jonah come to realize that YHWH is not going to carry through on the overturning that Jonah expects? By the record of his fuming and fretting, the audience is led to believe that it dawns on Jonah quite soon. He has watched the fervour of the Ninevites, at least in part, and he knows the nature of YHWH. Now there is a growing frustrated perplexity as to why God has pursued him so relentlessly to get him to Nineveh only seemingly to show him up as a sort of buffoon. He looks like a prophet who got it all wrong. His interpretation of 'Nineveh will be overturned' was in the judgment sphere; the possibility of reform in those same words carries an outcome that blindsides him (Sasson 1990: 267). Because he has not foreseen this – or ignored it – the confrontation of ch. 4 is all that much more heated on his part.

JONAH 4:1–4

Translation

4:1 And it was exceedingly troubling to Jonah, and he was burning.
2 And he prayed to Yhwh and he said, 'Please Yhwh; this was precisely my thinking when I was still in my own country. Therefore, I pre-emptively fled to Tarshish because I know you are a God of grace and compassion, long-suffering, and great in *ḥesed*, and changing regarding the evil.
3 So now, Yhwh, please take my life from me because my death would be better than my life.'
4 But Yhwh said, 'Is it good that you are in turmoil?'

Notes on the text

4:1. The semantic ranges underlying both *wayyēra'* ('and it was troubling') and *wayyiḥar lô* ('and he was burning') are wide. This is the first appearance of the verbal form of *r''* in Jonah. *wayyēra'* followed by *'el* is unique to Jonah, implying a more direct impact on him. It may suggest that he endures the misery rather than initiating it (Sasson 1990: 273–275).

2. 'And he prayed' is the same word used in 2:2[1], but here the lexical connotations of lament and complaint fit with the context.

The strong but polite *'ānnâ* Yhwh gives way to Jonah's justification. The latter commences with the rhetorical interrog. *halô'*, which establishes the certainty of a matter by virtue of posing it as a question, 'Is it not?' (Brown 1987: 201–219; Moshavi 2011: 91–105).

'ad-heyôtî ('when') combines the prep. with the inf. const. *qiddamtî* is a pi. form that is an auxiliary to the inf. const. (*librōaḥ*). *qedem* means 'before', both in terms of time and space; the verb means 'to do something first' (*IBHS* §36.2.1d).

yāda'tî, the qat. form, emphasizes Jonah's affirmation regarding Yhwh's nature: it has shaped his decision to refuse the mission. This expression precedes significant utterances (Trible 1996: 517).

kî followed by *yāda'tî kî* introduces the 'creed' regarding Yhwh and recurs through Israel's expressions of trust (Sasson 1990: 279–282). This is the only use of the shortened form of the divine name (*'ēl*) in the book.

3. *ṭôb . . . m-* is the comparative – 'better than'.

4. *hahêṭēb* is a hiph. inf. abs. that has come to be understood as an adverb (GKC §113k). It means doing something 'carefully and thoroughly'. The form occurs nine times outside Jonah, six of them adverbially (Deut. 9:21; 13:15[14]; 17:4; 19:18; 27:8; 2 Kgs 11:18), highlighting the diligence with which the activity is engaged (Timmer 2011: 125, n. 24). Here it precedes the verb for the sake of emphasis; see also v. 9.

The interr. particle that introduces Yhwh's rejoinder echoes Jonah's rhetorically shaped question from v. 1, especially since it follows 'and Yhwh *said*'.

Form and structure

There are a number of possible ways that ch. 4 may be divided. The MT (along with Mur) has three sections to the book, and the final one starts with 4:4. Another possible criterion for dividing the chapter is the reversal of Jonah's mood between vv. 1–6 and 7–11 (Sasson 1990: 270–272). While the MT has a paragraph break after v. 3, I have chosen to include v. 4 with this section to incorporate the rhetorical response from Yhwh to Jonah's declaration.

From a lexical/structural perspective, there is symmetry in the word counts for Jonah and for Yhwh in this chapter. Each utters 47 words and even the framing words are equal in number; Jonah speaks 39 words (vv. 2–3) as does Yhwh (vv. 10–11). They are going 'toe-to-toe' (Sasson 1990: 317; Lessing 2007: 347).

It is only in 4:2–3 that the narrator divulges a more extended content to Jonah's reluctance to obey Yhwh's command. The now-evident gap between 1:2 and 1:3 is filled with the details regarding Jonah's not-very-gracious view of Nineveh (Trible 1994: 203–204). The first phrases of Jonah's prayer of self-justification seem to be halting. It is only after 'therefore' that he launches full scale into why he fled. His statement is peppered with the 1 sg. pron. suff. *tî* – 'my word', 'my being', 'my land', 'I went early', 'I knew'.

Comment

4:1. The wide semantic range underlying *r*ʿʿ opens possibilities for probing further Jonah's response to what has just happened. Although it is syntactically distant and indefinite, God's relenting regarding his intended punishment (*rāʿâ*) is the subject ('it') of *wayyēra*ʿ. Those circumstances catch Jonah off-guard, particularly as they are contrary to his own sense of justice. God turns from the heat of his anger (3:9); that is the signal for Jonah's to start (Allen 1976: 227). Put bluntly, Jonah determines that Yhwh's mercy is 'unjust' (*wayyēra*ʿ) as opposed to right and good.

Generally, if something is displeasing, it is 'evil in the eyes of'. This situation is unpleasant 'to [*ʾel*]' Jonah, and his disposition shifts from the feisty person of ch. 1 and the grateful survivor of ch. 2 to utter perplexity and dejection (Sasson 1990: 273; see also Davies 1977b: 105–111). In combination with the impersonal construction 'and it burned to him', it indicates these circumstances have put him in a most uncomfortable place. When the experience is external to an individual, the 'burning' idiom represents an emotional reaction to the circumstance (*IBHS* §22.7b). The idiom is familiar to English speakers, who may express vexation as being 'burned up'.

In Neh. 2:10, the similar idiom refers to the dismay of Sanballat and Tobiah that Nehemiah was coming to intervene on behalf of the small community of Jews in Judah. The same combination characterizes Saul when he returns from battle with the Philistines and finds the women singing David's praise exponentially more than his own (1 Sam. 18:6–9). It leads to murderous brooding.

Understanding the complex tangle of emotions that accompany Jonah's perception is vital to unpacking the developments in this chapter. Part of the picture may be re-evaluating his life's prophetic work up to this point and seeing it disintegrating before his eyes. He knows what a spared Nineveh means. The expression returns in the developing conversation and is significantly more complicated than anger. The idiomatic figure of burning draws in his forthcoming physical discomfort, emotional distress and deep perplexity at what is happening. The composite picture includes chagrin, embarrassment and brooding along with anger, which fits better with the turn to prayer that initiates the next verse, and will serve as a better parallel towards the end of the conversation when YHWH describes Jonah as having compassion for the plant immediately after Jonah reaffirms that it is 'burning' to him. The narrator describes extreme distress that is visceral: Jonah feels heat.

2. Jonah's prayer in the aftermath of his preached message and Nineveh's response is a radical contrast to his prayer from the belly of the great fish. In ch. 2, Jonah offers thanksgiving for YHWH's mercy, but here mercy sets him at odds with YHWH. These are bitter and despairing words. Goldingay (2021: 406) observes that this is the only angry prayer in Scripture, but YHWH accepts it and responds to it.

'My word' on the lips of Jonah is a contrast; up to this point, the word of YHWH shapes the direction of the narrative. This pits Jonah's 'word' against that of YHWH, emphasizing the forthcoming conflict of perspectives (Magonet 1983: 21).

qiddamtî follows Jonah's reference to his prior patterns of thinking. In combination with the inf. const. ('to flee'), it intimates that he determined to pre-empt whatever the gracious and merciful YHWH had in mind for his prophetic message and its outcomes. This declaration is ironic: he fled west while *qedem* means east. Soon he will exit the city and sit on the east side.

His prayer is a masterpiece in logic – certainly YHWH cannot refuse it. First, he alludes to the fact that this has been his reasoning all along. 'Therefore', on the basis of that thoughtful consideration, he acted. Just to be certain, he reiterates in detail the bases: he did this 'because' he knew the revealed character of YHWH, fully articulated in Exod. 34:6–7 and echoing through subsequent articulations of his tradition (see Pss 86:15; 103:8; 145:8–9; Joel 2:13). Jonah shifts the components somewhat, starting with YHWH's graciousness and compassion, followed closely by being slow to anger and abounding in *ḥesed* and faithfulness (v. 6). At that point, Jonah digresses from Exod. 34:6–7. He compresses the weighty 'forgiving iniquity, transgression and sin' that is followed and balanced by 'visiting the iniquity' into one clause: 'changing [the verdict] regarding the evil'. This is a recipe for forgiveness, but Jonah emphatically does not want that mercy to extend to Nineveh. Thus, his affirmation of YHWH's grace, compassion and merciful love becomes an accusation.

3. After Jonah's declaration of his foundational belief regarding the character of YHWH, his expressed desire to die seems incongruous, particularly after his own harrowing experience, dramatic rescue and subsequent expression of thanksgiving. The radical shift is hinged to the Ninevites' entirely unexpected repentance (v. 1). It seems that Jonah continues to reason in terms of the implications for him; these will be complex. One matter that may be high profile is his apprehension about his own standing in Israel. It is apparent from 2 Kgs 14:25–26 that he had a significant voice in the court. Should the word get back that his prophetic voice was responsible for the divine reprieve granted to Nineveh, he might be treated as a traitor. Death at the hand of YHWH would be a lesser horror than death from his own countrymen under those circumstances. Even if the audience in Israel did not judge him so severely, the humiliation of returning as a 'failure' would be overwhelming. Jonah's self-perception as YHWH's prophet did not turn out at all how he anticipated. He had to acknowledge that the pronouncement (styled as the word that YHWH gave him to speak) had significant interpretive layers to it, and he missed them.

4. Jonah uses *ṭôb* ('good') as a value judgment weighing life and death. YHWH incorporates the same concept in *hêṭēb* but shifts the sphere to Jonah's tumultuous emotional state. This sequence recurs in vv. 8–9. This does not necessarily suggest that YHWH questions Jonah's motives or the credibility of his self-justification. While it could be making the point that Jonah's anger has no merit, especially given his affirmation of YHWH's nature (Stuart 1987: 503–504), YHWH may instead be probing the depths of Jonah's emotional response. Trible (1996: 519) points out that YHWH does not address the content of Jonah's prayer, does not hark back to his prior disobedience, does not lecture him on the logic of his appeal and does not command him to change. Instead, YHWH focuses on Jonah's current expression by asking searching questions. Those who pose it as 'have you the right to be angry?' may misunderstand it (Sasson 1990: 287).

Explanation

However we interpret the 'evil' in 4:1, it represents something radically awry with Jonah. The effects of his emotional roller coaster are evident as his reasoning, affirmation and despair crash against each other. We may attempt to sort them out, but in the end are left with at least two intersecting spheres. One is his own humiliation, shame and the wide-ranging implications of public 'failure'. His journey to Nineveh, with all its convoluted itinerary, is wasted energy, especially since both he and God know God was going to forgive them anyway (Jenson 2008: 82). The second is Israel's now dismal future. Nineveh overturned and destroyed in the geopolitical sense would have been reprieve for Israel and would have sustained the perception of its unique status as God's people. Nineveh overturned in the sense of spiritual reform would be ominous. Assyria would serve as YHWH's chastising rod (Isa. 8 – 10), a reality that rolls through the northern kingdom a generation later. Notably at this point, the *rāʿâ* for Jonah is 'great', whereas that adjective was never applied to the *rāʿâ* of Nineveh (1:2).

The unsettling reality is that Jonah's affirmation of YHWH's mercy, compassion, slowness to anger and *ḥesed* is the basis for his anger. He perceives that YHWH has put himself on the side of Israel's enemies (Wolff 1986: 160–168). We expect God to be 'on our side' and are thrown off-kilter when it turns out it is not that simple. A similar admonition is offered in the context of Joshua's encounter with the angel of YHWH, who presses him to hear another perspective (cf. Josh. 5:13–15). As we survey the wreckage of human political and religious manipulations, it is one story after another of presuming we know how God will function 'on our side'. Bad theology, however, is a recipe for despair. There is a subtle but very important distinction between God's being 'on our side' and being 'for us'. The former presumes stark lines between 'us' and 'them' and claims to know which side is right; the latter, an accurate translation of Ps. 124:1–5, refuses dichotomies that rest on human presumptions.

In a complicated bit of irony, Jonah's appeal to Exod. 34:6–7 identifies him with Moses, who put his own life on the line, pleading for Israel's life. Jonah puts his life on the line, pleading for Nineveh's destruction, which will mean Israel's continued existence, at least for a time. Exod. 34:6–7 is the precedent for Jer. 18:7–10, which expands the principle to repentant 'nations' rather than simply Israel. The severe theological dilemma is the extension of that mercy to nations that jeopardize Israel. For that reason, Nahum's message is equally important. It completes the Exod. 34 portrait that includes both long-suffering and ultimately punishing the iniquity. Nineveh was spared for a time – illustrating YHWH's mercy as well as his justice effected towards his own disobedient people (Youngblood 2019: 162–167).

YHWH remarkably turns his attention to this one single individual. Nineveh's sin and repentance are sidelined for the time as God addresses the miasma of despair, humiliation, frustration and vexation with a lesson tailored specifically for Jonah. The calculus of grace has broken down: although Jonah previously revelled in his own unmerited experience of YHWH's mercy, he is not able to transfer that equation intact to the vast and wicked city of Nineveh.

This prayer of Jonah has garnered a range of interpretive renderings. Against the backdrop of reading ch. 2 as good orthodoxy mediated through self-righteousness, now Jonah presumes he is the correct adjudicator of the moral world, whose good judgment has been slapped down by this demonstration of YHWH's mercy. From that perspective of wounded moral pride, he expresses his self-righteous arrogant challenges to God's character, even as he affirms it (Hoyt 2019: 500–501). While this interpretation does maintain a strong sense of moral rectitude – calling out that which is evil – it misses the deeply complex reality of whole-person responses to the unprecedented set of circumstances in which Jonah finds himself.

While the HB contains few prayers that ask YHWH to shorten or end life, that of Moses is one of those, and the plea is understandable (Num. 11:10–15). It is only when we begin to comprehend the extremity of biblical characters' circumstances that we allow them in grace to express the kinds of sentiments that erupt from us more than we care to admit. Job curses his existence and day of birth (Job 3) and Jeremiah his own bitter circumstances (Jer. 20:14–18). After Jezebel threatens to execute Elijah, he flees to Mount Horeb; as he is on the way he expresses his desire to die (1 Kgs 19:1–4). One possible reason for this may be somewhat the opposite of Jonah's situation. Elijah has just seen a powerful demonstration of YHWH's presence on Mount Carmel. King Ahab witnesses it as well. Elijah may well expect a radical turn on the part of the king and queen, but that does not happen. Instead, he feels entirely deserted and is in the desert of Beersheva to boot. Once he arrives at Sinai and hears words from YHWH to the effect that God is not finished with him, he resumes his work (1 Kgs 19:9–18).

In contrast to Elijah, who is convinced that his mission has failed and feels unable to proceed, Jonah is 'burning' because his words have been successful (Allen 1976: 229–230). Lessing (2007: 264) observes that Jonah pits his own word against YHWH's, but that may oversimplify the matter. Jonah pits YHWH's word against YHWH's action at this point. Perhaps he first rehearses the creed to demonstrate that he is up on his credentials and deserving of having been given a 'heads up'. Because YHWH has not seen fit to do that, Jonah threatens to 'resign' in the most dramatic way. He is theologically astute enough to recognize both the justice and mercy of God. The sticking point comes with the lack of clarity regarding a city whose stated wickedness is really off the charts

(Jenson 2008: 82). And that is the crux: Jonah puts himself in the place of determining when mercy is no longer 'deserved', a dangerous arrogation of God's sole prerogative to himself (Fretheim 1978: 234). In doing so, he ironically undermines his own oddly successful role in Nineveh's rescue.

Unavoidable questions arise at this point: How does this fierce sense of 'deserved' judgment appear in our contexts? How much do we attempt to limit the offer of God's mercy to those whom we approve and exclude enemies from any possibility of benefiting? How do readers respond after the destruction of enemies?

JONAH 4:5–11

Translation

5 And Jonah went out from the city, and he sat to the east of the city, and he made for himself there a shelter, and he sat under it in the shade until he would see what would happen in the city.

6 And YHWH Elohim appointed a plant, and he caused it to go up over Jonah to be a shade over his head to deliver him from his distress, and Jonah rejoiced greatly over the plant.

7 And God appointed a worm when the dawn came up the next day, and it smote the plant, and it withered.

8 And then when the sun rose, God appointed a harsh east wind, and the sun smote upon the head of Jonah and he was faint, and he asked with all his being to die, and he said, 'Better is my death than my life.'

9 And God said to Jonah, 'Is it good that you are in great turmoil about the plant?' And he said, 'It is good that I am in turmoil, exceedingly so!'

10 And YHWH said, 'You were troubled about the plant for which you did not labour and which you did not grow, which in one night came into being and in the next night perished.

11 And I, should I not have compassion on Nineveh, the great city, in which there are more than twelve thousands of human beings who do not know between their right and their left – and many animals as well?'

Notes on the text

4:5. The succession of verbs is straightforward, but the audience knows neither the time frame(s) within which Jonah's movements fit nor his expectations. If *wayyēṣēʾ* ('and he went out') is understood as a pluperf. ('and he had gone out', NIV), then this verse reorients the audience as to Jonah's whereabouts as soon as the opening exchange between Jonah and God starts: it serves as a flashback.

Jonah goes to the 'east' (*miqqedem*) of the city, a combined connection with and opposition to his prior fleeing 'first thing' (*qiddamtî*) to the west (v. 2; cf. 1:3).

A *sukkâ* ('booth') is insubstantial and temporary. Because 'booth' has added Western cultural connotations, 'shelter' is a better translation.

6. *wayĕman* ('and he prepared') is the 3 masc. sg. pi. wayyiq. from the root *mnh* (see 2:1[1:17]). *wayyaʿal* is another shortened hiph. lamed-hê verb.

The numerous proposals to identify the *qîqāyôn* are summarized by Robinson (1985: 390–403; see also Hoyt 2019: 508). It occurs only in this chapter and is most commonly identified as the *ricinus communis* (Latin), meaning 'castor-oil plant'. Two additional possibilities include a 'gourd' and some variety of 'wild vine or ivy'. Robinson suggests that the word was coined. Whatever its identification, it grows with miraculous swiftness and provides shade. That suggests reasonably thick foliage.

The hiph. inf. const. (*lĕhaṣṣîl*) from *nṣl* ('deliver') is followed by two prep. phrases that seem to pull in the opposite directions: *lô* ('*for* him') and *mērāʿātô* ('*from* his distress'). The former may be emended so that the 3 masc. sg. pron. suff. is attached to the verb form (*lĕhaṣṣîlô*) 'to rescue him'. This would follow the pattern in Exod. 18:9. On the other hand, this may echo *wayyiḥar lô* in v. 1 (Sasson 1990: 292).

The LXX reads the last clause as 'to shield [shade] him from his distress', instead of 'to deliver'. Underlying that reading may be a wordplay between the root *nṣl* ('to deliver' in hiph.) and *ṣll* (underlying the noun *ṣēl*, 'shade'). See also 4QXIIg, Vg and Tg (Gelston 2010: 64, 95*).

7. Elohim (God) is preceded by the def. art. The divine name changes with each appearance in this section.

tôlaʿat ('worm') is an indefinite object of God's 'appointing'. It does not directly act on Jonah as the previously appointed fish and plant have done but attacks the plant instead. *wattak* is the 3 fem. sg. hiph. from the root *nkh*, meaning 'to strike' or 'smite'. It has military connotations (*DCH* 5:684–690).

The prep. *bĕ-* with the inf. const. of *ʿlh* points to the time frame, starting somewhat before the break of dawn (*šaḥar*) on the following day (*lammaḥorāt*).

wayyîbāš ('it withered') may echo the use of *hayyabbāšâ* ('dry land') from 1:9, 13; 3:1 (Trible 1996: 521).

8. *wayehî* followed by *k-* plus the inf. const. changes the syntax: the appointment of the wind is happening at the same time as the worm is gnawing; and when the sun comes up, Jonah faces two sources of extreme discomfort. *zrḥ* ('to rise') is almost always used in conjunction with the sun.

The root *ḥrš* has multiple meanings (BDB 360–361; *DCH* 3:323–324). This adjective, *ḥărîšît*, is a **hapax**, and none of the possible meanings for the root is an obvious match. A primary meaning has to do with cutting in, engraving or ploughing; perhaps 'scouring' conveys the intention. 'To be silent' or 'dumb' (additional meanings of the root) do not seem to fit, although the Tg reads *šĕtîqtā'* ('quiet'), which could mean 'gentle' (Cathcart and Gordon 1989: 109). This wind is, however, destructive. *BHS* suggests reading *ḥārîpît* instead, but that has to do with reproach; it does not seem to remedy the interpretive problem. The syntax is further complicated because the fem. adj. is separated from the fem. noun (*rûaḥ*) by *qādîm*, a masc. noun. The only other passage where this occurs is Exod. 14:21, where the *rûaḥ qādîm* ('east wind') is modified by *ʿazzâ* ('strong').

šemeš ('sun') is both masc. and fem.; here the accompanying verb is fem.

ʿlp appears rarely and primarily in passive forms. The hith. can mean 'to cover oneself' (Gen. 38:14) or 'swoon away' (this passage and Amos 8:13). There are several occurrences in pu. as well (BDB 763; *DCH* 6:430; *HALOT* 836).

nepeš, normally translated 'life, soul, being', is used adverbially here. Jonah asks 'with all his being' to die (Timmer 2011: 129, n. 33).

9. *hahêṭēb* surfaces again (see v. 4) twice. *ʿad-māwet* ('to death') occurs only here. Thomas (1953: 220) suggests that is one of the alternative ways of expressing the superlative: Jonah is exceedingly angry, and he justifies his anger.

10. *ḥastā* is 2 masc. sg. qal from *ḥûs*, generally translated 'to have compassion', 'look with pity' or 'be concerned about' (*DCH* 3:174; *HALOT* 298). When *ḥûs* is used of human rulers, it applies to contexts of war or administration of justice, indicating a decision of a superior regarding subordinates. Complicating the matter is the fact that the only other uses of *lōʾ ʾāḥûs* (Jer. 13:14; Ezek. 24:14) are spoken by YHWH about his clear determination *not* to show compassion (Bolin 1997: 163–164).

ʾăšer governs two subordinate clauses. The first is 'for which you did not labour' and the second is 'which you did not grow [it]'. The pi. *giddaltô* may be associated with causation of a state of being (*IBHS* §24.1i), whereas hiph. operates more in the realm of causing action.

š- is a short form of *ʾăšer*. See *IHBS* §19.4 (n. 14). It serves as a conj. between independent clauses.

bin-laylâ (*ben* or *bin* in const. with what follows) represents a quality of something (GKC §128v). *ben* (or *bin*) may also be used of things that are inanimate. This expression means 'grown in a night'. It is rare that *bin* is used; see Deut. 25:2; Prov. 30:1.

11. YHWH's closing statement does not have an interr. particle. Nevertheless, it has characteristically been interpreted as a rhetorical question, continuing the preceding thread of YHWH's questioning. There are sufficient cases where the context warrants a question even without the particle (GKC §150a).

On the vocalization of the number, see GKC §97b.

ribbô preceded by the number could be calculated by multiplying 10,000 by 12 (BDB 914; *DCH* 7:402), but it is more fitting to interpret it as representing an exceedingly large number.

Bên-X *lĕ*Y expresses distinction between two classes, represented by X and Y respectively (*IBHS* §11.2.6c).

Form and structure

Wolff (1986: 163) puts 4:5 before 3:6–10, indicating that Jonah went directly out of town after his preaching stint. Vv. 5–10 in ch. 3 describe what he witnessed. Emending the text is not necessary, as the narrator has already used this flashback technique.

The narrative contrasts continue: Jonah sits in the shade of his booth in relative comfort (v. 6), while the king sits in ashes (3:6). The king is hopeful that Nineveh will be spared; Jonah is hoping to see its destruction (Magonet 1983: 20). Jonah's head is now protected, whereas in ch. 2 it was bound up by seaweed (2:6[5]). Jonah's delight over the plant is a surprise contrast from his morose state. As a contrast to the temporal ambiguities in preceding parts of this vignette, the point when the worm begins to gnaw is precise, and it does not take the plant long to wither.

Connections are also noteworthy: there is a phonological similarity between *ṣēl* ('shade') in v. 5 and *lĕhaṣṣîl* ('to deliver') in v. 6. The worm's 'striking' the plant (v. 7) will be paralleled by the sun's 'striking' Jonah's head (v. 8). The 'going up' of the dawn (v. 7) echoes the 'going up' of the plant over Jonah's head (v. 6). Jonah's 'to death' (v. 9) may echo his 'to life' (or 'throat') of 2:6[5]; it distinctly emphasizes the unequivocal assessment of his life from v. 8 – his death is preferable. YHWH poses a parallel between Jonah and himself, the plant and the city of Nineveh, and their respective concerns for each entity (vv. 10–11). The forms of *ḥûs* are the link. Just as *ʾādām* and *bĕhēmâ* are joined in 3:7 in the king's declaration, so also here in the King's closing question. 'The great city' circles back to the first description of Nineveh (1:2), where the primary characteristic was its wickedness. The radical shift to its population likewise links with 3:3; there the emphasis is on the urban magnificence under the dominion of God.

Comment

4:5. If this verse is a flashback, Jonah left town quite soon after it dawned on him that God was not doing anything immediately (3:10). His pent-up emotions explode in the recorded 'prayer'. It may be a distillation of repeated rehearsals of the issues both as he goes along and after he positions himself in his booth. On the other hand, it may indicate that he deliberately chooses to walk away from YHWH's probing question at the end of v. 4.

Whenever it happened, his departure initiates a series of subsequent actions on his part. Trible (1996: 519) calls them self-defeating 'diversionary tactics'. The main point of the sequence is his expectant posture regarding the outcome for the city, suggesting that he still is hoping YHWH will dole out the judgment that, in Jonah's mind, Nineveh certainly deserves. He knows what Nineveh's repentance means in the wider geopolitical sphere and expresses his dismay in the strongest terms. Perhaps at this point he hopes that his challenging YHWH, putting his own life on the line and appealing to divine justice may cause YHWH to rescind his intended mercy. Jonah has already seen YHWH change course and may hope it will happen again. YHWH's divine modification will be accentuated if the Ninevites' repentance ends up being fleeting and they return to their abominable ways (Youngblood 2019: 174); that would not be an unusual aftermath for a sweepingly emotional revival.

It may not be reading too much into the deliberative pace of Jonah's movements to suggest that he physically expresses the displeasure that has already been part of this communication to YHWH. The shelter is small and a temporary structure (see Isa. 1:8), occasionally used to symbolize transience of life (Job 27:18). Jonah has set it up rather hastily as the heat of the day will soon be upon him; he may not expect to be waiting there long. With the strong east wind eventually striking it, the construction likely does not hold up for long.

From this point on, the communication and interaction between YHWH and his prophet have everything to do with altering Jonah's perspective and broadening his vision. He seems to be still holding on to the expectation that there will be a cataclysmic overthrow. That has shaped his calling as a prophet: wickedness will be justly punished. Perhaps his exit is a precautionary move. An irony of the developing narrative is that YHWH promptly forgives Nineveh's wickedness but leads Jonah through circumstances that compel him to wrestle with his own *rāʿâ* (Jenson 2008: 88). See further below.

6. YHWH 'appoints' inanimate parts of his creation to do his bidding. Just as Jonah's 'responses' to YHWH have been actions – fleeing or walking out – so YHWH acts; this time he builds a plant to one-up Jonah's shelter. This is a plant that bursts into existence at YHWH's appointment, and it perishes just as quickly and for the same reason. *qîqāyôn* may include a pun on Jonah's name, which in Hebr. is ***yônâ*** (Sasson 1990: 292). It may also suggest a connection with the verb for 'vomit' (*qîʾ*) (2:11[10]).

Jonah's head is protected by the plant's leaves as it goes up over him. He has already constructed for himself a source of shade against the sun; YHWH gives him a better one, but it turns out to be temporary, even as the booth might have been. The juxtaposition of *ṣēl* ('shade') and *lĕhaṣṣîl* ('to deliver') carries further implications. Allegorical vignettes describe the physical shade provided by branches (Judg. 9:15; Ezek. 17:23; Hos. 14:8[7]). It is also a recurring figure for YHWH's protection (Pss 91:1; 121:5; Isa. 25:4), especially in conjunction with 'wings' (Pss 17:8; 36:8[7]; 57:2[1]; 63:8[7]).

Whereas the first appointee was the great fish, whose role was to deliver, we see the plant, the worm and the east wind as more ambiguous, symbolizing both deliverance and judgment. The divine name modulates with each appointment. YHWH appointed the fish, YHWH Elohim appoints the plant, 'the Elohim' appoints the worm, and Elohim, the wind. The first two, including the covenant name, turn out well for Jonah; the last two create more discomfort for him (Sasson 1990: 291). Walton (1992: 48) states that 'the use of the compound divine name serves to signal to the reader that Jonah is being treated like Nineveh'.

The recurrence of the frequently used *rāʿâ* makes a point: something about Jonah's reaction may be more than 'discomfort' or 'distress', unpleasant as those are. This is wrong, albeit understandable. The question will be how the plant will feature into this.

His joy at the plant's appearance is over the top; the cognate acc. signals that. Both his previous 'burning agitation' (4:1) and his exuberance here are described in superlative terms. Jonah seems to have been a mercurial personality. Both his delight and his vexation have to do with the mercy of YHWH. The plant not only protects him from the fierceness of the sun, but also hits the pause button on the burning misery in his own heart (Youngblood 2019: 177).

7. *tôlaʿat* is the most common Hebr. word for worm. Generally, the worm would consume or devour. Here it attacks, indicating the direct destructive contact that the plant will suffer, and underlying the confrontation between YHWH and Jonah (Sasson 1990: 301). While the plant is a sign of YHWH's mercy towards Jonah, the worm symbolizes his judgment. The creature appears in ominous contexts – Deut. 28:39; Isa. 14:11; 66:24 (Youngblood 2019: 177).

The rising of the dawn lyrically describes the slowly growing light prior to the appearance of the sun. In that welcomed coolness, Jonah is probably still sleeping. This time indicator is a reminder of Israel's hoary tradition: Jacob wrestled with a 'man' until the rising of the dawn (Gen. 32:25–27[24–26]). In the interval between the wrestling match and the rising of the sun (v. 32[31]), Jacob knew he had encountered God.

8. When God appoints the east wind, it is in the dry and hot desert. In that environment, the wind would carry particles of sand, capable of causing significant discomfort. That may underlie the unusual adj. *ḥărîšît*, with one of the root meanings being 'to cut'. A visual image of the effects of the word appears in Ps. 129:3 – 'they have ploughed furrows [*ḥārĕšû ḥōršîm*] on my back'.

The figure of the east wind is almost exclusively associated with God's intervention and judgment (Exod. 10:13 [twice]; Ps. 48:8[7]; Isa. 27:8; Jer. 4:11–12; Ezek. 17:10; 19:12; 27:26; Hos. 13:14–15). That may be a subtle message even as the narrative shifts focus to the heat of the sun. Joseph Karo, an eleventh-century Jewish commentator, suggests that God appointed it to demolish the *sukkâ*, so there was no shade once the sun was beating down on Jonah's head (Sasson 1990: 304). It is ambiguous, however, because the text never states that the hut was destroyed. The purpose of the wind was primarily to intensify Jonah's distress.

Walton (1992: 48–51) proposes that the object lesson of the plant likens Jonah to Nineveh. Both have impending calamity. Jonah's is the deadly heat and withering east wind; Nineveh's is the prophecy of forthcoming doom. To forestall the judgment, Nineveh repents; Jonah builds the shelter. In response, God forgives Nineveh. He also sends a plant to give succour to Jonah but then removes it. In its absence, the shelter – Jonah's attempt to protect himself – is to no avail. By removing the plant, YHWH does to Jonah what Jonah wanted YHWH to do to Nineveh – remove his grace and leave the city exposed to the *rāʿâ*. Jonah's frustration and despair in v. 3 is that God's mercy works for Nineveh. In v. 8, his response is because God's mercy has not worked for him. As a postscript, Jonah has not been pitying the plant but himself.

The image of the sun 'striking' is understandable particularly in the desert context, where temperatures easily exceed 100°F (nearing 40°C). Just as Jonah was 'burning' (v. 1), now YHWH brings to him another cause for 'burning'. The same language appears in Ps. 121:6, as YHWH is the shade that protects (v. 5) from the smiting of the sun. Two separate root meanings accompany the lexicon entries for *ʿlp* (BDB 763; *DCH* 6:430; *HALOT* 836). The first is 'to wrap oneself' (Gen. 38:14; Song 5:14); the second ('to feel faint') fits better here. The pu. masc. pl. qat. form appears in a description of sons fainting at the heads of Jerusalem's streets (Isa. 51:20) and trees figuratively fainting (Ezek. 31:15). The only other use of the hith. is Amos 8:13, describing the fainting of beautiful young women. Sasson points out the possible phonetic and semantic connections between this form and *hitʿaṭṭēp* ('to be faint') in 2:8[7] (1990: 316–317).

In the face of his life ebbing away, Jonah remembers and prays to YHWH. From his state of near collapse, Jonah does not directly ask YHWH as he did previously (v. 3). Instead, 'he asked his *nepeš* to die'. Jonah seems to engage in internal wrestling. Two verbs indicate this 'conversation'. He 'asked his life to die' and he 'said' that would be better. Jonah pronounces a value judgment on his life: he finds it wanting.

9. In response to Jonah's expressed desire to die, YHWH repeats his question, possibly to shake Jonah out of his interior dialogue. He presses Jonah about the 'validity' (*haḥêṭēb*) of his being 'overheated'. There is an added punch to 'Is it burning to you?' since Jonah is stricken by the blistering heat of the sun (v. 8).

YHWH refocuses the question: 'even about the plant, Jonah?' This essentially skewers Jonah, exposing his self-absorbed state. Previously, he proclaimed his frustration regarding justice and mercy and whether *he* thinks they are deserved. It turns out this small tutorial with the plant has revealed his world and responses as shrunken, circling primarily in the arena of self-interest. Jonah echoes the same phrase (*hêṭēb*) and adds, for good measure, 'it is burning to me to death'.

Wolff (1986: 172–173) notes that however Jonah answers God's question about the plant, he is trapped. If he says 'no' to the question, he admits his own anger is not justified. After all, he has no claim to the shade: it is God's surprise gift. But when he says 'yes', as he obliquely does, he admits God's prerogative to pardon Nineveh. Put another way, it does seem unjust to have a plant that serves him well suddenly removed, but he did not deserve the plant in the first place, just as Nineveh did not deserve mercy. A small mercy for Jonah in the form of the plant is snatched away. If YHWH takes Nineveh's extended period of grace away, it is the same – just augmented. How will the attributes of YHWH that Jonah previously reviewed fit with an about-face from mercy back to judgment? The plant over Jonah is a microcosm of an international situation. He tries to avoid the trap by returning to his desire to die.

10–11. Once Jonah responds in the sphere defined by a single plant, YHWH argues the case from the lesser to the greater. The two positions are accentuated by front-loading the personal pronouns 'you' (v. 10) and 'I' (v. 11). Jonah (you) and the plant are the 'lesser': if Jonah responds with deep emotion to the plant, how much the more YHWH (I), whose ongoing concern far outstrips momentary feelings of Jonah. The waw commencing v. 11 poses the ironic contrast between Jonah and YHWH. Whereas *ḥûs* ('compassion' or 'pity') fits the nature of YHWH, it rests much less comfortably on Jonah (Trible 1994: 218).

If Jonah's sentiment is anything akin to 'pity', it seems more like self-pity. He suffers because the plant withers. While he expresses joy over the plant (v. 6), the emotional response to its withering has only to do with the impact on himself. This constitutes a gap that the final question from YHWH will expose and fill in (Trible 1994: 221–222). There is no obvious reason for Jonah to be concerned for the plant itself. It is sufficiently fleeting as not to warrant extensive attention, and Jonah invests no toilsome labour in its brief existence. That is in marked contrast to the robust city to which YHWH's response is emotional.

ḥûs implies a welling up of feeling (Deut. 7:16; Ezek. 7:4; 9:10; Joel 2:17) and is often used in conjunction with eyes: it is a brief step to think of weeping. Centuries later, Jesus weeps over another unrepentant city (Luke 19:41–44). God intends his final self-portrayal to be as a compassionate sovereign, that sovereignty extending to the *way* he acts with the population of Nineveh. It is with a pity that suffers as he bears the weight of Nineveh's violence along with all the others (Fretheim 1978: 236–237). It also introduces a new element into the equation, shifting from theology of repentance and change to theology of pity and compassion.

There are some contexts where 'pity' may be too limiting an interpretation, especially when the object is inanimate. The level of emotional engagement may be expressed as 'troubled' or 'concerned about' (Bolin

1997: 160–161). It appears almost exclusively in conjunction with prophecies of disaster. Sometimes the point is to convey sympathy that is antecedent to action. Most often, however, the word appears with the negation *lôʾ ʾāḥûs* and indicates intensified alienation. This adds to the interpretive puzzle. The final utterance of YHWH does not have the interr. particle in Hebr. It has traditionally been translated and interpreted as a rhetorical question, one that indirectly affirms the sovereign albeit mysterious mercy of God but leaves the audience dangling (Trible 1994: 215–217). It also points to a positive interpretation of *lôʾ ʾāḥûs* (Wagner, *TDOT* 4:271–277).

Without the interrog. particle, however, this final statement could mean YHWH does not care about Nineveh (Bolin 1997: 163–164), or it could be evidence that the ways YHWH has treated the plant, Jonah and the city are inexplicable in the end (Cooper 1993: 158). Nevertheless, those interpretive directions do not fit well within the context of God's developing questions to Jonah through the chapter. It also unnecessarily attempts to knit together theological threads when they are better left in tension in the complex closure to the narrative.

Ben Zvi (2009: 2–13) asserts that rhetorical questions, with or without the particle, serve to strengthen assertions. In this context, the final verse provides a double ambiguous ending for the narrative. While readers do not know what happens to Jonah, there are significant far-reaching implications, among them an underlying statement to the effect that God will in the future judge the evil of Nineveh – as he does (Hoyt 2019: 515–521). If this book was intended to be oral discourse, this final question invites the audience into YHWH's challenge (Limburg 1993: 98).

Even as *ḥûs* links the two parts of this contrast together, the developments indicate how very different they are. The argument from the lesser (Jonah and his plant) to the greater (YHWH and the great city) includes a subtle but significant shift in the presentation of YHWH Elohim. In the final exposure of the divine responses to humans, he is not changing because the Ninevites changed (quid pro quo): he reacts out of pity, not tied to anything except his own tender divine nature.

For its part, the city is teeming with life; and Jonah's preaching, the manifestation of YHWH's compassion for Nineveh, features in its continued existence. There are two *ʾăšer* clauses that modify the city. The first is quantitative; the second, a qualitative description of those myriads of people. Nineveh's population figure is composed of two stylized elements, twelve and *ribbô*, both of which suggest larger than usual numbers. Even though ancient population estimates are speculative and vary considerably, the figure proposed by Olmstead (1923: 326) of approximately three hundred thousand for early seventh-century Nineveh is not unreasonable and accords well with this round large number. It is, however, possible that the number is both stylized and hyperbolic to convey to Israelites that the city of Nineveh exceeds (or exceeded) anything with which they were familiar. It is thus parallel to the earlier description that it was a 'great city to God' (3:3) and took a very long time to navigate on foot (Bolin 1997: 158–159). Repetition of words that use the consonants resh and beth (*harbēh*, *ribbô* and *rabbâ*) hammer home the large numbers involved in the potential destruction of Nineveh's population (Jenson 2008: 92). The root word means 'to be many'. The message is that the loss of the great city of Nineveh will result in catastrophic loss of life. How could Jonah desire that?

After the quantitative description of Nineveh, there is a further probing of the character of those myriads of people. That is the second *ʾăšer* clause, bringing further clarity on the issue at hand – or so it seems at first. The challenge, however, is discerning what they do not know and why that is important. The prep. *bên* ('between') is related to the noun often translated 'discernment'. It generally appears in contexts where the better choice between two options is obvious. The 'right' and 'left' pair is not that unusual in Scripture (Sasson 1990: 314–315). On a very basic level, a sentient person ought to be able to discriminate between 'right' and 'left'. Even this simple discernment task, however, is beyond the populace of the city. What does it mean?

If the wholesale repentance recorded in ch. 3 was substantial, this expression may not refer to the moral obtuseness of the city's residents. Perhaps it acknowledges that the population has not had the advantage of the moral instruction that Israel enjoyed in Torah (Jenson 2008: 93; Hoyt 2019: 514). Israelites were familiar with the admonition not to turn from the 'way' (*derek*) to the right or to the left (Deut. 5:32; 28:14; Josh. 1:7). Stuart (1987: 507–508) suggests that they did not have the wherewithal to make the kinds of decisions that would alleviate the 'trouble' in which they found themselves: they were trapped by their own disasters, without knowing how to extricate themselves. From another perspective, Sasson (1990: 315) suggests it may be a prosaic reflection of urban sociology; given the densely populated city, the people may not know their neighbours to the right or to the left. Amid the range of explanations for this seemingly unexceptional closure to the narrative, this one is both bland and not related to the general direction of the story. Instead, the expression may be hyperbole, a final declaration of utter need in a population that has thought itself powerful but is fundamentally inept in even the most basic ways.

The key themes of ch. 3 – repentance and turning – are not part of YHWH's closing words. Instead, 'many animals' are the final focus. This is in keeping with the robust experiences of the natural world throughout the book – the tempest, the sea and the fish – where Jonah has occasionally been the foreign element. In addition, the domestic animals play a significant role in the public demonstrations of penitence. The pairing of *ʾādām* and *bĕhēmâ* is not unique to this narrative; see Ezek. 14:13, 17, 19, 21 in the context of judgment, and Ps. 36:7[6] in the context of YHWH's saving them. Furthermore, animals are important in the economy and social structure of the city, representing livelihood and value (Stuart 1987: 508). How fitting that the book should circle around and include members of that creaturely realm within God's sovereign domain! They likewise do not know 'right from left' but he cares for them.

Readers shaped by Western world views tend to separate the animal and human domains and relegate the former to a less significant place than they are accorded in biblical texts. Shemesh (2010: 1–26) sets the final verse of Jonah within its wider literary and theological context, going back to the Sabbath commandment that provides rest for domestic creatures as part of the household. With this final verse, YHWH asserts his concern for the well-being of animals, recognizing that they suffer so frequently in conjunction with judgment against sinful humans.

Explanation

The final scene of this drama is worked out in the barren reaches east of Nineveh. Even though it is on display only briefly, the phenomenon of the east wind is a familiar one to inhabitants of the eastern Levant, and it was at God's beck and call. During the transitional periods between the dry and rainy seasons, the weather is characteristically less stable. The prevailing westerly wind pattern is reversed, and fierce hot winds sweep across the land from the east, south-east, south or even south-west, bringing very hot dry air that is often laden with fine dust particles. See further in Orni and Efrat 1971: 141–142; Baly 1974: 52–53. That is the backdrop for the steady drumbeat of the east wind as an instrument of judgment.

Jonah's positioning himself 'east' of Nineveh echoes Genesis traditions about the choice to go eastwards. Expelled from the garden, it seems that Adam and Eve headed eastwards since the cherubim were placed at that point (Gen. 3:23–24). Cain went away from the presence of YHWH, wandering to the east (Gen. 4:16). The same directional focus characterized Lot's choice when he left Abram to head towards the Jordan Valley and Sodom (Gen. 13:11). These intimate humanity's drift away from the presence of God and underlie the symbolism of Jonah's choice (Youngblood 2019: 173).

The progression of divine names through ch. 4 is a noteworthy part of the message. As the object of Jonah's affirmation of his belief in Israel's covenant-keeping God, the Tetragrammaton is repeated (vv. 2–4). The two are in relationship, tumultuous as it is. Once Jonah has exited the city to wait – likely for Nineveh's destruction – the Name is expanded to YHWH Elohim (v. 6), affirming both relationship but also perhaps subtly emphasizing that something much larger is going on. In this instance, YHWH Elohim mercifully appoints the plant; God cares for Jonah via the natural world. The next shift is to 'the Elohim' (v. 7), echoing how the king of

Nineveh referred to the divine being who, he hoped, would rescind the judgment (3:9–10). The king, working within his own polytheistic world view and language, was coming to grips with one supremely important member of the heavenly realm. In the microcosm of Jonah's circumstances, this name was likewise associated with judgment: the worm was appointed to do away with the plant that had benefited Jonah. The two final questions to Jonah bridge the name gap. Elohim asks the first, which has to do with Jonah's emotional turbulence over the plant. YHWH poses the last question, bringing in compassion for people. It may be going beyond the authorial intent to presume that the shift to Elohim at this point means Jonah is being treated as if he were outside the covenant (Hoyt 2019: 507–508; see also Walton 1992: 48–49).

YHWH is long-suffering with Jonah. He does not give up on his recalcitrant prophet but nudges him towards adopting a new posture, one that will be commensurate with *ḥesed*. That is the point of the questions, the implications of which echo for subsequent readers (Wolff 1986: 174–176). YHWH's tutorial for Jonah depends on the plant and, among other aspects, its brevity as a figure illustrating the fleeting nature of human life (Pss 90:5–6; 103:15–16; see also Matt. 6:30).

As the dialogue intensifies in the fourth chapter, *ḥûs* replaces *niḥam*. YHWH not only is free to change the verdict, but also highlights the emotional side of that change. Using this word, YHWH invites Jonah to see the world with an added lens, not simply from the judicial perspective (Craig 1993: 158–159). 'Eyes', often part of the idiom, first demonstrate profound grief: we weep. One wonders if Jonah weeps over the shrivelled plant or over his own seemingly meaningless and now very uncomfortable state. The rapid disappearance of the plant while he is sleeping may bring all of Jonah's self-doubt as YHWH's prophet back to the surface. That could be why he insists that death is a very real option. How can he live in a state of apparent rejection by YHWH (Sasson 1990: 317)? While we see *ʿad-māwet* ('to death') only this one time in the HB, the picture of utter despair reverberates into the deeply troubled words of Jesus in the garden. 'My *psychē* is deeply grieved . . . *heōs thanatou* (to death)' (Matt. 26:38).

Allen (1976: 234–235) imagines an audience for the entirety of the narrative being cleverly drawn by the narrator to side repeatedly against Jonah as they perceive his every spiritual failure, not realizing that they have been drawn into the very same judgmental stance that Jonah manifested. He was principled and consistent, but wrong. The bottom line is this: we and our enemies need grace and mercy. That playing field is level. 'Mercy triumphs over justice' (James 2:13b). The final verses of Micah (7:18–20) are read along with Jonah on Yom Kippur, the Day of Atonement. When Jonah fades from the narrative, each 'Jonah' in the audience faces the question 'Will I be like Jonah or like YHWH?'

Any hope of parsing God's intentions and purposes is beyond humans. It is not necessary to receive answers from YHWH to these kinds of questions. 'The hanging end of Jonah and the precarious nature of human existence which it metaphorically represents remain a haunting biblical witness to a theology that defies easy expression or analysis' (Bolin 1997: 178).

> uniquely, the book ends on a question – and that is what leaves us astonished and deeply affected. How many other sacred and eternal, inspired and inspiring books are there in which the last sentence is neither affirmation nor injunction, not even a statement, but, quite simply, a question? (Wiesel 1981: 154–155)

We, from the post-resurrection perspective, may be prompted to follow with further questions. To what extent is the honest narrative of Jonah's humanity, even blessed with the generous sovereignty of God, a caution to us? Are we busy fleeing, making excuses, or sulking? What is our response to a world shot through with outright evil and disaster (*rāʿâ*)? Like Jonah, we have been delivered and forgiven; we must guard from begrudging that grace to others (Luke 7:36–50) and instead be vessels that extend it freely.

MICAH

INTRODUCTION

The messages of Micah are often overshadowed by those of his contemporary, Isaiah. Nevertheless, the pronouncements of this prophet from 'outside the Jerusalem beltway' are powerful reminders of God's persistent call to transformed lives. While overshadowed by the volume and poetry of Isaiah, it is notable that Micah was the one whose words were brought to bear on the dicey situation described in Jer. 26:17–19.

My awareness of Micah beyond the 'Christmas verse' (5:2 in English) and the 'summary-of-ethics verse' (6:8) was nurtured by, of all things, field study in Israel. Teaching geography is an extraordinary way to enter the biblical text wearing a new set of lenses. Every time we studied the Shephelah (the foothills to the west of the Judean hill country), the vital role of the access valleys through that region became clearer. Even more, we realized the precarious place of the buffer-zone towns, sometimes pummelled from the west, sometimes from Judah to the east. Every time we read Micah from the top of Mareshah, pointing out Lachish to the south-west and the slopes of Tel Goded (Moresheth-Gath) just to the north, the anguish of this outside-the-beltway prophet rang out. This was a region that knew war, and it still does.

1. WHY APPROACH TO THE STUDY MATTERS

The primary issues under discussion in a study of Micah are all affected by the methodological lenses through which the text is viewed. Historical, rhetorical, literary and theological factors are interwoven in ways that will surface in the pages below. There is always a hermeneutical tension between units of discourse that were, at some point, presumed to be spoken into historically particular circumstances and the compilation of those oracles into larger written texts. When it comes to Micah, neither of those time frames is easily discerned. We will explore the possibilities below.

Closely related are the varied scholarly positions on the number of divisions within the text, their unity and coherence, both internally and across the dividers, possible authorship(s) and dates of the stages of compilation. These are important matters. Nevertheless, to front-load a text-focused discussion at the expense of a substantial understanding of the geographical and historical setting of the late eighth century BC would be to rob Micah of much of the force of his message(s). Thus, we commence with details of historical geography, particularly as they might have affected the fraying social fabric in Judah. Against that backdrop, the rhetoric carries even more heft, and the text speaks into generations to come of 'my people'. For a succinct survey of the interface of these matters, see Jenson 2008: 96–99.

2. THE GEOGRAPHICAL, HISTORICAL AND CULTURAL BACKDROP

'The word of YHWH that came to Micah, the Morashti, in the days of Jotham, Ahaz, Hezekiah, kings of Judah, which he saw concerning Samaria and Jerusalem' (Mic. 1:1). The first verse of Micah sends us immediately to a historical timeline and multiple maps. We want to know where Judah was vis-à-vis the surrounding nations and the more distant superpowers. We want to know when the named kings were reigning in Judah. We want to understand the historical, geographical and cultural implications of Jerusalem and Samaria. Finally, what is the meaning of 'the Morashti'?

2.1. Geography of the eastern Mediterranean

The land to which YHWH called Abraham and to which the children of Israel returned after 430 years in Egypt is strategically located on the international route of travel between geopolitical entities in Mesopotamia and those in Egypt. People groups living in and using Anatolia as a crossing point also found their way south into the land. This piece of real estate is bounded by the Arabian Desert to the east and the Mediterranean Sea to the west, meaning it was a narrow conduit for most international trade and military traffic. The recorded history of the first millennium BC is awash with conflict and conquest narratives. The campaigns of mighty rulers inevitably swept across the flat coastal plain on the western edge of the land.

The coast was (and is) marked by cosmopolitan populations, larger cities and foreign powers seeking access into the agriculturally rich interior of the country. As the coalition of Israelite tribes was transitioning to a monarchy, the coastal plain was the turf of the Philistines. The five cities associated with the Philistines were Gaza, Ashkelon and Ashdod on or near the coast, and Gath and Ekron, farther inland. The narrative of David and Goliath occurred in the region between the plain and the hill country inhabited by the Israelites; the name Gath echoes into Micah's opening chapter.

To the east of the accessible and vulnerable coastal region, an almost continuous spine of rugged hills runs from north to south through the country. When the tribes settled in the land at least half a millennium before Micah's time, the allotments for Judah, Benjamin and Ephraim were in the central hill country. The relatively rugged topography meant the inhabitants enjoyed a greater degree of security against attacks from outside, both from the east but particularly from the west. To access both Samaria and Jerusalem from the west meant plotting an itinerary along well-traversed routes into the interior; Samaria was more open in this regard than Jerusalem.

2.2. Narrowing the focus to Micah's region

The western foothills of the central mountain spine are called the Shephelah, the transliteration of the Hebr. word that means 'lowlands'. These foothills are cut through by five east–west valleys, providing means of access from the coast into the interior. Enemy forces used the staging ground of the Shephelah to launch attacks on cities in the hills, and particularly on Jerusalem. On those rare occasions when the small kingdom of Judah was not experiencing military pressure from enemies on the coast, they expanded in that direction to take and hold a defensive ring of cities. Because this region is so frequently viewed through military lenses, it works to think of the Shephelah as a buffer zone.

2.3. Cities of the Shephelah

Cities in this buffer zone were critical for the security of the kingdom of Judah. When Rehoboam, son of Solomon, strategically fortified towns in a defensive ring to protect the hill country and Jerusalem (2 Chr. 11:5–10), among them were cities on the lines of attack through the valleys of the Shephelah. Notable among these, both in the biblical record and outside, are Lachish, Gath and Mareshah. Each is strategically positioned along the western edge of the Shephelah and would feel the early brunt of any attempted aggression into the interior. Those three cities are identified with a good degree of confidence (Rainey and Notley 2006: 243). The most familiar of these is Lachish (Tell ed-Duweir). George Adam Smith described it:

> Her valley is the first in the Shephelah which the roads from Egypt strike, and Gaza stands at its lower end. Lachish has therefore through history played second to Gaza, now an outpost of Egypt and now a frontier fortress of Syria. In the Tell el-Amarna Letters we read of her in Egyptian hands. She is the farthest city Egyptwards which Rehoboam fortifies. Sennacherib must take her before he invades Egypt . . . War and commerce both swept past her. But this enables us to understand Micah's words about her. (Smith 1894: 165–166)

Gath heads the list of cities that Micah censured (Mic. 1:10). It was on the western end of the Elah Valley, about 8 miles (13 km) north of Lachish. Along with Adullam, Gath features in the narratives of David's rise to prominence (1 Sam. 17 – 2 Sam. 1). Mareshah is Tell Sandaḥanna, just several miles north-east of Lachish.

The other place names in Mic. 1:10–16 are much less certain from a historical geographical standpoint. In conjunction with the cities recorded in Josh. 15, Micah's list seems to follow a general north–south trajectory, moving from Gath to Lachish, and then abruptly turning back to Adullam and ultimately Jerusalem. Most were likely within a loop that represented the vulnerable border area (Suriano 2010: 438).

Micah is identified as 'the Morashti' (1:1; see also Jer. 26:18), indicating the importance of the location over the family name in his preaching context. No doubt 'Micah' was a common name. When he was 'at home', he would have been called 'Micah, the son of'. If, however, he is called to Jerusalem, noting his home town speaks volumes. This person is from the 'frontlines', like an embedded reporter in a war zone. Furthermore, this is a rural agricultural area. Those who live and farm in the valleys of the Shephelah are what we might think of as 'middle class'. Even apart from military threats, they would feel the sting of the unjust land grabs (2:1–2).

Both Moresheth-Gath and Mareshah are mentioned (1:14–15); the former was likely Micah's home town. The fourth-century *Onomasticon* of Eusebius locates Moresheth-Gath east of Beth-Guvrin (Eleutheropolis). The sixth-century AD Medeba Map places it just north of Eleutheropolis – the larger Hellenistic city that sprawled around OT Mareshah. The best location for Israelite period Moresheth-Gath is Tell el-Judeideh (Tel Goded), in the general vicinity of the Medeba Map's placement. It is a rise north of Beth-Guvrin. See Rainey and Notley 2006: 243 and Rasmussen 2010: 293.

2.4. Weaving together the geographical, historical and cultural fabric

The rule of David and Solomon over the united monarchy lasted about eighty years. The subsequent developments in both the northern and southern kingdoms are important for an understanding of the backdrop for Micah's prophecies. After the division in 931 BC, the northern tribes went through three-quarters of a century of severe political unrest and civil war. When Omri emerged on top, he relocated his capital to Samaria (1 Kgs 16:24), turning his political attention westwards and beckoning to more cosmopolitan influences as they streamed along the coastal highway. He made a marriage alliance with the Phoenician daughter of the King of Sidon (1 Kgs 16:29–33). The Omri dynasty embraced wholesale the wider Canaanite cultural trappings, dominant features of which were opulence and the worship of Baal. The title of Baal is associated with a variety of geographical locations, among them Baal Peor (Num. 25:1–5). The fact that Balak took Balaam to the top of Peor (Num. 23:28) for his own malevolent purposes is important with respect to Mic. 6:5.

Archaeological excavations in Samaria have revealed high-end architectural structures as well as imported ivories. These represent an upper class, the likes of which Amos roundly rebuked (3:15 – 4:1; 5:11–12; 6:4–6) in the eighth century. On the surface, economic and political security characterized the long reign of Jeroboam (II), son of Joash, in the mid-eighth century. It was, however, already rotting at the core (Hos. 7). By Micah's time, Samaria was on the cusp of destruction. The final years of the northern kingdom were fraught with strife as they spiralled downward (2 Kgs 15).

In contrast to Samaria, Jerusalem is more protected by rugged topography to the west. Nevertheless, subduing it was an objective of hostile forces on more than one occasion. Because routes through the Shephelah are ideal entry points, the cities in the Shephelah continue to be high profile. Their reported fortunes vacillated, depending on the character of the king. Jehoshaphat restocked the fortified cities of Judah (2 Chr. 17:2, 12, 19). Jehoram, son of Jehoshaphat, unwisely reversed his father's religious policies and suffered consequences, among them the encroachment of Philistines from the west. Although no cities are mentioned, the fact that Jehoram lost all his possessions and family suggests that the Philistines followed an open route from the coastal plain to Jerusalem, rolling over any possible defences (2 Chr. 21:16–17).

In the eighth century, Uzziah (Azariah in 2 Kgs 15) expanded the western front past Gath and to the coast, controlling the Shephelah and taking cities as far as Ashdod and Yavneh (2 Chr. 26:6–10). The biblical narratives do not reveal the less savoury side of this period, but it seems that systemic problems related to economic inequities were part of that picture. When Jotham took over from Uzziah, he did what was right, but the people continued to follow corrupt practices (2 Chr. 27:2). That one brief statement is the backdrop for the steady moral decline through Ahaz's reign that prompts Micah's stinging condemnations.

The extreme apostasy of Ahaz brought enemies from multiple sides. First the king of Syria attacked Judah and took captives. That was followed by a devastating blow from the northern kingdom; the numbers of those killed and taken captive are staggering (2 Chr. 28:1–8). This is called the Syro-Ephraimite War (734–732 BC). Even though Ahaz's people were shown mercy from Israel, it was not long until the Edomites invaded from the south-east, and the Philistines raided cities in the Shephelah. Ahaz unwisely appealed to the contemporary superpower, Assyria. Tiglath-Pileser III responded by imposing a heavy tribute on Judah (2 Chr. 28:16–21; Isa. 7:18–20; Rainey and Notley 2006: 230).

Assyrian aggression was not new. In the ninth century BC, Ashurnasirpal II swept through, leaving a swathe of terror and destruction behind him (*ANET* 276). In approximately 740 BC, Tiglath-Pileser III (Pul in 2 Kgs 15:19) essentially absorbed both Syria and Israel. When the coastal city of Ashkelon violated the treaty with Tiglath-Pileser (734 BC), he marched through Philistia and established his control as far as the Brook of Egypt (Rainey and Notley 2006: 226–229; Cogan 2015: 76–77). This was the time frame of the Syro-Ephraimite War. The north was subjected to Assyria as Tiglath-Pileser overthrew Pekah and installed Hoshea (*ANET* 283; Cogan 2015: 75). See Blakely and Hardin 2002: 11–64; esp. 41–45.

Tiglath-Pileser's successor, Sargon II, took Samaria (722 BC) and next absorbed Ashdod and Gath (*ANET* 284–286). The multiplicity of texts referring to the campaign to quell Ashdod suggests this was a major operation (Cogan 2015: 90–110). Isaiah describes in ominous terms the approach of the Assyrians to Jerusalem from the north (10:28–32), possibly a show of force by Sargon. Ahaz might have felt additional threats from the west if Sargon's Assyrian contingents raided towns in the Shephelah in conjunction with subduing Ashdod (Hoffman 2008: 89–92).

When Hezekiah took over from Ahaz, Sargon was still in power, and peoples of the Levant were keeping their treaties with Assyria. When Sargon died in 705 BC, however, there was political upheaval (Cogan 2015: 122). Multiple historical contexts could underlie the descriptions in Mic. 1:10–16. They include the devastation that Tiglath-Pileser III wrought, the rampages of the Philistines and the military incursions by Sargon's forces eastwards from Ashdod. Sargon would have been squeezing Jerusalem in a pincer movement, one part from the north (Isa. 10) and the other from the south-west.

The onslaught of Sennacherib (701 BC) is the best known of the Assyrian attacks. Early in his third campaign, Sennacherib boasted that he took Acco and Achzib farther north along the coast (*ANET* 287; Cogan 2015: 124). By the time he took forty-six cities of Hezekiah in Judah, complete with walled fortresses and villages, he had also brought Ashkelon and Ekron to their knees. Sennacherib further claimed he had taken more than two hundred thousand people in the large district of Judah and declared that he had Hezekiah trapped like a 'bird' in a cage because Hezekiah brought troops into Jerusalem (*ANET* 288; Cogan 2015: 124–125, 131–133). Hezekiah's responses included preparing Jerusalem for siege (2 Kgs 18 – 20; 2 Chr. 32; Isa. 22:9–11). The biblical text reports Sennacherib's forces in Lachish; from there he sent envoys to negotiate with Hezekiah in Jerusalem (2 Chr. 32:9–23). When all is said and done, Hezekiah was delivered for the moment, but Judah and Jerusalem were ravaged, he paid a hefty tribute and residents of Judean towns were treated brutally (Rainey and Notley 2006: 239–245; Borowski 2018: 33–40).

Sennacherib's records and the Nineveh palace reliefs of the collapse of Lachish (Cogan 2015: 133–134) in conjunction with the expansive and repeated biblical narrative of the siege of Jerusalem have focused attention almost solely on the events of 701 BC as the backdrop for Micah's opening prophetic lament. It may be, however, that a significant portion of Micah's prophetic warnings and condemnation fit the cultural decline before Hezekiah arrived on the scene. The nadir of spiritual darkness during Ahaz's reign brought the declaration of YHWH's impending judgment. That in turn served as a significant wake-up call to Hezekiah, so much so that in Jeremiah's day just about a century later, people were still talking about the reform of Hezekiah based on Micah's words (Jer. 26:17–19). In Hezekiah's first year, he saw what Micah's prophecies meant for Jerusalem. Nevertheless, by the end of Hezekiah's reign, an era had truly come to an end: the north was gone and Judah was a vassal of Assyria.

3. MICAH AMONG THE PROPHETS AND THE BOOK OF THE TWELVE – CANONICAL CONTEXT

On the prophetic timeline, Micah joins his contemporary, Isaiah, in the second half of the eighth century BC. Both were active during the reigns of Jotham, Ahaz and Hezekiah. While the name of Uzziah is not in Micah, it starts the list in Isa. 1:1. The transition to Jotham had already occurred due to Uzziah's leprosy. Nonetheless, because Uzziah was on the throne for fifty-two years, his is the definitive king's name in Isaiah's introduction. He is the only king of Judah named by Amos (1:1), as that prophet from Tekoa in Judah was called to head into the northern kingdom and prophesy at Bethel (Amos 7:10–17). Jeroboam (II), son of Joash, was king of the north; Amos named him as well (1:1). This was just about a generation before Micah arrived on the scene. On the surface, these were prosperous days for both kingdoms: 2 Kgs 14:25 references the words of Jonah, son of Amittai, prophesying the expansion of the northern kingdom that it enjoyed in the days of Jeroboam (II). Under the surface, however, the social fabric was fracturing (2 Kgs 14:26). Hosea's radical accusations of the northern kingdom were lived out and spoken during the days of the same four kings of Judah; Hosea also names Jeroboam (II). Even with the north on the cusp of destruction due to its pervasive evil, God mercifully sent warning voices to urge repentance. Micah's prophetic voice shifts the focus from the north to the south; he does not mention kings of the north. Instead, he sets the stage for waves of Assyrian aggression, the horror of which lies behind the pronouncements of Nahum that follow directly in the MT arrangement.

Isaiah and Micah depict the same perfidy of and tragedy for Judah and the Daughter of Zion. Both prophets see the wretched state of the small kingdom, the causes of the crises and the forthcoming consequences. In Isaiah's voice, the country is desolate, the cities are burned and foreigners consume the land (1:7). It gets more agonizing; the Daughter of Zion is abandoned (1:8) and YHWH rejects the multitude of sacrifices and rituals, asking who required them anyway (1:11–14). Sobering charges of doing evil (1:15–17), acting like a whore (1:21) and engaging in wholesale bribery (1:23) sound painfully like Micah. Woven early into each of their messages is the beacon of hope about the future of Mount Zion (Mic. 4:1–5; Isa. 2:2–5).

Micah has the central place in the BoT and 3:12 is near the centre of the compilation. Zion destroyed and reconstructed is a dominant theme. Before reaching that point, Samaria is on stage while Jerusalem is marginal. After ch. 3, it is the other way around. The declarations against Samaria and Jerusalem have almost identical words but, unlike Samaria, Jerusalem will not come to an end (Kessler 2020: 176–180).

4. THEOLOGICAL EMPHASES – MICAH AND THE COVENANT

4.1. The covenant Name

Micah's name is a foundational theological question: 'Who is like YHWH?' The elements of Hebr. are *mî* ('who'), the comparative particle *kĕ-* and *yâ*. Both *yâ* and the longer form, *yāhû* are part of theophoric names and represent the divine covenant Name YHWH (see Waltke 2007: 34–35). Micah could also be a shorter form of *mîkāʾēl*, which likewise involves the addition of a shortened form of the divine name (*DCH* 5:252). Micah's oracles have a steady subtext: there is no one like God. Micah repeatedly calls his audience to wake up to that fact and to sever their attachments to their own self-indulgences, paltry objects of worship and presumed security. It is abundantly clear that Micah's words are YHWH's words: at points their voices merge.

Who is like YHWH? The meaning of the name is encapsulated in the divine response to Moses' question at Mount Horeb: Who are you? YHWH declares that he is eternally self-existent (Exod. 3:14–15) – God of the fathers, God of the people in bondage and God of the *continuing* covenant with his chosen people. This declaration binds together the certainty of YHWH's unlimited power and authority with the reality of his covenant relationship. YHWH obligates himself to protect and nurture his people and keep his promises. God is fully and personally engaged with his people as well as being utterly transcendent.

4.2. YHWH's presence with the people

YHWH chooses to manifest his presence with his people, first in the tabernacle and later the temple. Jerusalem and the mountain of the house of YHWH were sacred space in the wider context of the land inheritance. Pollution of the Daughter of Zion – by idolatry and rampant injustice – was a terrible affront to the holiness of YHWH. That is the foundation for the horrifying declaration in 3:12.

The children of Israel were given carefully articulated instructions in Lev. 1 – 9 regarding the approach to sacred space. Awareness of the consequences experienced by Aaron's sons (Lev. 10) echoes into Micah 6:6–7: O YHWH, who may approach? Who may dwell? With what shall I approach? The covenant rituals built around sacrifice are not dismissed by Micah. What are dismissed are empty and noisy celebrations of sacrifice and superficial declarations of allegiance. Instead, the focus is on wholly transformed persons invited into YHWH's presence and called to faithfulness (Mic. 6:8; see also Amos 5:21–24; Isa. 1:12–17; Jer. 7:1–10).

God's covenant with Israel at Sinai was brimming with promises – blessings, land, freedom from bondage and God's unfailing covenant love. These people were God's kingdom of priests, a holy nation (Exod. 19:6) and were called to hear and obey God's Torah (Exod. 24:3–4; Deut. 4:1–2). Everything – geopolitics, social structures, worship – was to happen within this covenant context. Unswerving devotion and communication were foundational. When the people ignored or twisted YHWH's instructions and wounded others, it also deeply grieved YHWH. Clearly, those were serious concerns for the eighth-century prophets. They are particularly high profile in Micah, especially in the *rîb* ('dispute') discourse in ch. 6:1–8.

4.3. Covenant disputes

In previous scholarship, these discourses have been called covenant lawsuits based on the template in Deut. 32 – heaven and earth summoned as witnesses; accusation by YHWH of the guilty party; Israel's ingratitude with respect to the benefits bestowed by YHWH; declaration that empty ritual will not suffice; and exhortation to reformed conduct (Huffmon 1959: 285–295; Allen 1976: 364). Those formal characteristics, however, may be too much of a straitjacket (De Roche 1983: 563–574; Daniels 1987: 339–360; Bracke, *NIDOTTE* 3:1105–1106). Ben Zvi (2000: 28) does not read the summons in ch. 1 or the mention of 'witness' as signals of a forthcoming lawsuit, not least because of the emphasis there is on theophany. It is better to characterize the term as reflecting the grievance that one party has with another. In Mic. 6:1–8, YHWH is the wronged party.

As YHWH's appointed spokesperson, Micah warns the wicked of forthcoming judgment. He promises that the power brokers in the human realm will reap the consequences of what they have sown. Part of YHWH's supreme wisdom and power is his orchestrating the complex scenes of international politics: nations are his instruments to effect chastisement. There is a link in Micah's prophetic utterances between social, legal and economic abuses within the community and the dark threat of Assyria on the horizon. In Micah's context, the Assyrians are front and centre but the reader catches glimpses of the Babylonians biding their time in the wings. Chapters 4–5 provide a glimpse into the more distant future when both Assyria and Babylon will be significant players on the international scene.

4.4 Covenant infidelity and consequences

The depths of human wickedness are on full display across social categories. Micah is called to confront leadership at every level as they are complicit in the lax practice or malpractice of covenant care for community and land. Self-interest and neglect of those marginalized at every level rule the day. Lying and deception are high-profile transgressions in the context of abusing fellow humans. YHWH's chastisement will be measure-for-measure in full accordance with his covenant promises. Micah is unrelenting in his sarcastic dressing-down of purveyors of user-friendly religion at the expense of covenant fidelity.

4.5. Prophetic hope articulated and fulfilled

YHWH's interventions in history interweave through various time frames, designated 'last days'; 'in that day'; 'but now'. Looking forward and outward, YHWH's covenant is not restricted solely to the children of Israel: in the future, all nations will stream up to Mount Zion. This is echoed and developed richly in Isaiah's servant songs (Isa. 41 – 42). The place God has chosen to place his Name, the Daughter of Zion, is beloved by God and he will restore it beyond their greatest imagination. In the meantime, however, Micah's voice and YHWH's voice merge in expressing anger and anguish. The people are broken; they have broken the covenant; they are going to be broken completely by the force of superpower aggression.

Complex questions regarding disobedience, judgment, repentance, mercy and God's purposes rise to the surface in Micah. When and how are the prophetic declarations fulfilled? Mic. 3:12 prophesies the complete destruction of Mount Zion, but it is that very threat that Hezekiah takes to heart, changing his posture towards YHWH. His about-face is remarkable enough that it is remembered by the elders in Jeremiah's day. While Zion was eventually destroyed, the prophetic pronouncement was contextualized for its audience, purposeful for restoration of YHWH's people and contingent on their repentance (Chisholm 2010: 576–577).

4.6. The remnant

Even through judgment and destruction, YHWH will preserve a 'remnant' (*šĕ'ērît*), a term that has both negative connotations of impending judgment and hope of future restoration. The hope of a surviving remnant is evident in a wide range of ANE texts that are the backdrop for the HB (Hasel 1974: 50–134). The mercy of YHWH for his faithful people underlies the theological understanding of the term (Park, *NIDOTTE* 4:11–17). In Micah, the picture modulates from its first appearance to the final one in the book. The picture initially is a tattered bit of the flock that the Shepherd guides into safety (2:12). In conjunction with the roller coaster of forthcoming developments for Zion, the remnant displays vestiges of strength (4:6–7). By ch. 5, the remnant is a formidable presence among the nations (5:6–7[7–8]). *šĕ'ērît* appears predominantly in Isaiah (13 out of the 27 occurrences in the HB).

5. PROPHETIC RHETORIC: READING PASSIONATE POETIC DISCOURSE

There are multiple lenses through which to view Micah's prophetic utterances, starting with the interface between oral discourse characteristics and features that reflect literary artistry. The individual units of discourse range from challenges and commands to laments and embedded dialogues. At first read, they seem disparate and unconnected. Nevertheless, the whole of the text demonstrates linkages within units and from one section to another. These connections surface first on the level of phonological similarities that are *heard*. They also appear as semantic linkages. There are formal connections – repetitions, **chiastic** structures, introductory formulas – that anticipate subsequent generations of readers and 're-readers'. Ben Zvi (2000: 123–128) emphasizes the priority of readers' engagement with the text of Micah. Finally, there are thematic continuities. The recurrence of the remnant theme is one source of coherence (Cuffey 2015: 213–253).

Micah's words vibrate with vexation and pain. The turbulent poetry is raw and rugged. Especially in ch. 1, the short phrases and abbreviated sentences capture the real confusion of assault, battle, fleeing and fear. Micah howls as he pours out his grief (1:8); we hear his brokenness. What follows is likewise broken. Modern interpreters err in imposing grammatical and formal standards on the text. Andersen (1995: 147–148) criticizes the presumptions of the *BHS* editor, who attempted to restore the text of 1:10–16 in accordance with the standard ***qînâ*** metre. These are either real-time documentation of outbursts or a literarily brilliant composition. Weeping, loud cries, mourning, writhing in pain, nakedness and shaving hair are visceral responses to utter tragedy. At the same time, Micah states categorically that he is filled with the Spirit (3:8): his lament is seamlessly the lament of YHWH. Both intend to persuade the audience that they are in a precarious place.

Regular patterns in Hebr. grammar and syntax occasionally fade in the face of this complex and forceful poetry. Particles that would help knit together the syntax are absent. Shifting pronouns and tenses abound. The discourse intertwines both YHWH's and Micah's voices, using 'I' and 'my' for both. These self-references are followed by vocatives and then indictments in the third person. Alternating between sg. and pl. is a common feature of address to general audiences. There seem to be two audiences as the oracles develop. Initially, 'my people' indicates the victims of the leaders' crimes. By ch. 6, 'my people' are those accused of covenant violations. The messiness of the language, the ambiguities and multiple possible interpretations fit the situation, reflecting the ever-shifting sociopolitical cultural circumstances into which the prophet speaks. These are not static utterances. Together they awaken in the audience the same uncertain horror that permeates Micah's environment. They speak into our own confusion in the presence of mixed signals.

Characters that are part of Micah's backstory are 'described' solely through the snippets of dialogue embedded in the text. These brief clips sometimes collide, however, and readers are left to sort out who says what (cf. 2:6–7). Even the exchange in 6:6–8, closed unequivocally by the declaration regarding what YHWH seeks, is stunningly opaque in terms of who asks the series of questions and what their motives might have been. See Gordis 1949: 173–175. Personifications carry a profound emotional impact, especially when couched in accusations (Shaw 1993: 54–56). Some descriptions may be either figures of speech or literal: the gruesome description of cannibalism or human sacrifice (3:2–3) is one illustration. See the 'Comment' on this pericope. Nevertheless, in the face of these ambiguities, the summons and warnings are clear. Ben Zvi (2000: 58) observes that the befuddlement of twentieth- and twenty-first-century readers reflects distance from the text. Those reading the text whenever it reached its full form were 'proficient in Hebrew' and would likely not be flummoxed by features scholars have deemed grammatical and syntactical problems.

6. STRUCTURES AND IMPLICATIONS

The editor or compiler drew together under the superscription (1:1) what initially appear to be well over a dozen independent discourse units that alternate between judgment and hope. There are differences of opinion as to how these units work within an overarching structure. In one assessment, this structure consists of three sections: chs. 1–3, 4–5 and 6–7 (Andersen and Freedman 2000: 23–24; see also Jenson 2008: 96–97). Each section is dominated by accusation and judgment, but also includes a glimmer of hope. The imperative 'Hear!' commences the first (1:2) and last (6:1–2) of the three major sections. A variation on that three-part structure has the first section ending after 2:13 instead of 3:12. In this scheme, each section then starts with 'Hear!' (1:2; 3:1; 6:2), followed by oracles of doom and closing with a hopeful vignette (McComiskey and Longman 2008: 495). Cuffey (2015: 213–253) proposes an alternative structure, built around the fourfold alternation between doom and hope oracles and centred on the recurring theme of the remnant. The four sections are 1:2 – 2:13; 3:1 – 4:8; 4:9 – 5:14[15]; 6:1 – 7:20. Ben Zvi (2000: 69) likewise affirms a break after 2:13, noting that ch. 3 is more closely related to ch. 4. Goldingay (2021: 414–415) sees a major break at the point between 4:8 and 4:9. While each suggestion has merits, the observations below are based on a framework comprising three distinguishable units.

Rhetorical 'building blocks' connect both within the sections and across the 'boundaries' that separate those sections. All these discourse units rest within an **inclusio**. The book begins with Micah's name ('Who is like YHWH?') and the announcement that the sovereign YHWH is coming in judgment. It ends with a question that echoes that name: 'Who is like you?' The One who had hurled the Egyptians into the sea in judgment (cf. 7:15) would in the end hurl Israel's iniquities into the sea (7:18–20).

Significant internal connections establish continuity across these boundaries. The closure to the first three chapters of condemnation and judgment is the grim prediction of the fall of Jerusalem (3:12), but it is immediately followed by a radical shift to the exaltation and restoration of ruined Jerusalem and Zion and God's remnant (4:1–8). The promised Shepherd/King who will deliver the 'remnant of Jacob' (5:1–8[2–9]) reconnects with the wounded and scattered 'remnant' from 2:12–13 and 4:6–7. The pronouncement that God will cut off all idolatrous practices (5:9–14[10–15]) expands the condemnations in 1:5–7. The sobering municipal and social injustices (6:9–16) echo the same condemnations in 2:1–11. Both 4:1–5 and 7:11–12 promise return to sacred spaces.

7. WHEN WERE THESE ORACLES SPOKEN AND COMPILED?

Mic. 1:1, provided by the circles who edited the text, declares these discourses are the word of YHWH: they are authoritative for the generations to come. The introductory list of kings compels readers to take seriously the late eighth- and early seventh-century context in the southern kingdom. The next question is whether the details of Mic. 1:1 apply to the whole of the book: Are the sections of the book chronologically distinct? In general, the discourses in chs. 1–3 are ascribed to Micah although some scholars remove the brief statement of hope (2:12–13), thinking it would have robbed the judgment oracles of their power.

The fact that Mic. 3:12 was known and quoted as authoritative in Jeremiah's day (26:17–19) suggests that all or most of what preceded this declaration of judgment should have been known by Hezekiah's time at the latest. But then what? Do chs. 4–7 represent subsequent authorships beyond Micah's lifetime? The image of nations streaming to Zion (4:1–4) is peaceful and universal in scope; that may reflect a post-exilic context. The reference to Babylon (4:10) is further grounds for dating this material after the exile. Willis (1970: 77–90) surveys the possible explanations for the present arrangement of the book, ranging from its being a collection of independent units to its reflecting the final product of a long literary development adding to original oracles from Micah.

It is not known when the oracles of the eighth-century prophets were assembled. It might have occurred near the end of Hezekiah's reign, or it could have been as late as the second century BC. Just as the proverbs of Solomon were copied by the men of Hezekiah (Prov. 25:1), perhaps other valuable texts of the tradition were prepared for preservation during that geopolitically tenuous time as well. When they thought their heritage might be destroyed, they archived the important prophetic voices of their era. The elders who spoke up in Jeremiah's defence knew those words. See Waltke 2007: 8–16 for a summary of the views on date and authorship.

From a conservative perspective, Micah is responsible for all the discourse units. Even given that presupposition, there are approximately four decades and radically shifting circumstances between the accessions of Jotham and later Hezekiah. There is considerable latitude regarding which historical contexts sketched above are possible backdrops for Micah's words. The judgments against Samaria and Jerusalem, the broken postures of towns in the Shephelah and the looming threat of Assyria must lodge in some reality or realities, but which decades' events fit best? Is one historical context a sufficient backdrop? What follows is one loosely held reconstruction.

Samaria and Jerusalem seem to be under the same fundamental threats due to their transgression (1:5). Because Micah hails from the Shephelah, the focus narrows to that portion of Judah. The place identifications (1:10–16) may hold vague clues to circumstances that prompt the initial lament and even the subsequent two chapters. On the basis of the historical survey above, six options come to the surface, all of them connected in some way to military conflicts that affected Judah: (1) Tiglath-Pileser III's devastating sweep through the Shephelah and Negev (734 BC); (2) the Syro-Ephraimite horror and the attack on Judah by the combined forces of Pekah and Rezin (734–732 BC) that might have spilled over into the south; (3) Philistine raids into the Shephelah and Negev in the aftermath of that Syro-Ephraimite conflict (2 Chr. 28:18); (4) just before or right after fall of Samaria in 722 BC when Assyrian hostility might likewise have affected the south; (5) the Assyrian attacks on Ashdod, accompanied by guerrilla raids into the Shephelah (720–712 BC); (6) the most recorded events of 701, when Sennacherib attacked. An additional possibility may also gain some traction: it requires some rhetorical reading between the lines and has less direct connection with war. See below.

Micah's lament over the crisis for towns in the Shephelah (1:10–16) may be a wrenching response to the aggressive moves of Tiglath-Pileser III in that area. This is shortly after the transition to the reign of Ahaz, whose religious and political policies are tangled in the extreme and begin to bring YHWH's judgment. At just about the same time, the intertribal war between the north and south has catastrophic effects (2 Chr. 28:5–15). All of this unfolds under the dark cloud of Assyria's intervention, Edomite aggression and the Philistines' attack through the Shephelah (2 Chr. 28:16–18).

Hoffman (2008: 93–97) proposes a synthetic interpretation, involving both historical contexts and literary components. After Uzziah's death, the expansion westwards (2 Chr. 26:6–7) ceases. Ahaz loses territory and the Judean army abandons Shephelah towns (2 Chr. 28:18). The subsequent Philistine raids may be the basis for the Philistine rejoicing over Gath. The contrasting Judean response is lament (738–734 BC). This explains the absence of references to Assyrians but allusions to a Philistine presence. The destabilizing aftershocks of the ongoing skirmishes from 734 to 722 affect the whole of Judah. The prospect of Assyrian raiders plundering Shephelah towns in conjunction with the Ashdod campaigns traumatizes the population. If this is a 'geographic lament' lacking a singular historical context, it migrates across historical occasions. It may be that some of the wordplays on Shephelah town names are added to this 'wandering lament' in the horrific decade when they are the vulnerable targets of raids. Crossing the time frames blurs the 'lament' and 'prophecy' distinction intimated by the modulating tenses. The events of 701 are the culmination of the older prophecy/lament. In the end, it is uncertain when Micah enters the scene: he may witness the earliest threats as a young person. Whenever they occurred, the raids would leave the population uncertain whether to run, hide or capitulate. It may be that the cryptic personifications of the various named locations allude to this devastated state (Hoffman 2008: 93–94).

If a complex of these factors lies behind the lament segments of ch. 1, then further questions arise. First, what draws chs. 2–3 into this same historical frame? There may be the vaguest of hints regarding war atrocities, fleeting as they are. Second, if many of the strongest judgment oracles are directed at abuses during the reign of Ahaz, how and when is it that Hezekiah responds so strongly? Perhaps Micah's stern judgments continue to echo through Jerusalem as Hezekiah takes over in 716 BC. The geopolitical situation remains tense. Unlike Ahaz, Hezekiah heeds the warnings. One additional detail in Jeremiah requires consideration. Just after quoting Micah's words to quell the rising impulse on the part of priests and prophets to execute Jeremiah, the elders pose the rhetorical question 'Did Hezekiah put Micah to death?' This would suggest that Micah's closing volley against Jerusalem is stinging enough to be considered potential treason and warrant death (Jer. 26:17–19). That draws at least the final part of the first discourse unit into the fractious years between the fall of Samaria in 722 BC and Hezekiah's accession. If so, the rampages of Sargon through the region provide the best military context.

But that may not be the complete picture. Shaw (1993: 40–67) reads the text through rhetorical and discourse lenses, raising further questions. Should we be looking for a definitive military engagement at all? Do the place names instead lend themselves to a subtler and deeper social commentary? While there are allusions to what may be called war machinery, the wordplays address a wider range of troubling issues – coming and going from towns, shame, trappings of mourning, consequences of deceit and significant confusion. With both northern and southern kingdoms spiralling downward for several decades, ever-modulating social and political allegiances, and wholesale cultural anxiety, Micah may be reflecting the fragmentation of what is left of the tiny kingdom of Judah. They are engaged with their own crises, engendered by greedy and deceptive practices – as subsequent chapters make clear. Micah's accusations of these cities are of the same cloth as the condemnations that follow: they reflect what the towns of Judah are doing to themselves.

8. EXCURSUS: MICAH 4:1–5 AND ISAIAH 2:2–5

For a survey of the scholarship on literary dependence, see Waltke 2007: 213–220 and Andersen and Freedman 2000: 413–427. The possible explanations for the parallel passages in Micah and Isaiah may be distilled into the following: (1) Micah was the original author and Isaiah borrowed; (2) Isaiah was the author with Micah borrowing; (3) there was an independent source used by both; (4) the passage was inserted later into both books. In contrast to the preceding units, the liturgical style of this passage suggests that Micah and Isaiah were both quoting a piece familiar to their audiences, perhaps a song that the people would have known from the temple context (Willis 1979: 59). This would be an important rhetorical move to draw the audience in (Shaw 1993: 107).

Waltke points out the relationship of this **pericope** to the songs of Zion which are pre-exilic. Thus, it is quite possible that the symbolic elevation of Zion fits with an eighth-century context, contrary to those who contend it must be post-exilic. The same is true of the prospect of peace and breaking war implements, a theme missing in post-exilic material (Waltke 2007: 215–218).

The placement of the **pericope** in both Isaiah and Micah is instructive. In Micah, it is the hinge between the 'Book of Doom' (1:1 – 3:12) and the 'Book of Visions' (Andersen and Freedman 2000: 415–416), an intentional shift from condemnation to brief vignettes (4:6–14[4:6 – 5:1]) that echo and revisit the Zion focus of 4:1–5. In Isaiah, the discourse unit follows Isaiah's summons to hear YHWH's accusations against his faithless children, closed by a brief glimmer of hope (Isa. 1). After the invitation to 'walk in the light of YHWH', however, Isaiah abruptly returns to scathing condemnation and pronouncements of judgment. It may be that the pericope is more 'at home' in Micah.

Micah	*Isaiah*
In the later days,	In the later days,
the mountain of YHWH's house	the mountain of YHWH's house
will be established	will be established
as head among the mountains,	as head among the mountains,
and it will be raised above the hills;	and it will be raised above the hills;
and people [*ammim*] will stream to it.	and people [*goyim*] will stream to it.
Many nations [*goyim*] will come and say:	Many nations [*ammim*] will come and say:
Come, let us go up to the mountain of YHWH,	Come, let us go up to the mountain of YHWH,
and to the house of the God of Jacob.	and to the house of the God of Jacob.
He will teach us from his ways,	He will teach us from his ways,
and we will walk in his paths;	and we will walk in his paths;
for from Zion will go forth Torah,	for from Zion will go forth Torah,
and the word of YHWH from Jerusalem.	and the word of YHWH from Jerusalem.

Micah	*Isaiah*
He will judge between many peoples [*ammim*],	He will judge between nations [*goyim*],
and will settle disputes for powerful nations	and will settle disputes for many peoples [*ammim*] who are distant.
They will crush swords into cutting implements;	They will crush swords into cutting implements;
spears to knives for pruning.	spears to knives for pruning.
Nation will not take up sword against nation,	Nation will not take up sword against nation,
and they will not train for war any more.	and they will not train for war any more.
Every man will sit under his vine and fig tree;	
and no one causes them terror;	
for the mouth of YHWH of Hosts has spoken.	
For all the nations will walk,	
each in name of his gods;	O House of Jacob, let us walk in the light of YHWH.
But we will walk in the Name of YHWH for ever.	

9. TEXTS AND TRANSLATIONS

The critical notes in *BHS* and *BHQ* indicate that while the text of the MT is relatively well preserved, the meaning of a number of verses eluded the early translations. Variants from the LXX, Tg, Syr and Vg often range widely. When the LXX translators misunderstood the text, they attempted to make paraphrastic sense of it. The most significant of these appear in the 'Notes on the text' with suggestions as to the value and possible reasons for the alterations. Caution is in order regarding wholesale emendations. This is particularly applicable in addressing 1:10–16, where Micah might have been intentionally manipulating and distorting place names for the literary effects (Hoffman 2008: 91).

In addition to the ancient versions, there are fragments from Qumran. One small fragment (Mic. 5:1–2[2–3]) is similar to Jonah fragments in 4QXIIf and may likewise date from c. 50 BC (Fuller 1997a: 267–270). 4QXIIg contains fragments of Mic. 1:12–15; 2:3–4; 3:12 – 4:2; 5:6–7[7–8]; 7:2–3, 20. It comes from the last third of the first century BC (Fuller 1997a: 272, 313). 1QpMic contains citations of 1:2–9; 6:14–16; 7:17 (DJD

I: 77–80). The Minor Prophets Scroll from Wadi Murabba'at (Mur) includes significant portions of Micah (DJD IIa: 192–197; 2/2 Plates LXI–LXVI). See Waltke 2007: 16–17. The Greek Minor Prophets Scroll (8ḤevXIIgr) is tentatively from the later first century BC (DJD VIII: 19–26, 32–43).

10. OUTLINE

Part 1: Judgment on the horizon for Samaria and Jerusalem (1:1 – 3:12)
- I. Theophany
  - A. Identifications (1:1)
  - B. Summons to witness the coming of YHWH (1:2–4)
  - C. Culpability of Samaria and Jerusalem (1:5–7)
- II. Lament
  - Micah's posture of lament for Judah and Jerusalem (1:8–9)
  - Lament for towns in Judah (1:10–16)
- III. Condemnation and rescue
  - Woe to the powerful and covetous (2:1–2)
  - Humiliation: no part in the inheritance (2:3–5)
  - Dripping, denunciation, defilement, deception (2:6–11)
  - Remnant brought to safe haven by the Shepherd King (2:12–13)
- IV. Consequences of failed leadership
  - Skewed moral compass of leaders who devour people (3:1–4)
  - Shaming the false prophets (3:5–7)
  - Condemnation of leaders who have brought Jerusalem's ruin (3:8–12)

Part 2: Hope of restoration / hope of judgment (4:1 – 5:14)[15]
- I. To, from and within the safety of Mount Zion
  - A. Mount Zion restored as source of YHWH's instruction and justice (4:1–5)
  - B. Mount Zion as stronghold for the broken remnant (4:6–8)
- II. But for a time: tumult and attack
  - Interval of anguish for Daughter of Zion (4:9–10)
  - YHWH overturns the plans of enemy nations (4:11–13)
  - Siege and assault of the one judging (4:14)[5:1]
- III. YHWH's intervention planned from eternity and powerfully effected
  - One will go forth from Bethlehem as Shepherd (5:1–3)[2–4]
  - Deliverance from Assyria (5:4–5)[5–6]
  - The remnant in the dispersion (5:6–8)[7–9]
  - YHWH will cut off all objects of false hope (5:9–14)[10–15]

Part 3: Flawed covenant people will rise again (6:1 – 7:20)

I. Remembrance and ritual
   A. The charge of YHWH against his covenant people: remember! (6:1–5)
   B. Requirements for entry into YHWH's presence (6:6–8)

II. Fracturing
   YHWH cannot and will not countenance injustice (6:9–16)
   Lament for lost social and familial integrity (7:1–6)

III. Future restoration and retribution
   A. The Daughter of Zion will rise into YHWH's light (7:7–10)
   B. Return from distant places to the land (7:11–13)
   C. Security for YHWH's flock in the land (7:14–15)
   D. Reckoning for the nations (7:16–17)
   E. Who is like YHWH? (7:18–20)

TEXT AND COMMENTARY

MICAH 1:1

Translation

1:1 The word of YHWH that came to Micah the Morashti in the days of Jotham, Ahaz, Hezekiah, kings of Judah, which he saw concerning Samaria and Jerusalem.

Notes on the text

Goldingay (2021: 415) characteristically translates this introductory formula as the word 'became a reality' to the prophet. *dĕbar* ('word') is a collective sg., designating the whole collection of discourses (Waltke 2007: 34). *ʾel* is a more dynamic prep. than *lĕ*. The latter may imply that the prophet acquires the word (Andersen and Freedman 2000: 108).

ḥāzâ ('he saw') in prophetic revelation indicates the interface between the senses (Jepsen, *TDOT* 4:280–290).

The LXX adds 'and' between the names of the kings.

The prep. *ʿal* is used only once here, drawing together both Samaria and Jerusalem. The LXX has *peri*, 'concerning', but the force of the introduction may better suggest 'against'.

Form and structure

There are two *ʾăšer* clauses. The first is followed by *hāyâ ʾel* and indicates the spatial and temporal situatedness of Micah to whom the word has come. The second is followed by *ḥāzâ ʿal* and addresses content. The names of the three kings are presented in terse succession, not conjoined by the waw conj. The same pattern is evident in Isa. 1:1 and Hos. 1:1, both also eighth-century prophets.

Comment

The word 'was to' (*ʾel*) Micah, implying that it was embodied in Micah's experience and was present with him. As he speaks, Micah's words will be those of YHWH. He is assuredly not like a prior Micah whose understanding of Torah was slim at best (Judg. 17). The longer form of this name, Macaiah, appears in Jer. 26:18, where his words, recorded in 3:12, are quoted in defence of Jeremiah's outspoken preaching against Jerusalem and the temple. 'Micaiah' also identifies the prophet whose vision into the heavenly realms should have brought sober reassessment of the plans of Ahab and Jehoshaphat (1 Kgs 22). See 'Introduction' regarding the form of his name.

Identifying Micah's location rather than his family name is significant. It may be that Micah's audience is not in his home town. If it were, he likely would have been identified by his family name ('son of') to distinguish him from other individuals bearing the name Micah. He may be giving these messages in Jerusalem where his contemporary, Isaiah, is already very much in the public eye. Isaiah started prophesying towards the end of the reign of Uzziah. Micah was still known as 'the Morashti' to the elders quoting him in Jeremiah's day (Jer. 26:18). On the identities and geopolitical significance of the towns in the Shephelah, see the 'Introduction'. Mareshah and Moresheth-Gath (1:14) were about 35 miles (56 km) south-west of Jerusalem, on the frontlines of any enemy assault.

'Days of', followed by the kings' names in succession, represents a single epoch during which Micah's prophesying takes place. The absence of Uzziah is significant, suggesting the kingdom has begun its downward spiral. The absence of the names of any northern kings intimates the final dissolution of that kingdom; those years were fraught with assassinations as the north careered towards its end (cf. 2 Kgs 15). Hezekiah is particularly noteworthy: he repented at the preaching of Micah, even though we do not learn of that until the days of Jeremiah when Judah was itself on the cusp of destruction (Jer. 26:17–19). Because of the reference in Jeremiah, many scholars position Micah's prophetic warnings in the context of Hezekiah's reign. Nevertheless, we must not minimize the presence of Jotham and Ahaz in the list. See the 'Introduction'.

ʿal governs both Samaria and Jerusalem, suggesting they are under the same umbrella of judgment. See *IBHS* §11.2.13c. The place names serve as **metonymies** for all civic leaders, priests and priests who will in short order be indicted by Micah (Waltke 2007: 36).

Explanation

The vision establishes Micah's authority to give this prophetic word concerning the two errant capitals of the north and south. The title could be the product of editorial work on all the eighth-century BC prophets (Hosea, Amos, Isaiah and Micah) as they were possibly assembled towards the end of Hezekiah's reign. See 'Introduction'. We have no record of Micah's call, but the words of YHWH and Micah are interwoven seamlessly throughout the book.

A *ḥāzôn* implies visual divine communication – however that works – and often glimpses into the heavenly spheres to see the presence of God. The verb form appears in Exod. 24:11; Job 19:26–27; Isa. 1:1; 33:17. It is an extraordinary kind of seeing: there is no single English word that captures it. Micah *sees* the *word*, combining the visual with the articulated message. Hebr. often associates a range of sensory experiences with eyes (Waltke 2007: 36; see Jepsen, *TDOT* 4:280–290).

The introduction identifies the location and time of the prophetic activity, as well as the places and persons who will be the recipients of God's judgment. Micah's audience should recognize the dire circumstances. Assyria is looming on the horizon, and its presence is not benign. While there are undoubtedly lingering effects of the economic development during Uzziah's long reign, those are fading as Assyria under Tiglath-Pileser III flexes its international muscle. Ahaz and Hezekiah are compelled to negotiate changing political alliances and threats as Assyria rolls towards them, bringing Damascus, Gaza and finally the Galilee under its heavy hand. This is the sole mention of Samaria; the possible implications of the shift to focus primarily on the Judean Shephelah are addressed in the 'Introduction'.

MICAH 1:2–4

Translation

1:2Hear, all peoples; give ear, O land and its fullness;
the Lord YHWH is becoming a witness against you, the Lord from his holy temple.
3For now, YHWH is coming out from his place;
and he will come down and trample on the high places of the land.

4 and the mountains will melt under him, and the valleys will be split
like wax before fire, like water hurled down a slope.

Notes on the text

1:2. The shift from 2 masc. pl. impv. to 3 masc. pl. suff. on 'all' is not unusual (GKC §135r; J-M §146j).

On the form *ʾădōnāy* (the word for 'lord' with 1 sg. suff.), see *IBHS* §7.4.3e.

wîhî ('he is becoming') may be a juss. or a simple yiq. (see GKC §109k; *IBHS* §34.3d). The latter is preferred in this context; YHWH is coming to become the divine Witness in their presence. 1QpMic reads *YHWH* followed by a gap and then the letter hê (Gelston 2010: 95*). It possibly reflects *ʾădōnāy* after the Tetragrammaton and followed by the juss. form of the verb. The LXX reads *Kyrios.*

While the prep. *b-* may be translated 'be among you' (Goldingay 2021: 418), it is best read as 'against', particularly in contexts of testifying (Deut. 4:26; 30:19). YHWH will testify against them.

3. Translating *hinnēh* as 'behold!' is archaic for many readers. The word implies 'pay attention because *now* something is about to happen'. See Miller-Naudé and Merwe 2011: 53–81. The act. ptc. 'coming out' (*yōṣēʾ*) develops the sense of immediacy (see *IBHS* §40.2.1b) that is initiated by *kî-hinnēh*. The weqat. verbs 'will come down and will tread' continue the temporal immediacy. There have been emendations, based on some LXX versions and 1QpMic, that remove either *wĕyārad* or *wĕdārek*, indicating that one or the other has been added under the influence of other theophanic passages (Waltke 2007: 47–48).

1QpMic adds the def. art. to *ʾāreṣ*; this fits the Hebr. grammar of the const.

4. *wĕnāmassû* is a niph. form; see *IBHS* §21.2.1 on its being **middle voice**, 'and they will melt'. The LXX shifts the verbs that describe the effects of the theophany on the topography and omits 'split apart', which is a challenge.

muggarîm is a hoph. ptc. from *nāgār*. The pass. form is a **hapax**; the hiph. appears in v. 6. The root meaning is 'to pour down, hurl down'; this is overwhelming.

The labial (mem) assonance among the three words contributes to the sense of powerful flowing – *mayim muggarîm bĕmôrād*.

Form and structure

Ch. 1 is vast, sweeping from the reaches of heaven to individual beleaguered cities. The first part of v. 2 has rhythmic parallel structure. Each impv. – listen and 'give ear' – is followed by the intended audiences, the peoples and the earth. The second part of the verse signals a pause, waiting for the action that will give the platform for YHWH to serve as a 'witness' from 'his holy temple'. Two parallels shape the development: YHWH / the Lord and his holy temple are followed by YHWH and his place. These place indicators are not couched in a static declaration. Just as 'place' connects vv. 2 and 3, so the movement connects that place with the earth below: YHWH goes out, descends and treads.

Some scholars who were beholden to standard formal considerations emended the text to reduce the longer colons, but that is not necessary (Andersen and Freedman 2000: 133–134). The text as it stands vividly reflects Micah's ongoing participation in extraordinary visual revelation.

Comment

1:2. The introductory summons echoes the declaration of Micaiah ben Imlah (1 Kgs 22:28; 2 Chr. 18:27), and the same form is found in Job 17:10. The parallel summons to 'peoples, all of them' and 'the land and its fullness' distances each designated entity. It is a sweeping call to judgment on a universal scale.

The word, *ʿammîm* ('peoples'), indicates groups that share some commonality. That may involve kinship as well as culture, although blood relationship is not necessary to be considered part of this community. Both sg. and pl. may refer to a collective entity (O'Connell, *NIDOTTE* 3:429–432). The pl. and the parallel with 'earth and its fulness' point to a global audience.

The target of YHWH's testimony (*bākem*) is ambiguous. It may be the gathered nations, or it might have shifted to Israel, especially given the forthcoming accusations of Samaria and Jerusalem. 'Micah has pounced on his audience abruptly. The effect is dramatic' (Andersen and Freedman 2000: 139). That same strategy is employed by Amos as that eighth-century prophet captures the attention of his audience by pronouncing radical judgment on the small geopolitical entities round about, only to turn all his rhetorical powers against Israel itself in the chapters to follow.

While the initial summons has the trappings of a legal confrontation, that is soon sidelined by the overwhelming nature of the theophany. From his 'holy temple', from 'his place', the 'Lord' (*ʾădōnāy*) will bring heaven to bear on the earth. *hêkal*, a loanword from Sumerian meaning 'large house', indicates both 'temple' and 'palace', pointing to the interweaving in the ANE context of both deity and sovereignty, as well as the interweaving of God's dwelling in heaven and the earthly temple in Jerusalem (Ottosson, *TDOT* 3:382–388). Both emphases are significant (Ps. 11:4; Isa. 63:15; Hab. 2:20).

3. *kî-hinnēh* focuses on the reason for summoning the audience: they are about to witness the drama of YHWH's moving from his dwelling in the heavenly realms to appear as Witness, King and Judge. The major components of theophanies are based on the Sinai experience. YHWH descends amid swirling smoke and fire, shuddering mountain and thunder (Exod. 19:16–20); the heavens are in tumult (Ps. 18:8–16[7–15]). 'Go out' is used of YHWH going out to war to help David and Israel against the Philistines (2 Sam. 5:24); of YHWH going out to punish evildoers (Isa. 26:21; see also Zech. 14:3); of kings going out to war (2 Sam. 11:1); of Israel's military ventures against their enemies (Deut. 20:1; 21:10). The audience should have started quaking along with the mountains.

YHWH will 'tread the high places'. Divine actions, coming down and treading, signal the dreadful approach of the theophany from his place to accomplish his purpose. Micah elsewhere employs double verbal descriptions. See Crenshaw 1972: 44–45.

The verb 'to tread' appears in the contexts of the feet of Israel as they entered the land (Deut. 1:36; 11:24–25; Josh. 1:3; 14:9) and of treading olives and grapes in the press (Mic. 6:15; Amos 9:13). When YHWH God Almighty is the subject, treading the high places of the earth is one manifestation of his sovereign majesty (Amos 4:13). The image includes judgment, treading the winepress in anger and wrath (Isa. 63:3). 'High places' is suggestive. On the one hand, it includes those hills and mountains that surround God's people and provide them with a sense of security and stability (Ps. 125:2). These 'high places' are the 'backbone' of the land, reach down to the foundations (cf. 6:2) and yet are trembling (Mays 1976: 43). From another perspective, 'high places' represent false shrines in hilltops; see further on v. 5.

4. There is a remarkable spanning from heaven to earth, and the earth responds with appropriate seismic effects. The mountains melt and the valleys split open. These descriptors launch a pair of similitudes in the second line that connects with the listening audience. It would be more neatly coherent to have the figure of mountains melting followed directly by wax in the presence of fire. The result reflects a more 'logical' process – the mountains are 'shaken', following which the valleys 'melt like wax' and the water flows down. The overpowering nature of the theophany, however, quite possibly transcends logic.

Each figure in the tumultuous imagery jostles against the next one. As the valleys are 'split', the water courses through them. This image does not indicate the formation of valleys, but the bursting out of liquids, perhaps even from the great abyss (Andersen and Freedman 2000: 165–166). The same figure appears in Job 26:8 as he describes clouds that do not burst from the water in them. Here, the deep valleys will become coursing water channels, an image familiar on a much smaller scale to inhabitants of the Judean hill country during the rainy season. What they will see in this context will be terrifying in its immensity. Everything that is supposed to be firm is now fluid. YHWH's prophet draws together the profoundly cosmic realities of God's justice and power with real world geography.

Fire makes wax melt quickly, and then disappears. The verb always appears in a simile: hearts melt like wax (Ps. 22:15); as wax melts before fire, so the wicked perish (Ps. 68:3[2]); hills melt when YHWH appears (here and Ps. 97:5); the earth itself is flowing. How unlike the ever-enduring hills (Ps. 125:1)!

Explanation

While the covenant calls upon heaven and earth as witnesses (Deut. 4:26; 30:19; 31:28), here YHWH himself will be the Witness, a remarkable presentation of God's Person. Samuel calls God as his Witness (1 Sam. 12:5). In a particularly telling image, YHWH declares that he will be a witness to the truth against the false prophets, who speak lies to the people (Jer. 29:23; see also Mal. 3:5). Isaiah (3:13–14) indicates that YHWH is prepared to strive with and judge the people. From another perspective, the fickle people call YHWH as their sure and true Witness that they will do whatever he tells Jeremiah they should do (Jer. 42:5); they do not keep their promise! Through another set of lenses, Job longs for a Witness in heaven (Job 16:19).

'All peoples' and 'the fullness of the land' are served a comprehensive summons to listen to that divine Witness. This same cosmic scope resurfaces in 6:2. The third-person suffixes ('peoples, all of them' and 'her fullness') distance the summons, universalizing it. While the audience is a broad one, it is not further identified.

It is sobering to pause over the response of the entirety of creation to the appearance of the King. When God appears, nature itself is in tumult, reverberating with crashing thunder and shaking earth (Ps. 77:17–20[16–19]). When YHWH redeems his people from bondage, the sea and waters flee, the mountains and hills are mobilized, and the earth trembles (Ps. 114:3–7). Add to that the dimension of cosmic combat when YHWH 'goes out' to war on behalf of his people. The thunder of his chariots is deafening, the torrents of rain are accompanied by thunderous reverberations from the heavens, and he fights for his people (see Judg. 5:4–5). David implores YHWH to bend the heavens and come down amid smoking mountains with lightning as weapons (Ps. 144:5–6). Isaiah prays that God will 'rend' the heavens and come down (Isa. 63:19[64:1]). In Micah's vision, God's coming down radically alters both mountains and valleys. As he descends, he encounters first the tops of the mountains that become like wax, coursing like water through the newly cloven valleys. Just as YHWH 'descends' (*yarād*), so also the waters will course 'downward' (*môrād*; from the same Hebr. root). All nature erupts at his appearing in judgment. In his apocalyptic vision, Zechariah sees YHWH's going out to fight as a major seismic event reconfigures the terrain to the east of Jerusalem (Zech. 14:3–4). These dynamic images serve as a severe rebuke to dull hearts that find it difficult to bestir themselves when confronted with the prospect of God's presence.

The phrase 'high places' resonates with parallel descriptions of YHWH's assault on pagan world views (Crenshaw 1972: 39–41). The word of the sovereign YHWH comes to Ezekiel more than a century later (593 BC) when Judah is again saturated with all manner of false worship sites. The 'son of man' is told to prophesy against the mountains, the hills, the stream beds and valleys. Their high places and altars will be torn down, and corpses will be strewn about them (Ezek. 6:1–7). These were deeply embedded in the whole cultural fabric. Mount Zaphon features in a Ugaritic text about building a house (palace) for mighty Baal (*ANET*, 134). A brief plaster inscription found in Kuntillet 'Ajrud has the imagery of the El's coming as the mountains melt and the peaks grow weak (McCarter, *COS* 2:173). YHWH will reclaim that terrestrial territory as his own by treading on it.

Without too many hermeneutical gymnastics, the contemporary high places and altars may be identified in the upper echelons of financial districts and academia, to shame just a few. Several stanzas of Arthur Coxe's 1839 hymn put these fleeting powers in perspective:

> Oh, where are kings and empires now
> Of old, that went and came?
> But Lord, Thy Church is praying yet,
> A thousand years the same.
> For not like kingdoms of the world
> Thy holy Church, O God,
> Though earthquake shocks are threat'ning her,
> And tempests are abroad.
> Unshaken as eternal hills,
> Immovable she stands,
> A mountain that shall fill the earth,
> A house not made by hands.

MICAH 1:5–7

Translation

1:5 On account of the transgression of Jacob is all this, and on account of the sins of the house of Israel. Who is the transgression of Jacob? Is it not Samaria? And who is the high place of Judah? Is it not Jerusalem?

6 And I will make Samaria a ruin of the field, for plantings of a vineyard, and I will hurl down her stones into the valley, and I will uncover her foundations.

7 And all her images will be crushed, and all her prostitutes' payments will be burned in the fire; all her idols I will give to destruction. Because she gathered from harlots' hire; they will return to harlots' hire.

Notes on the text

1:5. The LXX, 8ḤevXIIgr and Tg MSS read 'sin' in the first line as sg., likely to sustain the parallel to *peša*ʿ. The prep. *bĕ-* is best translated 'on account of' or 'because'. Jacob's 'transgression' (*peša*ʿ) is the first word in the sentence, indicating the seriousness of the charge of rebellion. The range of meaning for *ḥaṭṭāʾt* includes 'sin', the 'sinner' and a 'sin offering'; it is the more extensive of the two terms. See Luc, *NIDOTTE* 2:87–93, for a summary of the Hebr. terms that signify the state of sin.

'All of this' is the subject of this nominal clause and points back to the theophany that will overwhelm them. Ben Zvi (2000: 30) calls v. 5 a 'Janus verse', both looking back but also pointing forward. This is the only place in the HB where a prep. phrase is the predicate with *kol-zōʾt*. See J-M §154; Andersen and Freedman 2000: 170.

The second occurrence of *mî* is replaced by *ûmâ* in 1QpMic. On reading *mî* as 'What?' and *mâ* as 'Who?', see GKC §137c and J-M §144b. In Exod. 16:8, Moses asks the people 'Who [*mâ*] are we?' in the face of their complaint. Having said that, retaining the meaning 'Who?' for *mî* is important. See 'Comment'.

hălôʾ is rhetorical and signals an obvious and emphatic answer forthcoming (Moshavi 2007a: 171–186).

The LXX, Syr and Tg read 'the sin of Judah' instead of 'the high places', and LXX adds 'house of' – all attempts to bring stronger parallelism between the first line and the last. Nevertheless, the MT reading is supported by 1QpMic and the Vg. Goldingay (2021: 418) translates *bāmôt* as 'great shrine'.

6. The word *ʿî* ('ruin') is used only five times: twice in Micah (here and 3:12), in Jer. 26:18 quoting Mic. 3:12, Ps. 79:1 (also referring to Jerusalem) and Job 30:24. The LXX has 'for guarding the fruits of the field' (cf. 3:12). The Syr has a 'field house'.

The word 'uncover' (*gālâ*) is the same one used elsewhere for sexual sin, repeatedly represented as 'uncovering the nakedness of' someone (e.g. Lev. 20:11, 17). The same expression is also used for prostitution (Ezek. 16:36; 23:18).

7. The hoph. form from *ktt* indicates complete destruction. In qal, it is used to describe Moses' pulverizing the burned remains of the golden calf (Deut. 9:21), the shattering of a potter's vessel (Isa. 30:14) and Hezekiah's destroying the bronze serpent (2 Kgs 18:4) and other images (2 Chr. 34:7). *pāsîl* and *ʿăṣāb* (the latter always in pl. form) are parallel terms referring to images and idols, whether of wood, stone, or metal. Whatever the composition of these objects, they were burnable. On the major Hebr. terms for idols and images, see Hadley, *NIDOTTE* 3:483–484, 644–646.

qibbāṣâ (pi. 3 fem. sg. 'she gathered') has been read as the equivalent of *qubbāṣû* (pu.) by the Syr, Tg and Vg.

On the possible roots and meaning of *ʾetnannêhā*, see *DCH* 1:669–670. It may be from *ntn*, 'to give', or *tnh*, 'to hire'. Waltke (2007: 53–54) presents and critiques the major suggestions. The Tg adds '*to the temple of those worshipping idols*' (Cathcart and Gordon 1989: 113; italics original).

Form and structure

V. 5 has two major parts. The first line compares Jacob and the house of Israel. See 'Comment'. *kol-zōʾt* rests between them, controlling both. They in turn point to the next two lines of the verse, an expanded set of rhetorical questions that address each of those political entities in turn. The pattern 'And who?' followed by 'Is it not?' appears twice, but the identities are not the same in each part. Micah often leaves an expected parallel to introduce something new. In this case, it is 'high places of Judah' instead of an expected 'sins of the house of Israel'. The developing parallels link 'transgression' with 'high place', Jacob (north) with Judah (south) and Samaria with Jerusalem.

There are four descriptive phrases in v. 6 that together indicate the utter destruction of Samaria. 'Ruin' and 'vineyard' are parallel entities in the agricultural context; 'her stones' and 'her foundations' represent urban and political devastation. There is a phonological parallel between *lĕʿî* ('into a ruin') in the first line and *laggay* ('into the valley') in the second. The 3 fem. sg. suffixes ('her stones' and 'her foundations') likewise are phonologically parallel. The term for 'uncovering', here used regarding the foundations, is a thematic link with the prostitution explicit in v. 7.

As a contrast to Yhwh's interventions, the first part of v. 7 shifts the grammar. It starts with all of Samaria's impotent images being crushed and all prostitutes' fees burned. Midway through the verse, the voice shifts from passive to Yhwh's active positioning of all her idols in the place of destruction.

wĕkōl recurs three times, stressing the comprehensive end of each of these sources of transgression for the people. The normal sentence structure is reversed for all three clauses, as the nouns emphatically precede the verbs, the first two of which are passive, subtly suggesting Yhwh's activity. In the third clause, Yhwh would deliver the idols of Shomron (Samaria) to *šĕmāmâ* ('destruction'), the sound parallel adding a further ominous tone.

Comment

1:5. The three most frequently used terms for covenant disobedience are 'iniquity'/'guilt' (*āwôn*), 'transgression' (*pešaʿ*) and 'sin' (*ḥaṭṭāʾâ*), in that order when they appear together. Micah uses the latter two here. In the political sphere, *pešaʿ* means 'treason', which in the religious context is idolatry. These two can never be divorced when the context is Israel's violation of the covenant.

'Jacob' and 'house of Israel' are synonymous and generally point to the entity of the northern kingdom. Samaria is the initial named culprit, specifically reiterating 'transgression of Jacob' and locating it in the central city of the north. Because the sanctuary for the northern kingdom was in Bethel and not in Samaria, the 'transgression of Jacob' was likely in the sphere of geopolitical rebellion (Goldingay 2021: 422). Nevertheless, the third and final line of the verse shifts the focus to Judah and Jerusalem. As Micah continues, 'Israel' and 'Jacob' cover Judah as well (Micah: 2:12; 3:1, 8, 9). This is distinct from a general pattern in the prophetic literature that distinguishes south (Judah) from north (Israel).

The use of *mî*, meaning 'who', is significant. It is more than an interchangeable interrogative with *mâ* ('what'). It personalizes the transgression and sin instead of simply enquiring 'What is?', and it may be an **ellipsis** for 'Who is responsible for?' Naming the city sets the culpability squarely on the leadership. There are canonical precedents for this. In Gen. 33:5, Esau enquires about Jacob's wives and children; in v. 8, his focus is on the approaching 'offering'. Both use *mî*. Deut. 4:7–8, using *mî*, poses two identity questions regarding 'the great nation'. David does the same, enquiring first about himself and second about his family and house; again, the word is *mî* (1 Sam. 18:18; 2 Sam. 7:18).

These rhetorical questions direct attention not only to the cities but also to the deity figures associated with those cities. The impending crisis is due to their idolatry. Shifting from the expected 'sin of the house of Israel' (or Judah) to 'high places' (*bāmôt*) moves towards the specificity of v. 7. It also looks forward to the ruin of the 'high place' of Jerusalem in 3:12. Their idolatry is coming under scrutiny. While the shift to Judah and Jerusalem is abrupt, it prepares for the focus on the Judean Shephelah in the last part of the chapter.

'High places' were worship sites that could be on hills or at the city gates, notably in the cities of Judah and here particularly in Jerusalem. In some cases, the worship was genuine, but syncretism persistently reared its head (Selman, *NIDOTTE* 1:670). Given the number of references to high places, they seem to have been a ubiquitous presence, sometimes innocuous, but more often a snare for God's people. See 1 Sam. 9:12–14; 1 Kgs 11:7; 2 Kgs 17:7–13; 23:5–8. A century after Micah, Josiah's reform shut down the high places in the cities of Judah and around Jerusalem (2 Kgs 23). At this point, Jerusalem itself was the epitome of the high places of Judah.

6. *wĕśamtî* points to the future, stating the consequences of the transgression. YHWH announces that he will make Samaria a 'ruin of the field'. The pronouncements about YHWH's coming (v. 4) are personalized and activated for urban Samaria. Its destruction would be so complete that plantings of a vineyard would grow where the walls and buildings had been. Under the enemy onslaught, Samaria's magnificent stone buildings would be reduced to the 'hill of Shemer' that Omri had purchased (1 Kgs 16:24). The return of the hill of Samaria to its former state would nevertheless carry a ray of hope. To be sure, the befouled political religious entity would be destroyed, but the agricultural image of a planted vineyard points to a fruitful future.

The use of 'hurl' or 'pour' is a link with the theophany in v. 4 – there melting mountains will be like water hurled down in a watercourse. Here, like an invader, YHWH will hurl Samaria's stones down the hill into the valley like the water pouring down a steep place (v. 4; see also Isa. 28:1–4). Only Mic. 1 uses this image of solid things pouring (Andersen and Freedman 2000: 178).

There are two intertwined aspects to the ruin of Samaria – the temple buildings, whose stones would end up in the valleys, and her prominent idols (v. 7). On the formidable buildings, both palatial and defensive, of the ninth-century Omri dynasty, see Mazar (1990: 406–409). YHWH would 'uncover her foundations'. The expression is freighted with sexual connotations; Michal accused David of lewdness in uncovering himself (2 Sam. 6:20). The image represents powerfully the spiritual lewdness and prostitution carried out in Samaria. V. 7 links Samaria's transgressions with prostitution to idols. Micah concentrates first on Samaria, describing the devastation. Nevertheless, this verse gives fair warning that Jerusalem's turn is coming: the destruction will reach her gates (v. 9).

7. *ʾetnannêhā* has a fem. suff., referring to Samaria's income from prostitution, likely in the context of idolatrous worship. It appears multiple times in Ezek. 16 regarding the salacious activities of the allegorical prostitute (vv. 31, 34, 41). It was hire paid for sexual services (Hos. 2:10–15[8–13]; 9:1), an exchange made quite clear in Micah by *ʾetnan zônâ* (twice) in the latter part of the verse. The syntax of the last line is challenging. It is uncertain what 'she gathered' (pi. 3 fem. sg.) from the harlot's hire. Was 'she' the city? Were they votive gifts of some sort? Were they material goods that accompanied treaties? A related question would be the extent of the harlotry connections. One implication of 'gather' is that the contents had been collected from rather far-flung places. Three times the text ties together the related ideas of idolatry and prostitution. The idols will be burned, which is likewise the prescribed punishment for prostitutes (Gen. 38:24; see also Lev. 21:9). The tangle of images, statues of idols and other objects of false worship is wound throughout the condemnation pronounced against the northern kingdom (2 Kgs 17:10–17). The cultural and religious backdrop for YHWH's judgments as spoken through the

eighth-century prophets was messy. His Name and character had been violated by the people's wholesale turn to the worship of Baal and the resultant bargaining posture – they would engage in ritual prostitution and appease Baal with gifts, and he was expected to provide accordingly.

The connection between images and idols and Samaria's 'earnings of prostitutes' intimates political alliances that came with religious strings attached. Hosea, another eighth-century prophet, condemned this short-sighted practice with specific regard to Assyria and Egypt (Hos. 5:13; 7:11; 9:3). Closer to Micah's time, when Ahaz tried it, the manoeuvre failed miserably (2 Chr. 28:16–23). Their 'earnings' would be burned with fire, the passive intimating that YHWH himself would intervene where the people failed (Deut. 7:5, 25; 12:3).

Nineveh (Nah. 3:4–7) was characterized as a harlot. Closer to home, Isaiah declared that the known harlot, Tyre, would return to her prostitutes' fees and would prostitute herself with all the kingdoms. Nevertheless, those 'fees' would not be hoarded away but would be given to YHWH (Isa. 23:15–18). That rather odd description connects with a further complication in this context. What she had gathered from the harlot's hire, 'they will return to the harlot's hire' (3 masc. pl. yiq. form). It seems that the artefacts and objects brought to the temple from afar specifically to purchase alliances and favour from the gods would be called out for what they were – payment for political favours in the guise of sexual services dressed up as religious entreaties. These would be burned, which would possibly melt them down so that they would return, as coinage, to the place from whence they came. It could have become an endless cycle (Hoyt 2019: 595). Fees from prostitution were forbidden to be given as gifts to the temple in Jerusalem (Deut. 23:18–19[17–18]), but perhaps the point was that these votive offerings brought to the high places in Samaria would be carried back to high places in Assyria by the triumphant Assyrian army. Hosea references Assyria's triumphant capture of the calf-idol of the northern kingdom (Hos. 10:5–6).

Explanation

Vv. 2–7 sweep from theophany through apocalyptic destruction to prophetic condemnation of idolatry. The 'high places' in v. 5 are historical locations, in contrast to the mythic allusions in v. 3, but the one interacts with the other. The ridges on which YHWH tramples are the familiar high places of Israel's worship. There is an additional parallel as fire both melts the mountains (v. 4) and destroys the images (v. 7).

YHWH's judgment would start with his covenant people. Micah's word is addressed to 'Jacob'. No doubt Judeans were assured about the sins of the north but were shocked at the same accusations directed at them. Nevertheless, Judah had their share of high places, starting with Solomon's constructions to accommodate his foreign wives (1 Kgs 11:7–8; see also 2 Kgs 15:4, 35). Among Hezekiah's reforms was the removal of high places (2 Kgs 18:4).

Samaria in the heyday of the Omri dynasty had palatial structures. The foundation stones that remain indicate elegant and sophisticated construction. Nevertheless, they would be destroyed and plants would grow in the soil where the foundation stones had lain. There are parallels between Isa. 28:1–4 and Mic. 1:3. Set at the head of a fertile valley, that pride of Ephraim would be hurled down and trampled underfoot. How fleeting in the long view are all the structures of human hands! While Sargon II did not raze the capital buildings (Rainey and Notley 2006: 234–235), the northern kingdom would no longer be a power broker. The Assyrian deportation and resettlement policies would undermine the identity of the northern kingdom. Josephus refers to the later destruction of Samaria by John Hyrcanus in 107 BC (*Ant.* 13.10.3). Herod later rebuilt the city and named it Sebaste (Rainey and Notley 2006: 345–346).

What a vision this is! Just as Micah prophetically sees mountains melting at YHWH's approach, he likewise sees the grand buildings of the capital sliding into the valleys and replaced by naked ruins, a metaphor for the utter loss of political power and vulnerable exposure. Time-lapse graphics in futuristic films may create the same kinds of effects, albeit faint in comparison.

Right from the start, Israel was to rid the land of the proliferation of Canaanite objects and images that would draw the people into idolatrous practices (Deut. 7:5). The verbs in Deuteronomy are different, but the objective was the same – removing temptations. The emphasis on prostitution may point to the Canaanite backdrop of Baal's supposed power over rain, fertility, healing and rising from the dead. To entice Baal to provide all these things, worshippers brought gifts to the shrines. The connection between the people's prostituting themselves to Baal and the image of the adulterous wife was dramatically lived out by Hosea. The covenant dispute of Hos. 4 is shot through with references to harlotry and prostitution. Israel's idols and carved images will be destined for destruction.

Reflecting the cultural degradation more than a century later, Ezek. 16 practically vibrates with the repeated emphases on prostitution, from the wanton use of gifts for harlotry (vv. 15–19) to the excessive and insatiable appetite lavished on Assyrians (v. 28) to utter mortification and nakedness (vv. 33–39). In the last section, YHWH declares that he will gather against her all those who have been her lovers (v. 37).

Lest we relegate these sobering matters to the shelves of ancient history, it is imperative to pause long enough to realize that the equivalent of 'high places', useless images and earnings from questionable means are all too evident in the fabric of our daily lives. Exploitation of sexuality continues unabated from the first millennium BC, and idols of all sorts reflect the insidious penetration of unbiblical world views into our lives. Where is our confidence lodged? What political party is presumed to 'save' us? What kind of rivals to the Master of the universe do we cosy up to? Whom do we fear? What are the secular temples that control our desires and fears? Does justice in the US Supreme Court carry more weight? How will the measure-for-measure principle so evident in Micah's words reverberate into the twenty-first-century Western church?

MICAH 1:8–9

Translation

1:8Over this I will wail and howl; I will walk stripped and naked; I will make wailing like the jackals and mourning as the daughters of the ostrich.

9For her wound is incurable; it has come to Judah. He has assaulted the gate of my people, to Jerusalem.

Notes on the text

With specific regard to 1:8–16, Schwantes (1964: 38) suggests that the text was seriously damaged and a portion of the right-hand side of the column was lost, necessitating significant reconstruction. Waltke (2007: 62–64) presents four guiding principles to address this challenging text, three of which have to do with maintaining the reading of the MT. The fourth eschews the tendency to find a pun in every verset.

1:8. 'Concerning this' (*al zō't*) starts Micah's description of intense mourning. It is used eighteen times in the HB. Of those, it commences a clause only five times. The first three verb forms in succession are coh., expressing resoluteness (GKC §48e; *IBHS* §34.5.1).

The root of *'êlîlâh* (hiph.) is *yll*, meaning to 'howl'. Like its English counterpart, 'ululate', it is onomatopoeic. Wailing is the best way to understand the noun and verb forms of *spd*. Some have suggested modifying the third verb, *'êlĕkâ* in MT, to either hiph. or pi., reading it as an intensive expression indicating continual going back and forth (Job 24:10; 30:28), accompanied by the deeply unnerving sounds. Some MSS omit the yod. The MT spelling is unique, perhaps to make it more akin to the form of the immediately preceding verb (Andersen and Freedman 2000: 193).

The LXX reads the verbs in v. 8 as 3 fem. sg., all referring to Samaria.

For the word translated 'stripped', the K is *šîlāl*, while the Q is *šôlāl*. Ascertaining the meaning of the word is difficult, as it is used only here and in Job 12:17, 19, where counsellors and priests are led away in this condition. BDB (1021) suggests the root *šll* means to 'draw out'. The *DCH* (8:305) offers three options: 'barefoot', '[led in] fetters' or 'mad'. The interpretation of 'chains' is echoed in the Tg (Cathcart and Gordon 1989: 114). The parallel adj. *ʿārôm* means to be exposed or bare. Gordis (1937: 183, n. 273) suggests that the K is a rare *šapʿel* form of *yll* ('to wail') and carries the sense of loud mourning through every clause of the verse. Just as the root *spd* is repeated, so also is *yll*.

For *kattannîm*, the LXX has 'dragons'.

9. The fem. sg. qal pass. ptc. *ʾănūšâ* ('incurable') is used adjectivally.

makkôtêhā, a pl. noun with the fem. sg. suff., may also be revocalized to read *makkat yāh*, a wound inflicted by YHWH. The emendation clears up a number of the gender challenges of the clause, maintaining the fem. sg. adj., *ʾănûšâ* and verb, *bāʾâ*, and explaining the shift to masc. for the last verb. YHWH is thus the divine agent inflicting the incurable wound (Waltke 2007: 67).

Gender and number shift to masc. sg. with the verb 'assault' (*nāgaʿ*) in the second line.

Form and structure

ʿal zōʾt is a hinge – another 'Janus verse' (Ben Zvi 2000: 33) – between what has preceded (v. 5) and the new literary form that follows. The repeated sound of the coh. ending *-ah* is part of the assonance conveying dismay and horror. Two clauses, each introduced by *kî*, articulate why the lament is so extreme. The threefold repetition of *ʿad* – 'to Judah . . . to the gate of my people . . . to Jerusalem' – is emphatic and ominous. The uncertainty increases as the identity of the approaching subject shifts from fem. sg. to masc. sg.

Comment

1:8. Three of the eighteen uses of *ʿal zōʾt* (Jer. 4:8, 28; Mic. 1:8) follow prophecies of judgment that prompt lament (Hoyt 2019: 601–602). Here, the forthcoming consequences for the towns in the Shephelah of Judah are hinged to the immediately prior judgments against Samaria, the crimes centring around idolatry.

What a spectacle! The normal mourning procedure involved removing ordinary clothing, donning sackcloth and sitting or lying in ashes (Esth. 4:1, 3; Jon. 3:6). The appearance of mourners included torn clothes (cf. Job 2:12; Joel 2:12–13). Loosening or removing the ritual sackcloth seems to be a more extreme measure. Micah engages in radical audible and visible mourning.

YHWH commands Isaiah to remove his sackcloth and sandals, walking *ʿārôm* ('naked') and *yāḥēp* ('barefoot') for three years (Isa. 20:2–4), specifically to signify the forthcoming captivity and exile of Egypt and Cush. That description does not necessarily imply that Micah walks barefoot as well: the word here is different. If the Q reading is followed, 'stripped' suggests war captives, and the possible meaning of 'led away in fetters' adds to this interpretation. Going naked may be a symbolic portent that the captives of Jerusalem will leave naked and shackled (see Mic. 1:11, 16) just as the captives of Egypt and exiles of Cush (Isa. 20:4) and just as humiliated warriors flee in defeat (Amos 2:16; see again Job 12:17, 19).

The identity of the creatures seems already to have been ambiguous to early translators. The LXX reading ('dragons') connected the word with *tannin* – a sea serpent of some sort (Gen. 1:21; Ps. 74:13; Isa. 27:1; Jer. 51:34) rather than *tan*, meaning the 'jackal'. There is some discussion as to whether the *bat-ya'ănâ* was indeed an ostrich. Some characteristics make it sound more like an owl, among them the fact that the ostrich does not wail. Instead, it booms. See Driver 1955: 12–13.

The accompanying noises are inhuman and eerie, sounding like night creatures of the wilderness. Jackals inhabit desolate areas and howl at night. The figure is particularly haunting in Isaiah's description of judgment against Edom (Isa. 34:8–14). As Edom lies wasted, thorns and thistles will overtake it along with wild birds and animals, among them jackals and wilderness birds (*bat-ya'ănâ*). Job uses the pair of creatures to describe his isolation (Job 30:29). The desolation and ruin of Babylon's pomp and splendour include wild creatures howling amid houses and palaces. Among them are jackals and *bĕnôt-ya'ănâ* (Isa. 13:19–22; see also Jer. 50:39–40). Nevertheless, the pair is also present as YHWH makes a way in the wilderness (Isa. 43:20). According to Lev. 11:16 and Deut. 14:15, the *bat hayya'ănâ* is an unclean bird.

9. The position in the sentence of 'incurable' emphasizes the deplorable state of 'her wounds', but the referent of 'her' and subject of the following fem. verb, *bā'â*, are uncertain. It may be a reference to Samaria, certainly severely wounded in the last decades of the eighth century. *bā'â* may be read as a prophetic future fem. because disaster as an abstract concept is the implied subject (Andersen and Freedman 2000: 197).

The severe implications of 'incurable' may be inferred from its use in 2 Sam. 12:15, where it describes the state of David and Bathsheba's first son after YHWH struck the child a mortal blow. The same combination of 'incurable wounds' appears in Jer. 15:18 as that prophet bemoans his miserable state. See also Isa. 17:11; Jer. 17:9, 16.

The verb *nāga'* ('assault') is forceful, carrying military connotations and implying that a blow is about to be struck (cf. Job 1:9). The same sequence 'came and struck' appears as well in Job 4:5. There are several interpretive options at this point. One approach has understood this as Sennacherib's threatening Jerusalem in 701 BC. The Assyrians, however, did not take the city at that point (2 Kgs 18:17 – 19:37). Furthermore, Isaiah's vivid description of the Daughter of Zion (1:5–9) leaves no doubt that Jerusalem was already seriously wounded, afflicted and damaged prior to the

Assyrian arrival. Another backdrop for Micah's description may be 2 Chr. 28 and the tangle of unsettling events during the reign of Ahaz. A third option raises the possibility that this passage does not specifically indicate a military attack. The city gate was the locus of judicial proceedings. Perhaps this is a metaphor for the complete internal rottenness and corruption that would bring inevitable destruction, given their disobedience.

Explanation

The prophet's voice is inextricably merged with that of YHWH throughout. The speaker repeatedly identifies the people as 'my people', indicating that both YHWH and YHWH's prophet lament in profoundly emotional and anguished compassion over the condemnation that is forthcoming. The disaster is judgment, but it is pronounced in sorrow: grief is the only possible response to judgment. YHWH is warning that he will do to Jerusalem and her idols what he has already done to Samaria (cf. Isa. 10:10–11; Hos. 8:4–6).

There are no subdued laments in this context. The process is *loud* and no doubt unnerving in the extreme. Comparison with animals of the night and their howling is designed to send shivers. This is the stuff of liminal and numinous spheres. Although howling and wailing are not part of Eliphaz's hair-raising description of a night-time encounter, the same trembling and dread are front and centre in his emotional response (Job 4:12–16).

Uncovering nakedness frequently carries suggestions of abhorrent sexual impropriety (Gen. 9:20–23; Lev. 18), but that does not apply in Micah's case. His 'nakedness' is symbolic: not being properly covered was unseemly (Exod. 20:26). The importance of maintaining covering even extended to hair. Shaving patches of the head signalled extreme lament and distress (Jer. 7:29; Ezek. 27:30–32; Mic. 1:16).

MICAH 1:10–16

Translation

1:10 In Gath, do not announce it; certainly do not weep. In Beth le-Ophrah, roll yourself in dust.

11 Cross over for yourself, O you who live in Shaphir, to shameful nakedness. The one who lives in Za'anan will not go out. The lament of Bet Ezel: he will take from you his standing ground.

12 For the one who lives in Maroth waits anxiously for good; for evil has come down from YHWH to the gate of Jerusalem.

[13]Bind the chariot to the horse, O you who live in Lachish. She was the first of the sin of the Daughter of Zion, for in her were found the transgressions of Israel.

[14]Therefore, you will give parting gifts to Moresheth Gath; the houses of Achzib to deception, for the kings of Israel.

[15]Until I bring to you the one who possesses, O you who live in Mareshah; let him come to Adullam, the glory of Israel.

[16]Make baldness and shave for your delicate children; make your baldness broad like a vulture, for they will go from you into exile.

Notes on the text

BHS notes that the text is corrupt from 10 to 15 (16a); all verses are 'mutilated'. While the profusion of significant early variants and textual emendations would seem to support that assessment, it may be premature. See the 'Introduction' for further observations regarding the rhetorical purposes embedded in inelegant – sometimes nearly incoherent – discourse. A number of the emendations presume a specific lament metre underlying the pericope but that is not warranted. 'The quest for poetic regularity has yielded a cleaner text, but only through heroic emendation, and the results express the individual scholar's expectations' (Andersen and Freedman 2000: 203). Only the major variants and emendations are noted below.

1:10. Gath somewhat resembles the Hebr. for 'tell' or 'announce': *bĕgat ʾal-taggîdû*. The first two letters of the verb (t and g) reverse those in the place name – Gat. Nevertheless, it already puzzled the translators of the early versions. In place of 'tell it not [in Gath]' the LXX reads 'do not exalt yourselves', possibly reflecting a textual variant since the Hebr. consonants underlying *taggîdû* may shift to *tagdîlû* or vice versa. The Syriac has 'do not rejoice', presuming an underlying *tāgîlû*.

The renditions of *bākô lōʾ-tibkeh* in a range of Greek MSS are varied; most of them attempt a pun based on a name. 'In Acco' is the most common substitute for the inf. abs.

The Syr and Tg render *bebêt leʿaprâ* without the lamed; they also have pl. 'houses'. The LXX seems to have understood *ʿprh* as *ḥprh*, meaning 'derision' (Waltke 2007: 72).

The Q is *hitpallāšî*, an impv.; the K is *hitpallāšity*, 'I rolled myself'. The LXX (and the equivalent in Syr) has *katapasasthe*, which may mean to sprinkle oneself with 'earth'. Aquila has 'roll oneself'.

11. In the first line, the number and gender shift. The impv. is fem. sg., fitting with *yôšebet* ('the one who lives'). In between, however, we find *lākem*, masc. pl. ('to/for you'). Attached in some way to that initial audience who dwell in Shaphir are 'nakedness' and 'shame'; the major sentence break (***athnach***) comes at this point. These two words are not linked in a construct relationship, and the order is unusual. 'Shame of nakedness' would be a standard way of expressing this humiliated state. One more shift away from the expected presentation is *ʿeryâ* instead of *ʿerwâ*, the usual word for nakedness. Both the LXX and the Tg for the verse depart significantly from the MT. The LXX deletes any sense related to *bōšet* ('shame'). The Tg elaborates:

> Make lamentation for yourselves bitterly over the slaughtered of your warriors. O Beth-zula, as for your desirable houses that you acquired by violence joining one to the side of the other, on this account the best of your land shall be taken away from you. (Cathcart and Gordon 1989: 114)

The impv. ('cross over' or 'pass by') is continued by the past tense – the one dwelling in Za'anan 'has not gone out'. The verse closes with an undefined subject who 'will take' or 'would have taken'.

The place name Shaphir seems to be related to an Aramaic root meaning 'to be pleasant' or 'beautiful' (Waltke 2007: 74).

Declaring that the inhabitant of Zaanan did not come out is a wordplay. The 'Z' in the English place name is the same Hebr. letter (ṣade) as the middle letter of *yāṣʾâ* ('she went out'). 'Going out' may (or may not) be connected to the name *bêt hāʾēṣel*. The subst. *ʾēṣel* indicates proximity or nearness, even though a denominative verb form means to 'withdraw' (BDB 69; *DCH* 1:363; Waltke 2007: 76–77). *BHS* notes suggest (without textual support) deleting and/or modifying the lines beginning with *mispad* and *yikkaḥ*, perhaps due to the absence of obvious wordplays in either of these lines. *ʿemdâ* is a **hapax**; it may mean 'standing ground' or some entity that stands.

12. The LXX reads *ḥālâ* as 'Who has begun?' based on the root *ḥll*. The Syr and Vg derive it from *ḥlh*, 'to be weak or sick'. Tg seems to understand the root as *yḥl* ('to wait') (Cathcart and Gordon 1989: 114). Roots with ḥeth and lamed are challenging; the best options here may be 'wait' (Andersen and Freedman 2000: 226; BDB 297).

yārad . . . lĕ- is unusual, but see Judg. 5:11, where it also refers to coming to the gates, pl. in that context. The sg. 'gate' of Jerusalem echoes v. 9. The LXX, Syr and Tg read 'gates' instead of the sg.

13. The command to 'harness' (*rĕtôm*) is a **hapax**; the LXX reads 'noise'. The word for 'steed' (*rekeš*) appears together with *sûs* in conjunction with the fighting forces of Solomon (1 Kgs 5:8[4:28]), which were the most fleet-footed (Esth. 8:10, 14). *lārekeš* ('to the steed') sounds like Lachish; 'ch' in the place name is the name letter as '*k*'. Micah continues the network of sound patterns. There is no particle representing the direct object, even though 'chariot' has a definite article.

While the verse starts with a masc. sg. impv., the subject is fem. sg. (*yôšebet*). The following fem. sg. pron. (*hîʾ*) may represent literary distancing, but it does not last long. Those sins were found 'in you' (*bāk*).

14. *šillûḥîm* may be identified as gifts or dowry (*DCH* 8:365). The city name mentioned is Moresheth-Gath. That sounds a bit like *meʾōrāśâ*, meaning one who has been 'betrothed' (see Deut. 22:23).

In place of Achzib, the LXX reads 'worthless houses', followed by 'became worthless'. The Tg embellishes the difficult Hebr.: 'The houses of Achzib *shall be delivered to the nations because of the sins that* the kings of Israel *committed by worshipping idols in them*' (Cathcart and Gordon 1989: 115; italics original).

15. *hayyôrēš* ('the one who takes possession') could be the subject except for the fact that the adjacent verb seems to be first person. This first verb, *ʾābî*, appears as *ʾābîʾ* in some MSS. For the shortened hiph. form of *bôʾ*, see also 2 Sam. 5:2; 1 Kgs 21:21; Jer. 19:15; 39:16. In each of those cases, the following word starts with 'aleph, so the two words together reflect *scripta continua*, with the one letter serving both words (GKC 3g [note]). The LXX reads 1 sg. for *ʾābî* (*agagō soi*), 'I will bring'. *BHS* suggests shifting to 3 masc. sg., 'the one who takes possession [by force] will come against you (*lāk*), O inhabitant of Maresha'. This makes the parallels between the first and second lines stronger, both employing the verb *yābôʾ*.

The Syr has the equivalent of *ʿad-ʿôlām* ('for ever') instead of *ʿad-ʿădullām* ('to Adullam') perhaps because the place name does not connect as well with the concept of 'glory of Israel'.

16. The ending on *taʿănûgayik* functions as 'an abstract subjective genitive denoting a verbal action affecting the construct' (*IBHS* §9.5.2). The connotations of the root include 'pleasure, merriment and joy'; *taʿănûg* means 'luxury'. See Prov. 19:10.

Form and structure

These verses present an intentional inventory of place names, but the purpose and effect are not clear. Many scholars propose radical emendations to preserve some sort of poetic metre. The MT is 'all but incomprehensible as it stands' (Andersen and Freedman 2000: 205), but that is part of the purpose. No matter the historical context, this is real-time lament over unspeakable calamity. The very messiness of the language fits the situation and expresses in the most compelling way not only Micah's horror but that of YHWH himself. These are outbursts of powerful grief, outrage and near hysteria. The message is refracted through disordered speech that sounds like turbulent gut-wrenching weeping. 'Irregularities' in the text mirror national confusion and instabilities; the grammar of the text as it stands is fragmentary. Micah might have deliberately distorted some place names to make them fit with a wordplay. These factors together suggest caution before engaging in wholesale emendations of the text (Hoffman 2008: 89–91).

Jerusalem and Daughter of Zion are at the centre (vv. 12 and 13) of this list with lament and judgment on both sides. Vv. 10–12 start with a lament and move towards the gate of Jerusalem; vv. 13–15 connect with the Daughter of Zion, work their way through additional threatened towns and the whole closes with a return call to mourning. It may be that Micah employs local taunts or gibes that represented local rivalries but were long since forgotten. Micah selects names that lend themselves to the semantic layering. Their usage would have been even more evident in the time of turmoil (Hillers 1984: 25–28).

Comment

See the 'Introduction' on the identity of the cities and possible historical contexts. The steady drumbeat of place names and corresponding dire effects are ominous. Some of the declarations involve puns, and some engage in more expansive phonological parallelism. There is a fine line between **assonance** and **paranomasia**. Of all thirteen names, five are associated with words of similar sound – Gath, Beth le-Ophrah, Za'anan, Achzib and Maresha. The word *yôšebet* appears five times in these verses, persistently focusing attention on the collective inhabitants of Shaphir, Za'anan, Maroth, Lachish and Maresha.

1:10. The beginning of each line stresses location – 'in Gath' and 'in Beth LeOphrah'. As each following clause expands these location indications, two patterns clash. In the first line, two instances of *ʾal* (the particle of negation) may suggest that both clauses admonish the audience not to speak or weep in each location. Thus, *bākô* is tweaked to read 'in Acco'. At the same time, because the second line that starts with 'in Beth LeOphrah' ('in the house of dust') develops something about rolling in dust, perhaps the main point of the first part is an emphatic 'don't tell' and 'don't weep' with no regard for location. That reads *bākô* as an inf. abs. with following verb (see GKC §113v on the inf. abs. separated by negation from the finite verb).

'Do not announce [it] in Gath' was not a novel introduction to this oracle. Just about three centuries earlier, David lamented the deaths of Saul and Jonathan on Mount Gilboa (1 Sam. 31 – 2 Sam. 1). 'O, how the mighty have fallen', he cried, and then warned against giving the Philistine inhabitants of the cities of Gath and Ashkelon cause for rejoicing: 'Tell it not in Gath!' (2 Sam. 1:19–20). The centuries-long hostility between Judah and the Philistine cities would be marked by continuing vigilance against giving to the enemy any cause for gloating. Just prior to Micah's day, the borders of Judah again extended west to include Gath (2 Chr. 26:6). At the time of Sargon, Gath was a Judahite city (Zukerman and Shai 2006–7: 742). Nevertheless, it was doubtless on the line of attack when the Philistines raided those western towns during the unstable reign of Ahaz

(2 Chr. 28:16–18). 'Tell it not in Gath' had a contemporary and dread-filled context.

Micah draws on this epic lament line and infuses it with new meaning: in this city, do not speak of a monumental disaster over which Philistines, perhaps newly lodged back in Gath, can again gloat. David's lament moves to the next formidable Philistine city, Ashkelon, but that does not fit Micah's context. David also urges the daughters of Israel to weep over Saul (2 Sam. 1:24); Micah's next line is a ban on weeping; he builds a rhetorical word texture with modified pertinent locations.

bākô could be read as a compressed rendition of 'in Acco'. That would put this member of the city list well outside Judah as Acco was on the Mediterranean coast north of Mount Carmel. It is more likely that it is an emphatic admonition *against* weeping, an irony that starts this lament of major proportions. David's lament was for the demise of the house of Saul; this is a much more catastrophic loss. Isaiah uses the same idiom (*bākô lōʾ-tibkeh*), admonishing the one living in Jerusalem not to weep (30:19). That, however, is in the face of hopeful developments. This is sheer disaster. Perhaps in extreme circumstances, numb silence is the only possible response, at least momentarily. Nevertheless, the author of Lamentations urges his audience to weep (*bākô tibkeh*) and with good reason (Lam. 1:2).

The next exhortation from Micah reflects another visceral response to tragedy – doing something with dust. But where and what? The location, Beth le-Ophrah, is not known and appears only here. See Suriano 2010: 434–436 for an exposition of the suggested reconstructions and possible identifications. The first issue is what to do with the lamed before Ophrah. The name may be a cobbling together from Bethlehem Ephrathah, which appears in 5:1[2]. That, however, is just south of Jerusalem and far afield from the Shephelah. Toponyms with *ʿpr* are typically rendered as Ophrah (e.g. Josh. 18:23). The physical nature of *ʿāpār* ('dust') may relate to the soil quality of the area (Aharoni 1979: 109; see also Andersen and Freedman 2000: 218). In this regard, Suriano (2010: 441) suggests that perhaps the *lĕ* signals a region as opposed to a specific place name – in other words, a dusty region. Although much later, Josephus (*J. W.* 4.8.1) mentions a Bethletepha, which preserved the lamed in between *bêt* and the next definitive word. The same linguistic/grammatic phenomenon is documented elsewhere. The place noted by Josephus was also in the lowlands (Suriano 2010: 439–440).

Regarding the 'dust' connection, we read in Jer. 6:26 that the 'daughter of my people' was commanded to put on sackcloth and *hitpallĕšî bāʿēper* (do something in or with 'ashes'). It is not entirely clear that the verb means 'roll'. In addition to this context, it appears only in one additional passage in Jeremiah (25:34) that does not contribute substantially to the discussion, and in Ezekiel (27:30): 'they will put dust on their heads and *hitpallāšû* with ashes'. Add to those data the fact that when Job's acquaintances arrived to be with him, they wept, tore their garments and tossed dust on to their heads heavenward (Job 2:12). Perhaps this was a sober ritual enacting the implications of death as returning to dust by symbolically covering oneself with it.

Thinking strictly geographically, it may be that just as the verse commences with a reference to a former Philistine city (Gath), it closes with a pun on *pelešet*, the blanket term for Philistia (Levin 2018: 449).

11. The expression 'naked, shamed' should be read with the preceding phrase, given the sentence division under *bōšet*. The degradation of the entire situation is too unseemly for sensitive eyes to behold. It may refer to a humiliating display, forcing broken people to parade naked. Images of such abuse are tragically too familiar from carefully documented travesties in mid-twentieth-century Eastern Europe and elsewhere. Perhaps the residents of Za'anan refused to come out and engage the forthcoming battle because of fear, or perhaps they came out unwillingly as captives. That is a contrast to the first part of the verse about Shaphir, whose departees would encounter a public and humiliating scene. The contrast could not be starker: the shame of nakedness will be their lot. Perhaps that is the reason for the admonition to 'pass by'.

The final two lines of v. 11 shift the balance, weighting the second part of the verse with an added two lines. The 'mourning' of v. 8 is repeated here. 'The mourning of *bêt hāʾēṣel*' seems to stand by itself as opposed to the previous descriptions of movement. One reading may be '[there is] mourning in the house next door', followed by a long pause: it is an ellipsis. Nothing further can be said. Or perhaps the 'house' that is nearby has some connection with the ambiguous 'his [or its] standing' (*emdâ*). Beth-ha-ezel does seem to be viewed as a contrast to Za'anan; the latter did not come, perhaps because of fear. The mourners in Beth-ha-ezel, however, have something taken from them.

Who will take what? While the subject may be the leader of an enemy force who will remove something that is 'standing' (*emdātô*), there are additional possibilities. The subject may be YHWH, who will remove *his* standing, a possible allusion to protection, perhaps an adumbration of some catastrophe for the temple. It may refer to an unidentified owner of 'the house' who is rescuing what he perceives to be a significant article (*emdātô*). Na'aman (1998: 516–527) suggests it may be related to an Assyrian word meaning 'tax', a pun intimating that they would no longer have protection (shade) from the Assyrian overlords. 'From you' (*mikkem*) is a bookend with *lākem* at the outset of the verse. Just who 'you' (pl.) refers to is not clear. Perhaps the anonymous 'you' are not able to stand because of shame, weakness and humiliation.

12. Each line in this verse starts with *kî*, providing explanations for the catastrophes. The successive lines contrast 'good' (*ṭôb*) with 'evil' (*raʿ*). The 3 fem. sg. qal verb is possibly from *ḥûl*, meaning 'to writhe'. See Judg. 3:25 where *ḥālâ* means 'wait'. Instead of implying waiting in hope, however, anxious writhing in inexpressible fear is part of this picture. *yôšebet* reappears, but the associated place name (Maroth) contrasts with the pleasantness of Shaphir. *maroth* sounds like *mārâ*, meaning 'bitter', contrasting their own bitter estate and the apparently unattainable good for which they long. Even though they wait for good, disaster (evil) will come down from YHWH.

13. In an irony of hermeneutics, because v. 13 is relatively clear, some scholars have declared that it has been redacted. The follow-up tongue-in-cheek observation, however, is that the redactors still left significant ambiguities (Andersen and Freedman 2000: 226). Generally, horses are harnessed to chariots, not the other way around. Both 'horse' and 'chariot' are collectives. Harnessing war chariots to the fastest horses indicates calling up the military forces, but it may also suggest hasty preparations for a swift evacuation.

The centrepiece is the description of the prominent involvement of Lachish in sin and transgressions related to the Daughter of Zion and Israel. Just what that 'first of sin' may be is not clear. It is also a challenge to determine why this sin of Lachish necessitated harnessing first-class steeds with chariots in preparation for some sort of military endeavour. V. 5 regarding Samaria shares terminology with this verse highlighting the Daughter of Zion. The twin terms of v. 5 (transgression and sins) are mirrored in reverse here (sin and transgressions). They 'were found' (*nimṣĕʾû*), intimating that it was YHWH who found them, and they were found in Lachish. It may be that reliance on military power instead of on YHWH was the crux of the transgression (Goldingay 2021: 427). See below under 'Explanation' for possible further elucidation from archaeological investigations at Lachish.

14. Following the connecting 'therefore', the verb shifts back to 2 fem. sg., 'you will give'. That serves the rest of the verse with its complicated semantic and structural features. The *šillûḥîm* may be identified as gifts or dowry (see 'Notes on the text'). *šillûḥîm* shows up two additional times in the HB; it is always pl. and could be interpreted as having something to do with marriage arrangements. The first instance is Exod. 18:2 (Jethro took Zipporah after 'her being sent' by Moses); the other is 1 Kgs 9:16, the record that Pharaoh captured Gezer, burned it, killed its inhabitants and then gave it, 'a parting gift', to his daughter. Perhaps this alludes to a conqueror taking away the city's inhabitants into exile just as a bridegroom takes away his bride and her dowry. Similarly, it may be the loss to invading enemies of the inheritance YHWH gave to his people (Jenson 2008: 116). A challenge, however, is that it is the father who gives a 'dowry', but the verb is fem.

Why did the transgressions of Israel linking Lachish and the Daughter of Zion (v. 13) prompt the kinds of consequences introduced by 'therefore'? The consequences included the obligation to give 'sent things' or 'parting gifts'. Who was obligated to give those gifts? The subject is feminine: Was it Jerusalem, the Daughter of Zion? The most significant implication may be that in each of the other biblical instances, there is a separation. Perhaps this suggests giving a parting gift because they are about to lose Moresheth-Gath (BDB 1019; *DCH* 8:365). It may be thought of as paying tribute (Waltke 2007: 82); that would explain the use of *ʿal*, 'against' (the loss of) Moresheth-Gath. A related possibility suggests it refers to a form of recompense, especially since the 'houses' of a place called Achzib seem to be part of the picture. Biblical mentions of an Achzib or something like it include Gen. 38:5 (the birthplace of Shelah); Josh. 15:44 (one of nine towns in the Shephelah district that also included Maresha); and Kozebah (1 Chr. 4:22, delineating descendants of Judah). Demsky (1966: 211–215) has suggested, comparing it with 1 Chr. 4:21–23, that the Hebr. 'houses of' may refer to factories worked by clans, all employed by the kings. This does not clarify the matter. In Micah's lament, the one who deceives is not identified, perhaps because he is a known quantity to Micah and his audience. 'Giving houses of Achzib' could be tribute payment or blackmail. In any case, if the initial verb governs this clause, these are given to 'kings of Israel' on account of Moresheth-Gath.

Achzib is related to the word for *deception*. The adj. *ʾakzāb* is used only here and in Jer. 15:18, where the waters of a stream are not trustworthy. Goldingay (2021: 420) opts for a less negative connotation of the word, translating it as 'disappointing', but that seems to reduce the force of the declaration. The verb appears in Isa. 58:11, describing sources of water that do not deceive (disappoint).

Because of the ambiguous syntax, however, 'the houses of Achzib' may not be a second object of 'you will give', with the implication that they are given to 'kings of Israel'. Instead, it may stand as a separate syntactically incomplete thought: 'the houses of Achzib are a deceitful thing [*ʾakzāb*] to the kings of Israel'. But who are these 'kings of Israel' and why would they deem houses in a place called 'Achzib' untrustworthy? Constructing a hypothetical context, perhaps the kings do not think this city along with the others will hold out against attack from the south-west. Reading between the lines, it may be that the two parts of v. 14 describe obliquely the double financial whammy that the leadership in Israel would suffer. On the one hand, they would have to pay tribute against the loss of Moresheth-Gath; on the other, they would lose revenues from Achzib (Waltke 2007: 83).

From another perspective, 'house' could imply 'estate'. Pressing further, it might have included the exchange of villages in a treaty. If so, that would explain the involvement of 'kings of Israel'. This could be political territory ceded to kings of the still-existing north. Micah would be playing on a military connotation of *šillûḥîm*, and it would imply a time frame before the fall of Samaria in 722 (Andersen and Freedman 2000: 232–234). See also Mic. 2:1–5.

15. Both parts of this verse are introduced by *ʿd*, albeit with different vocalizations. It has an ominous tone, suggesting the 'forthcoming' (*ōd*) movement 'towards' (*ad*) the destination – Jerusalem – even though it is not named at the end of the 'list'. Mareshah and Moresheth-Gath are ties that bind, and here is the final occurrence of *yôšebet*. The One who is the 'Glory of Israel' is contrasted with the 'kings of Israel' at the end of v. 14. The sound connections between *ʿădullām* and *ʿad-ʿōlām* are very likely an intentional part of the message.

The same individual is the subject of the first and second clauses: the one who would take possession (i.e. the conqueror) would come also to Adullam. Both Mareshah and Adullam were among Rehoboam's fortified cities (2 Chr. 11:5–10). Khirbet esh-Sheikh Madhkûr has been identified as Adullam (Rainey and Notley 2006: 243). The town would not have been on the regular line of attack from Lachish to Jerusalem. Why mention it, especially since there is less of an immediately identified assonance connection? If, however, the expression 'the glory of Israel' stands in apposition to Adullam, it may be an allusion to the earlier epic history of the place, a deliberate echo of David's flight from Achish when he was on the run from Saul (1 Sam. 22:1; 2 Sam. 23:13–17). That was a dark time for David; this would be even gloomier for David's descendants. Gath and Adullam serve as bookends of Micah's lament. In the current crisis of Micah's time, those who had been defending Judah would now be retreating from their defensive posts. Perhaps they too would take refuge in the caves that are a part of the Shephelah 'landscape'.

Another interpretive option shifts the focus; this may be an ironic reference to the conqueror becoming the 'glory of Israel' as he absorbed it into his dominion. The syntax continues to be rugged in the extreme, reflecting the reality of lament.

16. Each impv. commands an action that is indicative of extreme mourning – shaving, making bald heads and marking a noticeable bald place. These are public signs of their bereavement and are addressed to the cities, represented throughout as fem. (*yôšebet*) with the centrepiece being Jerusalem/Daughter of Zion (vv. 12–13). Something – at first the horror is left unspoken – was going to happen to their tenderly loved children. After the third command, however, the disaster is exposed: the children will be carried into exile. According to Deut. 14:1, the children of Israel were not to make 'baldness' (*qorḥâ*) between their eyes for the dead. That might have been a specifically focused pagan ritual (Waltke 2007: 85). Baldness on every head and sackcloth on every waist were outward manifestations that beauty and honour had vanished in the face of disaster (Amos 8:10; see also Isa. 3:24; 22:12; Jer. 47:5; Ezek. 7:18; 27:30–31).

The children 'of your delight' may refer to a mother's tender love for her children. On the other hand, it may be a swipe at children reared in her luxurious context, commenting on the spoiled and unprepared nature of that generation, whether the women or the children. A similar forthcoming situation may underlie the rebuke in Amos 4:1–3, where the complacent women who made oppressing the poor and indigent a pastime would be led away in humiliation. The lamentation in Amos 8:10 is likened to that of mourning an only son and is accompanied by sackcloth and baldness on every head. The devastating and visible implications of shaving are evident as well in Isa. 7:20. YHWH would bring Assyria as a figurative razor, sweeping away hair from head to toe.

The *nešer*, also translated 'eagle', is more accurately a griffin vulture (Kiuchi, *NIDOTTE* 3:200–201). As in other contexts, the key feature here is the stark white head. On the symbolic level, vultures are associated with death as they feast on carrion.

Explanation

This is an extraordinary literary unit, marked by complicated literary and linguistic patterns as well as abrupt disruptions to those patterns. What lies behind it? What is the audience of Micah supposed to 'hear'? Would they be concerned with personal circumstances and a given historical turmoil that combine to launch this, or is the 'open nature' of the text signalling that something else is intended (Ben Zvi 2000: 35)? Does an audience removed by two-and-one-half millennia have sufficient data to explore the historical circumstances?

In terms of the deeply emotional and protracted outburst, it is arguably the case that the text is not necessarily corrupt as supposed. Ancient versions already struggled with 1:10–16 because it is a raw reflection of someone (the prophet and YHWH) overcome with grief at the horrifying scenes rapidly unfolding. The emotional trajectory rockets through loud weeping, mourners covering themselves with dust, refugees quailing in shame and fear, panic, attempts at appeasement and signals of humiliation and abasement. The linguistic representations of this include rapid changes in tenses, moving from second to third person and back, and alternating between masc. and fem., all possibly indicating bursts of direct address to different parties at the same time (Andersen and Freedman 2000: 239–240). These complexities are not resolved: they should not be. This is an amalgam of utter horror as resistance against an enemy gives way, and waves of destruction overwhelm the people. Emending the text to make it 'clear' is the last thing readers should do. Schwantes (1964: 454–461) addresses the lament against the backdrop of early twentieth-century criticism, demonstrating that many of the textual difficulties are not impossible. Through a different set of cultural lenses, the mockery flung at each city may be based on something fundamental about the location that also would be its fate (Ben Zvi 2000: 36).

The closing verses of Micah's lament (vv. 13–15) reflect a general movement northwards from Lachish to Adullam (Suriano 2010: 438). While students of Micah have generally viewed the geopolitical tumult accompanying Sennacherib's arrival on the scene in 701 BC as the context for 1:10–16, we have already entertained the possibility that this entire first chapter may reflect the impact of the tumultuous events for both Judah and Israel (the north) several decades earlier as it also looks ahead to the darkness on the horizon. See the 'Introduction'.

Shaw's reassessment (1993: 40–67) of the rhetorical purpose of this pericope points him in a direction quite apart from military and cultic threats to Judah. The disaster as refracted through the often-opaque language is not military from the outside, but a series of pointed references to what is happening to Judah as it loses the allegiance of these Shephelah towns. The towns are accused of political disloyalty and rebellion, one possible interpretation of *peša'*. The scenarios depicted may together allude to economic and political alliances that are fracturing for a whole complex of reasons, evidenced in the wide-ranging declarations. Because the text does not represent a direct threat to Jerusalem, this could be prior to Sennacherib's time. Perhaps the absence of any reference to the fall of Samaria means these words were uttered before 722 BC. Further, it appears that the outcomes for both Samaria and Jerusalem are intertwined. They may be due to unwise economic alliances: the 'harlots' wages' of Samaria are an allusion to those fundamental socio-religious-economic connections. Shaw sees the beginning of this dissolution already in the time of Jeroboam II when the north began to experience loss of territory near the end of his reign (Isa. 9:11[12]). See also 2 Kgs 15:37; already in Jotham's reign, Rezin and Pekah were harassing Judah.

Lament customarily involves weeping; here Micah forbids it. In the juxtaposition of each of Micah's admonitions, we encounter the reality of contradictory utterances when emotional turbulence reigns. 'Don't weep,' but 'take on the appearance of radical mourning' is the first example. These responses that cover the emotional gamut continue. Radical alterations of appearance would accompany many of those who were living through this trauma.

The images of nakedness and shame have overtones of the degradation and humiliation of women; that fits with the cities being represented as feminine. The two terms for 'bare' and 'naked' recur in Ezek. 16:7, 22, 39 and 23:29, two chapters that are tragic allegories of shameful women representing YHWH's people. These images carry multiple levels of emotional anguish, as horrifying in the twenty-first century as they were in the eighth century BC.

The importance of Lachish (Tel ed-Duweir) cannot be overemphasized. In the wider geopolitical developments, two of the major store and chariot cities established by Solomon, Megiddo and Hazor (1 Kgs 9:15–19), were gone once the north left the monarchy. Shoring up his defences, Rehoboam's ring of fortresses included Lachish (2 Chr. 11:5–12). It was the Shephelah site that stood as a bulwark against incursions from Egypt and later Syria and Assyria. Hence the huge fortifications; Lachish was a gate into the interior. What happened at Lachish had military implications for Judah; making that connection may help us understand the command to harness the steeds.

Lachish was also 'the beginning of sin for the Daughter of Zion'. How so? Among other sins, Judah was tempted to switch her allegiance from YHWH to Egypt, and Lachish represented that geopolitical shift. Of equal significance is possible evidence that idolatrous worship flourished in Lachish until the reforms of Hezekiah. In the large inner gate area of Lachish, archaeologists discovered what is tentatively identified as a two-room shrine that had been intentionally desecrated, possibly indicative of a reform movement (Ganor and Kreimerman 2019: 211–236). Prior to that reform, the gate might have been a hub of cultic activity.

It takes some care in reading to hear the elements of dread through the linguistic, geographical and cultural veils. Once those have been somewhat penetrated, this cumulative picture is ominous in the extreme; contemporary audiences will do well to pause in the face of it. When judgment is forthcoming, YHWH's prophet is overcome with inexpressible anguish. It reverberates as each location faces uncertain horror. What a far cry from our tendency to hit pause or turn off the screen entirely when we are too troubled by images of suffering! Complacency cannot be our response – ever.

MICAH 2:1–2

Translation

2:1 Woe to those who devise trouble and those who work evil on their beds! In the light of the morning, they perform it, because it is in the power of their hand.
2 And they covet fields, and they seize; houses, they take. They practice extortion against a man and his household, a man and his inheritance.

Notes on the text

2:1. The introductory exclamation *hôy* has traditionally be rendered as 'Woe!' Nevertheless, there is an increasing tendency to translate it as 'Alas!' because of the number of funerary contexts in which it appears. Clifford's study (1966: 458–464) of the fifty-three OT appearances of *hôy*, mostly in the prophetic corpus, suggests a development over time of the significance of the term. In the ninth and eighth century, it was associated with mourning. In his assessment, this was the original use, thus best translated by 'Alas!' By the late monarchy and post-exilic period, it is related to bitter pronouncements of doom. See *IBHS* §40.2.4a and *DCH* 2:503–504. BDB (222–223) indicates that *hôy* should be distinguished from 'Woe!' (*ʾôy*) and reads it as 'Alas!' based on the number of prophetic passages involving lament (*mispēd;* Jer. 22:18; 34:5; Isa. 1:4).

The two participles that start the verse are followed by a yiq. form (v. 1) and weqat. forms continuing into v. 2. They should not, however, be read as future to the prophet's time: these are abuses that have taken place.

The LXX reinterprets the idiom *kî yeš-lĕ ʾēl yādām* with a translation that reads in English, 'because they did not lift to God their hands'. Joined to *ʾēl*, *yād* indicates the capacity of someone to do what he intends. Cross (*TDOT* 1:260–261) calls it a 'frozen idiom', the origins of which are lost. The idiom appears here and in Gen. 31:29; Prov. 3:27; Deut. 28:32; Neh 5:5. The latter two are negative statements – 'you will not be able to'.

2. The waw conj. initiates each clause; each verb form is weqat. 3 masc. pl., describing the wholesale theft.

wĕʾîš is represented without the waw in the LXX, Tg and Vg.

Form and structure

'Devising trouble [*ʾāwen*]' and 'doing evil [*rāʿ*]' are parallel, emphasizing the wickedness of planning these nefarious activities even while they are supposed to be resting. The standard idioms are 'devising evil' (*rāʿ*) and 'doing trouble' (*ʾāwen*); this is the only place in the HB where they are opposite. The shift draws attention to the activities. The first part of v. 2 addresses the violent seizure of property; there are three verbs with two objects. In contrast, the second part has only one verb with four objects, all in the sphere of oppression of people. The syntax suggests something is awry.

Comment

2:1. While Micah's cry may be his own mournful introduction (Allen 1976: 286; Andersen and Freedman 2000: 262), it heralds a forthcoming declaration of judgment. The same emphasis appears in the expanded set of pronouncements against truly evil persons in Isa. 5:8–24 (see also Isa. 10:5; 17:12; 29:15; 30:1; Hab. 2:6, 12, 15, 19). That suggests 'Woe!' especially because the backstories in these passages are the ongoing disregard of covenant stipulations. Both connotations are juxtaposed in Amos 5:16–18. First, those who mourn in the streets cry out *hô, hô* (v. 16); the modified spelling suggests that outbursts of emotion are represented by a range of vowel sounds. V. 18, however, commences with *hôy* to those desiring the day of YHWH, and what follows echoes with themes of judgment. The warning continues into Amos 6:1. These eighth-century prophets used the term with its rich texture: both lament and horror at the prospect of deserved judgment are part of the outburst. The unifying factor is death; it is what prompts lament and is the terrible end of judgment.

The semantic range of *ʾāwen* includes trouble, misery and sorrow, along with wickedness. This suggests that the despicable plans hatched during the night-time are intended to cause deep personal suffering. Some scholars question whether the subsequent clause, 'doing evil on their beds', was initially part of Micah's woe. Willis (1967: 534–541) reviews the range of suggested emendations to address the 'apparent illogicalness' in the sequence of the first line. After all, what evil could they 'do' while still in bed? Willis summarizes the uses of the verbal root *pʿl* with direct objects that have to do with iniquity, injustice and violence and demonstrates that, of its twenty-four occurrences, all have to do with execution of evil acts. In several cases, the expression 'upon his bed' refers to dreaming. Willis further (1967: 537–548) suggests that Micah describes people so consumed with their evil plans that they even dream about them. The bottom line is this: the process of planning is seamless with the execution. It is an integral part of who they are and what they do in the morning.

While 'morning' in English implies a general time frame from sun up to noon, in biblical Hebr., *bōqer* is a much narrower window of time following sunrise (Gen. 29:25; Judg. 9:33; 2 Sam. 23:4; 1 Kgs 3:21; 2 Kgs 3:22; Ruth 3:14). Thus, the light of the morning was important: with it, the darkness of evil should dissipate. That, however, was not so in the case of these schemers. Their plans could now be implemented. The pron. suff. on *yaʿăśû* is 3 fem. sg.; the referent is likely the abstract concept of trouble or wickedness since *ʾāwen* is masc. sg. It also points forward to the fem. *rāʿâ* of v. 3. There is no escaping the potentially crushing power that these planners of trouble have.

2. The dominant verb is 'covet'. Coveting activates desire; all three of the verbs that follow in this verse are premeditated crimes. Seizure follows directly on coveting, suggesting an immediacy, foregoing all supposed 'due process' in the acquisition of traditional inherited lands (Num. 36:7–9; see also Lev. 25:13–23; Num. 27:1–11; 33:53–54). This condemnation echoes Exod. 20:17, the expanded declaration prohibiting all manifestations of greedy desire (see also Exod. 34:24; Prov. 6:25; 12:12). In the articulation of the Ten Words, the last commandment names wife and household, lands and other property assets; these are in the crosshairs of the insatiable oppressors Micah describes. They have forgotten that the land belongs to YHWH (Lev. 25:23).

gzl ('to steal') carries connotations of violent seizure and theft of property – patrimonial lands and houses – as well as people from poor families (*DCH* 2:339–340). Robbed of their fields, these vulnerable people will be reduced to slavery. *nāśāʾ* ('to lift up') does not have a direct object, but is presumed to be the houses the rich oppressors have coveted: they simply take them. It could also be figurative for taking an owner away from his land as the land is appropriated (Andersen and Freedman 2000: 269, 272).

Whereas coveting motivates the seizure and taking in the first part of the verse, the second line has only one verb, 'they oppress'. The victims of that oppression are across the board, from the *geber* ('strong man') and his household to each individual (*'îš*), whose inheritance should have been guaranteed by the inheritance laws. The latter may include poor persons for whom the inheritance would be a lifeline: their inherited land may be all they have. The description fits well with the agrarian milieu. There are echoes in Micah's words of Ahab's coveting the field of Naboth and obtaining it by means of false accusations, a scheme set up by Jezebel (1 Kgs 21). That scene has ominous echoes here; Ahab was sulking *on his bed* (1 Kgs 21:4) after Naboth refused his attempts to acquire Naboth's field (Wolff 1981: 9). Isaiah condemns the same ugly practice; the first of his 'Woes!' is against those who join field to field, and house to house (Isa. 5:8). It also echoes the words of Hosea against the princes of Judah who play fast and loose with boundaries (5:10). It has an all-too-familiar ring to it as 'the fine print' often undercuts presumed assurances.

Explanation

The subject has shifted abruptly from looming external threats in ch. 1 to the internal unravelling of Judah's social fabric. Micah's accusations are not veiled generalizations: abuses and perpetrators are named. There is no squirming away from pointed references to covetousness and injustice. In each generation, faithful prophetic voices are called to address culpable parties in order effectively to combat injustices. This initial discourse of lament and woe sets the stage for the forthcoming attack on the false prophets.

The opening description is sinister: in the ANE mindset, night was an ominous time when evil abounded. It is no wonder that God's people are admonished to meditate on what is *good* during those hours of the night; see Deut. 6:7; Ps. 1:2. As Micah presents it, that pattern is upended: these people are so consumed with evil, they 'meditate' on it even through the night hours to be prepared to execute appalling schemes once day dawns. This is intentional evil in the extreme: they devote all their waking *and* sleeping hours to it. 'Devising evil on his bed' occurs in Ps. 36:5[4] as part of the description of the person who has no fear of God. Micah challenges his audience (including us) to discipline our desires and particularly ride herd on those thoughts that swirl about in our nearly sleeping hours. His words may be a clarion call to reconsider how we prepare ourselves for sleep: perhaps introducing the focusing disciplines of prayer and hymns of thanksgiving would be a start:

> Abide with me,
> Fast falls the eventide;
> The darkness deepens;
> Lord, with me abide.

Help of the helpless,
Oh, abide with me.
(H. F. Lyte, 1847)

If *ʾēl* is an oblique allusion to 'God', then this may indicate that these powerful evil persons presume to stand up as rivals to God (Waltke 2007: 95). Put in wisdom terms, 'the one who oppresses a poor person shows contempt for his Maker' (Prov. 14:31a). The picture that emerges at this point should be a forceful prod towards filling our minds with humble pleas for forgiveness and gratitude to God as we close every day.

The principle of ***lex talionis*** recurs throughout Micah and is a sober reminder that while humans think they are scheming to gain an advantage, YHWH is effectively orchestrating matters so that they will experience measure-for-measure justice. To the attentive audience, that pattern precludes the tendency to dismiss circumstances as simply coincidental. YHWH's responses echo in unavoidably parallel ways the criminal and wicked ways of his errant people.

It may be that in the heyday of Uzziah's prosperous reign, landed classes were adding to their holdings. Nevertheless, the temptation to expand wealth and property is ubiquitous. In that context, property was also appropriated by sneakily moving boundary stones. The persons who do that are deemed thieves (Job 24:2) and deserving of God's wrath (Hos. 5:10). Reading between the lines, Micah's words may also reflect increasing hostility between land farmers and officialdom in Jerusalem. Because Micah lived in the countryside, perhaps he felt it more.

The same greed underlies all attempts in all times and all places to seize violently what rightfully belongs to someone else. Amos spoke fiercely against it (2:6–7; 5:11–12). A century after Micah, Jerusalem had reached the depths of its injustice and violence; Habakkuk could only cry out 'How long?' (Hab. 1:2–4). The apostle Paul did not mince words: greed is idolatry (Col. 3:5). Adding possession to possession does nothing to assure one's future. Coveting leads to the worst kind of death – shrivelling of the heart. It is imperative that we escape our culture's obsession with self-gratification, the primary manifestation of inbred covetousness. Pronouncing 'Woe!' against these destructive ways is liberating (Wolff 1981: 56).

MICAH 2:3–5

Translation

2:3 Therefore thus says YHWH: I am now devising evil against this family, from which you will not be able to remove your necks; you will not walk proudly, for it will be an evil time.

[4]On that day, one will raise up a taunt against you, and a lament – a mourning lament: 'He *actually* said: "we are completely destroyed!" [But] this one has altered the portion of my people. [Back to quoting the grievance] "How he has taken away [what belongs] to me! He has divided our fields to an apostate."'

[5]Therefore, you will not have one who will cast the measuring line by lot in the congregation of YHWH.

Notes on the text

2:3. On *hinnî* (*hinnēh* plus pron. suff.), see 'Notes' on 1:3. The emphasis on immediacy is rendered with '*now*' (*IBHS* §40.2.1b), announcing YHWH's intent to respond in a timely manner to their perfidy.

mišpāḥâ ('family') was an eighth-century prophetic term, addressing the whole of Israel – even given the current divided kingdom (cf. Amos 3:1). See O'Connell, *NIDOTTE* 2:1139–1142.

rômâ is a **hapax**, used adverbially regarding how they walk. It may simply mean 'upright' or could have the connotation of 'haughtily' (*DCH* 7:450). The Greek text has 'suddenly'.

kî introduces the reason for their humiliation; *ʿēt rāʿâ* ('time of evil') is a designated time for disaster, and it is now upon them.

4. 'On that day' is a signal that recurs in 4:6 and 5:9[10] as well as here. See *IBHS* §17.5b. The substance of what is stated next is yet in the future. Nevertheless, the verbs move back and forth between qat. and yiq. The subject of *yiśśāʾ* is indefinite: it may be translated as 'someone will raise'. Whoever this speaker is, his role is to 'lift up a *māšāl*'.

nihyâ, a noun possibly related to the niph. of *hyh*, is a **hapax** in the HB. The early versions seem to have been challenged by this final word in the expression *wĕnāhâ nĕhî nihyâ*; Gelston (2010: 98*) suggests they were guessing at an already unknown word. Previous generations of scholars deemed its inclusion a matter of dittography (Stade 1886: 122–123; BDB 228), but excising it robs the taunt of its force. This passage and Ezek. 32:18 (regarding Egypt) are the only places where the qal of *nhh* is used. *nĕhî* appears primarily in Amos (5:16) regarding professional mourners and in Jeremiah as a parallel expression to *qînâ* (Jer. 9:9[10]; 31:15).

Several Syr MSS add waw to read *wĕʾāmar*, following the weqat. pattern of the preceding verb. Gelston (2010: 98*) suggests that the MT intentionally points to a break: the rest of the verse is a parenthetical quote of the complaint.

šdd means to 'violently ruin' and 'devastate' (cf. Hos. 10:2; Obad. 5; see a similar lament in Jer. 9:18[19]). The niph. is preceded by an inf. abs. (*šādôd nišaddūnū*). On the unusual vocalization of the finite verb, see GKC §67u.

yāmîr is a hiph. form from the root *mûr*, meaning he will 'alter, change, or exchange' (*DCH* 5:187), but it is cryptic. Who will change or exchange the 'portion' (*ḥeleq*) of 'my people'? Both the LXX and Syr read the equivalent of *yimmad* (*beḥevel*) instead of *yāmîr*, thus rendering it 'he has measured with a cord'. That may be the easy confusion between daleth (ד) and resh (ר) and the presumption of the root *mdd* (Gelston 2010: 98*).

The LXX (see also Syr) has the equivalent of 'there was no one hindering him [to turn him back]' for *ʾêk yāmîš lî*. The LXX and Syr often replace a positive question with a negative statement (Gelston 2010: 98*).

šôbēb is an adj. meaning 'back-turning'. Read here as a subst., it means 'apostate'.

BHS suggests reading *yĕḥallēq* (pi.) as *yĕḥullaq* (pu.), following the pass. form in the LXX.

5. Among the meanings of *ḥebel* are measuring line (see 2 Sam. 8:2; Amos 7:17). That underlies the implication of measured territory (*ḥebel naḥălâ*); i.e. inheritance (Deut. 32:9; 1 Chr. 16:18). 'One who casts the line [*ḥebel*] with the lot [*gôrāl*]' appears in this form only here. Both terms appear in the context of the original land allotment.

Form and structure

As YHWH begins to speak, verb combinations are awkward, perhaps to convey the layered interface between YHWH's speaking, the prophet's speaking and the aggrieved words of the 'lamenter'. There are sound and conceptual similarities with v. 1; just as they had devised and worked 'evil' (*rāʿ*) 'on their beds' (*al miškebôtām*), so YHWH would devise 'evil' (*raʿâ*) 'against this family' (*al mišpāḥâ*) and it would be a time of *rāʿâ*. The measure-for-measure is evident in the repetition of 'devise'. Just as they 'lifted up' property (v. 2), so a *māšāl* would be 'lifted up' against them. *yāmîš* connects with *lōʾ-tāmîšû* of the preceding verse. Within the verse, *yāmîr* and *yāmîš* resonate.

Comment

2:3. 'Therefore' links the prior accusations with the forthcoming judicial sentence that YHWH will pronounce. YHWH's response will be balanced and measure-for-measure. The word *rāʿâ* ranges from moral turpitude to disaster that has no connections with moral concerns. It serves well for Micah's articulation of the ***lex talionis*** principle.

'This family' has levels of meaning. First, it fits with the preceding emphasis on 'home' or 'household': inheritance is bound up with the family and clan structure. It refers to a social unit that is less than a tribe, often equivalent to a clan and generally more than the extended family. At this point, the 'family' comes to bear the brunt of YHWH's indictment, a noticeable shift from the preceding condemnation of the oppressing class.

The necks of the covenant 'family', the descendants of Jacob, would now be under the heavy yoke of evil. The shift from 'this family' to second-person address in the *ʾăšer* clause is not unusual; Amos 3:2 does the same in the address to the 'family' of 3:1. See also Isa. 5:8–10.

The reference to not removing 'your necks from there' implies a yoke. It was a common prophetic metaphor; see Isa. 9:3[4]; 10:27. The presence of a heavy yoke on their necks would prevent them from walking about with necks upright and 'outstretched' (*rômâ*). The adj. placed after the verb describes their visible state (GKC §118q).

The metaphor of the yoke suggests the foreboding presence of Assyria and the reality of Judah's subjugation to them. Fast-forward to Jeremiah's day when he was commanded to enact a similar geopolitical scenario by wearing a literal yoke (Jer. 27:1–7), indicating the heavy hand of Nebuchadnezzar on the small kingdoms surrounding Judah. See Isa. 3:16 for a parallel description of haughty women.

4. 'They will lift up a *māšāl*' appears in Hab. 2:6, accompanied by 'mockery' (*mĕlîṣâ*) and 'riddles' (*ḥîdôt*). Isaiah calls the taunt regarding the king of Babylon a *māšāl* (Isa. 14:4). Thus, it has a sharper tone than simply 'parable', particularly in the light of the prep. 'against you'. The taunt starts with an exaggerated characterization of their huffing, groaning and gasping, *wĕnāhâ nĕhî nihyâ*. That expression serves as a bridge between the person who is mocking them and the contents of a supposed grievance.

For the full effect of *ʾāmar* commencing the quote of the lament, we should hear the intonation. The following paraphrase, 'he *actually* said', captures it, with an implicit 'Can you believe he has the temerity to say this?' That is followed by a mocking rendition of 'we are utterly devastated'. With that in mind, the next tasks are to determine how much of what follows is the expressed grievance and whether the quoted lamenters are appropriately aggrieved. Have they indeed suffered wrong, or have they been the aggressors who are now experiencing a deserved comeuppance, and are not keeping quiet about it? The latter seems more likely: the mockery is directed at unsavoury rich land-grabbers who themselves now have been dispossessed. The lamenter uses 'we', as he presumes to speak for those now suffering their own utter ruin.

If the quote of the complaint stops after 'we are utterly ruined', the person who took up the taunt stops quoting and makes an accusation, here paraphrased as '[he says they are ruined? Hah!] *He* altered the portion of my people!' Through this interpretive lens, these accusatory words refer to the earlier serious misappropriation of the familial inheritance by those who are now bewailing their own devastation. 'My people' is used nine times in Micah (1:9, 2:4, 8, 9; 3:3, 5; 6:3, 5, 16). In six cases, they are the words of YHWH. It makes interpretive sense to have these words on the lips of the speaker who has raised the mocking accusation against the unscrupulous land-grabbers.

It may be, however, that the quoted complaint continues uninterrupted. If so, those bewailing their loss are making a patently false claim to be part of the covenant people and then expressing their dismay that *their* part has been altered. 'Heaven forfend; how could this be?' If the quoted complaint continues without pause through the whole verse, then this very question surfaces in the next line. 'How' (*ʾêk*) could be a deeply emotional exclamation in the face of the anonymous subject who will 'remove' *their* fields. On the socio-religious significance of *ḥeleq* and the implications for the whole of the community structure, see Tsevat, *TDOT* 4:448, and Van Dam, *NIDOTTE* 2:161–163. 'How could he do this?' Whom were they holding responsible? Is the undefined subject of 'alter' the same as the one who will 'remove' in the final part of the lament? Is it YHWH?

The final line of v. 4 voices dismay that the portion of 'my people' is not being handled justly. To wit, some anonymous subject will go so far as to divide 'our fields' (another way of indicating the portion) to a party who certainly should not have it – the 'apostate'. To whom does this collective 'apostate' refer? Behind that question, others linger. How many distinct voices are wound into this exchange? Is the figure accused of altering the portion the same as the one who will remove and divide up?

In Jer. 31:22, 'back-turning' modifies 'daughter' and is used in parallel with 'virgin of Israel'. See also Jer. 49:4. Jer. 3:14, 22 uses a related masc. form in a repeated appeal: 'return, O back turning children'.

Because there are additional instances in Micah where quoted lines from different sources merge, the best reading of this may be as follows. Someone starts the mockery by quoting the outlandish claim of the land-grabbers that *they* are ruined. He pauses to confront that claim. No, it was really those same nasty operators who removed the inheritance portions from YHWH's people. Then he returns to quoting to prove his point – yes, they really did say 'How could he remove our fields and give them to the apostate types?' Double close-quote: the complaint and the taunt.

One last identity conundrum surfaces: the 'apostate' may represent foreign entities – perhaps more than one – to whom YHWH will turn over parts of Judah's clan lands. These may be Philistines encroaching again, or it may be the Assyrians. On the other hand, because the sense of the word implies turning away from a prior allegiance to YHWH, it may be unpleasant incursions from the north bedevilling the south (2 Chr. 28).

5. 'Therefore' moves towards the result. Because of the dissolution of inherited lands and property ownership, any semblance of order as determined in the assembly is gone. 'Congregation of YHWH' is used six times in Deut. 23:3–9[2–8], in connection with a formal list of categories of individuals excluded from the assembled congregation of YHWH. That suggests the existence of an official procedural meeting in which tribal leaders presided as heads of the gathering. Outside the Pentateuch, the expression is used only here and in 1 Chr. 28:8. It seems there was an

official procedural meeting of tribal leaders that continued beyond the early days of Israel's existence in the land. The sons of Joseph, a large tribe consisting of descendants of both Ephraim and Manasseh, enquired of Joshua, 'Why have you given to me [collective sg.] an inheritance of one lot and one line [*gôrāl 'eḥād wĕḥebel 'eḥād*]?' (Josh. 17:14). While the terminology harks back to an earlier time, the practice might have continued, especially in cases of land disputes. Not having one who would carry out that tribal duty in the assembly would result in landlessness. If we read at least part of this in the context of ongoing hostilities between Israel and Judah, it may allude to a tribal 'land grab' by the north. See Hos. 5:9–10, where the princes of Judah are likened to those who move boundaries and upon whom the wrath of YHWH will descend.

Explanation

The expanding judgment pronouncement is hermeneutically significant, moving initially from Micah's sole focus on eighth-century land sharks (v. 2) to the culpable family. The significance of *rā'â* (evil, calamity, disaster) in the wider scheme of human choices and YHWH's responses cannot be overstated. When YHWH's people choose, in direct disobedience to his revealed Word, to walk in the way of evil as opposed to good, he responds measure-for-measure: repetition of the word indicates that. Just as Micah's culprits plot moral and social evil, YHWH will plot destructive evil against the whole 'family'. They seize fields, houses, inheritance; YHWH will overrule in the assembly any process for portioning out the land that, after all, belongs to God. Those who amass wealth in criminal ways will be cut off from any hope in the congregational allotment. The factor of increasing application – even in that immediate context – encourages readers through generations and across spatial contexts to make the same presumptions about YHWH's justice in their own circumstances. Renaud (1977: 396) suggests a further redactional location: the 'apostates' were the unfaithful Jews who stayed in the land after 587 and took the property of those who had been taken into exile.

The veiled allusion to the Naboth incident (1 Kgs 21) in v. 2 may resurface here with more menacing undertones. The framing and unjust execution of Naboth were heinous in the extreme. There is a distinct likelihood that his whole family perished as well. When Jehu was on the way to overthrowing the Omri dynasty, he and his chariot official Bidqar passed the former property of Naboth. He referenced YHWH's declaration that he saw the blood of Naboth and *the blood of his sons* and would repay (2 Kgs 9:21–26). That suggests that the whole of Naboth's extended family had perished: it was not just a land grab but one carried out with extraordinary brutality. It may explain the ferocity with which Jehu obliterated the whole house of Ahab (2 Kgs 10:1–17).

MICAH 2:6–7

Translation

2:6 'Do not speak drivel!', they drivel. 'They should not drivel concerning these things. Reproaches will not overtake.'

7 Is it said, O house of Jacob, 'Is the Spirit of YHWH short, if these are his works?' 'Do not my words do good with the one walking in integrity?'

Notes on the text

Because the Hebr. continues to be challenging, several principles guide the translation and interpretation of vv. 6–11. First, the MT is given preference because the versions themselves indicate its perceived difficulty from early on; second, the standard meanings of Hebr. words and expressions are preferred; third, the first-person referent of vv. 7–9 is likely YHWH; fourth, this is prophetic drama with dialogue of accusation and indictment embedded (Waltke 2007: 109–110).

2:6. *ʾal* with 2 masc. pl. juss. (*taṭṭīpû*) is a negative impv. intimating urgency (*IHBS* §34.2.1b). It marks the beginning of the abrupt outburst from Micah's opposition. *nṭp* ('to drip') dominates the exchange. The shift from second to third person signals the narrator's presence, interrupting his mocking quotation of the opposition's high-pitched prohibition against Micah's preaching; the ban against 'dripping' was uttered and repeated by 'drippers'. The LXX has the equivalent of 'Don't shed tears,' indicating the influence of 'drip'. The Tg returns to the root meaning 'prophesy'.

The root of *yissag* is possibly *swg*; this would be a niph. yiq. form meaning to 'turn back or turn away' (GKC §72dd; BDB 690–691). *kĕlimmmôt* could function adverbially (Andersen and Freedman 2000: 305), implying that turning back is done shamefully. *kalam* implies public humiliation and is used in parallel with *bôš* (Nel, *NIDOTTE* 3:658–660). An alternative possibility – requiring an emendation – reads 'it [reproach] will not overtake us', a hiph. form of *nśg*. That makes *kĕlimmmôt* the subject, even though it is fem. pl., while *yissag* is masc. sg. A further complication is that *nśg* occurs only in hiph. (BDB 673). The correspondence of person, number and gender is variable, especially when the predicate, the 3 masc. sg. form, starts the clause, as it does here (§GKC 145o). A related word, *tassēg*, occurs in 6:14. See *DCH* 6:124 for a succinct summary of the options.

7. The first question is introduced by *heʾāmûr*, used only here. It is a pass. ptc. with the interr. hê, rhetorically introducing what might have been a proverbial and well-known question bandied about by the opposition. It has been emended by some scholars to *heʾārûr* ('Is it cursed?').

Although there is no MS support for the emendation, a small scribal error may account for the shift. Based on parallelism in Job 3:3, Ehrman (1970: 86–87) claims that *ʾāmar* without emendation can mean 'cursed'. Driver (1887: 261–262) deemed its use 'singularly harsh', blunt and unclear as stated. That, however, is the point: this is not intended as a gentle discourse. While many claim the form as it stands is 'untranslatable' (Woude 1969: 247–248), it is not out of the question to retain the MT reading.

qāṣar is a stative verb as part of the idiom 'Is the Spirit of YHWH short'? See Prov. 14:29.

The LXX reads 'Do not *his* words [instead of "my words"] do good?'

Form and structure

Continuing the pattern from v. 4, these two verses likewise juxtapose quotations, this time from speakers who clearly are at odds. The embedded dialogue makes the presentation both powerful but also challenging because there is no textual indication of the shift in speakers. See Gordis 1949: 173–178. Micah adopts his opponents' scathing terms and turns them back on them. He also peppers them with two questions (v. 7b c) radically different in terms of presumed speakers and content but that share similar sounds. They both start with the interr. hê. The first, a quoted query about YHWH's short fuse, continues with 'if' (*ʾim*) 'these' are his works; the second shifts abruptly to a withering response from the voice of Micah and YHWH as to how it will be 'with' (*ʿim*) those who walk uprightly.

The use of *nṭp* in v. 6 forms an inclusio with v. 11, where the image of dripping wine and beer augments the sarcasm regarding false prophets.

Comment

2:6. Although the substance of what all the parties are doing is a form of prophetic activity, and most translations render *nṭp* with some lexical equivalent to 'prophesy', the translations 'to speak drivel' and 'to drivel' most closely represent 'drip' (Smith-Christopher 2015: 90). Goldingay (2021: 431) renders the word 'spout'. That is the sarcastic assessment of both sides in the polemic. To translate it simply as 'preach' misses the power of the verbal picture. Even in English, we use the expression 'dripping with sarcasm'. *nṭp* is generally not used regarding prophetic statements. Instead, we find it in contexts where liquid is dripping. The heavens dropped water (Judg. 5:4); mountains drip sweet wine (Amos 9:13); the lips of the strange woman drip honey [but she is bitter] (Prov. 5:3); the lips of both the beloved and the lover in Song of Songs drip sweet and precious liquids (Song 4:11; 5:13). Figuratively, the mountains will 'in that day' drip sweet juice (Joel 4:18[3:18]; see again Amos 9:13). If part of Micah's intent is to caricature the cadre of prophets assuring their audience of security and plenty, Amos 9:13–14 would be part of the backdrop with its emphasis on dripping delicious liquid refreshment.

'To drip' does accompany 'to prophesy' (*hinnābēʾ*) in some contexts. Ezekiel is told to set his face towards the south, 'drip to the south and prophesy to the forest of the field of the Negev' (Ezek. 21:2[20:46]). Shortly thereafter, his attention turns to Jerusalem with the same admonition: 'drip to the sanctuaries, and prophesy to the land of Israel' (Ezek. 21:7[21:2]). Amos quotes Amaziah's warning not to prophesy: 'Do not prophesy against Israel and do not drip against the house of Isaac' (Amos 7:16).

The same sentiment that Amaziah voiced was common among those who did not want to hear the word of YHWH. Micah's contemporary, Isaiah, calls out those who tell prophets and visionaries not to see or prophesy but to tell them things they want to hear (Isa. 30:10). Amos castigates his audience for compelling Nazirites to drink and for commanding YHWH's prophets not to prophesy, here using *nbʾ* (Amos 2:11–12). Commentators have posed numerous explanations as to why this word is used when sarcasm encounters prophecy, some focusing on the fact that intense speech can be accompanied by visible spitting (Mays 1976: 69; Wolff 1981: 51; Jenson 2008: 124).

The second part of the quoted prohibition adds *lĕʾēlleh*, meaning either 'to' some unnamed audience or 'concerning' significant issues. If the latter, they are fulminating in response to Micah's warning of impending judgment. It is an admonition not to mention such presumably unseemly matters. The prophetic 'camps' are divided as to how to talk about their identity as YHWH's entitled people.

The final clause of v. 6 is typical of false prophecy: both structurally and essentially, it does not cohere. The fact that it lacks coherence on the syntax level may be part of the message: false words do not hang together! It is either the continuing retort of Micah's opponents and their assurance that they will be immune to disaster, or a return to Micah's voice. If the latter, he quotes their false sense of assurance as the prelude to the incredulous questions of v. 7. See Neiderhiser 1981: 105; Jenson 2008: 124.

Another possible interpretation draws YHWH in as the subject. It requires filling in necessary prepositions and linkages, but this part of the protestation from Micah's opponents is that YHWH will never cause his people shame, presumably by deserting them (cf. Jer. 23:40) and removing them from the land that has been promised for ever. Micah does not agree with them.

7. Both *rûaḥ* ('spirit') and *nepeš* ('being') may be used with *qṣr* and can mean either short on patience or short on energy. At mid-verse, marked by the ***athnach***, there is a transition, but the absence of markers in the dialogue makes it difficult to determine who is speaking at this point (Gordis 1949: 173–178). Micah skewers the house of Jacob with their own

question, perhaps based on the presumption that God's Spirit could not be 'short'. It is, however, ambiguous. The first part of the question expresses their incredulity that YHWH could possibly be angry. It is founded on the basic theological affirmation that YHWH is long-suffering. As such, they feel entitled to security as his covenant people. These speakers style themselves as theologically literate. *ʾim* carries on the rhetorical incredulity: Could 'these deeds' (cf. v. 6), no doubt referring to the judgments Micah describes, possibly be ascribed to YHWH?

It may be that the next clause represents the continued claims of the false teachers. The content could be a self-congratulatory retooling from Ps. 125:4 – 'Does not YHWH do good for those who are good, and for the upright in their hearts?' (That is us, folks!) This seems, however, rather unlikely. Instead, in the face of the over-the-top protestations from the opposition, Micah, speaking for YHWH, offers a rebuttal, likewise posed as a question (*hălôʾ*). It brings the discussion back to the heart of the issue – obedience. For those who walk with integrity, it will 'go well' (*yêṭîbû*). Character lived out has consequences: the theme echoes through the psalms (Ps. 84:12[11]) and is evident in wisdom literature.

Explanation

Antagonism reverberates throughout these two verses. One side tries to silence the other. The identity of the members of the opposition is not clear, but a good possibility would be false prophets speaking on behalf of Micah's targets.

The rhetorical questions reflect different stances in this timeless theological controversy. It boils down to how to understand the character of YHWH in relation to the flagrant disobedience of his people. Should he be expected to mete out punishment or not? The verses immediately prior to this section present both accusations and consequences. The 'drivellers' are inclined to discount the certainty of those warnings of judgment. In other words, they are content to preach partial truths, a dangerous stance when the lives of the people are at stake.

Put in more contemporary terms, Micah's opponents are doing their cultural best to 'shut this man down'. Their presumption of 'immunity', saying 'How could YHWH possibly be angry? What's this short fuse?', is countered by a call for integrity from YHWH/Micah. Is Micah on his own? The pl. forms of the prohibitions uttered by Micah's accusers may suggest that there are others who remain faithful to YHWH. Who started the verbal altercation? There are not certain answers. By the time we get to v. 11, both parties are reported as using the term 'drip', so they are equally insulting.

Evident in the protestations of the 'house of Jacob' is a presumption of entitlement to security and ongoing well-being. All claim allegiance to

YHWH; the challenge is to work out which are the true and the false prophets. This is a timeless and timely challenge, but the people of YHWH are not left in the dark on the matter. The tests of the authentic prophet are quite clear: what they foretell has to come to pass within the covenant conditions (Deut. 18:21–22), and their words have to demonstrate complete allegiance to YHWH and his Torah (Deut. 13:2–6[1–5]). For further exploration of the presumed theological underpinnings of the pseudoprophets as refracted through Micah's words, see Woude (1969: 244–260). To be sure, these theological affirmations are firmly lodged in the covenant promises, particularly the election of the 'house of Jacob'. Added to that are the implications woven into Zion theology:

> The powerful take their prosperity as a sign of YHWH's favour, and as a confirmation of their righteousness. That wealth, however gotten, should contribute to a feeling of being right, to self-justification, is not restricted to Micah's time. Doubtless his opponents were sober, industrious and chaste citizens, and found satisfaction in living up to their selection of the precepts for a righteous life. Success and self-righteousness are an unshakable foundation for a theology against the prophetic work of judgment. (Mays 1976: 70)

These are influential people who have control of the economic and religious structures, and who know their way around the law in more ways than one (Jenson 2008: 123). Micah and his supporters are most likely in a minority, and probably an unpopular one. There is no room for their message of judgment. Nevertheless, Micah continues to hammer away at the unjustified confidence of those whose wholesale disregard of their covenant obligations is only matched by their unfounded sense of entitlement. How timely is that!

MICAH 2:8–11

Translation

2:8 And lately my people – as an enemy they are rising up. From the front of a
garment you strip off the insignia; from those passing by secure, those returning
from battle.
9 The women of my people you drive away from her luxurious house; from her
young children you take my glory for ever.
10 Get up and go! Because this is not the resting place; on account of defilement,
it will be ruined, and a sickened destruction.
11 If a person comes and lies, [with] a spirit of falsehood: 'I will drivel for you
for wine and beer', this is the driveller for this people!

Notes on the text

2:8. The use of *ʾetmûl* instead of *ʾetmôl* occurs only here and in Isa. 30:33. The juxtaposition of 'lately' or 'yesterday' with the yiq. verb form implies that their perfidy has been developing over some time (Andersen and Freedman 2000: 515). Towards that end, emendations are unnecessary: the anchor of *ʾetmûl* in past time is compelling.

The sg. 'my people' is matched by the 3 masc. sg. *yĕqômēm*. This pol. of *qûm* is rare, occurring only here and in Isa. 44:26; 58:12; 61:4. Isaiah's use of the word refers to places; Micah has people rising up – possibly a reflex. sense (*DCH* 7:231). Instead of *yĕqômēm*, Tg has the equivalent of 'delivered' (Cathcart and Gordon 1989: 116).

The lamed prep. is used in the comparative sense: the people are 'like' an enemy (*IBHS* §11.2.10d; see Deut. 9:21).

A *śalmâ* (*DCH* 8:156) is an outer garment and seems to have been synonymous with *śimlâ*; it was forbidden to keep it overnight (Exod. 22:8, 25–26; see also Deut. 24:12–13).

ʾeder is used only two times: here and Zech. 11:13. The original reading instead of *ʾeder* might have been *ʾăderet*, but the taw dropped out because the next word starts with the same letter. This may be a wordplay with 'honour' (*ʾeder*) being stripped away as garment is taken; *ʾeder* is unattested elsewhere as meaning 'garment'. See GKC §159; Allen 1976: 296–297; *DCH* 1:136–137. The LXX reads 'before his peace', understanding *śimlâ* within the semantic range of *šālôm*, and follows it with stripping off 'skin'.

tapšîṭûn in hiph. means to take off clothing (*DCH* 6:791), leaving a person naked; violence is woven into the imagery (Gen. 37:23).

The prep. *min* governs the next two participles that describe two categories of victims from whom the garment and honour are taken. The LXX has 3 masc. pl. ('they stripped') instead of 2 masc. pl. The direct object of the verb 'to strip off' would be the cloak (*ʾăderet* as modified).

The LXX reads 'removing hope' for 'those passing secure'. *šûbê* is a qal pass. ptc. in const., a **hapax**. The pass. indicates that the victims have been acted upon, but the perpetrators remain anonymous (Waltke 2007: 119). In place of *šûbê*, the LXX suggests something to do with a ruin or fracturing as the result of war. It may be that the root *šûb* ('return') modulated to *šbr* ('break') (Gelston 2010: 99*).

9. *grš* means 'forcible expulsion' (*DCH* 2:377–378); the pi. 2 masc. pl. describes the callous actions by the unnamed perpetrators. The LXX substitutes 'leaders of my people' for 'women of my people' and continues with the declaration that they have been expelled because of their evil deeds, a significant alteration of the sense of the MT (see Hoyt 2019: 641).

The word translated 'pleasant' or 'luxurious' (*taʿănūgêhā*) is rarely used. See notes on 1:16; Prov. 19:10; Eccl. 2:8; Song 7:7. The suff. on *taʿănūgêhā* is sg.; the same is true of their 'children' (*ōlālêhā*). The semantic range of *ʿôlĕlîm* includes unborn children (Job 3:16), those who use their vocal cords

(Ps. 8:3) and seek their food from their parents (Lam. 2:19), and children as distinct from adults (1 Sam. 15:3). While many emend the pron. suff. to pl., they are best interpreted as 'distributive singular' constructions, 'each from her own beloved (or luxurious) house(hold)' and 'each from her own children' (Andersen and Freedman 2000: 321–322).

For *tiqḥû hădārî lĕʿōlām* ('they take my glory for ever'), the LXX reads 'draw near the eternal mountains'.

10. The LXX reads *ṭomʾâ* as a noun, 'uncleanness'. Some versions of the MT vocalize the form as a 3 fem. sg.; others deal with it as a noun (Gelston 2010: 99*).

For *tĕḥabbēl wĕḥebel nimrāṣ*, the LXX reads 'corrupted with corruption'. It is important to distinguish *ḥebel* here from *ḥebel* as 'line' in v. 5. They are homonyms but not related. In this context the word, both in its verbal and noun forms, refers to corruption and destruction (*DCH* 3:149–152). The act. 3 fem. sg. pi. (*tĕḥabbēl*) may be retained instead of shifting it to a pass. form, *tĕḥubbal*. The subject could be either 'the resting place' (Waltke 2007: 121) or 'uncleanness'. *nimrāṣ* ('grievous') is a niph. ptc. modifying *ḥebel*.

11. Usually *lû* means 'if', with reference to a possibility that may not have actual likelihood (*IBHS* §38.2e). *hôlēk* often implies something ongoing; this would be the habitual activity of the false prophet (*IBHS* §37.6d). The LXX reads 'pursued' for *hōlēk* (ptc.).

The noun combination *rûaḥ wāšeqer* ('spirit and falsehood') is an 'adverbial modifier' (Hillers 1984: 36): it reveals what kind of person (*ʾîš*) this is.

Form and structure

The difficulty of the MT is indicated by the notable number of suggested alternative readings and emendations. See Jenson 2008: 125–126. It is a difficult text, lacking particles and modifiers and, by virtue of the word order, emphasizing the objects of the enemy's actions without clarifying what those actions were. The tortured syntax continues, with brief phrases capturing a series of appalling abuses of a hostile people. In general, that precludes discovering formal connections.

There is an overarching structural arc from v. 6 to v. 11: confronting prophets (6); questions (7); narrative of accusations (8–9); command (10); confronting prophets (11). See Andersen and Freedman 2000: 300. *wĕʾetmûl* is a rhetorical anchor, marking the shift from the series of questions in v. 7 to evidence. Its sound connects with *mimmûl*, which follows. Most of the accusations have *min*, indicating that *removal* of honour, security, homes and children characterizes the crimes. *lĕʿôlām* at the end of v. 9 is a painful contrast with *wĕʾetmûl* at the beginning of v. 8 (Goldingay 2021: 431). Either the grammar intentionally focuses the impact of the tragedy for each terror-stricken household, or it is one more example of the syntactical ruggedness of the emotion-wracked message.

Comment

2:8. When the pol. of *qûm* appears in Isa. 44:26, 58:12 and 61:4, the contexts have to do with rebuilding ruined places. Here, YHWH's hostile people are rising up; their actions are assuredly not in the sphere of rebuilding anything. The 'enemy' is one who is not faithful to the covenant relationship, fracturing entirely the sense of 'my people'. The specifics of their enmity follow as Micah shifts to addressing them directly as 'you'.

Both *ʾeder* (translated 'insignia') and *ʾăderet* are from the root meaning to be 'wide' or 'great'. The latter means a literal cloak, representing a significant personage (1 Kgs 19:13, 19; Jon. 3:6). The implicit sense of width is the basis for a figurative interpretation of 'glory' or 'majesty', ironic in Zech. 11:13, which speaks of the 'glorious' price at which the shepherd was priced. If Micah intends the figurative meaning, then in some way, something indicative of status – perhaps a visible insignia – is being stripped off or torn away from the outer garment. The cloak was integral to one's identity and it was a serious offence to strip it off. Because the word appears primarily in socio-legal circumstances, the tendency has been to limit the interpretation to abuse of the poor (see 2:2).

That may not fit the picture of violence against those returning from war that emerges in the next verses. A wide range of war refugees are being robbed of their remaining possessions and honour. Among them are those 'crossing' perhaps some territorial boundary, presumably in security as they make their way home. The gestalt of this description points to war victims or prisoners of war. Those 'crossing' should have been guaranteed safe passage (cf. Num. 20); robbing any kind of traveller was criminal on several levels (cf. Judg. 5:6). The incident recorded in 2 Chr. 28:12–15 is telling: the victims should have been protected. The word translated 'strip off' is also used for flaying and stripping corpses (1 Sam. 31:8–9). Hence, the translation of the LXX. There may be a subtext here about forceful military plundering (Shaw 1993: 80–82).

9. 'The women of my people' will bear the brunt of the dispossession from their homes. Micah focuses on one category among the tragic victims – the dispossessed women and their young children – and the impact of the catastrophe on them. 'My people' reappears here, this time as the social network in which the women and children have been secure until this point. These events have torn apart families. The malevolent people who have turned into an enemy drive out women, perhaps alluding to widows, and rob their children of YHWH's majesty and honour; it is YHWH speaking (1 sg. suff.). If this refers to orphaned children, they are for ever cut off from the line of covenant people as they are driven away. These are beloved households (including the family members) from whom the mothers will be separated.

10. The descriptive tone of the preceding verses shifts to impv. ('get up and go'), but it is not clear who issues the commands and to whom. Nevertheless, the point is clear: they do not belong in the land. Because Micah does not always include the def. art., its presence with 'resting place' is noteworthy. 'This is no longer *the* resting place'; in other words, the inheritance promised in the covenant is not theirs by default. That is because it has become utterly defiled.

Some commentators presume Micah is quoting the harsh commands of the wicked oppressors as they drive the people away. A more plausible alternative is that YHWH continues to speak and warns of what will essentially be measure-for-measure consequences for the land-grabbers. Just as they have driven away their victims, that will come around to them. Whoever the intended recipients are, they are to leave because the land is no longer their 'resting place', even though that was the covenant intent (Deut. 12:9; see also Ps. 95:11). How different from Isaiah's description of secure dwelling places and pleasant places to rest (32:18)! The corruption is expanded by the next agonizingly broken clause: it matches the state of the people and the land.

The implications of *ṭāmēʾ* frequently lie in the realm of ritual and ceremonial uncleanness of persons and animals; many instances appear in Leviticus. Nevertheless, those categories are not divorced from ethical matters. Murder and idolatry defile sacred space (Lev. 20:3; Num. 35:34; Jer. 2:7; Ezek. 8:5–18; 36:17–18), and defile both people and land. Hosea repeatedly uses the term when speaking of Ephraim and Israel (5:3; 6:10; 9:3–4). Micah here condemns social and moral defilement of sacred space. See Averbeck, *NIDOTTE* 2:372–373.

'On account of' may control both *ṭomʾâ* and *ḥebel*: 'on account of uncleanness – it is destroying, and [on account of] grievous destruction'. The sentence is not finished: the situation is too dreadful. Hoyt (2019: 654–655) has proposed an equally agonizing interpretation based on another possible meaning for the root *ḥbl* – 'suffer birth pains' (Ps. 7:15[14]; *DCH* 3:150; Fabry, *TDOT* 4:188–189). If that connotation also underlies this description, the land itself will face anguish. The land that should have been the 'resting place' brings ruin (cf. Lev. 18:25): 'on account of uncleanness – it is destroying'. The niph. ptc. strengthens the unspeakable nature of overwhelming destruction.

11. The 'acceptable prophet' whom Micah describes is anyone who encourages indulgence. Micah's declaration is spare and requires additional details to flesh out the hypothetical situation. It is unclear, however, just what those details and that situation may be. It involves an indefinite 'someone' (*ʾîš*) 'coming' (*hôlēk*), possibly claiming the presence of the spirit to give his utterances authority but lying baldly. *rûaḥ* ('spirit' or 'wind') is suggestive regarding the true nature of the individual's self-promotion. Just as wind is unpredictable, so also this liar. Add in a double dose of deception and the combination is lethal. Through more benign lenses, it may simply call him out for being full of 'wind' (see Job 6:26; Jer. 5:13). Above all, however, the element of deceit is unmistakable. This person lies: what he says is falsehood.

How the wine and 'strong drink' (*šēkār*) fit into the picture depends on how the next lamed prepositions are interpreted (see *IBHS* §11.2.10). This crowd-pleaser may be prophesying 'regarding'; notably that they will enjoy an abundance of those signature features of the fine life. Or he may be stating outright his fee: they can pay him in wine and strong drink. It is telling that *šeqer* and *šēkār* sound quite similar.

As Micah has done throughout this pericope, he abruptly shifts to quote the words of the self-promoting false prophet who claims to be ready to prophesy to them. Fittingly, that person claims to 'drip', and what he promises is liquid – both wine and beer. He is full, however, of a spirit of falsehood and his 'drippings' are lies. Micah's scathing declaration at this point drips with sarcasm: this is just the 'dripper' for this people. Allen (1976: 299) suggests that the blessing formula in Amos 9:13 might have been liturgically quoted by these prophets as a false promise.

Explanation

Micah is called to speak the truth against false purveyors of peace, whether inside and connected or not. The network of power brokers is woven with mendacity, resulting in abuses and fragmentation of all levels of society, especially when warfare shatters all structures that should have bolstered the people. The public mouthpieces for the status quo whom Micah is castigating appear again in Jeremiah as he encounters his false opponents (Jer. 23 presents one extended example).

The whole oracle is dominated by 'dripping', an image redolent with sarcasm. The false prophets may also have discredited themselves by their affinity for alcohol (cf. Hos. 7 and Isa. 5:11; 28:7–8). They say what the people, equally enticed by the prospect of dulled reality, want to hear. Flowing wine and strong drink are signs of the affluent and secure society to which they cling. Inside this prophetic framework the 'brewing' enmity and the violence against the vulnerable flourishes.

As a result of Micah's opponents preaching disastrous partial truths, the people have lost their moral anchor. The designation 'my people' includes both those who are among the people as enemies as well as their utterly broken returning victims. The focus on the plight of the victims accentuates the cruelty of those in power. The latter are also called 'my people', but it rings false because they have forfeited that position by their abuses. The ambiguity allows a wide interpretive net to be cast. Allusions to the tragic consequences of war devastation are embedded in the accusations. This is a horrifying picture of completely fractured social and covenant structures. Possibly the more threatening the geopolitical circumstances, the more brutally the powerful members of society protect their own position. The utter disintegration of 'my people, the house of Jacob' has reached the lowest possible point as they attack one another within the covenant community.

Women and children are forcibly removed from any place that would ensure security. Micah does not use the traditional terminology for marginalized people groups. Perhaps 'widows, foreigners and orphans' had become such jargon, so the expression had little meaning. This may also point in a subtle manner to a wider range of disenfranchised families. They are not generally among the marginalized but come from pleasant places. The wholesale brutalizing of women and children was a known image (Hos. 10:14; 14:1[13:16]; Amos 1:13; Ps. 137:9). Now all are dispossessed, including men of honour returning from war contexts. That may also be the purpose of saying the children are robbed of YHWH's honour: those good gifts with which YHWH has blessed his covenant people will be gone, at least for that time. To be sure, God's splendour and glory can never be diminished but it may seem so from the human perspective (see Ps. 106:19–20; Ezek. 1 – 3, 10 – 11).

All the aspects of war are very fresh in their memory; it is another glimpse into the disorder and mayhem depicted in 1:10–16. The eighth century was marked by ongoing hostilities between Israel and Judah along with threats from outside, but Micah does not report the battles; instead, he portrays the terrible effects on people. Whole populations are taken into slavery (see also Amos 1:6–7). YHWH's people attack their own kin, with leadership ravaging their citizenry in multiple ways. The discourse presumes very socially disruptive events (Shaw 1993: 92–93).

The echoes of 'resting place' are far-flung. Ps. 132 draws the concept to its centre point – Zion. The context is David's oath that *he* will not rest (vv. 3–5) until he finds a place for YHWH, a dwelling for the Mighty One of Jacob. V. 6 mentions Ephrathah, a name that surfaces in Mic. 5:1[2], and v. 7 returns to the theme of God's presence with them where they will worship: 'let us come to his dwelling place and worship at his footstool'. It continues with a petition (v. 8), 'Arise, YHWH, and come to your resting place' and then shifts to YHWH's own declaration (v. 14), 'this is my resting place for ever and ever'.

Micah's characterization of the false prophet as one who 'goes about' might have been an allusion to the changing professional circumstances for these prophets. Earlier voices claiming the prophetic mantle were often tied to a particular location. It is not so with Amos and Micah; perhaps this factor of stability decreases significantly in the eighth century (Andersen and Freedman 2000: 327). While it keeps these voices from being simply court figures for the powers that be, it also means they can be less accountable. The court prophets in Ahab's day succumb to the 'lying spirit' sent from the heavenly court; Micaiah, son of Yimlah, is witness to it (1 Kgs 22:21–23).

Again, these images are not to be left to moulder on the heap of eighth-century BC verbiage. They echo pointedly into the twenty-first century. The church must revisit the ways we bolster our own comfortable prosperity and security with selective preaching that is user-friendly and avoids repelling the paying congregation. Tragically, this may come at the expense of preaching the 'whole counsel of God' (Acts 20:27), and does irreparable damage to those whose lives are constantly threatened.

MICAH 2:12–13

Translation

2:12 I will certainly gather, O Jacob, all of you; I will certainly bring together the remnant of Israel. I will set them together as a flock in an enclosure, as a herd in the middle of pasture; they are in tumult from [fear of] men.

13 One who breaks through has gone up before them; they have broken through and have passed the gate. They have gone out through it. Their king has passed before them, and YHWH will be their head.

Notes on the text

2:12. Joining *ʾsp* with *qbṣ* is a standard idiom. Because these words share a significant semantic field, I have chosen the translation 'bring together' for the latter.

yaḥad serves as a syntactical 'bridge' between YHWH's promise to gather all the remnant and their placement together in a secure location.

'Flock' and 'herd' (*ṣōʾn* and *ʿēder*) are parallel references to domestic animals. *ʿēder* may include both cattle and sheep (*DCH* 6:285). Both terms are occasionally combined to mean 'flock of sheep' (Gen. 29:2; Mic. 5:7[8]).

The root of *boṣrâ*, *bṣr*, means 'to cut off, enclose, make inaccessible' (*DCH* 2:246–247). Mic. 2:12 is the only use of the noun form apart from a proper place name. Instead of *boṣrâ*, the reading may be *baṣṣīrâ*. The LXX reads 'in distress'; see also the Syr, Tg and Vg.

haddāberô has both the def. art. and a pron. suff. See GKC §127i. Waltke (2007: 134) rejects the suggestion to shift the final waw to the next word, thus reading *haddōber*.

The 3 fem. pl. hiph. (*tĕhîmenâ*), likely from *hûm* ('to confuse'), describes the collective 'flock' in the pasture (BDB 223; *DCH* 2:504; GKC §145c) that is in confusion. *hmh* (to 'murmur', 'growl', 'roar', 'make noise') and *hmm* have also been suggested as underlying the verb form. The LXX reads 'leap'.

The prep. *min* could be causative – they are in fearful tumult 'because of strangers' (*mē'ādām*) who have caused fear (Allen 1976: 300, n. 84). Another possibility is to read it as their not having anyone to care for them. That is based on reading the prep. as 'privative'; i.e. without a person to help (Waltke 2007: 135–136).

13. The first two verb forms shift to qat. The LXX reads *'ālâ* as a prep. instead of a verb. Sym, Syr and the Vg read it with a future sense, continuing from v. 12. Mur supports the qat. form. Further alterations are suggested for following wayyiq. forms.

Form and structure

The disaster at the end of ch. 1 is not the last word. The remnant would find refuge in Jerusalem. 'Gate' connects with 1:12 (the gate of Jerusalem). In addition, for the ***lex talionis*** justice noted in 2:3–5 to take place, the salvation indicated by v. 12 must occur. Five verbs propel v. 13 forward, but shift from sg., describing the 'breaker', to pl. as the focus changes to the flock who follow. Finally, subject and verb revert to sg.; this is their King.

The parallel constructions – gathering all of Jacob and gathering the remnant of Israel – in the first two clauses of v. 12 emphasize both activity and identity. Likewise, *ṣō'n* and *'ēder* are parallel constructions – 'flock' and 'herd'. In that parallel framework, *boṣrâ* as an enclosure is synonymous with being in 'the pasture' (*haddōber* – reading as modified).

Comment

The tone in these last two verses is so different that some propose this is another quotation from Micah's rival prophets. There are scholars who presume this is either a 'happy ending' added later, or Micah has included at this point another unrealistic statement from his feckless opponents. Ibn Ezra, a twelfth-century Jewish biblical scholar, was an early proponent of this position (Driver 1887: 264; Hillers 1984: 40). Through a different lens, some read these verses alternatively as a continuing judgment oracle, presuming the sheep are gathered for slaughter. Waltke (2007: 136–139) and Hoyt (2019: 659–660) summarize the scholarly opinions.

2:12. *yaḥad* is generally identified as an adv. modifying the preceding verbs. Nevertheless, Talmon (1953: 133–140) demonstrates that its use as a synonym for the covenant community in the DSS literature is already evident in the HB. If that implication fits for the eighth century BC, it may be read as the object of the verbs in this context.

'All of Jacob' is further elucidated as the 'remnant of Israel'. This is the first occurrence of 'remnant' (*šĕ'ērît*) in the book. An important implication is embedded in 'all of Jacob'. Even though the two kingdoms have been hostile, this anticipates the ideal reunified nation. YHWH promises to gather the remnant, the flock of sheep, together and place them in a protected, enclosed, inaccessible place.

It seems best to understand *boṣrâ* as an enclosure, synonymous with being in the midst of 'his pasture'. Isaiah references 'flocks of Kedar' and 'rams of Nebaioth' in the context of a future hope-filled gathering (Isa. 60:7). The only other use of *dōber* is Isa. 5:17 – 'and lambs shall feed in their pasture'. Having sketched that general pastoral scenario, it may be that the proper name Bozrah is designated as one of the shearing centres where noisy flocks would be a known phenomenon. Three locations carried that name (Gen. 36:33; Isa. 34:6; 63:1; Amos 1:12). If a name is intended, the most likely one for this context is the town in Edom. If the consonants of *ʾādām* in the next clause are revocalized to read Edom, that may strengthen the connection with Bozrah.

The tumult is akin to psalms of lament; see Pss 42:6[5], 12[11]; 43:5; 55:3[2]; 77:4[3]. See Isa. 17:12–13 regarding the terrifying and thunderous roar of nations.

13. Both the identity of the subject and the shifting verb tenses are challenging. For the sake of establishing a position, let us say that YHWH is the subject and thus the King and Shepherd. He is the One who breaks forth (masc. sg. qal act. ptc. *pōrēṣ*) and the subject of the qat. verb *ʿālâ*, representing a future singular event (Waltke 2007: 136). *ʿālâ* has military connotations, suggesting leading a campaign (see 1 Sam. 29:9). Wayyiq. forms follow, indicating a continuation of that time frame. The directional components are also complex. This Shepherd and King not only goes up; once the sheep are safely in the enclosure, he breaks forth, going in front of them. This is a 180-degree turn. Sheep imitate the movements of their 'Shepherd'; they have 'broken through' (*pārĕṣû*). The image of the flock modulates to an army of sorts, with YHWH's going 'before them' as their King at their head.

'Micah culls his vocabulary from the rich heritage of divine dealings with Israel' (Allen 1976: 303). When David was victorious over the Philistines, it was God who 'broke through' with the place name to memorialize it – Baal Perazim (2 Sam. 5:20). More expansively, there are echoes of the exodus – breaking out of bondage – that will reverberate forward into departure from the prison of exile (Jenson 2008: 130).

Explanation

Up to this point, the images of social abuses and war crimes have dominated; this message of hope is a necessary antidote. The images of Shepherd and King point forward to restoration after judgment; both recur in chs. 4 and 5. Given the dire judgment predictions, it is only logical that the prophet would also long to see in the future that God's covenant people would see the promises fulfilled. Rescue would come with a reversal of the threatened judgment.

Two contrasting images work together in v. 12. In the first, YHWH as Shepherd gathers his sheep to protect them in a safe enclosure. The representation of the people of God as a flock in its pasture is a familiar one. See Pss 74:1; 79:13; 95:7; 100:3; Jer. 23:1; Ezek. 34:31. No matter whether the historical context is intertribal warfare in the decades prior to 722 BC, ominous threats from increasingly aggressive enemies or the 701 attack of Sennacherib, the situation described in 1:10–16 has produced waves of displaced persons. Town after town has fallen and hordes of refugees are streaming towards a place of refuge, likely Jerusalem. Would they make it to and through the gates? That question is a segue to the second image of the King.

He reverses direction and goes forth to do battle on their behalf. This echoes Israel's long tradition of YHWH as their King (Exod. 15:18). Just as he broke through the waters of the Sea of Reeds and Israel passed through on dry ground (Exod. 14:29–31), so here he breaks through and leads them as their King as they pass through the gate. The image of YHWH's rule is linked with Jerusalem, expressed repeatedly in the psalms and notably in Isaiah's vision in the temple: 'My eyes have seen the King, YHWH of Hosts' (Isa. 6:5).

The word *šeʾērît* ('remnant') is parallel to *pelêṭâ* ('escaped remnant'), and appears most frequently in the prophetic literature, describing not only the remnant of God's people, but also other nations around Israel. It appears three more times in Micah (4:7; 5:6–7[7–8]; 7:18), and the theme is developed by his contemporary, Isaiah. The name of Isaiah's first child, She'ar Yashub ('a remnant will return'), echoes from its first mention in Isa. 7:3 into the future promises of restoration after the destruction wrought by Assyria (Isa. 10:20–22). Isaiah's prophetic word in 2 Kgs 19:31 links the 'remnant' (both *šeʾērît* and *pelêṭâ* appear in the verse) with 'going forth' from Jerusalem and Zion.

MICAH 3:1–4

Translation

3:1 And I said: Hear, O heads of Jacob, and rulers of the house of Israel. You are to know justice!

2 You hate good and love evil, tearing away their skin from upon them, and their flesh from on their bones.

3 And when they eat the flesh of my people, and their skin from upon them they strip off, and their bones they shatter, and spread [them] accordingly into the pot, and like flesh into a cauldron,

4then they will cry out to YHWH, but he will not answer them. And he will hide his face from them in that time because they have made their deeds evil.

Notes on the text

3:1. The LXX reads 'and he shall say' in place of *wāʾōmar* ('and I said'). See also the Syr.

While *hălôʾ* has traditionally been translated as introducing a rhetorical question that anticipates an affirmative answer, it may simply signal a strong positive assertion (Brown 1987: 201–219; Moshavi 2007b: 51–63). If a negative tone were intended, the following inf. const. would normally be accompanied by *biltî*, not *hălôʾ*.

2. The Tg shifts the image to removing belongings and precious wealth from people, softening the description (Cathcart and Gordon 1989: 117–118).

3. *waʾăšer* is a rel. pron., connecting the rulers and leaders with 'the flesh of my people' that 'they eat' (*ʾākĕlû*). *piṣṣēḥû* is a pi. intensive, better understood as breaking in pieces or dismembering.

The second *kaʾăšer* may be emended to *kišĕʾēr* ('like flesh') which is apparently how the LXX read it (*hōs sarkas*). That is a closer parallel with *bāśār* in the next clause. It might have come about as the result of **metathesis** of the second and third consonants of the form. See Allen 1973: 71 and Freedman 1983: 145.

The 'pot' (*sîr*) was a large cauldron, capable of holding sufficient 'flesh' to feed a significant group (Exod. 16:3; 2 Kgs 4:38-41). *qallaḥat* is used only here and in 1 Sam. 2:14, itself a context where sacrificial meat was prepared. See Honeyman 1939: 85.

4. *ʾāz* ('then') shifts the focus to an undefined time in the future. *bāʿēt hahî* intimates an 'appointed time' (Waltke 2007: 152). *BHS* suggests the phrase is an addition. The 'interruption', however, may be a subtle rhetorical feature.

wĕyastēr ('and he will hide') could be interpreted as either a juss. or a straightforward declaration about future consequences. Read as a juss., it carries a deeply emotional plea: Would that this would happen!

'Their deeds' is the direct object of *hērēʿû*, a 3 masc. pl. hiph. from *rāʿaʿ*. The causative aspect combines with the qat. form, emphasizing the process that they started in the past and continue into the present. They shape their actions with evil intent (Waltke 2007: 152).

Form and structure

The chapter overall is shaped by a broad chiastic structure. There are phonological and conceptual connections throughout.

A Rulers, leaders and heads (vv. 1–4)
  B Prophets (vv. 5–7) – with Micah as the counter (v. 8)
A' Rulers (vv. 9–12)

Pairing 'heads' and 'rulers' initiates the levels of parallelism that shape this section. It also connects with YHWH 'at their head' at the close of the preceding chapter (2:13), contrasting perfect leadership with flawed.

On a smaller scale, the structure of vv. 2–3 conveys the horror of the actions:

Skin torn from them   flesh from their bones
          Eating flesh
Skin stripped from them   their bones broken
          [cooking]
In a cauldron   in a pot

With the emendation suggested above (*kišēr* ['like flesh'] instead of *ka'ăšer*), the parallelism in the last line of v. 3 is more pronounced – they spread [dismembered pieces] like flesh in the pot and like flesh in a cauldron.

The structure of v. 4 has YHWH's non-response in the centre. The people, by contrast, have been active in word and deed:

They will cry   YHWH will not answer
He will hide his face   [because of]   their evil deeds

Comment

3:1. Micah's introductory statement 'And I said' is the only autobiographical statement in the book. Its authenticity has been the object of scholarly discussion, summarized by Waltke (2007: 144–146; see also Willis 1968b: 50–54; and Ben Zvi 2000: 73–75). Given the undercurrent of reported dialogue in ch. 2, followed by the far-ranging promises of YHWH at the end of that chapter, this resumes the prophetic challenges posed to the leaders. The prophet's voice will again merge with that of YHWH – 'Thus saith YHWH' (v. 5). Comparing this chapter's introduction with *wayyōmar*, which starts out Amos 1:2, Willis argues that this signals a division in the ordering of Micah's oracles.

The imperative to 'hear!' begins the charge; the particle *nā'* suggests a compelling plea in the light of what the prophet knows is forthcoming. The leaders are called 'heads' and 'rulers'. Throughout Israel's history, individuals called 'heads' functioned in both military and judicial roles, with the latter coming to more prominence (Bartlett 1969: 1–10). This means that the legal system at Micah's time was as corrupt as the other ruling classes. *qāṣîn* ('ruler') is used by Isaiah (1:10; 3:6–7; 22:3). Another possible interpretation is that this is an example of **hendiadys**; in other words, 'commanders in chief'. See also Josh. 10:24 and Judg. 11:6, 11, where the terms appear in military contexts. Notably, kings are not mentioned.

Micah continues to use 'Jacob' and 'Israel' to include the southern kingdom along with the more common northern association (see 2:12); Samaria and Jerusalem are not specified at this point. As Micah addresses the civic leaders, he may be in the temple courts, the place where the leaders would be gathered (Goldingay 2021: 445). If that is the case, there is an echo in the dramatic aftermath of Jeremiah's temple sermon just about a century later (Jer. 26:16–19).

Here Micah challenges the derelict leadership: they should know justice, the whole of covenant obligations incumbent on God's people to maintain the right order (Andersen and Freedman 2000: 351). This would apply particularly, although not exclusively, to the social and civil administrative functions. That they do not practise justice demonstrates that they are complicit in the crimes he articulates moving forward.

Micah no doubt encountered appointed officials, possibly sent from Jerusalem to oversee local affairs, in each of the Shephelah fortress cities (2 Chr. 11:7–9). Because the text reads 'the judgment', Shaw (1993: 109–113) suggests it could point to some leaders' rejection of a specific decision, not justice in general. The overtones of violence may imply armed encounters and perhaps even the repercussions of leaders having violated a treaty. Nevertheless, the continuation of the accusation suggests a wider application of the term.

2. Their studied ignorance of justice is evidenced by the complete skewing of their moral compass. 'Love' and 'hate' do not represent emotionally charged terms: they are reflected in the leaders' actions as authority figures (Goldingay 2021: 445). Hating good reflects a loss of moral anchor; loving evil manifests itself in the cruel actions that follow. The first three verbal forms are masc. pl. qal participles; they are directed at the prior addressees, continuing the accusation. 'You hate good and love evil' describes states of being, indicating the intrinsic nature of the leaders. The third ptc., 'tearing away', represents the vicious outcome of their natures.

The verb 'tear away' is used in Mic. 2:2 for 'tearing away' fields. That social oppression shifts here to a more hideous tearing – ripping skin from bodies and flesh from bones. The rulers have become subhuman. The question is whether this is an extended metaphor for their rapacious injustice or is more ominously literal. The two stages of this description may intimate something uglier than a simple figure of speech. Stripping skin is followed by removal of the flesh from the bones, no doubt by heavy-handed chopping. The victims are 'my people' (v. 3). 'Flaying', a gruesome war crime, was a standard weapon of terror among the Assyrians. Sargon II, contemporaneous with Micah, described how he flayed the presumptive king of Hamath, having defeated him at Qarqar (*ANET* 285).

Micah's audience might have seen these processes in action. Evidence from Assyrian inscriptions makes it quite clear that the practice continued unabated (Cogan 2015: 175–186). Did it seep into the tactics of Israel's leadership as well?

3. The qat. forms function to indicate habitual action (*IBHS* §30.4b). The broad categories of 'good' and 'evil' had raised expectations of a continuing balance, but evil dominates and re-echoes in the rest of this verse and the next one. 'Stripping off' links v. 3 with 2:8, where parts of garments were stripped off. These leaders prepare by skinning and 'chopping' (*piṣṣēḥû*). The pi. intensive of *pṣḥ* is onomatopoeic, reflecting the harsh sounds of shattering bones. Subsequently, they are 'spread out' (*pārśû*), arranged for cooking.

Both parts of the last line are controlled by the verb 'they spread' and the results are two emphatic parallel statements – [flesh] in the 'pot' (*sîr*) and flesh in another kind of vessel, called a *qallaḥat*. The pot was a large cauldron. The leaders of Jerusalem envisioned by Ezekiel used the term figuratively to refer to Jerusalem itself (Ezek. 11:3).

The images of stripping off the skin and chopping up the bones are repeated after Micah has put the crux of the matter squarely before his audience with the chilling picture of eating flesh. The systematic destruction is inescapable: their skin, their flesh, their bones. This process sounds like a very public event, here driven by depraved motives shaped by the unhinged morality. It is the epitome of callous violence. What does it mean? The image of 'eating flesh' is a biblical metaphor for severe injustice and oppression. See Pss 14:4; 27:2. Prov. 30:14 is particularly graphic: 'There is one – his teeth are swords; his incisors [a rare word, *mĕtallĕʿōtāyw*] are knives to eat the poor from the land and the needy from among humans.' The stated likeness of the simile (*kaʾăšer* followed by *kĕ*) may be the most effective way of emphasizing the cruelty of injustice: it destroys and devours a person entirely. Nevertheless, given the wider eighth-century BC context, the option of physical brutality is still 'on the table'.

4. The undefined nature of the future is ominous. In that time, YHWH will not answer their cries, even when they cry out in desperation. While *zʿq* can be a judicial term indicating appeal to a judge, it implies a very loud cry (*DCH* 3:127–128). Because these hardened leaders stopped their ears while their oppressed fellow Israelites cried out, the sovereign Judge will do the same. Divine silence closes the first half of the verse, and that is dreadful enough. Veiling of the divine face is even more appalling.

Micah articulates devastating consequences in keeping with the enormity of their cruelty. Their evil deeds reflect their completely skewed world view. Hearing the consequences should stop them short. They know this judicial principle that the measure of the punishment will fit the extent of the crime. It conveys a fundamental symmetry that recurs throughout the multiple prescriptions for the judicial system of Israel. The ***lex talionis*** principle is classically expressed in Exod. 21:23–25: 'life for life, eye for eye, tooth for tooth, hand for hand, foot for foot, burn for burn, wound for wound, bruise for bruise'. See parallels in Lev. 24:17–20 and Deut. 19:15–18.

These warnings are part of their heritage. 'My anger will burn against him [Israel] in that day, and I will forsake them and hide my face from them' (Deut. 31:17). And again, 'I will surely hide my face from them' (Deut. 32:20). Micah's contemporary, Isaiah, echoes these sober warnings: 'So when you spread out your hands in prayer, I will hide my eyes from you; yes, even though you multiply prayers, I will not listen. Your hands are full of blood' (Isa. 1:15; see also 8:17). They did not listen to the cries of the poor; God would not listen to them (Prov. 21:13). Even more forcefully, God is actively against those who do evil (Ps. 34:17[16]). Habakkuk knew that God's eyes are too pure to look at evil (Hab. 1:13).

Explanation

Even prior to Sinai, Jethro advised the appointment of judicial leaders for the Israelites, chosen based on their fear of YHWH and their integrity (Exod. 18:13–27). There is a systemic structure embedded in Torah for ensuring the proper application of judicial rulings. If locally appointed judges (Deut. 16:18) were uncertain in particularly gnarly cases, they had recourse to the Levitical priests, who would enquire in the presence of YHWH (Exod. 28:30; Deut. 17:8–13). The verb 'to know' implies not only intellectual mastery but also deep affirmation of justice for the whole range of God's people. In the ninth century, after the nearly disastrous alliance with Ahab, Jehoshaphat turned to the matter of judicial reform, fitting given his name. He established judges, with major officers centred in Jerusalem. They were also installed in the fortified cities. At the same time, the priestly involvement increased (2 Chr. 19:4–11). At first, this was salutary, but in time they succumbed to the corruption of power. As Hosea puts it, 'the judgment' will be against the priests and the royal house because of wholesale corruption (Hos. 5:1–4). Micah calls out the same twisted world perspective in the leaders he knows.

A century later, Jeremiah cites the example of Josiah: 'He judged judgment for the poor and needy. "Is not this to know me?" declares YHWH' (Jer. 22:16). The psalmist Asaph joins his voice to those decrying systemic injustice:

> Until when will you judge unjustly and show favour
> to the wicked?
> Do justice for the weak and the fatherless;
> do the right thing for the afflicted and the poor.
> Rescue the weak and the needy;
> from the hand of the wicked save them.
> (Ps. 82:2–4)

Loving evil and hating good has everything to do with hardened hearts. These are not abstract conceptual expressions: they have an impact on how we treat one another daily. Micah surveys the character of Judah's leaders and finds it wanting. This is a steady prophetic drumbeat in the eighth century BC. Amos adjures his audience to hate evil and love good (5:15); the context makes it clear they have been doing the opposite. Isaiah's pronouncement goes one step further: they not only love what is evil, but have gone about redefining the foundational categories of good and evil (Isa. 5:20); they make decrees and laws that implement systemic injustice (10:1–2).

The violence of 'stripping off' basic garments described in the previous chapter (2:8) turns here to ripping away the skin and flesh of the oppressed. The picture is of a wild carnivorous creature. This goes even beyond violent mutilation. Instead of caring for the people as good shepherds, leaders are shepherds who eat the flesh of their charges. Micah does not skirt the violence: multiple times he confronts his audience with the spectre of bloody pieces of flesh severed from both skin and bones and tossed into a steaming cauldron. The cannibalism metaphor is particularly powerful because it does not allow the audience to remain passive (Shaw 1993: 119).

The same cooking imagery recurs in the parable in Ezek. 24:3–12 (see also Ezek. 11:7–11); debased injustice sadly persisted in characterizing the people and their leaders. The details of Ps. 94:3–7, 20–21 point directly at those oppressing the sojourner, the widow and the orphan. Symbolism is one interpretive possibility. Eccl 5:7[8] describes the unsavoury circumstances when social and judicial structures are completely awry: 'the tearing of justice and righteousness' results in the oppression of the poor.

More gruesome scenarios suggest themselves. Perhaps Micah is referring to the utterly degraded state to which occupants of Jerusalem descended when they were under siege: they resorted to cannibalism. That is an unsavoury part of their national narrative as well. The northern kingdom experienced it under dire siege straits (2 Kgs 6:24–33); Ezekiel prophesied that Jerusalem's population would sink to that debased state (5:10); Jeremiah wept over it in the aftermath of Jerusalem's siege and destruction loomed on the horizon (Lam. 2:20).

There is another, even more harrowing, possibility. Perhaps that brutality was already cloaked in some sort of religious garb. This butchery *might have* been part of a cult of human sacrifice that was followed by disposing of the flesh. It would have followed the same procedures as animal sacrifice, where parts were eaten as part of the ritual. While this seems too extreme even to consider, there are connections to note. Ahaz, on the throne at this time, made his sons 'pass through the fire' (2 Kgs 16:3; 2 Chr. 28:3), an intentional act of the king. Mic. 3:3 continues the dismembering theme with a reference to 'eating the flesh of my people'. Hosea addresses sacrifice that is displeasing to YHWH (8:13), part of which he characterizes as 'sacrifices of humans' (*zōbḥê ʾādām*) in the context of serious sin in the worship context (13:2). It would be difficult to claim that this is anything but individuals arriving to sacrifice to Baal (Andersen and Freedman 2000: 354). The volume of the accusation ratchets up with the horror of Ps. 106:34–39; see also Isa. 57:5. On the cusp of Jerusalem's collapse before the Babylonians, Jeremiah intimates the same appalling practice (Jer. 19:4–5). The bizarre and obscure circumstances surrounding the Moabite king's sacrifice of someone's son (2 Kgs 3:27) affirms the reality of a human sacrifice that was expected to be (and was) efficacious.

Lest we think our sophisticated culture is far advanced beyond such things, we must pause. Perhaps we ought not to dismiss these pictures as simply extended metaphors, for we are capable of the same atrocities. We witness dismemberment of humans in the womb, primarily in the name of a societal 'greater good'. Human flesh was cheap in Europe in the 1940s and was subject to experimentation, melting down and other horrors that ought to sicken us. Our hermeneutical compass may need to be adjusted to face our own contemporary realities.

MICAH 3:5–7

Translation

3:5 Thus YHWH says concerning the prophets who lead my people astray, who bite with their teeth and then call out 'Peace!' But when he does not give to their mouths, then they sanctify war against him.

6 Therefore, it will be night for you without a vision, and will turn dark for you without divination, and the sun will set upon the prophets and the day will darken over them.

7 Those who see visions will be ashamed and the diviners will be abashed; they will all cover the upper lip because there is no answer of God.

Notes on the text

3:5. The verb *tā'â* means 'to err' (*DCH* 8:656–658). The hiph. masc. pl. ptc. appears frequently in the prophetic literature. Isaiah uses it to address utter moral degradation to which leaders and false prophets contributed (3:12; 9:14[15]; 30:28). YHWH's people suffer the consequences.

nšk generally refers to the lethal bite of a serpent (Gen. 49:17; Num. 21:6–9; Prov. 23:32; Amos 5:19). Apart from Micah's vivid imagery, it is never used for eating food. The Tg revises the image to giving a banquet to the false prophets (Cathcart and Gordon 1989: 118).

The implications of *qr'* include making an announcement or declaration. Its parallel position with *qdš* in the following line may invest it with the sense of sacred proclamation (Waltke 2007: 160).

6. Following the LXX (also represented in the Vg), many scholars emend *ḥāšēkâ* (3 fem. sg. qal qat.) to a noun, making it parallel to 'night' in the initial clause. It is, however, possible to read it as a qal inf. const., 'with a feminine shape' (Waltke 2007: 162).

qĕsōm is likewise a qal inf. const. from the denominative verb *qsm* (*DCH* 7:272); it is not necessary to modify it to *qesem*. It should be translated 'without their having divined it' (Andersen and Freedman 2000: 374). The prep. *min* means a separation from – 'without'.

When *bāʾâ* (3 masc. sg. qal qat. from *bô*) is used with the sun, it means 'to set' (*DCH* 2:102). It and *qādar* ('to be dark') appear in the weqat. form, indicating the future for the false prophets.

The Tg modifies the description to focus on the shame and embarrassment that will prevent the false prophets from prophesying and teaching (Cathcart and Gordon 1989: 118).

7. The Tg substitutes 'teachers' for 'diviners'; it surfaces again in v. 11. Two synonymous verbs, *bôš* and the stative verb *ḥāpēr*, express humiliation and are frequently paired to express public disgrace (Ps. 71:24; 83:18[17]; Isa. 1:29; Jer. 15:9).

The verb *ʿāṭâ* ('to wrap or cover'; *DCH* 6:349) is used both literally and figuratively of a garment (*beged*, *mĕʿîl* or *śalmâ*) covering one's body (see Ps. 104:2, Isa. 59:17; Jer. 43:12). The precise nature of the action in this context is unclear: *kullām* may mean 'entirely', or it could refer to all the parties involved. If the former, this would imply wrapping in one's cloak right up to the upper lip to cover the face (Andersen and Freedman 2000: 375).

Form and structure

These three verses shift the focus from the brutality of civil leaders to the prophets. The rhetoric moves from accusation (v. 5) to declaration of the sentence (v. 6) to the consequences (v. 7). There are word pairs in each verse, but the relationships among them are ambiguous. In v. 5, the pairs are prophets and leading astray, teeth and mouth, peace and war, declaring and sanctifying. Some are synonymous; others pose antitheses. Declaring peace is countered by sanctifying war in the next line. The first line of v. 6 consists of two parallel declarations that are echoed in the second line. Night is followed by darkness; the setting sun, by the darkening of the day. All emphasize the encroaching gloom.

Comment

3:5. YHWH's declaration is 'against' the prophets. These individuals are commissioned to speak *for* YHWH; here, they are accused of leading people astray, and thus YHWH speaks *against* them. This overarching condemnation of these prophets is followed by graphic descriptions of their responses to two categories of audience members. If their demands are met, they proclaim peace; if not, they sanctify war.

'Biting' is intentional hyperbole. It is again reminiscent of Ahab's seizing Naboth's vineyard and Jezebel's subsequent false accusation with a sanctioned blasphemy charge (1 Kgs 21). 'Fees' for prophetic 'services' were part of the culture (see 1 Sam. 9 – 10 and 2 Kgs 4). A homonym, *nešek*, means 'interest' charged on a loan (*DCH* 5:778). It may be related, construing it as something 'bitten off', as it were. Prohibitions regarding this practice regarding fellow Israelites employ a cognate accusative that may be translated 'you shall not bite off interest' (Deut. 23:20–21[19–20]). That provides a fitting background to the practices condemned by Micah.

The image of these prophets concocting their announcements of 'peace' to 'bite' an edible bribe points to something more sinister: it recalls the rapacity evident in v. 3, and is freighted with undertones of death and irreparable damage, the opposite of their prophesied 'peace'. See Ps. 140:1–3 on evil and violent people who stir up war with tongues of serpents and venomous lips. One swathe of the audience feeds the ravenous appetites of the false prophets, who are biting with their sharp teeth to grab at food.

The biblical proportions of *šālôm* are rich and multifaceted, including physical well-being, social and societal harmony, economic security and freedom from aggressive assault (Jenson 2008: 135; *DCH* 8:365–370). The popular prophets, however, eviscerated the concept by making thin promises bereft of the obedience that underlies the right order prevailing through the whole of their lives.

The waw in *wa'ăšer* ('but when') should be read as an adversative, introducing the refusal on the part of one lone individual to succumb to the prophets' greedy manipulation. This singular individual 'would not give [*lō'-yittēn*] upon [*al*] their mouths'. The prep. *ʿal* may not have to do with actual eating (putting food 'into their mouths') but refers to speaking. In other words, this individual does not cave into the false prophets' demands: 'on their mouths' refers to what they have said. Because he refuses to go along with the established bribery pattern, he becomes the target of their hostility.

The second statement is particularly strong: the false prophets 'sanctify' a declaration of war, a formal procedure for dedicating war and warriors. Torah established procedures for going to war, among them the involvement of the priests (Deut. 20:2). During the tumultuous transition to the monarchy, Saul presumptuously took upon himself that priestly duty that Samuel should have performed (1 Sam. 13:8–12). See Jer. 6:4, 22:7 and 51:27–28, where YHWH would sanctify Israel's enemies against her. Joel draws together the same two verbs 'summon the nations' and 'sanctify war', following which the image of swords and spears being retooled is reversed (Joel 4:9–10[3:9–10]). Here, given their upside-down morality – calling evil good and good evil – the attack on a lone defender of righteousness becomes a 'cause'. By their own doing, they make a sham of the prophetic role. What an absolute perversion of the entire concept of being set apart in relationship to the holiness of God. How very timely!

6. The word order is important. 'Night' comes immediately after 'therefore', and there are no finite verbs in the first line. Instead, the sense of prevailing darkness is conveyed by a pair of inf. const. forms. As a result of their perfidy, night and darkness will prevail; that is YHWH's judgment and how very sober it will be! The imagery moves from the numinous realm of visions and divination into the basic experiences of day shading into night, described with finite verbs. Just as the sun goes down and darkness settles, so also it will be for these diviners and visionaries. There will be *nothing*, neither the truth of the prophetic vision nor the possibly 'shady' results of divination. The verse closes with 'the day' darkening over them, but how that day is to be understood is ambiguous. Perhaps it signals the light that both illuminates the physical world and characterizes that which is good. Those shrouded in the darkness of night and self-deception will lose the capacity to see that day. The image is a familiar one. Following his admonition to exercise justice for the destitute and oppressed, the psalmist castigates those who are bereft of knowledge and understanding, walking instead in darkness while the very foundations of the earth tremble (Ps. 82:5).

7. Micah shifts his focus to the social outcomes for fraudulent visionaries and diviners. When they are revealed as charlatans, the cultural shaming is powerful. No surprise: they are frauds, and their prophetic declarations are not coming true.

The visionaries and diviners enact their shame by covering their lip. That response may be the same as Job's pause and declaration after God's first speech. Speaking from a posture of humility, he said, 'I put my hand over my mouth' (Job 40:4b). When Ezekiel's wife died, YHWH commanded him not to engage in the normal mourning rituals, one of which was covering his lip (24:17–22). Interpreting this specifically as moustache is based on the description of Mephibosheth's mourning the whole time David was absent. He 'did not do something' (the verb is *lôʾ-ʿāśâ*) to his lip (2 Sam. 19:25), suggesting he did not trim his moustache. Covering the lip was also the posture of lepers who cried out 'Unclean!' (Lev. 13:45). Both leprosy and mourning put an individual on the margins of society, subject to humiliation and shame; likewise, exposure as fraudulent is a blow to honour.

Just as YHWH will not answer the cries of flagrantly disobedient people and will hide his face from them (v. 4), so God is not answering the false prophets or those who wait for their words. Instead of YHWH, or YHWH Elohim, Elohim appears alone here. That may signal Micah's unwillingness to associate the covenant Name with these unsavoury persons (Waltke 2007: 165), or it may serve as a hint as to the real 'source' of the false prophets' prognostications (Hoyt 2019: 683). 'Answer' is a noun (BDB 775; *DCH* 5:409); there is no reply from God/god. This creates an 'envelope' around vv. 5–7.

Explanation

The prophets are supposed to guide all the populace, including the heads of state, into righteousness and justice, but they have failed miserably. Micah's outrage mirrors YHWH's wrath at the evil the deceitful prophets are bringing to his people. These prophets are soothsayers who 'prophesy' good outcomes when it pays well. 'Good', however, is not 'true'. There is sadly a long history of false prophecy in Israel. Elijah confronted the phenomenon in the northern kingdom in the ninth century (1 Kgs 18 – 19). The same was true in Jeremiah's time: by avoiding the touchy subject of the people's sin, the prophets sealed their fate (Lam. 2:14; see Jer. 6:14; 11:7). This steady usurpation of the good office by charlatans may be why Micah does not call himself a prophet (Jenson 2008: 135). Israel should have known better: Torah includes clear instructions on how to recognize false prophets (Deut. 13:2–6[1–5]; 18:15–22).

Divination was widely practised in the ANE, sometimes with accompanying omens such as arrows, lots and dreams. Just slightly more than a century after Micah's time, the King of Babylon paused to 'consult' (*liqsōm-qāsem*) the spiritual realm to determine whether to attack Jerusalem or Rabbath-Ammon first; he engaged other mechanisms as well (Ezek. 21:24–29[19–24]). Divination and magic share the same objective – accessing the divine. Israel absorbed some of these practices, and the fine line between divination and magic is not always clear. When divination occurs in conjunction with falsehood, however, it is clearly reprehensible. This is evidenced by the strong condemnation in the Pentateuch (Lev. 19:26–31; Deut. 18:10–14) and prophetic oracles. Zech. 10:2 draws together *tĕrāpîm* who speak wickedness and diviners who see falsehood. The multiple parallel terms describing these forbidden practices and their practitioners hint at the wide array of mechanisms that were employed. To make the matter more ambiguous, *qesem* seems to carry a positive valence in Prov. 16:10 – an oracle on the lips of the king. See Horsnell, *NIDOTTE* 3:945–951. Caught up in the fray between cultural 'parties' – two groups against each other – YHWH's people will be ravaged (see Jer. 6:13–15; 8:14–15; Ezek. 13:10–16). It all is totally unwarranted. Depending on the historical context, this may even have pitted Israelite against Israelite. If Micah was addressing the last decades of the fracturing northern kingdom, there was intertribal hostility (2 Chr. 28:9).

The prophets' bad reputation by the time of Zechariah (13:2–6) is a carry-over from the steady stream of deceit uttered by false prophets in the last days of the southern kingdom. They lulled the people to sleep instead of issuing wake-up calls, telling them what they wanted to hear and undermining Jeremiah's warnings and pleas for repentance. It was they who spearheaded the idolatry and false self-dependence that led to the exile. Parts of Jer. 23:9–40 echo into Zechariah. Seventy years later, following a brutal exile, the people were still trying to put their lives back together.

The true prophetic voice and those who claimed allegiance to YHWH but insidiously planted false expectations and theologies in the minds of their audiences sometimes blurred together. We are reminded of Balaam, who did receive revelation from YHWH (Num. 22 – 24), and of the prophets surrounding Micaiah ben Imlah, who also had revelation from the heavenly court (1 Kgs 22). That Micah the Morashti would pronounce against the visionaries of his day a darkening of their prophetic abilities suggests that they had indeed experienced revelation from YHWH at some point. God's covenant people have constantly to be on their guard against the half-truths that lull them to sleep with cheap promises of *šālôm* that are divorced from godly repentance (Waltke 2007: 170–173). May God spare us from the sober consequences of crowd-pleasing preaching!

When the writing prophets spoke, they were outside the social institutions that had offered support to prior generations of prophets. It was, therefore, dangerous to speak truth that ran contrary to a party line. Add to that the inherent complexity of fraud, self-deception and gullibility on the part of both visionaries and their audiences. Many people no doubt believed what these prophets said, especially if they grounded it in declared allegiance to the covenant. This would reach the depths of depravity when they rationalized the kinds of injustices that were occurring: recall the 'orthodox trial' of Naboth (1 Kgs 21). At some points, the false prophets sound more 'correct' than Micah does, an illustration of the sobering fact that every orthodoxy is subject to corruption when its adherents succumb to moral self-deception (Andersen and Freedman 2000: 366–367).

The temptation to proclaim peace when the people's moral compass is askew is sometimes terribly strong; it is an easy message to preach. Jeremiah (Jer. 23) and Ezekiel (Ezek. 7:25; 13:8–10) faced this same wave of false prophets. Woe betide any population that follows culturally acceptable prophets whose words are determined solely by the desires of the audience! The matter is complicated: the psalmist struggled with competing cultural winds as well; he lived among those who hated peace, and when he spoke of peace, they spoke of war (Ps. 120:6–7).

MICAH 3:8–12

Translation

3:8 However, I, I am full of power, with the Spirit of YHWH, and judgment and might – to declare to Jacob his transgression and to Israel his sin.

9 Hear this, O heads of the house of Jacob and rulers of the house of Israel, those who abhor justice and twist everything that is straight;

10 the one who builds Zion with bloodshed, and Jerusalem with injustice.

[11]Her heads for a bribe will judge; and her priests for a price will instruct; and her prophets for silver will give divination; yet upon YHWH they lean, saying, 'Is not YHWH in our midst? Evil will not come upon us.'

[12]Therefore because of you, Zion will become a field that is plowed, and Jerusalem will become a ruin, and the mountain of the house will become forested high places.

Notes on the text

3:8. *wĕʾûlām* ('however') introduces the contrast between the false leaders Micah has just condemned and his own person. *kôaḥ* ('power') is separated from the rest by *rûaḥ yhwh* ('the Spirit of YHWH'). *rûaḥ yhwh* is omitted from Sym, and by numerous text critics as well. It interrupts the sequence of *kōaḥ . . . ûmišpāṭ ûgebûrâ* ('and judgment and might') but is in Mur and represented in Syr, Vg and Tg.

9. The masc. pl. pi. ptc. from the root *tʿb* means 'those who abhor' (*DCH* 8:655–656). The yiq. form closing the verse conveys the sense that they have customarily done this and can be expected to continue.

10. The subject of this clause is sg. – 'the one who is building Zion'. The LXX, Tg and Vg have read it as pl., which fits better with the preceding verse (Goldingay 2021: 442). 'Blood' is pl. (*dāmîm*) and implies bloodshed in abundance, often in the context of violence. See *DCH* 2:446. The parallel word in the next clause is *ʿawlâ*, denoting 'severe injustice'.

11. Verb forms return to 3 masc. pl. yiq. The nouns are also pl. Each has the 3 fem. sg. pron. suff. (her); these are representatives of the leaders in Jerusalem.

The *bêt* prep. implies 'in exchange for'.

yišāʿēnû appears only in niph. and means to support oneself or lean upon (*DCH* 8:517–518). While it does have a physical sense in terms of leaning on a spear (2 Sam. 1:6) or another person (2 Kgs 5:18), most frequently it implies trust.

12. *tēḥārēš* is a niph. pass. form of *ḥrš* ('plough'). *ʿiyyîn* seems to be interchangeable with *ʿiyyîm*, the form that is in Jer. 26:18. Goldingay (2021: 443) indicates that *iyyîn* is the Aramaic form of the pl., corrected by Jeremiah. As it stands, it phonologically connects with *Ṣîyôn*. For *lĕbāmôt*, the LXX reads 'grove of a thicket'. The Tg reflects a similar downplaying of the connotations of *bāmôt*, with '*a thicket of the forest*' (Cathcart and Gordon 1989: 119; italics original).

Form and structure

The qualities that follow Micah's declaration that he is 'full' pile up together, syntactically illustrative of the 'fullness'.

'Heads of the house of Jacob' and 'leaders of the house of Israel' echo v. 1. 'Hating good and loving evil' is more specific; they abhor justice and twist that which is upright. Each clause of v. 11 front-loads the culprits (her heads, her priests, her prophets). The verbs come last (judge, teach, divine); in between are datives of means (bribe, price, silver). This repeated structure emphasizes the cumulative abuses. The shift to third person creates distance. The pronouncement of judgment is a threefold superlative: Zion, Jerusalem and the mountain of the house.

A Masoretic note beside 3:12 indicates that this is the midpoint in the verse count of the BoT. Both the text of Micah, especially with 'the days to come' (4:1), and the whole compilation look forward to judgment and restoration.

Comment

3:8. The 1 sg. pron. in addition to the 1 sg. finite verb *mālēʾtî* emphasizes Micah's declaration. The subject–verb combination essentially has two objects, both the Spirit of YHWH as well as the list of attributes. Micah is filled with the Spirit, and that filling entails the qualities of strength, justice and might. All are necessary to accomplish his mission. It may be that 'Spirit of YHWH' is embedded in the list of attributes to indicate their inseparability from the Spirit. These three characteristics may together be a hendiatreis, pointing to one extraordinarily mighty quality; Micah would need it in his ongoing preaching against sin (Waltke 2007: 167, 174–175). The prominence of justice stands out against the backdrop of the flagrant injustices Micah has just condemned.

gĕbûrâ may be distinguished from *kôaḥ*, as it comes from the language of warriors' courage in battle (Judg. 8:21; Isa. 3:25; Jer. 9:22[23]; see also Mic. 7:16). In Isa. 11:2, the shoot from Jesse is characterized by *gĕbûrâ* along with wisdom and understanding, counsel and might, knowledge and fear of YHWH. Micah's prophetic word comes with nothing less than divine power. The somewhat awkward syntax contributes to the force of the message. Everything about his false opponents is empty darkness – no visions, nothing. Micah, on the other hand, is brimming with power and the Spirit of YHWH infusing and undergirding everything he is called to declare as he confronts Jacob with his transgression and Israel with his sin. See 'Comment' on 1:5. This filling gives him YHWH's power against the power of crooked and unjust leaders who, no doubt, will do everything they can to maintain their power. While Micah himself is vulnerable, YHWH's Spirit is not.

9. Micah repeats the same summons with which he called the leaders in 3:1 – 'Hear this, you heads of Jacob and leaders of Israel!' This is the whole nation; there is no political nuance between northern and southern allegiances. The accusation of v. 1, veiled as a rhetorical question regarding their knowledge of justice, sharpens at this juncture. They *know* justice, but they scorn it. It is as if they have not grasped the previous message: with different words, he accuses them of the same moral depravity. Hating good and loving evil are now represented as abhorring and despising justice and twisting everything that is straight. The description fairly leaps into the twenty-first century.

These are strong, emotionally wrenching, words. The noun form of the verb translated 'despise' or 'abhor' includes both ethical infractions such as lying, as well as ritually abhorrent practices, the epitome of which is idolatry. The masc. pl. ptc. describes their ongoing loathing of justice. The structure of the second line of the verse plants justice and uprightness in the middle, tragically enveloped by those who loath and twist. They pervert everything that is straight. *yĕšārâ* (a fem. sg. noun) is much more common as an adj., modifying 'way' or 'path (Andersen and Freedman 2000: 381).

10. 'Bloodshed' and 'injustice' together issue the strongest indictment against this builder of Zion, for whom shedding human blood to accomplish his purposes was a matter of course. If a singular 'builder' is intended by *bōneh*, it may be an oblique reference to one of the named kings in the introduction, although there is no def. art. on the ptc. Of the three, Ahaz's career was marked by unsavoury activities in the extreme (2 Kgs 16; see 2 Chr. 28:13), and those may lie behind the accusations and dire warnings of Micah. If so, no wonder Hezekiah takes Micah's words to heart and shifts course when he comes to the throne (Jer. 26:18). Having said that, there may be an ominous pointer in Isa. 22:9–11 to activities closer to Hezekiah himself that are not pleasing to YHWH. Vv. 9–10 sound initially like accolades but v. 11 contains a rebuke: 'you' (pl.) did not look to the One who planned all this. See 'Explanation'. While Hezekiah's religious reform turns the tide for the period of his reign, it does not take long for the ugly spectres of injustice, paralysis of the law, violence and destruction to become the definitive features of Jerusalem's cultural scene (Hab. 1:2–4). Habakkuk echoed Micah's outcry, using the same expressions: 'Woe to the one who builds a city with bloodshed and establishes a town with iniquity' (2:12).

Regardless of which monarch may be in view, the horror of the overall scene escapes us unless we pause to reflect. Zion is God's holy mountain; Jerusalem is the city of the great King (Ps. 48:2–3[1–2]). The image of blood dripping from its stones and iniquity seeping through its foundations is utterly discordant. The imagery graphically portrays the wholesale effects of injustice at every level. The leaders and people are alike culpable. In the next verse, Micah articulates the crimes.

11. Each of the guilty groups is named in succession; their identity appears before their crime. While prophets and judicial heads are charged more than once in this chapter, this is the only place where priests are named. The yiq. verbs imply the incessant nature of these reprehensible activities. It comes down to money at every level. Bribes get judicial preference from the heads, entirely contrary to the injunctions against showing partiality in judgment, either to rich or poor (Exod. 23:1–8; Deut. 10:17–18; 16:18–20; 27:25; see also Prov. 17:23). In the wider culture, awash in practices that are in effect bribery, the admonitions in Torah and Proverbs are unique (Grisanti and McCann, *NIDOTTE* 4:75–76). The priests and Levites were responsible for teaching, and were to do so in the place YHWH would choose (Deut. 17:8–13). It was a sober responsibility to be conducted in God's presence. Micah, however, accuses them of issuing instructions simply for a price. Torah is bought and sold. Finally, Micah returns to the false prophets who engage in divination if there is sufficient silver offered to them, a reprise of 3:6. Even though their official activities are tainted in the extreme, all three categories of leaders presume to lean on YHWH. That trust may be directed to another person (2 Chr. 16:7; Ezek. 29:7) or to YHWH (2 Chr. 13:18; 14:10[11]; 16:7–8).

They reach the nadir when they claim that YHWH is obviously in their midst, so how can anything evil happen? It is dependence on the place, but that is the place they have polluted. The attitude resurfaces in Jeremiah's day when the people brazenly break the covenant and then intone 'the temple of YHWH' three times to assure their security (Jer. 7:3–15). While apostasy to other gods is heinous, false reliance on YHWH in the face of flagrant disobedience is the most insidious. Their confident question 'Is not YHWH in our midst?' and the accompanying presumption of security may sound like good traditional thinking. After all, it is a refrain through Ps. 46 (vv. 6, 8, 12[5, 7, 11]). It is not going to pass muster with Micah.

12. 'Therefore' echoes the judgment pronounced against the visionaries and diviners in v. 6. At this juncture, 'because of you (pl.)' is comprehensively directed at those leaders whom Micah identifies as culpable. They cover the gamut: political governance, prophetic guidance and sacerdotal functions are all interwoven in their social structures. They build Zion and Jerusalem with injustice; now they will 'unbuild' the city as it reverts to a ploughed field and a heap of ruins. Ploughing along with 'field' suggest an intentional cultivation process in place of the urban and temple context. This declaration echoes the judgment against Samaria, soon to be reduced to a heap of rubble in the field (1:6). The parallel is unmistakable.

Three location names are specified as objects of YHWH's judgment. Together they completely disturb the presumed security of God's sanctuary in Jerusalem. A part of the city is Mount Zion; that in turn is where YHWH's residence is established – 'mountain of the house'. The first two will return to uncultivated status.

The pl. *bāmôt* as the descriptor of 'mountain of the house' is appropriate in this context; it echoes the initial condemnation in 1:5. The extent of its ruin would be indicated by overgrowth of shrubs and trees. The destruction of high places is a familiar image: a generation prior to Micah,

Hosea warned the northern kingdom of the same end (Hos. 10:8). Isaiah declares that YHWH will come down – echoing Mic. 1:3 – to do battle on Mount Zion, on its hills. It may be that Micah uses the term 'mountain of the house' instead of 'temple' because the description is so disturbing. The threat of return to forested and uninhabited land carries images of wildness, danger and uncleanness (Isa. 13:19–22; Jer. 9:9–10[10–11]; 50:39).

bāmôt is the same term Ezekiel uses for cultic sites on mountain tops where multiple deities are worshipped (Ezek. 6:1–7). Instead of the mountain where YHWH alone has his dwelling – 'the mountain of the house' – the temple is filled with detestable images (Ezek. 8:8–18). Mount Zion becomes a high place just like all the others surrounding it. It is telling that Micah does not add YHWH to 'mountain of the house': it no longer merits that identification. It will be well on its way to becoming a forest, a location of wildness, danger and death. How different from the glory of the house of YHWH!

This is the passage that the elders of Jerusalem cite, with some minor modifications, when they rein in the death threats of the prophets and priests against Jeremiah. They declare that when Micah spoke these words in the days of Hezekiah, the king feared YHWH, pleaded for mercy and did not put Micah to death (Jer. 26:18–19). Whether it was the Assyrian attack of Sennacherib or prior hostilities, YHWH's judgment as prophesied by Micah was forestalled. Nevertheless, in the aftermath of Nebuchadnezzar's destruction in 587/586 BC, Jerusalem was indeed 'ploughed as a field' and reduced to rubble.

Explanation

Early in his prophetic ministry, Isaiah utters a brief but stinging rebuke regarding Jerusalem's filth and bloodguilt; nevertheless, he anticipates the time when they will be cleaned up (4:4). There may be a connection between Micah's description of building Jerusalem and Isa. 22:10–11. In the time of Hezekiah, when the ominous presence of the Assyrians was looming, significant structural changes were made to enhance the security of the city, especially in terms of its water supply and walls for the western hill expansions that had occurred in the preceding decades when refugees began flocking into the city. While those strategic plans were important and viewed through a favourable lens in the historical narratives recalling the work of Hezekiah to defend the city (2 Kgs 20:20; 2 Chr. 32:3–5, 30), Isaiah gives a more measured picture. The efforts to construct the wall involved breaking down houses to make the wall secure, perhaps the Iron Age equivalent of eminent domain, and perhaps without compensation. Evidence of this activity remains in the archaeological footprint in the Jewish Quarter of the Old City of Jerusalem.

There is an additional interpretive lens through which to view these statements. If Micah's accusation was directed to Ahaz, who had no qualms about passing his sons through the fire and absorbing pagan altars and practices (2 Kgs 16:3), perhaps 'building with bloodshed' means laying foundation stones accompanied by human sacrifice (Andersen and Freedman 2000: 382–383). It sounds too horrific even to consider, except that we have veiled allusions to human sacrifice for geopolitical purposes (cf. 2 Kgs 3:25–27).

The leaders in Micah's 'crosshairs' constitute the top strata of Israel's national identity. The corrupt collusion weaves an inescapable snare. The prophets proclaim a message presumably from YHWH (cf. v. 5); the priests teach it as God's truth; the leaders use the 'revelation' to unjustly grab benefits for themselves. Isaiah, Micah's contemporary, is more specific about the presumably powerful leadership that YHWH will remove from Jerusalem: they are valiant men, military leaders, judges, prophets, diviners, elders and counsellors of various stripes and allegiances (3:2–4). What courage it takes to engage those types! No wonder Micah reminds his audience of the power and might of the Spirit of YHWH (v. 8)! The grim reality of corrupt leadership in Judah continues unabated. From the crucible of Babylon, Ezekiel is called to witness these same failures of leadership (chs. 8, 13, 14). In our twenty-first century, we daily face the ugly spectre of corruption at every turn. Only sacrificial prayer can turn the tide. And drain the swamp.

Among the utter tragedies is the fact that the powerbrokers persuade themselves that they are safe in this racket because they are in proximity to the dwelling place of God. Just as they stole the lands of Israelites through oppression and extortion (2:2), now their prime 'real estate holding', the mountain of the house itself, will be ruined. Justice will be done in that sense. But that place cannot be left permanently in ruins: it is the dwelling place of YHWH Almighty. Ps. 132 remembers David's faithfulness in his desire to find a dwelling place for the Mighty One of Jacob (132:5, 7) and resting place for YHWH (132:8, 14). The designations Ephrathah and 'fields of the forest' appear in this context (132:6). The final dismal verse of ch. 3 is the launch for the next chapter's vision of hope for the mountain of YHWH.

Filled with strength, YHWH's Spirit and a mighty sense of justice, Micah states the indictment. How very different from his contemporaries who speak only when they feel sufficiently filled with food and drink! How can we be certain of that empowerment? A major component must be that we are so infused with the Word of God that we cannot contain it even if we try (Jer. 20:9). That means we can smell falsehood and corruption and are not swayed by smooth words. Note Acts 4:31: the apostles were filled with the Spirit and spoke boldly (see also Acts 13:46). Likewise, Paul condemns the ever-present compulsion both to hear only what we want to hear and to feed that appetite: 'For the time is coming when people will not endure sound teaching but having itching ears, they will accumulate for themselves teachers to suit their own passions' (2 Tim. 4:3).

How very timely this message! In a culture that is confounded by competing structures for presenting and shaping our experienced reality, God's people are summoned, as Micah was, to heed this 'stirring call to reason, to morality and to reality' (Allen 1976: 315). We must evaluate our lived experiences by the timeless truths of God's Word, read, memorized, pondered, repeated, applied.

MICAH 4:1–5

Translation

4:1 And in the days to come, the mountain of the house of YHWH will be established at the head of the mountains; it will be lifted up above the hills, and peoples will stream to it.

2 And many nations will come, and they will say: Come, let us go up to the mountain of YHWH, to the house of the God of Jacob so that he may teach us his ways, and we may walk in his paths. For from Zion Torah will go forth, and the word of YHWH from Jerusalem.

3 And he will judge among many peoples and will adjudicate for strong nations far off. And they will hammer their swords into cutting implements and their spears into knives for pruning. Nation will not lift up sword against nation, and they will no longer learn war.

4 And each person will sit under his vine and under his fig tree, and no one will cause dread, for the mouth of YHWH of Hosts has spoken.

5 Though all the peoples continue to walk, each in the name of his god, we will walk in the name of YHWH our God for ever and ever.

Notes on the text

The parallel text in Isaiah underlies many of the *BHS* notes. This frequently involves shifting *gōyīm* and *ʿammîm*. See the comparison in the 'Introduction'.

4:1. *wĕhāyâ* introduces an ideal forthcoming narrated future that, as with many waw- plus *hyh* forms, is only loosely connected with the preceding discourse (*IBHS* §32.2.6c).

'In the days to come' (*bĕʾaḥărît hayyāmîm*) is used fourteen times in the HB. It points to an 'envisioned' future, distant from the speaker's perspective (Waltke 2007: 192).

The LXX omits *bêt* ('house') and simply has the equivalent of the mountain of YHWH. It renders *nākôn* ('established') twice and has 'they shall hasten' for *wĕnāhărû* ('they will stream'). *nākôn* is a niph. masc. ptc. from *kûn*, 'to be firm'. *wĕniśśā'* is a niph. masc. ptc., continuing the sense of *nākôn*. The pass. forms intimate that YHWH is the power behind this transformation.

2. The qal masc. pl. impv. *lĕkû* ('come') is followed by a 1 pl. coh., *wĕnaʿăleh* ('let us go up').

'Let him instruct us' is juss. with the pron. suff. It is a prayer, followed by a coh. exhortation – 'let us walk' (*wĕnēlkâ*).

3. *bên* means 'among' instead of 'between' in this context; there are multiple nations involved. *rab* and *ʿāṣûm* are frequently used together, indicating strong and mighty numbers of people. Zech. 8:21–22 expresses the same intent on the part of many peoples and strong nations to seek YHWH in Jerusalem.

hôkîaḥ is a hiph. qat. form of *ykḥ*, meaning to 'decide, judge, reprove, rebuke, correct' (*DCH* 4:209–210). The verb is often used in concert with *špṭ*.

The prep. *lĕ-* could be either 'on behalf of' or 'against' mighty nations even from far away – *ʿad-rāḥôq*. The phrase is not in the parallel passage in Isa. 2. Although it is not as common to render the lamed prep. as 'against', it fits the context better (see *IBHS* §11.2.10).

The 3 masc. pl. pi. of *ktt* means to 'hammer into pieces' (*DCH* 4:478). The meaning of *ʾittîm* is uncertain. They were cutting instruments made of iron (1 Sam. 13:20–21; Isa. 2:4; Mic. 4:3; Joel 4:10[3:10]) and must have been small enough that retooled swords would work for the makeover. Byington (1949: 52) suggests they were 'hoes'. The words translated 'hoe' (both verb and noun form) in Isa. 7:25 are from *ʿdr*, used only in that passage and Isa. 5:6. Perhaps smaller implements were attached to long wooden poles.

mazmērôt, the product of their reworked spears, occurs only as a pl. in the same passages as above, along with Isa. 18:5. 'Raise' (*yiśʾû*) is a pl. verb with the collective sg. subject (*gôy*).

4. *ʾîš* is distributive (each person), used with the pl. verb.

maḥărîd is the hiph. masc. sg. ptc. from *ḥrd* ('to tremble'). The same term is used in Lev. 26:6, promising peace and the release from paralysing fear when the people are obedient to the covenant.

5. In conjunction with the waw introducing the second clause, *kî* may best be translated 'though' (GKC §159bb; see also 7:8). Together they set up the contrast. Nevertheless, Goldingay (2021: 443) rejects that option, and it is not a common rendering of the particle. *kôl* followed by *ʾîš* indicates the reality of distinctions within the universal tendency of humans to seek after the divine. The expression is used only here in the HB. Instead of 'in the name of his god', the LXX has 'his way'. The Tg interprets the expression: they '*shall be guilty because they worshipped idols*' (Cathcart and Gordon 1989: 120; italics original).

Form and structure

On the macro level, the following connections and contrasts between the previous chapter(s) and chapter 4 are noteworthy:

> absence of holiness (esp. 3:10–12) / *God*'s 'house' (4:1)
> wicked 'heads' (3:1, 9) / 'head' of the mountains (4:1)
> bloodshed built Zion (3:10) / Torah going out from Zion (4:2)
> 'refugees' to Jerusalem (2:12–13) / pilgrim nations to Zion (4:1–2)
> injustice (2:1–2; 3:1–11) / YHWH's justice (4:3)
> false peace (3:5) / real peace (4:4)
> priests' 'instruction' (3:11) / YHWH's instruction (4:2)

There are word pairs throughout that hint at totality: mountains and hills, peoples and nations, ways and paths, swords and spears.

Comment

4:1. Hope for the future necessitates God's intervention to reverse the current state: there will be restoration after the catastrophe that closes ch. 3. This points to a significant 'turning point within history when YHWH will bring about his will' (Allen 1976: 324). After the forthcoming judgment that devastates Zion, the iconic mountain will not only be restored, but will draw many nations to it. 'In the days to come' need not have eschatological implications in this context: there is no sense of termination. Likely contributing to the association with the 'end', is the frequent translation in the LXX of *ʾaḥărît* ('after' or 'end') as *eschatos* ('last'). See Buchanan 1961: 188–193 and Willis 1979: 54–71.

The yiq. form of *hāyâ* followed by *nākôn* indicates that the mountain of the house of YHWH will be established with certainty (see *IBHS* §37.7.1b). 'Hills' (*gĕbāʿôt*), parallel to *hārîm* ('mountains') in more than half its occurrences, are generally lower in elevation. They also are associated with pagan worship: the phrase 'on every hill and under every green tree' is illustrative (Deut. 12:2; 2 Kgs 17:10; Jer. 2:20). See Selman, *NIDOTTE* 1:805.

The elevation of Zion is a multifaceted figure. From a purely geographical perspective, the temple area, while higher than the City of David, is lower than the mountains that surround it. For it to be elevated about the hills, 'lifting up' would be necessary, not an impossibility in that seismically active region. Zechariah envisions geophysical tumult in his apocalyptic vision of 'the day of YHWH' (Zech. 14:3–5). Further, Zion has been humiliated; the restoration of YHWH's favour and presence there will mark a transformation of cosmic proportions. The geographical description is a 'political and religious metaphor communicating the prestige and authority of the God who dwelt in the temple' (Jenson 2008: 145). As a result, peoples and nations will stream to Jerusalem.

While the terms have overlapping semantic ranges, *gôy* usually signifies 'nation' or some other geopolitical entity, while *ʿam* is a group related by blood ties (Andersen and Freedman 2000: 403). *wĕnāhărû* is a denominative verb, used infrequently and only figuratively (Jer. 51:44); the noun means 'river' or 'stream'. Although water rushes downward, here many nations and peoples are 'flowing towards' (*ʿâlâw*) the presence of YHWH, reminiscent of the pilgrimages to Zion for the three annual festivals. *ʿâlâw* may also be understood as 'upon it [the stream]'. There is a second meaning for *nhr*, 'to be radiant or shining' (see Jer. 31:12; BDB 626; *DCH* 5:632), which may hint at their radiance in the presence of YHWH. The parallel in Isaiah has *ʾēlāyw*, which works better with the verbs of 'going' in the next verse.

'Going up' to Jerusalem has a long tradition; the psalms of ascent (120–134) are an expression of that pilgrimage, sung as the children of Israel made their way to Jerusalem for the festivals (cf. Ps. 122:3–4). Ps. 48:2–3[1–2] declares that Mount Zion is beautiful in elevation, the joy of all the earth.

2. The encouragement to 'go up' points to the notion of approaching YHWH in his heavenly dwelling, represented on earth by the temple. The expression Mount of YHWH echoes Sinai from which Torah was given. 'God of Jacob' does not appear elsewhere in the prophets, but it does occur in the psalms of Zion (46:8[7], 12[11]; 76:7[6]; 84:9[8]).

The root *hlk* occurs three times in this verse; the first two instances signify movement on the part of peoples and nations towards YHWH's presence on Mount Zion. This is a mutual invitation to go up to his 'house' on his holy mountain. Those who gather in the throng are intent on learning from the ways of YHWH. The words for 'way' (*derek*) and 'path' (*ʾōraḥ*) are basically synonymous; the latter is more frequent in poetry. 'God's ways' include the recitals of his acts in history on behalf of his covenant people along with his statutes, precepts and requirements for the covenant people. Learning God's ways will inevitably transform them: they will conduct themselves appropriately in accordance with being God's representatives. That is how Torah will go forth from Jerusalem: it will be embodied.

3. Attention shifts from the nations who will learn the ways of YHWH to the activities of YHWH himself. In previous chapters, injustice has been high profile, but these declarations affirm that a time is coming when injustice will be set right on a global level. If the lamed prep. is interpreted as 'on behalf of' strong nations, it implies YHWH will take the part of the mighty and powerful, not the first expected outcome. Nevertheless, this prospect could mean their powerful force will not allow them to get away with heavy-handed brutality. International as well as intertribal disputes will be under the purview of the Judge of all the earth. Not only will the internal bribery and wickedness of the contemporary leaders (ch. 3) cease, but God's perfect arbitration will eradicate international aggression. YHWH will judge and adjudicate. The same two verbs appear in Isa. 11:3–4 in the description of the shoot from the stump of Jesse. When the Spirit of YHWH rests upon him, in righteousness, he will judge for the poor and the meek. On YHWH's 'holy mountain' there will be no one hurting or causing destruction, because the knowledge of YHWH will cover the earth (Isa. 11:9). That kingdom scene appears in Isa. 25:6–8 – YHWH of Hosts will prepare a banquet on this mountain and abolish death for all peoples on this mountain. Seeing well beyond his Babylonian context, Daniel envisions the stone becoming a great mountain and filling the earth (2:35, 44–45).

The second half of the verse describes the results. The sociocultural landscape will shift when YHWH judges: no geopolitical entity will engage in hostile actions. It will be necessary to hammer war weapons sufficiently to reshape them into tools. Swords and spears represent the major components of Israel's military equipment. The agricultural implements are not as easily identified. See 'Notes on the text'. The occurrence of *mazmērôt* in Isa. 18:5 is in a context that has to do with trimming 'small tendrils' (*hazzalzallîm*). That word is a **hapax**, which makes it likewise difficult to pinpoint. *zll* means 'to shake', so the suggestion is that these are small branches. The implement necessary to trim them would necessarily be long enough to reach twigs. Former spears would work well. The entire arsenal will be reconstituted. There is a radical refocusing from hostile aggression to stewarding the land, a faint echo of Eden. It will be global disarmament. For the opposite in the day of judgment, see Joel 4:10[3:10].

4. The radical demilitarization means the elimination of dreaded external threats and an accompanying reduction in taxes that support the national defence budget. The security of God's people will be assured (Jenson 2008: 147). 'Dwelling' is the traditional image for well-being. Dwelling under their own vine and fig tree communicates prosperity in that secure place (see Zech. 3:10). 'Vine and fig' are the ideal representation of *šālôm*. It intentionally echoes the security and expansive kingdom during the Solomonic era (1 Kgs 5:4–5[4:24–25]) and was part of a tantalizing Assyrian offer to the beleaguered defenders of Jerusalem (2 Kgs 18:31; Isa. 36:16). It is also an explicit contrast to the illegitimate snatching of land evident in 2:1–2. Added to that, no one will terrify them, because they will be free from the anxiety of war-torn regions.

The promise is guaranteed by God's own faithful Word – because 'the mouth of YHWH of hosts has spoken'. Isaiah uses the same expression (1:20; 40:5; 58:14). Unique to Micah is the addition of Saba'oth. *ṣebāʾôt*, often translated 'Almighty' or carried across as 'Saba'oth', means 'armies'. These 'hosts' can be human participants in warfare but also the hosts of heaven, often the objects of idolatrous worship (Deut. 4:19; 17:3;

2 Kgs 17:16). Most significant, however, is its incorporation into the Name of God, indicating his sovereign control over all these forces of the heavenly realms; they are *his* army (see 1 Sam. 17:45). Among a 'host' of additional references, Judg. 5:20 indicates that the stars from heaven fought against Sisera. They do God's will (Ps. 103:19–22).

5. Micah's contemporary reality includes those who do not declare allegiance to YHWH in Zion. The human quest for the divine does cross all boundaries, but it does not obliterate those boundaries. Each individual will choose to 'walk in name of his god'. This closure recognizes that not *all* the nations will be streaming towards the mountain of YHWH at this time. There will be those, represented by *ʾîš*, who will persist in walking in the names of their gods. The LXX reads 'in his way', which is somewhat more ambiguous in terms of their choice. The contrast is emphatic, introduced by 'but we'. Micah and those who are faithful to YHWH will walk in the Name of YHWH. 'Name' embodies the nature and character of the sovereign of the covenant (Exod. 34:6–7) and evokes confidence in God's truth. It is a **metonymous** representation of YHWH, who dwells in the sanctuary, protects the people and is jealous for his reputation. See Ross, *NIDOTTE* 4:147–151.

There is a temporal indicator at this point that balances the 'in the days to come' of the opening declaration. God's faithful people will walk in the Name of YHWH 'to the distant future [*lĕʿôlām*] and beyond [*wāʿēd*]', pointing to the ideal future. In addition to its use (twelve times) in the psalms, the expression appears in Exod. 15:18 in the culmination of the song of Moses and the Israelites: YHWH will reign 'to the distant future and beyond'.

Explanation

Prophetic hope reverberates through this oracle as it envisions these events in the historical future. Historical realities, such as Zion and Jerusalem, are part of the picture. At the same time, it rests above the current scene, merging the realities of the revelation on Mount Sinai with the Mount of YHWH, the temple on Zion. The certainty embedded in *nākôn* draws in other realities, the throne of God established in the heavens on the foundation of justice and righteousness (Ps. 89:15[14]) and the throne of David (78:67–72). Even in a geopolitical context fraught with war, cruelty and destruction, it transcends those circumstances with the prospect of tranquility. On the larger scale of Micah, 4:1–5 is the 'end' of the story, situated in the centre of the book (Andersen and Freedman 2000: 430).

These 'days to come' have a temporal 'thickness' (Waltke 2007: 192) that includes restoration from exile all the way to new heavens and new earth, depending on the context in which the expression occurs (Gen. 49:1; Num. 24:14; Deut. 4:30; 31:29; Isa. 2:2 // Mic. 4:1; Jer. 23:20; 30:24; 48:47;

49:39; Ezek. 38:16; Dan. 2:28 [Aramaic]; 10:14; Hos. 3:5). In this context, the envisioned future is built around the Torah's going forth from Zion. The images of peoples streaming to Zion followed by Torah's going forth join the imagery of the river whose streams are a cause for rejoicing to Zion (Ps. 46:5[4]). All provide nourishment, renewal and restoration, and point forward to the water flowing from the throne of God (Ezek. 47:1–12; Rev. 22:1–2). Jeremiah, despite his grim circumstances, likewise looks forward to a time when all nations will gather to the throne of YHWH in Jerusalem (3:17–18). YHWH loves Zion, the holy mountain where he founded his city. 'Glorious things of Thee are spoken, Zion, city of our God' (Ps. 87:1–3).

In the ANE, establishing the residence of a god at the top of a mountain conveyed multiple messages. Among them, the deity was victorious over chaos, this location was presumed to provide a means of access into the god's presence and the 'sacred space' indicated that the deity dwelt with this people. In that wider world-view context, it was important that the mountain of YHWH's dwelling would be higher than all the others. It powerfully symbolized his sovereign rule over all creation, a reality that was yet in the future (Waltke 2007: 195).

The dominant entreaty through Ps. 119 is that YHWH will teach his servants his ways, his Torah, his precepts and his decrees so that their (our) conduct will be blameless and pure. Even more, the psalmist finds great delight in living within that world view, seeing wonderful things in YHWH's Torah (v. 18) and singing about his decrees (v. 54). Ps. 24:3–4 articulates significant criteria for ascending the 'Mount of YHWH'. They include above all clean hands and pure hearts. The future pilgrimage to Mount Zion echoes Israel's three annual pilgrimages to Jerusalem, enjoined in Torah, for appearing before YHWH. Here, Israel will be joined by a multitude from the nations.

Transformed by God's word, living Torah-bearers will then be testimonies. YHWH's way is perfect, and his word is true (Ps. 18:31[30]); he makes our way reflect that same quality (Ps. 18:33[32]). We must be armed with God's teaching (Torah) so that we 'walk in his ways'. Ps. 86:11 is a daily prayer:

> Teach me, O YHWH, your way,
> that I may walk in your truth.
> Unite my heart to fear your Name.

From a NT perspective, we are privileged to be 'living epistles' (2 Cor. 3:2–3). See also Isa. 51:4 – the law will go out and effect justice, righteousness and salvation. This transformation, if authentic, will affect for good all aspects of culture: education, artistic endeavours, politics and economics.

Rather than 'learning war', the nations will pursue Torah and the Word of YHWH. Martial skills will be unnecessary in this peace that will be founded on God's teaching, not on the empty promises of false prophets. The same prophetic hope for the obliteration of all war equipment appears in Isa. 9:3–4[4–5] and Ps. 46:10[9]. While much of the Western church has been graciously spared the terrors of physical combat, individually we nonetheless harbour a subtler arsenal of aggressive weapons. Among them may be 'our barbed tongues, our sharp tongues, and our cutting words', all very much in need of retooling (Wolff 1981: 176).

Everyone dwelling securely 'under his own vine and fig tree' further implies that contentment will characterize this future state. How radically different this is from the greed described in 2:1–2! The endless compulsion to obtain more will no longer be part of the embedded world view, nor will it be supported by systemic structures that encourage it. Curbing the human tendency towards self-indulgence will eradicate the hostilities that result from personal, social and international covetousness. This is guaranteed by nothing less than YHWH's unchangeable Word.

The intent to 'walk in the Name YHWH' is a public declaration of allegiance based on knowledge of YHWH's unfailing covenant character and the truthfulness of his Word. It is a declaration of faith and faithfulness through all generations of God's people. This affirmation is a contrast to nations who choose to stay with their own idolatrous world views and have not joined the pilgrim throng to Jerusalem.

MICAH 4:6–8

Translation

4:6 In that day, declares YHWH, I will surely gather those who are limping, and those
who have been driven away, I will certainly bring together – whom I have caused
evil.

7 And I will make the limping a remnant and those far removed a powerful
nation, and YHWH will rule over them on Mount Zion from now and for ever.

8 And you, O watchtower of the flock, stronghold of the Daughter of Zion, unto
you it will come; the former dominion will come, the kingdom to the Daughter
of Jerusalem.

Notes on the text

4:6. *nĕʾum* always appears in const., most frequently followed by the divine Name as a prophetic voice speaks the oracle. Used 376 times in the HB, most of them in the writing prophets, it indicates a formal utterance. Translating it with the archaic 'saith' is appropriate.

ʾōspâ is the 1 sg. coh. of a qal pe-'aleph verb; see GKC §68gh on the form. This may also be a wordplay on both *ʾsp* and *ysp* ('to add/increase'), suggesting an emphasis on gathering in this context (Andersen and Freedman 2000: 433).

The qal fem. sg. ptc. of *ṣlʿ* is a personification of Judah as an injured and broken flock. Its parallel, the niph. fem. sg. ptc. of *ndḥ*, is likewise descriptive of those who will be driven into exile.

The verb of the final clause is the 1 sg. hiph. qat. form of *rʿʿ*, meaning 'to harm, injure, or destroy' (*DCH* 7:530).

7. *weśamtî* (1 sg. qal weqat. form) plus *lĕ-* expresses the resultant consequence for the direct object (*haṣṣōlēʿâ*): 'I will make the lame a remnant'. The root and meaning of *hannahălāʾâ* (niph. fem. sg. ptc., a **hapax**) are unclear. It has been variously translated; the LXX has 'thrust back, driven away'. The Hebr. form may be from *hlʾ* (BDB 229; *DCH* 2:543–544), possibly understood as 'the far-offed one' (Hillers 1984: 54). The adv. *hālĕʾâ* means 'to be farther away' (cf. Gen. 35:21; Jer. 22:19; Amos 5:27). See Waltke 2007: 222 for a review of the attempts of early versions to address the meaning.

8. For 'tower of the flock', the Tg reads 'O anointed One of Israel', no doubt shaped by the rest of the verse as well as the forthcoming allusions in 5:1[2]. It continues with an expansion: '*who* have been hidden away because of the sins of the congregation of Zion.' 'Hidden' may reflect an interpretation of *ʿōpel* as meaning 'dark' (Cathcart and Gordon 1989: 120).

The double subject of both *tēʾteh* and *bāʾâ* (3 fem. sg. qal forms) is 'dominion', including both 'former dominion' and 'kingdom', even though there is an ***athnach*** under *tēʾteh*. The Tg shifts the adjective 'first' or 'former' to modify 'dominion' in the second part of the verse. The root of *tēʾteh* is *ʾth* (*DCH* 1:454; GKC §68f). It is an archaic form, meaning 'to come', suggestive of the theophany of Deut. 33:2. The *daghesh* in the taw is due to the final *kā* on *ʿādêkā* that immediately precedes this verb. The masc. sg. pron. suff. refers to *ʾttâ*, 'you'. Waltke (2007: 232–233) reviews the attempts to address the complicated sentence structure.

Form and structure

This segment, commencing with 'in that day', fits inside the prior framework ('in the days to come'). It introduces an intermediate temporal framework as a mediating link, and holds out hope for the Daughter of Zion with a return to the imagery of both Shepherd and King. The verbs from 2:12–13 – gather and bring together – recur in v. 6, pointing much further into the future. There are three developments through vv. 6–7: YHWH will gather; he will transform; he will rule. V. 8 initiates an intricate sound and semantic pattern that shapes the text to 5:1[2]. The outer framework is composed of 'and/but you' (*wĕʾattâ*), both here and in 5:1[2]. In between, vv. 9 and 14[5:1] commence with *ʿattâ* ('now'), v. 10

drives it forward with *kî-ʿattâ* ('for now') and v. 11 starts with *wĕʿattâ* (either 'and now' or 'but now'). In each case, the 'now' sections all address Jerusalem in contexts of disaster that will be turned around. The absence of specific historical anchors contributes to its ongoing affirmation by successive generations of readers. The units are woven together, binding the past with the future. Each depends on the details of the preceding ones, and together they provide hope for a readership that is still under duress (Ben Zvi 2000: 120–123).

Comment

4:6. 'In that day' introduces the scenario in vv. 6–8; it serves as a mediating link between the previous vignette and the future glory described in the next verses. It starts with YHWH's declaration that he will gather. This regathering echoes the promise in Deut. 30:1–4: those who had been driven away will be restored and regathered. The imagery ('lame' and 'those thrust out') and language of gathering and assembling recall the sheep from 2:12–13. The word translated 'lame' is used only here, in Gen. 32:32[31] (Jacob limping), and Zeph. 3:19, which reads 'at that time, I will save the limping, gather those thrust out'. The immediate referents of 'those banished or thrust out' are exiles.

A third description extends and disturbs the parallel: the rel. pron. with the conj. (*wĕʾăšer*; 'even those whom') introduces the previously mentioned broken and scattered ones as being in that condition because of YHWH. He does not remove himself from involvement with the just punishment that has come upon them. YHWH's acknowledgment is 'I brought about the evil'– when his people do evil, YHWH responds in measure. The promise, however, looks beyond the forthcoming consequences of their persistent disobedience. The Shepherd will most surely gather and bring them together, even this unwieldy collection of battered sheep and exiles far away.

7. Those 'far removed' is parallel to 'those driven far away' in the preceding verse. After the first affirmation that YHWH will make those broken ones a remnant, the next clause is a surprise. That remnant, once far away, will become a 'mighty nation': YHWH will transform the remnant. When YHWH establishes his dominion on Mount Zion, he will reign over the remnant, providing everlasting protection – 'from now and to the distant and unbounded future'.

8. The tone switches at this point to addressing personified locations, Migdal Eder and the 'Ophel of the Daughter of Zion'. The verse is a hinge between the preceding promise to bring back and transform the remnant and the next developments. *migdal* means 'tower', generally with reference to a security feature of cities and towns. Being joined with *ʿēder* suggests a powerful symbol for the people.

'And you' commences the verse; it will return in the address to Bethlehem (5:1[2]). Common to both will be the rule of a king who is clearly related to the Davidic line. There has been considerable discussion on how to understand Migdal Eder and Ophel in conjunction with Daughter of Zion. In the past, many interpreted them as separate towns around Jerusalem (Waltke 2007: 230). More likely, they are two names for the same general location. The tower will provide protection for God's bruised flock that has been thrust out of Jerusalem. Echoing the end of ch. 2, this suggests that Jerusalem itself with YHWH in its midst will be their strong tower. Thus, a specific location is not the point. See Zech. 10:3, which declares that YHWH of Hosts will visit 'his flock' (*edrô*), the house of Judah.

In Jerusalem geography, the Ophel was a section south of the temple mount. The verbal root of Ophel means 'to swell'; that fits with the topographical bulge at this point. The term always appears with the definite article ('the Ophel'), generally in conjunction with a fortifying wall. It might have been a later name for the Millo, the outer part of the reconstruction work that David did near the crest of the Jebusite city after he conquered it (2 Sam. 5:6–9; 2 Chr. 11:5–8). Solomon's Jerusalem building activities also included building the Millo (1 Kgs 9:15, 24; 11:27). In Micah's day, Hezekiah repaired the walls of the city of David, raised towers and strengthened the Millo (2 Chr. 32:5). 'Millo' means 'fill' and likely took its name from the massive supporting structure built up around the narrow neck of bedrock that connects the City of David with what became the temple mount. Jotham built the wall of the Ophel (2 Chr. 27:3). When Manasseh rebuilt the outer wall of the City of David, west of the Gihon, it encircled the Ophel (2 Chr. 33:14). Temple servants living on the Ophel (Neh 3:26; 11:21) repaired the wall opposite the water gate to the east and the projecting tower, and the men of Tekoa worked from the projecting tower to the wall of the Ophel (Neh. 3:27). Both 'tower of the flock' and 'Ophel' are symbols of strength.

The term 'Daughter of Zion' introduces a personification of Jerusalem/Zion (2 Kgs 19:21) that expresses the tender and vulnerable relationship between God and God's chosen dwelling place. It appears in conjunction with God's disappointment, sorrow and punishment (Isa. 1:8; Jer. 6:2) as well as promise for deliverance (Isa. 52:2–3; 62:11).

The verse is shaped by pairs: Migdal Eder and Ophel; will come and will enter; 'former dominion' and 'kingdom'. The two verbs appear together prior to the two subjects indicating dominion. It is helpful to untangle them. Having done that, it is still unclear to what 'former dominion' refers in Israel's historical context. In addition to 'kingdom', it may be a subtle pointer to David and connect with Bethlehem and 'origins of old' (5:1[2]). The return to and recovery of Jerusalem will involve YHWH as King and perhaps a human appointee.

Explanation

The initial emphasis is on regathering the wounded and broken flock. The intertextual connection with Jacob's limping (Gen. 32:32[31]) is not to be missed: YHWH wounded Jacob's hip in the night-time wrestling match. These wounded sheep are Jacob's descendants. Just as YHWH blessed Jacob, YHWH will care for them. Faithful to his covenant, YHWH has brought the disastrous consequences of their disobedience upon them; now restoration is the focus. The figure of the Shepherd King is evocative of both tender care and power. Its initial referents are the exiled, broken and chastised people of YHWH. In the future, his gathering will extend to a wider range of the broken and excluded; they will rejoice on his holy mountain (Isa. 56:4–8).

YHWH promises to transform this broken remnant into a mighty nation. The term 'remnant' is significant in prophetic judgment oracles because it contains the kernel of hope. It is the small but surviving community that will continue the living memories and traditions promised to the patriarchs. It is therein that their strength lies (Waltke 2007: 227). YHWH will rule over them (anticipating ch. 5) on Mount Zion 'from now and to the distant future'.

The former dominion will come back. YHWH always reigns, but Israel does not always experience it. There are thematic connections with Isaiah's 'little apocalypse'. In that day, YHWH will punish, and he will reign on Mount Zion (24:21–23). YHWH has made the city a heap of ruins (25:2), but YHWH of Hosts will prepare on this mountain a feast (25:6–7).

MICAH 4:9–10

Translation

4:9 Now, why are you crying out a cry? Is there no king in you? Has your counsel perished, that writhing has gripped you as one giving birth?

10 Writhe and thrust forth, O Daughter of Zion, as one giving birth, because now you will come forth from the city, and you will dwell in the field. And you will come to Babylon. There you will be delivered. There YHWH will redeem you from the hand of your enemy.

Notes on the text

4:9. A few MSS of the LXX and Tg add the waw to *ʿattâ*.

The root meaning of *rûaʿ* is 'to raise a shout, either in triumph or distress'. The verb is a 2 fem. sg. hiph. It may intimate a call to arms (cf. Hos. 5:8), but here better fits with a scream of distress (*DCH* 7:451–452); both are loud and intended to disturb. The noun *rēaʿ*, appearing only here and Job 36:33, is a 'roar' or a 'shout' (BDB 929; *DCH* 7:513).

The syntax of the second line following the ***athnach*** is awkward. The interr. hê first introduces a question about the absent king. The next clause, starting with *ʾim*, may be an additional question, in which case *ʾim* is disjunctive (GKC §150c). That suggests the king and counsellor are two separate offices, and both have been rendered useless (see also *IBHS* §40.3b on questions marked by *ʾim*).

'Writhing' (*ḥîl*; a masc. sg. noun) is the subject of *heḥĕzîqēk* (3 masc. sg. hiph. with 2 fem. sg. suff.), which means to 'seize'. The impv. form appears in the next verse.

10. Two fem. sg. impv. forms *ḥûlî wāgōḥî* are directed to the Daughter of Zion, Jerusalem. The first connects with the use of *ḥîl* in the preceding verse. Isaiah uses the image frequently (13:8; 23:4–5; 26:17; 45:10; 66:7–8). The root of *gōḥî* is *gyḥ* ('burst forth'; *DCH* 2:344).

Form and structure

V. 9 introduces the first of the series of '(but) now' clauses (also vv. 11 and 14[5:1]), drawing attention back to the current crises. V. 10 continues the emphasis on 'now'. They are embedded within the framework of the homonym (4:8; 5:1[2]) 'and you'. While each of the oracles briefly draws the focus back to the crisis of 'now', it also ranges far ahead with a fuller hopeful prophecy.

The similitude 'like one giving birth' connects vv. 9 and 10. The two rhetorical commands of v. 10 sound like gasping (giving birth), and press ahead into small snippets, compressed future events, that move the inhabitants of Zion out and away.

Comment

4:9. 'Now', also in v. 10 ('for now') and 11, 4:14[5:1], signals transition to the current and foreseeable realities; it captures a definitive moment in Zion's history. The realities span from severe suffering to deliverance; they are marked by outcry and writhing in agony. The outcry is intense. The Daughter of Zion writhes in agony, likened to one giving birth; that pain compels her to scream. The semantic fields related to giving birth are rich in the HB. Fabry (*TDOT* 4:188–189) notes possible connections between cords and pregnancy; undoing knots loosens the unborn child to travail and birth pangs. There is an alternative possible interpretation. Instead of 'Why are you crying out in such distress?' it may be translated 'Why are you suffering such harm?' reading it as *tārôʿî rōaʿ* (see Prov. 11:15).

See, however, Exod. 32:17, where Joshua interpreted the roar of the people as war in the camp.

Micah's rhetorical questions may be sarcastic: Should not the presence of a king or an adviser in their midst ameliorate distress? If the 'adviser' is synonymous with 'king', this is the only place in the HB where that is so (Andersen and Freedman 2000: 445). More likely they are separate and refer to the utter failure of a human governing system at that point. The question could be raised as to when that might be. To be sure, this critique is fitting in the final throes of the northern kingdom and the perilous accompanying circumstances of the south. The reign of Ahaz could be a more likely time frame than that of Hezekiah, but the description is vague and applies across the generations of the Davidic dynasty – and beyond.

From another perspective, Micah may be expressing his incredulity at their utter disregard for YHWH as their King and Counsellor. The ambiguity in the text allows for multiple possibilities. Does Israel have a King and Counsellor? Yes: it is YHWH. But do they have one now? No. Because king and counsellor are rendered ineffective, she (the Daughter of Zion) is in wretched straits. Fierceness of childbirth pangs is a fitting image for their helpless and agonizing despair. The image continues into the next verse. Despite the anguish, however, the standard image of childbirth pain is not entirely discouraging because it points ahead to new life after pain that is endurable, made so by hope.

10. Just like labour pains, their agony intensifies; the language expresses that. It seems that the interpretation of 'bursting forth' fits the birthing scene best: Zion is urged by a midwife figure to bring the child through the pain of delivery (Waltke 2007: 241–242).

The image leaves no doubts as to the gripping agony. They are left without any king, whether human or divine, bereft of direction and any sense of where to turn in these tumultuous times. The repetition of 'like one in childbirth' emphasizes their vulnerable position. Neither the city nor the womb is any longer a safe haven. Jerusalem is called a *kiryâ* in this context, parallel to *ʿîr*, but possibly conveying the sense of a smaller city, as Jerusalem was.

What happens next is ambiguous. The yiq. form followed by weqat. verbs stretch out the process. The three successive clauses may be a capsule statement of the journey into exile and all the implications linked with eventually being in Babylon. On the other hand, it may simply refer to dispersion (Jenson 2008: 152–153). Micah emphasizes the pain of each stage of going, whether into exile or some other form of expulsion. First, they will exit, being thrust out of the city. Then, the conditions will be rugged at best; they will be 'camping' (*šākantĕ*) in the field. The verb means to 'stay' or to 'dwell' and implies an extended time in tents. YHWH's dwelling place in the midst of his people in the wilderness was a *miškān*, the tabernacle or tent. 'Field' is the qualifier that indicates the radical shift in their circumstances – from city to tents in the field. How different from the urban comforts to which they were accustomed! Zion becoming a ploughed field (3:12) echoes here.

The final stage will bring them to Babylon, the place of punishing exile, which they will enter. 'There' is mentioned twice. The first is in conjunction with 'you will be delivered'. The text does not say 'delivered from' Babylon, but simply 'delivered'. With the second reference to 'there', the subject shifts: 'there YHWH will redeem you'. Deliverance prior to redeeming is unusual, but both occur in the context of Babylon. Once the period of exile in Babylon is completed, they will be delivered and redeemed from the hand of their enemy. Exodus terminology is woven into this verse. The people are disabused of the notion that redemption will come to them in their own familiar surroundings. It will happen in a foreign land, a surprising reversal of expectations.

Explanation

The image of the king cannot be tainted by a contemporary sense of 'figurehead'. The king represented the power of the kingdom, even if it was a smaller entity. Absence of the royal figure unsettled the populace. Hosea captures the people's disdain for an apparently impotent regent (Hos. 10:3; 13:10). Likewise, a kingdom bereft of wise counsellors is in dire straits. Micah's juxtaposition of king and counsellor in the rhetorical questions suggests a possible parallel, especially if the questions allude to their disregard for YHWH as their ultimate sovereign. Micah's contemporary, Isaiah, prophesies of the forthcoming Child who will be the perfect King and Counsellor, reigning on David's throne for ever (9:5–6[6–7]).

Through a different interpretive lens, this also includes a hopeful expression: their King is still in their presence, even 'now'. The childbirth imagery points both to their pain and their joy. It indicates the devastation of their present circumstances and the forthcoming need to leave the city, while at the same time heralding future deliverance. Just about a century later, Jeremiah poses the same question (Jer. 8:19), even in those desperate days.

YHWH will 'deliver' (imaging the divine 'Midwife'), but it will be through a long and dark route into exile before redemption. Even in the darkest moments of exile, disaster and defeat, YHWH is present. Because of this reference to Babylon, there are those who suggest this segment was added long after Micah's time. There are redemption and exodus echoes in Isa. 43:14–19 and 48:16–21, frequently reckoned an exilic text for the same reason. Nevertheless, naming Babylon does not have to be an indicator of exilic or post-exilic composition. It is not depicted here as the ruling power that takes them into exile, but simply as the place where they will go. Already in 2 Kgs 17, Babylon is specified as one of the destinations of those uprooted from the northern kingdom in 722 BC.

Because the exiles did not necessarily settle in the city but were in communities along canals (Ps. 137; Ezek. 1 – 3), 'Babylon' means both the city and the countryside. A subtext here may be the danger of settling too comfortably in Babylon to the point of needing deliverance from the insidious encroachment of the world views that characterized that cultural setting. The close of the verse indicates the nature of that place of danger: deliverance and redemption are necessary. YHWH will redeem 'from the hand or your enemies'. They are unnamed, but are nevertheless a serious threat.

MICAH 4:11–13

Translation

4:11But now, many nations have gathered against you. They are the ones saying: 'Let her be profaned; may our eyes gaze on Zion.'

13But they do not know the thoughts of YHWH; they have not understood his counsel, that he has gathered them as fallen grain to the threshing floor.

14Rise up and thresh, O Daughter of Zion, for I will make your horn iron, and your hoof I will make bronze, and you will crush many peoples. And I will devote for destruction to YHWH their unjust profit, and their might (wealth) to the Lord of all the earth.

Notes on the text

4:11. The niph. of *neʾespû* may be read as a pass., implying that they are gathered by YHWH for his purposes. It could also be **middle voice**: they 'gathered themselves' (*IBHS* §23.2.1; 23.2.2).

teḥĕnāp refers to extreme profanation that brings judgment. It along with *wĕtaḥaz* ('gaze') are fem. sg. and may be either qal statives or juss. forms. The latter is likely: that is what the mockers want to happen to the 'Daughter of Zion', the implicit subject of *teḥĕnāp*. The LXX reads 'rejoice' in place of *teḥĕnāp*.

The subject of *wĕtaḥaz* (3 fem. sg.) is 'our eyes' [pl.]. The Syr, Tg and Vg read the equivalent of the sg. 'our eye'.

12. *ʿāmîr* is synonymous with *ʿōmer*, which means both fallen grain and a measure that is one-tenth of an ephah. On dry and liquid measures, see Fuller, *NIDOTTE* 1:382–388, for details on all the standard measures in the Israelite period; see also Powell, *ABD* 6:897–908. *ʿāmîr* is used only in four prophetic oracles (this verse along with Amos 2:13; Jer. 9:21[22]; Zech. 12:6). 'Threshing floor' (*gōren*) has the locative hê attached to it.

13. The root of *dôšî* is *dûš* ('thresh'). Normally the fem. sg. impv. would be *dûšî*, matching the preceding verb (Waltke 2007: 254). The 2 fem. sg. hiph. qat. form of *dqq* ('crush') continues the previous two imperatives.

The LXX, Syr and Vg have the equivalent of 2 fem. sg. for the MT *haḥăramtî* ('I will devote to destruction'). The second person fits better with the context and may preserve an archaic 2 fem. sg. form, adding the *î* at the end (GKC §44h). The 1 sg. points to YHWH as the subject.

*beṣa*ʿ means 'wealth' acquired by generally violent means (Exod. 18:21; Isa. 33:15; Ezek. 22:12–13). It, along with *ḥêlām* ('their wealth'), may refer to plunder (see Num. 31:9; Zech. 14:14) that had been carried off from Israel; now they were taking it back.

Form and structure

There are two sections with *ʾsp* and *qbṣ* (vv. 4–8, 11–13) that surround vv. 9–10. All are glimpses of Zion, first in its vulnerable state but followed with a vision of restoration.

There are echoes in these verses from previous sections. Many nations will come, this time with nefarious intentions. They will be gathered, just as the Shepherd gathers the flock. They are not cognisant that the counsel of YHWH will overturn theirs.

Comment

4:11. This oracle shifts their temporal attention once more. The question is just what 'now' implies in this context. It seems that Micah's audience is drawn back from temporally distant Babylon to the immediate threat of mighty Assyria. The gathered nations are also verbally aggressive. Their declaration is powerful, and because Micah is representing their cruel taunt, it has correspondingly rough syntax.

The niph. of *neʾespû* implies either that they are gathered by YHWH for his purposes, or that they gathered themselves. The two are not exclusive, because their military aggression was under the sovereign control of YHWH. The present ptc. (*hāʾōmrîm*) emphasizes the very audible taunt that follows. Any attack on the temple will profane it utterly. The prospect of pagan nations calling for the defiling of the Daughter of Zion seems unlikely to some scholars: Would these mighty nations not be more interested in destruction or plundering? Early on, the LXX shifts the expectation to their rejoicing at seeing the city fall. Ben Zvi (2000: 119), however, suggests that the text presents these events through the eyes of members of the covenant community and does not reflect the world view of the nations. Having said that, no doubt the nations are sufficiently aware of Israel's own perception and fears regarding their temple to adopt the expression as part of their expected triumph. Gazing into the interior of the temple (the house of YHWH on Zion) profanes it. *ḥzh* followed by *bĕ* can take on the connotation of gloating (Obad. 12; Mic. 7:10). The power of the eyes is turned against Zion.

12. 'But they' contrasts their insolent boasting with the plans of YHWH. They neither know nor do they understand his plans or his counsel. *maḥšĕbôt* ('thoughts') is a neutral term, used with reference to the purposes of both YHWH and humans, which, in many cases, can be quite at odds (cf. Isa. 55:7–9). The parallel term *ʿēṣâ* ('counsel') is a contrast to the absent and failed counsellor of v. 9.

The parallelism between their breathtaking lack of knowing and understanding is augmented by the statement of YHWH's purpose. It prepares for the next dire verses, where an empowered Daughter of Zion will enact those purposes. While the hostile nations gather and maliciously devise public shaming and trouncing of YHWH's people, he has gathered them like a swathe of fallen grain to the threshing floor. YHWH is the Harvester and Israel the thresher; see also Isa. 41:15. The simile of gathered grain to the threshing floor is fitting: the temple site was previously the threshing floor of Aravnah (2 Sam. 24:24–25; 2 Chr. 3:1), and the threshing floor is a metaphor for the place of judgment (Isa. 21:10; Jer. 51:33; Hos. 13:3). The irony is that they will be marching towards their annihilation.

13. *qûmî* (qal fem. sg. impv.) is preparatory: she is to 'rise' to thresh. Embedded in these orders are images of the Daughter of Zion's unexpected superiority over seemingly invincible enemies amassed against her. The imagery is apocalyptic: she is represented as a ferocious beast, rising to thresh, crushing the enemy forces like heads of grain. YHWH will make the weaponized 'attire'.

The attackers will be pulverized. In the process, she will gore them with her horn of iron. That aggressive action suggests that she will protect herself as she is threshing (Waltke 2007: 255). Hooves of bronze are the ultimate threshing machine. Iron and bronze together signify invincible might and power. This image is a radical contrast to the wounded and lame creatures of the gathered remnant upon whom YHWH brought ill (4:6–7). This will be utter destruction, the means to accomplish it given by YHWH. The Daughter of Zion, reconstituted as a terrible threshing animal, will pound them to powder. That goes far beyond what would be expected from normal threshing. The same verb is used multiple times for crushing false idols. Key examples include the golden calf (Exod. 32:20; Deut. 9:21); the enemies crushed by David (2 Sam. 22:43); the idols and the altar destroyed by Josiah (2 Kgs 23:6, 15); and the Asherah image crushed by Asa (2 Chr. 15:16). The 'many nations' of v. 11 will become the crushed 'many peoples'. On symbolism of horns, see Deut. 33:17; 1 Sam. 2:10; 1 Kgs 22:11; Ps. 75:11[10].

Once the threshing is completed, YHWH commands that the wealth gained by violence be devoted by destruction to himself. Retaining the MT reading with the first person *haḥăramtî* ('I will devote to destruction') is an instance where the identities of YHWH and Jerusalem merge; the conflict with Jerusalem is indeed conflict with YHWH. The grammatical oddity contributes to the ambiguity (Ben Zvi 2000: 117). The implications of this action are far-ranging. Forms of *ḥrm* ('to devote to destruction') appear most frequently in conjunction with Israel's preparation to enter the land and encounter that which was utterly antithetical to the sanctity of YHWH's people and land (Deut. 7:26; 13:18[17]; Josh. 6:17; 7:1–15). In most of the cases, these were material goods. When persons were involved, they generally had engaged in outright rejection of God and God's ways. YHWH ordered the destruction of materials so that they could not be used or abused by people. Giving all the devoted items over to God protected the Israelites. See Naudé, *NIDOTTE* 2:276–277. It was also a confession that YHWH is the Lord of the whole earth (Mays 1976: 111).

'Their unjust gain' and 'their wealth' gained through violence are sandwiched between YHWH and the 'Lord' (*ʾădôn*) of all the earth, as if to say there will be no way for them to retain any of it. In the sacred space of God's presence, that which is vile will be destroyed. 'Lord of all the earth' is used six times in the HB. All of them appear in extraordinary contexts. In Josh. 3:11, 13, the ark of the Lord of all the earth crosses the Jordan. Two of Zechariah's apocalyptic visions identify the 'Lord of all the earth' as a major figure (4:14; 6:5). Using imagery echoed in Micah 1:4, Ps. 97:5 describes the powerful theophany: the Lord of all the earth will come with brilliant light and fire, melting mountains like wax.

Explanation

In contrast to the many nations who come for instruction (4:2), these nations are coming for war. They declare their intent both to defile Zion and to make it a public spectacle at which their eyes will gaze in triumph. The same insolence is vividly described in Lam. 2:16, prayed against in Ps. 129:5 and condemned in Obad. 12. Contempt for YHWH and his people is the object of YHWH's rebuke in Ps. 2:2–3. The same level of profanation appears in Jer. 23:11: both prophet and priest are polluted and defiled, and YHWH found their evil in his house.

Whereas the prior oracle (4:9–10) looks far forward from Micah's time to the exile to Babylon, this one returns to Micah's own historical context and the feared enemy desecration of the Holy Place. Even though the historical allusions are vague, the vignettes of Zion are lodged in experiences that are terrifying. Enemies who revile their opponents are a reality in all times and places of war. It serves to dehumanize the foe; how ironic that Israel will become like a ferocious animal against the aggressors.

The nations think they have planned this but, as the next verse makes clear, God has gathered them there for his purposes. There is a vital parallel with ch. 2: human intentions are reversed by God's plans. 'They do not know the thoughts of YHWH, and they do not understand his counsel' (4:12). The attendant good news at this point is that even though evil seems so overwhelmingly destructive, it can never be finally successful, for God transforms it. Those who dwell in darkness, however, do not and cannot understand this (cf. Dan. 12:10). The repeated message of Scripture is that God is in the business of reversing the tragedy. It culminates in the incarnation, death and resurrection of the second Person of the Trinity. That has a familiar ring: Rom. 8:28–39 continues to encourage the faithful believer, especially when current circumstances seemingly hide the face of God. The Lord of Hosts is still firmly on his throne. When evil seems to triumph at every turn, from the thick fabric of lies and deceit to the murder of unborn children, the knowledge that justice and righteousness are the foundation of his throne (Ps. 89:15[14]) is a beacon of hope – light that penetrates even the deepest darkness.

YHWH first commands the Daughter of Zion to act, and then promises to equip her to accomplish his purposes. The same continues to be true for God's people. We are to rise up in obedience, faithful to keep his instructions, and trusting that God's Spirit will provide whatever is necessary. It may be that the tasks are grim ones, reflecting severe conflict in the spiritual realms. In Dan. 10, the warring dark powers reach from the heavens into every earthly turmoil. The brutal evil we see daily is an imprint of cosmic war; it requires vigilance and powerful prayer intervention. Hence, Paul's admonition to put on the *full* armour of God and to stand, stand, stand firm (Eph. 6:10–20). Daniel, a 'treasured' person (10:11, 19), heard the same admonition: stand and be strong. We must stand against *everything* false and contrary to the knowledge of God, taking every thought captive to Christ (2 Cor. 10:3–5), ordering our lives by God's truth and praying faithfully that the burning arrows of the evil one will be extinguished.

MICAH 4:14[5:1 ENGLISH]

Translation

4:14[5:1]Now, you will be banded together, O daughter of a troop; he has placed a siege against us. With a rod, they will strike against the cheek the one judging Israel.

Notes on the text

4:14[5:1]. The words translated 'banded together' and 'troop' come from the root *gdd*, which can mean to 'cut into' or 'penetrate', on the one hand, or 'band together' on the other (*DCH* 2:316). When the 2 fem. sg. hithpol. yiq. form, *titgōdědî*, means 'cut oneself', it is with specific reference to forbidden religious practices (Deut. 14:1; 1 Kgs 18:28). The noun form, *gedûd*, is a military term and may anticipate an impending invasion of Jerusalem (cf. Mic. 1:9).

The LXX introduces the 'daughter of Ephraim' into the framework and interprets *gdd* as 'to hedge in completely', likely reading *gdr* ('fence') instead of *gdd*. It also renders 'the one judging' (*šôpēṭ*) as if it were a repetition of *šebeṭ* ('rod' or 'tribe'): 'with a rod [*rabdō* for *šebeṭ*] they shall smite on the cheek the tribes [*phylas* for *šebeṭ*] of Israel'. The Tg, Syr and Vg understand the verb as related to 'troop' or 'band' (Cathcart and Gordon 1989: 121).

Form and structure

There is extensive discussion as to how this verse fits with the rhetorical development in the whole book. Does it belong with what precedes? There is a space in the MT between it and 5:1 which would suggest that. Willis (1968c: 529–547) sorts through the array of scholarly opinions and makes a case that it begins the next section because it continues to set the stage for the forthcoming contrast. This interpretive position is represented in the English chapter division. See also Waltke 2007: 262 and Allen 1976: 339. It may be an independent unit but serves as a connector with both the preceding and following material (Hoyt 2019: 723–724). Hillers suggests that it is an incomplete oracle (1984: 62).

This one verse is rich in sound plays: *titgōdĕdî* ('you will be banded together') is followed by *bat-gĕdûd* ('daughter of a troop'); *šebeṭ* ('rod') is followed shortly by *šôpēṭ* ('the one judging'). The syntax is rugged. The three finite verb forms run the gamut, starting with fem. sg. impv., shifting to masc. sg. qat. and followed by masc. pl. yiq.

Comment

4:14[5:1]. After the brief survey (vv. 12–13) that ranges far ahead, the reality of the current siege returns with 'but now', picking up from v. 11. The uneven syntax conveys the unsettled nature of the situation. The humiliation described in v. 14 jolts the reader after the triumphant closure of v. 13. It is challenging to identify relationships among the major players. *titgōdĕdî* generally refers to forbidden religious practices. Through that set of lenses, it could imply engaging in self-mutilation as an extreme mourning practice (Allen 1976: 341), or perhaps as an apotropaic measure to ward off the impending assault. On the other hand, it is used in Jer. 5:7 with the sense of gathering in a throng, perhaps figurative for penetrating some spatial context. It may be another way of referring to a king who has been rendered, to all intents and purposes, impotent in the face of the crisis (Mays 1976: 114; Waltke 2007: 265). Or it may refer to their disdain for YHWH. Both possibilities surface in connection with 4:9. The text continues to be open to multiple ways of reading it (Ben Zvi 2000: 119–120). Willis (1968a: 533) interprets this figure as a clear reference to a military endeavour that is failing, perhaps because its leadership is trusting in human resources.

The ambiguities continue. The 'Daughter of Gedud' is apparently a city under siege. The unidentified representative speaker is with those under siege; perhaps it is Micah at this point. We do not know who set up the siege from the outside. An unidentified 'they' attacks someone who is prominent enough to be 'judging' (*šōpēṭ*) Israel. This attack was accomplished with a *šebeṭ* ('rod'), playing on the sound similarities with 'judge' (*šôpēṭ*). *šōpēṭ* is preceded by *ʾēt*, an indication of the direct object.

Both the attacking subject and the object of the smiting are opaque characters. All we know is that 'with the rod, they struck on the cheek the one judging Israel'. This action is a blatant insult (1 Kgs 22:24; Job 16:10; Lam. 3:30). If Daughter of Gedud is another allusion to Zion, it is the last one for Micah. 'Daughter of Zion' is a frequent moniker for Jerusalem. Given the root meaning of 'to cut into', perhaps 'Daughter of Gedud' is a foreboding figure: they are about to be penetrated and slashed. The battle will be lost; Jerusalem will be lost. 'Strike the judge of Israel on the cheek' indicates complete humiliation. In the next verse, attention shifts to Bethlehem.

Explanation

While the general interpretive focus for this verse is on Jerusalem's vulnerability in the face of attack, Shaw (1993: 140–153) suggests that Daughter of Gedud means 'daughter of a raid' and refers to those who are outside Jerusalem besieging it, some of whom may be disaffected Israelites. Because the language is so cryptic, locating the vignette in a possible historical context is again challenging. Among the options are the forty-six towns lost by Hezekiah to Sennacherib; insults lobbed by the Assyrian spokesmen to the Jerusalemites (2 Kgs 18:13–37); the later siege and exile when Nebuchadnezzar was attacking Jerusalem; or the fate of Zedekiah. Recognizing the surplus of meaning embedded in the poetic brevity, it is likely that Assyria is in the forefront and continues as the paradigmatic enemy well beyond the eighth century (Jenson 2008: 155). That interpretive strategy will return in ch. 5.

MICAH 5:1–3[2–4]

Translation

5:1[2]But you, Bethlehem Ephrathah, being insignificant among the clans of Judah; from you for me will go out one to be ruling Israel; and his goings forth from beginning, from the days of eternity.

[2[3]]Therefore, he will give them until a time that she who is in labour has given birth; and the rest of his brothers will return to the children of Israel.

[3[4]]And he will stand and shepherd in the strength of YHWH, in the majesty of the Name of YHWH our God; and they will dwell, for now he will be great unto the ends of the land.

Notes on the text

A very small fragment from Qumran Cave 4 (4QMic) has ten letters that correspond to parts of 5:1–2[2–3].

5:1[2]. 8ḤevXIIgr does not include Bethlehem. On that basis, some scholars have suggested that Bethlehem was a later addition, and the original reading was *bêt-ʾeprātâ*, 'house of Ephrathah'. Bethlehem, however, appears in the Syr, Tg and Vg. The LXX reads 'Bethlehem, the house of Ephrathah'. 4QMic reads *lî* ('for me') *yēṣēʾ* as *lô* ('for him') *yēṣēʾ*.

môṣāʾôt as a fem. pl. noun occurs only here (and perhaps in 2 Kgs 10:27; see Q); it means 'goings forth', possibly suggesting 'origins' (*DCH* 5:185). A related masc. noun (*môṣāʾ*) appears frequently, generally meaning a place from which something or someone goes forth. Here, the waw conj. and the masc. sg. pron. suff. connect directly with the Ruler who would 'go forth' for YHWH.

qedem has both spatial and temporal implications (*DCH* 7:186–187). In terms of time, it is parallel to *rēʾšît*, indicating the 'beginning' (Prov. 8:22).

2[3]. *ʿēt* is frequently used to designate time for a customary practice; e.g. the time when kings go forth (*lʿēt ṣēt*) in 2 Sam. 11:1. It appears with the demonstrative pron. 'in that time', indicating a known and expected practice.

The subject of *yĕšûbûn* is 'the brothers'; thus, the pl. The **paragogic nun** works phonologically given the following vowel sound. It also may suggest emphasis (GKC §47m). It is not necessary to emend *ʿal* to *ʾel* (with *BHS*); *ʿal* can mean 'to' (*IBHS* §11.2.13; J-M §133bf), implying return to the prior state of being.

3[4]. *wĕyāšābû* is a qal 3 masc. pl. verb the root of which is *yšb*, 'to dwell'. The implication is that they will be secure. The Vg, Syr and 8ḤevXIIgr read *wĕyāšūbû*, presuming the root to be *šûb*, 'to return'.

Form and structure

Phonological and conceptual repetitions weave through this section. 'But you' follows the previously ominous repetition of 'but now', continuing the homonymic patterns with *wĕʾattâ* and *wĕʿattâ*. *yēṣēʾ* ('he will go forth') is followed by *môṣāʾōtāyw* ('his goings forth').

'Being' the smallest among the clans of Judah is juxtaposed with 'being' the ruler of Israel.

The figure of giving birth continues from 4:9–10. *yĕšûbûn* ('they shall return') and *yāšābû* ('they shall dwell') of v. 3 connect with sound similarity.

The last of the sequence of (*wĕ*) *ʿattâ* (see 4:9, 10, 11, 14) appears in v. 3 as *kî-ʿattâ*.

Comment

5:1[2]. Countering the steady drumbeat of 'but now' (*wĕʿattâ*) and the threatening events directly on the horizon, we now read 'but *you*' (*wĕʾattâ*). Rather than Jerusalem's (Daughter of Zion and city of David) being under threat, Micah visits another city of David, Bethlehem, and calls it Bethlehem Ephrathah. These proper names together serve as appositions that define 'you', bringing the focus into the geographical context. In Ruth 4:11, the two names are used in parallel for the same town. David's father, Jesse, was identified as an Ephrathite from Bethlehem (1 Sam. 17:12). Gen. 35:16–19 indicates that Rachel died 'on the way to Ephrathah; that is, Bethlehem'. See also Ps. 132:6; Ephrathah is mentioned in this psalm that extols the 'resting place' David vowed to build for YHWH. When Matthew cites this text, he adds an explanatory note – 'Bethlehem in the land of Judah' (2:6). It may be that the addition of Ephrathah was to distinguish this Bethlehem in the tribe of Judah from a second town, also called Bethlehem, in the tribe of Zebulun (Josh. 19:15).

When *ṣāʿîr* is used in the same context as *bĕkôr*, it can be translated as 'younger'. The word appears twenty-two times and the great majority of them are in contexts where 'younger' is the appropriate translation, accompanied by a sense of inferiority (Waltke 2007: 267–268). That comparison is not explicitly in this context, however, and *ṣāʿîr* does not have the def. art. (as it does, for example, in Judg. 6:15). Thus, 'insignificant' or 'least' is a better interpretation (Andersen and Freedman 2000: 465). It is followed by *lihyôt* ('to be'), which precedes the somewhat awkward shift from a town name, Bethlehem, to a kinship label. *lihyôt* does not work, strictly speaking, as a comparative ('too small to be among'); if that were the grammatical construction, it would be *mihyôt* (Waltke 2007: 268).

One basic meaning of *ʾelep* is 'thousand', often read into the socio-military contexts of taking the census (cf. Num. 1 and 26). This military connotation continues into the narratives of Israel's calls to arms (1 Sam. 8:12; 10:19; 1 Chr. 13:1). Rather than a literal thousand men, it seems to have been the largest unit under the control of one leader (Exod. 18:21; Num. 1:16; Josh. 22:14). In addition, it can describe the geographical territory held by those within a kinship unit in the social structures of Israel (Judg. 6:15; Amos 5:3). The social and military contexts are related in that the census was taken to address inheritance allocations as well as military preparedness (see Num. 1:16). See Jenson, *NIDOTTE* 1:416–418.

The importance of Bethlehem Ephrathah in Judah is highlighted again with 'from you' commencing the next clause. The syntax is awkward: there are three pronouns, and the order of the words is unusual. Instead of the verb (*yēṣē'*) in the first place, two prep. phrases precede it. 'From you' connects with Bethlehem, and 'for me' refers to YHWH. 'To go out for me' is found nowhere else in the HB. Even though the subject of 'he will go out' is undefined at this point, it undoubtedly signifies the Ruler. Nevertheless, he will serve YHWH; hence, the emphatic position of *lî* prior to *yēṣē'*.

The repetition of *lihyôt* in this clause is thought by some scholars to be a matter of dittography, but that is not a necessary conclusion. Both intimate ongoing 'being', not limited in time. The contrast in the parallel is striking; 'being insignificant' is juxtaposed with 'being ruler'. This may be used in parallel with 'king', particularly in the sense of political dominion. This individual will rule for Israel.

lihyôt seems to function as a further description of Bethlehem Ephrathah's insignificant place in Judah, intended to set the stage for the dramatic declaration. Micah's audience is kept in partial suspense. At the same time, the more important connection begins to surface: just as the mention of Bethlehem brings David to mind, so also does 'insignificant among the clans of Judah'. Against the sociomilitary backdrop, Bethlehem was not just small; its size prevented it from contributing in a major fashion to military readiness, a matter perceived to be vital in the tenuous circumstances facing Judah. Matthew's paraphrase of this verse reads 'rulers' instead of 'clans' (Matt. 2:6). The robust implications of *'elep* replace the narrower sense of *gĕdûd* from the preceding verse.

YHWH himself goes forth to war on behalf of his people (see notes on 1:3; along with 2 Sam. 5:24; Isa. 26:21; Zech. 14:3). The concept also echoes the birthing imagery from the previous chapter. The 'goings forth' of this promised Ruler have a very long history: *miqqedem* ('from the beginning') references the whole span of eternity past after that boundless beginning (Prov. 8:23; see also Isa. 46:10). It is echoed in 'from the days of eternity'. 'Days of eternity' may be used within a historical framework; in this case, it will echo for Micah's audience the glory days of David's reign (Isa. 63:9, 11; Amos 9:11; see Allen, 1976: 343–344, n. 29). At the same time, 'from the days of eternity', specifically with the prep. *min*, reverberates from the eternal past into the unending future (see Ps. 93:2).

2[3]. The interpretive ambiguities in what Micah says abound. How do we understand 'therefore' in this context? It follows directly on both the locational and the transcendent identity of the Ruler in v. 1. There are echoes of the line of David and declarations of his existence from eternity past. It is against this rich backdrop that Micah continues with reference to 'time' (*ēt*) and 'now' (v. 3). The promise of some sort of deliverance must be placed in a context that would have meaning for Micah's audience.

Who is the subject ('he') who will give, and who are the recipients? Is the subject YHWH, the Ruler, or perhaps even the wounded judge from 4:14[5:1]? Even though Micah generally includes the divine Name when he means YHWH, though it is not present here, that seems to be the best interpretation, given that 'for me' in v. 1 reflects YHWH. Does 'them' recall the clans of Judah already on the radar screen from v. 1? Does it point forward to 'the rest of the brothers' or, more broadly, 'the children of Israel'? Both appear as the verse continues. And what does *ntn* ('give') mean in this context? Does it mean to give them up ('abandon', NIV)? Or does it mean to establish ('place' or 'set') them securely somewhere? Because the identity markers that precede 'therefore' imply power, it does not seem likely at first blush that 'giving them up' will be the next step. It may indeed be the case that there will be an undefined and difficult interval before the appointed 'time' (*ēt*). YHWH will place and sustain them in that interval, even though the events described in 4:9–11 may feel as if YHWH has abandoned them. Whatever it is, it occurs until a 'time'. Contrary to the infinity of time of the preceding verse, this narrows into a specific point. *ʿēt* appears with the demonstrative pronoun, 'in that time'. In the poem of Eccl. 3:1–8, the word points to specific seasons for the events of life. Here, the anticipated point in time is when the one giving birth will give birth! The qat. form implies an accomplished event. Perhaps this is a way of indicating the specific fulfilment of 'from you, he will go forth' (*yēṣēʾ*) in v. 1. It is, however, more likely that the figure refers to the Daughter of Zion, echoing the birthing anguish from 4:9–10.

This could be a literal 'woman' (*yôlēdâ*) birthing a child; that prompts a quest for the identity of the child. It may, however, be symbolic, pointing to the remnant. Those going forth in that context are going initially into difficult places, but the hopeful note is that they will return. Either concurrently or as a result of this birth, the 'rest' (*yeter*) of his brothers will return. *yeter* is not used specifically to designate 'remnant'; the 'remnant' (*šĕʾērît*) includes those who will return from exile, fulfilling the promises regarding restoration. Instead, *yeter* means 'the rest' of the widely spread diaspora, particularly from the north.

'His brothers' could mean specifically brothers of the one born or brothers of the Ruler. More likely, it refers more broadly to Israelites, perhaps those who have been estranged, exiled and removed as a remnant to another location. (See the recurrence of 'a remnant shall return' in Isa. 10:20–23; 11:10–16.) It suggests that the estranged northern and southern tribes will be united as they are transformed, reflecting a long-term deep yearning of YHWH's people.

3[4]. Each of the verbs in this verse is a weqat. form, continuing the focus on the future events associated with 'the time'. The masc. subject of 'and he will stand' picks up from *yēṣēʾ*: *he* will come forth and *he* will stand. 'Standing' implies stability and continuity; that firm posture enables the Ruler to shepherd. There is no explicit object of *rāʿâ*, but the flock of

Israel is understood. The Ruler is empowered by YHWH's attributes of strength and majesty. The underlying meaning of *gʾh* is to 'be high'; because the noun is abstract, it conveys the concept of majesty – that which is far and above.

The qualities of power and majesty are linked together as the Ruler stands and shepherds. His authority is surely established in the Name of YHWH. On Name, see 'Explanation' on 4:5. There are echoes again of David, whose name YHWH promised to make great (2 Sam. 7:9). The extent of the Shepherd's greatness is defined by 'to the ends of the land'. The noun *ʾereṣ* ('land') lacks a definite article, perhaps suggesting that the greatness of the Ruler and the concomitant security will extend well beyond the known boundaries of 'the land' as it was defined for Israel. This expression recurs in promises about the future royal rule (Deut. 33:17; Pss 2:8; 72:8; Zech. 9:10).

Explanation

It seems counter-intuitive, but the greatness that comes directly through the power of God results in peace and security: he will be their peace (5:4a[5a]). While that brings a logical closure to this section as stated, the interpretive complexities will be addressed in the next 'Comment' section. Their secure dwelling in the land presupposes their return. It also points ahead: ***kî-*** *ʿattâ* ('for now') indicates the idealized future time (so assured that it is represented as the present) when the One ruling will be great.

MICAH 5:4–5[5–6]

Translation

[5:4[5]] And he will be the One of peace.

As for Assyria, when he comes into our land, and when he treads our palaces, he [the Ruler] will raise up for us against him seven shepherds and eight princes of men.

[5[6]] And they shall break the land of Ashur with the sword, and the land of Nimrod at her entrances; and he shall deliver from Ashur when he comes into our land, and when he treads into our territory.

Notes on the text

5:4[5]. *wĕhāyâ* characteristically introduces or advances discourse (*IBHS* §32.3.6). In older translation parlance, that was expressed as 'and it shall come to pass'.

This first three-word line is marked by the ***athnach*** at the end, indicating a break. Although the verse seems abruptly to shift from the first declaration to the rest of the verse, *wĕhāyâ* appears four times in ch. 5, each instance beginning a new unit.

As a 'nominative absolute' (*IBHS* §4.7), *ʾaššûr* is set off from what follows. It may be translated 'as for Assyria', and is followed by two successive clauses introduced by *kî*, translated 'when' or 'if'.

The 3 masc. sg. yiq. forms *yābôʾ* and *yidrōk* present the aggressive future actions of the collective enemy.

Instead of 'our palaces' (*ʾarmĕnōtênû*), LXX has 'on our land'. The Hebr. equivalent would be *beʾadmātēnû*, which does fit better with the similar clause in 5b, 'entering our borders', and may be explained in terms of copying changes. 8ḤevXIIgr, Tg and Syr read as the MT.

The consonantal structure of *hăkēmōnû* could be either 'we will raise up' or 'he [the Ruler] will raise up for us'. While the vocalization supports the former, the latter provides a better understanding of the continuing role of the Ruler: the One who is *šālôm* will also 'deliver' (*wĕhiṣṣîl*) from Assyria (5b). See Andersen and Freedman 2000: 474–478.

nĕsîkê ('princes') is used infrequently (Josh. 13:21; Ps. 83:12[11]; Ezek. 32:30). Chiefs of tribes were possibly intended. The root *nsk* means both 'to pour out' (its more common usage) and 'to instal' (Ps. 2:6). The meanings are likely related as installations of rulers involved libation and anointing processes. The rhetorical 'seven shepherds and eight leaders' is the largest of this kind of pattern. One of equal magnitude appears in Eccl. 11:2, and the pattern recurs in Ugaritic texts (Cathcart 1968: 513).

5[6]. *rāʿû* may be from *rʿʿ*, one meaning of which is 'to break' along with the more familiar 'to be evil' (BDB 949–950; *DCH* 7:531–532). They (the leadership team) will break Assyria's power by bringing disaster on the land. The phonological and semantic linkages are rich; in v. 3, *rʿh* means to shepherd.

bipĕtāḥêhā ('her openings') may be read as *bappĕtīḥâ*, meaning 'with the unsheathed sword'. The latter is used in pl. only in Ps. 55:22[21]; see also Ezek. 21:33[28]. While the ancient versions were clearly puzzled by *pĕtāḥêhā*, as evidenced by the alternative translations, emendation is not necessary, given that the point of attack in ANE contexts was always the entrance. See Waltke 2007: 736 for the range of interpretive options. The LXX has 'with her moat' instead of 'her openings'.

Form and structure

The first three words of v. 4 have a distinct position in the printed edition, balanced between what precedes and what follows. The editors were perplexed as well. In the Aleppo Codex, it rests in the middle of a **parashah**.

The seven–eight pattern is emphatic, indicative of completeness and sufficiency. See 'Comment'.

There is wordplay with 'shepherds' (*rō'îm*) who will 'break' (*wĕrā'û*) Assyria with the sword. The consonants resh and 'ayin also connect with evil and disaster. The second line repeats the essence of the line from v. 4 regarding Assyria's coming into the land and treading either palaces or borders. This is a chronological flashback.

Comment

5:4[5]. *wĕhāyâ* ('and it shall come to pass') may start a new train of thought that continues directly into the material on Assyria. At the same time, *zeh* points back to the One who will be the consummate Ruler, joining his identity with what is yet to come. This may also be an independent rel.clause, translated 'He will be the One (*zeh*) of peace' (*IBHS* §19.5). Parallels in Ugaritic texts suggest the construction links vv. 1–3 with what follows in 4–5 (Cathcart 1968: 511–512). See further examples in Judg. 5:5 and Ps. 68:9[8], where *zeh sînai* is best translated 'the One of Sinai'. Ben Zvi (2000: 125) calls this another 'multivalent, multiduty, Janus expression'.

While the image of ruling Shepherd now gives way to another scene, it reminds the reader of 4:6 ('in that day') and the promises that follow. *šālôm* connotes much more than absence of hostility; instead, it indicates the state in which matters have been set right, primarily by recompense or retribution. That implies a struggle, following which rightful victory has been won (Nel, *NIDOTTE* 4:130–135). *šālôm* includes ongoing protection and security. Understanding that may help link this clause both with what precedes and what follows.

The explicit mention of Assyria at this point may connect with previous allusions to siege (4:11, 14[5:1]). It is not necessary to emend *'armĕnōtênû* ('our palaces/fortresses') to *'admātēnû* ('our land') on account of the verb *drk* ('trample'). Enemies overrunning the land would gleefully trample over structures that symbolized the power centres of the vanquished people. See also the image of fire devouring citadels and fortresses (Hos. 8:14; Amos 1:1 – 2:5) and Joel's symbolic locust plague streaming through city walls and windows (2:9). While Assyria may be a **metonymy** representing all enemies of Israel, it is the clear and present threat. Although *BHS* suggests the clauses regarding Assyria's coming into the land and trampling the fortresses are out of place because they are repeated at the end of v. 5, they provide the transition back to the current threatening circumstances. These circumstances are not minimized.

The seven shepherds (*rō'îm*) will work in concert with the Ruler who will stand and shepherd (*wĕrâ'â*) in the strength of YHWH (v. 3). Aligned with them are the eight *nĕsîkê 'ādām* ('princes of men'). The 'seven and eight' defensive forces are raised up 'against him'; i.e. against Assyria. The seven in the pattern points to perfection, completeness and totality, further suggesting a natural association with the divine and holiness (Jenson, *NIDOTTE* 4:34–37). Those qualities are woven through the additional allusions and symbolisms in this passage. We see lesser versions of the numerical pattern in Prov. 6:16–19; 30:18–31; Amos 1:3 – 2:3. There are extra-biblical examples – twelve in Ugaritic texts and four Aramaic examples (Andersen and Freedman 2000: 479). The figurative point is that when defenders are raised up, they will be an entirely sufficient and formidable number (Willis 1968a: 541). The mechanism for moving this leadership coalition into position in a time of crisis is not specified.

Allen (1976: 347–348) suggests that vv. 4–5 reflect an earlier popular war song, intended to fuel enthusiasm for defence of national honour in the face of aggression. While its national echoes had died away in the face of overwhelming Assyrian might, Micah revives it here but weaves into it a more solid foundation. They would no longer depend on their own human ingenuity and leadership, but on YHWH and his appointed Ruler.

5[6]. Even though the word *rāʿû* is homonymic with the word for 'shepherding', if 'break' is the intent here, the contrast is vivid. The tables are turned; the leaders respond to Assyria's invasion and trampling with the sword. The parallelism is clear: the two direct objects, preceded by *ʾet*, are the land of Assyria and the 'entrances' of the land of Nimrod, the vulnerable points in any attack. However the deliverance was effected, the rescuers would head to Assyria and take back captives, just as a shepherd rescues the flock from marauding animals. The closure to v. 5 echoes the initial depiction of the Assyria threat in 4b. This does not need to be read as an accidental repetition. Instead, the ominous hostile presence on the horizon is real; they enter the land and trample the territory. Transgressing boundaries was a serious violation of what God had ordained in terms of inheritance, whether family holdings or ethnic entities (Deut. 19:14; 32:8; Hos. 5:10). In this context, *gĕbûl* indicates the whole region and not simply a boundary; it is synonymous with *ʾereṣ* ('land'). Nevertheless, in the centre of this small chiasm is the deliverance provided by the Ruler, the One who will sustain *šālôm*. The centre of the vision looks to a future that is undefined, especially if the 'lands' of Assyria and Nimrod are in view and the multiple shepherd leaders will be the ones responsible. As is common in Micah, the culmination of the 'story' is not always at the end.

Explanation

These two verses picture Assyria's invading and carrying off a significant part of the population. A deliverer or deliverers will go to Assyria and return with restored captives, raising the question 'When?' While the invasion details match painfully well with multiple historical hostile incursions into the land, deliverance from the jaws of Assyria is still an unfulfilled hope. In Micah's immediate future, Assyria demonstrably has the upper hand. Even though they do not take Jerusalem, Sennacherib boasts of defeating those forty-six fortified cities. The depiction on the walls of one of Sennacherib's palace rooms of his capture of Lachish with its formidable fortifications is unmistakable evidence of trampling fortresses and boundaries. Micah's home town was within eyeshot of Lachish. Isaiah references the boastful claims of the king of Assyria against Zion and Jerusalem: he removes the boundaries and plunders their treasures (Isa. 10:12–13), but his day of judgment at the hand of YHWH will come.

Nevertheless, the shepherds qua princes raised up against the enemy are not only sufficient defenders but will also go on the offensive against Assyria and Nimrod. It is best to interpret these as two scenarios that merge under the figures of shepherds, weaving together present with future. Assyria is an archetype of all hostile forces.

Shaw (1993: 156–160) suggests a geopolitical backdrop in the form of a multinational (small nation states) coalition, represented by the seven–eight pattern, against the looming threat of Assyrian aggression several decades prior to Sennacherib. Because instability was the order of the day after Uzziah's death, Micah speaks into the constantly shifting realities on the ground.

Hillers (1984: 69) offers another scenario for these verses. It involves reading 'our land' instead of 'our palaces', an emendation noted above. It also requires that the final word of v. 4 be Aram instead of *ʾādām*. That is a possible consonantal shift, based on the daleth (ד) and resh (ר) interchange. With those emendations as backdrop, it may be that the Assyrians indeed invade the land; crossing the Euphrates means coming into the idealized land of Israel. Israel then musters leaders of Aramean mini-states to help; hence, 'seven shepherds, and eight leaders of Aram'. The region of Aram (Syria) is the buffer zone between the superpower in Mesopotamia and Israel proper.

The curtain falls on the oracle of hope and salvation for the Daughter of Zion, for a time known as the Daughter of Gedud (4:14 – 5:5[5:1 – 5:6]). Considering these promises within the framework of 4:1–6, we are reminded that the hope of universal renewal will not occur before the appointed Ruler, eternally existent, is born. The task of this Shepherd King will be to reunite all the children of Israel and keep them securely in his kingdom; he will indeed be the One of peace. Confronting the unbridled hostility between Jews and Gentiles, Paul revisits this imagery of peace and restoration of unity and vastly expands the application. In the care of the Shepherd Ruler brought forth by YHWH, the dividing wall of hostility will be eradicated (Eph. 2:14).

The echoes of Pss 2 and 110 in these verses flesh out the picture even more. YHWH declares, 'I have installed [*nāsaktî*] my King on Zion, my holy mountain' (Ps. 2:6); among those leaders who will be raised up for the people are princes (*nĕsîkê ʾādām*; Mic. 5:4[5]). This is a rare word: the verb form meaning 'set up' or 'instal' occurs only twice (Ps. 2:6; Prov. 8:23) and the noun, always pl. ('princes'), only four times (Josh. 13:21; Ps. 83:12[11]; Ezek. 32:30; Mic. 5:4[5]). YHWH further promises that he will make the Son's inheritance extend to the 'ends of the earth' (Ps. 2:8); the forthcoming Ruler will be great to the ends of the earth (Mic. 5:3[4]). Connecting with Mic. 5:5[6], the Son will 'crush them with a rod of iron' (Ps. 2:9). See also Ps. 110:5–6; the verb *māḥaṣ* ('to crush') is used twice.

MICAH 5:6–8[7–9]

Translation

5:6[7] And the remnant of Jacob will be in the midst of many peoples like dew from YHWH and like abundant showers on grass, which does not wait for anyone or tarry for the children of men.

7[8] And the remnant of Jacob will be among the nations in the midst of many peoples like a lion among the creatures of the forest, like a young lion in the sheepfold, which, when it crosses through, will trample down and tear apart, and there will be no one who will rescue.

8[9] May your hand be lifted against your foes and may all your enemies be cut off.

Notes on the text

5:6[7]. *šĕʾērît* is a fem. noun, but linked with Jacob it is governed by the masc. form of the verb. Based on the parallels between vv. 6 and 7, the LXX and Syr add the equivalent of 'among the nations' after 'remnant of Jacob' in v. 6. The root *qwh* appears primarily in pi. with a sense of waiting; a related word is *tiqwāh*, 'hope'. A second meaning, however, is 'to gather' or 'to collect' (*DCH* 7:211–212).

7[8]. There are seven words for 'lion' in Hebr. (see Job 4:10–11 for four of them); the two most common appear here. *ʾaryēh* simply means 'lion', while the *kĕpîr* is a young lion, but old enough to hunt its prey, which in this case are vulnerable sheep within the sheepfold. See Stallman, *NIDOTTE* 1:513–517.

bĕhēmâ most often refers to a domesticated animal, particularly cattle.

ʾăšer ʾim occurs six times in the HB (Gen. 13:16; 28:15; Num. 32:17; Job 9:15; Isa. 6:11; Mic. 5:7[8]). When it is followed by qat. verb forms, *ʾăšer ʾim* indicates actions that exist in the future state as completed (GKC

§106o). It should be translated 'when', not 'if'. The subjects and verbs are sg., but together graphically image the collective destructive power of the remnant. The three qal 3 masc. sg. verbs in succession represent a horrifying crescendo. When the lion and young lion 'pass by' (*ābar*), they 'trample' (*rāmas*) and 'tear' (*ṭārap*). Their prey have no chance of survival. The hiph. masc. sg. ptc. implies ongoing absence of help: there is no one to deliver (*maṣîl*).

8[9]. *tārōm* is a qal 3 fem. sg. juss. from *rwm* ('to lift up'; see BDB 926; *DCH* 7:442) as is *yikkārētû* (niph. 3 masc. pl. from *krt*, 'to cut off').

Form and structure

These are the second and third instances of *wĕhāyâ*, intimating another perspective on the future. The lens first is trained on the apparently benign circumstances of the 'remnant of Jacob'. The next *wĕhāyâ* introduces a more fearsome view, dominated by rapacious lions.

Vv. 6 and 7 are parallel expressions on the surface. The cadence of the repeated description in the first part of each is followed by pairs of similes in the second lines. The verb forms appear in the third line of each verse. In v. 6, they are all yiq. forms; in v. 7, the form shifts to qat. The striking parallels could lull the audience into presuming the similes are conveying the same message. Nevertheless, a surprising ambiguity underlies the structural similarity: Are these images intended to carry the same basic message about the remnant or an antithetical one? The extra 'among the nations' in v. 7 may hint that something a bit disruptive is coming.

V. 8 initiates the theme of 'cutting off', a steady drumbeat through the next section.

Comment

5:6[7]. The remnant of 2:12 and 4:6–7 has been a scattered and vulnerable entity. Here, the remnant is 'in the midst of many peoples', suggesting a wide dispersion. Remembering that the Assyrian resettlement policy exchanged a range of population groups, the dispersion of the Israelites extends much farther than Assyria and later Babylon. See Isa. 11:11. In this imagery, the remnant is not fleeing or broken; nevertheless, depending on the interpretation, it may still need to be rescued.

It is first described as dew and rain. There is ambiguity, however, right from the outset in the way this first simile functions. It may be that the focus is on the herbage of the fields that awaits dew and rain (Andersen and Freedman 2000: 485). The first simile includes an important datum: the dew is from Yhwh. Furthermore, just as dew is evident in profusion, so also the remnant. The abundance of showers upon the herbs or grass

(*ʿēśeb* and *dešeh* are used synonymously) is also an extraordinarily good circumstance. These two expressions regarding dew and the abundant rain as blessings appear together only in Deut. 32:2.

Connecting the two meteorological similes with the description of the consequences is the rel.pron. *ʾăšer* ('which'); it refers to dew and rain, not to the grasses. Two parallel descriptive verbs follow: 'it [or he] does not wait' and 'it [or he] does not tarry'.

Even though it rarely rains between April–May and October in the land, the moisture from dew is sufficient to keep the vineyard, orchard and olive crops maturing through the summer. It is refreshing in the early morning and often so abundant as to run from surfaces into the ground. Dew is evidence of God's blessing (Gen. 27:28; Deut. 32:2; 33:13, 28; Isa. 26:19). This first pair of similes may present the Israelites themselves functioning among the nations just as these blessings do. This fits with the covenantal obligation of Abraham's descendants to be a source of blessing to the nations. On the other hand, the image may suggest that the remnant itself is waiting for deliverance from their wide dispersion just as people in that part of the world long for moisture.

The second meaning of *qwh* underlies the noun *miqweh*, a place where water is collected. It may imply that these blessings, like the remnant, neither collect nor linger. This is the outcome for the nations among whom the remnant abides. Dew and rain do not stay in the place where they fall. Instead, they evaporate, run off or gather in pools. This is the meteorological backdrop: any place where water lingers is a source of hope, but the point of the simile may be that dew and rain do not linger long enough to gather in pools.

To be sure, both verbs imply intrinsic hope as the sentiment that accompanies waiting. The time frame intimated by the yiq. forms is one of expectation for future blessing of dew and rain that will come only from YHWH in YHWH's time. The inability of humans to prolong the present blessings of dew and rain redirects the focus to YHWH, the source.

A challenge remains: How do we address the negations in relation to the subject of these verbs? The 'remnant' is a fem. noun whereas these verbs are masc. sg. Who is *not* hoping and waiting? Are readers to understand that the refreshing moisture of dew and abundant rains leaves before the benefits are realized? Is this likeness then transferred to the temporary presence of the remnant? Or is it suggesting that the remnant is, in their dispersion, waiting but not receiving help?

The above discussion rests upon the idea that 'dew' and 'rain' are positive figures. There is at least one instance where 'dew' serves as a threatening image. In 2 Sam. 17:12, Hushai counselled Absalom to gather his forces before confronting David's army in order to fall upon them 'as dew falls on the ground'. Hosea mentions dew (along with morning clouds, smoke and chaff) as he chastises Israel for their fleeting faithfulness (13:3). In sum, it is an ambiguous figure.

7[8]. The verbatim repetition of the position of the remnant of Jacob in the midst of many nations sets the reader up for a surprise. The initial expectation is the next set of similes, both introduced by 'like', will carry the same positive valence if indeed the first set is positive. That is not the case. Just as with the dew and rain, the relation of the remnant to the lions is important. The position of the remnant has shifted radically: they are no longer the fearful sheep (2:12); they are like lions, and are rapacious and threatening creatures as evidenced by the description that follows.

One possible interpretation would be that, to the surprise of those who persist in viewing Israel as weak and helplessly beleaguered, the remnant is now likened to a lion that passes through, tramples and tears at its victims. Each verb intensifies the violence that follows their initial passing through. A second interpretation puts the remnant in the same tenuous position as they were regarding the dew and refreshing rain – waiting but not certain. Here they are in the midst of lions and, for the time being, there is no possibility of deliverance. This final word on the matter ('and there is no one delivering') helps us revisit both sets of similes and see that Israel's place as the remnant is still more than vulnerable. In this interpretive framework, they are still waiting.

8[9]. Whether the remnant is a powerful force in dispersion or are suffering and waiting for their much-needed deliverance, their rescue comes abruptly in this verse. These petitions intimate a radical reversal, but from where? Whose hand? Micah may directly invoke the intervention on their behalf of YHWH's hand (power), lifted to cut off the enemies of the remnant. On the other hand (an unavoidable pun), it may be a plea that the remnant's hand will be lifted in strength, perhaps enabled by the Ruler. The best option seems to be the Ruler, first introduced in v. 1 and tantalizingly described through v. 3. He is the key figure through this whole segment, even though he waits off-stage in the wings while the remnant is still in exile in Assyria, Babylon or points well beyond. When his hand is uplifted, however, he is no longer backstage.

The appeal that the enemies be cut off sets the stage semantically for the next section. It is all about YHWH's cutting off everything that is evil. The niph. form appears frequently along with 'he will surely die' when there has been a severe violation of holiness: the guilty party will be 'cut off' (Lev. 7:20–27). That death sentence, 'you shall surely die', was first issued by YHWH Elohim in Gen. 2:17.

Explanation

With these two sets of similes, the place and role of the remnant shift dramatically, but the implications are ambiguous, perhaps reflecting ongoing realities for dispersed people groups. The tension between the benign and malign images is important – and real.

The great nations of Micah's day, notably Assyria and Egypt, are frequently represented as powerful lions. Tearing and carrying off prey is a prophetic motif (Isa. 5:29; Hos. 5:14; Nah. 2:12[11]). Isaiah and Hosea press the image further: there is no prospect of one who rescues from the lions. As a counterweight, the descendants of Israel are represented as powerful lions, victorious against their foes (Gen. 49:9; Num. 23:24). YHWH of Hosts is likewise a fearless lion coming down to do battle on Mount Zion and its heights (Isa. 31:4). The multifaceted remnant lion points ahead to the Lion of the Tribe of Judah, victorious through brokenness and suffering. Despite their current subjugation to Assyria, eventually, through the work of the Ruler (5:1[2]), Israel will ultimately overcome *all* 'Assyrias'. Isaiah echoes this same theme (Isa. 10:5–19).

MICAH 5:9–14[10–15]

Translation

5:9[10]And in that day, an utterance of YHWH, I will cut off your horses from your midst, and I will destroy your chariots.

10[11]I will cut off the cities of your land, and I will tear down all your fortifications.

11[12]I will cut off sorceries from your hands, and soothsayers will not be among you.

12[13]I will cut off your carved images and your standing stones from your midst. You will no longer bow down to the work of your hands.

13[14]I will pluck up your *asherim* from your midst, and I will destroy your cities.

14[15]And I, with anger and wrath, will exact vengeance on the nations who have not heard.

Notes on the text

5:10[11]. *mibṣār* ('fortress') is from *bṣr*, meaning 'to cut off' in the sense of an enclosure that cuts the inhabitants off from threats (see 'Comment' on 2:12).

11[12]. *kĕšāpîm* ('sorceries') and *mĕʿônĕnîm* (variously translated as 'soothsayers', 'mediums' or 'whisperers') seem to be among the more esoteric of the magic arts; see the comprehensive list of forbidden practices in Deut. 18:10–14. *kĕšāpîm* is used only in pl. *mĕʿônĕnîm* is a pol. masc. pl. ptc. from *ʿnn*; an alternative form occurs without the mem (Isa. 2:6). See Horsnell, *NIDOTTE* 2:735–738, for a broad survey of the major terms.

12[13]. The word for 'idols' is the pl. form with pron. suff. (*pĕsîlêkā*). Both *pesel* and *pāsîl* are masc. sg. forms. See Carpenter, *NIDOTTE* 3:644–649. Micah also targets 'your standing stones' (*maṣṣēbôtêkā*). The root *nṣb* simply means 'to stand'.

While the meaning of *hištaḥăweh* is presumed to be 'to bow down', the root and conjugation are still under discussion. The traditional understanding is that the root is *šḥh* and is a hithpal. See Waltke 2007: 324 for recent suggestions based on Ugaritic.

13[14]. The Tg reads 'your enemies' instead of *ʿārêkā* ('your cities'). This is a nearer parallel with *ʾăšērîm*. Even closer is the emendation suggested in the *BHS* notes – some form of created idols (*ʿăṣabbêkā*). Willis (1969a: 355) follows the interpretation that the Hebr. consonants (*ʿr*) represent a cognate form in Ugaritic that is synonymous with *pesel*. That avoids the apparently unnecessary repetition of cities (v. 10) and keeps a tighter parallel with the *ʾăšērîm*. *ʿăṣabbêkā* have already made their appearance in 1:7 along with *pĕsîlêhā*.

Form and structure

Almost every line is introduced with 'and I': four of them are a steady hammer of 'and I will cut off', followed by specific objectives, and subsequently echoed with synonyms for the forthcoming destructive action and its target. See Willis 1969a: 353–368. This is the last in the sequence of the *wĕhāyâ* oracles, the culmination of the series of vignettes peering into the future. It is introduced by 'in that day' and followed with the declaration that YHWH is speaking. The fourfold repetition of 'and I will cut off' moves the focus from physical defences that YHWH will destroy to the idolatrous strongholds in their hearts.

The repetition of 'from your midst' (vv. 9, 12, 13) keeps the focus on the problem of Israel's misplaced trust. Likewise, the repetition of the 2 masc. sg. pron. suff. conveys by sound as well as semantics the dreaded truth that 'your' presumed sources of security will be entirely removed. The parallelism in v. 9 between 'cut off' and 'destroy' is accentuated by the sound parallel between *miqqirbekā* ('from your midst') and *markĕbōtekā* ('your chariots').

The abrupt shift at the end from 'you' (apparently Israel) to 'the nations' may be a signal to pause and rethink to what extent that final condemnation also applies to Israel (Ben Zvi 2000: 138–139).

Comment

5:9[10]. The last time we encountered 'in that day' was in 4:6. That was a declaration of YHWH, just as it is here, indicating a shift in focus. At this point, the tone changes abruptly from the precarious presence of the remnant in foreign lands (vv. 6–7) and the destruction of their enemies (v. 8) to judgment.

'Cutting' has a wide semantic range that has implications for understanding the force of YHWH's declaration. As a qal verb, it often appears in conjunction with cutting the covenant (*bĕrît*), a powerful image establishing YHWH's relationship with his people (Jer. 34:18, referring to Gen. 15:9–10). V. 8 employs the niph.: behind the pass. is the hand of YHWH. Now, YHWH will cut off and destroy everything in which they place their confidence. The hiph. is frequently translated 'annihilate' or 'destroy', particularly regarding things or persons who are tainted with wickedness.

This radical shift has prompted some to suggest that the enemies of Israel are now in the crosshairs instead of Israel. This would not be unusual. In other words, when YHWH declares, 'in that day', it will be the time of God's future judgment on enemies who are, without question, idolaters. On the other hand, this series of pronouncements certainly could apply to Jacob's waywardness: it is better to interpret it in that framework.

Each occurrence of 'I will cut off' is followed with a second clause that vividly describes further consequences. YHWH's first target is the war machinery – horses and chariots – in which people are so prone to trust. This false dependence was strongly prohibited (Deut. 17:16–17) and roundly condemned (Ps. 20:8[7]; Isa. 31:1). Micah already issued Lachish an ominous challenge to harness the team of horses to the chariots in what would be a futile attempt to thwart an enemy onslaught (1:13). The elimination of horses and chariots may also reflect cultic expressions that have surfaced. In Josiah's reform almost a century later, one of the targets of the purge includes the horses and chariots dedicated to the sun (2 Kgs 23:11).

10[11]. When horses and chariots fail, the populace retreats within the walls and presumes themselves secure. YHWH will cut off the cities of the land and tear down the fortresses. 'Tearing down' was the first step in reducing a city to a heap of rubble and a ruin (cf. 1:6 and 3:12). Cities and fortresses are almost interchangeable, as major cities must be fortified. Walled cities and fortresses are the last resort for a besieged people. Once inside substantial walls, they can subsist only as long as food supplies and water hold out. Long-term sieges wear the populace down (see 2 Kgs 6:24–31). Hosea states the message of YHWH's judgment against Ephraim in the same terms: their warriors in whom they trust will fall tumultuously and the fortresses will be destroyed (Hos. 10:13–14). Prior to Jerusalem's destruction in 587 BC, Nebuchadnezzar besieged the city for two years (2 Kgs 25:1–4).

11[12]. The objects of God's judgment shift at this point from physical war machines and apparently solid defensive structures to practitioners in the shadowy spiritual realms. These latter are much more insidious and dangerous. YHWH will cut off sorceries from their hands, and they will not have soothsayers – some kind of shadowy practice. All forms of magic practices are strongly condemned in the Torah (Lev. 19:26–31; Deut. 18:10–14). Nevertheless, there is ample evidence that the people succumbed to the insatiable temptation to consult with powers from the 'other side' through the centuries they were in the land. During the period of the Judges, Abimelekh held tenuous control over the city of Shechem until a usurper, Ga'al, took the city. Abimelekh's forces set an ambush outside the city and when they rose up from the ambush, Ga'al described one company as coming from the direction of the 'soothsayers' tree' (Judg. 9:37). A whole range of suspect practitioners were engaged by Manasseh (2 Kgs 21:6). Hosea takes the people to task for enquiring of a piece of wood (Hos. 4:12); Isaiah expands that image with brilliant sarcasm (Isa. 44:9–20). Several centuries later as the kingdom of Judah is collapsing, Ezekiel castigates women who sew amulets into their clothing to trap people (13:18–20).

Jeremiah denounces these two categories of people, among others, because they are outright liars (27:9–10). See also 2 Kgs 9:22; Isa. 47:9, 12; Nah. 3:4. Removing the sorceries from their hand means 'from their power'. They will become ineffectual when they try to use them.

12[13]. The focus of Micah's condemnation moves again, this time to visible idols made with hands (see Ps. 115:4–8). *pesel* is the generic label for these forbidden objects, which were to be destroyed. It appears in the articulation of the Ten Words (Exod. 20:4; Deut. 5:8) and in the legal and prophetic passages that forbid the making and worshipping of images (Deut. 4:16, 23, 25; Isa. 40:19; 42:17; 44:9). *pesel* may be used in conjunction with *tĕmûnâ*, a pictorial representation. An alternative form, *pāsîl*, is used in this context as well as Mic. 1:7. These images could be of wood or stone and could be overlaid with gold or silver. The cognate verb means to 'hew' and is used six times, four of them with reference to Moses' cutting out the second set of stone tablets (Exod. 34:1, 4; Deut. 10:1, 3). See also 1 Kgs 5:32[18] regarding the hewn stones for the temple. On the major Hebr. terms for idols and images, see Hadley, *NIDOTTE* 3:483–484, 644–646.

The 'standing stones' are more ambiguous in the experience of God's people. The meanings include a pillar or monument, such as Absalom set up for himself (*maṣṣebet*; 2 Sam. 18:18); the memorial stones Jacob set up on several occasions (*maṣṣēbâ*; Gen. 28:18–22; 31:13; 35:14); twelve pillars in conjunction with the altar and ratification ceremony (*maṣṣēbâ* as a collective; Exod. 24:4); and standing stones in conjunction with Canaanite altars (Exod. 23:24; 34:13; Lev. 26:1; Deut. 7:5; 12:3). It seems that Jacob adopted a wider Canaanite practice that then narrowed to a ceremony in sacred space. Outside that space, it is viewed with approbation. Altars and standing stones are Israel's response to agricultural bounty, but YHWH will break them down (Hos. 10:1–2). As with the horses, the images and standing stones are said to be 'in your midst'. They are embedded into the very fabric of society, a presumed source of security. As noted earlier, there seems to be some sense in which the latter are perceived with less approbation. In conjunction with a future day, Isaiah mentions an altar in Egypt and a 'standing stone' for YHWH at the border (Isa. 19:19). Nevertheless, the temptation to attribute to these objects a form of power is insidious. A radical shift is necessary: they are adjured no longer to worship anything made with their hands. See Ps. 115:4; Isa. 44:9–20; 46:5–7; Hos. 14:4[3]; Rom. 1:21–25.

Because YHWH will have already cut off the imagery that surrounds them, they will no longer be able to bow down to them. *ʿôd* is an adverb meaning 'still'. With the negation, it means 'no longer'. The series of 'I will cut off' closes at this point: the work of their hands will no longer exist.

13[14]. Each of the next verbs – 1 sg. wayyiq. forms – represents a further judgment. 'Uprooting' (*ntš*) means drastic action to rid the people permanently of the evil that is 'in their midst'. The objects of YHWH's uprooting are the 'Asherim'. The identity and description of the Asherah are complicated. Several seemingly related nouns surface in condemnations of the idolatrous practices of Israel, including Asherah, Astarte, Ashtoreth. Broadly speaking, these pointed to a Canaanite deity, presumably the wife of El and 'mother of the gods'. As it insidiously makes its way into the Israelites' worship spaces, the goddess is represented by a figure of a tree or a pole (Judg. 6:25; 1 Kgs 16:32–33; 2 Kgs 13:6; 17:16). There are multiple reasons why these need to be 'uprooted'. They are a ubiquitous threat as indicated by the expressed plurality (Deut. 7:5; 12:3; Isa. 17:8; 27:9; and numerous other passages). In the Isaiah passages, the pl. form appears in conjunction with *ḥammānîm*, 'incense altars' (*DCH* 3:256) or 'sun pillars' (BDB 329). Oddly enough, the pl. of the fem. noun is generally *ʾăšērîm*, as here (with suff.). See Hadley, *NIDOTTE* 1:569–570.

The last line is YHWH's parting shot: he will bring about utter destruction. The verb implies completion of the process that began with the prior *krt* decrees. If the object is read as 'your cities', this draws attention back to v. 10. It brings closure to the judgment against Israel before the next verse moves to the nations.

14[15]. Shifting focus, now the nations are the target. While vengeance has negative connotations in the twenty-first-century environment, in the Israelite covenant world view, it is a positive concept because YHWH is the Authority behind it. It means that wrongs will be addressed, and justice done. Vengeance is YHWH's prerogative, and that is as it should be. 'Anger' (*ʾap*) and 'wrath' (*ḥēmâ*) occur frequently in conjunction with YHWH's execution of vengeance: he is always the subject of *ʾap* (Waltke 2007: 329). When Israel is disobedient, YHWH effects disciplinary vengeance (Isa. 1:24–26; Jer. 5:9, 29). Just as frequently, however, God's vengeance is turned against the nations: the familiar names of Assyria, Babylon and Egypt recur. They heavy-handedly wield power and, in the process, dishonour YHWH and harm his people. See Peels, *NIDOTTE* 3:154–156.

The sins of the nations are not catalogued. They do not need to be: the prophet has been called to deal with YHWH's people. Nevertheless, Israel's enemies have been severely oppressing them, and that warrants judgment from the sovereign, covenant-keeping God of Israel. The offence is summarized succinctly: they have not heard or followed the basic parameters of right and wrong in the sphere of human existence. As a result, YHWH will exact vengeance in anger and wrath. The absence of a parallel suggesting measure-for-measure here is noteworthy. Earlier Micah emphasized that because Israel did not heed YHWH's covenant instructions, when they cried out, YHWH would not hear them. In the case of the nations, there is no mention of reciprocity. The nations simply have not heard.

Explanation

In this chapter, Micah has seen far into the past and gazes into his future, articulating critical points and places along the way. These temporal elements, marked by the repeated *wĕhāyâ*, define the present for Israel, but it is not always clear just how. In the meantime, the main thrust continues to be against their hard-hearted defiance of YHWH and his covenant. That brings to the fore again the question regarding the political and religious context(s) for this discourse. To be sure, there are sobering connections with the whole historical sweep in which God's people struggle to remain faithful; that is the point of timeless prophetic discourse. Nevertheless, the egregious idolatries in the days of Ahaz, coupled with the unsettling political uncertainties and accompanying temptations to cobble together 'safety nets', may beckon us to that time frame. Sadly, it is unlikely that the people suddenly put all these things away in Hezekiah's reform movement!

Training another lens on the matter, although the mechanisms change, the desire to have an advantage over one's opponent still motivates unseemly activities. Ancient Israel was tempted by a range of divination options, presumably to access secret information; those who inhabit Western twenty-first-century cultures succumb to other means, some of them not particularly ethical. Examples may include insider-trading activities, computer hacking in any number of venues or pay-offs, otherwise known as bribery. Micah continues to remind his audience that placing their trust in false sources of knowledge and security, especially accompanied by wholesale disobedience, is folly in the extreme. Does that render all defences unacceptable? Surely not: Nehemiah is a parade example of 'trust and defend!'

It is tragically instructive that immediately after Isaiah's presentation of nations streaming to Zion to learn and walk in the ways of YHWH (Isa. 2:2–5), the same picture of present reality takes over again. They fill the land with unacceptable practices, with horses, chariots, idols and the work of human hands (Isa. 2:6–8). Whether they represent primarily the military stockpiles on which the people are tempted to rely, or bring in misdirected worship practices as well, the presence of these tempting distractions is ubiquitous.

Nevertheless, a time is forthcoming for Israel when they will finally realize that neither alliances with political superpowers nor their own military might will be worth trusting in (Hos. 14:4[3]). Echoing Micah's oracle here, Zechariah speaks of YHWH's future eradication of those same tokens of war from Israel in the messianic future (Zech. 9:9–10). May it be so – soon! In these final verses, Micah's repetitive rhetoric emphasizes the appalling and comprehensive nature of this judgment. Jeremiah's series of verbal hammer blows against Babylon does the same: YHWH will 'shatter' every level of human existence (Jer. 51:20–23).

Why such apparently harsh treatment of the nations? Their sins are not listed. How are they supposed to obey when they are not privileged with Torah? It is clear, however, that there are universally applicable moral obligations. The same principle informs our understanding of God's judgment as articulated in the first chapter of Amos. Most of those crimes are in the category of 'war crimes', and the condemnation of those foreign nations implies that they transgressed foundational understandings of goodness in pursuit of their own greedy aspirations. Truthfulness and justice give way to cruelty. That is a severe violation of God's holy character. Despising, destroying and degrading his image-bearers requires vindication.

The prospect of God's fury against sin in all geopolitical, systemic, familial and personal contexts creates significant discomfort in many circles. The Western church of the twenty-first-century would rather sidestep God's vengeance and focus exclusively on God's mercy, compassion and forgiveness. As wonderful as those attributes are, a representation of the Master of the universe focusing solely on attributes that are comfortable renders him impotent in the face of virulent evil that never rests. It remakes the sovereign Lord into a culturally acceptable trope. Those whose lives have been repeatedly endangered in totalitarian regimes, however, may find great solace in the promises that YHWH will enable them to triumph over their oppressors (cf. Ps. 118:7–13). He performs vengeance to protect them. Interrupting this steady drumbeat is a powerful and comprehensive statement: 'you will no longer worship the work of your hands'. That encompasses all that has gone before and applies to every possible construction on which they rely.

MICAH 6:1–5

Translation

6:1 Hear therefore that which YHWH is saying: rise up! engage the mountains in a disputation, and let the hills hear your voice.

2 Hear, O mountains, the charge of YHWH; and enduring ones, the foundations of the earth, for YHWH has a dispute with his people, and he will contend with Israel.

3 My people, what have I done to you? And how have I wearied you? Answer me.

[4]For I brought you up from the land of Egypt, and from the house of bondage I redeemed you. And I sent before you Moses, Aaron and Miriam.

[5]My people, remember what Balak, king of Moab, counselled, and what Balaam, son of Beor, answered him; [remember crossing] from Shittim to Gilgal, in order to know the righteous acts of YHWH.

Notes on the text

6:1. The impv. (*šimʿû*; 'Hear!') followed by *nāʾ* indicates a logical development from the preceding conditions (*IBHS* §34.7). 'Therefore' is a good translation option because it steps away from the possibly meek tone of 'please'.

The clause starting with *ʾēt ʾăšer* ('that which') articulates what they are to hear (*IBHS* §10.3.1).

In the clause *rîb ʾet-hehārîm* ('engage the mountains in a dispute'), *ʾet* may mark the direct object: the mountains are engaged as participating witnesses in the strife. The consonantally similar prep. *ʾēt* means 'with' or 'in the presence of'; Williams (2007: 127–129) surveys the wide range of nuances of the prep. Allen (1976: 362, n. 2) reads the clause as 'present the case before the mountains', indicating that *ʾēt* must have this latter meaning; see also BDB 86 (*ʾet* II, 1c.). Allen references Gen. 20:16 and Isa. 30:8. Neither of those passages, however, is helpful, and are the only illustrations of the shift from meaning 'with' to 'in the presence of'. See 'Comment'.

wĕtišmaʿnâ is a qal fem. pl. juss. with *haggĕbāʿôt* as the subject. 'Let the hills hear your voice' identifies Micah as the mediator of YHWH's word.

2. The adj. *ʾētān* is used subst. to refer to things that are permanent. It has the def. art., setting it apart as a voc. followed by 'foundations of the earth', likewise a voc. While there are attempts to emend *hāʾētānîm* to *haʾăzînû* to fit better with the syntactical pattern preceding it, the MT reading works as it designates more specifically the abiding nature of those 'foundations of the earth'.

ykḥ ('decide', 'prove', 'argue') primarily appears in the hiph.; it is used only here in hith. (*DCH* 4:209–210). Even though it is the reflex. conjugation, this is not a reciprocal exchange: that would necessitate a pl. verb. This is entirely YHWH's doing.

3. The lamed prep. has a range of implications, including 'to', 'for' and 'against'. The last is a lamed of disadvantage (*IBHS* §11.2.10d; Williams 2007: 107).

The impv. (*ʿănēh*; 'answer') in the *rîb* context suggests something more pointed than 'answer me!' 'Testify against [*bĕ-*] me!' is the implication. See 1 Sam. 12:3; Isa. 3:9; 59:12.

helʾētî ('I have wearied') is a 1 sg. hiph. qat. form of *lʾh* ('to be weary'). The only other place where God is the subject of that verb is in Job's accusations detailing the ways God has afflicted him (Job 16:7). The LXX adds 'In what have I grieved you?' after 'What have I done to you?'

4. *kî* ('for', 'because') is both disjunctive and connective; there is a literary pause waiting for their answer, but it is not forthcoming.

Both *pdh* and *g'l* mean 'to redeem'. Here YHWH declares that he redeemed his people from being servants, using the somewhat less frequent *pdh*. It suggests the payment necessary to remove them from slavery. *g'l* carries a greater sense of kinship and household as loci for the redemption transactions (Hubbard, *NIDOTTE* 1:789–794).

5. *'ammî* ('my people') is a voc.: it is YHWH's summons, this time not to answer but to 'remember'.

mâ . . . ûmeh ('what . . . and what') function in sequence, compelling the audience to face up to the distasteful details embedded in the next two clauses.

Form and structure

The discourse commences with the conventional summons to witness the covenant accusation. The word *rîb* shapes these first verses; it is the 'dispute' of YHWH against the people. The people are interrogated by YHWH. His four questions will be matched by four questions from the people. The pericope is a mixture of judicial and emotional language. The voice moves from the impv. addressed to witnesses to words directed to God's people.

There are no textual variants regarding the recitation of God's covenant intervention on behalf of Israel. It was their national narrative and not subject to uncertain transmission.

Comment

6:1. The force of YHWH's speaking fuels the admonitions to rise up, strive and again 'hear'. Nevertheless, it is unclear just when YHWH's direct address to the people begins. It may not be until v. 3, starting with 'My people'. In the interval, 'rise up!' is addressed to Micah, strategically placed in the position to summon the parties to the *rîb*. *rîb* is the emphasis in these first two verses, and is intertwined with the mountains and the hills as witnesses. In both verb and noun forms, *rîb* represents a dispute against the offending party by the side that has been wronged. See the 'Introduction' regarding the covenant 'dispute' (*rîb*) nature of this discourse and whether it should be characterized as a 'lawsuit'. Traditionally, judges were expected to adjudicate the disputation process (Exod. 23:2; Deut. 19:17; 21:5). In the prophetic oracles, YHWH brings the charge, mediated through the prophets, against Israel. The accusations are followed by judgment. In this passage the characteristic pattern shifts: there are no accusations, and the summoned mountains and hills recede into the background.

The first occurrence of *rîb* is an impv. following directly on *qûm* ('rise up'). The question is how to understand the 'role' of the mountains in this process. If *ʾet* is a direct-object marker, the role of the mountains as witnesses is more than simply their abiding presence. It also fits well with the voc. in the next verse: 'Hear, O mountains'. This command is followed by a parallel: 'Let the hills hear your voice', suggesting that Micah's own words were to be resounding.

2. The impv. 'Hear!' is repeated but now the subjects are the mountains: they are to hear the dispute YHWH is bringing in the context of his covenant. One of the points of this description is to build up the grandeur of these witnesses; this is serious (Allen 1976: 365). Mountains and everlasting foundations of the earth join the 'hills' of v. 1. *ʾêtān* appears in conjunction with waters that are ever in place (Exod. 14:27); people who were firmly established being led away (Job 12:19); an 'enduring nation' (Jer. 5:15) and even objects (Gen. 49:24). See also Deut. 21:4 and Amos 5:24 regarding a never-failing stream.

rîb recurs in the second clause. YHWH's strife is 'with his people'; most frequently *ʿim* carries the connotation of presence and fellowship with. On occasion, however, it is used in adversarial contexts such as this one (Williams 2007: 126). Here it is repeated: YHWH has a complaint against his people and against Israel, the purpose of which is to set things right. The impact of this must not be lost: former covenant 'partners' will now be in a legal contest.

3. YHWH speaks directly at this point. With two brief questions, he shapes the contours of the case. In the usual exchange of accusations in a dispute, 'What have I done?' expects a list of offences, no matter whether justified or not. While YHWH invites them to accuse him, he also commands them to testify. The people do not, or at least their answer is not recorded. Of course, there is nothing they can say that could even begin to pass muster as a valid accusation.

YHWH's first question plays with the range of implications of the lamed prep. It could be interpreted as 'What have I done *for* you?' As it turns out, that will be the sole focus of God's 'defence'. They are called to remember what they have so completely forgotten: that YHWH has repeatedly acted on their behalf. On the other hand, it equally could read 'What have I done *to* or *against* you?' (*IBHS* §11.2.10d; Williams 2007: 107).

4. Because the people cannot answer, YHWH moves forward to present *his* case, summarizing what he has 'done for' them. YHWH did not just bring the people 'out' of the land of Egypt and the house of bondage. That expression occurs 76 times. Being 'brought out' was a major emphasis of the initial declaration at Sinai (Exod. 20:2; Deut. 5:6). Here, the verb is 'brought up' with all its implications, both the rescue from Egypt as well as the conclusion of the journey in the land. The verb *ʿlh* ('to go up') is used in the context of their redemption from Egyptian bondage 42 times (Waltke 2007: 351). There is a telling sound connection as well; *helʾētî* ('[how] have I wearied you?') in the preceding verse is here contrasted with *heʿĕlītîkā* – YHWH brought them up.

YHWH's historical recital initially focuses on three heroes (v. 5); YHWH sent leaders to go before them. *ʾet* is used only prior to the name of Moses, the first in the list. This may indicate they are to be considered as closely bound together in their work. Naming Moses, Aaron, Miriam may be intended as a contrast to the dismal current leadership. See also Josh. 24:5, 1 Sam. 12:6–7, Ps. 105:26 (recitals of covenant history), where Moses and Aaron are named. Micah adds Miriam to their names, indicating her significance for the redemption narrative. It began with her stationing herself on the banks of the Nile to watch over the basket containing the infant Moses (Exod. 2:1–10). It continued as she prophetically taught the children of Israel to sing of their redemption (Exod. 15:20). The work of Moses, Aaron and Miriam was prophetic, implied by 'sent'; each was a true prophet in contrast to the perfidious Balaam of the next verse. This is the only place in the prophetic writings where Aaron is noted. The only other mention of Miriam outside the Pentateuch is 1 Chr. 5:29[6:3].

5. In the context of covenant history, 'remembrance' means reflecting on the past for the sake of transformation in the present. See Allen, *NIDOTTE* 1:1100–1106. It seems they might have little trouble remembering their iconic figures of Moses, Aaron and Miriam. To recall the less savoury parts of their journey towards the Promised Land is a more painful focus, but it is necessary. There are several layers to this command to remember. Each is a separate piece.

'Remember' presumes YHWH's people will recall his faithful provision *between* Egypt and the Promised Land. These provision narratives are associated with Marah, Rephidim, Sinai, Kadesh, forty years in the wilderness, Edom, Sihon and Og and Moab. Notably, Micah does not mention those events. He calls them instead to 'remember' the backstory behind the arrival of Balaam and his oracles that ended up blessing Israel. Balak's part in the initial hiring and engagement of Balaam to pronounce an effective curse on Israel is styled as 'counsel', but that does not capture the meaning of the word in this context. Micah makes a point of stating that Balak was the king of Moab. That means he presumed he was calling the shots. Thus, *yʿṣ* ('counsel'; 3 masc. sg. qal) in this narrative suggests that Balak gave orders according to his royal will and expected Balaam to respond appropriately, especially as he offered a significant remuneration for Balaam's services (Num. 22:17; 24:11). To state it another way – they are to remember the intention of Balak. The second focus of the call to remember simply says that Balaam 'answered' him, but that description is freighted with layers of meaning. No matter what Balaam and Balak intended, YHWH turned the anticipated curse into a blessing (Num. 22 – 24;

Deut. 23:4–6[3–5]; Josh. 24:10). The reversal is remembered multiple times in the text; it is important, and they are to remember it. Furthermore, the actual contents of Balaam's blessings contain remarkable theological declarations about the future of God's covenant people.

Equally memorable, but soberingly so, is what Balaam later counselled 'under the table'. The debacle at Baal Peor was a terrible curse (Num. 25 and 31:1–16; also referenced in Ps. 106:28–31). This was one of the lowest points for Israel: it matches the golden calf for heinous idolatry. Although they are not mentioned here, the semi-nomadic Midianites were culpable as well. Notably, Moses, the true prophet of YHWH, is entirely absent from the Balaam narratives: Moses and Balaam are never in direct conflict over the Word of YHWH. Balaam himself is an ambiguous figure until Num. 31:1–16. That ambiguity serves Micah's purposes well. The challenge for eighth-century Judahites is how to determine true from false prophets. Balaam's presumed allegiance to YHWH (Num. 22:7–21) does not prevent him from introducing deception and flagrant disobedience into his message when it serves him financially (Num. 31:14–16; 2 Peter 2:15–16). Just as Balaam mixes truth with utterly destructive advice, so Micah's contemporaries, the false prophets who mix truth with falsehood and then accuse *Micah* of 'dripping' (Mic. 2:6).

Evidence of the lasting impact of the Balaam traditions is found in the Deir 'Alla inscription, which names that unseemly prophet. The inscription was found in a Late Bronze temple but is generally dated to the eighth or seventh centuries BC, contemporaneous with Micah (Rainey and Notley 2006: 115). The implications of this event seem to have been taken seriously, even to Micah's day. YHWH uses an unwilling Balaam against the king, at least until he is threatened with loss of his fee. Even then, Balaam's prophetic utterances reach far into the future beyond the abominable advice he gave the king (Num. 24:17).

Even though Shittim is the location of the worst apostasy after the golden calf (Num. 25:10), YHWH does not renounce them at that point. Nevertheless, Israel is on probation: they are to remember that it was a suspended sentence (Andersen and Freedman 2000: 558). This part of the narrative reverberates into the prophetic messages as well. Fast-forward to the mid-eighth century: Hosea reminds his audience of their shame at Baal Peor (Hos. 9:10). Now, Micah is called to convey those same uncomfortable truths to the generation of wicked King Ahaz. The connection with prophetic fees echoes from the Balaam narrative to Micah's context.

'From Shittim to Gilgal' is an extraordinarily pithy summary of the fulfilment of God's promise. Both place names have the definite article ahead of them, and both names have meanings drawn from the geographical context. *šittîm* means 'acacias'; *gilgāl* refers to a 'circle [of rocks]'. In Num. 25:1, the Israelites are encamped at *hašittîm* when they give into the appalling activity with the daughters of Moab at Baal Peor, the result of Balaam's wicked advice. Abel Shittim (Num. 33:49; Josh. 2:1) is the last stop before, and *haggilgāl* (Josh. 4:19–20) the first place mentioned after, crossing the Jordan. At Gilgal, YHWH commands Joshua to circumcise the Israelites because the practice had lapsed during the forty years in the wilderness (Josh. 5:2–9); this is essential because it is the sign of the covenant with Abraham (Gen. 17:9–14).

The move from Shittim to Gilgal represents a radical accomplishment of YHWH's purposes despite their flagrant disobedience. Nevertheless, Gilgal is not an entirely benign location in their history. To be sure, Samuel anoints Saul as king before YHWH at Gilgal (1 Sam. 11:14–15), and Israel returns there to sacrifice (1 Sam. 13:7–15). Perhaps because of those early traditions, however, the people begin to engage in inappropriate worship (Hos. 4:15; 12:12[11]; Amos 4:4), and YHWH 'began' to hate them there (Hos. 9:15).

As the people set up the commemorative stones, this event is linked with crossing the Sea of Reeds. Both crossings take place 'on dry ground', bookending all the incidents in between with God's miraculous deliverance and fulfilment. They are to remember, and the peoples of the land will also know YHWH's mighty hand and fear him (Josh. 4:19–24). Micah closes his recital of covenant history with the same intent as those commemorative stones. It is 'in order to know' that YHWH has worked on their behalf. The substance of the 'righteous acts of YHWH' is his deliverance of his people. Ps. 103:6–7 declares that YHWH's works of righteousness and justice are of a piece with what he reveals to Moses and the children of Israel. They are to know and remember that YHWH keeps his covenant. That should serve as a trenchant summons for present audiences: obedience is essential. This is the closing statement of YHWH's case, and sets the stage to go forward into the next aspect of the accusations regarding the broken covenant relationship. The scenery on the stage shifts to the sanctuary. God has gone to indescribably great lengths for them: they are called to 'answer' him. What will their response be?

Explanation

The biblical pattern embedded in the covenant statement involves heaven and earth summoned as witnesses (Deut. 4:26; 30:19; 32:1; Isa. 1:2–3). In the wider cultural context, natural phenomena (viewed as gods) were called as witnesses to treaties. At the end of the day, however, the summons that starts the chapter does not move into the expected accusation and indictment. Instead, it continues with questions that invite a response from the people. It is a confrontation the end of which attempts to move towards some sort of rapprochement. How strongly we maintain that depends on the interpretation of vv. 6–8. Micah does, however, overturn a formal and known genre.

There are additional dimensions to the appeal directed to the mountains and hills. This would be a familiar concept to Micah's audience. At the end of his life, Joshua renewed the covenant with the Israelites gathered at Shechem. He set up a large stone and declared that it was a witness because it 'heard all the words of YHWH' (Josh. 24:25–27). As the 'foundations of the earth', mountains have stood as silent witnesses for a long time. There is also a geographical dimension to consider. The testimony would echo through the mountains and hills. They would be alive, as it were, with the mighty voice of YHWH. Furthermore, it might be that engaging the mountains would also remind those attending to the accusing voice that mountains had been favourite places for false worship, Ba'al Pe'or and Ba'al Hermon being two examples.

In the prior oracles, 'my people' are victims of hardened leadership; here, they are held responsible for the dismal state of affairs. With the opening question, the divine pathos is evident: God asks for evidence against himself. That connects directly to the recitation of God's acts and calls to obedience. While the exodus is the primary example, their journey to the land is of equal importance, as it fulfilled the Abrahamic promise.

While Micah's audience resides in the eighth century BC, they share an unbroken connection with the generation of the exodus and Sinai. This is Israel's national narrative, with lasting implications: '*we* were there' (Deut. 29:14–15; see also 4:10–13; 5:3); each generation was to 'tell the next generation' (Pss 78:4; 145:4); recitals of salvation history included God's covenant grace, *and* the people's rebellion (examples being Pss 78; 105 – 106). The relationship established at Sinai and Israel's national narrative of redemption are likewise the narrative of the church. The bond of covenant *ḥesed* and the obligations to love YHWH with all our hearts and love his people fully and unreservedly are changeless.

As the people were on the threshold of the Promised Land after forty years in the wilderness, they almost forfeited that (again) by succumbing to the effects of Balaam's counsel. Counsel can be bad! At the outset of the great hymns of Israel's faith, the psalmist pronounces a blessing on the person 'who does not walk in the counsel of the wicked' (Ps. 1:1). Walking implies constancy; the accompanying postures of standing and sitting cover all the bases, evil is to be avoided at all times and in all places, and notably when it is filtered through what passes itself off as wise advice. This whole picture should cause God's people to take stock. Golden-tongued mouthing of snippets of covenant language is not sufficient. How easily do we succumb to preaching an easier and more 'profitable' form of the message?

YHWH is vindicated by the righteous acts on behalf of his people. During the unsteady period of transition to the kingship, Samuel likewise confronted the people with the '*righteous acts* of YHWH', chronicling deliverance after deliverance (1 Sam. 12:6–11). The same expression is embedded in their sung tradition (Ps. 145:7). Israel's sins are, however, also part of the sweeping historical narrative. Above all else, they are persistently ungrateful for those 'righteous acts' and have a long track record of rejecting them. This same amnesia plagues the church.

The pivotal point between this section and the next is what they are to remember particularly about Sinai. Following the great Passover redemption, they experience YHWH's presence at Sinai, are taught how to *approach their holy God* and *how to live justly* in relationship with YHWH and each other. Both emphases will feature prominently in the next section. How *are* they to enter the sanctuary?

MICAH 6:6–8

Translation

6:6With what shall I come before YHWH, [when] I bow myself before God of the height? Shall I come before him with burnt offerings, with year-old calves?

7Does YHWH desire a thousand rams, ten thousand torrents of oil? Should I give my firstborn for my transgression? the fruit of my belly as a sin offering for my soul?

8He has told you, O *Adam*, what is good. And what does YHWH seek from you except doing justice, and love of *ḥesed* and being careful to walk with your God.

Notes on the text

6:6. The first *bammâ* ('With what'?) is followed by three more specific queries introduced by interrogative hê. *ʾăqăaddēm* (pi. 1 sg.) is a derivative from *qedem*, meaning 'front'.

The niph. *ʾikkap* is a **hapax**, from the root *kpp*, meaning 'to bend, bend down, or be bent' (*DCH* 4:455). Possible implications of the niph. include middle, passive or reflex. action (*IBHS* §23.2;23.4). The last fits best in this context. The root is used only four additional times (Pss 57:7[6]; 145:14; 146:8; Isa. 58:5), and in each case conveys a posture of humility.

7. *hăyirṣeh* (3 masc. sg. yiq. form with the interrogative hê) means 'Will he accept?' 'Thousand' (*elep*) and 'ten thousand' (*ribĕbôt*) together convey numbers beyond calculation (*IBHS* §15.2.5).

8. *higgîd* is the hiph. 3 masc. sg. qat. form of *ngd* (to 'announce' or 'declare'); *dôrēš* ('seeking') is a qal masc. sg. ptc. YHWH's people should know the answers to their questions because he told them – repeatedly – what is 'good' (*ṭôb*).

This is the only place where *ʾādām* is used as a voc. They are *ʾādām*, created in the image of God.

mâ . . . ûmâ introduce each accusative clause. *kî ʾîm* (GKC §163d) can best be understood as YHWH's seeking 'nothing but' the following character components – which end up being everything.

The word translated 'humbly' is a **hapax**. It is a hiph. inf. abs. from *ṣnʿ*. A masc. pl. subst. adj. (*ṣĕnûʿîm*) from the same root appears in Prov. 11:2 in an antithetical parallelism declaring that the opposite of 'pride' (*zādôn*) is indeed wisdom. The context suggests that maintaining an accurate self-perception is an appropriate interpretation. While the early versions reflect uncertainty on the meaning of *haṣnēaʿ*, its use in 1QS 5:4 and 8:2 suggests possibly leaning towards an interpretation of 'skilfully' or 'wisely' (Hyatt 1952: 236–237). See further in 'Comment'.

Form and structure

YHWH has posed questions to his people; now they respond in kind. Each possibility is more exaggerated than the previous one. As a contrast to the escalating and frantic backdrop, the simple 'he has told you' is followed by three comprehensive characteristics.

Comment

6:6. The focus shifts to questions from the covenant people, perhaps posed by a representative personage, a 'would-be worshipper' (1 sg.), who wants instruction on the appropriate posture for entering the sanctuary. At least they know they are not to appear empty-handed (Exod. 23:15), but what are the additional requirements? Coming into the sanctuary means coming before the divine King. It requires preparation. *ʾăqaddēm* is repeated in the second iteration of the question. It is as if to say, 'Really, take this question seriously! I want to know what to bring.' The niph. *ʾikkap* intimates bowing oneself entirely in recognition of the vast chasm separating the human petitioner from the transcendent and majestic God. The speaker refers to YHWH as the God of the height – the height of heaven.

A whole burnt offering (*ʿôlâ*) was costly. Both the whole burnt offerings and year-old calves were meaningful and demanding sacrifices (see Lev. 1:3–4). The latter were required in the ordination of the priests (Lev. 9:2, 3, 8). At the same time, these animal sacrifices were manageable. That will not be the case as the frantic questions continue to tumble from the lips of this would-be worshipper. It is important to note at this point that *ʿôlâ* does in several contexts include human sacrifice (2 Kgs 3:27; Jer. 19:5).

At first read, these questions express honest concern for fulfilling their obligations in terms of approaching their holy covenant God; we will return to that option. On the other hand, what follows seems intentionally overdone as the proposed 'fee' for the privilege of gaining access to the King escalates. It may represent sarcasm on the part of the people or their hypothetical representative, or it could express Micah's own caustic hyperbole that he will subsequently dismiss.

7. The hypothetical worshipper works himself into a frenzy to find out what will please YHWH. A basic knowledge of Torah in this case is dangerous: it supplies the categories, but the questions skew those categories terribly. Escalating hyperbole is the order of the day – a thousand rams, ten thousand torrents of oil, the firstborn child as a sin offering.

The ram (*ʾayil*) is the male leader of a flock and thus a valued animal. It was sacrificed as part of the ordination of Aaron and his sons (Exod. 29 and Lev. 8); it was also one of the options for the guilt offering (Lev. 5:15, 16, 18, 25), the burnt offering (Lev. 9:2), the fellowship offering (Lev. 9:4, 18, 19) as well as additional ritual occasions. It is a known 'item' and readily pulled into this frantic query. There may be additional echoes: a ram caught in a thicket served as the substitute for Isaac, the chosen son, on Mount Moriah (Gen. 22:13). A ram was among the animals cut in two as part of the covenant ceremony with Abram (Gen. 15:9).

These exaggerated amounts could suggest that the petitioner is a king for whom these numbers may actually be possible. If so, a traditional backdrop for this query could be the legacy of Solomon at the dedication of the temple: according to the account in 2 Chr. 7:5, he offered twenty-two thousand sacrifices from the herd and one hundred and twenty thousand from the flocks.

Oil was a staple of the tabernacle and temple procedures. Modest amounts were mixed in with grain offerings (Lev. 2:5–7), and it also maintained the perpetual lamps (Exod. 27:20–21). A special recipe was used for anointing (Exod. 30:22–33), and the ordination ceremony required this oil along with rams. Relatively small amounts were sufficient for each of these. A *naḥal* is understood to be a 'torrent', not simply a river. Just as one thousand rams is excessively superlative, so also are 'ten thousand torrents' of oil. From the perspective of the HB, these are unimaginably large numerical designations. (This same expression – no doubt sung with loud enthusiasm – in 1 Sam. 18:7 unsettled Saul when he heard it in accolades for David.)

The sentence structure shifts. The petitioner poses the radical question, introduced by 'Should I give?' (*haʾettēn*). The apex of the shrill questions is the suggestion that YHWH could require the sacrifice of 'my firstborn son', the 'fruit of my body' (*pĕrî biṭnî*). *beṭen* generally refers to 'belly'. While it frequently refers to the woman's womb (*DCH* 2:141–142), the expression here echoes Ps. 132:11 as YHWH promises David that one from his own body (*pĕrî biṭnĕkā*) will sit on his throne.

There is some question whether 'my transgression' and 'my sin' refer to the moral state of the petitioner or to the offering brought to address that guilty condition. While *ḥaṭṭaʾt* commonly means 'sin offering' as well as 'sin', this would be the only place where *pišʿî* is used to indicate the offering. The terms may be adv. accusatives (*IBHS* §9.5.2), describing the most important characteristic of the firstborn when the worshipper brings it (Waltke 2007: 360–361).

Firstborn sons were to be dedicated to YHWH and then redeemed, not offered as sin offerings (Exod. 13:11–16). These are all exceedingly extravagant suggestions. How ought they to be interpreted? The hypothetical questioner recognizes that something dramatic is necessary to deal with transgression and sin. See 'Comment' on 1:5 regarding the implications of *ḥaṭṭāʾâ* and *pešaʿ*. The scenario echoes in an ominous way Abraham on Mount Moriah (Gen. 22) and the ambiguous vow and fulfilment of Jephthah (Judg. 11). It reverberates forward to Ezekiel 16:20 and 20:21–26 with unimaginable insinuations. It is what the evil kings Ahaz and Manasseh do at the lowest ebb of the southern kingdom's existence (2 Kgs 16:3; 21:6; see Ps. 106:37–38 and possibly Hos. 13:2). In the two instances noted above (2 Kgs 3:27; Jer. 19:5), the term 'burnt offering' (*ʿôlâ*) is used regarding the sacrifice of sons. Micah would know the horrendous circumstances of Ahaz's reign firsthand.

This is unthinkable for twenty-first-century Western Christians. Nevertheless, viewed from the cultural framework of Ahaz's day, offering a child would not necessarily be viewed as brutality. Instead, it is offering the father's dearest treasure to YHWH. The closer the bond between father and the child – and the firstborn would be in that place – the more valuable the sacrifice. If Micah's audience senses the alarming absence of YHWH, they may think this is an antidote (Andersen and Freedman 2000: 524). Pressing this to an extreme interpretive possibility, perhaps the voice is that of the king: he speaks on behalf of the people, especially in the face of national crisis. If Ahaz is that representative speaker, offering a child fits: he is already known for passing his son through the fire (Andersen and Freedman 2000: 553).

8. The calm and direct response in v. 8 departs from the driving rhythm of the preceding questions. The substance is simple: all of YHWH's moral requirements are available to be known. What he has already told them is to have ongoing implications in their lives; that is what YHWH will look for. The three-part 'creed' in the second part of the verse articulates the key components of 'good'. Bound up in these initial declarations are implicit accusations. They have not heard what God has told them. They have not paid attention to Torah other than a few handy categories to give themselves the proper jargon. Deut. 10:12 would have been a touchstone for them if they had paid attention. In reality, however, they are bankrupt.

The voc. *ʾādām* reminds them of the human condition, and presses these requirements to the whole of humankind. It may also be a subtle but compelling reminder that if they are thinking of any version of human sacrifice, they will be savaging a bearer of the image of God. The absence of 'my people' potentially carries both positive and negative connotations. Now the addressees are a universal audience, through all times and places. At the same time, the shift from YHWH's Name and the designation of relationship may point to an intentional distancing (Hoyt 2019: 764). See Hos. 6:6–7, and the use of *ʾādām* in that context.

Each directive employs an inf. const. to shape the verbal idea, followed by the object. Micah shifts a common idiom: instead of 'doing *ḥesed*', the customary expression, YHWH's command, simply translated, is to 'do justice' and 'love *ḥesed*'. The latter is unique to this passage and seems at first glance to be a tautology. It appears in 1QpMic and 1QS, where the main thrust of it has to do with the quality of relationships between people. It may be that the two nouns in construct indicate 'love of the *ḥesed* type' or 'faithful love' (Hyatt 1952: 232–239).

The first two components are embodiments of God's own nature (Ps. 100:5), characterized by perfect justice and unfailingly loyal and steadfast covenant love. That is a succinct definition of *ḥesed*. As image-bearers of God, they are to mirror his character, which is what YHWH is 'seeking'. A follower after God must be 'doing' justice – in other words, constantly living in accordance with every judicial and moral requirement of Torah and doing so on behalf of others. Equally comprehensive and challenging are 'loving' *ḥesed* and 'walking' with circumspect awareness that one is not the centre of the universe; 'walking' is the common metaphor to indicate conduct. However we translate *haṣnēaʿ*, the third requirement 'to walk carefully' may be a deliberate corrective to the possibly insincere self-abasement of the enquirer in v. 6.

'Love' is the language of the covenant; adding the implications of faithfulness embedded in *ḥesed* means a double dose. It signals motives as well as actions that are based on lasting spiritual commitment, especially in relationships where those who are vulnerable are delivered from threats and have their needs unfailingly met. The point is that even the most egregious sins, as envisioned by the frantic questioner, can be turned around with practise of these character traits. Together all three of these will be the basis for the recital of rebuke that follows.

The challenge in translating *haṣnēaʿ* has consumed an inordinate amount of attention at the expense of the main point, which is the admonition 'to walk with your God'. Walking in all his ways is coupled with fearing YHWH (Deut. 10:12). This is a tenet of Torah that echoes into wisdom literature. Ps. 86:11 distils the admonition

> Teach me your way, O YHWH,
> that I may walk in your truth.
> Unite my heart to fear your Name.

That admonition may echo into the next verse.

Explanation

There is a wide range of interpretive possibilities regarding this section. From one angle, vv. 6–7 could reflect Micah's sarcastic depiction of the people's insincere and exaggerated claims that they are eager to approach God. To wit, having heard the reprise of YHWH's unfailing provision for them, they are determined to show that his implicit accusations are just plain wrong. With these questions, they make it quite clear that they fully intend to keep their part of the covenant relationship, exaggerated as their claims will be. Micah is having none of it.

Some have proposed that the initial question in v. 6 has parallels with the 'entrance liturgy' as worshippers contemplate coming into the sacred precincts (Allen 1976: 369), especially Pss 15 and 24 (who can 'ascend', 'stand', 'dwell' with God on Zion?). To be sure, characteristics of personal righteousness shape the responses in the psalm contexts, but neither priests nor temple ritual are mentioned here. See Ben Zvi 2000: 150–151 for a substantial critique of that approach to 6:6–8. As noted above, the questions may be satirical. They start with the presumed desire to know how to approach the deity with whatever he may want. The increasing exaggeration in v. 7, however, tips off the audience that these are not sincere questions. Their affirmations of God's transcendence and the need to bow in humility are feigned.

On another hand, these questions may represent the people's honest frantic appeal in dire circumstances. They were on the cusp of utter destruction by Assyria. Perhaps the failure and bankruptcy of the priesthood (see ch. 3) has belatedly dawned on them (Willis 1968c: 273–278). In YHWH's preceding admonition to 'remember', the one area he has not addressed is the cult. How is a person to approach the holy presence? Does YHWH now reject costly gifts as acceptable means of atonement? What are they to do? The beauty of the ambiguity through these two verses is this: it reflects with a painful realism the messy range of emotions on the part of God's people. Some are no doubt honestly wondering how possibly to get back into YHWH's good graces; others may be cynically posing the questions; still others may be motivated by raw fear. And everything in between.

This is an ongoing theme in the prophets. Isaiah roundly condemns the tangled web of sacrifices, incense and iniquity (Isa. 1:12–17). Jeremiah likewise declares that frankincense, burnt offerings and sacrifices are unacceptable in the face of the people's outright rejection of YHWH's Torah (Jer. 6:19–20). Parts of Ps. 50 bolster that claim. Nevertheless, a more robust reading of the entirety of Ps. 50 makes it eminently clear that obedient ritual practice is of a piece with fearing God and renouncing sin (cf. Ps. 66:13–20). What may be called the sanctuary requirements are not dismissed: they are part of the covenant stipulations for approaching God. Atoning sacrifice is necessary for sinful people (Lev. 17:11; Heb. 9:22). Nevertheless, without living in accordance with the justice requirements of the covenant relationship, these cultic observances are insufficient.

While these questions could reflect Micah's disgusted reflection of their insincerity, the crescendo from reasonable burnt offerings and calves to highly inflated numbers may express their terror at the approach of an enemy before whom there is no human hope of survival. In this frame of mind, perhaps they are enquiring as to whether the ultimate in sacrifice, a human offering, will forestall the disaster. It amounts to their offering what they perceive as being the definitive bargaining chip. Sadly, they do not comprehend that they are not in a position to bargain, and the covenant relationship does not reduce to quid pro quo.

Unthinkable as that seems at first, it would be an indication that the wider cultural milieu has seriously penetrated their religious thinking. After all, the Moabite king Mesha seemed to presume that the sacrifice of a son on the wall was necessary, misguided as that might have been (2 Kgs 3:27). The cult was Canaanite in origin. Perhaps the biblical practices of dedication and redemption (Exod. 13) as well as substitution (Gen. 22) were supposed to address obliquely a practice that was always hovering around the people. As we have already seen, by the time of the writing prophets the people were engaged in an unsettling steady drumbeat of sacrificing their children (Ps. 106:37–38; Isa. 57:5; Ezek. 16:20; 20:31; Hos. 13:2; Amos 2:1). It was practised by kings Ahaz and Manasseh (2 Kgs 16, 21), even though the *kings* should have been the moral leaders. There is no doubt that YHWH is outraged; and yet, there is another narrative to consider. In the exceedingly challenging situation with the Gibeonites, there was measure-for-measure taking of life to rectify an old wrong (2 Sam. 21). In sum, perhaps Mic. 6:7 ought not to be considered a preposterous offer (see Shaw 1993: 174–175; Andersen and Freedman 2000: 538).

A third possibility may be worth noting. Could it possibly be that this reflects their awakening despair in coming to realize there is never enough a *person* can do in the face of God Almighty? Unlikely as it may seem at first blush, their response *could* indicate contrition and desire to please YHWH. They know that sacrifice is necessary to approach YHWH and overcome their own grievous sin. If so, these are honest questions. If the Torah does not present a clear remedy for the severe sin of rebellion, what are they to do? The brief review of history has reminded them of the need for God's mercy to cover apostasy (Exod. 34:7; Andersen and Freedman 2000: 559).

There are echoes in Amos of the same inadequacy of human efforts to cobble together an approach to God, dramatic as those may be. Although the perspective and message of Amos are tailored to the middle of the eighth century BC in the seriously deficient northern kingdom, the absence of any moral anchor holding the people's waywardness in check was pretty much the same down south.

> I hate, I despise your festivals, and I do not take sensory delight
> in your gatherings.
> Even though you offer up to me whole burnt offerings and your
> grain offerings,
> I do not desire them.

And I will not look at the peace offerings of your fatlings.
Take away from me the tumult of your songs; the song of your harps I will not hear.
Let justice roll like waters, and righteousness like an unending stream.
(Amos 5:21–24)

Hosea likewise readjusts the perspective of his audience:

For *ḥesed* I desire, not sacrifice,
and knowledge of God rather than burnt offerings.
(Hos. 6:6)

Jesus (Matt. 9:12–13; 12:7) reiterates Hosea's declaration as he confronts Pharisees harping on about what they regard as infractions of requirements of ritual Torah. See also Hos. 8:13.

In sober contrast to the hyperbole preceding it, the succinct response of v. 8 references fundamental and interwoven concepts they should have known. YHWH does not respond directly; instead, a voice speaks for him, declaring and distilling the substance of all of Torah. It may be that the stated 'requirements' are specifically aimed at the reigning king. One requirement of Israel's kings is that they read Torah (Deut. 17:18): when Joash was crowned, Torah was handed to him (2 Kgs 11:12). Pss 72 and 101 carry a steady drumbeat on justice and *ḥesed* in Israelite culture (Shaw 1993: 177–178).

The Community Rule (1QS) may give further insight into interpreting these requirements. The phrases *ʾahabat ḥesed* ('loving *ḥesed*') and *haṣnēaʿ leket* ('walking circumspectly'), unique to the HB, appear several times in this document. The *yaḥad* ('community') was to be characterized by 'truth and excellent humility and love of *ḥsd* [*wʾhbt ḥsd*]' (ii.24). Subsequently, similar constellations of attributes are articulated in Column v: 'charity and justice and love of *ḥsd* [*wʾhbt ḥsd*] and wise decorum [*whṣnʿ*] to walk [*lkt*] in all their ways' (v.4); and again, 'truth and humility and love of *ḥsd* [*wʾhbt ḥsd*]' (v.25). The full sequence recurs in viii.2, 'to do truth and righteousness and love of *ḥsd* and to walk with wise decorum'. The inf. const. forms 'doing' and 'walking' are bookends, just as they are in Mic. 6:8 (Parry and Tov 2014. 1: 2–35). Rather than being separate characteristics individually shaped by 'doing, loving and walking', they all joined in a fully orbed description. Justice is oriented particularly towards maintaining the well-being of the community: it is central to the prophetic messages. Notably, the trait of humility is represented in these excerpts by a word distinct from *haṣnēaʿ*. Thus, the latter might have carried significantly richer connotations than 'walking humbly'. Perhaps, being aware of one's position, the best interpretation is 'wisely'. See again Hyatt 1952: 232–239, as well as a critique of his word-study process by

Hoyt (2019: 765–766). No doubt the members of the Qumran community drew from the well of Mic. 6:8. Through the NT lens, Jesus challenges the hypocrites of his day, the Pharisees, to tithe diligently even of the smallest spices, while doing justice, loving mercy and being faithful as well (Matt. 23:23). This declaration of Jesus echoes Mic. 6:8.

Additional canonical connections are significant. Two incidents in Samuel indicate the persistent need for these prophetic admonitions. After the people request a king, Samuel summons them and preaches a powerful farewell sermon that reminds them of God's good acts on their behalf, warns them against disobedience and admonishes them to serve YHWH and walk in the good and right way (1 Sam. 12). Later, when Saul tries to cover up his disobedience regarding the Amalekites and their king, Agag, Samuel's response makes it painfully clear that costly and highly emotional ceremonies are insufficient if their entire hearts are not given over to YHWH (1 Sam. 15:22–23).

The people's question 'With what?' presupposes they can *bring* something, a life that will substitute for theirs in its death. YHWH's response is an adumbration of Paul's words: they and we are to be living sacrifices (Rom. 12:1–2), fully transformed in every way. Cultic language merges seamlessly with moral rectitude. Speaking through Hosea, YHWH declares that he will restore Israel and 'betroth' her 'in righteousness and in justice, in *ḥesed* and in compassion', and adds 'in faithfulness' and the promise of 'knowing' YHWH (Hos. 2:21–22[19–20]).

It is not an exaggeration to say that *ḥesed* summarizes all relationships within our theological understanding. Unfailingly loyal covenant love characterizes God's love; it should be equally manifested in our love for God and for one another. In response to Jesus' summary of the 'law and the prophets' (Mark 12:28–34), the scribe responds that these two great commandments are more important than all whole burnt offerings and sacrifices. That comment echoes Mic. 6.

In the light of the admonition to remember, it may be worthwhile to pause again to commit the following passage to memory:

> Teach me your way, O YHWH,
> that I may walk in your truth;
> unite my heart to fear your Name.
> (Ps. 86:11)

MICAH 6:9–16

Translation

6:9 The voice of YHWH! Let him call to the city. [It is] sound wisdom; let him have regard for your Name. Hear, O tribal leaders, and assembly of the city!

[10]Can I overlook any longer the house of wickedness, the treasuries of wickedness or the despicably scanty ephah?

[11]Can I be pure with wicked scales, or with a bag of deceitful stones?

[12]Her rich men are filled with violence, and her inhabitants have spoken falsehood, and their tongue is treachery in their mouth.

[13]And also I, I have made you weak by smiting, ravaging [you] because of your sin.

[14]And you, you will eat but not be satisfied; and it will be dark in your midst. You will reach, but you will not bring into security; and those whom you do deliver, I will give over to the sword.

[15]And you, you will sow and not reap; you will tread the olive and not anoint with oil, and from the new wine, you shall not drink wine.

[16]And the statutes of Omri have been kept, and every deed of the house of Ahab – you have walked according to their counsel, so that I am giving you to horror, and her inhabitants to hissing, and you will bear the reproach of my people.

Notes on the text

With good reason, *BHS* indicates that this is a confused text from v. 9 all the way to v. 16. Allen's footnotes on the textual options are helpful (1976: 375–376).

6:9. The yiq. verb *yiqrāʾ* ('let him call') could be a juss. It follows both *qôl yhwh* and the indirect object *lāʿîr*. It may be that *qôl* (or *qôl yhwh*) is an exclamation and 'he' is the subject of *yiqrāʾ* (Andersen and Freedman 2000: 545–546; GKC §146).

The clause *wětûšiyyâ yirʾeh šěmekā* (lit. 'sound wisdom, he/it will see your name') is difficult. The LXX reads 'and he will save those who fear his name', suggesting an original text that read *wěhôšîaʿ yirʾē šěmô*. The Tg, Vg and Syr likewise render *yirʾeh* as 'fear'. While *yirʾeh* ('to see') could be revocalized to *yirāʾ* ('to fear'), there is no direct evidence to support that (Gelston 2010: 106*).

There are two interpretive options for the end of v. 9. The first follows the MT: 'hear [heed] the rod [*maṭṭeh*], and the One who has appointed it. [v. 10] Yet'. This reading seems strained, but does continue the focus on good sense and proper regard in the presence of YHWH, who wields a chastising rod (Gelston 2010: 106*). A second rendering, 'Hear, O tribal leaders, and the assembly of the [v. 10] city,' seems to work better in the overall context. The consensus of the early versions is to understand *maṭṭeh* as 'tribe' instead of 'rod'.

ʿôd ('yet') is awkward at the beginning of a sentence. It could be YHWH's saying he will not neglect 'any longer' the blatant abuses that are occurring. The LXX has read *ʿôd* as *ʿîr* ('city'). Given the similarity between daleth (ד) and resh (ר), along with waw (ו) and yod (י), especially in the context of MSS, *ʿîr* could easily interchange with *ʿôd*, especially influenced by the proximity of the verb meaning 'to appoint'. In that framework, *maṭṭeh* is read as a collective voc., calling to tribal leaders and the 'assembly' (*môʿēd*) of the city. An additional redivision of words and a minor alteration of consonants, from *yʿd* (the root of 'appoint') to *wʿd*, permits the noun *môʿēd*, a governing body within the urban context. On the other hand, Goldingay (2021: 470) prefers to keep the equivalent of 'rod' followed by an indirect question regarding who might appoint it. It is still not clear to whom the fem. suff. attached to the verb refers.

10. For *haʾiš* in the MT, the LXX has 'not fire'; see also the Vg and Syr. *haʾiš* could be from the root, *nšh*, meaning 'to forget' (*DCH* 5:776–777). Some scholars have interpreted the word in this manner. It is an abbreviated form of what would be expected as the 1 sg. yiq. (*haʾešeh*). 'Expected' because this is a verb that is not used frequently: there are no other occurrences of qal yiq. forms. On the other hand, it may simply be an interr. particle followed by a modified form (*ʾiš*) of *yēš*, meaning 'Are there?' See also 2 Sam. 14:19 (Gelston 2010: 106*).

Another approach involves emending *bêt* ('house') to *bat* as a parallel to the measure of the *ʾêpâ* (a dry measure) at the end of the verse. The *ʾêpâ*, in construct with *rāzôn*, a masc. sg. noun, is characterized by being lean. *Rāzôn* is used only twice in addition to this passage. In both Isa. 10:16 and Ps. 106:15, it means a wasting disease. The root, *rzh*, means 'to be or grow lean'. See *DCH* 7:458–459.

zĕʿûmâ is a fem. sg. qal pass. ptc. from *zʿm*, 'to be indignant, to denounce, to curse'. In conjunction with the Balaam narrative (Num. 23:7–8), it means to curse. The passive form appears in DSS texts that address those associated with Belial (*DCH* 3:125–126). A literal rendition of this phrase would be 'the ephah of accursed scantiness'.

11. The qal 1 sg. with the interr. *haʾezkeh* (MT) is awkward. The Vg changes YHWH's question to a declarative statement, 'and I will justify'. The LXX, Syr and Tg shift it to third person (Gelston 2010: 106*). *zkh* means 'to be pure', with an extended meaning of being justified or regarded as just and righteous (*DCH* 3:103–104). It occurs twice in Job as Eliphaz, later echoed by Bildad, asks how a human being can possibly be pure (15:14; 25:4). The only other place this applies to God is Ps. 51:6[4]. *mirmâ*, a fem. noun meaning deceit or treachery, is parallel to *rešaʿ*. The related verb *rmh* means 'to beguile' or 'deal treacherously' (*DCH* 7:494–495). The 'weights' were calibrated stones kept in a bag.

12. The rel.pron *ʾăšer* lacks an antecedent: it is likely the city (v. 9) as suggested by the 3 fem. sg. pron. suffixes, 'her' wealthy ones (*ʿăšîrêhā*) and 'her' inhabitants (*yōšbêhā*).

13. *wĕgam-ʾănî* (*IBHS* §39.3.4d) followed by the first-person qat. form is emphatic. Although the LXX (Aquila and Theodotian), Syr and Vg read *heḥĕlêtî* ('to be weak or sickly') as some form of 'begin' (*haḥillôtî*), the MT reading works. The combination of *ḥlh* and *nkh* appears in descriptions of God's justified punishment, accompanied by a form of *šbr*, indicating 'brokenness' (Jer. 10:19; 14:17; 30:12; Nah. 3:19; see Allen 1976: 376, n. 58; GKC §114n). The hiph. prophetic qat. form with the inf. const. means 'I will cause [you] to be weakened or sick by smiting'. It is followed by an inf. abs., 'to destroy' (*hašmēm*) them on account of their sins.

14. *yešḥăkā* is a **hapax** and was variously interpreted by the ancient versions. Some Greek versions are based on 'to be dark' (*ḥšk*), particularly a dread of impending darkness. The Vg understood it as 'humiliate' (*šḥh*). It is not clear on what textual basis the Syr reads 'dysentery' and the Tg 'sickness' (Gelston 2010: 107*). Those interpretations may be related to the connection with 'inward parts' (*bĕkirbekā*). Additional conjectures include 'emptiness caused by hunger' (BDB 445), 'fever' (*DCH* 8:319) and 'gnawing hunger' (Jenson 2008: 177). Each option is dependent on some facet of the context. A good case can be made for interpreting the word as a severe digestive ailment. The reading of the Syr may reflect the root meaning of *šāḥōaḥ*, which is 'to be bent over'. Someone eating but not being sated may be in that condition because they suffer from dysentery. Both Tg Jonathan and **Rashi** understood the word as a 'violent disorder of the bowels' (Ehrman 1973: 103–105).

Some presume the root of *wĕtassēg* is *nsg*, meaning 'reach' or 'seize'. Others read it as a variant spelling (*taśśēg*) of the hiph. form of *śûg*. That would echo 2:6, the claim on the part of false prophets that disaster will not overtake them. See summaries in Allen 1976: 376, n. 60, and Waltke 2007: 402–403.

taplîṭ could be the hiph. form of *plṭ*, used only here and in Isa. 5:29. Both the hiph. and pi. mean 'bring to security' (*DCH* 6:691–692).

16. The 3 masc. sg. hith. *wĕyištammēr* is at odds with *ḥuqqôt*, a fem. pl. noun. The LXX, Syr and Vg read the equivalent of the 2 masc. sg. *tišmôr*, which also matches the subsequent verb form. The MT reading, however, possibly refers collectively and reflexively to the inhabitants of the previously mentioned city. They are keeping (for themselves) the 'statutes of Omri'. Because the verb is distant from that entity, it is a masc. form.

lĕmaʿan is followed by the inf. const. of *ntn* with 1 sg. suff. The first direct object is 'you', while the second implicit one is 'her inhabitants' (referencing the city). Together they are given over to (*lĕ-*) the shame of appalling destruction.

Form and structure

The challenges of the text may be the result of Micah's characteristic rough syntax or a product of transmission issues. This is especially true in v. 9 and its possible continuation into v. 10. Reading the MT as it stands, vv. 10–12 are YHWH's accusations; vv. 13–15 spell out the sentence under the covenant. Micah shifts from the indictment in the third person to the judicial sentence, each aspect addressed to 'you'. Vv. 14 and 15 set up a series of contrasts between their hopeful positive actions and the negative outcomes.

The shifting pronouns are part of the message and should not be levelled for the sake of smooth reading. The sg. seems to signify the people, and the pl. refers to leaders. Vv. 9 and 16 are thus addressed to leaders, whereas 13–15 focus on the people. All of them need disciplinary measures; the strata of their social structure are indicated by the pronoun shifts. There is a singular wicked person; that may be the king ('he'). The wealthy oppressors ('they'), leaders ('you' pl.) and finally the people ('you' sg.) represent the decreasing stature and power of each (Andersen and Freedman 2000: 557–560).

Comment

6:9. The hypothetical exchange over how to approach Yhwh gives way to his public summons. Perhaps *qol* ('voice') here functions like *hinneh* ('Look!') – to get attention. See 'Notes' on 1:3. It is significantly more dramatic than 'Thus saith Yhwh', compelling as that ought to be. The opening evocation is followed by the impv. 'Hear!', which echoes vv. 1 and 2. The whole is a wake-up call to the unnamed city.

Goldingay (2021: 470) handles the unwieldy *wĕtûšiyyâ yirʾeh šĕmekā* by suggesting an ellipsis in this second line. Just as the voice of Yhwh calls to the city in the first line, so here 'discernment [*tûšiyyâ*] [calls to the one who] regards your Name'. Nevertheless, it is not entirely clear how the phrase functions in the wider context of the verse. Mays suggests it is a later addition (1976: 146). It could be Micah's own aside, directed to Yhwh ('your Name'), positioned between the warning that Yhwh is summoning the city's leadership and the forthcoming impv. to 'Hear!' (Jenson 2008: 174–175). Appealing to 'common sense' or 'sound wisdom' (*tûšiyyâ*) and fearing Yhwh gives the audience a heads up. This is serious.

Hearing will not be easy: the accusations are severe. That may help us determine how to translate what follows 'Hear!' While both interpretive options (see 'Notes') are weighty, the balance tips towards its being a direct summons to urban leaders initiating the indictment against the city, its assembly and tribal leaders, probably of Judah. To be sure, dread is the optimal 'posture' at the prospect of the 'voice of Yhwh', but an indefinite admonition to have regard for the Name maintains the MT reading.

10. Emending the first word of this verse to 'city' and reading it with the preceding verse means that the awkwardness of *ʿôd* ('yet') starting the verse is no longer a problem. It directs attention to the city, and what follows are urban activities that constitute grave injustices.

There are still interpretive challenges. The prophet's words burst forth; the broken syntax mirrors the injustices that break all bounds. There are no prepositions to help position elements of the sentence. The first word they are to 'hear' is YHWH's self-referential question, but what is he asking? The rhetorical question implies YHWH's incredulity at and refusal to overlook their appalling greed. The multiple means of acquiring ill-gotten gains follow in the rest of this verse and the next. They may be referencing municipal and royal stockpiles (the 'house' and the 'treasuries'), all gained by virtue of systems that aided and abetted dishonest dealings. Fittingly, the chapter closes with condemnation of the '*house* of Ahab' (*bēt-ʾaḥʾāb*).

Read in that framework, YHWH is appalled at their greed, encapsulated in 'house of wickedness' (*bêt rāšāʿ*) immediately followed by 'treasures of wickedness'. It is not necessary to delete 'house of wickedness' before 'treasuries of wickedness', although that is an emendation suggested in the *BHS* notes. Together they convey the excess of accumulated evil. *ʾôṣār* was a place for storing goods and came also to mean the stored goods.

The *ʾêpâ* was a dry measure, particularly for grain; its liquid equivalent was the *bat*. In the pre-exilic period, the *ʾêpâ* was approximately 18 pints (10 l); the *bat* was approximately 39 pints (22 l). See Fuller, *NIDOTTE* 1:382–388, and Powell, *ABD* 6:897–908, for details on all the standard measures in the Israelite period. There was reprehensible cheating in terms of measuring the basic food source of grain. If *bêt* is read as *bat*, the parallel between *bat* and *ʾêpâ* is echoed in the next verse with two deceitful methods of weighing produce.

The *ʾêpâ* in construct with *rāzôn*, a masc. sg. noun, is characterized by being lean; this is a scant measure. YHWH further exposes the excessive cheating. The pass. form of *zĕʿûmâ* ('denounced' or 'accursed') appears in DSS texts that address those associated with Belial (*DCH* 3:125–126). Pronouncing a curse against a powerful extortioner is more than simply venting. It is presumed that those words are uttered in the presence of YHWH, who will indeed vindicate his oppressed children.

Greedy merchants who cheat with false measures are an abomination to YHWH (Deut. 25:13–16). It is sobering to pause and absorb the truth that the *people*, not just the practice, are an abomination. In that social structure, the victims have no human recourse. How could YHWH overlook the blatant dishonesty? The word for 'evil' (*rešaʿ* or *rāšāʿ*) occurs twice in this line and once more in v. 11. These are truly evil and egregious practices, and they echo through every century after Micah into the present.

11. YHWH poses two questions; the second starts v. 11. Both have to do with YHWH's apparent 'standing' in the face of the appalling abuses. Many translations shift the force of the verb to the practitioners of duplicity in the marketplace; in other words, 'Can I acquit [these wicked people]'? The force of this question, however, is this: 'Can *I* [YHWH] be pure when there are evil scales and false weights'? That interpretation keeps the focus on the perception that YHWH would tolerate such abuses.

Either way, YHWH will not tolerate those who engage in shady business practices whether they be weighing with devices that are out of balance or using a bag full of falsely labelled stones for weighing produce. In a context where accurate measuring devices are absent, rigging the weights and scales may easily avoid detection. Hosea calls out the same pernicious evil (12:8[7]). One can imagine all the ways that merchandising is altered to favour the seller; it is an ongoing problem. A century later, Habakkuk is aghast at the prospect that YHWH can even look on evil: '[You] are too pure of eyes to see evil, and you are not able to look at wrong' (1:13).

12. Two characteristics – violence and deceit – stand out as YHWH zeroes in on the city's rich inhabitants. The very apparatus with which they speak has been hardwired to utter deceit! Both tongue and mouth are indicted. Violence is a strong word; YHWH views as violent the systemic injustices built into the economic realm whereby the wealthy amass what they now hold in 'wicked treasuries'. It does not take a rocket scientist to apply the warning in these accusations to our own contexts.

13. YHWH is unquestionably the originator of these judgments. In response to the characters of the rich and unscrupulous merchants, YHWH will act. The horrifying nature of the punishment is also not left to question. Their apparent financial successes gained at the expense of the folk they have trampled will come to a crashing halt. Disasters will overwhelm YHWH's people when they refuse to hear and obey the Torah (Deut. 28:58–61). The vivid descriptions of sickening disaster from both Jeremiah (7:33; 19:7–9) and Ezekiel (chs. 5–7) a century later leave no doubt that in the wake of fierce enemy attack, there are no places untouched by plague, death and devastation. There is a hopeful adumbration; Gelston (2010: 107*) connects it with Isa. 53:10.

14. Just as God has said 'I, even I, will act,' here he emphasizes their state with the personal pron. *ʾattâ* along with the second-person finite verbs 'you, you, will eat but not be satisfied'. This is the first of a series of judgments that echo the covenant curses, called 'futility curses' (Hillers 1984: 82), continuing to drive home the consequences of disobedience. Micah's words are grounded in Lev. 26:26, these judgments reverberate in the pre-exilic prophets (Isa. 9:19[20]; Hos. 4:10) and surface again even after the exile. Haggai chastises the Judean population for having their priorities all wrong, focusing on their own self-satisfaction instead of rebuilding God's temple. As a result, they will be 'eating but not to satisfaction' (1:6). The consequences of malnutrition may underlie *yešḥăkā*. On the other hand, the prospect of impending darkness is equally fitting. That ominous threat has already appeared regarding darkness for those passing themselves off as visionaries (3:6). Now, darkness will be 'in their midst'. It will shape their whole existence.

The text is ambiguous as to what they will reach or overtake, and what will happen next. If they are expecting to reach some beleaguered group of people to rescue them – perhaps the city or a group of refugees – Micah dispels that notion. Addressing them directly, he says, 'you will not bring [them] into security'. The hiph. of *swg* appears in five other places

(Deut. 19:14; 27:17; Prov. 22:28; 23:10; Hos. 5:10). If that is the correct underlying root, it may shed light on Micah's implications. All the passages have to do with moving a boundary stone. That action is most assuredly in the category of the land theft that Micah has already condemned and is the rural counterpart to the cheating and stealing in the urban context. When they attempt to continue that process, they will not be successful and will lose to the sword any presumed profit (Hoyt 2019: 774–775). Micah concludes with an emphatic grim addition: any who may be brought into a secure place, YHWH will give over to the sword, implying complete annihilation.

15. Each clause addresses the covenant-shaped consequences of their disobedience. All are lodged in their agriculturally based economic and social structures. They will not reap a harvest from their sown fields. The variety of grains, providing the primary sustenance of 'bread' (*leḥem*), are harvested between the middle of April and the end of May. *tidrôk* ('tread') covers both olives and grapes, even though olives are generally not trodden. Both crops are harvested and prepared in late September and into October. It may be that 'treading' olives indicates desperate circumstances. The yield is too small to employ the larger machinery of the press. Olive oil is a staple, used as food, medicine, fuel for ordinary lamps as well as in the temple, and in additional ritual contexts. There will not be sufficient for anointing with 'oil' (*šemen*) whether for skincare or for official installations. Generally, *tîrôš* is the product of treading. They will have grape juice (*tîrôš*) but in the end no wine. The same grim outcomes shape Amos's words (5:11). These crises could be due to drought, locust plagues, or enemy invasion.

16. What are the 'statutes [*ḥuqqôt*] of Omri'? The meaning of the related verb is 'to inscribe' (*DCH* 3:303–304); *ḥûqqâ* (fem. sg.) suggests a well-established custom. Micah accuses the people of keeping those customs and every deed of the house of Ahab. 'House of Ahab' could imply the dynasty, even though it is Omri's dynasty. It may be another veiled allusion to the house of Ahab seizing Naboth's inheritance; see 'Comment' on 2:2. The expression may also indicate the ongoing effects of that dynasty, permeating the southern kingdom well into the reign of Manasseh (2 Kgs 21).

Note the irony in this. The people have not kept the statutes, decrees, precepts and Torah of YHWH, but it seems they have bound themselves to those of the Omri dynasty. That may be the implication of the reflex. *yištammēr*. Furthermore, even though they need to be reminded of the righteous acts of YHWH (6:5), they seem to have no trouble walking in step with the house of Ahab, heinous as that counsel is. The shift to second person may be a way Micah directs attention more explicitly to the culpable leadership (Waltke 2007: 405).

The term translated 'counsel' may better be understood as 'operative plan'. It is less democratic than twenty-first-century Western culture might construe it. It is used often of God's providential purposes; the word appears with increasing frequency in Isaiah, Micah's contemporary. Here, the purposes of the Omri dynasty presume to turn upside down the redemptive plan of YHWH. Micah already has given his readers a glimpse of the connotations of this word. The related verb *y'ṣ* appears in conjunction with what the people are to remember about Balak, king of Moab. He gave 'counsel' to Balaam; in other words, he told the prophet what he was expected to say to go along with Balak's plan. It was not the other way around (6:5).

Both English ('hissing') and Hebr. (*šĕrēqâ*) are onomatopoeic. The word appears primarily in Jeremiah (19:8; 25:9, 18; 29:18; 51:37), always in company with 'horror' (*šammâ*), as Jerusalem and the southern kingdom were gasping their last before the onslaught of Nebuchadnezzar. This evidence of 'reproach' will be borne publicly. In sum, this is a recipe for utter disaster: horror and humiliation will be their lot in the wake of destruction. The chapter closes with 'my people', an inclusio with 6:2.

Explanation

The parenthetical appeal to 'sound wisdom' in company with the fear of YHWH echoes predominant themes in Proverbs where the incessant emphasis is on truth and honesty in all dealings. Against that practical theology backdrop, v. 9 begins the catalogue of injustices, a terrible contrast with the lofty aspirations of v. 8. To review the eighth-century BC context, the economic development under Uzziah likely had a dark underbelly of shady dealings in the realm of commerce, even though short measures and dishonest scales are an abomination to YHWH (Prov. 11:1; 20:10, 23; see Lev. 19:35–36; Deut. 25:13–16). Amos condemns the wholesale exploitation and abuse of the poor in the northern kingdom just about a generation before Micah's time (5:11; 8:4–6). Lying lips are equally an outrage in YHWH's sight (Prov. 12:22). If YHWH overlooks any of those activities, he will not be faithful to his covenant but will instead be complicit. That is unthinkable.

All of it together is an evil swamp that swallows its victims, and each characterization reverberates with YHWH's contempt for the practitioners. It is not simply a figure of speech that the measures and weights are called 'wicked', a personal and moral judgment usually reserved for the practitioners. YHWH views them as of one piece (Jenson 2008: 175). Lest we are tempted to excuse ourselves from those expressions of divine contempt, we pause to contemplate the ways in which cheating and lying nibble at our own integrity on an everyday basis. Do we want to escape an obligation? Just create a half-truth excuse, and another and another. Do we feel trapped by our own overconfident promises? Just ignore the requisite demands that are now forthcoming. Do we want to smother uncomfortable truths about deceit and injustice that swirl endlessly around us? Listen for a sufficient amount of time to the dominant voices that do just that with their own thick blanket of deceit. Political, commercial and financial structures, and the media – perhaps the equivalent of false prophets – are all in collusion.

The reputation of Samaria and the house of Ahab continues to echo even beyond the time of Micah. The Divine Judge will punish. That should not come as a surprise: they ought to know the implications of the broken covenant (Lev. 26:14–26; Deut. 27:11–36; 28:15–65). After witnesses, questions and answers, here is the verdict. Enemies will overrun the country; food will be scarce and famine will result; and all expectations of economic flourishing are dashed. The whole economy is gutted as productivity grinds to a halt. In Manasseh's day, YHWH's prophets warn that he will stretch over Jerusalem the measuring line of Samaria and the plumb line of the house of Ahab in judgment (2 Kgs 21:13).

It is beneficial to pause for reflection at this point. These are sobering words for a twenty-first-century Western culture that remembers very little but is instead bent on 'cancelling' everything that does not fit the correct sociopolitical posture. Among those aspects that are intentionally put into the dustbin of history are the authority of God's Word and the recitals of his unfailing providential provision, often mediated through significant persons. Having cast aside the moral anchor encapsulated in 'Hear, O Israel', 'love the Lord your God' and 'love your neighbour as yourself', there is little basis for ethical behaviour in any social or political sphere, especially when every sector has succumbed to an ideology that celebrates the rule of self. We as God's people are called to 'remember' and 'know' the righteous acts of our sovereign covenant Lord on our behalf. How forgetful we are of God's faithfulness! This chapter reminds us of those failings. It also reminds us to be vigilant in resisting the beguiling tug of wider cultural practices and values. Otherwise, we slide with shocking rapidity into destructive and self-serving patterns.

MICAH 7:1–6

Translation

7:1Wailing to me! For I have become like the gatherings of the summer, as the
gleanings of the grape harvest. There is not a cluster to eat, nor the first fig that
my soul desires.

2The godly person has perished from the earth, and there is no upright one
among men. All lie in wait for bloodshed; each hunts his brother with a net.

3[Their] hands do evil well; the prince demands, one judging [does so] for
payment, and the person of high standing, he speaks the desire of his soul. And
so they weave it together.

4The best of them is like a briar; the upright [worse] than a hedge. The day of your watchmen . . . your visitation has come. Now, their confusion will be here.
5Do not believe in your companion; do not trust your intimate friend. From the one who lies in your embrace, keep the openings of your mouth,
6Because a son treats his father with contempt; a daughter rises against her mother; a bride against her bridegroom; the enemies of a man are the people in his house.

Notes on the text

7:1. *ʾallay lî*, an onomatopoeic interjection, is used only here and in Job 10:15 ('If I have done evil, woe to me!').

Instead of *kĕʾospê* ('like the gatherings'), the LXX reads 'as the one gathering', likely because the speaker is sg. (*hāyîtî*) ('I have become') and presumed to be the person gleaning and not the 'gatherings' themselves.

The terms *qayiṣ* ('summer') and *bāṣîr* ('grape harvest') are used in parallel in Jer. 48:32 and here.

A *bikkûrâ* is a fig that has ripened early (*DCH* 2:172); hence, 'first'. It is not expected at the end of the season. It is also not intended to be a collective: Micah was hoping for individual finds. The masc. pl. form *bikkûrîm* is used more frequently (BDB 114). The verb *ʾwh* occurs only in pi. (this passage) and hith.; it means 'to desire' (*DCH* 1:149).

2. Neither *ḥāsîd* (a person characterized by *ḥesed*) or *yāšār* ('upright') carries the def. art.: they are generic terms that go together (cf. Job 1:1).

yeʾĕrōbû (masc. pl.) implies an ambush with the intent to shed blood with violence (*DCH* 1:365–366). For *yeʾĕrōbû*, the LXX reads 'they judge', perhaps influenced by the mention of 'the judge' in v. 3. For *yāṣûdû* (3 masc. pl. from *ṣûd*), the LXX reads 'they afflict'. The Tg paraphrases, adding 'innocent blood' for *lĕdāmîm*. It also reads *yāṣûdû ḥērem* as 'deliver . . . to destruction', adopting the more common meaning of *ḥērem* and working it into the understanding of the verb (Cathcart and Gordon 1989: 126; Gelston 2010: 107*). A second meaning of *ḥērem* is something that has slits or is perforated (BDB 357; *DCH* 3:319); it fits with *ṣûd*, 'to trap with a net'. This refers to hunters' nets (here and Eccl. 7:26) or those of fishermen (Ezek. 26:5, 14; 32:3; 47:10; Hab. 1:15–17).

3. *lĕhêṭîb* (inf. const. from *ṭôb*) means 'to do well'. The LXX reads the first clause as 'they have prepared their hands for evil'. Syr and Vg have taken the same interpretive route. It is not necessary, however, to emend *ʿal*, either by dropping the ʿayin and joining the lamed to the next word, *lĕhāraʿ*, or by changing the inf. const. to a finite verb. Instead, this could be Micah's spare allusion to their clapping their hands *over* the evil they are carrying off so well.

hašōpēṭ baššillûm ('the one judging for payment') does not have a finite verb. The LXX reads 'the judge speaks peaceful words', interpreting the root meaning as 'peace' rather than 'payment'. The meaning of *yĕʿabbĕtûhā* (pi.), a **hapax** as a verb, is derived from the uses of a related noun (*ʿăbōt*) which primarily refer to a twisted cord or rope (Exod. 28:14, 22; Judg. 15:13–14; 16:11–12). The masc. pl. is intended to indict all the offenders; the fem. sg. pron. suff. likely refers to 'desire' (*hawwat*) with the overtones of evil corruption that are woven together. There are additional meanings cited for *hawwâ*, among them 'destruction', 'ruin', 'wind', 'evil word' (*DCH* 2:502–503).

4. The pron. suff. on *ṭôb* indicates the superlative: the *best* of them is like a briar. The second parallel clause regarding those who are upright has a slightly different structure, prompting an emendation to fit the same superlative structure (*kimĕsûkâ* instead of *mimmĕsûkâ*). *mĕsûkâ* is a **hapax**, but similar in sound to *mĕśûkâ*. Both roots, whether spelled with a samekh or *śin*, mean 'to hedge' in the sense of providing an obstruction to the path. See Job 1:10; Hos. 2:8[6].

The 'day of your watchmen' is without a nearby verb; it begins the thought that is carried on by the more specific 'your visitation' and completed with the 3 fem. sg. qat. form *bāʾâ*. Followed by 'now', it intimates that the visitation is viewed as a fait accompli.

5. The adj. *ʾallûp* is used subst. to mean someone who is a close friend, in between a 'neighbour' (*rēaʿ*) and a brother or other family member. See also Prov. 16:28; 17:9. Jer. 13:21 uses the term to indicate allies.

6. In the repertoire of Hebr. words for 'fool', *nābāl*, an adj. used subst., is the strongest. It represents a person with the most egregious lack of moral character, one who utterly rejects God. The verb – used here – means to treat someone as that kind of fool (*DCH* 5:593).

Form and structure

The beginning of ch. 7 laments the curses pronounced in 6:11–15 and the breakdown of society at every level. It may be that the speaker is Zion, or perhaps a representative of the land and the people, not solely the prophet Micah. Reicke (1967: 349–367) reads the chapter as a liturgical unit possibly related to the autumn festivals. The initial indictment references the public sphere (vv. 1–3), but the fracturing is evident in the closest private relationships as well (vv. 5–6).

In these verses, there is a brief **chiasm**: Micah's woe and his soul's desire are the end points within which we have summer fruit, gleanings of the vine, grape clusters and 'first fruit'. See Jenson 2008: 179. On a smaller scale, the centre of v. 3 is the set of three corrupt officials. The outer 'ring' is shaped by the practice of evil. Inside are the evil administrators. In v. 6, four parallel and escalating sets of discord shatter the family relationships, the last of which is a comprehensive declaration of unbridled strife.

Comment

7:1. The repeated labial sound in *ʾallay lî* ('wailing to me'), is reminiscent of the traditional Middle Eastern ululation, a penetrating cry heard at times of both mourning and joy. Micah returns to a lament (see 1:8), describing his own utter disappointment in terms familiar to his audience. They know the dashed expectations when those who gather and glean come up with nothing. A subtext here is that the harvesters themselves ignore the laws of gleaning that are designed to provide for the poor: some should be left. It is yet another indication of the fractured social structures.

There is some ambiguity in the first two agricultural similes, both introduced by 'like'. The masc. pl. const. *ʾospê* is unusual; with reference to the produce, we would expect the sg. *ʾāsîp*. This pl., however, matches the fem. pl. noun in the following simile. It could be that Micah likens himself to the one who is gathering and gleaning but finds nothing. This is the way the LXX read it; it fits with a wider canonical pattern of expecting fruitfulness in conjunction with the blessings of YHWH. On the other hand, closer attention to both similes in tandem opens a second possibility. It may be that Micah likens himself to that 'nothing', to the *gatherings* of summer, which in this case are slim. In other words, there is nothing left in his emotional place: he is empty because what his 'soul' (*nepeš*) longs for is absent. While the grain harvests are in spring and early summer, the grape and fig harvests come in the late summer and early autumn. Not one grape or fig remains. That is how Micah describes himself (or Zion), and it is also a transition to the next verse: not a righteous person is left.

The same ambiguity is evident in the first set of similes regarding the presence of the 'remnant' in ch. 5. They are like either the dew and rain (5:6[7]), which should bring refreshment, or the ground awaiting those blessings but being disappointed when both rain and dew are transitory.

Lev. 26:5 promises a fully fledged grape harvest when the people are obedient. How different this is! The absence of even a cluster of grapes to eat or a first-ripe fig speaks of the utter devastation of YHWH's judgment. Up to this point, the images imply the close of the harvest season. The figs that have ripened early are an infrequent delicacy for which Micah longs, but there are none. The symbol conveys the utter moral failure of God's people. See Num. 28:26 regarding the 'day of first fruits' when these were offered to YHWH. See also Hos. 9:10 and Isa. 28:4 for the other two uses in sg. The preceding chapter foretells the destruction of the olive and grape harvests (6:15); now Micah laments that forthcoming event.

2. A *ḥāsîd* was one characterized by *ḥesed* and all that implies. The following parallel expression bemoans the absence from the land of anyone who was upright from among all of humanity. In the second line, both their 'corporate' (*kullām*) guilt and 'individual' (*ʾîš*) culpability are emphasized, each having the first position in the parallel clauses. The first clause represents the macro level: they *all* lie in wait for bloodshed. The focus shifts seamlessly from the land's lack of productivity to the social vacuum. Just as there is no remnant of desirable fruit of the land, upright people are likewise gone. Unfailingly loyal 'covenant love' (*ḥesed*) is the hallmark of God's people; the same word is in 6:8, summoning the people to 'the love of *ḥesed*'. The tragic absence of good people allows rapacity and violence to flourish.

Earlier Micah condemns them for building Zion with bloodshed (3:10). There is a persistent subtext regarding physical violence visited on vulnerable people. Ambushes and traps have a particularly insidious character because they involve 'brothers' who will be reduced to hunted animals. While this clearly extends beyond immediate family relationships, the bond that should characterize them is also severely violated. Further, it implies intentionally vicious conflict among equals whether they share kinship bonds or are members of the 'house of Israel'.

3. Refracted through the uneven nature of the Hebr., the extent and horror of the corruption that Micah confronts are clear. The unsavoury characters are all leaders of one stripe or another – the prince who demands, the one who judges and the one of high standing ('the great one'). These have already been called out for their parts in the systemic net of fraud (chs. 2 and 3).

The overarching description is blunt: 'concerning the evil [their] hands do well', the ironic point being that they have mastered the art of doing evil. Those hands are not only invested in the work of evil, but clap in glee at their unsavoury accomplishments. Micah censures each category of corrupt administrators with a stinging description of their 'expertise'. *šillûm* ('payment') comes from *šlm*, the root representing a fundamental and complete state of well-being, often achieved by having made recompense. The word appears elsewhere only in Isa. 34:8, where it is used in parallel with YHWH's vengeance, and Hos. 9:7. Hosea declares that when the days of visitation and the days of recompense come, Israel will know it. In the context of Micah, the payment ironically is a wholesale bribe. The more common word for bribe is *šōḥad* and the practice is reprehensible (see Mic. 3:11). 'The one who judges for payment' is likely intimately connected, not only syntactically, but possibly even to the point of working in collusion with the 'prince' (Hoyt 2019: 785). The word translated 'desire' may connote evil intentions, as it does in Ps. 52:9[7]; Prov. 10:3; 11:6. It appears quite innocuously in v. 1, but has a related stronger meaning of engulfing ruin or destruction; see 'Notes' above. The demonst. pron. *hûʾ* points back emphatically to 'the person of high standing', giving extra weight to his position. To add insult to injury, 'they' twist all of this. What the prince demands is not articulated, leaving the field wide open; there is no end to the extent of his overreach. The esteemed individual could be a general allusion to the previous two official types, making the uncomfortable observation that self-gratification is the defining motive behind everything they say. On the other hand, this may be an oblique reference to the king. It is certain that his word causes things to happen. The figure of twisting cords in the final verb is apt: each of the offending parties is woven into that web of corruption. They know how to work the system from their own vantage points. See its use in Ezek. 3:25 – an undefined 'they' would put cords on Ezekiel and bind him. In the prophet's declaration, they are all culpable, as they speak out of their own selfishness, not out of a posture of responsibility.

4. These disgraceful characters are so pervasive – just like fast-spreading briars in a field – they have succeeded in setting up obstacles to proper and godly conduct. Micah dismisses them abruptly and turns from description to forewarning. The pronouns shift to second person. The dreaded day is coming. The listening audience would be familiar with watchmen, whose role is crucial. Woe betide an appointed watchman if he does not warn the people of impending danger! But woe betide the people when they ignore the warnings! 'Visitation' suggests the worst. There is no comfortable interval. What the prophets have been announcing – God's judgment – is arriving. Hosea emphasized the same dreaded immediacy (9:7–8).

'Now' is filled with foreboding. Those who have been obstructions in the whole tangle of injustice will end up in their own tangled confusion. The metaphor of the net is appropriate for the web of organized crime that Micah has described. There is a wordplay between the thorn 'hedge' (*mĕsûkâ*) and 'confusion' (*mĕbûkâ*). The noun translated 'confusion' is used only twice, here and in Isa. 22:5. In Isaiah, the combination of the words is even more ominous. It is a day of *mĕhûmâ ûmĕbûsâ ûmĕbûkâ* – a day of tumult and trampling down and confusion. Related words occur in Exod. 14:3, describing the confusion of the Israelites as they were leaving Egypt, and Esth. 3:15, a picture of a city turned upside down after the shock of Haman's edict. 'Watchmen' refers to the prophets who issue warnings to YHWH's people, a role most fully developed in YHWH's charge to Ezekiel about a century later (3:17; 33:7).

5. The corruption described in 7:3 brings about the societal problems of vv. 5 and 6. Not only are the leaders indicted and the populace in general warned of coming judgment, but the disorder also hits increasingly closer to home. They are admonished not to believe and not to trust, synonyms reflecting the tragic state of suspicion at every level. Distrust ruptures relationships with neighbours and family members. Most heart-rending is the warning against speaking freely to one's wife, 'the one who lies in your bosom'. The admonition not even to trust her is emphasized as the clause begins with 'from'. 'Guard the openings of your mouth' is a striking image of words captured mid-air before they are sounded.

6. For a son to treat his father as a fool is the height of insolence and disobedience to the Torah (Exod. 20:12). It results in speaking with rudeness and contempt in place of honour. It is also a shameful violation of cultural norms, additional examples of which are evidenced in the Code of Hammurabi 192, 195 (*ANET* 175). Not to be outdone, a daughter will rise against her mother, followed by the bride against her bridegroom. In the last case, there is an **ellipsis**: the verb is assumed.

This is family anarchy with all the siblings engaged. The parallel is precise – sons and daughters against fathers and mothers. Even a bride, one joining with hope and joy a new family, will be swept into the same destructive interaction patterns. These are unthinkable, indicative of complete disintegration of the social fabric.

Explanation

When Jesus comes into Jerusalem at the beginning of Passion Week, he specifically seeks out seasonally early figs (Mark 11:12–14), perhaps to enact Micah's prophetic declaration in his own context. Their absence reflects the disappointing fruitlessness of Israel. There are parallels with the kingdom parables of Jesus, as he frequently begins with agricultural motifs and shifts to *persons* (Andersen and Freedman 2000: 568).

The 'prince' and 'judge' seem to be the middle level in the administrative hierarchy that is awash in kickbacks and corruption. The suggestion of hierarchy embedded in the label 'the great one' may intimate they report to him. The metaphor of bound cords that are part of a net is appropriate for the web of payoffs and political influence that Micah has described. The tightly woven conspiracy defies any attempts to untangle the components of deceit, violence and corrupt betrayal. Those in power are intent on keeping the web intact.

The current community's citizens and leaders are ruinous thorns, ripping all who come into contact with them. Thorn hedges were used to define boundaries. In that context, they represent a means for property protection but, ironically, here are the opposite, serving as obstructions to just and right conduct at every level of the social structure. The images convey the worst kind of entanglement. Even the 'good' and the 'upright' are absorbed into what turns out to be corruption and 'boundary grabbing'.

The figure of the watchman hovers in the gloom. In the Israelite context, watchmen were a vital part of community security, particularly in terms of warning against enemy military threats. The verb intimates close watching for potential danger and then sounding the alarm. This 'day of visitation' will test the watchmen's faithfulness. Tragically, in Micah's context, many of the prophets are anything but faithful watchmen. This prophetic role is epitomized in Ezekiel's call to be a watchman for the house of Israel, meaning in his context the southern kingdom of Judah (3:17–21; reiterated in 33:1–9). It was not an enviable task: he had to call out their sins or himself be in jeopardy.

A generation prior to Micah, Hosea observes the same ugly violence in Israel's social fabric: even priests band together like robbers to lie in ambush and murder (Hos. 6:8–9). Isaiah declared YHWH will remove any semblance of leadership; as a result, oppression and insolence will carry the day (Isa. 3:1–5). The implications for social structures when the 'righteous', *ḥāsîd*, and the upright are taken away are sobering (Isa. 57:1–13). The upshot is mockery, transgression, deceit, rampant idolatry and even slaughtering children in the valleys (v. 5).

A hermeneutic of suspicion flourishes when evil abounds and when there are no moral anchors. How are God's people to know whom to trust among their elected officials, appointed spokespersons, advisers, judges and church leaders when deception and falsehood are rife? Absence of trust and trustworthiness shatters all foundations of civility.

Not only will suspicion be the order of the day (v. 5), but outright discord will reign in the fabric of the family, signalling disintegration of traditional authority structures. Just about a century after Micah, Jeremiah addresses the same fundamental issue: 'Let each one be on guard against his neighbour. Don't trust any brother, because every brother will certainly deceive, and every neighbour will spread slander' (Jer. 9:3[4]).

These patterns of dysfunctional family strife are unsettling enough for us as we buck our cultural tide, awash with intergenerational mockery in our various media venues. We try to hang on to the fifth commandment to nurture parental honour in some vague form (Exod. 20:12), but cultural sludge has dulled our senses. We respond with shock when we discover the severity of the punishment when a son rebelled against his father (Lev. 20:9; Deut. 21:18–23). Lest we dismiss those injunctions entirely as being simply the 'old' covenant, Jesus reaffirms the persistent tendency in us to wreak havoc in our families, particularly turning against our parents (Matt. 10:21; Luke 12:53).

MICAH 7:7–10

Translation

7:7 But I, to YHWH I will look. I will wait for the God of my salvation. My God will hear me.

8 Do not rejoice, my enemy, against me; though I have fallen, I will rise. Though I sit in darkness, YHWH is a light to me.

9 I will bear the wrath of YHWH, for I have sinned against him. When he argues my case, and he has done me justice, he will bring me out to the light, and I will see his righteousness.

10 And let my enemy see, and may shame cover her. The one who says to me: 'Where is YHWH your God?' My eyes will see it. Now you will become [a place] for trampling, like mud outside.

Notes on the text

There are no significant variant readings in the ancient versions.

7:7. The waw is disjunctive.

8. *śmḥ* is a common word for 'expressing joy', but with a subset of passages it connotes arrogant exultation regarding someone (*DCH* 8:161). See also Pss 35:19, 24; 38:17[16]; Isa. 14:8; Obad. 12. *ʾōyabtî* ('my enemy') is a fem. sg. ptc. with the 1 sg. pron. suff. from the verb *ʾyb* ('to be an enemy'). It most frequently serves as a subst., often with suffixes as here, 'the one who is enemy to me'. Both *nāpaltî* ('I have fallen') and *qāmtî* ('I will rise') are qat. forms, representing the future event as assuredly complete as that in the past (*IBHS* §30.5.1e). *ʾēšeb* shifts to the yiq. form, a subtle allusion to the ongoing challenges they will face.

9. *zaʿap* ('wrath') is emphatically the first word in this verse. The qal 1 sg. yiq. verb *ʾeśśāʾ* ('I will bear') indicates that this state will continue for an indefinite period of time.

10. *wĕtēreʾ* ('let [my enemy] see') is a plea (juss.). There is no direct object. See GKC §75p on the unusual vocalization and tone; the same appears also in Zech. 9:5 regarding Ashkelon's seeing and being afraid.

The 3 fem. sg. suff. on *ûtĕkassehā* ('may [shame] cover her') (pi.) refers to the enemy.

hāʾōmĕrâ ('the one saying') is a fem. sg. ptc. standing in apposition to 'enemy'.

ʾayyô is the interr. *ʾayyēh* ('Where?') with the 3 masc. sg. suff., anticipating YHWH.

Form and structure

The voices of YHWH and Micah merged in the preceding condemnations of vv. 1–6. V. 7 stands as a pivot between the expression of despair about the cultural nadir and the hymnic pieces that make up the rest of the chapter. Micah declares his allegiance and trust. Following that affirmation, Micah's identity merges with suffering Zion's falling before her enemy, sitting in darkness, bearing the wrath of YHWH and longing for the future when she would see it all set right.

There is significant discussion as to whether v. 7 concludes the preceding unit or commences the next (Hoyt 2019: 797–798). Waltke (2007: 430) indicates that it belongs to both. See again Reicke 1967: 349–367 on the liturgical nature of ch. 7, exemplified by distinct lamenting voices that share characteristics with psalms of lament, and are bound together as a unit. If 7:8–20 is a liturgical hymn, then the modulation between second and third persons is not at all unusual. In the sung context, the prophet addresses the people and YHWH, and speaks for YHWH as he addresses his audience in return. This is preparatory for the final hymn of praise for YHWH's faithful 'acts of righteousness'.

Comment

7:7. The disjunctive waw marks the shift between judgment on the day of their visitation and Micah's declaration of purpose. Their day of watching is upon them (v. 4). He too will watch, but his watching will be 'in YHWH' and results in hope. The contrast is dramatic: Micah declares his intention to be countercultural ('but I') as he continues to oppose the leaders and false prophets. He affirms his hope in the God of his salvation, the God who will hear him. *yešaʿ* means 'salvation'; the root *yšʿ* appears fifty-six time in Isaiah alone (Hubbard, *NIDOTTE* 2:556–562). A caution is in order lest that concept be lodged solely and always in some very future day. In the Israelite world view, it includes the promise that deliverance will come, presumably in their own lifetime's experience. In addition, it implies God's presence with people in their suffering, not necessarily rescue out of it. In Exod. 14:13, 30 and 15:2, the paradigm is set for the rest of Israel's experiences as YHWH's chosen people.

8. Micah, voicing the lament of Zion, warns the enemy not to rejoice. The Assyrians come first to mind as the consummate enemy for Israel and Judah: in the late eighth century BC, Nineveh was on the cusp of victory over Zion, and it was a dark time indeed. On the other hand, 'the enemy' is anonymous with good reason: there will be a succession of enemies. Zion anticipates that YHWH will hear and respond in accordance with his characteristic faithfulness.

Micah and Zion also know dark days will continue to be ahead; nevertheless, though they will sit in darkness, YHWH will be their light. Dwelling in darkness is a familiar figure for seemingly interminable despair. Isaiah likewise depicts the distress, gloom and thick darkness that envelop children of Israel. Nevertheless, in a radical turnaround, those people walking in darkness see a great light; it will shine (Isa. 8:22 – 9:1[2]).

9. *zaʿap* indicates raging anger; see 2 Chr. 16:10; 28:9; Prov. 19:12; Isa. 30:30; Jon. 1:15 (raging of the sea). The inhabitants of Zion confess that YHWH's anger is deserved: they will bear it. The city has sinned against YHWH. The clause is the equivalent of a parenthetical note regarding the wrath of YHWH that will come to an end, lasting only until the time when he will act. YHWH will 'plead my case' and 'do my justice' (*mišpāṭî*).

While Micah expects the same judicial process (the 'disputation', *rîb*) be applied, the personnel are noticeably altered. YHWH is not only the supreme sovereign judge: he becomes the defence lawyer in the process. The defence is robust. The echo of Mic. 6:8 is unmistakable in 'doing justice'; here Zion depends on YHWH himself to demonstrate that characteristic fully. The previous darkness will be a thing of the past: YHWH 'will bring me out' to the light. Finally, Micah and Zion will see YHWH's righteousness. It is directly joined with being in the light. There are echoes from the exodus imagery, particularly as they have been called to remember YHWH's righteous acts on their behalf, starting with his bringing them up from Egypt (6:4–5).

10. Micah pleads that the enemy be compelled to experience the full implications of what they will witness, both for Zion and for themselves. As Zion sees the righteousness of YHWH effected for YHWH's people, the enemy will also see. What they see is not stated; the absence of a direct object hints at the indescribable vastness of the forthcoming vindication. They will not stand before it but will be especially shamed as they are reminded of their previous mocking words. This is not a simple matter of feeling a bit of embarrassment: the crushing humiliation will be measure-for-measure.

The enemies of God's prophets caused them untold public humiliation and heaped insults upon their God; Micah illustrates it by quoting their taunting question 'Where is your God?' Asking 'Where is YHWH your God?' seems to have been a stock taunt. It was part of the exchanges between the messengers of Sennacherib and Hezekiah (2 Kgs 18:33–35; see also Ps. 115:2). It was intended to be an egregiously insulting slur. There is no need to expand this: the pause at the ***athnach*** is sufficient. Instead, there will be more 'seeing', and it is not a pretty sight for the enemy.

The interface between Micah and Zion culminates in 'my eyes' (his and Zion's) seeing the humiliation and degradation of the enemy. 'Now' implies that vindication will be imminent in the time frame of the oracle. Trampling is a familiar figure from Mic. 5:7[8]; it is one of the activities of the remnant as they are in the midst of the nations.

The noun *mirmās* indicates what the enemy will become – a trampled place, like the muddy streets outside (*DCH* 5:490). Mud in the streets is used to describe the lowest and most contemptuous point to which one can descend (see Ps. 18:43[42]; Zech. 10:5).

Explanation

Micah binds together both YHWH and Elohim in this affirmation of his trust. With his single affirmation 'My God will hear me' Micah echoes truths that are laced through the psalms of trust: he knows YHWH hears his cry and inclines his ear (Ps. 86:1–7); because YHWH is for him, he has nothing to fear from people (Ps. 118:6–9); his help comes from YHWH, who made heaven and earth (Ps. 121). And so many more!

Micah's cultural context was shot through with abuses of the most sordid nature, but he keeps his focus. So must we. Our armour against the tidal waves of corruption lies in the full assurance that YHWH God Almighty is firmly on his throne, and justice and righteousness – foundations of that throne (Ps. 89:15[14]) – will prevail. That assurance gives us courage and confidence as we repeatedly don the requisite armour (Eph. 6:10–20) and refuse to be submerged in the swamp. One stanza from 'For All the Saints' is a great encouragement:

> And though the strife is fierce, the warfare long;
> Steals on the ear the distant triumph song;
> And hearts are brave again, and arms are strong. Alleluia!
> (W. How, 1864)

At the same time, the prophet is no stranger to the mockery and gloating that are lobbed at folks who have the courage of their convictions. Micah is fully aware that the opponents, of whom there are likely a significant number, are waiting and rubbing their hands in gleeful expectation. 'Enemy' is frequently used in parallel with *śônēʾ*, 'one who hates'. We can just imagine the pundits of the day preparing their verbal banquet for the receptive audience.

Micah is a realist; he does not expect God suddenly to sweep away all the disastrous effects of the people's sins. Darkness and night are figures for disaster that is palpable, but light eventually pierces that darkness. Micah's unassailable conviction that YHWH is his Light gives him confidence to persevere. Punishment for Zion will be followed by restoration; darkness, by light. And the light of YHWH will be sufficient illumination for Micah in that darkness.

> For lo! There breaks a yet more glorious day;
> The saints triumphant rise in bright array;
> The King of Glory passes on His way. Alleluia!
> (W. How, 1864)

As in the psalms of lament and the book of Lamentations, the reality of deserved suffering is not minimized, but hopeful expectation shapes the closure to this liturgical sentiment. These truths that are embedded in the psalter encourage God's people through the generations:

> YHWH is my Light and my Salvation.
> From whom shall I be afraid?
> (Ps. 27:1)

> YHWH is for us a Refuge and a Fortress,
> a proven Help in troubles.
> Therefore, we will not fear
> though the earth tremble and mountains
> fall into the heart of the sea.
> (Ps. 46:2–3[1–2])

The prospect of knowing, remembering, reciting and seeing the righteousness of YHWH echoes through Israel's psalm tradition. A steady refrain is 'his righteousness endures for ever' (Pss 111:3; 112:3; 119:142). Singing these truths was and is a gift; it helps the flagging memory and bolsters enfeebled spirits. All the prophets were certain of final vindication and the triumph of YHWH's sovereign good purposes, even in the face of unspeakable present horrors (see Isa. 60:1–5; Ezek. 37 – 39; Hab. 3; Zech. 14).

Earlier, YHWH rebuked them for not remembering 'the righteous acts of YHWH' (6:5). Now, they will be more than a memory: Zion will see them. Through these verses, Zion's culpability and their vindication before YHWH are both parts of the picture. They have been the victim of aggression both from enemies outside and fractious elements within (Andersen and Freedman 2000: 583). It is not too much of a stretch to think Christologically, both in terms of justice being done *for* Micah and his people along with their *seeing* the righteousness of God, fulfilled in the righteousness of Christ as applied to YHWH's chosen people.

MICAH 7:11–13

Translation

7:11[There is coming] a day to build your walls; that day the boundary will be distant.

12That day he will come to you from Assyria, and the cities of Egypt, and from Egypt to the River; and sea from sea and mountain of the mountain.

13But the land will become a desolation because of its inhabitants – from the fruit of their deeds.

Notes on the text

7:11. *gĕdērāyik* has a 2 fem. sg. pron. suff. *gādēr* means 'wall' or 'fence', suggesting in this context a large building project. For *yirḥaq-ḥōq*, the LXX reads 'he will rub out your laws', most likely influenced by one of the possible meanings ('statute') of *ḥōq*. See 'Comment'.

12. The subject of *yābô*ʾ ('he/one will come') is ambiguous. *minnî* is a rare poetic form of *min* (see GKC §90l; it is a particle that serves as a noun in the const. state). Its combination with *lê-* occurs twice, representing 'coming from'. The LXX reads the equivalent of *yābô*ʾ*û* (pl. instead of sg.), suggesting possibly the return of exiles. The Tg explicitly indicates 'the exiles' (Cathcart and Gordon 1989: 127).

māṣôr is used to refer to Egypt only in poetry (see 2 Kgs 19:24 = Isa. 37:25; Isa. 19:6). It is likely intended as a pun with the proper name Mizra'im (Egypt), as well as a noun (*ṣar*) meaning 'distress' or 'trouble'.

The LXX avoids the first *māṣôr* and reads 'your cities'; the second *māṣôr* is read as 'from Tyre' (*miṣṣôr*).

The LXX wrestled with 'sea from sea and mountain of the mountain' (*wĕyām miyyām wĕhar hāhor*) as is evident from 'days of water' in conjunction with the first, followed by 'and turmoil' in place of the mention of mountains.

13. It is not clear whether the waw is conjunctive or adversative. Neither successfully knits this verse with what precedes it. *hāyâ* followed by *lĕ-* implies 'becoming'.

Form and structure

This is the second of the four sections in the liturgy of ch. 7. The tone shifts to the events of a forthcoming day, described in three separate brief vignettes. *yôm* starts each of the first three clauses. (That) day is clearly the focus. V. 11 is shaped by the two mentions of *yôm*, followed by one more in v. 12. While it is tempting to standardize the three occurrences to *hayyôm hāhû'*, that is not necessary. They are all different, emphasizing the particulars of each instance. Each development includes a significant facet of the promises for YHWH's people. The first is to rebuild for security; the second is to expand; and the third is their return to fill the expanded inheritance. Word choice in each case is important.

The string of geographical locations does not seem to have a controlling structure. It also has only one verb. While the first line initially seems to deal with locations from which 'he' (or 'they') will come to Zion, the structure of the subsequent lines could imply that the entire verse is dealing with the boundaries of this extended territory. In other words, the movement of returning exiles is not in view. Instead, the third day indicates the extent to which the expanded authority will reach.

Comment

7:11. The building activity initially refers to rebuilding the broken walls of Zion. While *gādēr* can mean 'wall', suggesting a large building project, the more common word for the wall of a city is *ḥômâ*. The use of *gādēr* allows conceptual flexibility, necessary in conjunction with *yirḥaq-ḥōq*. Like *gādēr*, *ḥōq* has multiple layers of meaning. It frequently is understood as 'statute' or 'decree', something 'inscribed' (*ḥqq*). See 'Comment' on 6:16. Legal stipulations were cut into substantial surfaces such as stone. Statutes have authority; *ḥōq* may be a **metonymy** representing the extension of authority. On the other hand, it may mean an inscribed boundary stone, a figure for marking the distant limits of the expansion of Israel in that day.

The focus shifts from the wretched end of the enemy to Micah's affirmations regarding the long-awaited 'day'. It is multifaceted: a 'day' to build, 'that day' to expand and 'that day' for return (v. 12), parallel expressions of renewal. In the geographical context of the Levant, enclosures, both walls and fences, were made of stone. This day to rebuild 'your walls' follows the tragedy of the destruction of Zion. The psalmist asks why YHWH broke down its walls (*gĕdērêhā*; Ps. 80:13[12]; cf. 89:41[40]). Micah addresses the city with the promise that her walls will be rebuilt, a turn of fortunes for the ruined Zion of 3:12. At the same time, the absence of the name may suggest expansion to additional cities, especially if this first vignette about building walls is linked with a second that figuratively describes expanded authority, represented by *ḥōq*.

12. The ambiguous subject of *yābô'* could be the collective group of exiles who will return to the rebuilt city from the far-flung regions that shape the rest of the verse. There is a steady drumbeat that God's people will return from Egypt and Assyria (Isa. 11:11; 27:12–13; Hos. 11:10–11; Zech. 10:10). Isaiah's prophecies are introduced by 'in that day'. From another perspective, *yābô'* may be a way of initiating the description of the extensive territory: 'coming' is not understood as movement from one place to another. Instead, what follows gives a rough approximation of boundaries rather than locations from which returnees are coming. 'It is coming' from Assyria and the 'cities of Egypt'. If 'cities', however, is read as another instance of 'to' (*'adê* exchanging with *'ārê*), then this first line articulates geopolitical boundaries – Assyria to Egypt. The next line turns it around and says, 'from Egypt to the River'. It is possible that the repetition of *māṣôr* should be read as 'from Tyre'; see the LXX. That would presume a geographical note including the region of Phoenicia to the north-west.

How the final line works is just as much a conundrum. The awkwardness of the language at this point fits with the rest of Micah's unusual expressions. Literally, it reads 'and sea from sea and mountain of the mountain'. It is likely that the two mentions of 'sea' refer to the Sea of Salt (Dead Sea) and the Mediterranean. Thus, everything in between will be part of their expanded territory. No doubt this is an intended echo of the halcyon days of the united monarchy, now only a wistful memory for the shrunken southern kingdom. In the royal psalm traditionally ascribed to Solomon, the king's dominion will extend from sea to sea, and from the River to the ends of the earth (Ps. 72:8). Zechariah echoes the same phrase regarding the rule of the coming King (Zech. 9:10): it will encompass the whole earth (Mays 1976: 162).

But what are the respective mountains if indeed the expression has geographical referents? One viable option recognizes two locations called Mount Hor, the one mentioned as part of a northern boundary of the 'land of Canaan' (Num. 34:7), and a southern Mount Hor, where Aaron died (Num. 20:23). Thus, both the sea and the mountains that define this space locate it within the broader 'from the River' to Egypt. The expression 'mountain of the mountain', however, does not necessitate a *name* of Hor. It may be that this draws attention to the 'hill country' (*hāhār*) between the two seas.

This description of territorial extent is unique in several respects. Mazor is an unusual designation for Egypt. Because there are two reversed sets that name northern and southern geopolitical entities, the odd reference to sea to sea and mountain to mountain may be intended to indicate something on the east–west axis. Casting back through the liturgical tradition, Ps. 133 comes to mind. Unity among brothers and sisters is like dew on Mount Hermon in the north, spanning to Mount Zion, '*the* mountain' (*hāhār*).

YHWH's promise through Ezekiel assures his people that he will gather them to feed on mountains, in ravines and in all inhabited places (Ezek. 34:13). From a non-geographical perspective, this may be a **merimus**, implying 'everywhere', or it reflects a superlative – 'the highest mountain' (Shaw 1993: 194; Jenson 2008: 185).

13. The referent of *hā'āreṣ* may be the land of Israel or it may reflect a global perspective. If the latter, it may describe the judgment of the rest of the earth while Israel has been safely regathered. In that case, the whole earth will become a desolation. It may, however, be better to read it as an interlude between the triumph of vv. 11–12 and the renewal of vv. 14–17 (Andersen and Freedman 2000: 588). The waw conj. in that reading is an adversative, 'but'. At some point, the land will become desolate on account of those who lived there, 'her inhabitants'. The desolation will be the consequence of their deeds.

Explanation

Just what rebuilding activity is in view is impossible to determine. Although Zion is likely the referent, it is not named at this point. To be sure, Jerusalem underwent numerous destructions. Presuming that this looks ahead to Nehemiah's work (Mays 1976: 161) is too limiting. When 'expansive boundaries' (*yirḥaq-ḥōq*) are mentioned, they are set for vast regions such as the sea (Jer. 5:22), waters (Job 26:10) or the heavens (Ps. 148:6). The immensity of each of those may be a hint of expectations for the land of Israel in the future in this verse. This is the only place where *ḥōq* is used with apparent reference to the land.

The expansion of a future entity may hark back to the idealized reign of David. The details are unclear at key points, and Micah may simply be describing significantly expanded territory, rather like Isa. 26:15. The 'from . . . to' pattern is repeated to emphasize the extent of the boundaries on both north-east and south-west. The 'River' without any proper name attached generally means the Euphrates; examples include Gen. 31:21;

Num. 22:5; Josh. 24:2–3; Isa. 7:20. There may be another layer of historical inclusion as well: Egypt afflicted Israel at the beginning of their journey to the Promised Land, and Assyria was the cause of the northern kingdom's leaving it (Waltke 2007: 456–457). Perhaps the first geographical statement addresses returnees from these places and the second uses the same pattern but shifts to boundaries – a cleverly interlaced net.

MICAH 7:14–15

Translation

7:14Shepherd your people with your staff, the flock of your inheritance, who dwell alone in the forest, in the midst of Carmel. They will graze on Bashan and Gilead as in the days of old.

15As in the days of your going out from the land of Egypt, I will show him wonders.

Notes on the text

7:14. The verb *rʿh* ('to shepherd' and 'to graze') can be both transitive (as this masc. sg. impv.) and intransitive, as at the end of the verse. In the latter case, *yirʿû* functions as a juss.: 'may' they be able to graze there. The direct object is 'your people'. In apposition is 'the flock of your inheritance'.

šōknî ('dwelling') is a qal ptc. that maintains an early case ending (GKC §90lm; *IBHS* §8.2e), likely indicating a close connection with the word that follows. It also appears in Deut. 33:16; Jer. 49:16; Obad. 3.

15. The 2 masc. sg. suff. on *ṣēʾtĕkā* ('your going out') may refer either to YHWH or to Micah as representative of Israel 'going out' of Egypt. The LXX reads 'from Egypt' instead of 'from the land of Egypt'. The yiq. causative form of *rʾh* ('to see') points to the future when YHWH will again show his mighty interventions on their behalf. The 3 masc. sg. pron. suff. on the verb is a collective referring to YHWH's people as those who will see.

niplāʾôt is a fem. pl. niph. ptc. that comes to serve on its own as a noun, parallel to *peleʾ*, meaning 'something beyond understanding'.

Form and structure

In the third liturgical poem, the tone shifts from description to petition. The persons speaking, spoken to and spoken about are elusive. The first line of v. 14 interchanges the parts of the imagery. We would expect 'flock' to be the object of 'shepherding with the rod' and 'people' to be linked with 'inheritance'.

Comment

7:14. The plea 'to shepherd' is voiced by either Micah or the re-gathered people and addressed to YHWH as Shepherd. 'Your people', 'your staff' and 'your inheritance' emphasize the relationship, now precious.

The preceding verses pose the expanded geographical framework within which the restored people will flourish again. Here the focus is on the protective and nurturing relationship between the Shepherd and his people (his flock) in the most secure parts of those regions. The implications of *naḥălâ* as 'inheritance' are rich and wide-ranging. It includes family and kinship ties to the tribal lands that have been allotted to them (Num. 32:18; Deut. 4:21; 15:4; 19:14). Those point both to the land as a whole, promised by YHWH to Israel, and to Israel who are bound to YHWH as his inheritance for ever (Deut. 32:8–9). See Wright, *NIDOTTE* 3:77–81. In that land context, the tribes acquired inheritance portions that were assigned by YHWH through casting lots (Josh. 14:1–2; 23:4). The word used for 'staff' here (*šēbeṭ*) also means 'tribe'; the same interchange is true of *maṭṭeh* ('staff' and 'tribe').

God's flock will dwell alone in the forested region. Being set apart in isolation means they are safely away from the threats posed by outside marauders (see Deut. 33:28). The Hebr. word *karmel* may refer to the proper name given to the prominent mountain jutting into the Mediterranean Sea, as well as to any region fruitful with growth. It is often in parallel with *ya'ar* ('forested land') and in opposition to *midbar* ('wilderness'). Because this discourse unit mentions *karmel* in conjunction with two additional place names, it may be that Mount Carmel is in focus. Being in the 'midst of Carmel' suggests enjoying the bounty of that elevated expanse of land with its excellent soils and good rainfall. Its elevation also means that significant parts of it are off the international routes that traverse the land, either for commercial or military purposes. The summit of Mount Carmel is heavily forested. On several occasions, Isaiah uses *karmel* in conjunction with the proper names Lebanon (29:17; 35:2) and Sharon (35:2), suggesting that Mount Carmel may be intended. Isa. 10:18 includes both *ya'ar* and *karmel*. Nevertheless, the term is also used in parallel with 'the hill country' (2 Chr. 26:10) describing the regional developments of Uzziah. That would suggest a location farther south, perhaps near the districts noted in Josh. 15:48–52, 55–57 (Rainey 1982: 57–62).

By way of contrast, Gilead and Bashan are in Transjordan, both fruitful regions but much more open. It is no wonder that the two-and-one-half tribes asked to stay in Transjordan: they saw it was excellent for livestock (Num. 32:1). Nevertheless, these geopolitical areas frequently end up being battlegrounds. The tribes of Reuben, Gad and half of Manasseh settle there but are among the first to suffer repeated invasions by the armies of Syria (1 Kgs 20:26–27; 22:1–36; 2 Kgs 9:15; 10:32–33). By the late eighth century, Gilead along with most of Galilee is firmly in the hands of Tiglath-Pileser III (2 Kgs 15:29–30). Nevertheless, as this promise looks to the future, it also maintains the unbreakable connection with 'the days of old'. The current interval is tumultuous, but Micah reiterates the hopeful declarations of 2:12–13; 5:4–6[5–7].

15. 'As in the days' connects this declaration to the end of the previous verse and expands on the central facet of that 'days of old' narrative. Micah, representing the gathered worshippers, is the speaker in v. 14; thus, his voice may continue, addressing YHWH initially, saying 'in the days when you went forth from the land of Egypt'. Ps. 68:8[7] remembers God 'when you went out before your people'. Nevertheless, this is unusual; the narrative is generally YHWH's *bringing* the people out. Because that is so and because YHWH is clearly the speaker for the next clause, it may be YHWH's voice that starts the verse. In that case, the 2 masc. sg. refers to Micah. He is reckoned across generations as a part of Israel with whom YHWH made the covenant (Waltke 2007: 442).

YHWH declares, 'I will show him wonders', shifting the person from second to third. This is not insurmountable: Micah's patterns of syntax, like those in the psalms, are redolent with this feature. *niplāʾôt* and *peleʾ* both refer to YHWH's acts in redemption and judgment, but the fuller form of the word appears in those contexts more frequently.

Explanation

These verses draw on long-standing traditions of YHWH's relationship with his people. They resonate around reassuring figures of the Shepherd in contrast to vicious leadership. YHWH takes Israel and the people as his special inheritance. We see this concept already in the historical books (1 Sam. 10:1; 1 Kgs 8:53; 2 Kgs 21:14), repeated in the prophets (Isa. 19:25; 47:6; Joel 2:17) and laced into the psalms (Pss 33:12; 68:10[9]; 78:62, 71; 94:5, 14; 106:40). See also v. 18. Now his flock appeals to their Shepherd to keep his promises to nurture them.

The question of the time frame(s) for these discourse units surfaces again. Because geographical regions that were significant for the northern kingdom are named, this may suggest that at least some of the audience would have been concerned about northern-kingdom issues. Tiglath-Pileser III conquered Gilead and Bashan (2 Kgs 15:29–30), whose restoration would be a beacon of hope for a beleaguered northern audience. In addition, the absence of Jerusalem and Judah is notable (Shaw 1993: 207–218).

Micah's audience has already been admonished to 'remember' (Mic. 6:4–5) the vast span of that journey from Egypt to the Promised Land, all of which was shaped by YHWH's daily provision for them (Deut. 8:1–18).

A significant part at the end of that journey involved the battles against Sihon and Og whereby all the Transjordanian territory, including Gilead and Bashan, was acquired and settled. YHWH now promises wonders will be forthcoming just as in those past days. As with all of God's majestic deeds and attributes, his 'wonders' (*niplāʾôt*) are also part of the sung repertoire of God's people. Ps. 98:1 starts out with 'Sing a new song to YHWH, for the wonderful things he has done.' The verses that follow give the details, which never grow old – his righteousness, his holiness, his *ḥesed* and *ʾĕmûnâ* ('faithfulness') for Israel. Ps. 100, and especially v. 5, follows suit.

MICAH 7:16–17

Translation

7:16 Nations will see and be ashamed of all their might; they will place hand over mouth; their ears will be stopped.

17 And they will lick dust like the serpent, like crawling things of the earth. They will tremble from their enclosures to YHWH our God; they will dread, and they will fear you.

Notes on the text

7:16. There is not an object to indicate what the 'nations' (*gôyîm*) see. 'Hand over mouth' (*yād ʿal-peh*) is reminiscent of the false visionaries and diviners who covered their lips in shame (3:7). *ʾōzen* is a fem. dual form; the qal 3 fem. pl. verb means their 'ears' were deaf, and it suggests their own intentionality in that process.

17. The pi. form of *lḥk* ('lick') appears infrequently; it implies to consume generous amounts (*DCH* 4:532), not just timidly to poke one's tongue at something. Balaam prophesies that Israel will lick up the produce of the land (Num. 22:4). Flames lick up the water in the trenches that Elijah dug on Mount Carmel (1 Kgs 18:38).

The only other place *zōḥălê* ('crawling things') is used is Deut. 32:24 with reference to venomous crawling creatures of the dust (*zōḥălê ʿāpār*). Like snakes, the nations headed for refuge.

misgĕrōtêhem ('their closed off places') is from *sgr* ('to close').

Form and structure

These are sensory responses – seeing, speaking, hearing. In v. 17, two similes convey the humiliation. In the second half of the verse, verbs of shuddering, dread and fear characterize their posture. The phonetic similarity between 'seeing' and 'fearing' bookends these two verses. In between are multiple manifestations of shame and dread.

Comment

7:16. The preceding verse closes with 'wonders' shown to Israel. This verse commences with nations *seeing* and responding with shame. The reaction echoes that of Zion's enemy (v. 10). In neither case is there a direct object, but one is not necessary. The point is, they see their own bankruptcy in every way. They had depended on their own might, but with that paltry power removed, their only response could be shame at their previous posturing and current exposure, an ancient empire with no clothes. Their reactions engage their senses of vision, speech and hearing. Perhaps covering their mouths is not only because they have nothing to say: it may be to stifle cries of horror, astonishment and defeat. It is a vain attempt to contain overpowering dread. Likewise, they will refuse to hear any more: it is too overwhelming.

17. Part of the humiliation of licking up dust is the amount that will be consumed. See 'Notes'. Their despicable and disgraced position is emphasized: they will be like things that crawl away into the earth to hide, emerging with trembling from their hiding places. Deut. 32:24 references the venomous crawling creatures of the dust that God will use for judgment against Israel. In Micah, these are parallel to the serpents licking the dust. Like these horrid creatures, the nations have crawled into hiding places. While they presume to escape the coming judgment, they will be forced to emerge. When they do, abject horror will overwhelm them and they will tremble and be in dread before 'YHWH our God' and will fear 'you'. 'Dread' and 'fear' compound the terror in the presence of YHWH.

Explanation

Not only will the nations react with gestures of shock and dismay, but they will find themselves figuratively reduced to states of unspeakable humiliation. The symbolism in the specific reference to the serpent echoes powerfully the curse in Gen. 3:14 where the serpent in the garden will 'eat' dust as it slithers along on its belly. Other instances of 'licking dust' to depict utter humiliation include Ps. 72:9; Isa. 49:23. To be sure, the enmity between the seed of the serpent and the offspring of Eve means some of the 'dust' it will devour will be the fallen remains of Adam returned to dust (3:19). Nevertheless, in the coming days the curse of Gen. 3 will be overturned and evil, viscerally powerful as it is, will be reduced to nothing – finally. Hos. 10:8 describes evil persons pleading with the mountains and hills to fall on them and cover them, an image that Jesus, on his way to the cross, evoked for those mourning and wailing along the way (Luke 23:30). Much worse is to come. In the final cataclysmic judgments, all the mighty ones of the earth will, like the crawling things, slither away to hide in caves and among the rocks. When they summon the mountains to fall on them, it will be in the vain hope that they will be hidden from the 'face of the one sitting on the throne and the wrath of the Lamb' (Rev. 6:15–16).

MICAH 7:18–20

Translation

7:18Who is a God like you, forgiving iniquity and passing over transgression for the remnant of his inheritance? He has not kept hold of his anger for ever, because he delights in *ḥesed*.

19He will return, he will have compassion on us; he will subdue our iniquities. And you will cast into the depths of the sea all their sins.

20You will give truth to Jacob and *ḥesed* to Abraham, which you swore to our fathers from the days of old.

Notes on the text

7:18. *nōśē'* (masc. sg. act. ptc.) has a wide range of meanings: 'to lift, bear, carry, support, sustain, endure, take away, carry off, forgive' are all possibilities (*DCH* 5:758).

YHWH does not seize or strengthen (*lō'-heḥĕzîq*) his anger. This qat. verb may suggest a present time frame (*IBHS* §30.5.1c nos. 19–21). While *ḥāpēṣ* is a stative verb, it serves here as a pred. adj. that is front-loaded in the clause.

19. *yāšûb* ('he will turn') acquires an adv. sense that governs the following verb, *yĕraḥămēnû*: 'he will have compassion again' (GKC §120g). *kbš* implies 'subduing by force' (*DCH* 4:361); BDB (461) suggests the figure 'tread down'. The Akkadian *kabāsu* can mean 'to forgive', an interpretation that would follow well on the preceding divine intent to be compassionate (Gordon 1978: 355).

Some versions (LXX, Vg, Syr, Tg) continue the 3 masc. sg. 'and he will cast', but the shift to 'you' is an indicator of relationship and the anticipated consequences.

The pron. suff. on 'sins' at the end of the verse is 3 masc. pl. (*ḥaṭṭ'ôtām*), although LXX, Syr and the Vg read 'our sins' to maintain consistency with the 1 sg. pron. suff. in the previous line.

Form and structure

These final verses include the comprehensive three terms for sin and are followed by seven ways to express YHWH's all-encompassing forgiveness (Mays 1976: 167). In the closing verse, Micah again captures the attention of his audience by separating and reversing the order of the two theological underpinnings of the covenant ('truth' and *ḥesed*) as well as the patriarchal names ('Jacob' and 'Abraham') with whom they are associated.

Comment

7:18. The expression 'forgiving iniquity' echoes Exod. 34:7, where it is directly followed by 'transgression and sin'. Micah extends the spiritual largesse. God 'even' (*we-*) passes over transgression. Both participles, 'forgiving' and 'passing over', suggest ongoing grace for the remnant of YHWH's inheritance. Micah's echo of Exod. 34:6 adds the emphasis embedded in Ps. 103:8–12: he does not always chide or keep his anger for ever. Micah puts it in his own unique idiom: YHWH does not 'seize or strengthen' his anger endlessly. *kî* marks a contrast between YHWH's attributes of anger and *ḥesed*. They are not even addressed in the same categories. Anger is put into a temporal sphere that ends. *ḥesed* is the object of YHWH's delight that is ongoing.

'Who is a God like you?' Micah's name is embedded in this rhetorical question (see 'Introduction'); the question presumes the answer 'there is none like you'. What makes YHWH truly great is the unparalleled and boundless offer of forgiveness. It is not power, might and majesty, although all those characteristics are intrinsic to the Person of God. No, it is giving a second chance, and a third and a hundredth.

Labelling wrongdoing and disobedience in the HB is important, given the nature of covenant expectations. The three most frequently used terms are 'iniquity', 'transgression' and 'sin'. They occur together thirteen times, with 'iniquity' standing in the first position, followed by 'transgression' and 'sin'. 'Iniquity' is primarily a religious term, and it serves as a summary word for all sins against God. 'Transgression' has a narrower range, stemming from a political context in which it had implications of rebellion. That carries over into the rebellion of YHWH's people against the covenant. 'Sin' is the term with the broadest meaning, appearing in both social and religious contexts; it includes missing (the mark), erring and failure in addition to the theological implications of disobedience (Luc, *NIDOTTE* 2:87–93).

19. Three yiq. verbs in succession drive forward into the boundless future the continuing description of YHWH's covenant faithfulness. *yĕraḥămēnû*, a derivative verb, carries with it the nurturing that is bound up with bearing children, a powerfully emotional and visceral feeling.

Further, YHWH does not just look the other direction regarding our transgressions. The image of YHWH's subduing sins by treading on them is unique in the HB; recognizing their foul nature, he grinds them into the ground to eradicate them and any of their lingering effects. This fits well with the subsequent image of casting them into the depths of the sea. For good measure, God – now addressed as 'you' – will cast those sins into the 'deepest places of the sea' (*mĕṣulôt yām*). Primarily used in poetic texts, this expression indicates both the depths of the sea and deep human distress (Ps. 88:7[6]). Jon. 2:4[3] echoes the horror of the experience of the deep sea with its waves and breakers. See also YHWH's destruction of Pharaoh's army (Exod. 15:4–5). In Ps. 103:11–12, YHWH sets immeasurable distance between our iniquities and us; here they are buried in the depths of the sea. In the same manner as we saw in v. 9, Micah identifies fully with the people ('our iniquities'). The image of hurling sins appears also in Isa. 38:17; in that case YHWH casts them behind his back.

Two additional matters bear mention. First, for people in the ANE, the sea was a fearsome place: the Abyss and abode of all evil. Such epic creatures as Rahab, Leviathan and the *tannîn*, a sea serpent, were presumed to dwell there (see Job 9:13; 26:12–13; Pss 74:13–14; 89:11[10]; Isa. 27:1; 51:9). Its darkness and inherent danger along with the complete inability of humans to control any aspect of it make its waters an ominous figure. When YHWH casts all the sins of the people into the sea, it is a powerful representation of God's power to send all that horror back to its 'source', a fitting end to it.

Second, there is in Judaism a compelling symbolic action that is drawn specifically from this passage. On the first day of Rosh HaShanah (the New Year), observant Jews gather at a body of water and symbolically cast the sins of the past year into the water, appealing to YHWH for mercy and forgiveness. In addition to the depths of the water engulfing those sins, the water itself purifies.

20. The two theological foundations of the covenant are generally presented as *ḥesed wĕʾĕmet* ('covenant love and truth'), often accompanied by *rāb* ('great'). This capsule statement points back to Exod. 34:6. Among the many examples are Pss 25:10; 40:12[11]; 57:4[3]; 61:8[7]; 85:11[10]; 86:15; 89:15[14]; 115:1; 138:2 – and those are only in the psalms. Micah has reversed the two weighty terms, another means of recapturing audiences lulled by familiar expressions. Both faithfulness and truth are intertwined in *ʾĕmet* – a related form is *ʾĕmûnâ* ('faithfulness' and 'trustworthiness'). See Moberly, *NIDOTTE* 1:427–433. YHWH is faithful because his character is thoroughly truth. No false motives or directives can flow from that. The combination of *ḥesed* and *ʾĕmet* is sufficient to undo all the wiles of the evil one – in any place and at all times.

The powerful theological force of *ʾĕmet* and *ḥesed*, in conjunction with Jacob and Abraham, closes the book. Pairing 'truth' with Jacob carries a hint of irony: a derived implication of his name is 'deceiver', and he lived up to his name. Just as Micah's previous historical allusions are brief but profound, so also here. These attributes of God are timeless: God will faithfully keep the oath he swore to 'our forefathers'. The oath on behalf of the descendants of Abraham, Isaac and Jacob has been 'from days of old'. It is part of the comprehensive picture of the activities of the Ruler in Mic. 5:1[2].

Explanation

The incomparability of God is the foundational theme of all parts of God's revelation. Who is like you, O God? No one. His chosen people, his kingdom of priests and holy nation experienced God's power on their behalf in the exodus (Exod. 15:11). They were bound to YHWH at Sinai (Exod. 19 – 20). The psalms repeatedly affirm there is none like Israel's God: his glory and mighty works are marvellous (Pss 71:19; 77:14–16[13–15]; 86:8–10; 96:4; 97:9).

Key themes from the whole of Micah are wound together here: remnant, inheritance, desire, *ḥesed*, iniquity, transgression, sin and 'from the days of old'. Steadfast and unfailing 'covenant love' (*ḥesed*) undergirds God's grace and mercy; it leads to his forgiving and pardoning. It is God himself in Jesus who ultimately bears, carries, endures all the consequences of our sins. He wins by sacrifice; he is victorious through lonely suffering; he is God with us even as he tramples our sins and hurls them to the depths. This is a remarkable picture of unquestioned victory – victory over sin, the deadliest enemy.

> If you, O YHWH, should keep iniquities; O Lord, who could stand?
> But with you is forgiveness, in order that you will be feared.
> (Ps. 130:3–4)

What a ride we have been on with this prophet! And what a way to draw this revelation of God's love and justice to a close! God is truth and God's faithfulness is to 'for ever and beyond'. Our part is to mirror those qualities to the best of our ability, with the unfailing help of God's Spirit and on our knees. We sing, 'Great Is Thy Faithfulness', and are reminded of the title of Johann Sebastian Bach's Cantata BWV 70: Wachet! Betet! Betet! Wachet! The title is a small chiastic structure: 'Watch! Pray! Pray! Watch!'

BIBLIOGRAPHY

COMMENTARIES

Achtemeier, E. (1996), *Minor Prophets I*, NIBC, Peabody: Hendrickson.

Alexander, T. D., D. W. Baker and B. Waltke (1988), *Obadiah, Jonah, Micah*, TOTC, Leicester: Inter-Varsity Press.

Allen, L. C. (1976), *The Books of Joel, Obadiah, Jonah, and Micah*, NICOT, Grand Rapids: Eerdmans.

Alter, R. (2019), *The Hebrew Bible: A Translation with Commentary, Prophets*, vol. 2, New York: Norton.

Andersen, F. I., and D. N. Freedman (2000), *Micah: A New Translation and Commentary*, AB 24E, New York: Doubleday.

Armerding, C. E. (2008), 'Obadiah', in *EBC* 8:421–550.

Baker, D. W. (2006), *Joel, Obadiah, Malachi*, NIVAC, Grand Rapids: Zondervan.

Barton, J. (2001), *Joel and Obadiah: A Commentary*, OTL, Louisville: Westminster John Knox.

Becking, B. (ed.) (2016), *Obadiah*, New Readings: A Biblical Commentary, Sheffield: Sheffield Phoenix.

Ben Zvi, E. (1996), *A Historical Critical Study of the Book of Obadiah*, BZAW 242, Berlin: de Gruyter.

——— (2000), *Micah*, FOTL 21B, Grand Rapids: Eerdmans.

——— (2003), *The Signs of Jonah: Reading and Rereading in Ancient Yehud*, JSOTSup 367, London: Sheffield Academic Press.

Bewer, J. A. (1912), *Jonah*, ICC, Edinburgh: T. & T. Clark.

Bickerman, E. J. (1967), *Four Strange Books of the Bible: Jonah, Daniel, Koheleth, Esther*, New York: Schocken.

Block, D. I. (author and ed.) (2013), *Obadiah*, Exegetical Commentary on the Old Testament: A Discourse Analysis of the Hebrew Bible, Grand Rapids: Zondervan.

Bolin, T. M. (1997), *Freedom Beyond Forgiveness: The Book of Jonah Re-Examined*, JSOTSup 236, Sheffield: Sheffield Academic Press.

Calvin, J. (1847), *Jonah, Micah, and Nahum*, A Commentary on the Twelve Minor Prophets, vol. 3, tr. J. Owen, Edinburgh: The Calvin Translation Society (first published in Latin in 1559).

Cary, P. (2008), *Jonah*, BTC, Grand Rapids: Brazos.

Coggins, R. J. (1985), '"Judgment Between Brothers" – A Commentary on the Book of Obadiah', in R. J. Coggins and S. P. Re'emi (eds.), *Israel Among the Nations*, Grand Rapids: Eerdmans, 65–102.

Cuffey, K. H. (2015), *The Literary Coherence of the Book of Micah: Remnant, Restoration, and Promise*, London: Bloomsbury T. & T. Clark.

Fretheim, T. E. (1977), *The Message of Jonah: A Theological Commentary*, Minneapolis: Fortress.

Goldingay, J. (2021), *Hosea–Micah*, Baker Commentary on the Old Testament Prophetic Books, Grand Rapids: Baker.

Hillers, D. R. (1984), *Micah: A Commentary on the Book of the Prophet Micah*, Hermeneia, Philadelphia: Fortress.

Hoyt, J. M. (2019), *Amos, Jonah, & Micah*, EEC, Bellingham: Lexham Press.

Jenson, P. P. (2008), *Obadiah, Jonah, Micah: A Theological Commentary*, New York: T. & T. Clark.

Keil, C. F., and F. Delitzsch (1900), *The Twelve Minor Prophets*, vol. 1, Edinburgh: T. & T. Clark.

Lessing, R. R. (2007), *Jonah*, St. Louis: Concordia.

Limburg, J. (1988), 'Jonah', in *Hosea–Micah*, Interpretation, Louisville: Westminster John Knox, 137–157.

——— (1993), *Jonah: A Commentary*, OTL, Louisville: Westminster John Knox.

McComiskey, T. E., and T. Longman III (2008), *Micah*, EBC, Grand Rapids: Zondervan, 491–551.

Magonet, J. D. (1983), *Form and Meaning: Studies in Literary Techniques in the Book of Jonah*, Sheffield: Almond.

Mays, J. L. (1976), *Micah: A Commentary*, OTL, Philadelphia: Westminster.

Millard, A. R. (2009), 'Obadiah', in *ZIBBC* 5: 90–99.

Niehaus, J. (1993), 'Obadiah', in T. E. McComiskey (ed.), *The Minor Prophets: An Exegetical and Expository Commentary*, vol. 2, Grand Rapids: Baker, 495–541.

Nogalski, J. D. (2011a), *The Book of the Twelve: Hosea–Jonah*, SHBC, Macon: Smyth & Helwys.

——— (2011b), *The Book of the Twelve: Micah–Malachi*, SHBC, Macon: Smith & Helwys.

Page, F. S. (1995), *Amos, Obadiah, Jonah*, ed. B. K. Smith and F. S. Page, NAC 19a, Nashville: Broadman and Holman, 171–288 (both Obadiah and Jonah).

Petterson, A. R. (2015), *Haggai, Zechariah, Malachi*, AOTC 25, Nottingham: Apollos; Downers Grove: InterVarsity Press.

Raabe, P. (1996), *Obadiah: A New Translation with Introduction and Commentary*, AB 24D, New York: Doubleday.

Renaud, B. (1977), *La Formation du Livre de Michée*, Paris: Gabalda.

Renkema, J. (2003), *Obadiah*, HCOT, Leuven: Peeters.

Sasson, J. M. (1990), *Jonah: A New Translation with Introduction, Commentary, and Interpretation*, AB 24B, New Haven: Yale University Press.

Shaw, C. S. (1993), *The Speeches of Micah: A Rhetorical-Historical Analysis*, JSOTSup 145, Sheffield: Sheffield Academic Press.

Simon, U. (1999), *The JPS Commentary: Jonah*, Philadelphia: Jewish Publication Society.

Smith, G. A. (1929), *The Book of the Twelve Prophets*, 2 vols., New York: Doubleday.

Smith, J. M. P. (1911), *The Book of Micah*, ICC, New York: Charles Scribner's Sons.

Smith-Christopher, D. L. (2015), *Micah: A Commentary*, Louisville: Westminster John Knox.

Stuart, D. (1987), *Hosea–Jonah*, WBC 31, Waco; Word.

Sweeney, M. A. (2000), *The Twelve Prophets*, vol. 1: *Hosea, Joel, Amos, Obadiah, Jonah*, Brit Olam, Collegeville: Liturgical Press.

Timmer, D. C. (2021), *Obadiah, Jonah, Micah*, TOTC 26, London: Inter-Varsity Press; Downers Grove: InterVarsity Press.

Trible, P. L. (1994), *Rhetorical Criticism: Context, Method, and the Book of Jonah*, GBS, Minneapolis: Fortress.

——— (1996), 'The Book of Jonah', in *NIB* 7:463–529.

Waltke, B. K. (2007), *A Commentary on Micah*, Grand Rapids: Eerdmans.

Watts, J. D. W. (1969), *Obadiah: A Critical Exegetical Commentary*, Grand Rapids: Eerdmans.

Wolff, H. W. (1981), *Micah the Prophet*, tr. R. D. Gehrke, Philadelphia: Fortress.

——— (1986), *Obadiah and Jonah: A Commentary*, tr. M. Kohl, Minneapolis: Augsburg.

Youngblood, K. J. (2019), *Jonah: God's Scandalous Mercy*, 2nd ed., ed. D. I. Block, Zondervan Exegetical Commentary on the Old Testament: A Discourse Analysis of the Hebrew Bible, Grand Rapids: Zondervan.

ADDITIONAL REFERENCE WORKS AND VOLUMES

Aharoni, Y. (1979), *The Land of the Bible: A Historical Geography*, tr. and ed. A. F. Rainey, Philadelphia: Westminster.

——— (1981), *Arad Inscriptions*, tr. J. Ben-Or, ed. and rev. A. F. Rainey, Jerusalem: Israel Exploration Society.

Aharoni, Y., M. Avi-Yonah, A. F. Rainey and Z. Safrai (1993), *The MacMillan Bible Atlas*, 3rd ed., Jerusalem: Carta.

Alter, R. (1981), *The Art of Biblical Narrative*, New York: Basic.

——— (1985), *The Art of Biblical Poetry*, New York: Basic.

——— (2019), *The Art of Bible Translation*, Princeton: Princeton University Press.

Baly, D. (1974), *The Geography of the Bible*, rev. ed., New York: Harper and Row.

Bartholomew, C. (2015), *Introducing Biblical Hermeneutics: A Comprehensive Framework for Hearing God in Scripture*, Grand Rapids: Baker.

Bartlett, J. R. (1989), *Edom and the Edomites*, JSOTSup 77, Sheffield: Sheffield Academic Press.

Berlin, A. (1983), *Poetics and Interpretation of Biblical Narrative*, Sheffield: Almond; repr. Winona Lake: Eisenbrauns (1994).

——— (2008), *The Dynamics of Biblical Parallelism*, rev. and expanded, Grand Rapids: Eerdmans.

Benoit, P., J. T. Milik and R. deVaux (1961), *The Caves of Murabbaʿat*, DJD IIa/b, Oxford: Clarendon.

Cathcart, K. J., and R. P. Gordon (tr.) (1989), *Targum of the Minor Prophets*, Translated with a Critical Introduction, Apparatus, and Notes, The Aramaic Bible, vol. 14, Wilmington: Michael Glazier.

Clark, G. R. (1993), *The Word* Ḥesed *in the Hebrew Bible*, JSOTSup 157, Sheffield: Sheffield Academic Press.

Cogan, M. (2015), *The Raging Torrent: Historical Inscriptions from Assyria and Babylonia Relating to Ancient Israel*, 2nd ed., Jerusalem: Carta.

Craig, K. (1993), *A Poetics in the Service of Ideology*, Columbia: University of South Carolina Press.

Crenshaw, J. L. (1971), *Prophetic Conflict: Its Effect on Israelite Religion*, BZAW 124, Berlin: de Gruyter.

Davies, P., and D. J. A. Clines (1993), *Among the Prophets: Language, Image and Structure in the Prophetic Writings*, JSOTSup 144, Sheffield: Sheffield Academic Press.

Day, J. (2000), *Yahweh and the Gods and Goddesses of Canaan*, LHBOTS, Sheffield: Sheffield Academic Press.

De Moor, J. C. (1987), *An Anthology of Religious Texts from Ugarit*, Leiden: Brill.

Dobbs-Allsopp, F. W. (1993), *Weep, O Daughter of Zion: A Study of the City-Lament Genre in the Hebrew Bible*, BibOr 44, Rome: Editrice Pontificio Istituto Biblico.

Edelman, D. V. (ed.) (1995), *You Shall Not Abhor an Edomite For He Is Your Brother: Edom and Seir in History and Tradition*, Atlanta: Scholars Press.

Gelston, A. (1987), *The Peshitta of the Twelve Prophets*, Oxford: Clarendon.

——— (2010), *The Twelve Minor Prophets*, Stuttgart: Deutsche Bibelgesellschaft.

Glueck, N. (1967), *Ḥesed in the Bible*, tr. A. Gottschalk, introduction G. A. Larue, Cincinnati: Hebrew Union College Press.

Gordis, R. (1937), *The Biblical Text in the Making: A Study of the Kethib–Qere*, Philadelphia: Dropsie College for Hebrew and Cognate Learning; repr. New York: KTAV (1971).

Gordon, C. H. (1949), *Ugaritic Literature: A Comprehensive Translation of the Poetic and Prose Texts*, Rome: Pontifical Biblical Institute.

Grayson, A. K. (1976), *Assyrian Royal Inscriptions*, vol. 2, Records of the Ancient Near East, Wiesbaden: Otto Harrassowitz.

Hasel, G. F. (1974), *The Remnant: The History and Theology of the Remnant Idea from Genesis to Isaiah*, 2nd ed., Berrien Springs: Andrews University Press.

Herodotus (2004), *The Histories*, tr. G. C. Macaulay, ed. D. Lateiner, New York: Barnes & Noble Classics.

House, P. R. (1990), *The Unity of the Twelve*, JSOTSup 97, Sheffield: Almond.

Jastrow, M. (1950), *Dictionary of Talmud Bavli, Yerushalmi, Midrashic Literature and Targumim*, New York: Pardes.

Jones, B. A. (1995), *The Formation of the Book of the Twelve: A Study in Text and Canon*, SBLDS 149, Atlanta: Scholars Press.

Josephus, *Antiquities of the Jews, Books IX–XI*, tr. R. Marcus, LCL, Cambridge, Mass.: Harvard University Press (1990).

Kaufmann, Y. (1960), *The Religion of Israel*, abridged, tr. M. Greenberg, Chicago: University of Chicago Press.

Kugel, J. L. (1981), *The Idea of Biblical Poetry: Parallelism and Its History*, New Haven: Yale University Press.

Laniak, T. (2007), *While Shepherds Watched Their Flocks* <www.ShepherdLeader.com>.

Lauterbach, J. (1933), *Mekilta d-Rabbi Ishmael*, 3 vols., Philadelphia: Jewish Publication Society.

Levine, E. (1978), *The Aramaic Version of Jonah*, 2nd ed., New York: Sepher-Hermon.

Magness, J. (2011), *Stone and Dung, Oil and Spit: Jewish Daily Life in the Time of Jesus*, Grand Rapids: Eerdmans.

Mazar, A. (1990), *Archaeology of the Land of the Bible: 10,000–586 B.C.E.*, New York: Doubleday.

Neusner, J. (2004), *Judaism and the Interpretation of Scripture: Introduction to the Rabbinic Midrash*, Peabody: Hendrickson.

Nogalski, J. (1993a), *Literary Precursors to the Book of the Twelve*, BZAW 217, Berlin: de Gruyter.

——— (1993b), *Redactional Processes on the Book of the Twelve*, BZAW 218, Berlin: de Gruyter.

Olmstead, A. T. (1923), *History of Assyria*, New York: Charles Scribner's Sons.

Oppenheim, A. L. (1964), *Ancient Mesopotamia: Portrait of a Dead Civilization*, Chicago: University of Chicago Press.

Orni, E., and E. Efrat (1971), *Geography of Israel*, 3rd rev. ed., Jerusalem: Keter.

Parry, D. W., and E. Tov (2014), *The Dead Sea Scrolls Reader*, 2 vols., Leiden: Brill.

Provan, I. W., V. P. Long and T. Longman III (2015), *A Biblical History of Israel*, 2nd ed., Louisville: Westminster John Knox.

Rainey, A. F., and R. S. Notley (2006), *The Sacred Bridge*, Jerusalem: Carta.

Rasmussen, C. G. (2010), *The Zondervan Atlas*, Grand Rapids: Zondervan.
Redditt, P. L., and A. Schart (2003), *Thematic Threads in the Book of the Twelve*, Berlin: De Gruyter.
Schrader, E. (1885–8), *The Cuneiform Inscriptions and the Old Testament*, tr. O. C. Whitehouse, 2 vols., London: Williams and Norgate.
Scott, R. B. Y. (1968), *The Relevance of the Prophets*, rev. ed., New York: Macmillan.
Sharp, C. J. (2008), *Irony and Meaning in the Hebrew Bible*, Indiana Series in Biblical Literature, Bloomington: Indiana University Press.
Siddall, L. R. (2013), *The Reign of Adad-Nirari III: An Historical and Ideological Analysis of an Assyrian King and His Times*, Leiden: Brill.
Smith, G. A. (1894), *The Historical Geography of the Holy Land*, London: Hodder & Stoughton; repr. London: Fontana Library (1966).
Sternberg, M. (1985), *Poetics of Biblical Narrative: Ideological Literature and the Drama of Reading*, Bloomington: Indiana University Press.
Thiele, E. R. (1965), *The Mysterious Numbers of the Hebrew Kings*, Grand Rapids: Eerdmans.
Tiemeyer, L.-S., and J. Wöhrle (2020), *The Book of the Twelve: Composition, Reception, and Interpretation*, VTSup 184, Leiden: Brill.
Timmer, D. C. (2011), *A Gracious and Compassionate God: Mission, Salvation and Spirituality in the Book of Jonah*, NSBT 26, Apollos: Nottingham; Downers Grove: InterVarsity Press.
Tov, E. (1990), *The Greek Minor Prophets Scroll from Naḥal Ḥever*, DJD VIII, Oxford: Clarendon.
Walton, J. H. (2018), *Ancient Near Eastern Thought and the Old Testament: Introducing the Conceptual World of the Old Testament*, 2nd ed., Grand Rapids: Baker.
Watts, J. W., and P. R. House (1996), *Forming Prophetic Literature: Essays on Isaiah and the Twelve in Honor of John D. W. Watts*, JSOTSup 235, Sheffield: Sheffield Academic Press.
Wiesel, E. (1981), *Five Biblical Portraits*, South Bend: University of Notre Dame Press.
Williams, R. J. (2007), *Williams' Hebrew Syntax*, 3rd ed., rev. and exp. J. C. Beckman, Toronto: University of Toronto Press.
Wyatt, N. (1998), *Religious Texts from Ugarit: The Words of Ilimilku and His Colleagues*, Sheffield: Sheffield Academic Press.
Xenophon (1922), *Anabasis*, tr. C. L. Brownson, LCL, Cambridge, Mass.: Harvard University Press; repr. 1968.

CHAPTERS AND ARTICLES

Aharoni, Y. (1970), 'Three Hebrew Ostraca from Arad', *BASOR* 197:16–42.
Alexander, T. D. (1985), 'Jonah and Genre', *TynB* 36:35–59.

Allen, L. C. (1973), 'More Cuckoos in the Textual Nest: At 2 Kings xxiii.5; Jeremiah xvii.3,4; Micah iii.3; vi.16 (LXX); 2 Chronicles xx.25 (LXX)', *JTS* 24:69–73.

——— (1997), זכר, in *NIDOTTE* 1:1100–1106.

Andersen, F. I. (1995), 'Linguistic Coherence in Prophetic Discourse', in A. B. Beck, A. H. Bartlett, P. R. Raabe and C. A. Franke (eds.), *Fortunate the Eyes that See*, Festschrift for David Noel Freedman, Grand Rapids: Eerdmans, 137–156.

Anderson, B. A. (2010), 'Poetic Justice in Obadiah', *JSOT* 35:247–255.

Assis, E. (2014), 'Structure, Redaction and Significance in the Prophecy of Obadiah', *JSOT* 39:209–221.

Averbeck, R. E. (1997a), זבח, in *NIDOTTE* 1:1066–1073.

——— (1997b), טמא, in *NIDOTTE* 2:372–373.

Baer, D. A., and R. P. Gordon (1997), חסד, in *NIDOTTE* 2:211–218.

Ballard, R. D., and L. E. Stager, D. Master, D. Yoerger, D. Mindell, L. Whitcomb, H. Singh and D. Piechota (2002), 'Iron Age Shipwrecks in Deep Water off Ashkelon, Israel', *AJA* 106:151–168.

Band, A. J. (1990), 'Swallowing Jonah: The Eclipse of Parody', *Proof* 10:177–195.

Bartlett, J. R. (1969), 'The Use of the Word *r'ōš* as a Title in the Old Testament', *VT* 19:1–10.

——— (1982), 'Edom and the Fall of Jerusalem, 587 B.C.', *PEQ* 114:13–24.

Ben Zvi, E. (1996), 'Twelve Prophetic Books or "The Twelve": A Few Preliminary Considerations', in J. W. Watts and P. R. House (eds.), *Forming Prophetic Literature: Essays on Isaiah and the Twelve in Honor of John D. W. Watts*, JSOTSup 235, Sheffield: Sheffield Academic Press, 126–156.

——— (1999), 'Wrongdoers, Wrongdoing, and Righting Wrongs in Micah 2:1', *BibInt* 7:87–100.

——— (2009), 'Jonah 4:11 and the Metaprophetic Character of the Book of Jonah', *JHS* 9:2–13.

Biddle, M. (2007), 'Obadiah–Jonah–Micah in Canonical Context: The Nature of Prophetic Literature and Hermeneutics', *Int* 61:154–166.

Blakely, J. A., and J. W. Hardin (2002), 'Southwestern Judah in the Late Eighth Century B.C.E.', *BASOR* 326:11–64.

Block, D. I. (1985), 'Israel's House: Reflections on the Use of *byt yśr'l* in the Old Testament in the Light of Its Ancient Near Eastern Environment', *JETS* 28:257–275.

Bolin, T. M. (1995), '"Should I Not Also Pity Nineveh?": Divine Freedom in the Book of Jonah', *JSOT* 67:109–120.

Borowski, O. (2018), 'Sennacherib in Judah – the Devastating Consequences of an Assyrian Military Campaign', *ErIsr* 33:33–40.

Bracke, J. M. (1997), ריב, in *NIDOTTE* 3:1105–1106.

Brody, A. J. (1998), *'Each Man Cried Out to His Own God': The Specialized Religion of Canaanite and Phoenician Seafarers*, HSM 58, Atlanta: Scholars Press.

Brown, M. A. (1987), '"Is It Not?" or "Indeed!": *HL* in Northwest Semitic', *Maarav* 4:201–219.
Brueggemann, W. (1981), '"Vine and Fig Tree": A Case Study in Imagination and Criticism', *CBQ* 43:188–204.
Buchanan, G. W. (1961), 'Eschatology and the "End of Days"', *JNES* 20:188–193.
Butterworth, M. (1997), נחם, in *NIDOTTE* 3:81–83.
Byington, S. T. (1949), 'Plow and Pick', *JBL* 68:49–54.
Carpenter, E. (1997a), גמל, in *NIDOTTE* 1:871–873.
——— (1997b), פסל, in *NIDOTTE* 3:644–649.
Carpenter, E., and M. Grisanti (1997), שק, in *NIDOTTE* 3:1270.
Carroll, R. P. (1990), 'Obadiah', in R. J. Coggins and J. L. Houlden (eds.), *A Dictionary of Biblical Interpretation*, London: SCM, 496–497.
Cathcart, K. J. (1968), 'Notes on Micah 5,4–5', *Bib* 49:511–514.
Chisholm, R. (2010), 'When Prophecy Appears to Fail, Check Your Hermeneutic', *JETS* 53:561–577.
Clements, R. E. (1975), 'The Purpose of the Book of Jonah', *VTSup* 28:16–28.
Clifford, R. J. (1966), 'The Use of *Hôy* in the Prophets', *CBQ* 28:458–464.
Collins, C. J. (1995), 'The *Wayyiqtol* as Pluperfect: When and Why', *TynB* 46:117–140.
Cooper, A. (1993), 'In Praise of Divine Caprice: The Significance of the Book of Jonah', in P. R. Davies and D. J. A. Clines (eds.), *Among the Prophets: Language, Image and Structure in the Prophetic Writings*, JSOTSup 144, Sheffield: Sheffield Academic Press, 144–163.
Crenshaw, J. L. (1972), '*Wĕdôrēk ʿal-bāmŏtê ʾāreṣ*', *CBQ* 34:39–53.
——— (1986), 'The Expression *mi yodeaʿ* in the Hebrew Bible', *VT* 36:274–288.
Cross, F. M. (1966), 'An Aramaic Inscription from Daskyleion', *BASOR* 184:7–10.
——— (1974), אל, in *TDOT* 1:260–261.
——— (1983), 'Studies in the Prosody of Hebrew Verse: The Prosody of the Psalm of Jonah', in H. B. Huffmon, F. A. Spina and A. R. W. Green (eds.), *The Quest for the Kingdom of God: Studies in Honor of George E. Mendenhall*, Winona Lake: Eisenbrauns, 159–167.
Daniels, D. R. (1987), 'Is There a "Prophetic Lawsuit" Genre?', *ZAW* 99:339–360.
Davies, G. I. (1977a), 'New Solution to a Crux in Obadiah 7', *VT* 27:484–487.
——— (1977b), 'The Use of *R*ʿʿ Qal and the Meaning of Jonah IV 1', *VT* 27:105–111.
Demsky, A. (1966), 'The Houses of Achzib. A Critical Note on Micah 1:14b', *IEJ* 16:211–215.
De Roche, M. (1983), 'Yahweh's *Rib* Against Israel: A Reassessment of the So-called "Prophetic Lawsuit" in the Pre-exilic Prophets', *JBL* 102:563–574.

Dozeman, T. B. (1989), 'Inner-Biblical Interpretation of Yahweh's Gracious and Compassionate Character', *JBL* 108:207–223.
Driver, G. R. (1938), 'Linguistic and Textual Problems: Minor Prophets, II', *JTS* 39:260–273.
——— (1955), 'Birds in the Old Testament', *PEQ* 87:5–20.
Driver, S. R. (1887), 'Notes on Difficult Grammar Texts', *Expositor* 5:259–269.
Dyck, E. (1990), 'Jonah Among the Prophets: A Study in Canonical Context', *JETS* 33:63–73.
Ehrman, A. (1970), 'A Note on Micah II 7', *VT* 20:86–87.
——— (1973), 'A Note on Micah VI 14', *VT* 23:103–105.
Emerton, J. A. (2001), 'Looking on One's Enemies', *VT* 51:186–196.
Fabry, H.-J. (1980), חבל, in *TDOT* 4:188–189.
Ferguson, P. (1996), 'Who Was the "King of Nineveh" in Jonah 3:6?', *TynB* 47:301–314.
Freedman, D. N. (1977), 'Pottery, Poetry, and Prophecy: An Essay on Biblical Poetry', *JBL* 96:5–26.
——— (1983), 'Discourse on Prophetic Discourse', in H. B. Huffmon, F. A. Spina and A. R. W. Green (eds.), *The Quest for the Kingdom of God: Studies in Honor of George E. Mendenhall*, Winona Lake: Eisenbrauns, 141–158.
——— (1990), 'Did God Play a Dirty Trick on Jonah at the End?', *BR* 6:26–31.
Fretheim, T. E. (1978), 'Jonah and Theodicy', *ZAW* 90:227–237.
Frolov, S. (1999), 'Returning the Ticket: God and His Prophet in the Book of Jonah', *JSOT* 86:85–105.
Fuller, R. (1997a), 'The Twelve', in E. Ulrich, F. M. Cross, R. E. Fuller, J. E. Sanderson, P. W. Skehan and E. Tov (eds.), *The Prophets*, vol. 10 of Qumran Cave 4, DJD XV, Oxford: Clarendon, 221–318.
——— (1997b), איפה, in *NIDOTTE* 1:382–388.
Ganor, S., and I. Kreimerman (2019), 'An Eighth-Century B.C.E. Gate Shrine at Tel Lachish, Israel', BASOR 381:211–236.
Garr, W. R. (1983), 'The Qinah: A Study of Poetic Meter, Syntax, and Style', *ZAW* 95:54–75.
Glazier-McDonald, B. (1995), 'Edom in the Prophetical Corpus', in D. V. Edelman (ed.), *You Shall Not Abhor an Edomite for He Is Your Brother: Edom and Seir in History and Tradition*, Archaeology and Biblical Studies 3, Atlanta: Scholars Press, 23–32.
Goitein S. D. (1937), 'Some Observations on Jonah', *JPOS* 17:63–77.
Gordis, R. (1949), 'Quotations as a Literary Usage in Biblical, Oriental and Rabbinic Literature', *HUCA* 22:157–219.
Gordon, R. P. (1978), 'Micah VII 19 and Akkadian *Kabāsu*', *VT* 28:355.
Gray, J. (1953), 'The Diaspora of Israel and Judah in Obadiah v. 20', *ZAW* 65:53–59.
Grisanti, M. A. (1997a), ים, in *NIDOTTE* 2:461–466.
——— (1997b), שמה, in *NIDOTTE* 3:1251–1254.

Grisanti, M. A., and J. C. McCann (1997), שחד, in *NIDOTTE* 4:75–76.

Hadley, J. M. (1997a), אשרה, in *NIDOTTE* 1:569–570.

——— (1997b), עצב, in *NIDOTTE* 3:483–484.

——— (1997c), פסל, in *NIDOTTE* 3:644–646.

Halton, C. (2008), 'How Big Was Nineveh?', *BBR* 18:193–207.

Hamilton, V. P. (1997), נשא, in *NIDOTTE* 3:160–163.

Handy, L. K. (2004), 'Of Captains and Kings: A Preliminary Socio-Historical Approach to Jonah', *BibRes* 49:31–48.

Harris, R. L. (1980), *gillûl*, in *TWOT* 1:163–164.

Hasel, G. F. (1980), זעק, in *TDOT* 4:112–122.

Hassler, M. A. (2016), 'The Setting of Obadiah: When Does the Oracle Concerning Edom Transpire?', *JETS* 59.2:241–254.

Hayden, R. E. (1997), אפר, in *NIDOTTE* 1:483–484.

Hoffman, Y. (2008), 'The Wandering Lament: Micah 1:10–16', in M. Cogan and D. E. Kahn (eds.), *Treasures on Camels' Humps: Historical and Literary Studies from the Ancient Near East Presented to Israel Eph'al*, Jerusalem: Hebrew University Magnes Press, 86–98.

Honeyman, A. M. (1939), 'The Pottery Vessels of the Old Testament', *PEQ* 71:76–90.

Horsnell, M. J. A. (1997a), כשף, in *NIDOTTE* 2:735–738.

——— (1997b), קסם, in *NIDOTTE* 3:945–951.

Hrushovski-Harshav, B. (1971), 'Prosody, Hebrew', in *EJ*, 595–623.

Hubbard, R. L. (1997a), גאל, in *NIDOTTE* 1:789–794.

——— (1997b), ישע, in *NIDOTTE* 2:556–562.

Huffmon, H. B. (1959), 'The Covenant Lawsuit in the Prophets', *JBL* 78:285–295.

Hyatt, J. P. (1952), 'On the Meaning and Origin of Mic 6:8', *ATR* 34:232–239.

Innes, D. K. (1969), 'Some Notes on Micah, Chapter II', *EvQ* 41:10–13.

Jenson, P. P. (1997a), אלף, in *NIDOTTE* 1:416–418.

——— (1997b), שבע, in *NIDOTTE* 4:34–37.

Jepsen, A. (1980), חזה, in *TDOT* 4:280–290.

Judisch, D. (1999), 'The Historicity of Jonah', *CTQ* 63:144–157.

Kaltner, J., R. Graybill and S. L. McKenzie (2020), 'Jonah in the Book of the Twelve', in L.-S. Tiemeyer and J. Wöhrle (eds.), *The Book of the Twelve: Composition, Reception, and Interpretation*, VTSup 184, Leiden: Brill, 164–175.

Kessler, R. (2020), 'Micah in the Book of the Twelve', in L.-S. Tiemeyer and J. Wöhrle (eds.), *The Book of the Twelve: Composition, Reception, and Interpretation*, VTSup 184, Leiden: Brill, 176–185.

Kidner, D. F. (1970), 'The Distribution of Divine Names in Jonah', *TynB* 21:126–128.

Kitz, A. M. (2000), 'The Hebrew Terminology of Lot Casting and Its Ancient Near Eastern Context', *CBQ* 62:207–214.

Kiuchi, N. (1997), נשר, in *NIDOTTE* 3:200–201.

Konkel, A. H. (1997a), זר, in *NIDOTTE* 1:1142–1143.

——— (1997b), נכר, in *NIDOTTE* 3:108–109.

Krause, J. J. (2008), 'Tradition, History, and Our Story: Some Observations on Jacob and Esau in the Books of Obadiah and Malachi', *JSOT* 32:475–486.

Kronholm, T. (1999), נשר, in *TDOT* 10:77–85.

Landes, G. M. (1967a), 'The Kerygma of the Book of Jonah: The Contextual Interpretation of the Jonah Psalm', *Int* 21:3–31.

——— (1967b), 'The "Three Days and Three Nights" Motif in Jonah 2.1', *JBL* 86:446–450.

——— (1982), 'Linguistic Criteria and the Date of the Book of Jonah', in B. Levine and A. Malamat (eds.), *Eretz-Israel: Archaeological, Historical and Geographical Studies*, vol. 16, Jerusalem: IES, 147–170.

Lawrence, P. J. N. (1986), 'Assyrian Nobles and the Book of Jonah', *TynB* 37:121–132.

Lemanski, J. (1992), 'Jonah's Nineveh', *CJ* 18:40–49.

Lessing, R. (2002), 'Just Where Was Jonah Going?: The Location of Tarshish in the Old Testament', *CJ* 28:291–293.

Levin, Y. (2018), '"Tell it Not in Gath" (Micah 1:10): What Is Gath Doing in a List of the Destroyed Towns of Judah?', in I. Shai, J. R. Chadwick, L. Hitchcock, A. Dagan, C. McKinny and J. Uziel (eds.), *Tell it in Gath: Studies in the History and Archaeology of Israel: Essays in Honor of Aren M. Maeir on the Occasion of his Sixtieth Birthday*, Zaphon: Münster, 445–460.

Levine, E. (2002), 'Justice in Judaism: The Case of Jonah', *RRJ* 5:170–197.

Lichtheim, M. (1997a), 'The Report of Wen-Amun' (1.41), *COS* 1:89–93.

——— (1997b), 'The Shipwrecked Sailor' (1.39), *COS* 1:83–85.

Lindblom, J. (1962), 'Lot-Casting in the Old Testament', *VT* 12:164–178.

Lipinski, E. (1973), 'Obadiah 20', *VT* 23:368–370.

Lubeck, R. (1988), 'Prophetic Sabotage: A Look at Jonah 3:2–4', *TrinJ* 9:37–46.

Luc, A. (1997), חטא, in *NIDOTTE* 2:87–93.

McCarter, P. K. (1976), 'Obadiah 7 and the Fall of Edom', *BASOR* 221:87–91.

——— (2000), 'Kuntillet 'Ajrud: Plaster Wall Inscription' (2.47D), *COS* 2:173.

Marcus, D. (1999), 'Nineveh's "Three Days' Walk" (Jonah 3:3): Another Interpretation', in S. Cook and S. Winter (eds.), *On the Way to Nineveh: Studies in Honor of George M. Landes*, ASOR Research Books 4, Atlanta: Scholars Press, 42–53.

Master, D. M. (2009), 'Micah', in *ZIBBC* 5:120–147.

——— (2013), 'Samaria/Sebaste', in D. M. Master (ed.), *The Oxford Encyclopedia of the Bible and Archaeology*, vol. 2, Oxford: Oxford University Press, 329–336.

Mazar, E. (2018), 'Is This the Prophet Isaiah's Signature?', *BAR* 44:64–73, 92.

Merwe, C. H. J. van der (1993), 'Old Hebrew Particles and the Interpretation of Old Testament Texts', *JSOT* 60:27–44.

Miller, C. L. (2007), 'The Relation of Coordination to Verb Gapping in Biblical Poetry', *JSOT* 32:41–60.

Miller-Naudé, C. L., and C. H. J. van der Merwe (2011), '*Hinnēh* and Mirativity in Biblical Hebrew', *HS* 52:53–81.
Moberly, R. W. L. (1997), אמן, in *NIDOTTE* 1:427–433.
Moshavi, A. (2007a), 'הלא as a Discourse Marker of Justification in Biblical Hebrew', *HS* 48:171–186.
——— (2007b), 'Syntactic Evidence for a Clausal Adverb הלא in Biblical Hebrew', *JNSL* 33:51–63.
——— (2011), 'Rhetorical Question or Assertion? The Pragmatics of הלוא in Biblical Hebrew', *JANES* 32:91–105.
Muilenburg, J. (1961), 'The Linguistic and Rhetorical Usages of the Particle *kî* in the Old Testament', *HUCA* 32:135–160.
Na'aman, N. (1974), 'Sennacherib's "Letter to God" on His Campaign to Judah', *BASOR* 214:25–39.
——— (1998), '"The House-of-No-Shade Shall Take Away Its Tax from You" (Micah I 11)', *VT* 45:516–527.
——— (2011), 'Textual and Historical Notes on the Eliashib Archive from Arad', *TA* 38:83–93.
Naudé, J. A. (1997), חרם, in *NIDOTTE* 2:276–277.
Neiderhiser, E. A. (1981), 'Micah 2:6–11: Considerations on the Nature of the Discourse', *BTB* 11:104–107.
Neiman, D. (1963), 'Sefarad: The Name of Spain', *JNES* 22:128–132.
Nel, P. J. (1997a), כלם, in *NIDOTTE* 3:658–660.
——— (1997b), שלם, in *NIDOTTE* 4:130–135.
Nogalski, J. D. (1998), 'Obadiah 7: Textual Corruption or Politically Charged Metaphor?', *ZAW* 110:67–71.
——— (2007), 'Recurring Themes in the Book of the Twelve: Creating Points of Contact for a Theological Reading', *Int* 61:125–136.
——— (2012), 'Not Just Another Nation: Obadiah's Placement in the Book of the Twelve', in R. Albertz, J. D. Nogalski and J. Wohrle (eds.), *Perspectives on the Formation of the Book of the Twelve: Methodological Foundations, Redactional Processes, Historical Insights*, BZAW 433, Berlin: de Gruyter, 89–107.
——— (2017), 'Intertextuality and the Book of the Twelve', in *The Book of the Twelve and Beyond: Collected Essays of James D. Nogalski*, Atlanta: SBL Press, 217–239. Original publication (1996) in J. W. Watts and P. R. House (eds.), *Forming Prophetic Literature: Essays on Isaiah and the Twelve in Honor of John D. W. Watts*, JSOTSup 235, Sheffield: Sheffield Academic Press, 102–124.
O'Connell, R. H. (1997a), משפחה, in *NIDOTTE* 2:1139–1142.
——— (1997b),עם, in *NIDOTTE* 3:429–432.
Ogden, G. S. (1982), 'Prophetic Oracles Against Foreign Nations and Psalms of Communal Lament: The Relationship of Psalm 137 to Jeremiah 49:7–22 and Obadiah', *JSOT* 24:89–97.
Ottosson, M. (1978), היכל, in *TDOT* 3:382–388.
Park, S. H. (1997), שאר, in *NIDOTTE* 4:11–17.

Peels, H. G. L. (1997), נקם, in *NIDOTTE* 3:154–156.
Pons, M. V. (2014), 'The Origin of the Name Sepharad: A New Interpretation', *JSS* 59:297–313.
Powell, M. A. (1992), 'Weights and Measures', in *ABD* 6:897–908.
Prince, J. D. (1897), 'The Word MZWR in Obadiah 7', *JBL* 16:176–177.
Raabe, P. R. (1995), 'Why Prophetic Oracles Against the Nations?', in A. B. Beck, A. H. Bartlett, P. R. Raabe and C. A. Franke (eds.), *Fortunate the Eyes that See*, Festschrift for David Noel Freedman, Grand Rapids: Eerdmans, 236–257.
Rad, G. von (1959), 'Origin of the Concept of the Day of Yahweh', *JSS* 4:97–108.
Rainey, A. F. (1982), 'Wine from the Royal Vineyards', *BASOR* 245:57–62.
——— (1983), 'The Biblical Shephelah of Judah', *BASOR* 251:1–22.
Reicke, B. I. (1967), 'Liturgical Traditions in Micah 7', *HTR* 60:349–367.
Robinson, B. P. (1985), 'Jonah's Qiqayon Plant', *ZAW* 97:390–403.
Robinson, R. B. (1988), 'Levels of Naturalization in Obadiah', *JSOT* 40:83–97.
Röllig, W. (1999), 'Baal Shamen', in K. van der Toorn, B. Beckling and P. W. van der Rollig (eds.), *Dictionary of Deities and Demons*, Grand Rapids: Eerdmans, 149–151.
Ross, A. P. (1997), שם, in *NIDOTTE* 4:147–151.
Ryken, L., J. C. Wilhoit and T. Longman III (1998), 'Day of the Lord', in *Dictionary of Biblical Imagery*, Downers Grove: InterVarsity Press, 196–197.
Schultz, R. L. (2003), 'The Ties that Bind: Intertextuality, the Identification of Verbal Parallels, and Reading Strategies in the Book of the Twelve', in P. L. Redditt and A. Schart (eds.), *Thematic Threads in the Book of the Twelve*, Berlin: de Gruyter, 27–45.
Schwantes, S. J. (1964), 'Critical Notes on Micah 1:10–16', *VT* 14:454–461.
Scott, R. B. Y. (1965), 'The Sign of Jonah', *Int* 19:16–25.
Selman, M. J. (1997a), במה, in *NIDOTTE* 1:670.
——— (1997b), גבעה, in *NIDOTTE* 1:805.
Shemesh, Y. (2010), '"And Many Beasts" (Jonah 4:11): The Function and Status of Animals in the Book of Jonah', *JHS* 10:1–26.
Shiloh, Y. (1993), 'Jerusalem', *NEAEHL* 2:705–712.
Sieges, A., and N. R. Werse (2020), 'Obadiah in the Book of the Twelve', in L.-S. Tiemeyer and J. Wöhrle (eds.), *The Book of the Twelve: Composition, Reception, and Interpretation*, VTSup 184, Leiden: Brill, 151–163.
Smith, G. V. (1997), זיד, in *NIDOTTE* 1:1094–1096.
Smith, L. P. (1952), 'The Book of Micah', *Int* 6:210–227.
Snyman, F. (1989), 'Cohesion in the Book of Obadiah', *ZAW* 101:59–71.
Stade, B. (1886), 'Miscellen', *ZAW* 122–123.
Stallman, R. C. (1997), ארי, in *NIDOTTE* 1:513–517.
Strawn, B. A. (2010), 'Jonah's Sailors and Their Lot Casting: A Rhetorical-Critical Observation', *Bib* 91:66–76.

——— (2012), 'On Vomiting: Leviticus, Jonah, Ea(a)rth', *CBQ* 74:445–464.

Stuart, D. K. (1976), 'The Sovereign's Day of Conquest', *BASOR* 221:159–164.

Suriano, M. J. (2010), 'A Place in the Dust: Text, Topography and a Toponymic Note on Micah 1:10–12a', *VT* 60:433–446.

Swart, I., and C. Van Dam (1997), חמס, in *NIDOTTE* 2:177–180.

Talmon, S. (1953), 'The Qumran *yḥd* – a Biblical Noun', *VT* 3:133–140; repr. in *The World of Qumran from Within*, Jerusalem: Hebrew University Magnes Press, 1989.

——— (1978), הר, in *TDOT* 3:427–447.

Thomas, D. W. (1953), 'A Consideration of Some Unusual Ways of Expressing the Superlative in Hebrew', *VT* 3:209–224.

Thompson, J. A., and E. A. Martens (1997), שוב, in *NIDOTTE* 4:55–59.

Tsevat, M. (1980), חלק, in *TDOT* 4:447–451.

Van Dam, C. (1997a), איד, in *NIDOTTE* 1:371.

——— (1997b), גורל, in *NIDOTTE* 1:840–842.

——— (1997c), חלק, in *NIDOTTE* 2:161–163.

Van Groningen, G. (1980), עם, in *TWOT* 2:676.

Wagner, S. (1980), חוס, in *TDOT* 4:271–277.

Wakely, R. (1997), נדר, in *NIDOTTE* 3:37–42.

Walsh, C. (2015), 'The Metaprophetic God of Jonah', in I. D. Wilson and D. Edelman (eds.), *History, Memory, Hebrew Scriptures*: A Festschrift for Ehud Ben Zvi, Winona Lake: Eisenbrauns, 259–272.

Walton, J. H. (1992), 'The Object Lesson of Jonah 4:5–7 and the Purpose of the Book of Jonah', *BBR* 2:47–57.

——— (2009), 'Jonah', in *ZIBBC* 5:100–119.

Way, R. J. (1997), צום, in *NIDOTTE* 3:780–783.

Wendland, E. R. (1996a), 'Text Analysis and the Genre of Jonah (Part 1)', *JETS* 39:191–206.

——— (1996b), 'Text Analysis and the Genre of Jonah (Part 2)', *JETS* 39:373–395.

Werse, N. R. (2013), 'Obadiah's "Day of the Lord": A Semiotic Reading', *JSOT* 38:109–124.

Willis, J. T. (1967), 'On the Text of Micah 2,1a*a–b*', *Bib* 48:534–541.

——— (1968a), 'Micah IV.14–V.5 – a Unit', *VT* 18:529–547.

——— (1968b), 'A Note on ואמר in Micah 3:1', *ZAW* 80:50–54.

——— (1968c), 'Review of *Micah 6:6–8*, by Theodor Lescow', *VT* 18:273–278.

——— (1968d), 'Some Suggestions on the Interpretation of Micah I 2', *VT* 18:372–379.

——— (1969a), 'The Authenticity and Meaning of Micah 5:9–14', *ZAW* 81:353–368.

——— (1969b), 'The Structure of Micah 3–5 and the Function of Micah 5:9–14 in the Book', *ZAW* 81:191–214.

——— (1970), 'Fundamental Issues in Contemporary Micah Studies', *ResQ* 13:77–90.

——— (1979), 'The Expression *be'acharith hayyamin* in the Old Testament', *ResQ* 22:54–71.

Wilson, R. D. (1918a), 'The Authenticity of Jonah', *PTR* 16:280–298, 430–456.

——— (1918b), '*mnh*, "To Appoint," in the Old Testament', *PTR* 16:645–654.

Wiseman, D. J. (1979), 'Jonah's Nineveh', *TynB* 30:29–51.

Woude, A. S. van der (1969), 'Micah in Dispute with the Pseudo-Prophets', *VT* 19:244–260.

Wright, C. J. H. (1997), נחל, in *NIDOTTE* 3:77–81.

Zukerman, A., and I. Shai (2006–7), '"The Royal City of the Philistines" in the "Azekah Inscription" and the History of Gath in the Eighth Century BCE', *UF* 38:729–778.

INDEX OF SCRIPTURE REFERENCES AND ANCIENT SOURCES

OLD TESTAMENT

Genesis

Exodus

INDEX OF AUTHORS

INDEX OF SUBJECTS